SOLDIERS
OF LIBERTY

To Patrick Cahir

SOLDIERS OF LIBERTY

A STUDY OF FENIANISM
1858–1908

EVA Ó CATHAOIR

THE LILLIPUT PRESS
DUBLIN

First published 2018 by
THE LILLIPUT PRESS
62–63 Sitric Road, Arbour Hill
Dublin 7, Ireland
www.lilliputpress.ie

Paperback ISBN: 978 1 84351 752 8
Hardback ISBN: 978 1 84351 713 9

A CIP record for this title is available from
The British Library.

1 3 5 7 9 10 8 6 4 2

Set in 10 pt on 14 pt Sabon by Marsha Swan
Printed in Poland by Drukarnia Skleniarz

Chronology

Martyrs'. Clerkenwell explosion kills twelve innocent people. Clan na Gael founded in New York.

1868–9 Reorganized IRB emerges, now led by the Supreme Council.

1869, 1871 Fenian amnesty campaign leads to two amnesties for the prisoners.

1876 Whaling ship *Catalpa* rescues military Fenians from Australia.

1879 onwards, IRB overshadowed by land agitation and Parnell's Home Rule movement.

1882 Phoenix Park Murders, new British secret service undermines IRB.

1884 IRB assists at founding of GAA. Feud splits Clan na Gael into pro- and anti-Sullivanites, the latter led by Devoy and Dr Cronin. Alliance between Clan and IRB breaks down.

1885 John O'Leary returns from exile and spearheads cultural initiative for a weakened IRB.

1881–5 Dynamite war by Irish-American bombers in Britain.

1888–9 *Times* Commission sits. Pigott's forgeries are unmasked, while Le Caron reveals that he has been spying on Fenianism for twenty years.

1889 Dr Cronin murdered in Chicago.

1891 Death of Parnell, when IRB and GAA split into pro- and anti-Parnell factions.

1895 Clan na Gael split leads to founding of INA by Sullivanites, now under Lyman, which divides IRB in turn.

1898 Commemoration of the centenary of the United Irishmen.

1900 Clan and IRB gradually reunite, attempts to revive the IRB continue.

1907 Death of O'Leary, return of Tom and Kathleen Clarke from America, revival of the IRB gains momentum.

Illustrations

Acknowledgments

This book began with an invitation from Sheila Foley and the committee of the Kickham Country Weekend, Mullinahone, to lecture on the Tipperary Fenians. I received great encouragement not only from Sheila, but also from our south Tipperary circle of friends, including the late Col Eoghan Ó Néill of Lisronagh, the late Liam Ó Duibhir of Clonmel and Dr Thomas McGrath of Ballingarry.

I am proud to acknowledge the help and inspiration of the late Mrs Mary Hanrahan of Ballycurkeen, Dr Martin Mansergh, Jerome Devitt, Dr Brian Sayers, Diarmuid Ó Mathúna, Gearoid Foley, Henry Cairns of Bray, the late Tess Kearney, Sean Dougan, Charles McLauchlan of Manchester, Matt Doyle, secretary of the National Graves Association, Caroline Timmons, Seumas Brennan of the Academy Hotel, Dublin, the staff of the Mermaid Arts Centre, Bray, Aidan McGowan, John Roche, Dr Proinsias Ó Drisceoil, June Jackman of Pimlico, Doreen and the late Tom Powell of Chiswick and Ingrid di Palma of Maida Vale, London. Michael Kelleher of Bray Public Library continued in his role as my favourite research assistant, ably assisted by Robert Butler and Kate Brazil. The late Pat Casey of the Old Dublin Society and my son Patrick Cahir acted as photographers. Aidan Lambert of Dublin and Mike Ruddy of Tennessee, USA, lent illustrations.

I was facilitated by the staffs of the National Archives of Ireland, the National Library of Ireland, the Dublin City Library & Archive, Cork Central Library, Bray Public Library, Dingle Public Library, the National Archives for England and Wales, London, the British Library, the British Newspaper Library, Colindale, London, the Bodleian Library, Oxford, Maida Vale Public Library, Hammersmith Public Library, Paddington Public Library, St Mary's Cemetery, Kensal Green, London, the New York Public Library and Calvary Cemetery, Queen's, New York.

However arduous, my pursuit of Irish history was never boring, especially when Tony Hocking diverted his coach of unsuspecting tourists to locate a Fenian grave. Colleagues Mick Nolan (Galvins) and P.J. Hammond gave important support. Great credit is due to publisher Antony Farrell, editor Djinn von Noorden and the Lilliput team. Publication was facilitated by a grant from the Northern Ireland Commemorative Fund of the Department of the Taoiseach. Finally, apologies and thanks to Dr Brendan Ó Cathaoir, Patrick Cahir, Dr Katharina Ó Cathaoir and Emer Nagle, whose lives were somewhat overshadowed by the Fenian movement.

Contents

*Towns and villages in Munster and Kilkenny where Fenian 'circles'
were active from the 1860s (hand-drawn by author).*

Introduction

Between 1845 and 1852 Ireland experienced the last major Famine in Western Europe, which accelerated an ongoing economic transformation. The cataclysm reduced a population of over eight million to six and a half million people. Accompanied by the abortive Young Ireland Rising and the failure of the Tenant League, this culminated in a relentless exodus, which decreased Ireland's population to four and a half million by 1901.[1]

Irish Catholicism was alien to the Protestant ethos of the host countries. Immigrants experienced a cold welcome and were slow to gain middle-class status in North America. John Mitchel led nationalist writers in politicizing the concept of exile, which reinforced their separate identity through his *Jail Journal* and *The Last Conquest of Ireland*. Allied to hatred of England, this spurred immigrant communities to support change at home.[2]

Communal remembrance of Famine evictions fed Irish-American support for Fenianism, threatening the British Empire on a transnational basis. This also motivated the Irish in Britain and, to a lesser extent, Canada and Australasia.[3]

In Ireland, the more fortunate tenant farmers consolidated their holdings, turning to cattle, sheep and butter production for export to Britain. Commercial farming replaced subsistence agriculture, augmenting a growing middle class. Strong farmers and merchants embraced such opportunities, while a burgeoning railway network facilitated export.[4]

The new consumer goods were distributed by hundreds of shop assistants, commercial travellers and transport workers, recruited among the non-inheriting sons of farmers and shopkeepers. These young, urban Catholics were marked by Famine memories and the unceasing depopulation. Together with local artisans, whose livelihood was threatened by cheap English imports, they questioned Ireland's role of supplying manpower and agricultural produce for the British Empire. Lacking access to higher education, they were excluded from the professions and a career in politics, but rejected the status quo and sought an outlet for their talents. Influenced by Thomas Davis and the *Nation*, with older mentors having participated in the Young Ireland movement, these men demanded a more democratic society.

During the mid-1850s small groups of men and women in Munster and south Leinster cherished the conviction that the defeat of the 1848 Rising was not final. James Stephens followed in the footsteps of Wolfe Tone by appealing to the 'men of no property' – tradesmen, mechanics and clerks, when establishing the Irish Republican Brotherhood and its American sister organization, the Fenian Brotherhood, in 1858–9. Alongside John O'Mahony and Michael Doheny, Stephens failed to win middle-class support, forcing them to entrust important positions to men of humble origin, as Dublin Castle recorded contemptuously. The IRB was therefore more egalitarian than its predecessors.[5]

This study disagrees with R.V. Comerford's interpretation of Fenian cadres as convivial associations of young men, asserting their autonomy like other Europeans, rather than motivated by revolutionary zeal. Early leaders, having been minor Young Irelanders, imitated their patriotic socializing as a cover for revolutionary activities and to boost morale. Creating cohesion through a nationalist counterculture was essential, when simultaneously challenging the British Empire, the Catholic Church and the Irish middle class. Rather than enjoying 'patriotism as a pastime', activists experienced police harassment and detention in unhealthy jails. This was often followed by the loss of their livelihood, culminating in the emigration of whole families and, sometimes, illness and death of the released suspect.[6] The lives of the Munster and Kilkenny Fenians explored in this study support the conclusion that an ardent, transnational desire for change animated the members of the IRB, the Fenian Brotherhood and their successors.[7]

In 1863 the IRB launched the *Irish People* newspaper, which revived national self-confidence and propagated democratic values in an age of rapidly increasing literacy.[8] It depicted Irish revolutionaries as part of a European struggle against entrenched *anciens régimes*, pointing to the American Republic as an alternative role model. Although shut down by Dublin Castle in 1865, the *Irish People* exercised a long-term influence: John O'Leary taught its tenets throughout his life, as did Charles Kickham in *Knocknagow*, the most popular novel of nineteenth-century Ireland. The paper provided future activists with a political education and inculcated self-reliance and persistence.[9]

The Catholic Church increased its influence, expecting the British Empire to reward it as a guarantor of social stability, while resenting the privileged position of the minority Church of Ireland. The hierarchy was aware that its flock remained disadvantaged, but rejected Fenian plans for an independent Ireland as utopian and likely to end in bloodshed. It guarded its political hegemony, copper-fastened by denominational education. Cardinal Cullen opposed the concept of a separation of church and state promoted by the *Irish People*. The IRB intellectuals were brave, if foolhardy, to defy him, although their rejection of the confessional state has been vindicated.

Flying in the face of contemporary economics, which counselled Irishmen to attract British investment, and seize career opportunities within the empire, the IRB insisted on an alternative vision. Republican leaders perceived themselves as educators of 'the people' in line of succession to Tone and Davis. John O'Mahony, Michael Doheny, John O'Leary, Thomas Clarke Luby and their female relatives realized that opposing the British Empire meant a long march towards nationhood.[10] They conceived of Ireland as a spiritual entity and subscribed to a Christ-inspired ethos of devotion and sacrifice, which could culminate in bearing witness on the scaffold. Interpreting their lives as a patriotic pilgrimage, these leaders resembled Polish separatists of the early nineteenth century, reacting to the iron grip of Tsarist Russia.[11] The Quaker Alfred Webb, later an MP of the Irish Parliamentary Party, experienced a conversion to nationalism when observing Luby, O'Leary and Kickham, 'great and pure intentioned men' in the dock.[12]

Webb became convinced that 'there must be something radically wrong, as there was, in a state of things when such men could thus rise up and submit themselves to such a doom'.[13]

Unlike their Young Ireland predecessors, the Fenians embraced physical force separatism from the beginning. Despite Stephens's failure to instigate an insurrection, the transnational persistence of Fenianism forced British politicians to focus on Irish concerns, resulting in a land bill, which initiated overdue agrarian reform. O'Mahony and Stephens made considerable progress with rebuilding national self-belief and in organizing Irish America. P.S. O'Hegarty concluded that the Fenian movement represented the greatest threat experienced by the British Empire since 1798.[14]

After numerous habeas corpus arrests and the swift suppression of the 1867 Rising, the demise of the IRB appeared imminent. But the rescue of Colonel Thomas Kelly and his aide-de-camp in Manchester, during which a policeman was tragically killed, and a trial leading to convictions of dubious validity refocused attention on the IRB. The executions of Allen, Larkin and O'Brien, the Manchester Martyrs, which a panicked government allowed to go ahead, created support among all strands of Irish nationalism and a pantheon of Republican martyrs mirroring the Catholic saints emerged, which helped to counteract the condemnation of the hierarchy. When the IRB became eclipsed by Parnell and his party during the 1880s, it continued to maintain a presence through cultural and sporting activities, which embodied its alternative vision of Ireland.

The Irish diaspora enabled Fenianism to operate on a transnational level. Agents travelled within and across nation states, utilizing ethnic networks and evolving technology for effective communication. The movement appealed to the Irish masses in the transatlantic world through the radical press, while sympathizers lobbied Washington to intervene on behalf of imprisoned activists. Although aggravating Anglo-American tensions after the Civil War, detainees, who were naturalized US citizens, failed to provoke a rupture, which would have benefitted them. Instead, a liberal consensus between the two powers emerged, marginalizing Irish concerns.

The classic Fenian strategy of waiting for an international war involving Britain to initiate the insurrection, as advocated by the early leaders, led to much frustration and 'incoherent conspiracy' or, in Desmond Ryan's phrase, 'fighting among themselves like a bag of cats'.[15]

Talented activists left to invigorate the Irish Parliamentary Party and the Land League, driven by pragmatic considerations rather than a renunciation of physical force. The IRB never recaptured its mass appeal of the 1860s, but dedicated followers kept it alive by infiltrating organizations likely to advance its ethos. Although disastrously fragmented between 1882 and 1900, the IRB inspired numerous small and often short-lived initiatives, which helped to transform Ireland's cultural landscape, while slowly beginning to replace disheartened, superannuated men with dedicated revolutionaries.

As security experts like John Mallon and Sir Nicholas Gosselin retired, they bequeathed Dublin Castle their (mistaken) conviction that the IRB was in irreversible decline. But it remains doubtful that even with generous resources the police would have gained an inside track on the likes of Seán MacDiarmada or Tom and Kathleen Clarke. The new leadership, crystallizing after 1900, had learned from past mistakes and colleagues straying from its rigid standards were ruthlessly sidelined.[16]

Throughout its history, Fenianism was never monolithic. Given the influence that the Fenian Brotherhood and later Clan na Gael exerted in US politics, tensions between the aspirations of some Irish-American leaders and the requirements of the home organization were unavoidable. During a period of stagnation in the 1870s, a minority in the US adopted what contemporaries called 'scientific' warfare. This was credited with superseding conventional armies to redress the balance of power in favour of determined revolutionaries. The dynamite war of 1881–5 caused panic in British cities but proved unsuccessful and divisive. It was rejected by most IRB leaders. John O'Leary, as the mentor of W.B. Yeats, T.W. Rolleston and others associated with the Irish literary revival, propagated an idealistic version far removed from Rossa's 'skirmishers' or the seamy underbelly of rural Fenianism, enmeshed in agrarian combinations. ✗

Despite Colonel Kelly's ambitions for the March Rising, William Mackey Lomasney's sporadic guerrilla tactics in Cork in 1867 and the later ideas of Bulmer Hobson, the IRB persisted with planning a traditional insurrection, which contemporaries considered the hallmark of an emerging nation. Such efforts culminated in the Easter Rising. Fenianism was pivotal in creating an independent Irish state, but its physical force legacy, which continued to reverberate, led to its relative neglect by historians until recently. We must, however, evaluate Fenianism as a product of its age, when the majority of people enjoyed few democratic rights and this country's position within the British Empire was ambiguous.

The history of the IRB from 1858 to 1908 can be divided into five phases, beginning with its leadership under Stephens, which lasted until the Fenian Brotherhood split, and the trials of the *Irish People* staff in 1865–6. Secondly, the Rising of 1867 and its aftermath led by the Irish-American officers was followed by the reconstruction of the organization and its focus on the amnesty campaign between 1868–71. Thereafter, the IRB gradually stagnated and was overtaken by the land and Home Rule agitations, which more active personnel joined. It was further disrupted by the Irish-American dynamite campaign and British secret service infiltration. The concept of the Fenian spirit, of dedicated idealists, intent on handing on the separatist tradition, also developed. Ongoing efforts at revival continued between 1885–98 with little apparent success. These only began to bear secretive fruit in the fifth phase after 1900.

A factual account of this secret movement requires a balancing act between voluminous official documentation, for instance by Sir Thomas Larcom, undersecretary between 1853–68, and the reminiscences of revolutionaries in the radical press in Ireland and America. By 1866 the British administration tended to overestimate the Fenian threat, as informers on both sides of the Atlantic inflated membership numbers to boost their importance and income. Police officers like Thomas Talbot gained promotion and monetary rewards by displaying zeal. Although he must have been alert to the extemporizing nature of the Fenian organization, this is strangely absent from his reports.

In the aftermath of the 1867 Rising the administration suspected Colonel Kelly of planning an attack in London via the sewage system and precautions were taken. Fenian recollections reveal that the Kelly section was engaged in bitter infighting and only received limited support from America. While Colonel Kelly's letters, reprinted in the transatlantic press, taunted the authorities with their inability to recapture him after 18 September 1867, his followers were barely able to stay operational in England.[17]

John Devoy penned the most wide-ranging memoirs, recalling an impressive panorama of personalities. This must be approached with caution, however, as all those with whom he had clashed were dead by then and unable to dispute his version. Devoy was celebrating Irish independence, for which he had worked throughout his life, and tended to inflate IRB membership and the achievements of key players. Controversies, for instance, the IRB/INA split, were glossed over in his and other accounts. John O'Mahony's recollections demonstrate his commitment, but lack any analysis of how he contributed to the split of 1865. John O'Leary and Thomas Clarke Luby are too discursive, while James Stephens's unreliable account varies according to circumstances.

In a vivid style with strong emotional appeal, Jeremiah O'Donovan Rossa depicted a vanished rural Ireland, elucidating the motivation of his Munster contemporaries and exaggerating IRB strength. Like most leaders, he blithely underestimated the obstacles to be surmounted in fighting the British Empire. Joseph Denieffe's factual memoir pays tribute to their female supporters, who accepted contemporary subordination to male relatives. Their contribution was very much taken for granted by the imprisoned conspirators.[18]

Desmond Ryan became the first historian of Fenianism in the Irish state, co-editing the Devoy correspondence, a primary source, which sheds light on Clan na Gael from 1871 to 1928. William D'Arcy provided an excellent overview with *The Fenian Movement in the United States* (1947). Breandán Mac Giolla Choille urged in-depth studies at local level to demonstrate the extent of the movement, while warning that writing the history of Fenianism 'will prove a formidable task', requiring 'hard work and patient sifting'. The present study, which explores the sesquicentenary of the Fenian Rising, attempts to meet his challenge by investigating the experience of largely forgotten middle-ranking and local leaders through archival research to elucidate, in the words of Leopold von Ranke, *'wie es eigentlich gewesen ist'* (as it really happened).[19]

Recent accounts by Owen McGee and Máirtín Ó Catháin portray the IRB in Ireland and Scotland, while Brian Jenkins has recorded the British reaction in forensic detail.[20] Marta Ramon's magisterial biography of James Stephens, Matthew Kelly's *The Fenian Ideal and Irish Nationalism, 1882–1916,* and *The Dynamiters: Irish Nationalism and Political Violence in the Wider World, 1867–1900* by Niall Whelehan have further enriched our understanding.[21]

The title *Soldiers of Liberty* was chosen as it recurs in the writings of contemporaries. The more idealistic among the Fenians portrayed themselves as soldier-citizens of an embryonic Irish Republic. American Brotherhood directives from the 1860s described the qualities of a soldier of liberty as readiness for action, devotion, 'obedience, patience and strict sobriety'.[22] On his cenotaph in Glasnevin Cemetery, Michael Davitt paid tribute to John 'Amnesty' Nolan as 'a true soldier of Irish liberty', a phrase repeated on the Terence Bellew McManus/John O'Mahony monument. A spirit of service in the cause supported the elite of the IRB throughout the nineteenth century and can be traced in Munster and elsewhere.[23]

Subtitled *A Study of Fenianism, 1858–1908,* this book began as a prosopography of leaders from south Tipperary and Kilkenny, where the IRB had its roots. Furthermore, the three founders of the movement, James Stephens, John O'Mahony and Michael Doheny, hailed from this region. The IRB spread to Cork, but was initially weak in Dublin and for some the city by the Lee remained the real Fenian capital during the 1860s, given its large membership in proportion to the population. Even after the axis of power shifted to Connacht and Ulster during the 1870s, many prominent officers were natives of Munster. In the 1880s Cork constituted the only town in Ireland where O'Donovan Rossa could enlist old Fenians for his dynamite campaign.[24]

When exploring motivation and aims, references to more than 1000 members from Munster and Kilkenny were explored and mini biographies assembled. Their family and friendship networks were of the utmost importance in enlisting members, creating a sense of community and maintaining commitment, sometimes over several generations, especially when the IRB declined. Rather than a continuity of Republican organizations, the 'apostolic succession' lay in the choice of personal successors. In Kilkenny, for instance, John Haltigan, a former Young Irelander, had enrolled his sons in his Fenian 'circle'. Among their followers was Richard De Loughry, an iron founder and friend of James Stephens. Before the last members of the Haltigan family, decimated by imprisonment and emigration, left Kilkenny, they initiated P.J. O'Keeffe, an orphaned teenager, who subsequently led the local IRB, including Peter De Loughry, son of Richard. A cousin of John J. Breslin, who had been instrumental in the escape of Stephens from the Richmond bridewell in 1865, Peter in his turn would make the key used to free de Valera from Lincoln jail. John

Devoy was very aware of these friendship and kinship alliances and cultivated them when detained in Dublin during 1866, which facilitated his subversive contacts in the US on release.[25]

While large numbers of men left the movement after imprisonment in the 1860s, in some regions a core membership remained, which conspired for decades, often on several continents. 'Crossing the path of the British car of conquest' frequently led to tragic lives, but the commitment of such leaders ensured the survival of the Fenian ideal into the twentieth century. Nameless female Republicans can also be glimpsed, whether providing meals for destitute prisoners or swiftly hiding rifles from the constabulary. Among those gradually emerging into the political arena were Ellen O'Leary of Tipperary and Mary Jane O'Donovan Rossa of Clonakilty, forerunners of the redoubtable Maud Gonne, the only woman sworn into the IRB.[26]

The history of a movement that failed to dissolve in the face of considerable obstacles, including a resounding defeat in the field, to remain active from 1858 to 1924, is worth recording. It is not only a fascinating tale in which I have attempted to let the dramatis personae speak for themselves, but also of great genealogical significance, as can be seen in Appendix I. A sister of Edward Duffy of Loughglynn, Ballaghadereen, Co. Roscommon, herself an activist, described the challenges facing the historian of Fenianism: 'The history of Fenianism, if properly written by a person with enough of honour to "set down nought in malice", would be a strange history of suffering and heroism, deceit and truthfulness.'[27]

SOLDIERS OF LIBERTY

CHAPTER I

In the Shadow of the Famine
The Birth of Fenianism, 1845–60

The repeated failure of the potato crop resulted in the Great Famine, the greatest catastrophe of modern Irish history. Fuelled by longstanding social and agrarian problems, it caused enormous suffering with the loss of more than two million people through death and emigration. Thousands identified with Jeremiah O'Donovan Rossa of Rosscarbery, who recalled:

> Coming on the harvest time of the year 1845, the crops looked splendid. But one fine morning in July there was a cry around that some blight had struck the potato stalks. The leaves had been blighted, and from being green, parts of them were turned black and brown, and when these parts were felt between the fingers they'd crumble into ashes. The air was laden with a sickly odour of decay, as if the hand of death had stricken the potato field, and that everything growing in it was rotting.[1]

Distress was prevalent in the south west, where the Skibbereen district gained an international notoriety. Limited public relief works commenced in the autumn of 1846. Since Cromwellian times, Rossa's family had suffered a series of evictions, followed by the demise of the local linen industry. After the blight had destroyed his potatoes for the second time and the wheat was seized for the rent, Denis Donovan became a ganger on the relief works. When he fell ill, Jeremiah O'Donovan Rossa, his fifteen-year-old son, replaced him to retain these wages. Denis died on 25 March 1847. No wake was held for fear of infection, but neighbours attended the funeral.[2]

3

Afterwards Rossa assisted in burying Jillen Andy, who had starved to death.
He never forgot this coffin-less interment and how her handicapped son pined
beside the grave until he died some weeks later. Rossa also caught Famine fever,
but recovered. As a Fenian convict during the 1860s, he recalled these 'scenes of
youth, that nursed my hate of tyranny and wrong ... and help me now to suffer
and be strong'.[3] His 'Jillen Andy' is the most moving poem to emerge from the
Famine experience:

> *Four men bear Jillen on a door – 'tis light,*
> *They have not much of Jillen but her frame;*
> *No mourners come, as 'tis believed the sight*
> *Of any death or sickness now, begets the same.*
>
> *And those brave hearts that volunteered to touch*
> *Plague-stricken death, are tender as they're brave;*
> *They raise poor Jillen from her tainted couch.*
> *And shade their swimming eyes while laying her in the grave.*[4]

During the summer of 1847 the Donovan family came close to destitution.
The widow surrendered the land in return for residence in an unoccupied house,
where they survived on charity. Later that year, London decided that the starving
would be solely supported by Irish poor rates, increasing the tax burden on landlords and tenant farmers. Pervasive social disintegration enabled proprietors
to consolidate holdings, as resistance against ejectment was unlikely: between
1846 and 1854, from 250,000 to 500,000 people were evicted.[5] Contemporaries
witnessed the shanty towns of the homeless, where those who failed to obtain
a workhouse place endured a slow death. In Connacht, the families of Michael
Davitt, Dr Mark Ryan and John O'Connor Power experienced similar hardships, before emigrating to industrial England.[6]

Thousands abandoned Ireland for a new life abroad and emigration to
North America continued at record levels into the 1850s.[7] In 1848 a relative
sent the eldest Donovan brother a ticket for Philadelphia, enabling him to earn
enough to bring out the family. Rossa, the only one left in Ireland, described
the sundering of kinship ties when bidding farewell to his mother and siblings:

> At Renascreena Cross we parted. There was a long stretch of straight even road
> from Tullig to Mauleyregan over a mile long ... Five or six other families were
> going away, and there were five or six cars to carry them and all they could carry
> with them, to the Cove of Cork. The cry of the weeping and wailing of that day
> rings in my ears still. That time it was a cry heard every day at every cross-road
> in Ireland. I stood at that Renascreena Cross till this cry of the emigrant party
> went beyond my hearing.[8]

During the decade ending in 1851, the population of Ireland fell from 8,175,124 to 6,552,385 people; by 1871 only 5,412,377 remained. In scenes of universal dispossession and departure almost an entire generation vanished; 'only one out of three Irishmen born about 1831 died at home of old age – in Munster only one out of four'.[9] Munster lost nearly 50 per cent of its people between 1841 and 1871.

While the transformation from subsistence economy to commercial agriculture signalled the exodus of the cottier class, the Famine also produced winners, for instance better-off farmers, who increased their holdings by evicting sub-tenants. This worsened tensions within the Catholic community. When solicitor Timothy McCarthy Downing told a public meeting that strong farmers treated their cottiers more harshly than the (Protestant) gentry had, his audience cheered.[10] Rossa blamed England for seizing the harvest: 'As in the case of my people in '45, the landlords came in on the people everywhere and seized the grain crops for the rent – not caring much what became of those whose labour and sweat produced those crops. The people died of starvation, by thousands. The English press and the English people rejoiced that the Irish were at last conquered.'[11]

The situation was more complex, however. Denis Donovan did not feature on the Anglo-Irish Lord Carbery's rent roll, but was an undertenant of the mother of Dr Daniel Donovan, medical officer of the Skibbereen Union. This kinswoman ordered the seizure of Donovan's wheat and demanded his eviction in 1847. Nevertheless, Rossa continued to blame 'perfidious Albion', relating how a previous Lord Carbery, to conciliate this former Gaelic ruling family in return for a peaceful life, became godfather to the future Mrs Donovan, whom he presented with a lease for part of Rosscarbery.[12] Three other houses besides Denis Donovan's featured in this document, and Dr Donovan's mother, like thousands of head tenants, was shedding the mass of impoverished smallholders. Rossa added, in a neutral tone, that wealthy relatives refused to assist his family.[13]

As a result of the Famine, the Cork merchants amassed fortunes by speculating in foodstuffs and astute farmers and professionals prospered. In 1842 a property-less Timothy McCarthy Downing commenced legal practice in Skibbereen to acquire 3446 acres with a valuation of £1375 by 1878.[14] Henry O'Shea, the father-in-law of Katharine, Parnell's beloved, belonged to those 'who exploited landlords bankrupted in the Famine by buying up estates at knockdown prices'.[15] Between 1851 and 1871 the production of beef, sheep and butter increased, while the acreage dedicated to grain shrank. Britain required agricultural produce and such profits multiplied as Ireland's population declined.[16] The emerging middle class of strong farmers, professional men and priests supported the British connection and absorbed its values. Their consumption of goods from the new stores rose, facilitated by an expanding railway network, but this prosperity did not extend to labourers and artisans in declining trades like nail-making.[17]

Mitchel interpreted the Great Famine as a diabolical plot to convert Ireland into a vast farm to feed Britain's industrial population, dispersing unruly Irishmen, while leaving adequate numbers for enlistment in the British army. He rejected the English interpretation of a 'dispensation of providence'. Blight had been prevalent throughout Europe, 'yet there was no Famine save in Ireland. The British account of the matter, then, is first a fraud – second, a blasphemy. The Almighty, indeed, sent the potato blight, but the English created the Famine.'[18]

Contemporaries were dismayed that Ireland continued to export grain in 1846, while legal restrictions hampered imports. Although close to the centre of the empire, this island endured inadequate relief measures, causing unnecessary deaths. James F.X. O'Brien believed that 'a native government' would have protected the people, while Isaac Butt realized that London's policies undermined the Union.[19] Mitchel's belief in British genocide was widely disseminated, but is discredited by modern research. Even if exports had been prohibited, the cottiers, who were most affected by the destruction of the potato, lacked the means to purchase alternative food, while the distribution of relief was hampered by a rudimentary infrastructure.[20]

On arrival in Britain and North America, the Irish were less than welcome, frequently clustering together in traumatized exile. The US had absorbed the immigration of the largely Protestant and professional United Irishmen, but their Catholicism marked the Famine Irish as aliens, who found solace in their ethnic neighbourhoods and church. During his childhood in industrial Lancashire, Michael Davitt listened to the Irish community in Haslingden recalling the Famine and absorbed a hatred of landlords, a widely shared experience given the number of Fenian officers born abroad.[21]

There was a perception that those forced to leave Ireland might yet return to gain justice. In 1852 G.H. Moore of Moore Hall warned the government to 'beware that the race they have banished across the Atlantic does not some day come back again'.[22]

For the remainder of the nineteenth century, many exiles, especially those who failed to prosper, nursed a sense of grievance. Rossa wrote of the isolation of older emigrants in America, who remained 'strangers in a strange land'.[23] This poignant remembrance of the old land can be seen in Calvary Cemetery, New York, where countless memorials record the place of origin of the Irish in considerable detail, a practice not shared by other Europeans.[24]

The Famine left its mark on contemporaries. Charles Kickham recalled his dismay at the 'severe distress' in Mullinahone and observed his father, a shopkeeper, lending money to emigrants. Kickham deplored the loss of the rural population; the hope that Ireland might 'yet be something else besides grazier land for bullocks' became a main theme, culminating in *Knocknagow*, a celebration of a vanished community.[25] John Sarsfield Casey, born in 1846, witnessed the aftermath of the Famine during his childhood in Mitchelstown. He, as well as Brian Dillon in Cork, Michael Cavanagh of Cappoquin, Patrick Neville Fitzgerald, Ballinacurra West, Co. Cork, William Lundon of Kilteely, Co. Limerick and James F.X. O'Brien of Dungarvan, the last two future MPs, were among thousands radicalized by the Famine.[26]

There was widespread fear that the Irish would vanish from their home-land: John O'Mahony wrote that the island was the 'ancestral birthright' of the exiled, 'disinherited sons of the Clanna Gaedhail', who should 'possess its soil' and not 'the land-jobbers who now devour its people and their fruits'.[27] The O'Mahonys, bilingual in Irish and English, but suffering a financial decline, straddled two worlds. They commanded anachronistic Gaelic allegiance while under increasing pressure from anglicization and modernization. When the Kingston Estate near Mitchelstown terminated their lease for Loughananna in 1840, O'Mahony attributed this to the radical politics of his ancestors. He felt 'for the other victims of the Irish land law by the poignancy of his own grief and indignation', recalling the Famine 'with tears in his manly eyes'.[28]

The Rising of 1848

Daniel O'Connell, the dominant figure of Irish politics, was in failing health. Heated debates about physical versus moral force with the Young Irelanders, a group of intellectuals associated with the *Nation*, which endeavoured to create a cultural, non-denominational Irish identity, led to their withdrawal from the Repeal Association in July 1846. Forming the Irish Confederation, they remained constitutionalists and only Mitchel supported the radical ideas of James Fintan Lalor, who postulated that title to the land derived from the people, advocating agrarian reform and separatism.[29] By February 1848, Mitchel, who had abandoned the Irish Confederation's hope that the landlords would join their cause, founded the *United Irishman*, based on Wolfe Tone's appeal to 'the men of no property'.[30] He initiated a 'public conspiracy' to depose British rule in Ireland. The swift overthrow of the monarchy in France and the spread of revolution across Europe encouraged the Young Irelanders to expect peaceful change at home. The clubs of the Irish Confederation began to mobilize.[31]

Tried for his inflammatory rhetoric under the new treason-felony act, Mitchel was sentenced to fourteen years' transportation. Confederate Club members demanded his rescue and a Rising – in vain. Mitchel interpreted his conviction by a packed jury as illegal, while his willingness to suffer for his principles united nationalists. The Young Irelanders decided on a Rising after the harvest, but were surprised by the suspension of habeas corpus. William Smith O'Brien, MP, their leader, discovered that the club membership in Kilkenny, where they hoped to inaugurate the insurrection, had been grossly exaggerated. Touring Kilkenny and south Tipperary in search of support, the hesitant leadership met desperate peasants, but the urban middle class and the Catholic clergy hampered their efforts.[32]

The Rising culminated in an episode on 28 July 1848 when John Blake Dillon, a co-founder of the *Nation*, escorted British soldiers through a barricade in Killenaule, Co. Tipperary, aware that a confrontation would prove fatal to the insurgents, who included James Stephens. The following day in Ballingarry, the rebels under Smith O'Brien failed to storm the Widow McCormack's house, where a group of constables had barricaded themselves.[33] During the brief outbreak, Michael Doheny and John O'Mahony participated as leaders, while Charles Kickham and John O'Leary were involved on the periphery.[34]

Stephens and Doheny walked through Munster, hoping to escape abroad, the latter demonstrating his commitment by writing '*A chuisle geal mo chroidhe*', addressing Ireland as a beautiful, sorrowing woman, reminiscent of James Clarence Mangan's 'Dark Rosaleen'. Expressing regret at their failure, Doheny concluded that he would persevere in his devotion to the nation regardless of consequences.[35]

On the borders of West Cork and Kerry, Doheny and Stephens contacted Timothy O'Sullivan More of Templenoe and influential members of the McCarthy clan of Kilfadda More, Kilgarvan, to receive help from Dr Timotheus McCarthy, his niece, the poetess 'Christabel', and Timothy McCarthy Downing of Skibbereen.[36] Stephens arrived in Paris in September 1848, while Doheny settled in New York. Henceforth, they aimed for a secret conspiracy.[37]

During the autumn of 1848 O'Mahony organized guerrilla warfare in south Tipperary and Waterford, but was frustrated by his undisciplined followers. Their attacks on constabulary barracks involving John Savage and Philip Gray, a Confederate Club member from Dublin, Michael and Richard Comerford of Carrick-on-Suir, and Felix O'Neill of Lisronagh, Clonmel, failed. Amidst recriminations, O'Mahony's campaign fizzled out.[38] Attempts by O'Mahony,

Gray and O'Leary to rescue Smith O'Brien and his companions, then on trial in Clonmel, ended in failure and O'Leary's arrest.

Daniel O'Connell had gained financial support from Irish exiles, proving the relative ease with which Dublin and New York could be linked. American republicans provided Famine relief, while Irish immigrants interpreted the US narrative of manifest destiny to include their homeland. They began collecting money in January 1848, urging the Young Irelanders to militant action. The Irish Republican Union of New York took the lead in lobbying US politicians in this presidential election year, while the Irish Confederation despatched emissaries to New York. An Irish Brigade was to support the insurrection, but the collapse of the Rising, inexplicable to immigrants, led to the IRU considering an invasion of Ireland via Canada. British officials gathered intelligence and monitored the arrival of potential combatants from the US, leading to the arrest of naturalized citizens, which foreshadowed tropes of the Fenian period.[39]

British press coverage added insult to injury: on 2 August 1848 the *Times* derided 'the fifty-first Irish rebellion', mistakenly portraying Smith O'Brien as cowering 'on all-fours among the cabbages' during the police fusillade. A later editorial claimed that his pardon was due to the insurrection having been 'a paltry riot in a cabbage-garden ... not even a pig was injured'.[40] Such racial stereotyping was galling. Famine survivors also experienced shame, as there had been no sustained resistance. Mitchel, O'Mahony and Davitt shared contemporary convictions that 'manly' citizens resolutely opposed tyranny unlike Irish peasants, who proved themselves unfit for self-government by behaving like slaves. Others, having violated communal ethics to survive, sought to excuse themselves by blaming outsiders, foremost the British administration.[41]

The 1849 Attempt

On his release John O'Leary resolved to found 'a secret, oath-bound society' dedicated to separatism. Junior members of the Confederate Clubs remained at large and began to conspire in Dublin, Cork, Clonmel, Waterford and Kilkenny. They sought help from Doheny in New York, as did Stephens, who wrote 'that what you so forcibly advocated in your letters, is already afoot in Ireland – *a secret organization*'.[42]

O'Mahony had joined Stephens in Paris, but refused to risk his followers' lives in such uncertain circumstances. O'Leary and James Fintan Lalor moved from Dublin to Waterford, Tipperary and Limerick, where the conspiracy was centred. Adherents were mostly urban tradesmen, labourers, the sons of shopkeepers and small farmers. Joseph Brenan, a member of the Irish Confederation and follower of Mitchel, and Thomas Clarke Luby, the son of a Protestant clergyman from Co. Tipperary, were among the leaders. Luby, a graduate of Trinity College, Dublin, had initiated his revolutionary career in 1848 by joining the Rising with the support of his parents, who shared his Young Ireland ideals.[43]

The secret society movement extended over 'a large area of Munster and south Leinster', resembling the early strongholds of Fenianism. The Rising was planned for 16 September 1849, with simultaneous attacks in counties Cork, Limerick, Clare, Kilkenny and Waterford; it was rumoured that British soldiers would make common cause with the rebels. But the only outbreak occurred in Cappoquin, where Joseph Brenan and James F.X. O'Brien led an unsuccessful attack on the constabulary barracks. Elsewhere, Fintan Lalor was among those arrested. Released in poor health, Lalor planned the publication of a radical newspaper, but died on 27 December. Six hundred secret society men, including John O'Leary, followed his coffin in semi-military formation through Dublin.[44]

The conspiracy of 1849 foreshadowed the Irish Republican Brotherhood. Separatist and oath-bound from the beginning, its members had been politicized in the Confederate Clubs. Many, like O'Leary, Luby and John Savage, remained eager for revolutionary action. Others, Charles Kickham among them, initially supported the constitutional tenant right agitation. But their more conservative and socially elevated seniors, including Smith O'Brien, Dillon and Gavan Duffy, rejected physical force as counterproductive under present circumstances.[45]

The Tenant League

The Irish Tenant League under Charles Gavan Duffy and Frederick Lucas was founded in response to the increasing taxation of the farming class. It campaigned for lower rents, fixity of tenure and compensation for improvements for those evicted, supported by the Catholic clergy of Kilkenny, Waterford and Tipperary. The league formed an alliance with the Catholic Defence Association, which opposed the Ecclesiastical Titles Bill of 1851, prohibiting Roman Catholic prelates from using their titles. This independent parliamentary party, pledged to demand religious equality and agrarian reform, achieved resounding success in the general election of 1852.[46]

The Irish party fragmented after barrister William Keogh and banker John Sadleir broke ranks and accepted government office in Lord Aberdeen's Peelite-Whig coalition. The split led to unedifying election scenes as priests opposed each other, while church discipline terminated the involvement of curates supporting

the league. Archbishop Cullen, however, approved of Sadleir and Keogh's eleva-
tion, aiming for concessions for his church. In November 1855 'the quietude
that comes of baffled hopes and defeated endeavour' settled over Ireland, as a
disillusioned Gavan Duffy sold the *Nation* and emigrated to Australia.[47]

In February 1856 the Tipperary joint-stock bank collapsed. John Sadleir, its
founder, had indulged in unsuccessful speculation, and committed suicide. The
failure of both bank and Tenant League created a bitter legacy and a distasteful
example of office-seeking. Michael Davitt wrote of 'a people betrayed by both prelates and parliamentarians', while John O'Leary concluded that[48] 'the period between
the collapse of the Tenant League and the rise of Fenianism was the "deadest" time
in Irish politics within my memory'.[49] With hindsight, A.M. Sullivan lamented that
this failure provided Fenian agents with an 'irresistible argument'.[50]

British observers imagined that Ireland had achieved the necessary tran-
quillity for economic growth. In reality, not only did the grievances of the
tenant farmers continue to fester, but the Catholic Church, as enforcer of social
control, considered itself undervalued by the state. For most Catholics, access
to the professions remained restricted and higher positions were the preserve of
the Protestant minority.[51]

In 1849 the Irish Republican Union, founded as the first North American
organization to prepare for revolution in Ireland, was being incorporated into
the New York state militia. Doheny served among its officers to continue his
separatist commitment but John Blake Dillon and Richard O'Gorman wrote to
William Smith O'Brien in 1852 that they were prioritizing professional success,
having abandoned politics:[52]

> You will hardly be surprised that O'Gorman and myself, in view of such facts,
> should regard the regeneration of Ireland as an object too remote and difficult
> to excite in us any lively interest – In truth, no Whig feels more thoroughly the
> conviction than I do at this moment that Ireland is not at present capable of
> existing under a respectable government of her own formation.[53]

O'Mahony's hope that the French Republic would support Irish independence
died after Napoleon III seized power. In November 1853 he left for New York,
where he suffered a nervous breakdown.[54]

Thomas Francis Meagher and John Mitchel escaped from the penal colony
of Van Diemen's Land to New York. Mitchel's arrival, in particular, reinvigorated
his compatriots. Reacting to the broken state of the Irish nation with defiance,
he founded the *Citizen*, which serialized his *Jail Journal* from January 1854.
Proclaiming that Ireland had 'a destiny to achieve, and wrongs (how matchless
and how bitter!) to avenge', he longed for an armed expedition to Ireland.[55]

When Britain entered the Crimean War as an ally of Constantinople in 1854, the Russian minister in Washington, aware of the might of the British navy, declined Mitchel's request for support. Mitchel regretted Irish-American apathy, following various futile schemes since 1848, when revolutionary funds had been squandered by their promoters. Realizing that the Crimean War would not provide an opportunity for insurrection, he 'quietly withdrew'. After a controversy with Archbishop Hughes of New York reduced the circulation of the *Citizen*, Mitchel relocated to Tennessee.[56]

The Emmet Monument Association

By early 1855 Michael Doheny and John O'Mahony responded by forming the secret Emmet Monument Association.[57] Its purpose was readily understood by Republicans, for the name alluded to Robert Emmet's speech from the dock, in which he concluded that 'my memory be left in oblivion and my tomb uninscribed, until other times and other men can do justice to my character. When my country takes her place among the nations of the earth, then, and not till then, let my epitaph be written. I have done.'[58]

The EMA offered basic military training and claimed to have enrolled 30,000 men. The committee planned on issuing bonds to raise funds and negotiated with Russian representatives, receiving assurances of aid for an invasion of Ireland, which was envisaged for September 1855. The resources of the British secret service demonstrate the obstacles the EMA would have to overcome, however. From 1854 onwards, Parliament had granted the Foreign Office an annual £32,000 for espionage, although this was reduced to £25,000 p.a. after 1858. In June 1855 Joseph Denieffe, an EMA member in New York, was returning to Kilkenny due to a family crisis. He was surprised to learn from Doheny and James Roche, a former editor of the *Kilkenny Journal*, that the EMA had not yet established any contact with separatists in Ireland. Denieffe was immediately made its agent.[59]

Returning to his native city after an absence of four years, Denieffe noticed a prevalent atmosphere of 'gloom and sadness'.[60] He appeared unaware of the mass grave of 970 persons at the Kilkenny Workhouse on the Hebron Road, which he passed every day on his walks. Communal silence continued to cover the victims, half of them children, until 2005.[61] He commented on the loss of indigenous industries. During his childhood Kilkenny had contained 19,071 people, which had declined to 13,235 by 1861. An anonymous emigrant of the 1840s, returning fifty years later, corroborated Denieffe by depicting the defunct distillery, flour mills and blanket manufacture.[62]

Denieffe sought out survivors of Young Ireland, chiefly John Haltigan, the foreman printer of the *Kilkenny Journal*, who introduced potential recruits, most notably Edward Coyne and James Cody of Callan. Such contacts were often disguised as participation in sport, for instance, greyhound coursing with Haltigan in Co. Kilkenny, which contradicts Comerford's thesis of young men seeking associational recreation.[63]

Aged twenty and seventeen respectively, these two played an important role in promoting the movement and were prototypes for future regional IRB leaders. Cody's family farmed at Crochtabeg, while Edward Coyne was the son of a publican. On completion of their national school education, both trained as shop assistants, which required organizational skills and a smart appearance. Cody became the foreman of a draper's shop and Coyne managed his family business. Members of the emerging Catholic lower-middle class, they were eager to participate in politics. Coyne, a natural leader, attracted followers in Callan, while James Cody had friends in rural Kilkenny and south Tipperary. Denieffe, too, was energetic and had achieved a senior position as a tailor.[64]

James Cody, Callan, CSO/ICR /16 (NAI).

John Haltigan's only contact in Dublin introduced Denieffe to activists from 1848–9, notably Philip Gray, Peter Langan, Garrett O'Shaughnessy and Thomas Clarke Luby. Denieffe organized clusters of potential insurgents in Kilkenny, south Tipperary and Dublin, but his arrangements were unavoidably provisional. He received the *Citizen* from New York to keep himself informed. Reading of dissensions, Denieffe and Haltigan concluded 'that all was up for the present'.[65]

In 1855 British consuls in the US warned Sir Thomas Larcom, the permanent undersecretary in Dublin Castle, that Thomas Francis Meagher, Michael Doheny and a member of the Emmet family were preparing a 'filibustering expedition' in association with secret societies in Ireland. The plotters were also discussing a Canadian raid and had 'letters from the Irish constabulary', assuring them that it would change sides once the invasion force landed. William Halpin, a leading separatist in Cincinnati, was among those arrested at the behest of the British consul. Lord Wodehouse in the Foreign Office instructed the police in Ireland and London to ascertain the numbers of returning emigrants and identify any subversives among them.[66]

By December British officials realized that the conspirators 'are fighting among themselves and are likely to squander any funds they may collect' during their conference in New York. When the Crimean War concluded the following year, the EMA disbanded, but thirteen representative members maintained contact in case of future opportunities. At home, Denieffe continued to communicate with Haltigan. Although the Indian Mutiny raged from 1857 to the following summer, the EMA coterie failed to act.[67]

James Stephens returns

Stephens was born in Kilkenny in 1825, probably as the extramarital child of a relative of his adoptive parents. Before the Rising he worked as an engineer on the Waterford to Limerick railway. Stephens recalled that the conviction of Irish independence being achievable never left him, despite seven years of exile.[68] In February 1856 Lord Desart alerted Dublin Castle that he had returned to Kilkenny. Others, suspected of having taken a seditious oath, were also said to be coming back. The authorities, however, concluded that no secret societies existed in Kilkenny.[69] During his 3,000-mile walk, Stephens discovered little interest in insurrection among the bourgeoisie, but

> artisan and labourer spoke to me with enthusiasm of the [Confederate] Club days and hoped to see them again before they died. I saw eyes light up to the

glow of indescribable ardour when I spoke to them of their brothers beyond the seas, of the new and greater Ireland in the Western Republic, and reminded them that the cause which braved so many dangers had got enough life left in it to rise once more, in the near future, to the position it deserved to enjoy.[70]

Stephens visited former 1848 men, including Joseph Rivers of Tybroughney Castle, Carrick-on-Suir, a connection of O'Mahony. When Stephens stated that unless the 'land were given to the Irish people [independence] was not worth the trouble or sacrifice of attaining', Rivers accused him of socialism. Stephens may have picked up socialist ideas in France, but had no intention of alienating potential supporters. He realized that an urban-rural divide prevented mechanics and labourers from joining tenants against their landlords and henceforth dealt with this issue solely in aspirational terms.[71]

He called on William Smith O'Brien, his former commander, who had recently been permitted to return to Cahirmoyle, Co. Limerick, where he prepared Gaelic manuscripts for publication. Retired from politics, Smith O'Brien remained the elder statesman of Irish constitutionalism. He blamed a lack of commitment by the urban middle class and the Catholic clergy for his defeat in 1848. A social conservative, Smith O'Brien mistrusted popular movements. An exasperated Stephens reflected that this aristocrat lacked faith in the 'men of no property' who 'had deserved better leaders'.[72]

After roaming through the countryside, Stephens informed his associates that 'the cause was not at all dead, but sleeping'.[73] He ignored the numerous military garrisons, but underlined working-class support for a revolution:

My 3,000 mile walk through Ireland convinced me of one thing – the possibility of organizing a proper movement for the independence of my native land. I found, of course, many circumstances to discourage me throughout my tour: the hostility of the aristocracy, the apathy of the farmers, the pigheadedness of the *bourgeoisie*; but the labourers and the tradesmen were on the right track, and the sons of the peasants were very sympathetic ... I came to the resolve that the attempt was not only worth trying, but should be tried in the very near future if we wanted at all to keep our flag flying; for I was sure as of my own existence that if another decade was allowed to pass without an endeavour of some kind or another to shake off an unjust yoke, the Irish people would sink into a lethargy from which it would be impossible for any patriot [to rouse them].[74]

Stephens taught French in influential families, including that of John Blake Dillon and John David Fitzgerald, the attorney general. Both Dillon and John O'Leary refused to participate in Stephens's revolutionary project when approached, considering it hopeless.[75] After renewed contact with his radical associates in New York, Stephens responded on 1 January 1858:

> I proceed to state the conditions on which I can accept the proposed cooperation of our transatlantic brothers, and the great personal responsibility devolving on myself ... I undertake to organize in three months from the date of his return here at least 10,000, of whom about 1500 shall have firearms and the remainder pikes. These men, moreover, shall be so organized as to be available (all of them) at any one point in twenty-four hours' notice at most ... Nor do I hesitate to assert that, with the aid of the 500 brave fellows you promise, we shall have such a prospect of success as has not offered since – I cannot name the epoch in our history.[76]

He refused to be 'worried or hampered by the wavering or imbecile' and acted as a 'provisional dictator'. Stephens argued that the people had never been tested as revolutionaries, due to the improvised manner of the Young Ireland Rising.[77] He, O'Mahony and Doheny decided that a disciplined, armed organization was required before an insurrection could take place. His backers were to provide around £100 per month, but the US ad hoc committee, consisting of O'Mahony, Doheny, James Roche, Michael Corcoran, Thomas J. Kelly and Patrick O'Rourke, lacked organized support, struggling to raise the first instalment during a recession. Nevertheless, they appointed Stephens as 'chief executive of the Irish revolutionary movement' with 'supreme control and absolute authority ... in Ireland'.[78]

The Irish Republican Brotherhood was founded on 17 March 1858, when Denieffe returned to Dublin with £80 and the document of authorization. Stephens, Thomas Clarke Luby, Joseph Denieffe, Peter Langan, Garrett O'Shaughnessy and Owen Considine were the first to take the IRB oath:[79]

> I, AB, do solemnly swear, in the presence of Almighty God, that I will do my utmost, at every risk, while life lasts, to make Ireland an independent democratic Republic; and that I will yield implicit obedience, in all things not contrary to the law of God, to the commands of my superior officers; and that I shall preserve inviolable secrecy regarding all the transactions of this secret society that may be confided to me. So help me God! Amen.[80]

Luby drafted the oath to allay the scruples of Catholics, whose church punished membership of secret societies with excommunication, explaining the reference to 'the law of God'.[81] Of these first members, two hailed from Kilkenny, two from Dublin, one from Tipperary, as did the Luby family, indicating a South Leinster/Munster base reminiscent of the Confederate clubs. As a security precaution, the conspirators did not use a specific name for some years, but referred to 'our movement' or 'the organization'. According to Luby, the names 'Irish Revolutionary Brotherhood' and 'Irish Republican Brotherhood' remained interchangeable until 1866, when the latter version began to predominate.[82]

COLONEL JOHN O'MAHONY, HEAD CENTRE OF THE FENIAN ORDER.—Photographed by Bancalow.—[See Page 122.]

Col O'Mahony, 99th NY, 'Head Centre' of the
*Fenian Brotherhood (*Harper's Weekly*).*

Within hours of founding the IRB, Stephens and Luby departed on their first organizing tour. In Kilkenny city, Haltigan 'was set to work' before they proceeded to Tipperary, where 'they were well received' and became guests of the idiosyncratic Fr John Kenyon of Templederry, friend of both Mitchel and Luby. In Cork, James Mountaine, a shoe manufacturer and former Young Ireland sympathizer, became the first to take the IRB oath. He and his friend Brian Dillon were motivated by the ongoing drain of emigration. Others, who 'wouldn't accept the defeat of 1848', included John Lynch, William O'Carroll, a baker, Michael O'Brien, a shop assistant from Ballymacoda, Mark Adams, a middle-aged engineer with Beamish and Crawford and James O'Mahony, a shopkeeper in Bandon.[83]

This first tour became a blueprint: organizers started from Dublin and canvassed Kildare, Carlow and Kilkenny on their way to Clonmel or Carrick-on-Suir, finishing in Cork. Stephens and Luby walked considerable distances to save money. Stephens's modus operandi consisted of secret visits to influential nationalists in the towns to outline his transatlantic plans; his confident manner was often successful.[84]

Family and friendship networks were vital when approaching potential recruits. Stephens visited Denis Mulcahy, who farmed 107 acres in Redmonds-town near Clonmel. A friend of John O'Mahony, Mulcahy had been an activist in Limerick and Kilmallock in 1848–9, while his brother John had organized in Co. Cork. Denis subsequently became the secretary of the Clonmel Tenant Protection Society. Now an old man, he allowed Stephens to hold meetings in his home. His daughter Catherine was a supporter, while Denis Dowling Mulcahy, an only son, became leader of the Clonmel district. Young Denis approached other strong farmers, who were rare among the IRB, and enrolled Felix O'Neill. He and O'Mahony also succeeded in changing Charles Kickham's mind after he rebuffed Stephens's offer.[85]

Great secrecy was observed, as nationalists in each town recommended others living further afield to Stephens 'and so, the good cause spread'.[86] In May 1858 James O'Mahony of Bandon directed him to Donal Óg McCartie of Skibbereen, a leading member of the Phoenix National and Literary Society, founded in 1856. Jeremiah O'Donovan Rossa had chosen the name of this mythological bird, which rises from its own ashes. The fifty members of the Phoenix Society hoped to revive the nation after the Famine. Stephens swore in McCartie, who informed Rossa that Irish-Americans would help them win independence with an invasion force of 5–10,000 men and sufficient arms for the fighters at home.[87]

Until 1853 Rossa had worked in the shop of Mortimer Downing of Kenmare and Skibbereen, a relation and former Young Irelander. Patrick and Denis, two of Downing's sons and Rossa's close friends, joined the IRB along-side Mortimer Moynahan. The latter was the chief clerk of Timothy McCarthy Downing, a lawyer, whose initial client interviews he conducted, while sizing up recruits and swearing them into the IRB at night.[88] Rossa, Moynihan and MacCartie, the West Cork leaders, approached prospective members at community events. In Skibbereen, for instance, Rossa joined a funeral to speak to Corly-Batt McCarthy-Sowney, an influential older man. Near the entrance to Abbeystrewery Cemetery was an unmarked mass grave, where a boy, appar-ently dead, had moaned during the Famine when struck by the gravedigger's spade and been rescued. Lame for life, 'Johnny Collins' became the Skibbereen workhouse messenger. McCarthy-Sowney joined the Fenian movement in this emotive place. He owned a mill between Drimoleague and Bantry and delegated his teenage grandson to swear in the sons of farmers, who brought grain to their mill.[89] Visiting Ireland in December 1860, John O'Mahony was very impressed with McCarthy-Sowney, who wanted his lands back, as well as compensation for 200 years of rent paid.[90]

Bitter memories of Cromwellian confiscations and impoverishing fines imposed on Catholics, who refused to attend the Protestant church, fuelled Fenianism. Rossa, McCartie and Moynahan 'enrolled into the movement many of the most influential farmers' in West Cork, for they wanted men who could persuade their neighbourhoods to join an insurrection.[91] It is likely that Rossa incorporated the remnants of agrarian societies, decimated by the Famine, given the number of small farmers enrolled. This was certainly the case in Connacht, where Rossa assisted Edward Duffy in converting Ribbonmen to the IRB some years later. In Clare, Edmond O'Donovan forged such links in the Tulla district.[92] Rossa concluded, rather optimistically, that within a few months they had obtained 3000 members. Stephens and Rossa also organized in Kenmare, where William Steuart Trench managed Lord Lansdowne's estate. The locals appeared cowed by the agent's system of spies and IRB progress was modest, although supported by E.F. Donnelly and Humphrey Murphy, leaders of a recent tenant revolt against Trench.[93]

While Stephens and Luby toured the country during the summer of 1858, established 'circles' were disintegrating, lacking 'communication and supervision', as the promised funds from New York failed to arrive. Stephens resolved to travel to America to regularize support.[94] During the difficult early years, Luby and O'Leary believed that Stephens's charismatic leadership was vital, 'for without him nothing could have been done, and with him everything was done that could well be done under the circumstances'.[95] Denieffe recalled:

> At this time Stephens was at the highest notch in my estimation. He was grand. I would undertake anything for him. He seemed to have me under a spell. He was the only practical man I had met in the movement up to that time. ... He was abstemious, frugal – in fact, in adversity his greatest qualities were shown to perfection. He was all that could be desired as a leader.[96]

To maintain secrecy, the organization had adopted a European cell system and the first four letters of the alphabet denoted IRB rank: an 'A' was a colonel or 'centre' of a Fenian 'circle'; a 'B' was a 'sub-centre' or captain and a 'C' a sergeant, while the ordinary foot soldiers were 'Ds'. In theory a potential leader would set up his 'circle' by recruiting nine 'Bs', who each swore in nine 'Cs', who in turn would enlist nine 'Ds', resulting in a unit of 820 men. In reality, however, the size of 'circles' varied considerably.[97]

The cell structure and custom of swearing in members on a prayer book were reminiscent of the United Irishmen. The authorities began to treat men arrested with such an item as IRB organizers. The Fenian oath was administered with great stealth in the backrooms of public houses, sheds and fields:[98]

> No witness of the taking of the oath was ever present. Only the man who administered the oath and the man who took it could give definite information of the act, and no member was supposed to know any other man in the circle outside his own section, numbering not more than ten. The first rule, the swearing in, was always strictly adhered to, but the other was utterly disregarded. Every man knew all the members of his own circle and practically those of every other circle in the town. And the organization would not have grown so rapidly were it not for that fact. Touching elbows with fellow members at public demonstrations and having 'a pint' with others was a great factor.[99]

That each officer should know only his immediate superior and the nine men he had sworn in was illusory in a close-knit Irish context. For the proposed insurrection, Fenian recruits would have to act in concert, which meant assembling in groups. Former Young Ireland members were accustomed to patriotic songs, conviviality and outings to heritage sites. This built confidence through brotherhood and broke down the customary deference towards the upper classes and clergy, whose pretensions to regulate such activities were rejected by the IRB. Perfect secrecy was conceivable only among a dedicated core. The early leadership consisted of survivors of 1848–9, who had avoided emigration, and young idealists of limited means. Traumatized by the Famine, followers betrayed their uncertainty by a lack of discretion, surrounded by the majority, who accepted contemporary reality.[100]

Cheap railway excursions enabled the masses to attend public events. The consecration of a church in Kilkenny, for instance, was utilized by the Fenians, who kept their men massed separately from the crowd and introduced the regional leaders to each other to encourage them. [101]

The earliest reference to sport as a cover for seditious activity dates to a hurling match in the barony of Clanwilliam, Tipperary, in 1666. The Munster IRB adopted this method, ostensibly playing football, 'but really to accustom the men to act in bodies' for the Rising.[102] Cricket served a similar purpose: in October 1864 excursionists from Carrick-on-Suir and Clonmel and groups from Kilkenny and Mullinahone assembled in Callan before continuing to Dunamaggin for a match. Two hundred Fenian visitors and 800 locals picnicked under the leadership of Rody Kickham of Mullinahone, Edward Coyne, James Cody and 'a butcher from Callan named Lanigan'.[103] As magistrates and police had been alerted, the planned meeting was abandoned.

The Phoenix Arrests

The relationship between Stephens, this 'most autocratic of democrats', and the other heirs to the Young Ireland tradition was tense.[104] The nexus of Sullivans and Healys, while recalling historical dispossession and the Famine, considered Fenian methods unrealistic and remained convinced that clerical opposition would abort IRB efforts. Widespread poverty facilitated the authorities when offering rewards for information. The Sullivan brothers argued that membership of a secret organization sufficed to convict, while evidence of overt treason was required for constitutional agitation.[105]

During the summer of 1858, A.M. Sullivan, editor of the *Nation*, visited Bantry, his birthplace, where it was whispered that he, Smith O'Brien and Mitchel were leaders of the Phoenix Society. Although Sullivan had rejected Stephens's advances, many locals disbelieved his public denial as tactics. Sullivan derided the secrecy practised by the conspirators as 'absurdly inefficient'.[106] By 16 September the local resident magistrate was gathering information and on 4 October Sir Thomas Larcom heard from William Steuart Trench that 3000 persons had joined the Phoenix Society in Skibbereen and 700 in Kenmare. John Caulfield, sub-inspector of police in Bantry, commented that the conspirators were keeping 'alive a spirit of hatred to the English crown and government' since 1847. They were procuring weapons and received funding from America. Caulfield believed that A.M. Sullivan hoped to be prosecuted, as this would increase the circulation of the *Nation*, which was barely breaking even.[107]

Fr John O'Sullivan, parish priest of Kenmare, wrote privately to Lord Mayo, the chief secretary, on 5 October, informing him that 'an extensive conspiracy was being organized' from Bantry and Skibbereen.[108] Although its membership had been greatly exaggerated, Fr O'Sullivan denounced the Phoenix club and pressurized a young man into revealing its oath, which he enclosed. He learned the names of members and, with the help of their parents, convinced these youths to withdraw. He may also have tried to curry favour with Lord Lansdowne, as he hoped to build a convent in Kenmare.[109] Bishop Moriarty instructed Fr O'Sullivan to 'warn the people' and he and the priests of Bantry and Skibbereen condemned seditious activities from 3 October on. Fr O'Sullivan's intervention proved decisive in halting the conspiracy in Kerry, but when he pleaded for clemency for the Phoenix boys, Dublin Castle ignored him.[110]

As the authorities took this affair seriously, Bishop Moriarty urged A.M. Sullivan to publish sensible advice. On 25 October Sullivan consulted with William Smith O'Brien, the subject having been discussed in the press. The latter announced in the *Nation* that he had never joined a conspiracy, considering it counterproductive. Sullivan agreed, urging idealistic youngsters to withdraw from the 'mischievous' plot.[111] This formed the basis for Stephens's subsequent denunciation of Sullivan as a 'felon-setter'.[112]

During September William Hort, R.M., investigated inconclusive rumours that a 'democratic association' was being organized in Callan, Co. Kilkenny, which had apparently been more successful in Carrick-on-Suir and Mullinahone. On 31 October Fr John Salmon, parish priest of Callan, urged magistrates to intervene during Mass.[113] On 7 November the congregation in Ballingarry, Co. Tipperary, was told that if Fr Philip Fitzgerald, who had witnessed the 1848 insurrection at Farrenrory, or his curate heard that any of them were involved in sedition, the authorities would be informed. The clergy was alert to whisperings of conspiracy, 'particularly in the towns in the south of Ireland' and warned: 'They might think of '48 – what destruction they caused on themselves ... And that the Commons was the laughing stock of all Ireland and that Mr Smith O'Brine [sic] was the laughing stock of all the people of England and that they were directed by their bishop to denounce from the church any person who would join any such society and not to give them the rites of their church.'[114]

On 3 December Dublin Castle issued a proclamation that secret societies existed in Ireland, offering rewards for information. Within days, thirty Phoenix men were detained in Skibbereen, Bantry, Killarney, Kenmare and Macroom. It emerged that a spy had infiltrated their organization. Newspaper reports described those arrested as respectable, if misguided young men with 'at least a good English education'.[115] Three of the Phoenix leaders worked as clerks for Timothy McCarthy Downing of Skibbereen, who also came under suspicion. In Kenmare, Steuart Trench rejoiced that few tenant farmers were involved, as the conspirators consisted mostly of tradesmen, shop assistants and clerks. There was a notable exception: Florence O'Sullivan Jr, a trainee apothecary in Killarney, was the son of a middleman in Kenmare.[116]

The *Times* condemned 'this confederation of fools', which aimed for 'an invasion of Ireland by American filibusters' and demanded action from the government. It opined that the Famine had benefited Ireland as the 'helpless portion of the population', which previously 'rendered improvement impossible', was removed by 'death or emigration' and a redistribution of property and new investment had taken place.[117] The Famine had succeeded in subduing 'the aspirations of the Irish nation to a degree never known before ... The people ... were enfeebled bodily and mentally by the dreadful struggle they had passed through.'[118] It took years to restore their confidence.

The *Times* blamed the ungrateful Irish:

How deep-rooted are the evils with which we have striven to contend, and how ill the race in whose destiny we are so deeply interested profits by the opportunities of prosperity or the teaching of adversity. Time was when England, in the plentitude of ignorant generosity, was willing to take upon herself the blame of spendthrift landlords and barbarous peasants, of the recklessness, the extravagance, and the folly of centuries ... If the Irish cannot be content with their lot, the fault we are now convinced is theirs, not ours.[119]

This editorial displayed profound incomprehension, considering 'priests and people' systematically opposed to 'regeneration', while attributing the clergy's dismay at Famine deaths and emigration to their loss of income. The *Times* believed Catholic practices like holy days a distraction 'from the details of daily labour' in the modern world.

Martin Hawe, a respectable but almost bankrupt leather merchant, was one of the leaders in Kilkenny. He had sworn in Patrick Callaghan, a clerk with the Slieveardagh Mining Company, on a visit to Callan in the summer of 1858. Callaghan, a lukewarm member, became alarmed when Fr Salmon, the parish priest, refused to hear his confession and turned informer.[120] Hawe, Coyne, Thomas Mangan and William Kavanagh, two nailsmiths of Callan, and Denis ('Denny') O'Sullivan, a national school teacher in Ballydonnell, Co. Tipperary, were among those arrested on 3 January. The last named was the Callan-born grand-nephew of the Gaelic diarist Humphrey O'Sullivan. Given local sympathy with them, Fr Salmon restrained a protesting crowd when the prisoners were removed to jail.[121] Resident Magistrate Hort and the Earl of Desart conducted an inquiry, but Callaghan knew little of importance, apart from having taken an oath 'to renounce all allegiance to the queen of England ... and fight at a moment's warning, to make Ireland an independent democratic Republic'; all except Hawe were soon released.[122]

Fr Salmon continued to denounce secret societies and founded a Christian men's association with 150 members, who were to read religious books under his supervision. (It soon became moribund as the IRB revived.) The constabulary considered the Phoenix Society almost defunct by 12 December 1858, largely due to the priest's intervention. The arrests halted Fenian recruitment in Nenagh, where 'respectable' former Young Irelanders had been approached. One leader confided to the police that they could now abandon this 'foolish and insane project'. By 16 January 1859, Fitzmaurice, R.M. for Skibbereen, was convinced that all was over, as Stephens, the leading organizer, had fled abroad.[123] The *Times* agreed: 'The Phoenix Association, if it ever existed, has been crushed, not by the arrest of a few young men, but by the combined force of public opinion, and the unanimous declaration against it of the most patriotic men in Ireland.'[124]

The evidence against Jeremiah O'Donovan Rossa, Patrick and Denis Downing, William O'Shea, Mortimer Moynahan and companions was slight, but they continued to be detained.[125] Some were released on bail and visited Queenstown (now Cobh) to meet Baron Poeri and the Neapolitan revolutionaries of 1848. Sent into American exile by the King of the Two Sicilies, they had seized their ship to land in Cobh before continuing to England to a hero's welcome. Rossa contrasted his treatment with British adulation for foreign nationalists.[126]

The jury at the first trial of schoolmaster Daniel O'Sullivan Agreem in Tralee failed to agree. Catholic jurors were excluded from the second prosecution in March 1859. The defendant dismissed his counsel in protest and was found guilty and sentenced to ten years amidst a general outcry against jury-packing, which abandoned a precept of the liberal state. Bishop Moriarty of Kerry, expressing 'abhorrence and contempt' for the Phoenix Society, interceded for some suspects and John David Fitzgerald, the attorney general, felt Dublin Castle should oblige, 'for we owe to him mainly the exposure and suppression' of these conspirators.[127]

Stephens in America, 1858–9

Mitchel, Doheny and O'Mahony persisted with their devotion to an idealized concept of Irish independence. Doheny, however, had developed a drink problem. He wrote to William Smith O'Brien that autumn, convinced of having sacrificed financial success for 'the old hope and old cause and I now busy myself in endeavouring to reanimate the Gaelic'. O'Mahony was his closest friend: 'We eat away our hearts in bitter memories and bitterer hopes.'[128] The *Nation* reported about 'the Irish exiles':

> Michael Doheny resides on Long Island, and divides his brain between law and literature. He is an exceedingly able man, a fast friend, and a forcible enemy. He has had great experience in politics, and is a powerful and ready speaker... He also, I understand, in conjunction with John O'Mahony, conducts the Gaelic department of that journal [the *Irish-American*]. This is quite a feature. We have the original Gaelic side by side with the English translation, and accompanied with such notes as the patient research and accumulated knowledge of O'Mahony can alone present.[129]

The *Nation* praised O'Mahony's recent, scholarly translation of Seathrún Céitinn's *Foras feasa ar Éirinn*, but failed to mention his introduction, denouncing Dublin Castle and its 'killing by famine'. The paper alluded to Richard O'Gorman's successful legal career, blessed by 'the goddess of fortune, dressed with briefs and ribboned with red tape'.[130] Doheny reflected despondently:

I would like to be gay and happy but I cannot. My days are becoming shorter and shorter and between me and the night hope is fast disappearing and a dark horizon closing in and in. Oh! It is a sad sad thing to be thus descending the hill, so far away from all the sympathies that fed and fired one's youth. It is a terrible thought that one must lie down to sleep at last in foreign soil. And yet methinks that with me at least it is better so. I doubt if I could sustain the sight of Ireland now.[131]

Stephens hoped to access the fund collected during 1848, part of which had been used for legal expenses and in facilitating the leaders' escape from Van Diemen's Land. It was administered by a directory of Young Ireland exiles, including Meagher and Judge Emmet. Mitchel had settled in Knoxville, Tennessee, and founded the *Southern Citizen*, which serialized *The Last Conquest of Ireland (Perhaps)* during 1858–9. Stephens approached Meagher and Mitchel, recommended by Fr Kenyon if not the influential John Blake Dillon.[132]

James Stephens (courtesy NLI).

Mitchel recalled that Stephens demanded that he and Meagher should head the organization in the US to appeal for money 'and remit all to him. This was cool. I questioned him closely upon the progress he had made in Ireland; and he had assured me that he had *then* (nine years ago) 15,000 sworn confederates (they were not called Fenians) all armed with rifles. I did not believe him.'[133]

When Meagher and Mitchel met Stephens again in Washington, he peremptorily demanded that they join his conspiracy. Disbelieving this 'most plausible gentleman', who pronounced himself 'the only representative and standard-bearer of the Irish national cause', and with the British Empire at peace, the Young Irelanders felt that their fund would be wasted. They 'arrived at the conclusion at which many others have since arrived, that he was a *humbug*'.[134] The interview terminated when Stephens lectured Mitchel and Meagher on their national duty. Stephens and Mitchel 'seem to have been mutually repellent from the beginning', despite their shared contempt for constitutionalism. Having failed to win over any senior 1848 leader, the money remained out of Stephens's reach to intensify his antagonism towards the old *Nation* elite.[135]

News of the Phoenix arrests constituted a transatlantic setback and the IRB's financial resources remained modest up to 1864, when only £1500 had been received from America. From 1864–6 the Fenian Brotherhood sent £32,500, of which £7000 was seized by Dublin Castle. The conspiracy was run on £25,500 and the voluntary contributions of its Irish members. On the North American continent less than £100,000 was collected, an inadequate sum when compared to the funds at the disposal of the British.[136]

In spite of his customary inability to appreciate the talent of others, Stephens believed, 'since the day I became a soldier of liberty', that O'Mahony was the most outstanding patriot, whose intellectual gifts and devotion to the nation qualified him as Stephens's potential successor. Both men were democrats, according to Stephens:

> In a word, the only countries I recognize over the earth are toil and privilege; the one of these I shall struggle for, the other against, with all the faculties of my being, while I can exercise them. O'M's [O'Mahony's] love of universal justice is not less than mine, and he would willingly battle for it in any land; but if it came to the case put, between England and Ireland, he should tear up and cast away from him the most sacred treasures of his soul to bring himself to do what I could do so easily.[137]

Stephens felt irritated by the leadership ambitions of many Irish-Americans, whom he considered mediocrities at best. Nevertheless, they appointed him 'chief executive of the Irish revolutionary movement' with 'supreme control and absolute authority over that movement *at home and abroad*' and he, in turn, made O'Mahony his American deputy in January 1859:[138]

> I ... hereby appoint John O'Mahony, formerly of Kilbenny [sic] County Limerick, and of Mullough, near Carrick on Suir, Ireland, supreme organizer and director of said IRB in America. *With him alone as chief centre shall any communication be held from home*, and I hereby notify to the members of the Brotherhood in America, *that any one writing to Ireland* after having been made acquainted with this order, *shall be looked on and treated as a traitor.*[139]

The scholarly O'Mahony was familiar with the Gaelic tales of Fionn Mac Cumhaill and the Fianna, a band of warriors sworn to protect Ireland, associated with Slievenamon in Co. Tipperary. Another probable inspiration was O'Mahony's friend John O'Daly, founder of the Ossianic Society, which published the Fianna poems.[140] O'Mahony called the US wing of the revolutionary movement the 'Fenian Brotherhood', a name set to capture the popular imagination, making it synonymous with Irish separatism. Doheny received no appointment, which must have rankled. A democratic organization, the Brotherhood administered a pledge instead of an oath:[141]

> I ... solemnly pledge my sacred word of honour, as a truthful and honest man, that I will labour with earnest zeal for the liberation of Ireland from the yoke of England, and for the establishment of a free and independent government on Irish soil; that I will implicitly obey the commands of my superior officers in the Fenian Brotherhood; that I will faithfully discharge the duties of membership as laid down in the constitutions and bye-laws thereof; that I will do my utmost to promote feelings of love, harmony, and kindly forbearance among all Irishmen; and that I will foster, defend and propagate the aforesaid Fenian Brotherhood to the utmost of my power.[142]

O'Mahony, the 'head centre', described his American organization as 'neither anti-Catholic nor irreligious. We are an Irish army, not a secret society,' but met with opposition from the Catholic Church. His task was to enrol men and collect funds for an invasion of Ireland. In 1848 Doheny had been a regional leader and O'Mahony an influential gentleman, while Stephens was an unknown recruit, yet he contrived to dominate Fenianism from the outset.[143]

In December 1858 the Foreign Office requested information about possible Irish plots, 'especially the alleged intention of a regiment of militia to make a seditious excursion to Ireland'.[144] Consul Edward Archibald wrote from New York that the Irish poor supported these schemes 'to gratify anti-English feelings' and a few made a living by administrating such funds. On 21 March 1859 Archibald reported that the St Patrick's Day celebrations had showcased the political importance of the Irish and collections were made for imprisoned members of the Phoenix Society. The conspirators lacked a definite plan of action, unless England was drawn into an international war. In May, Archibald stated that some of the Phoenix men, 'of whom James Stephens (alias "Shook" or "Shuke") is undoubtedly one', were in New York. The 69th Regiment had paraded in their honour and Doheny spoke, more violently than reported in the press.[145]

Thomas Clarke Luby (courtesy NLI).

Convinced that the IRB would receive regular subsidies henceforth, Stephens concluded his organizing tour and left with donations of £600 in gold. But suspecting that O'Mahony lacked the crucial skills and ruthlessness for successful leadership, Stephens made a decision, which would prove disastrous. He decided to appoint a deputy leader:[146] 'O'Mahony must swear to remain here till we are up at home; and I must also swear him not to allow any man to force him to give up his position. The supreme control over the organization in America I have already given him. An active man by his side would enable him to make this effective. Who can I appoint?'[147] His doubts were shared by A.M. Sullivan, who described O'Mahony as engaged in 'Gaelic studies, and lived and dreamed a great deal in ancient Ireland', rather than developing Irish-American networks to increase his influence.[148] On arrival in France, Stephens consulted with O'Leary and Luby, instructing the latter to replace the IRB vow of secrecy with a promise to obey one's officer, who would immediately command silence. This calmed the religious scruples of members after the Phoenix arrests, allowing them to claim that they did not belong to a secret society.[149] The 'Paris' version of the oath ran: 'I, AB, in the presence of Almighty God, do solemnly swear allegiance to the Irish Republic, now virtually established; and that I will do my very utmost, at every risk, while life lasts, to defend its independence and integrity; and, finally, that I will yield implicit obedience in all things, not contrary to the laws of God, to the commands of my superior officers. So help me God! Amen.'[150]

In characteristically buoyant style, Stephens claimed that the IRB was holding its own despite the recent debacle and castigated their American critics, writing to O'Mahony: 'Who will be base enough to say now that these men – our brothers – are not to be relied on. Cowardly slaves and knaves alone believe it. Let God be thanked for the day on which you and I, and a few other intelligent men, decided on taking our stand, come weal or woe, by the people of Ireland! The woe, I firmly believe, has passed away forever: the weal is coming fast, with laurels and the songs of triumph!'[151] Such florid rhetoric was accompanied by exhortations that 'to produce anything better than disastrous massacre [of an insurrection], a good deal must be done on your side'.[152]

The 'head centre' was to obtain numerous letters of introduction to meet people and impress audiences during his forthcoming tour. Knowing how careless O'Mahony was about his appearance, Stephens 'commanded' him to dress smartly. He also decided that donations should be transmitted via John O'Leary, despatched to assist O'Mahony during the summer of 1859.[153]

A.M. Sullivan raised subscriptions in the *Nation* to provide lawyers for the Phoenix detainees. In early 1859 Stephens and his Irish-American supporters started the 'Irish patriotic defence fund' to support revolutionary activities with O'Mahony as treasurer, but its ambiguous name misled the public into believing they were helping the prisoners. P.J. Meehan, the Limerick-born editor of the influential *Irish-American* newspaper, and T.D. Sullivan, its Dublin correspondent, exposed Stephens's duplicity. O'Mahony, always sensitive when truth and honour were concerned, broke off his recruiting tour to return to New York, where O'Leary witnessed 'the horrible anguish inflicted on O'Mahony by these accusations and insinuations', which were detrimental to the Fenian Brotherhood.[154]

O'Mahony detested the disunity prevalent since the death of Daniel O'Connell: every leader maintained his own set, 'an incongruous and bickering mass of discordant factions', fighting for supremacy; he felt entitled to command after his family's sacrifices since 1798 and his own 'persistent and continuous action'. O'Mahony responded to A.M. Sullivan's accusations that the Phoenix sympathizers had been misled into believing him a protagonist, 'the low bred fool! What use would his name be anywhere.' The 'head centre' was unwittingly stoking the very dissensions he deplored.[155]

John O'Leary (courtesy NLI).

By July the Co. Cork Phoenix prisoners had been detained for eight months. Dublin Castle, believing that the evidence was slight and the movement petering out, repeated its offer that in return for pleading guilty, these detainees and Daniel O'Sullivan, the only one convicted, would be liberated. From the safety of Paris, Stephens ordered the prisoners to reject any arrangement involving an admission of guilt. This message failed to reach Rossa, Mortimer Moynahan and William O'Shea, who accepted the offer, believing that the Cork IRB suffered from terminal 'disorganization'.[156]

They were freed by the newly elected Liberal government under Lord Palmerston. William O'Shea and Patrick Downing emigrated to the US, where they continued their Fenian commitment. In Skibbereen, Rossa's shop had failed. A.M. Sullivan believed that swift suppression in West Cork, Kerry and Callan exposed the Phoenix Society as a paltry affair and 'many treated it with great derision'. Dublin Castle remained ignorant of its full ramifications and Robert Anderson, an advisor on Fenianism, became convinced that lack of diligence at the highest level allowed Ireland to drift into conspiracy.[157]

The collapse of the movement should have followed. It says much for the animus of Famine exiles and the self-confidence of members at home that the IRB did not enter a final decline, for Edward Coyne, Martin Hawe, Denis O'Sullivan, Dan McCartie and Jeremiah O'Donovan Rossa were among those who stealthily resumed revolutionary activities.[158]

Since the Young Ireland leaders declined to support him, Stephens instructed Luby to spread his version of the negotiations with Mitchel and Meagher and to brand A.M. Sullivan a 'felon-setter' – an individual who alerted the authorities to dedicated patriots, causing their arrest. The IRB learned to consider Sullivan a second 'Sullivan Goula', named after the Phoenix informer. The editor of the *Nation*, a rival for the leadership of the nationalist community, was henceforth hounded. Stephens treated 'the Young Ireland party' as enemies, illustrating his inability to cooperate with equals or analyse the failings of his organization.[159]

The IRB attempted to harness the distress and bitterness of post-Famine communities outside the British jurisdiction. But while Stephens complained about inadequate contributions, O'Mahony required funds to build up his Brotherhood. By 1860 the organization was still unknown in rural America and lacked support in the cities of the Midwest. Middle-class people showed little interest, others had become cynical about freeing Ireland, their hopes having been raised several times in vain. O'Mahony and Doheny tried to stimulate interest through their newspaper, the *Phoenix*, but headed a tiny group in comparison to the Ancient Order of Hibernians, for instance. They had to satisfy demanding constituents and operated more democratically than Stephens.[160]

O'Mahony sent a series of envoys to monitor progress in Ireland. James Cantwell, a native of Tipperary who had been present on the Commons in Ballingarry in 1848, was among Stephens's inner circle in New York. By March 1860, however, his presence led to friction. Cantwell described the 'considerable disorganization' of the IRB, though Stephens exhibited an '*iron will* and thorough confidence' to hold it together 'under any circumstances for seven years if necessary'.[161] Tensions continued and in August Luby informed O'Mahony of the irritation of IRB men in Munster with 'the great promises and little performance' of their American allies, who 'seem so ready to censure shortcomings', which they themselves had caused. Responding to critics like John Mitchel, Stephens prompted Luby to collect the signatures of twenty-five 'centres' in Ireland, expressing confidence in 'James [Stephens] and John [O'Mahony]', which were sent to New York. It confirmed that support for the early IRB was located in Munster and Leinster. However, ground had been lost in north Tipperary and Waterford.[162]

Table 1. *Signatories to a vote of confidence in Stephens and O'Mahony, August 1860*

Leader	Location	Co.
Peter Langan	Dublin	Dublin
Thomas C. Luby	Dublin	Dublin
Joseph Denieffe	Dublin	Dublin
Charles Beggs	Dublin	Dublin
John Haltigan	Kilkenny city	Kilkenny
Martin Hawe	Kilkenny city	Kilkenny
Edward Coyne	Callan	Kilkenny
Thomas Purcell	Bray	Wicklow
James W. Dillon	Wicklow town	Wicklow
Brian Dillon	Cork city	Cork
William O'Carroll	Cork city	Cork
James O'Mahony	Bandon	Cork
T. P. O'Connor	Laffana	Cork
Eugene McSwiney	Tomes, Macroom	Cork
Daniel McCartie	Skibbereen	Cork
Mortimer Moynahan	Skibbereen	Cork
O'Donovan Rossa	Skibbereen	Cork
Denis O'Shea	Kenmare	Kerry
Michael Comerford	Newtown, Carrick-on-Suir	Tipperary
John O'Kavanagh	Carrick-on-Suir	Tipperary
Denis D. Mulcahy	Redmondstown, Clonmel	Tipperary
James O'Connell	Clonmel	Tipperary
William O'Connor	Grange, Clonmel	Tipperary
William Butler	Waterford city	Waterford
Thomas Hickey	Coolnamuck	Waterford
Total: 25	Munster: 16	Leinster: 9

(Source: *Rossa's Recollections*, 297–8)

In November 1860 Cantwell wrote to O'Mahony from Templemore that the IRB had potential, but was badly managed and required money. Hoping for a European war next spring, he urged that preparations 'must commence *at once*', otherwise the home organization could collapse, except for 'some super-human effort which I cannot see'.[163]

Alerted to the Phoenix conspiracy, Dublin Castle sent Sub-Inspector Thomas Doyle of the constabulary to covertly monitor Irish communities in New York, Boston, Philadelphia, Pittsburgh and Cincinnati until January 1861. He concluded that only a minority contemplated insurrection, as 90 per cent considered this hopeless, although many felt deep hatred towards England and the landlord class. 'Irresponsible' militia associations had been drilling for years, according to Doyle. In 1860 Colonel Doheny claimed 25,000 trained members in the US, which was a gross exaggeration. Nor were the majority of Irishmen in New York supporters:[164]

> If John O'Mahony could muster strength he would, I am convinced, be willing enough to encounter risk to hazard his own life in the attempt to become the Garibaldi of Ireland. But he is without strength or adequate resources: the Fenians who would go to Ireland are comparatively few and there are thousands of the Irish race in their country who do not look upon the movement as deserving of serious consideration.[165]

Fenian balls and excursions served to keep up interest and raise funds. In November 1860, for instance, Doheny lectured in Boston, accompanied by Colonel Corcoran and 150 unarmed members, who paraded with a military band and American flags. The policeman predicted that some Irishmen would join a Rising regardless of success, but unless Britain became involved in a war, the Fenian Brotherhood seemed 'doomed to die out'. Nor did O'Mahony contemplate an invasion of Canada.[166]

The Papal Brigade

In 1859–60 British statesmen and newspapers affirmed the right of Italians to choose their own government, advocating that they should rise or be despised as 'men who do nothing but howl and shriek in their fetters'.[167] During this politically unstable period, Piedmont-Sardinia with its ally, Napoleon III of France, defeated the Austrian Empire. In 1860 Garibaldi invaded the Kingdom of the Two Sicilies and marched on the Papal States. English volunteers participated, but enthusiasm for Italian revolution was underpinned by evangelical Protestantism and opposition to Roman Catholicism. One thousand Irish volunteers rushed to defend the Pope's temporal power, illustrating their close identification with the Catholic Church, although it blocked Italian unity. After a brief campaign, members of the Papal Brigade, including Rody Kickham of Mullinahone and John Gleeson of Borrisoleigh, were rapturously welcomed home.[168]

In an age of restricted male suffrage, plebiscites were used to voice popular concerns. Given British support for Italian self-determination, Irish nationalists decided to 'take England at her word'. On 14 April 1860 A.M. Sullivan inaugurated the national petition, assisted by Daniel O'Donoghue, the nationalist MP for Tipperary. It appealed to Queen Victoria for a referendum on the restoration of the Irish Parliament, defunct since the Act of Union in 1801. This plebiscite was infiltrated by IRB canvassers, eager to gain recruits. One of them was John Kenealy, whose father had been among thousands of farmers threatened with ruin after the collapse of Sadleir's bank. As a teenager, Kenealy migrated from the Kanturk district to Cork to learn the clothing trade. By 1860 he was a commercial traveller, met Stephens, rejected constitutionalism and became an IRB leader in Cork with contacts in London, Liverpool and Manchester. The petition movement attracted energetic young men, often employees of the large drapery stores in Dublin. Some had arrived from Munster, already sworn into the Brotherhood.[169]

Bold Fenian Men, 1861–5

On return from New York, Stephens pleaded various excuses to remain in Paris, while Luby represented him in Ireland. In late 1860 O'Mahony arrived in the French capital, anxious to assess the condition of the IRB and for Stephens to resume organizing.[1] O'Mahony proceeded to Dublin, where he risked arrest for his 1848 activities. The 'head centre' met Luby, John Martin and Fr John Kenyon of Templederry, who had just returned from visiting Mitchel in Paris. Fr Kenyon detested Stephens and preferred Luby to conspire under O'Mahony, their mutual friend. Mitchel, too, distrusted Stephens 'as incapable of telling the truth' and considered Fenianism 'a fraud'.[2]

In Dublin, Luby introduced the 'head centre' to his new recruits, for until recently there were only fifty followers in the capital; artisans and former Young Irelanders, whom Denieffe had enlisted in 1855. Cornelius O'Mahony, a national school teacher from Co. Cork who was attending a training course in Dublin, introduced Luby to James Joseph O'Connell O'Callaghan of Kanturk. A shop assistant in Arnotts, O'Callaghan was to become a leading IRB recruiter to form a Dublin 'circle' of 1100 Fenians. Enterprising men were in demand as assistants in the new department stores, but lacking capital and higher education, could rarely advance much further up the social ladder.[3]

Luby escorted O'Mahony to Kilkenny, which was likely to impress as a Fenian hub. He met the leaders in Cork, including William O'Carroll and James

O'Mahony of Bandon, an enthusiastic Gaelic scholar, who accompanied him
to Skibbereen, where O'Donovan Rossa and the West Cork men expressed
dissatisfaction with the lack of progress. These 'conceited leading spirits of the
Skibbereen school' confirmed O'Mahony's discontent with the management of
the IRB. West of Bantry the Fenian advance was permanently stalled, due to the
vigilance of Fr John O'Sullivan of Kenmare.[4]

O'Mahony also consulted with Denis Dowling Mulcahy, whose father had
been a comrade since 1848, and Charles Kickham.[5] The *Nation* reported his
arrival in Carrick: 'John O'Mahony, esq, arrived on Saturday at eight o'clock p.m.,
at his sister's residence, Mrs Mandeville, Ballyquirkeen House, near Carrick-on-
Suir, attended Mass on Sunday last at Ballyneale Chapel. When Mass was over,
he was scarcely able to make his way out of the chapel from the immense number
of friends and lovers of liberty who flocked together to meet him.'[6]

O'Mahony tried to gain Luby's support for a restructuring of the IRB,
proposing a council of advisors to represent Stephens during absences. Luby,
ever the loyal lieutenant, declined to negotiate without 'the captain'. Stephens
eventually arrived, but instead of admitting that his two years abroad had
damaged their movement, blamed O'Mahony for failing 'to obey orders and
send over money'.[7] The latter responded ineffectually, whereupon Stephens
denounced 'his shortcomings, feebleness and insincerity and wound up by
reminding him how he, Stephens, had dragged him out of obscurity and put
him in a position he never dreamed of'.[8]

Stephens blundered when humiliating the proud 'head centre,' for such
incidents rankled.[9] Nevertheless, it was agreed that at least 5000 trained men
with officers were needed as a nucleus for the army of liberation, with 50,000
rifles to equip the IRB. A fixed deadline had been abandoned, acknowledging
the immense obstacles to be overcome. David Sim concluded that during these
pervasive disputes the IRB perceived itself as an economic victim of the Fenian
Brotherhood, its paymaster, which felt entitled to direct policy.[10]

O'Mahony returned to New York, where the Civil War had broken out in
April 1861, dividing the Brotherhood into Federal and Confederate combatants. Stephens was slow to keep the 'head centre' informed. O'Mahony, far
more accountable as a leader, fretted about progress and remained vulnerable
to criticism. Having only Stephens's wildly optimistic letters to rely upon, he
sent further envoys.[11]

O'Mahony was an idealist and scholar who never adopted American values,
based on material success, and lacked the necessary ruthlessness to dominate the
Brotherhood. O'Mahony realized that upholding separatist goals against the
triumphant British Empire would be a long struggle. He was inspired, according

to Stephens, by: 'The memories of times gone by and hallowed by the deeds of the men of his blood, the language, the literature, the monuments, speak to him as to no other. The study of these – the spur to which, in other men, is distinction or material recompense – in him finds ample motive and guerdon in this passionate love.'[12]

Mitchel expressed approval of the movement in May 1861, but warned O'Mahony that 'it is not so widely spread or so efficaciously armed and prepared as you would wish, and as I would wish – but still so far as it goes, and to the extent of the organization, it is good'.[13]

Mitchel described his meeting with Daniel O'Donoghue, 'The O'Donoghue of the Glens', in Boulogne. This promising MP, a relative of the Liberator, had told Mitchel, that he would shortly present the national petition to queen and Parliament. If rejected, O'Donoghue mooted withdrawing from Westminster to found an organization, seek foreign aid and prepare for revolution. Mitchel believed in his sincerity and suggested cooperation to O'Mahony. O'Donoghue did not form a coalition with Stephens. The latter's intransigent attitude was a disincentive for talented leaders, as G.H. Moore also avoided collaborating with him.[14]

Infiltrating the National Brotherhood of St Patrick

On St Patrick's Day 1861 Thomas Neilson Underwood of Strabane, a barrister and descendant of a United Irishman, initiated the National Brotherhood of St Patrick. This constitutional society fostered social occasions of a patriotic kind and was intended as a meeting point for nationalists. Although popular, it lacked clearly defined aims and a strong leadership, making it vulnerable to infiltration. In Kilmallock, for instance, the Brotherhood consisted of fifty members. A minority wished to promote purely cultural aims, leading to their withdrawal from this society, which metamorphosed into the Kilmallock IRB.[15] In Tipperary town no organization existed prior to 1861, when schoolmaster Thomas Dogherty Brohan established a branch of the NBSP, inviting John O'Leary, the most prominent 1848 man, to become its figurehead. The latter expressed disdain about futile petitions for reform and suggested the Wolfe Tone approach, which if unsuccessful, was at least honourable. Brohan and his followers concurred and met Stephens, who initiated them into the IRB in the summer of 1861. Brohan proved a valuable organizer and subsequently wrote for the *Irish People*.[16]

In May 1861 the O'Donoghue presented the national petition of 423,026 signatures to Parliament. Canvassing such multitudes for support was a considerable achievement, but the government had little interest in Irish issues. Queen Victoria, who lacked sympathy for the Irish people, failed to exercise a unifying influence and ignored the petition. This played into the hands of Fenian organizers, who pointed to her 'contemptuous silence' as 'disdain for a people' who would not fight for their right to choose their government.[17]

IRB recruiting agents tended to exaggerate membership numbers. O'Connell O'Callaghan claimed, when enlisting John Devoy, that there were 15,000 Fenians in Tipperary and 20,000 in Cork. Devoy, however, considered figures of 3000 and 4000 more realistic.[18] Some, casually enrolled by friends, undoubtedly lacked commitment, but the Comerford thesis of 'patriotism as a pastime' appears unlikely, given the penalties. The semi-military constabulary, the vigilant eyes and ears of Dublin Castle, was distributed throughout the country and gathered information about anything unusual, for instance, the arrival of strangers. According to Superintendent Mallon, persistent shadowing to coerce suspects to either abandon Fenianism or leave the country was used from 1863. Employers were routinely alerted to the politics of their staff, resulting in the dismissal of IRB members, whose emigration increased disenchantment with the British state.[19]

Fenians resented the control that Dublin Castle and the Catholic Church exerted over their circumscribed lives. The authorities may have opposed these peer groups, fearing that increased self-confidence would lead to demands for greater rights. The charismatic Stephens projected visions of a more democratic Ireland, instead of stultifying middle-class domination or enforced emigration for dissidents.[20]

The McManus funeral

During the 1850s, nearly 60 per cent of the US army was made up of Irish immigrants. The Irish in the north perceived liberated African Americans as competition in the labour market, while the Catholic Church did not condemn slavery. Many Irish felt that slaves were better off than small farmers in the old country. Confederate residents constituted only 5 per cent of the Irish-born in America, but accepted slavery for economic reasons. Initially, there was a reluctance to enlist, although thousands defended the Union and earned citizenship with their blood. The American Civil War necessitated a postponement of the planned Fenian invasion.[21]

Stephens informed O'Mahony that he was not 'deluded by the lunatic dream, that a mob, however numerous' would spell success, but considered 100,000 trained men at home, whom he could arm with O'Mahony's help, a necessity for the Rising, combined with a Fenian Brotherhood contingent of a thousand at least. Stephens warned that until such forces were available, 'a descent on the Irish shores' would prove counterproductive.[22]

In San Francisco, an impoverished Young Irelander and boyhood friend of Charles Gavan Duffy died on 15 January 1861. Terence Bellew McManus had been a shipping agent in Liverpool, where he supported Repeal and later the Irish Confederation. Unexpectedly joining Smith O'Brien for the Rising, McManus sacrificed an income of £1000 p.a. Convicted of participation in the siege of the Widow McCormack's house, McManus had been transported to Tasmania, but escaped. He repudiated efforts to include him in a British pardon, preferring to die in exile as an unrepentant rebel.[23] Californian Fenians conceived the idea of returning his body to Ireland, possibly influenced by the magnificent reburial of Napoleon I in Paris or the Duke of Wellington's funeral procession to St Paul's, London, in 1852. The impressive obsequies of Daniel O'Connell in 1847 formed another precedent.[24]

The funeral project provided a focus for the Fenian Brotherhood, which was losing ground since the outbreak of, the Civil War. 'This may be made the turning point in our future,' O'Mahony believed. Stephens showed little interest initially, but Doheny, O'Mahony and Thomas Francis Meagher formed an 'obsequies committee' in New York. Meagher, a prestigious leader of the Irish-American community, approached Archbishop John Hughes, who agreed to preach a 'sermon, upholding the right of an oppressed people to struggle' for freedom in (old) St Patrick's Cathedral during the Requiem Mass.[25] 'Dagger' Hughes stressed that McManus died a good Catholic, but limited Fenian propaganda by ordering that the remains be stored in Calvary Cemetery in Brooklyn and not in the accessible cathedral downtown.[26]

O'Mahony marshalled thousands, who escorted the coffin like a 'great, silent army' to the steamer in a solemn procession of thirty-two pall-bearers with each representing an Irish county. Michael and Mary Jane Doheny, James Roche, Michael Cavanagh, Captain Frank Welpley, 69th New York National Guard and Captain Michael Smith were among the Fenian Brotherhood delegates from California and New York to accompany the remains. When Doheny saw the Irish coast rising out of the mist for the first time in thirteen years, he wept bitterly.[27]

William Delany, Bishop of Cork, blocked clerical participation in the funeral, but William Keane, his counterpart in Cloyne, permitted the use of the church in Cobh, which was draped in black. A local committee received the remains and the American escort on landing, surrounded by a vast crowd. Their address of welcome highlighted that Britain refused Ireland the right of selecting its government, while promoting this principle in Europe. An uprising and the hope that the Famine exiles might yet return were hinted at.[28]

In Cork city thousands paid their respects. An American reporter felt he was experiencing a revival of the Irish nation: 'The multitude that attended the funeral was more imposing for numbers, and of dignity and devotion than anything of the kind I ever witnessed in Ireland ... No such demonstration ever took place in Ireland since '48, and it was an index of anti-English feeling.'[29] Stephens estimated that 8000 men marched in Cork, with more than 80,000 onlookers, supported by the Cork trades' associations, which had been politically dormant since 1848. Rossa was deeply impressed and made contacts among the IRB from Kerry, Limerick, Tipperary and Waterford. At the railway station in Blackpool, 'the entire procession' marched past the coffin 'with heads uncovered', before the remains departed for Dublin.[30]

In July William O'Carroll had alerted O'Mahony to 'the frenzied movement' of Doheny and James Roche. Michael Cavanagh, O'Mahony's private secretary, warned Stephens that Michael and Mary Jane Doheny and Roche were intent on provoking an impromptu uprising by using a landmark as an emotional gathering point:[31] 'They thought it would arouse the country if the remains were taken to Slievenamon or some such historic place on the way between Cork and Dublin, and the people called upon to rally around, for God and for country.'[32]

Given that the IRB was ill-prepared for action, Stephens armed Rossa and the Cork delegation with revolvers.[33] The train called at numerous stations in Munster to allow sympathizers to participate. In Kilmallock, thirty IRB members, 'wearing crêpe on their arms ... waiting at the station and when they heard the train was coming, but discovered it was not going to stop ... went down on their knees to pray for the soul of the man whose body was now being whisked past them'.[34]

At midnight there was a lengthy halt at Limerick Junction, where multitudes crowded onto the platform. This was the most likely location for an attempt to seize the coffin and Stephens had posted Thomas Dogherty Brohan and 'his select Tipperary band of one hundred young men' to control the masses.[35] At Stephens' signal Brohan's men knelt to pray for the repose of the rebel's soul and 'the deliverance of the living' followed by all present 'and while the whole crowd was on their knees' the train departed. Rossa and Luby were in agreement, 'so solemn a ceremony I do not think I ever witnessed'.[36] Informed by Stephens, O'Mahony considered this 'a grand and most convincing report, not alone of the extent and discipline of our organized brothers in Ireland, but of the patriotism and national vitality of the whole Irish people'.[37]

On arrival in Dublin before dawn, a procession of several hundred men with members of the NBSPB carrying flaming torches conveyed the coffin to the Mechanics' Institute in Abbey Street.[38] No church was available, as Archbishop Cullen objected to a public funeral, suspecting that the organizers planned to proclaim their separatist aspirations, which they shared with McManus.[39]

Dr Cullen's 'principal concern was for the progress ... of the Roman Catholic Church' and he feared the NBSP as an IRB front. In Liverpool, for instance, it had launched itself at a meeting to raise funds for the McManus funeral. Fr Patrick Lavelle of Mayo informed the archbishop of the honours rendered to McManus by the clergy in America and Cobh, while the sister of the deceased wrote twice, requesting Catholic rites. Dr Cullen delayed his veto of any clerical involvement until the last moment.[40] The IRB placarded Dublin with a statement by Fr Lavelle to counteract him. Due to tensions between the archbishops of Dublin and Tuam, Fr Lavelle could defy Dr Cullen with impunity. The priest described McManus, a good Catholic and patriot, as being denied the honours given to any political time-server, who wished 'to sell his creed and his country together to the first buyer for prompt payment!'[41] (He was alluding to Sadleir and Keogh, who had accepted office under the Liberals.)

Until the final procession to Glasnevin Cemetery on 10 November, the remains reposed in the Mechanics Institute, where the American delegates were welcomed with a carefully choreographed speech. Their spokesman responded that, if 'the principle for which he [McManus] strove, and suffered, and died in a foreign land, had pined away into a mere souvenir, or even an aspiration' this funeral would be 'an empty pageant'. On the contrary, the delegates declared it 'a source of eternal pride and pleasure' to inform Irish America of the patriotic 'feeling manifested by the people' as the cortège passed through Cork: '... the vindication is the more complete from the fact of that magnificent demonstration having been worked out, from beginning to end, by the people alone'.[42]

While the 'McManus obsequies committee' appealed to its collectors to forward subscriptions, large crowds 'consisting principally of respectable artisans, their wives and families', queued to view the coffin, on which Fr Kenyon placed a 'massive silver crucifix' of Irish manufacture, presented to Miss McManus.[43] A tradesman had constructed a then fashionable 'funeral car', fourteen feet long, resembling 'a pyramidical cenotaph' with an oblong platform nine feet from the ground for holding the coffin. Draped in black with white crosses, this 'extremely handsome' vehicle was drawn by six black horses. The *Freeman's Journal*, the leading Catholic newspaper, publicized the instructions of the funeral committee to wear black crêpe armbands and to observe 'the most profound silence'.[44]

The committee reassured devout Catholics that in New York, 'Irish priests have chanted the funeral Mass' with Archbishop Hughes. McManus should be honoured 'because he was a bright example of what an Irish soldier should be – calm, brave and single-minded', having 'lost all in the brave endeavour to save the lives of our people, and give liberty to our country'.[45] This appeal, probably written by Stephens, concluded by comparing McManus's sacrifice to the crucifixion: 'Come to his funeral, ye people of Ireland, and prove to the world that you still love the old cause for which he suffered. Let every town and hamlet bestir itself on this occasion, for it is fitting that the people for whom he died should bear him in their midst to their last resting place. Come with us, and place him in the great city of the dead [Glasnevin].'[46]

The surviving Young Irelanders expected to dominate what they quite reasonably interpreted as a commemoration of their past and were dismayed that a clique of 'obscure, unknown, irresponsible fellows' had commandeered the funeral.[47] These included Joseph Denieffe and Maurice O'Donoghue, a native of Kilmallock, who was a leader of one of the Dublin 'circles'. For the emergent IRB, McManus was a martyr and precursor, a link in the chain of the Republican succession: 'In our minds out there the spirit of Irish liberty went hand in hand with the spirit of the dead.'[48]

Fr Kenyon was to give the oration, but when his address on nationality transpired to be merely 'aspirationist', Stephens composed the eulogy.[49] Tensions between the former Young Irelanders and the 'professional revolutionists', as Smith O'Brien described the Fenians, continued: 'During the week that preceded the funeral all sorts of intrigues were carried on … Every effort was made to take the management of the business out of the hands of the Fenians, by playing upon the religious fears of Miss McManus.'[50]

The decisive clash between the Fenians and their opponents, who included Fr Kenyon, the O'Donoghue, John Martin and James Cantwell, occurred the night before the burial. Luby, with Stephens in the background, responded firmly to this challenge, while the sister of the deceased, on being appealed to, declined to support the Young Irelanders. This ended Luby's friendship with Fr Kenyon and made him bitter about the Young Irelanders.[51] On 10 November 1861 the obsequies concluded with a final procession, as recalled by an anxious Luby:

> But the moment had come. The coffin was borne out and placed in the hearse. The word was given. The leading bands struck up a funeral march, gradually taken up by bands at intervals all along the line, and the vast procession moved slowly in the direction of the Custom House, every man wearing a crêpe badge of mourning. Of course the several trades and societies … bore aloft their various banners. Horsemen, selected from our own Brotherhood, in semi-military

costume ... with marshals on foot, bearing white wands, preserved order all along the whole line of march. In fact the Metropolitan Police that day abdicated their functions and left the preservation of order completely to ourselves, and never was order better maintained in Dublin streets than on that proud day.[52]

Miss McManus as chief mourner was supported by Mrs Doheny, Fr Kenyon and John Martin.[53] John Haltigan, Edward Coyne, Felix O'Neill and Edward Hollywood acted as pall-bearers. 'The celebrated Hollywood', as Stephens described him, was a Dublin silk-weaver and the only artisan member of a delegation to the French Republic in 1848. Felix O'Neill had spent some years in voluntary exile in France after that Rising.[54]

Towns with a strong IRB presence sent representatives. They were led by the Cork deputation, including James Mountaine, John Lynch, James O'Connor and Michael O'Brien, followed by Tipperary with Patrick Sheedy and Thomas Dogherty Brohan, Peter Gill, the editor of the radical *Tipperary Advocate*, the Carrick-on-Suir men with James Meagher, their 'centre' and John Haltigan and Patrick Mansfield Delany of Kilkenny. Also present were Charles Kickham, Felix O'Neill and Denis Dowling Mulcahy as delegates for Clonmel and Edward Beverage and James Russell for Limerick city. Callan sent the ubiquitous Coyne and Cody, and Ennis, Michael Considine, its tradesman-orator. The Thurles group included Dr Hanley, Andrew Ryan of Gortakelly Castle, Borrisoleigh, and a Kickham relative, Lieutenant Crean of the Papal Brigade.[55] There were representatives from Carlow, Portarlington, Kells, Trim, Navan, Monaghan, Manchester and Glasgow, while Edward Duffy was the most prominent leader from Connacht.[56]

The attendance suggested that enthusiasm for the IRB was prevalent in Munster and Leinster. The democratic character of the proceedings was under-lined by the trades' societies, such as the drapers' assistants, carpenters, tailors and bricklayers and the occupations of prominent participants, ranging from James Mountaine, a shoe manufacturer, and John Lynch, a publican, both of Cork, to several shop assistants, such as Michael O'Brien of Ballymacoda. In contrast to the majority of Irish people, who worked on the land, only three substantial farmers, Felix O'Neill, Denis Dowling Mulcahy and Patrick Mansfield Delany played leading roles, underlining the urban and artisan char-acter of the movement. The *Kilkenny Moderator* demonstrated the snobbery of the age, when deriding the funeral in comparison with the processions of O'Connell and the Young Irelanders. This attitude also explained why the establishment continued to underestimate Fenianism:

> When we look back to the O'Connell gatherings or even the Young Ireland 'Confederation' assemblies, and remember the array of names, of borough

magistrates, professional men and traders, accustomed to put forward as representing Kilkenny on such occasions, we cannot but view in the most ludicrous light, this miserable farce of 'an imposing demonstration'.[57]

John Blake Dillon, T.D. Sullivan, Dr George Sigerson, physician and litterateur and Isaac Varian of Cork, a Young Irelander, were among the distinguished personalities present. Four priests accompanied the cortège: Fr Kenyon, Fr Ashe, a Capuchin from Dublin, Fr Courteney of Birmingham and Fr Lavelle, who recited the *de profundis* at the graveside, the chaplain of the cemetery being absent on Archbishop Cullen's orders. Fr Lavelle addressed the crowd, predicting that 'this day will be memorable in the annals of Irish history':[58] 'I am proud to say that, though the patriot may have died, the spirit that he evoked has outlived him, and will raise Ireland from the degradation in which she is placed. Here lies a true Christian, a true patriot having pledged his life for your interests, after having sacrificed all for you; and I hope that the lesson will not be lost upon you.'[59]

Captain Smith, chairman of the American delegation, delivered the oration, which Stephens had composed, by torchlight. It portrayed McManus as yearning to be 'a soldier bringing freedom' or die in exile. The funeral constituted a test of whether the people had abandoned their quest for nationhood in the aftermath of the Famine. But the multitudes awaiting the cortège in Cork and Tipperary demonstrated that they were as 'true as any of their predecessors'. Smith concluded by praising the intelligence and power of the people, advocating self-reliance and hinting that independence, 'the day for which our fathers yearned, struggled, fought and suffered cannot now be very far off'. These proceedings became the blueprint for others, most memorably the O'Donovan Rossa funeral in 1915.[60]

Luby considered the McManus obsequies an extraordinary event, the work of a stateless people. They surpassed Napoleon's second burial, which was carried out by a powerful nation. During this 'great Fenian demonstration from first to last', 20–30,000 spectators witnessed thousands of earnest young men, marching in military formation.[61] It was an amazing display of what could be achieved without middle-class leadership, giving, as A.M. Sullivan lamented, 'the Fenian chiefs a command of Ireland which they had never been able to obtain before' and, in opposing constitutionalists, 'they henceforth assumed a boldness of language and action never previously attempted'.[62] The latter, who could offer no viable alternative, were dismayed, while Luby rejoiced that the Young Irelanders 'could no longer keep up their pet fiction, that 'twas idle to attempt rousing the Irish people to any fresh effort for the restoration of Irish national independence – a fiction which, ever since their fiasco in '48 had allowed them still to pose as patriots, and yet keep their precious skins safe'.[63]

Mourners from rural areas spread the word. Extraordinary enthusiasm broke out and members of the NBSP transferred to the IRB en masse. But afterwards 'marked men' were dismissed by their employers and a reluctant O'Mahony had to divert resources to aid them on arrival in New York, for any impression that the American body lacked funds would dishearten the IRB.[64]

The IRB after 1861

The American delegates returned home in January 1862 with positive accounts to lecture in Irish-American cities on the need to support the revolutionaries who were awaiting a conflict between the US and Britain. Nevertheless, funds received by the IRB remained modest. From 1862 onwards there was a marked increase in Fenians joining the Federal forces, whose commanders facilitated O'Mahony's representatives to recruit for the Brotherhood. The attendant expense led to a financial hiatus, which worsened his relationship with Stephens. The latter disapproved of O'Mahony encouraging Irish enlistment in General Corcoran's legion, ending in thousands dying 'in a cause which was not Ireland's'.[65] When remittances stalled, Stephens sent Luby to New York on 12 February 1863, instructing him to suspend or supersede O'Mahony, if necessary, a proceeding never contemplated by Luby, who returned to Dublin with modest donations.[66]

George Archdeacon, Liverpool (courtesy NLI).

Poor harvests during 1859–64 caused economic hardship, in particular for smaller farmers and shopkeepers, and led to increased emigration, while workhouse admissions rose from 46,000 in February 1859 to almost 67,000 people in February 1863.[67] Such conditions facilitated IRB recruitment. John O'Leary recalled that by 1862–3 the organization was flourishing in the Belfast area and spreading in Connacht. It also developed a presence in Britain, including London, Manchester, Birmingham, Glasgow and Dundee.[68] George Archdeacon, formerly a Young Ireland leader in Manchester, returned from the US in 1862. He became the Fenian chief of Liverpool, Britain's gateway to the Atlantic. Archdeacon rejected constitutional agitation for tenant right, favouring the development of Irish resources, an alliance with Irish America and independence. The local police considered him 'almost of the lowest order' and engaged in any revolutionary movement 'since 1848'.[69]

While Stephens advocated a silent conspiracy to prepare for insurrection, this was often negated by the noisy displays of his followers. Possibly as the result of low Irish self-confidence after the Famine, one of the difficulties facing the leadership on both sides of the Atlantic was the impatience of their rank and file to see immediate results. One may otherwise question the benefit of nationalist demonstrations in Cork against the Prince of Wales's marriage in 1863, which focused official attention on James Mountaine and John Lynch. In Skibbereen, Rossa risked arrest when organizing similar protests. By pleading guilty in 1859, Rossa became liable to imprisonment, if convicted again, but considered that these displays kept the movement alive by inspiring confidence in the masses.[70]

From 1863 the IRB spread to Clare, due to the efforts of Edmond O'Donovan and his brothers, sons of John O'Donovan, the great Gaelic scholar. Edmond enlisted his uncle, Henry Broughton, a farmer near Broadford, as the local 'centre', as well as organizing in O'Callaghan's Mills, Scariff and Tulla. O'Donovan converted John Clune of Quin, a prominent Ribbon leader, to the IRB, which led to an influx of agrarian society men. Edmond further ensured their loyalty by providing some modern rifles. Both Edmond and John O'Donovan Jr had developed a keen interest in weapons and military engineering, which they disseminated on tours of Munster. Devoy exaggerates, however, when claiming that Clare 'was one of the best Fenian counties in Ireland'.[71]

There were links between the Clare and Limerick city Fenians, but Co. Limerick remained poorly organized. Kilmallock formed the exception, where William Henry O'Sullivan, the owner of a hotel and public car establishment, presided over a Fenian stronghold, sheltering IRB men among his forty employees.[72]

(Left) *Edmond O'Donovan, FP 398;* (right) *John O'Donovan Jr, FP 400 (courtesy NAI).*

To the beleaguered Sullivan brothers of the *Nation*, the conspiracy appeared to proliferate alarmingly after 1862, with 'sympathizers all over the British Empire; a numerous membership in the United States; and friends in many other parts of the world; so that – for a time – its adherents might have parodied the British boast and said that the sun never set on the Fenian Brotherhood'.[73]

T.D. Sullivan and John O'Leary portrayed the IRB as consisting of respectable mechanics, clerks and shop assistants and a few medical and law students, augmented by labourers and farmers' sons. What motivated them? Given the dangers of joining a secret society, it could hardly be short-term personal advancement, although prominent members possessed energy and talent.[74]

James J. O'Kelly's family, for instance, migrated to London to join his uncle, John Lawlor. This distinguished sculptor and secret Fenian worked on the Albert Memorial, where he hid IRB members among his employees. James, who would become a celebrated journalist, art dealer and MP, and his brothers Stephen and Charles, successful sculptors, were arrested as suspects. Aloysius, the youngest O'Kelly, has been rediscovered as a significant Irish painter and nationalist. Edmond O'Donovan, their friend and fellow conspirator, became an intrepid explorer and author of *The Merv Oasis. Travels and Adventures East of the Caspian during the Years 1879–80–81* (1882). He and James J. O'Kelly served as early war correspondents, sympathizing with the Sudanese insurrection against Egyptian and British domination in 1883–4.[75]

These young men were less deferential than the Young Irelanders. Politics remained the preserve of the wealthy, but in 1865 Michael Heffernan Dunne of Callan, a suspect since 1858, mocked the establishment by posing as candidate for Kilkenny, a daring act for a nailsmith, when MPs were invariably 'gentlemen'.[76] The *Irish People* carried his address, which urged the electors to seize this unique opportunity to send 'a mechanic to Parliament, in preference to some titled humbug', though Heffernan Dunne embraced physical force: 'Nearer to home, and on more improved principles I intend serving my country.'[77]

His parody of an election campaign, supported by John Haltigan, James Cody, James Hetherington, the Mullinavat 'centre', John Kavanagh, a relieving officer of the Kilkenny poor law union, Rody Kickham, cousin of Charles and others excluded from the franchise was an IRB propaganda exercise.[78] On 6 July during a meeting at Knocktopher, Heffernan Dunne declared himself a Fenian before a crowd of a thousand. Three cheers were given for O'Mahony, for 'he is our government', while the annual congress of the Fenian Brotherhood represented the Irish Parliament *in embryo*. At the market house in Callan, Heffernan Dunne quoted Thomas Davis in his 'democratic address' to indicate that the IRB would rise 'in rude, but fierce array'. Supporters of George Bryan, the future MP, were ignored as merely working for 'lucrative situations' for their clique. The constabulary looked on, crestfallen, while 'Rory of the Hill', an insurrectionary ballad by Charles Kickham, was played.[79]

The intellectual qualities of the IRB leadership exerted an enormous appeal in an age of limited educational opportunities for the working class. Stephens, Luby and O'Leary were widely travelled, had enjoyed a classical education, spoke French and conversed knowledgeably about art and science. They made stimulating teachers. Joseph Denieffe recalled that mixing with them 'was equal to a course of lectures on history, literature and poetry, not of English only, but of all the nations that had any to boast of in ancient or modern times'.[80]

During his tours, Stephens explored places of natural beauty and historic interest, such as the Killarney region, to inspire his followers that their country was worth fighting for. When solvent, he was not averse to a little luxury, for instance, dining in Eccles Hotel in Glengarriff. Denieffe considered his months in Paris, which included sightseeing, when attending what Stephens had hoped would become a course of military studies for IRB officers, among the highlights of his life.[81]

On 19 October 1863, O'Mahony, while preparing for the Fenian Brotherhood's first national convention, alerted his friend Charles Kickham to his resignation as 'head centre' and the only authorized channel of communication between his Brotherhood and the IRB. He informed Stephens, who had appointed him in 1859, that '[this condition having been] repeatedly violated to your knowledge I consider myself perfectly discharged'. Only if unanimously re-elected, would O'Mahony resume office, submitting to[82]

> the control of my constituents, through their representatives, but *to none other*. Neither shall any party outside of these states be permitted henceforth to interfere with its internal or external action, except within those limits assigned to the command of the CE [chief executive] of the IRB. All secret emissaries sent here to interfere with and interrupt the action of the F[enian] B[rotherhood] by maligning its officers and misdirecting its private members, will be treated as traitors and enemies, no matter *who* sustains them or *who* sends them hither.[83]

O'Mahony complained that Stephens had scapegoated him for 'the inevitable consequences of his own desertion of me during the most trying crises' and henceforth 'as chief officer of the American organization, my powers must be put upon an even level with his authority over the Irish. I will no longer consent to be accountable to him for my official conduct.'[84]

Both chiefs continued to harbour grievances. O'Mahony resented slights and was in need of reassurance from friends, including Kickham and Edmund O'Leary, John's half-brother. While Stephens wrote in a patronizing manner, invariably dramatizing his own role, neither he nor O'Mahony welcomed inspectors from the sister organization. Furthermore, letters from William O'Carroll in 1861 indicate that the 'head centre' attempted to establish his own source of information inside the IRB, independent of Stephens, which O'Carroll's tactful and loyal response foiled.[85]

The first national convention of the Fenian Brotherhood, which took place in Chicago between 3 and 5 November 1863, perceived the 'genius, eminent purity, and disinterestedness' of O'Mahony as a guarantee that Irish independence was obtainable and he was unanimously re-elected.[86] Secret resolutions declared the Republic 'virtually established' and acknowledged Stephens as 'the supreme organizer of the Irish race', while limiting his power to European Fenianism. O'Mahony's endorsement as the foremost leader in the US greatly offended Stephens.[87]

The convention aligned the Brotherhood with American democratic practice. It decreed annual elections for its officers, while instituting a central council of five men to assist O'Mahony, in addition to the positions of national treasurer and assistant treasurer to deal with the funds collected, although ultimate accountability rested with O'Mahony and Stephens respectively. The organization adopted a constitution and was divided into 'circles', and, when these attracted a large membership, 'sub-circles' under the control of 'sub-centres' and 'centres', supervised by 'state centres' in those parts of the Union where Fenianism flourished.[88]

O'Mahony stressed that the restructuring of the Brotherhood was to deflect criticism by the Catholic Church, which proved unsuccessful, as the condemnation of the 1864 Fenian bazaar by Bishop Duggan of Chicago demonstrated. O'Mahony's keynote address outlined the progress made, for in 1858 the Brotherhood had consisted of only forty men in New York. Five years later he claimed that it stretched from the Atlantic to the Pacific and from Canada to the Mississippi. In reality, the organization was powerful in New York, the cities of the eastern seaboard and the Chicago region. In Canada, for instance, it existed only in Montreal and Toronto. Although the Civil War delayed the planned invasion, the Brotherhood was gaining thousands of members in the Federal armies. This proved a fallacy, however, as Fenian enthusiasm often lacked a framework, while the 'fighting Irish' suffered a terrible dichotomy by dying for the Union.[89]

James Gibbons of Philadelphia, the owner of a printing business, who had joined the Brotherhood in 1859 and subsequently became a member of its central council, compared the Fenians to silkworms, whose death leaves splendid raw materials behind. He prophesied that Ireland would yet be freed by 'the sorrow-stricken exile'.[90] Delegates included Major Patrick Downing, on behalf of the Army of the Potomac, and his brother, Captain Denis Downing, who was acting as proxy for the 'centre' of the Rappahannock 'circle' of the Federal forces. Denis, a survivor of the bloody battles of Fredericksburg, Chancellorsville and Gettysburg, had a leg amputated four months earlier, but insisted on enduring the long train journey to Chicago. There were also representatives from Canada and a proxy for General Michael Corcoran, detained by military duties. Charles Kickham attended on behalf of the IRB.[91]

The Fenian Brotherhood stressed the need for unity and a well-prepared descent on Ireland, a task made imperative due to the rapid depopulation at home. O'Mahony censured the Young Irelanders, who had led him into revolution in 1848, but held aloof from it ever since. The Brotherhood conceived the Chicago resolutions as its declaration of Irish independence, pledging to hold annual conventions until this had been achieved.[92]

Some leaders in the Illinois region considered O'Mahony an obstacle to rapid progress. These 'men of action' organized the 'Great Irish National Fair', a fundraising bazaar in Chicago, which had not been authorized by O'Mahony. They appealed to the public in Ireland to donate artifacts of sentimental or historical interest through the *Irish People* newspaper.[93] The response was overwhelming. Henry Clarence McCarthy, a leading Chicago dissident, travelled to Dublin to collect the items, while secretly urging Stephens to intervene to salvage the Fenian Brotherhood. Stephens believed that O'Mahony, his main ally, had metamorphosed into 'our standing drag-chain and stumbling-block', disillusioning the Irish membership through inadequate funding. The IRB felt reassured by 'sensible' Henry Clarence McCarthy, unaware that Sir Robert Peel, the chief secretary, had been alerted to his arrival and ordered him to be shadowed.[94]

Stephens, appointing O'Leary, Luby and Kickham as a 'Fenian executive' should a crisis arise during his absence, accompanied McCarthy to Chicago, where the Fenian Fair opened on 28 March 1864. It ran for a week and donations featured 'a "King O'Toole" cane, which would make a very passable bludgeon', 'some very elegant Limerick lace shawls', 'shamrocks in their native earth', which reduced some emigrants to tears and 'earth taken from the grave of Wolfe Tone'.[95] Objects associated with Republican heroes like Lord Edward Fitzgerald, commander of the United Irish Army of 1798, were treated almost like Catholic relics: 'Mr Mooney has also sent a piece of the noble martyr's coffin' and John O'Clohessy provided a window shutter handle from Wolfe Tone's home in Dublin. The *pièce de résistance*, however, was the silver and bog-oak crucifix of the McManus funeral. It had been donated by his sister and cost $1000. Irish-Americans and fellow citizens of various ethnicities contributed, the Polish Central Committee sending a painting with the title *Order Reigns in Warsaw*, a reference to the uprising of 1863. Fenian intentions were unwisely revealed by stating that the money would be 'devoted to the natural purposes of the Brotherhood'. The fair proved a resounding success, but despite promises that it would benefit the IRB, Stephens received only $14,000 of the $54,000 realized.[96]

He was dismayed that the Fenian Brotherhood membership had been over-estimated by 30,000, when it consisted of 10,000 civilians and 10,000 Federal soldiers. Stephens toured and raised funds, but felt that the organization and its revenues would need to increase greatly. A consummate salesman, Stephens supported the dissidents, who had assimilated American values, prioritizing material success over idealistic motivation. The 'men of action' disdained O'Mahony's abortive efforts in 1848, echoing Stephens's attitude towards Smith O'Brien and his lieutenants.[97]

The dissidents claimed to have rescued the Brotherhood from stagnation, portraying O'Mahony as an initially adequate figurehead, although indecisive, suspicious and liable to act despotically. Even Kickham admitted that O'Mahony bore grudges, advising him to 'subdue the Celtic devil of revenge within you'. He also suffered from short-sightedness, then considered unmanly. The Chicago faction reacted with impatience when the gentlemanly O'Mahony refused to visit cities whose Irish communities had not expressly invited him and shrank from aggressive, American-style fundraising.[98]

Stephens's suggestion that paid officers should promote the Fenian Brotherhood was adopted. He effected the appointment of Henry Clarence McCarthy as 'deputy head centre' with responsibility for those propaganda and fundraising tasks that O'Mahony found distasteful. The latter consented, although suspecting Stephens and the dissidents of plotting to depose him. Prominent Fenians in the Midwest anticipated that, once the insurrection broke out, McCarthy would supersede O'Mahony as war leader. Stephens failed to grasp that by encouraging this clique, he undermined O'Mahony's power base as well as his own.[99]

Valid misgivings

Stephens announced that, should tensions between Britain and Austria over the future of the Schleswig-Holstein territories in Northern Germany lead to war, he would initiate the Rising. Otherwise, 1865 would be the year of action. Proclaiming his decision from American platforms, he tactlessly ignored O'Mahony's valid misgivings and limited the American Fenians to little more than a year to organize an invasion. Considering the logistics of smuggling weapons to Ireland and evading the British fleet with a Fenian expedition, this deadline was fraught with difficulties. Stephens subsequently explained his motivation:[100] 'What the people wanted here, as well as in Ireland, was a fixed time for action, and not to be dragged on as they had been for years, without knowing when the time for action would come. To the statement then made, much of the progress since made is to be attributed.'[101]

Stephens's cry of 'war or dissolution in '65' galvanized the movement, but O'Mahony, considering this policy ill-advised, resolved to sabotage him. In 1868 O'Mahony recalled that:

> I made no unfounded statements to the men at the head of our associated brothers here. I never concealed from them any of the obstacles that impeded my work at this side. I never pandered to their impatience and their rashness, by holding out false hopes to them. I never made them reckless promises with respect to any matter that happened to be beyond my immediate reach.'[102]

He considered resigning, but perceived himself the guarantor of revolutionary probity. O'Mahony's life centred on Fenianism and it is likely that by 1864 he overestimated his influence at home, where Stephens had developed a considerable following.[103]

Michael Scanlan, Chicago (courtesy Dublin City Archive).

When Stephens returned to Ireland in August 1864, after almost six months in the US, the IRB was less prepared for insurrection than he cared to admit. American support depended on a favourable report. Luckily for Stephens, O'Mahony's envoy was very much under his spell. Philip Coyne, a tailor, had settled in St Louis and drilled with the Emmet Guards of the state militia since 1858. Captain Coyne commanded this unit, part of the 1st Missouri militia, on behalf of the secessionist governor, when forced to surrender to Federal troops at Camp Jackson on 10 May 1861. Two years later Coyne was deported from St Louis to the Confederacy for covertly operating a mail service for the rebels. His brother Edward, the 'centre' for Callan, was present in October 1863, as Stephens wrote successfully to General Corcoran to use his influence to ensure Philip's return.[104]

O'Mahony believed that Michael Scanlan, a native of Co. Limerick, and the poet laureate of American Fenianism, had made 'the first open attempt' to undermine him, while preparing for the second national convention of the Brotherhood. In an unauthorized circular, Scanlan issued the 'final call', urging all branches to transmit outstanding funds, implying that the Rising was imminent. O'Mahony countermanded the order, but suspected that 'circles' supporting the dissidents retained large sums, unknown to the central treasury. He refrained from opposing his critics to avert an open rupture.[105]

William R. Roberts (courtesy Dublin City Archive).

During the national congress in Cincinnati from 17 to 20 January 1865, delegates rejected allegations about Stephens and his supporters, while O'Mahony decided to support the cause by remaining in office. His control continued to slip as the number of central councillors was increased to ten, now led by the president of the council, who also acted as 'deputy head centre'. Councillors included Henry Clarence McCarthy, Michael Scanlan, James Gibbons, P.W. Dunne, Patrick O'Rourke and Patrick Keenan, the latter two joint treasurers.[106] There were, however, two vacancies on the council, which were not immediately filled, for reasons only known to Henry Clarence McCarthy and his clique.[107]

Although fifty 'circles' had become extinct during the Civil War, since the Chicago convention of 1863 the membership had increased from sixty-three 'circles' with 15,000 men to almost 300 'circles' with approximately 75,000 enrolled. Fenian revenues were multiplying, but the cost of setting up new branches was considerable. Stephens had declared that the Rising would take place in 1865 and P.W. Dunne's resolution that they would hold the next convention in (liberated) Ireland was greeted with unanimous acclamation. They authorized the 'final call', signalling the countdown to insurrection, should the Fenian council and O'Mahony consider the time right. In addition to weekly dues, the congress requested an additional levy of $5 per member. A scheme of issuing bonds, reminiscent of that proposed by the EMA in 1855, was in preparation.[108]

Envoy Philip Coyne presented an unexpectedly favourable report, covertly written by Stephens, claiming that the IRB had 'from 80,000 to 85,000 men', with 15,000 of these from Cork city and county and 30,000 based in Dublin, south Leinster and the south riding of Tipperary. To avoid alerting the constabulary, Coyne had interviewed a few leaders in Dublin and Stephens escorted him on brief visits to Cork and Belfast. Pleading lack of funds, 'the captain' then sent Coyne to stay with his family, whose familiarity with the IRB strongholds of Callan, Kilkenny, Mullinahone and Carrick-on-Suir reinforced a favourable impression. Much of this report was hearsay, as Stephens had chosen interviewees who would support his rosy picture.[109]

But as neither the Cincinnati convention nor O'Mahony were fully convinced by these assertions it was decided to send further military envoys to Ireland. At its first meeting in New York, the new central council elected William Randall Roberts, a native of Mitchelstown who had made his fortune as a department-store owner, as well as P.J. Meehan to fill its vacancies. Meehan constituted a controversial choice, having drawn attention to the disingenuously named 'Irish patriotic defence fund', implying that the Brotherhood was involved in financial wrongdoing in 1859.[110] O'Mahony had since perceived Meehan as 'a malignant, personal enemy', as well as 'one of the most envenomed opponents of the Fenian movement since '59, nor had any journalist at either side of the ocean done more than he to vilify its leaders and obstruct its progress, with the exception of his friend and *confrère*, Alexander M. Sullivan, of the Dublin *Nation*'.[111] O'Mahony accepted Meehan's unanimous election by the councillors, who were led by Henry Clarence McCarthy, as they needed broad-based nationalist support. The Fenian chief was determined 'to complete the work I have entered on'.[112]

O'Mahony's worst flaws as a leader were his inability to read character or heed warnings about dubious individuals like 'Red Jim' McDermott. Colonel Downing urged him to be more selective in his friendships and to retain as much authority as possible, for should 'anything go wrong, it is you only, and those concerned, who will have to bear the burthen thereof'. O'Mahony, however, continued to excuse McDermott's apparent tactlessness, enjoying his effusive declarations of loyalty.[113]

After the Cincinnati congress, considerable moneys began to be transmitted to Ireland and Stephens acknowledged receiving £1158 between 30 January and 18 March 1865. He protested to O'Mahony about 'the danger to which your indiscretion exposes us', for Quinlan, the American courier, declared himself a Fenian and drunkenly 'threatened to shoot folk' during a dispute on the boat from Liverpool.[114] 'Still intoxicated', Quinlan left O'Mahony's letters on board to rush to the *Irish People* office, strictly out of bounds to avoid police attention. Luckily, Quinlan met a quick-witted IRB man, who retrieved the documents to convey them to Stephens. Shortly afterwards, Quinlan was arrested. This episode illustrates the character of many Fenian foot soldiers, which consisted of determination and naivety.[115]

In April Colonel Thomas J. Kelly arrived in Ireland for a tour of inspection lasting three months. He was followed by General F.F. Millen of the Mexican army, who had offered his services to the Fenian Brotherhood, having previously contacted the British consul in New York, intent on betraying O'Mahony.[116]

The Confederate surrender that month created opportunities of utilizing thousands of veterans before they returned to civilian life. The Fenians hoped to exploit American power by harnessing US grievances to Irish separatism. Eighteen British-built cruisers of the Confederacy had destroyed a considerable amount of Yankee shipping, prolonging the war. This contravened British law, which prohibited such sales to belligerents. Washington now demanded $15,500,000 in damages for the 'Alabama claims', named after the most lethal Confederate ship. Although Anglo-American tensions continued with Fenian sabre-rattling serving as a bargaining tool for US politicians, the matter was settled by international arbitration in 1872, enhancing Gladstone's statesmanship. The new, harmonious Anglo-American relationship sidelined Irish nationalists. Additionally, 634,703 of the 1,556,000 men who had fought for the Union, had been either killed or wounded, while the Confederacy numbered 483,000 of its 800,000 soldiers among the casualties: America was war-weary.[117]

O'Mahony had instructed Colonel Kelly 'to inspect professionally, with his own eyes', the level of IRB preparedness, independently of Stephens. This would delay the Rising by three months and Stephens and his followers, who had refrained from emigrating as action appeared imminent, were furious.[118] Colonel Kelly reported to O'Mahony on 31 May 1865 in pseudo-business terms, which failed to conceal his meaning:

> The state of trade was represented to be in such a condition that all the available funds of the firm were deemed to be essential immediately, and that it would be too late for your house to invest after I had made full reports in July. Of course I insisted on complying with the directions your firm gave me to the fullest extent, although I am forced to the conclusion that from the immense emigration taking place we will lose our best customers and workmen if we do not open the factory this fall. I *know* that the Union must go to pieces after this year if work is not supplied to the hands. I talk frequently with all hands and I find that large numbers are remaining with the *promise* of employment.[119]

Colonel Kelly stated that they needed to import arms ('if the machinery can be furnished') and officers capable of planning a campaign ('skilled mechanics are indispensable, more especially draughtsmen and designers') to ensure success. On 21 June he recorded inspecting the Dublin IRB in spite of the 'extraordinary vigilance' of the police. He believed that membership estimates were essentially correct, while many local leaders resented his investigation as doubting Philip Coyne's report. In both Dublin and Cork, members were in danger of losing their livelihood due to loyalist employers and the Catholic clergy, for his inspection attracted attention. In small country places, Colonel Kelly had to proceed cautiously to avoid exposing their best men. Nevertheless, the leadership was looking 'forward to business this year' and the members recalled how O'Mahony had promised that the Rising should take place at the end of the Civil War.[120]

Many had staked everything on this and property was being sold and rent withheld, while others, who could emigrate after losing their jobs, remained in expectation of action. Should they fail to rise, the exodus from Ireland would reach unprecedented levels, Colonel Kelly warned. The IRB would probably collapse by December 1865 amidst bitter denunciations of O'Mahony. He outlined the Fenian infiltration of the British military and potential supportive action by the IRB in England:

> The contingencies in our favour are immense. The knowledge possessed of the whereabouts of the immense stores of material and supplies; the various local arrangements being made to seize them, the work done and being done within the garrison (a good deal of which I have seen); the fact of about half the militia being ours; the immense organization lately done in England (sixty new centres being appointed within two months) which can be so terribly used for a diversion – all these, if properly used, and leaders and means are furnished, leave but little doubt on my mind as to the success of the project.[121]

Colonel Kelly volunteered to remain in Ireland as a vote of confidence in the Rising. Stephens, however, expressed anger that yet another 'inquisitor' had been sent: 'Well, I considered Captain Kelly's mission the deadliest blow ever aimed against us. How earnest and intelligent men could have even contemplated such a move at such a stage of the work is deepest mystery to me.'[122]

Stephens urged that in future funds should be transmitted via agents in Paris, while Fenian representatives could buy weapons for at least 80,000 men in Birmingham. Ideally, he would like 300 cannons and £300,000 to purchase arms, but was willing to settle for less. Stephens claimed to have more than 200,000 men sworn in at home, but lacked precise figures. He concluded in an uncharacteristically humble manner, apologizing for his bad temper, due to the trials endured in 'so high and holy a cause', before sending Rossa to New York on 24 June to plead for immediate insurrection.[123] This was supported by F.F. Millen, who offered to stake his life on Stephens's analysis of the situation, although he had not started inspecting. Millen believed that the majority would join the uprising and urged O'Mahony to authorize the 'final call', preferably this year and failing that, next spring. He warned that they were running a race against emigration and there might not be enough of the nation left to fight if they failed to act.[124]

O'Mahony responded by sending American officers to assist the IRB with its final preparations. Other committed Fenians, on being discharged from the Union armies, travelled to Ireland at their own expense.[125] Among these was John James O'Connor, a native of Valentia Island in Kerry, whose family had emigrated to Massachusetts during the Famine. Colonel O'Connor had distinguished himself in the battles of Bull Run, Antietam and Spotsylvania. A committed organizer, he stayed in Cahirciveen, where the IRB was weak, although suffering from unhealed wounds. Initially Colonel O'Connor's unobtrusive manner deflected attention from his activities.[126]

The early arrivals in July 1865 numbered a group under Captain Patrick Magrath of Chicago, who was assigned to fight in Kilkenny under John Kavanagh, the local 'centre'. Colonel John W. Byron, a native of Clogheen, Co. Tipperary, had commanded the 88th Regiment and, briefly, the Irish Brigade. Released from a Confederate prison camp at the cessation of hostilities, he travelled through Tipperary, Waterford and Limerick in preparation for the Rising, inspecting British fortifications and IRB units.[127] John Daly remembered that in Limerick city around August, Colonel Byron wished to ascertain their strength. The Fenians assembled among the populace walking the course before the horse races. At every jump an IRB officer waited, surrounded by his 'circle', when the number of Fenians in Limerick city was found to be 1600.[128]

The hesitant central councillors selected plenipotentiaries before making the 'final call'. O'Mahony sent P.J. Meehan, a moderate nationalist, and P.W. Dunne, who demanded action to Stephens with introductions and a draft for £500. On 22 July, Meehan unwittingly lost the documents in Kingstown (Dun Laoghaire). They fell into the hands of Dublin Castle, providing evidence of a transnational conspiracy, whose personnel operated across national frontiers. During their leisurely stay, the plenipotentiaries confirmed the reports of their predecessors and urged O'Mahony to send 300 experienced officers and money to buy arms, while omitting any mention of their misadventure, which left them open to pressure from Stephens.[129]

The 'head centre', still fearing that Fenianism was abandoning long-term success for precipitate action, felt overruled by the positive accounts of 'six successive envoys': 'The organization here under me was like a wild unbridled horse' over which O'Mahony had lost control. He could only hope for the best.[130]

On 5 August O'Mahony and Roberts issued the 'final call'. Stephens and Henry Clarence McCarthy, the deputy 'head centre', had arranged a secure method of transferring funds, but omitted to inform O'Mahony. Terminally ill with consumption, McCarthy died that August; during the subsequent confusion, the 'head centre' sent £6000 in the only manner known to him, leading to its confiscation by Dublin Castle.[131]

Dunne and Meehan, when departing from Cobh in mid September, assured John Kenealy, organizer of the Cork IRB, that the Fenian Brotherhood was preparing to land 30,000 men. Kenealy responded that 5000 of these with arms for 40–50,000 Irish members would be sufficient, being familiar with 'American exaggeration'. As arrests were likely after the loss of Meehan's documents, Kenealy resolved with Stephens to appoint 'sub-centres' for the Cork region. Nevertheless, even this methodical member retained seditious documents at home, but managed to divert the attention of the police to the wrong trunk, thereby preventing numerous arrests.[132]

Table 2. *Stephens's report on IRB strength, Dec. 1864*

Region	Number of men
Greater Dublin area, parts of Wicklow, Wexford, Kildare, Carlow, Kilkenny city & county, most of south riding, Tipperary	28,729
Cork county & city	15,536
Belfast & Ulster	6283
Connacht	3764
Total	54,312
Total with additional members for regions unvisited	80,000 to 85,000

(Source: Stephens to O'Mahony, 11 Dec. 1864, Fenian Brotherhood Collection, CUA)

CHAPTER 3

The Irish People, *1863–5*

In 1831 the government established a national system of primary education based on a curriculum, which omitted Irish history to facilitate anglicization. Nationalists, who feared an erosion of identity, protested, although welcoming the growth of literacy, which would reach 53 per cent within twenty years. In 1842 Thomas Davis, Charles Gavan Duffy and John Blake Dillon founded the *Nation*, an instantaneous triumph as a popular guide in 'national affairs, political, literary, industrial, and artistic'. The Young Irelanders sought to unite their country by depicting an ancient nation, whose distinguishing spirit survived, contradicting British convictions that it was incapable of self-government.[1] Doheny felt 'as if a light had streamed down from heaven, fresh from God, to give the people hope, comfort and assurance', while John O'Leary, on reading Davis, experienced something akin to a religious conversion, realizing 'that for weal or woe my fate must be linked with that of my country'.[2]

The *Nation* was read aloud in Charles Kickham's home from the beginning, as an uncle had been the first subscriber in Mullinahone. For Kickham and his friends, John and Ellen O'Leary and Thomas Clarke Luby and his wife Letitia, the *Nation* provided an idealized concept of nationality to which they committed themselves wholeheartedly. It proved immensely influential in attributing any difficulties to British domination, to be overcome by developing national self-confidence through Ireland's unique cultural heritage.[3]

After 1847 emigration turned Irish nationalism into a transatlantic phenomenon, as alienated immigrants immersed themselves in their ethnic culture, which disseminated the writings of Young Ireland. In an age of rapid economic change, the growth of print media facilitated radical newspapers, while the transmission of news was further accelerated by the completion of the transatlantic telegraph cable. Working-class papers, combining Irish Catholic sensibilities with a secular outlook, were in demand. Editors had to avoid challenging the political leadership of the hierarchy, however, as the demise of the *Universal News* and Martin O'Brennan's *Irish News* in London, as well as that of the *Glasgow Free Press*, were to demonstrate.[4]

O'Mahony, Doheny and James Roche set up the earliest Fenian newspaper, the New York *Phoenix*, in June 1859. Its prospectus urged separatism rather than the ongoing constitutional farce and pleaded for brotherhood among Irishmen to remove British usurpation, using all legitimate weapons 'to restore the soil of the island to the Irish people'.[5] Observers considered the *Phoenix* animated by 'a ferocious hatred of England', preaching 'self-reliance' and the confiscation of landlord property. It advised on guerrilla warfare with pikes and the manufacture of gunpowder, but ended in August 1861, as Doheny and Roche prepared to depart with the McManus remains.[6]

Roche remained in Dublin, fell out with Stephens and established the weekly *Galway American*, supported by Thomas O'Neill Russell, author and Gaelic revivalist. Galway lacked a newspaper, while its transatlantic port might facilitate a Fenian invasion. The *Galway American* and, a little later, the *Irish People*, were modelled on the *Phoenix*: tropes included separatism, Irish-American military prowess and covert endorsement of physical force. The US served as a Republican role model. While the *Galway American* did not have a definitive position on peasant proprietorship, it devoted more space to agrarian issues than the *Irish People*, inviting readers to share their (negative) encounters with landlords. Unlike the IRB intellectuals, the pragmatic Roche advocated immediate action. He grasped, influenced by active Ribbon societies in Connacht, that any movement evading this question would not attract the peasantry, thereby losing vital support. Both Roche and O'Neill Russell were leading members of the NBSP, but failed to induce the US government to endorse it.[7]

Published in Galway from 12 April 1862 to June 1863, the paper relocated to Dublin as the *United Irishman and Galway American*, the official organ of the NBSP. When Roche clashed with Stephens on the issue of free speech, the latter ordered a boycott of the NBSP and its paper, which collapsed in April 1864. Roche and O'Neill Russell were forced to emigrate to the US.[8]

Founding the Irish People

Luby and O'Leary, who had become acquainted at James Fintan Lalor's sickbed in 1848–9, must have known that Lalor wrote in the *Felon* that any profits accruing from a radical newspaper should be dedicated to insurgency.[9] Stephens, however, 'had always hitherto held that newspapers were an abomination, and that, for good or ill, he needed them not, asserting, and no doubt believing, that he could mould public opinion in Ireland far better by his secret propagandism than by any paper'.[10]

Until November 1863 the IRB depended on travelling organizers and the distribution of occasional pamphlets to spread its message, but a growing membership required effective communication. Fenian 'circles' tended to disintegrate when left to themselves. At times, Stephens needed to restrain over-enthusiastic followers, who might foment a local outbreak, resulting in wholesale suppression. He realized that the people could not be converted to separatism by 'a whispering campaign'.[11]

During 1862 the *Nation* continued to voice its disapproval of O'Mahony and the Fenian Brotherhood. When A.M. Sullivan, editor of the *Nation*, denounced the 'head centre' as 'a maniac or a moral assassin', Charles Kickham defended this leading Gaelic scholar while opposing a premature revolution in the *Irishman*, the only newspaper open to the IRB. O'Mahony had impressed Kickham during his visit to Tipperary in 1861 with 'his calm, statesman-like wisdom' and 'the gentle kindliness of his disposition'.[12] Kickham emerged as a talented polemicist. When the *Irishman* changed ownership, it could no longer be depended upon and the rivalry between Stephens and Roche precluded access to the *United Irishman and Galway American*.[13] O'Donovan Rossa recalled that 'there were so many newspapers now attacking our work, so many peaceable and constitutional patriots publicly and privately thwarting the spread of it, that it was considered absolutely necessary to have an organ'.[14]

The pragmatic Stephens established his own paper, surmising with characteristic optimism that every member would buy a copy, thereby supplementing the uncertain remittances from America. Although Michael Davitt and Richard Pigott queried the wisdom of a secret society publishing a newspaper, the authorities could hardly remain in ignorance for much longer.[15] During the summer of 1863, Stephens began touring his Munster strongholds, in particular Cork and Tipperary, to solicit loans and subscriptions (at 8*s*. 8*d*. per annum). His prospectus declared the 'title of paper, the *Irish People*. I need say nothing of its principles. The tone of the paper shall be elevated and calm – prudent and wise, in short. The matter and style, I dare assert, shall be found superior to anything yet offered to the Irish people. Size of the paper – at least that of the thing called the *Irishman*.'[16]

Stephens intended raising £1000 through subscribers, but less than a quarter of this was collected. Rossa probably facilitated him by donating the insurance money he received after the tragic death of his second wife. John O'Leary discovered almost immediately that Stephens lacked sufficient capital and 'had a weekly struggle to bring out each number', depending on incoming payments with O'Leary and Rossa making up the shortfall from private funds.[17] Due to the by now permanently strained relations between Stephens and O'Mahony, Kickham, on excellent terms with the 'head centre', appealed to him for financial support. On 18 January 1864 Kickham thanked O'Mahony for a donation, believing it 'more than probable that if it were not for this timely aid we should have gone down before now'.[18] He had learned from Stephens how vital the *Irish People* was to the success of their movement; unfortunately, it needed another, immediate contribution of £300:

> In fact, our ship is at this moment among the breakers, and if you cannot come to our assistance we are lost. If you cannot raise £300 within *one week* after the receipt of this letter all is over. Write at once to all your friends. Let them beg or borrow the money. Keep back the monthly remittance to pay it – and if necessary let the proceeds of the Chicago Fair go for the same purpose.[19]

Kickham felt 'overpowered when I think how much depends upon your response to the appeal I have made to you. I have implicit trust in you. I expect a reply from you that will heal old wounds, and save the good old cause from the peril which threatens its very life.'[20]

O'Mahony sent the funds. Writing to him on 11 December 1864, Stephens acknowledged the drain on their limited resources, for the paper was 'at once a great weakness and a great strength'.[21] Given the Fenian Brotherhood's failure to provide adequate support, Stephens depicted the heroic struggle to establish the *Irish People* as having kept a disheartened IRB together, although 'we could barely, and by almost incredible efforts succeed in bringing out the paper from week to week'.[22] It became a rallying point at a reasonable cost, but contrary to Stephens's estimated circulation of 15,000 copies in Ireland and 10,000 in Britain and America, creating a profit of £5000 per annum, lack of funds, a perennial problem for radical publications, persisted throughout the existence of the *Irish People* from 28 November 1863 to 16 September 1865. Its weekly circulation never exceeded 10,000 copies, although these were passed around and organizers like Devoy saw to it that influential men, for example, national schoolteachers, received the paper gratis.[23]

Financial constraints led to wages being paid to those in greatest need and O'Leary and Kickham soon relinquished putative salaries. Offices were rented at 12 Parliament Street, close to Dublin Castle, which was probably coincidental. There, editing and typesetting were carried out, before the paper was printed at Pattison Jolly in nearby Essex Street, returning to the office for folding and dispatch to the country, where shopkeepers acted as its agents.[24]

Aware of their literary talent, Stephens had summoned John O'Leary from London and Charles Kickham from Mullinahone. Luby, Stephens's perennial assistant, gave practical advice, having worked on the *Irish Tribune* in 1855.[25] While Stephens engaged this triumvirate as joint editors, he intended to write the leading articles himself, before discovering that transmitting ideas in writing was a wearisome process in contrast to his fluent persuasiveness as an organizer. Stephens's struggles with 'Isle, race, and doom', his first editorial, were a case in point. He hoped to convey that Ireland's great natural beauty, as epitomized by the Golden Vale, Slievenamon and the Lakes of Killarney, coupled with her tragic history, made her a land worth fighting for.[26] Stephens's bombastic language and disjointed ideas negated this and he relinquished journalism soon afterwards. [27]

Denis Dowling Mulcahy, the bibliophile 'centre' for Clonmel, acted as sub-editor, while John Haltigan left his Kilkenny 'circle' to become the registered printer and as such, responsible for the contents of the paper. He was accompanied by his teenage son James, John 'Fireball' Neville and Edward Martin as printers and Jeremiah O'Farrell, the future office caretaker. All had been dedicated IRB members in Kilkenny. They were paid half a crown more than other typesetters, perhaps as a form of danger money. Stephens appointed Rossa as business manager with James O'Connor, who had been one of the Cork city 'centres,' and Michael Moynahan of Skibbereen, a brother of Mortimer, the 1858 Phoenix leader, as his assistants. During Rossa's absences on recruiting tours these book-keepers took charge of the office. Cornelius (Con) O'Mahony, a native of Macroom and former teacher, combined clerical duties for the *Irish People* with acting as Stephens's secretary, while James O'Connor's young brother, John, became the office messenger.[28]

Mulcahy and Haltigan were excellent choices, but their removal from Clonmel and Kilkenny respectively contained drawbacks. Mulcahy had been intensely security conscious and exercised strict discipline, according to the informer Pierce Nagle.[29] This was now relaxed, with unfortunate consequences. Haltigan remained a leading organizer, frequently recruiting in Callan and south Kilkenny and cooperating with John Morris, the Carlow 'centre', which distracted him from his responsibilities in Dublin. Rossa's appointment was of dubious value. Although enthusiastic and popular, his lack of prudence and method proved detrimental to the paper's finances. R.V. Comerford has suggested that Stephens removed prominent leaders from their power bases, making them reliant on IRB salaries to bring them under his control in Dublin. With the exception of Rossa, the men selected were suitable and it is unlikely that Stephens would act in quite such a Machiavellian manner; but it was a mistake to allow the functions of the operational and literary IRB staff to overlap, which unwittingly facilitated legal prosecution and endangered the paper.[30]

Fenians visiting Dublin and idle sightseers were drawn to the *Irish People* office. Denieffe lamented that 'all the precautions taken ... were now ignored' and 'soon we saw detectives hovering around like birds of prey'. The earliest police report on the *Irish People* from December 1863 confirm that the authorities were unaware of the extent of the conspiracy until then.[31]

Denis Dowling Mulcahy (courtesy NLI).

The supremacy of the people

The *Irish People*, the name chosen by Stephens, revealed his central theme, the sovereignty of the people as the source of legitimate power. He echoed Giuseppe Mazzini in his conviction that the working class embodied greatness and virtue, in contrast to the contemporary belief in the superiority of aristocracy and bourgeoisie.[32] Praising the people as the 'trunk and core' and the 'flower and fruit', Stephens proclaimed in his first editorial, 'Isle, race, and doom': 'Our faith in the present generation of the Irish people is boundless, especially in the young men: never have the youth of this country been moved and pervaded by a nobler spirit of patriotism – never been more compact of the stuff of martyrs and heroes.'[33]

The Fenian paper championed the workers: 'If at times the soul is staggered and appalled by the long agony of the people, it speedily takes nerve and hope from the spectacle of their sublime tenacity. Mark, we write emphatically of the *people* – the hoodwinked and misled, the duped and victimized *toilers* of this land.'[34] Aristocratic patriots were 'great exceptions', 'which strongly confirms the fact, that the real glory of our cause must be sought for in the action of the people alone'.[35]

Stephens believed that the working classes should be taught 'their rights and duties, power and dignity'.[36] This would create a revolution, as the 'overthrow of tyranny has always been the work of the people. It is by their combined and determined efforts that rulers are made and unmade. America and France have furnished us with glorious examples of this. But ... blood was shed before freedom came; and so it must be in Ireland.'[37]

The political education of the masses had been initiated by Wolfe Tone, a 'great organizer and teacher' and continued by Robert Emmet. But they were succeeded by false teachers of the parliamentary kind, who disheartened the people. A mystical belief in the nation, which cannot be extinguished unless the Irish are exterminated, suffused the paper, for 'the wellspring of nationality is the heart of the people'.[38] The Fenian journalists did not acknowledge the Young Irelanders as important predecessors, pronouncing them incapable of appreciating the people, although

> *they* had not accepted the foreign rule; and yet their leaders could or would not see. The people *alone* never counted for anything with those leaders; and this is precisely the point upon which we are at issue with them. We believe that Ireland will be virtually saved by the people alone. We say *virtually* saved, because we believe when the people *begin the work*, a large proportion of the middle classes, particularly the educated young men, will be with them. But if the people *alone* did not begin the work, it would never be begun. Therefore the fate of Ireland depends upon the people.[39]

The paper blamed the failure of the last insurrection, 'the abortion of '48', on the 'unparalleled incapacity' of its leaders. The Young Irelanders attempted 'to screen themselves' from criticism for 'their subsequent desertion of the national cause' by slandering their followers as 'a worthless, cowardly people, for whom it was useless and absurd to struggle any longer'.[40] Constitutional politicians like Charles Gavan Duffy, who had compared the state of Ireland to a corpse on the dissecting table when withdrawing to Australia, were condemned: 'The physician who pronounces a living patient to be dead must be an incompetent physician. The leaders who pronounce a living nation to be dead must be incompetent leaders. The convalescent patient should decline the further professional services of the incompetent physician. The convalescent nation should do likewise by the incompetent leaders.'[41] The people were blameless, having lacked guidance, but now realized, presumably through the teachings of the IRB, that the nation stood 'upon the brink of an abyss' and faced 'utter extirpation'.[42]

In his third and final editorial, Stephens denounced constitutional nationalists opposing him as 'felon setters'. Although West Britons deemed the native Irish racially inferior and lawless, Stephens interpreted their violence as resisting British law, which had 'murdered so many millions' of them. True Irishmen detested all informers, who were employing a new technique to alert the administration by posing as patriots, simultaneously censuring anyone who tried to organize an uprising. Stephens concluded by threatening the 'felon setters': 'As to the warnings and denouncings, the people can denounce and warn, too. *This is the first note of warning to all whom it may concern.*'[43]

Stephens never relinquished his bitterness over the Young Ireland elite's failure to support him. Even O'Leary, whose relationship with the 1848 leaders remained cordial, believed that these predecessors lacked consistency, for 'if we were the fools they seemed to take us to be then, what had they been but a very few years before?'[44] The McManus funeral demonstrated the power of the working class without 'traditional leaders', as Stephens had succeeded in excluding the Sullivans and Grays, successors of the Young Ireland leadership, who controlled the nationalist press.

The *Irish People* claimed that John Mitchel was out of touch to advise 'his countrymen *not* to think of sending the dead patriot's remains to Ireland, as that island was not in a fit condition to receive them. But he found he was mistaken, and exclaimed triumphantly – "Surely, the touch of that dead hand will rouse the young men of Ireland to *conspire* at last!"'[45] Mitchel had also 'declared his disbelief in the possibility of a military organization in Ireland. We trust the day will arrive when he will discover his error on this point also.'[46]

In an age of denominational tensions, the *Irish People* followed the *Nation* in 'its strife with sectarianism'.[47] It recalled that in the past the most outstanding patriots had been Protestants, underlining that 'Catholicity and nationality' were not inevitably linked. How Protestants could be won over to separatism was not discussed, however. Although the IRB was overwhelmingly Roman Catholic, it did have Protestant members, including John Edward Kelly of Kinsale, who fought at Kilclooney Wood in 1867, and P.J. Kain of the *Erin's Hope*, later an Episcopalian pastor in Woodbridge, New Jersey.[48] The *Irish People* stated 'our belief is that Protestants and Catholics should act for themselves in politics, independently of clerical dictation; and that good Irishmen may kneel at different altars, and, at the same time, join hearts and hands in the cause of their country'.[49]

Recurring themes were the futility of constitutional agitation, the anti-national attitude of the upper classes and the tragedy of emigration. Daniel O'Connell's 'moral force' teachings, for instance, were derided as 'repeal associations and confederations fulminating fierce denunciations against the Saxon from conciliation halls, music halls, and other vocal regions'.[50]

The IRB considered this downright mischievous, for even when 'honestly and ably conducted, parliamentary agitation is a delusion and a snare'.[51] Neither did it matter whether constitutional politicians were honourable, as they formed an inevitable minority in Parliament, 'the place of all others where no good thing could ever come to them'.[52] The *Irish People* urged its readership to join a secret conspiracy instead.[53]

O'Connell's conciliation policy and the failure of the 'men of station' to act decisively had created a lack of self-respect among the people, which resembled enslavement by training them to act 'like a beggar or a dog, to pray and whine'.[54] In contrast to the *Nation*, the Fenians perceived the propertied classes as Britain's garrison:

> Twenty years ago Thomas Davis appealed to the aristocracy to save the people with their own hands. We make no appeal to the aristocracy. For we know that, though we spoke with the tongues of men and angels, our appeal would be in vain ... They are the tools of the alien government, whose policy it is to slay the people, or to drive them, like noxious vermin, from the land.[55]

The *Irish People* left itself open to charges of assassination by declaring that 'no false delicacy must prevent us from trampling upon [the propertied classes]'.[56]

After receiving a free pardon in 1856, William Smith O'Brien returned to his Cahirmoyle estate.[57] Multitudes travelled from Limerick, some in their own carriages, to welcome him home. Smith O'Brien regretted a changed Ireland, where acceptance of British rule had superseded the desire for a native legislature. The *Irish People* commented: 'He was right, as far as the classes represented by the highly respectable crowd whom he addressed were concerned.' The upwardly mobile were eager to discard reminders of the Famine, but the working class had not 'abandoned the old faith, forgotten the wrongs and robberies of seven centuries' to embrace the Sassenach, for they 'were as true as ever'.[58]

The paper was critical of the larger tenant farmers, who prospered due to rising prices for agricultural products and became pro-British with 'a great horror of anything and anybody that might cause a "disturbance" in the country'.[59] Kickham commented that 'as a class, those men of bullocks are about the worst men in Ireland', possessing 'no more souls than the brutes which they fatten for the tables of our English masters'. Such 'boors in broadcloth' might ape 'gentility', but, lacking true refinement, were despised 'even by the smallest of the small gentry'. Kickham preferred 'communing with better men', namely the 'hardy, honest sons of labour'.[60]

Emigration

The prosperous farmer lacked empathy with the cottier, who required adequate pay, but was considered 'little better than an extortioner to expect two shillings a day for cutting the harvest'.[61] Larger tenants wished the land labourer to hell or America, for 'his cabin and cabbage plot were very much in the way', regardless of rural depopulation. A decline in agricultural profits formed a salutary lesson for such farmers, as 'no prosperity can be permanent … as long as we remain in the grip of England'.[62] Famine conditions were no longer needed to remove the people, as the legal system controlling access to the land accomplished this effectively. The children of small- and middle-sized farmers were forced to emigrate and many labourers only stayed until they could afford a ticket for America. British rule was at the root of this exodus, according to the *Irish People*.[63]

Many were concerned that depopulation would reduce Ireland to 'a mere feeding-ground for cattle'. At the Kilkenny agricultural show of 1863, Lord Carlisle, the viceroy, had proclaimed the destiny of Ireland as 'the fruitful mother of flocks and herds', supplying British markets.[64] On 15 August he was bitterly opposed by Kickham and a gathering of 700 people, who renewed their 'vows never to cease till we have achieved the independence of Ireland'. Lord Carlisle, in turn, denigrated this protest as the 'shrilly voices on the summit of Slievenamon'.[65] In the final issue of the *Irish People* Kickham appealed to his countrymen to 'get this island into their own hands' or perish, with 'the remnant of our race wanderers and outcasts all over the world … Our only hope is in revolution.'[66]

These fears were echoed by Thomas Dogherty Brohan, who described how potato plots had been turned into sheep walks near Cashel, where ruined houses taunted survivors of the Famine. The population of this town fell by 2709 between 1841 and 1861.[67] As long as emigration continued, the IRB risked losing many young men, who might fight in an insurrection. Stephens voiced disapproval of 'deserting' Ireland and dedicated followers were reluctant to leave for America until forced out by economic necessity.[68] The *Irish People* warned that 'emigration today is almost a crime', hinting that patriots should 'live in a manner not unworthy of men, who are ready one day to die for Ireland!'[69]

The editorial staff also blamed British rule for the sufferings of emigrants. Nineteenth-century Ireland experienced low levels of illegitimacy and prostitution, while a rising middle class valued its 'respectability', as manifested in the 'purity' of its women.[70] The *Irish People* commented on a letter by Bishop Lynch of Toronto to the bishops of Ireland, which described 'a large proportion' of the Irish in North America as 'pariahs', having suffered 'social degradation and the loss of their souls ... as the inevitable results' of emigration. Both in Canada and the US, hospitals, jails and poorhouses contained an inordinate proportion of Irish people and the bishop criticized the unjust laws of their homeland, which caused this flight abroad.[71]

Kickham contrasted the dire poverty of such emigrants, 'absolutely penniless' on arrival, with other nations. Bishop Lynch acknowledged that respectable girls with relatives or savings did well and became a credit to the Catholic Church; others, however, were forced to take the first unsuitable job and fell by the wayside. Pointing to the multitudes of Irish women in Canadian jails, the bishop lamented that the city of Montreal 'was comparatively chaste until 1852–3, when numerous bands of girls were brought from the poorhouses of Ireland'.[72] Some had been taken in by charitable families, but their workhouse upbringing made them inept servants and they left. Kickham asked his readers whether the Fenians, denounced by church and state, had caused this, before pointing to Drs Cullen and Moriarty, the 'spiritual guides of the Irish people', but among 'the chief props of a system the most fruitful of crime and misery that the world has ever seen'.[73] Bishop Lynch agreed privately that the ragged Irish, evicted 'to give place to cattle', felt estranged from their priests, whose 'fierce denunciations' of Fenianism were in contrast with 'scarcely a word of reproof for the exterminators of the poor'.[74]

Kickham also quoted Archbishop Cullen, preaching in Clonea, Co. Waterford: 'Wherever the British flag floats, there will be found divines to lift the standard of the church. It was a special dispensation of God to disperse the Irish people over every country of the globe.'[75]

Kickham juxtaposed Dr Cullen's brand of ecclesiastical imperialism with the report of a prison chaplain, who stated that in Protestant Liverpool 60 per cent of jailed prostitutes were Irish Catholics.[76] Kickham exclaimed 'England robbed us of land and liberty. Her rule has been a rule of rapine and murder,' which did not spare the chastity of destitute females, who sank into 'the foul sea of pollution, making night hideous with their shrieks and blasphemies – for they try to drown remorse in drunkenness – till they are prostrated by unnamed diseases … into the hell of the damned'. Was 'the island of saints henceforth to be known as the island of harlots', Kickham thundered.[77]

The *Irish People* discussed how poverty forced women into prostitution, a topic ignored by contemporaries. Francis J. Balfe wrote that, although Roman Catholics made up only 10 per cent of the population of England and Wales, they comprised almost one third of prisoners in 1863. It was 'in no sense a blessing' that Irish emigrants had been driven out by misgovernment and were despised by the Catholic clergy in Britain.[78] 'A Tipperary Girl' stated that as well as personal destitution, the necessity to help 'famishing friends in Ireland' coerced women to become street walkers. She concluded that the root cause was 'Saxon misrule'. Writers from Dunamaggin and Kilkenny city described the Catholic clergy as the 'garrison of the English government', desirous of winning land and power, but ignoring drunkenness, usury and how Irishmen were driven to enlist in the military.[79]

Artisans and clerks struggled for democratization against the constabulary and the Catholic clergy, who alerted employers to their politics to trigger dismissal. In Rath near Skibbereen, Simon Donovan, a national teacher, lost his post for voicing Fenian views. His father, also a schoolmaster, was warned not to shelter him or risk unemployment, so Simon emigrated to America. The letter-writer recalled Skibbereen being looked down upon for its 'pitiful donkey-eating people' during the Famine, but since they had become revolutionaries, the middle classes 'vehemently denounced' them.[80]

Irish-American soldiers

Even before 1848, many believed that any insurrection, which lacked leaders from the gentry, the traditional officer class, was doomed to failure. It was a British cliché that the Irish made good soldiers but could conquer only under English officers.[81] A nation was often judged by its military abilities and 1848 'made Irishmen the sad mockery and laughing-stock', undermining the spirit of the 'fighting Irish'. Having suffered defeats by the Maori, the 'arrogant' British depicted them respectfully. Irishmen, tired of the 'insults of their Anglo-Saxon masters', should try to administer 'a sound drubbing' to win similar esteem.[82]

Thousands of Famine immigrants had joined the US forces to escape urban poverty before the Civil War, when the *Irish People* revived martial confidence through its reports:[83] 'Young men, not equal to those whom we have yet available in Ireland, have led, in the present American war, with valour and devotion never surpassed, through battles terrible beyond all precedent, the companies and regiments of the Federal armies.'[84] It stressed the advantages of American democracy, where talented labourers became officers, 'a living example of what a people's army can do – an army officered exclusively by men sprung from the ranks of the people ... a large proportion of whom are Irish-born'.[85]

At least 180,000 Irishmen participated in this conflict, including 20,000 fighting for the Confederacy. The chief instance of a citizen promoted through merit was General Michael Corcoran, a founding member of both the EMA and the Fenian Brotherhood, designated by O'Mahony to lead the invasion of Ireland. Corcoran had gained military experience officering Irish-American volunteer units during the 1850s. In October 1860 he was arrested for refusing to parade the Irish 69th New York militia in honour of the Prince of Wales, then visiting New York. Corcoran demonstrated his loyalty towards the Union and avoided punishment by volunteering with his regiment at the outbreak of the Civil War, while gratifying Irish America, having snubbed Queen Victoria's heir.[86] The *Irish People* exulted that

> the career of this man, sprung from the ranks of the people, and of the people, should be a bright encouragement to us all. How ridiculous it would have appeared some fifteen years ago to prophesy that the 'raw Irish youth', with only as much education as the village school was able to afford him, was destined to command a legion in the field? Here is a glorious example for the manhood of Ireland.[87]

William O'Shea of Bantry and two of the Downing brothers from Skibbereen, whose military training consisted of drilling with the Phoenix Society in West Cork, had been promoted from the ranks. Captain O'Shea of the 42nd New York Tammany Volunteers was wounded at Gettysburg on 3 July 1863, where he displayed considerable bravery, while his brother David fell. Willie, the youngest son of John Mitchel, was among the Confederate casualties.[88] Patrick Downing survived to become colonel of the 42nd Regiment, but his brother Denis had to have a leg amputated at Gettysburg. He declared himself 'perfectly recovered' and his courage as a disabled man gained the admiration of Kickham.[89] The *Irish People* concluded proudly:

Captains O'Shea and Downing, and Major Downing, underwent a long imprisonment in Cork Gaol, in '58 and '59, on a charge of being United Irishmen, or
belonging to an oath-bound society conspiring to destroy English government
in Ireland. They belong to the Irish people, and while there exists a large supply
of such material available in England and Ireland, we must have trust in the
ultimate success of the cause of our country'.[90]

The paper preached that the Fenian invasion of Ireland needed to take place
sooner rather than later, for 'countless thousands' had been trained in this ferocious war, eager to demonstrate their valour 'in nobler battles at home'. These
veterans would 'turn their eyes and hearts fondly towards the land of their
birth' to rescue Ireland 'from the clutches of the tyrant', assisted by the IRB.[91]

Such statements reinforced revolutionary morale, while increasing psychological pressure on Dublin Castle. But the battlefield carnage was horrendous.
Michael Corcoran, who had been taken prisoner at the first battle of Bull Run in
1861, became a hostage of the Confederates to ensure the safety of their privateers, captured by the US authorities. After an exchange of prisoners, he returned
to New York in August 1862 to be promoted to brigadier general. His death in
December 1863, the result of a brain haemorrhage, was a severe blow for the
Brotherhood. While the total number of Fenian losses is unknown, O'Mahony
lamented in 1865 that whole 'circles' within in the US Army had become defunct.[92]

Capt. Denis Downing (courtesy NLI).

In May 1864 a bloody war of attrition against the Confederacy began, and, within a fortnight, the Union armies had suffered 18,000 casualties. The South found it almost impossible to replace the 10,000 men, who were sacrificed as the Federal Army approached Richmond, the Confederate capital.[93] Major Patrick Downing led the 42nd New York infantry, including Captain William O'Shea, who was 'killed in action 12 May 1864 at Spotsylvania', aged twenty-six. Two of the Downing brothers also failed to survive the war and the third, Denis, returned to West Cork to die at the age of thirty-two. The *Irish People* covered the obsequies of Patrick O'Regan of Rosscarbery, who had been among the earliest Fenians, later enlisting in the Union Army with his brothers. It became one of John O'Mahony's most depressing duties to attend such funerals in Calvary Cemetery, New York.[94] At the outbreak of hostilities Stephens had pondered the paradox that many Fenians would enlist to gain military experience, only to die in the process: 'How many of the best of our race shall be sacrificed in this way? And they, poor dupes and victims, shall be all the while dreaming that they are serving their native land!'[95]

The paper urged 'national self-reliance' rather than depending on foreign allies, traditionally France or Spain. During the late 1830s, Mazzini had developed the concept that Italians alone would save Italy, which was copied by the Young Irelanders and echoed by the Fenians: 'The Irish people for the first time in history have taken for their motto – *ourselves alone*.'[96]

In the 1850s, when England was embroiled in conflict, separatists had missed opportunities through lack of preparation. The *Irish People* advocated perseverance in organizing the masses as 'the grandest exemplification of intelligence and heroism,' without which 'no nation ever became permanently great'.[97] Steadfastness could generate respect, sometimes resulting in support from unexpected quarters. Men, who had grown disillusioned or impatient because of the mammoth task ahead, were reprimanded and urged that the only way forward was by secret organization:[98] 'All nations, that have won independence, made preparation for the struggle by silent work, not by noisy demonstrations.'[99]

Statements that the Fenians intended 'to rid the land of robbers, and to render every cultivator of the soil his own landlord, the proprietor, in fee simple, of the house and land of his father'[100] were noted by Dublin Castle, where Robert Anderson as legal adviser commented on 'brilliantly written articles', inciting the people to revolution.[101]

John O'Leary believed that independence would not be won by men valuing comfort, money and reputation, but by those willing to pay the price of 'pain, poverty, disease and obloquy'. The Fenian intellectuals saw themselves in the context of a European struggle for democracy, referring to Poland, Italy and

Hungary. They also lauded the Maoris' fight against colonial oppression in New Zealand.[102] O'Leary quoted Daniele Manin, who had united the citizens of Venice in 1848 to resist the Austrians for seventeen months: 'To save one's country, a man must be prepared to expose himself to everything, even to the curses of his contemporaries.'[103]

Manin, 'the soul of the Venetian Republic', led the heroic resistance against the Habsburg Empire to gain the admiration of opponents of Austrian imperialism. Having sacrificed everything for Venice, Manin surrendered and went into exile with his ally, General Guglielmo Pepe of Genoa: he died in Paris in 1857. Manin's vision of a united Italy remained unrealized during his lifetime, but posthumously he became a hero of the Risorgimento. It is not known if O'Leary ever met Manin; Stephens, however, was in contact with Italian nationalists, notably General Pepe, during his years in Paris.[104]

Separatism the only solution

Inspired by James Fintan Lalor, the *Irish People* advocated peasant proprietorship, but failed to elaborate how this could be achieved.[105] It consistently denounced efforts to address the grievances of the farming classes through legislation: 'Any tenant right measure, likely to be conceded by the British legislature, will assuredly prove a delusion and a humbug. The only way for us to settle the land question satisfactorily is to win national independence. Then the people could establish a peasant proprietary. This is the true and only remedy for our agricultural population.'[106]

Once independence was won, all other blessings would follow. It was pointless, for instance, to agitate for the disestablishment of the Church of Ireland, which formed an integral part of British rule. This liberally endowed Church (although its members amounted to a mere one-eighth of the population) was 'an ever present memorial of the injustice and wrong perpetrated upon' Irish Catholics. It divided the country into a clique of Protestant ecclesiastical dignitaries and proprietors and the majority of the population. Likewise, any tenant right bill wrung from Parliament would prove 'fraudulent and delusive', for only an Irish legislature could grant peasant proprietorship. Under foreign domination, there would be no 'justice for Ireland'. Kickham and O'Leary failed to discuss a scheme for land redistribution, probably due to apprehensions that this would deepen divisions within the Catholic community and distract from the goal of independence. During the Land League period, Kickham was to remark that the tenants would 'go to the gates of hell' for the land, with O'Leary adding 'and so they have'.[107]

IRB propagandists resented the condescending pronouncements of the *Times*, echoing Mitchel's accusation of genocide. W.E.H. Lecky, the outstanding contemporary historian, similarly deplored 'the ceaseless ridicule, the unwavering contempt, the studied depreciation of English newspapers' towards the Irish.[108] To Luby, Kickham and O'Leary the solution was obvious: 'Ireland's connection with England must be promptly severed, or else that the Irish people must cease to dwell in the land of their fathers.'

The *Irish People* did not condemn British attitudes outright, but exposed prevalent prejudice by clever quotation, for example, when reprinting an article from the *Saturday Review*, which considered that 'Ireland has no snakes or vermin except among its peasantry and clergy', who formed 'the raw materials of treason and sedition'.[109] The *Review* perceived emigration as likely to improve the Irish: 'Just as the Red man and the Bushman and the Maori melt away before the sure and certain advance of the superior race, so will the worse elements of Irish humanity yield to the nobler and civilising elements now at work in Ireland.'[110]

This journal exulted at the departure of the agrarian 'midnight assassin' to the American Civil War 'to enrich Virginian fields with hireling blood'.[111] Such racism must have created sympathy for Rossa's outburst of how 'those English savages rejoice over the manner in which they destroy us. They thank God we are gone, "gone with a vengeance", they say. What a pity we haven't the spirit to return with a vengeance.'[112]

Exploring the reasons for this exodus, the editorial team quoted the *Morning Star*, which held that small farmers would continue to leave a country where at best they could earn two shillings a day, while in America the average wage was five or six shillings. Irish conditions compared unfavourably with those in Britain and its colonies. English tenants in crisis could receive outdoor relief, while an Irish peasant had to give up his land to enter the dreaded workhouse. This loss of means and social status drove many abroad.[113] As was then customary, the *Irish People* copied and commented on articles from other publications, for instance, the *Irish Times*, which had suggested that a quotation from the *Principles of Political Economy* by John Stuart Mill should be hung over the gates of Dublin Castle,[114] 'when the inhabitants of a country quit the country en masse because the government will not make it a place fit for them to live in, the government is judged and condemned'.[115]

The *Irish People* was written in a lively, sometimes humorous style, although contributions could be repetitive. Its detailed coverage of the activities of O'Mahony's organization boosted morale. This paper responded to the accusation of being the organ of the Fenian Brotherhood by denying that the

American auxiliary existed in Ireland, which was factually correct, for the Irish Republican (or Revolutionary) Brotherhood operated here, or even 'the Irish Republic virtually established'.[116]

No *priests in politics*

The Fenians were astute enough to realize that if they were linked to the Risorgimento, their considerable popular influence would dissolve. When Mitchel attacked the pope's temporal power as despotism in 1854, his *Citizen* declined. The Risorgimento was anathema to Irish Catholics, who clung to the papacy for historical reasons. Fr Lavelle had declared himself anti-Mazzini and anti-Carbonari, while the *Nation* paradoxically upheld the Papal States against Italian nationalism. The *Irish People* decided to ignore this great movement as much as possible.[117]

Its editorial team was adept at exposing the follies and inconsistencies of its opponents. Aware that the Catholic Church prohibited membership of secret societies on pain of excommunication, the *Irish People* informed readers that Pope Pius IX had prayed publicly for the success of the conspiracy-based Polish insurrection of 1863–5. Nevertheless, the Irish hierarchy continued to condemn secret organizations at home, choosing to support the British state.[118] O'Connell's 'liberty is not worth the shedding of a single drop of blood' doctrine, so popular with the clergy, was undermined by the pope himself, when he appealed for volunteers to defend the Papal States against Italian nationalists in 1860. Pius IX stated that it was 'no use reasoning with a robber', a maxim the *Irish People* adopted with relish.[119] The Foreign Enlistment Act made it illegal for British subjects to enrol men in the Papal Brigade, but the priests had turned recruiting agents in a way 'that *secrecy, discipline* and *silent action* were the soul of the movement, which was planned and executed in a manner that Wolfe Tone himself might have envied'.[120] Charles Kickham concluded that 'it would be difficult to convince the people not to follow the good example set by their spiritual guides'.[121]

During penal times, priests had often been the only educated advisers of the Catholic population, which was unnecessary nowadays. The IRB leadership also considered that priests owed their first allegiance to the church, which could force them to withdraw at a critical moment, with disastrous consequences. The Fenian elite recalled the failure of Fr John Kenyon to lead local Confederates in 1848, when suspended by his bishop, as well as clerical interference with the Tenant League. They urged that priests should be excluded from participation in politics – for their own good.[122]

The *Irish People* pursued a spirited campaign for the separation of church and state, 'no priests in politics', claiming that the clergy was guided by expediency, 'on the side that was neither the honest nor the national one'.[123] However beneficial this novel concept might prove, the leadership was foolhardy in challenging the hierarchy, accustomed to a pivotal role in politics since O'Connell's campaign for Catholic Emancipation.

Archbishop Cullen, consolidating the position of his church and aligning its practice with Rome, would not relinquish political influence. He had experienced the expulsion of Pio Nono from the Papal States in 1848, which traumatized him to the extent of equating revolution with social catastrophe. He denounced Garibaldi, the hero of the Risorgimento, as 'a fortunate marauder'.[124] Dr Cullen was convinced that the Fenian insurrection must fail, ending in condign punishment of its foot soldiers, but 'Stephens and the real delinquents' would evade the law, just like Mazzini and Garibaldi. He mistakenly suspected the British of encouraging the IRB in preparation for savage repression.[125]

The archbishop distrusted both the Young Irelanders (his treatment of Charles Gavan Duffy was a case in point) and Dublin Castle. Identifying the Tories with the Orange faction, which he detested, Dr Cullen clung to the Liberals, but gained little in return. He ignored Catholic teaching, which permitted armed resistance to oppression as inapplicable to Ireland. In Kerry, Bishop David Moriarty was similarly convinced that Ireland's future lay within the empire, but met with opposition from the local IRB.[126]

As O'Leary was an agnostic and Luby a nominal Protestant, Kickham, the only devout Catholic among the senior staff, was chosen to present the Fenian position. Stating that British rule was destroying the Irish nation, which justified revolution, Kickham asked: 'Is it not then the duty of the Irish patriot be he priest or layman to teach the people that they have a right to judge for themselves in temporal matters? We have over and over declared it was our wish that the people should respect and be guided by their clergy in spiritual matters.'[127] But when 'priests turn the altar into a platform' to denounce reading the *Irish People* as a mortal sin and 'call upon the people to turn informers, and openly threaten to set the police upon the track of men who are labouring in the cause ... we believe it is our duty to tell the people that bishops and priests may be bad politicians and worse Irishmen'.[128]

Many priests, if confined to a spiritual role, 'would be worthy of respect and veneration' but knew little of politics after years of seclusion in a seminary. Nevertheless, they became community leaders on ordination and 'then the altar is turned into a platform, and vulgar political tirades substitute for sermons'.[129] This diminished respect for religion. The *Irish People* advised: 'It is quite possible for a priest (and even a bishop) to be mistaken.'[130] In the contest for the hearts and minds of the Irish people, the IRB accused the hierarchy of lacking patriotism by hampering opposition to British tyranny. Dr Cullen denounced the *Irish People* as 'the organ of the friends of violence' and worked for an official condemnation of Fenianism by Pope Pius IX. This did not happen until 12 January 1870 and proved ineffectual.[131]

The clergy counselled prudence, but if their flock had favoured independence, it would have been compelled to follow suit. While the urban and rural poor sympathized with Fenianism, the dominant farming class stood aloof. As the faithful generally accepted the hierarchy's political influence, the forthright views of the *Irish People* 'alarmed and shocked'.[132]

The National Association

The Catholic hierarchy had rejected the non-denominational queen's colleges of 1848 as 'godless' and initiated the Catholic University under John Henry Newman in 1854, but it struggled and the Catholic 'university question' continued throughout the nineteenth century.[133] Dr Cullen promoted denominational education as an insurance policy against social unrest. He condemned Fenianism in several pastorals.[134] In England, popular support for Italian nationalism, partly animated by anti-Catholicism, was accompanied by frenzied adulation of Garibaldi. Dr Cullen, like Dr Manning, the English primate, feared that Irishmen would conclude, 'if a revolution be so praiseworthy elsewhere, why not get up one at home?'[135] He asked: 'If it was a glorious thing for Garibaldi to collect a fleet at Genoa, and invade a country … and dethrone its king, why should not a head centre of the Fenians in America collect an army, and endeavour to overthrow the government of this empire?'[136]

By 1864 the Archbishop of Dublin took the IRB challenge so seriously that he, together with John Blake Dillon and P.J. Smyth, founded the National Association as an alternative, promoting tenant right and denominational education. The *Irish People* speculated (correctly) that the association would fail, in spite of Dr Cullen urging the clergy to use 'their influence in obtaining members and associates'.[137] The Fenians denounced this new body for 'deluding the Irish people', who had grown indifferent to elections, depriving Archbishop Cullen of a Whig alliance in Parliament with the customary sinecures 'for respectable "Cawtholics"'.[138] The National Association proved disunited and the Fenians considered only John Blake Dillon a formidable opponent.[139] When he ran for Tipperary in the 1865 general election, supported by Dr Cullen and Archbishop

Leahy of Cashel, the *Irish People* denounced the former rebel for discrediting separatists: 'Here, it will be said, is another of the "pack of fools" who attempted to get up a rebellion in Ireland coming to help England govern that unfortunate country. Who can believe that Irish men are disaffected, when the very rebel leaders of a few years ago become members of the foreign Parliament?'[140]

In Clonmel, IRB men created 'uproar' and prevented the future member for Tipperary from speaking. Charles Gavan Duffy deplored this 'senseless and stupid policy which the Fenians borrowed from the Chartists', of a 'mob' silencing a distinguished patriot.[141] Kickham concluded that any political party, which did not enjoy the support of Dr Cullen, would be penalized, suspecting that his grace would exclude 'all who will not join his agitation from the sacraments'. The archbishop also warned that parents, whose sons attended the Protestant Trinity College, Dublin, were 'unworthy of the sacraments'. The *Irish People* recalled that Dr Slattery, the previous Archbishop of Cashel, and a son of the Liberator had been among its students: 'It will surprise Irish Catholics to learn that Daniel O'Connell ought to have been excluded from the sacraments.'[142]

Archbishop Cullen was not a talented politician; the *Times*, for instance, accused him of deepening the denominational divide, but he displayed commendable zeal when campaigning for the sick and old, immured in the workhouses.[143] Dr Cullen was keenly aware of the preferential appointment of Protestants to local government posts, despite the multitude of Catholic rate payers. In his detestation of the Poor Law system Dr Cullen's views were in perfect unison with those of his erstwhile critic, Charles Kickham, who described the workhouse as 'that recruiting depot of hell'.[144]

The *Irish People* faced persistent clerical opposition. In Clonmel, for instance, a Franciscan reminded his audience that 'any one reading that paper was excommunicated', while fathers who allowed it into their homes 'were damned'. Financial pressure was brought to bear on those buying it, including the dismissal of national teachers and the cancellation of tradesmen's contracts.[145] In Clogheen, Co. Tipperary, Fr O'Gorman 'hunted down all there who ... became agents for the *Irish People*' to stop its distribution; no further editions would be sent from Dublin unless a seller, whose livelihood this priest could not threaten, was found. In Co. Waterford a clergyman successfully blocked the renewal of licences for publicans who sold the *Irish People*.[146] In England, Archbishop Manning and Bishop Ullathorne of Birmingham were similarly engaged in opposing the *Universal News* in its final, radical phase.[147]

Writing under the pseudonym 'Jim Long', Denis Dowling Mulcahy recorded that clerical eagerness to condemn Fenianism was not accompanied by a desire to prevent the exploitation of the poor. In Clonmel, for instance, working men were forced to pay 150 to 200 per cent interest to moneylenders, which the priesthood ignored, while squeezing contributions from poor members of their flock.[148] This attitude can be glimpsed in the painting *Mass in a Connemara Cottage* by Aloysius O'Kelly (a brother of James J. and Stephen O'Kelly, both London IRB members), portraying an immaculately dressed priest, far removed from the lives of his deferential, toil-worn congregation. Only a few young men form an exception with straight backs and defiant stares.[149]

The *Irish People* published a letter from Midleton, which hinted that Fr John Fitzpatrick, the parish priest, was selfish and had benefited from the Famine when serving in Skibbereen.[150] In *The Felon's Track*, Doheny recalled a cleric, who had denounced him, O'Mahony, Meagher and McManus in Killusty chapel, culminating in the 'fervent wish that *he might live to see our blackened corpses dangling on the gallows'*. Although this priest failed to procure their arrest, he had become Archdeacon of Cashel and his family was rewarded by the authorities with 'very lucrative berths, in inland offices'. Little wonder that the archdeacon feared attacks on the propertied classes, but did he ever recollect the thousands forced to leave Cashel due to 'benignant' British rule, the *Irish People* wondered. A letter to the editor portrayed Catholic Emancipation as facilitating the rise of the middle classes and the clergy, who abandoned under-privileged co-religionists to their fate.[151]

'Original poetry'

A quality paper, the *Irish People* covered music, drama, book reviews, (nationalist) Irish history and politics. Its outstanding columns were 'answers to correspondents', 'original correspondence' and 'original poetry'.[152] Davis had considered the Irish language integral to the teaching of history, but accepted that it would have to be introduce gradually in national schools. Few of his colleagues were willing to learn Irish. Despite Rossa's enthusiastic scholarship, the *Irish People* did not feature a Gaelic language section, unlike its New York namesake or the *Nation* from August 1858 to July 1860. This may be due to its readership of urban artisans and clerks, who knew little Irish.[153]

The old *Nation* succeeded in assembling a gifted circle of poets, but above all, had been blessed by Davis's talent for writing inspiring ballads. John O'Leary, a cousin of Eva of the *Nation*, agreed that a national literature, albeit in English, was indispensable and used the 'answers to correspondents' column to advise aspiring poets. In an age of limited educational opportunities, this was an uphill struggle. A writer signing himself 'Z', for instance, was told that 'your poetry is emphatically of the kind that neither Gods, men, nor [newspaper] columns allow. It is ... profoundly mediocre.'[154]

Most would-be contributors failed to develop beyond repetitive nationalist rhetoric. An exasperated O'Leary exercised quality control: 'We are constantly receiving cart-loads of verses which look as if the writers had showered down a certain number of words on paper, and cared not how they came together.'[155] He revealed his feelings by quoting one line, which 'most pithily describes our editorial condition at the present time – "We are persecuted well"'.[156] Despite the quality of its literary pages, the *Irish People* failed to produce a major poet. O'Leary was unfortunate that his paper had less than two years to establish an intellectual coterie, which was a factor. The *Irish People*'s only lasting contribution to the ballad tradition consisted of John Keegan Casey's 'The Rising of the Moon', commemorating the insurrection of 1798.[157] It concludes:

> *Well, they fought for poor old Ireland*
> *And full bitter was their fate.*
> *Oh! What glorious pride and sorrow*
> *Fill the name of Ninety-Eight.*
> *Yet, thank God, e'en still are beating hearts*
> *In manhood's burning noon,*
> *Who would follow in their footsteps,*
> *At the Rising of the moon.*

Rossa published 'The Soldier's Tale', also known as 'The Union of Macroom', which relates the familiar story of eviction and admission to a workhouse:[158]

> *With neither house nor bed nor bread,*
> *The workhouse was my doom,*
> *And on my jacket soon I read,*
> *The Union of Macroom.*

The protagonist enlists in the British army and is troubled by his actions during the Indian mutiny: 'And many a sultry day I spent blowing Sepoys from our guns.' In confession he learns that membership of the Papal Brigade, the British or US forces constituted no sin, but he is 'cursed, outlawed and banned' by his Church, after joining the Fenians 'to strike a blow'.[159] It is regrettable that Rossa wrote so little for the paper, given his literary ability. This poem constituted effective propaganda in the style of a traditional ballad.

Kickham's most memorable verse had already appeared elsewhere, but he contributed a tale, 'The Lease in Reversion', which showed that creating misery was not a landlord monopoly.[160] Large farmers, when motivated by greed, were eminently capable of doing so. Kickham, a perceptive critic of class divisions, knew of many land labourers, forced to survive on one meal per day. He pointed to the injustice of the poor never possessing any 'of their native soil', as '*cruel landlords* and *ambitious tenants* have blotted out every trace of our once numerous cottiers'.[161]

Ellen O'Leary, poet and a sister of the editor, shared his aspirations. Like the old *Nation*, the *Irish People* staff held social evenings, when policy discussions took place.[162] Ellen was often present and contributed patriotic verse, utilizing themes such as emigration or the privileged lives of landlords, paid for by the sufferings of the poor. Miss O'Leary quietly defied accepted norms, which confined women in politics to the role of society hostess or patriotic poetess. Stephens described her as 'the lady had a bright and intellectual face, and her manner was elegant without being affected'.[163]

In January 1864, the birth of the eldest son of Albert Edward, Prince of Wales, threw the *Times* into a patriotic frenzy, claiming that providence had favoured 'the British Isles' above all others. Their inhabitants enjoyed wealth and an unprecedented rule of law, threatened only by foreign 'quarrels and confusion'.[164] Britain resembled the 'happy isles' of classical mythology. The *Irish People* disagreed, wondering if Ireland were part of the US, would it still endure periodic famines or if it belonged to France, would farmers lack security of tenure, given that several million French citizens owned their land. Instead, the paper observed, the Irish benefited from British law with its packed juries. It concluded: 'But we are a united people, and what's England's is ours as what's ours is most certainly England's.'[165]

*Ellen O'Leary (courtesy National
Graves Association).*

Ellen O'Leary's poetry treated this subject with sarcastic outrage, commenting in a tone worthy of Mitchel, that 'our great oracle the *Times* having declared that the happiness and prosperity of the British Isles, including, of course, Ireland, at this moment is such as to have no parallel in history ... Truly, our happiness came on us unawares, and we lived in *unblissful* ignorance of possessing it.'[166]

In 'The Isles of the Blest', she used a hyperbolic style to mimic such inflated claims, contrasting the utopia of the *Times* with the misery of Ireland, where the last major Famine in western Europe had ended only twelve years previously:

> Yet 'tis strange, passing strange, and most wonderful, too,
> 'tis wondrously strange, and yet wondrously true,
> In hundreds, in thousands, as though from a pest
> House, our sons sail away from 'the isles of the Blest'.
> They say, the base traitors – who'd believe such false tales? –
> Though fruitful our isles, common food often fails;
> That men, starved amidst plenty, were ground and opprest,
> In the home of the happy, 'the Isles of the Blest'.[167]

As a polemicist, Ellen O'Leary elaborated tropes discussed by the *Irish People* in an almost masculine tone. In 'The Emigrants', she depicted the misery of those forced to leave Ireland 'to earn their daily bread'.[168] O'Leary's social concern stands, however, in uneasy contrast to traditions in Tipperary town that her family was severe on tenants of the very property, which underpinned John and Ellen's commitment to separatism.[169]

The fifteen-year-old Fanny Parnell wrote poetry for the *Irish People*, an acceptable way for a lady to supplement her income. Perceiving her work as propaganda, 'Aleria' studied the paper. According to Jane McL. Côté, her biographer, Miss Parnell's invariably masculine tone arose from an unconscious desire to express action and defiance in verse, then a male prerogative.[170] In 'The Poor Man to his Country', she voices determination to spurn emigration and comfort abroad in favour of fighting tyranny at home:

> Stern suffering doth but knit me closer still unto thy breast;
> And shame it is thy sons on foreign shores should seek for rest,
> 'tis shame to leave thee in thy direst need, unhappy land!
> Nor lift, to save thee from the tyrant's gripe, one helping hand.
> O brethren, prove the mettle of your swords by noble deeds.[171]

It is not known how Fanny came to be a nationalist, but she insisted on attending Rossa's trial in 1865 and 'could hardly restrain her tears and ... pictured herself as the next occupant of the dock'.[172] Although cultivating the conventional image of gentle femininity when fundraising for the Land League and her brother, Charles Stewart Parnell, during the 1880s, her *Land League Songs* adopt an equally forceful Fenian tone, 'to the persecutor of the poor, the hunter of the priests, and the shooter of women and children – William Buckshot Forster – these poems are respectfully dedicated by the author, Fanny Parnell'.[173]

Mary Jane and Jeremiah O'Donovan Rossa
(courtesy NLI).

Mary Jane was the convent-educated daughter of Maxwell Irwin, a respected shopkeeper and Young Irelander in Clonakilty. Timothy Warren Anglin, her cousin and godfather, was forced to emigrate to Canada during the Famine, where he edited the *Freeman* and became speaker of the House of Commons, 1874–9. On meeting Rossa, Mary Jane began to contribute poetry to the *Irish People*. In 'Irish Missioners – the Bridge', she took up the theme of a destitute woman driven to prostitution. The title is an allusion to Dr Cullen's statement that the Irish diaspora would spread the faith. The girl reassures her family back home that she is doing well, but commits suicide to avoid discovery of her 'fall':[174]

> 'Gainst the span of the dark-tinted bridge,
> Where the rough severed waters unite in a ridge
> Like a furrow of snow, when the late morning sun

Looked down thro' the city smoke misty and dun –
A chill form was floating there, a white face appearing there,
Lost, doubly lost, and no being in hearing there,
Under the arch of the dark-tinted bridge.[175]

Mary Jane became Rossa's third wife on 22 October 1864. John O'Leary recalled her as 'giving, I then thought, great promise of a future which, I am sorry to say, has never arrived', due to the demands of an erratic husband and large family.[176]

Other contributors included John Walsh of Cappoquin, a national teacher who signed his love poems 'Kilmartin', Ellen Forrester of Manchester, mother of Arthur, a future assistant of Michael Davitt, while the youthful John Locke of Callan featured as 'Vi et armis'.[177] Dr George Sigerson, surgeon, poet and translator from the Irish, did not join the IRB, but contributed to the Fenian paper as a member of the Kickham/O'Leary literary circle.[178]

'Original correspondence'

The first significant article for the 'original correspondence' column was written by Charles Kickham, escorting his sister and her baby to their new home in America. He was horrified at 'the *number* of our people flying from this suffering land'.[179] In an immediate, appealing style, Kickham described familiar, heartrending scenes, such as the departure of the emigrant ship from Cobh. He alluded to Republican heroes and incidents as if establishing a separatist reference map of Ireland, 'the sombre night comes down upon us as we pass Spike Island; and I think of John Mitchel'.[180] In touching, if somewhat sentimental, language Kickham described how the emigrants, hearing two musicians strike up, 'fell into a closely packed procession, and marched slowly round the vessel after them'.[181] When the music ceased, one of them remarked, as if waking from a dream: '"Begor, boys, I thought the daisies were under my feet." And the daisies and shamrocks were under all their feet during all that hour. We are a soft-hearted race heaven help us.'[182]

Kickham met 'that true son of old Ireland, and my dear and valued friend, John O'Mahony. He is in good health and spirits, and labouring earnestly as ever for the old land. Yet, far away from old Kilbeheny and the lordly Galtees, his life must be a life of suffering indeed, if he be not upborne by the proud thought that he is suffering ... [in a] holy cause.'[183] Kickham represented the IRB at the first general convention of the Fenian Brotherhood, deploring the opposition of the Catholic clergy in America, which might prove fatal to the Irish nation. In a very modern way, he felt that priestly dictatorship damaged the church, 'those politi-co-ecclesiastical autocrats who attempt to throw dust in the eyes of the people'.[184]

Readers contributed to the 'original correspondence' section, acquainting the editor with local issues. The anti-clerical James F.X. O'Brien, a Young Irelander and Fenian in Cork, wrote as 'De L'Abbaye'. Its foremost contributor, however, was Thomas Dogherty Brohan, the 'centre' for Tipperary town, alias 'Harvey Birch'.[185] He appealed to the less sophisticated through his deceptively simple tales of a peddler from Clanwilliam Barony, accompanied by his dog, called 'Dan, and I think he is a more harmless animal than Daniel O'Connell that humbugged the people'.[186] The peddler was a farmer's son, whose father had supported O'Connell at his parish priest's behest. Their landlord retaliated by evicting the family, which scattered, the father dying in Cahir workhouse and his sisters becoming servants until they had earned their fare to America. The son took to the roads, carrying the *Spirit of the Nation* in his pack, while his dog growled at the priest, a signal that an anti-national individual was approaching. Harvey Birch's popular stories illustrated IRB tenets.[187]

Eighteen-year-old John Sarsfield Casey contributed a letter, depicting 'Mother Ireland', 'an unfortunate old woman', whose 'large potato garden' was in a broken-down state, foreshadowing the popular Tommy Makem ballad 'Four Green Fields'. Separatists should spread their message by socializing with working men on Sundays, their only free day, reminding them of longstanding grievances and the Fenian solution. Casey advised leaving such groups of potential insur-gents with a propagandist follow up:

> Irishmen, you who are aware of your country's wrongs, will you do nothing for pity, for mercy, for your country's sake? Sunday is an idle day with all. Travel six, eight, or ten miles through the country; impart a knowledge of Ireland's wrongs and hopes to your ignorant, though well-inclined countrymen; purchase an extra number of the *Irish People*; give it to them, and by so doing you will be conferring a lasting favour on your motherland – poor Granua Wail.[188]

In contrast to the Comerford thesis of patriotism as a pastime, Casey's approach is astute in engaging with these peer groups unobserved by parents, employers and other authority figures to win recruits.

Ellen Eliza, daughter of John Callanan, a former Young Irelander of The Hill, Clonakilty, did not hide her identity under a pseudonym, unlike most female correspondents, when contributing well-regarded letters in 1864–5. In dignified language, this friend of Mary Jane O'Donovan Rossa objected to Fr Leader, parish priest of Clonakilty, instructing the electors to be guided by county gentlemen, who would select wealthy candidates for the 1865 election. Ellen Eliza urged readers to think for themselves, while adding that only those who profited from parliamentary electioneering still bothered to vote. When an anti-Orange Order demonstration led to 'tumultuous gatherings' in Clonakilty in July 1865, John Callanan burned a picture of William III from his window, assisted by Ellen Eliza. Illustrating how unquestioningly the female leadership accepted Victorian ideas of respectability, Mary Jane told Rossa that she would cut her friend after her unladylike public appearance in night attire.[189]

The editorial staff provided its readership with an education in democracy and had an 'open university' effect. James I.C. Clarke, James J. O'Kelly and James Clancy, London 'centres', studied the *Irish People* and were impressed by its 'virile, direct' style. Clarke, a future playwright, published his first nationalist poems in this paper and all three were to become journalists on the *New York Herald*. Dogherty Brohan, James Haltigan, James O'Connor and Hugh Byrne of Wicklow ('Hugo del Monte'), benefited from contact with this literary elite.[190] Devoy recalled that Thomas Clarke Luby was generous with his recommendations:

> His advice on reading was well worth taking, as he was a thoroughly well-read man and a most competent judge of literature. He wrote more than any other member of the *Irish People* staff and his articles, although characterized by fine literary skill, were so plain and direct that the uneducated man could understand them as well as the person of culture, and therefore they made a greater impression than those of John O'Leary, who was a bit too philosophical and sometimes wrote over the heads of his readers.[191]

How influential was the *Irish People* ultimately? It never rivalled the circulation of the *Nation* at home, but was embraced by the Irish in Britain, who endured a hostile environment. In Liverpool, where George Archdeacon's paper shop constituted an unofficial IRB office, a further seventeen newsagents sold the *Irish People*. Distributors were also appointed in Birkenhead, Leeds, Chesterfield, Bolton, Sheffield, London and Glasgow. In Britain, A.M. Sullivan lamented, it almost succeeded in 'annihilating the circulation of the *Nation* in many places'. (The short-lived *Irish Liberator*, the organ of the NBSP in England, but controlled by the London IRB, had collapsed by July 1864, despite support from Thomas Clarke Luby.) The *Irish People* was posted to Canada and the US and promoted by John O'Mahony as 'our Irish organ' – a list of 500 American subscribers is extant.[192]

The Fenian weekly presented an alternative reality to the British state, featuring Tone and Emmet as role models. The leaders legitimized themselves by claiming political power as the right of the common people, but were unable to overcome the power of the Catholic hierarchy.

Devoy conceded that the Fenian paper was inferior to 'the old *Nation* of Duffy and Davis', although mobilizing the people and disseminating ideas, which 'have endured ever since. It prepared the way for all that has since happened and inspired the people with a new spirit. The fighting Land League would not have been possible but for it.'[193]

The anti-clerical tone of the *Irish People* resonates in *A Portrait of the Artist as a Young Man*, where Mr Casey, the old Fenian turned Parnellite, goaded beyond endurance in the Christmas dinner scene, shouts:

> Didn't the bishops of Ireland betray us in the time of the union when Bishop Lanigan presented an address of loyalty to the Marquess Cornwallis? Didn't the bishops and priests sell the aspirations of their country in 1829 in return for Catholic Emancipation? Didn't they denounce the Fenian movement from the pulpit and in the confession box? And didn't they dishonour the ashes of Terence Bellew McManus?[194]

The New York Irish People

O'Mahony responded to the seizure of the Dublin paper with a New York edition running from January 1866 to October 1872. Initially, it avoided denunciations of the senate wing and published stories by Kickham, articles on Irish history and a serial, 'The men in the gap', lauding Stephens, O'Mahony and O'Donovan Rossa. The *Irish People* featured a weekly column by Fr Lavelle to reassure devout Catholics, refuting Bishop Moriarty and denouncing Garibaldi as the pro-British enemy of both Irish separatism and the pope. The Fenian Brotherhood described itself as a democratic organization, opposing class distinctions on the British '*divide et impera*' system. Its paper supported national self-determination and the right of the people to the land, but lacked the ironic wit of the original.[195]

A correspondent gloated over its denunciation in London and quoted a review in the *Times*:[196] 'In the midst of all this purely entertaining matter we have a glimpse of what may be called "business",' referring to Fenian plans. 'All the leading English journals consider the Irish People fully up to the mark as an organ of the Fenian Brotherhood.' The government have issued orders to the postal authorities to prevent your circulation in Great Britain as much as possible.'[197]

Sir George Grey conceded that Fenian agents from America distributed copies secretly. He considered the government justified in suspending habeas corpus to facilitate an effective suppression.[198] Dublin Castle knew that the *Irish People* reached Ireland, 'to disseminate treason throughout the country', but Lord Wodehouse, the Lord Lieutenant, and the home secretary learned that, while the police could seize the paper, the post office was not entitled to confiscate it in transit.[199] The *Irish People*, on the other hand, felt the power of the radical press vindicated, when excluded from 'the Isles of the Blest' after exposing the British government. It urged readers to post it to Ireland by wrapping 'it in the half sheet of some other paper, leaving the name of the other paper exposed, and it may thus escape detection', adding, 'our cause is just, and God will defend the right'.[200]

Linking the transatlantic community of activists, Irish publications were 'perfectly notorious' for copying seditious news from US papers under cover of legitimate reporting to avoid prosecution. In tandem with the *Irishman* as successor to the Dublin *Irish People*, its New York namesake opposed the senate wing, which used the *Irish-American*, allied to the *Nation* of the Sullivan brothers, for its mouthpiece.[201] News from the various counties and the Fenian prisoners, obituaries and appeals, for instance, to aid the charitable Nun of Kenmare, or George Archdeacon, who had fallen on hard times, focused immigrants on the 'old country'.[202]

From January 1868 on, O'Mahony rehabilitated himself by publishing his recollections in the *Irish People*, copied by the *Irishman*, the *Glasgow Free Press* and the *Universal News* of London, the latter two papers of the migrant Irish in Britain. O'Mahony edited the *Irish People* for two years, beginning in December 1868.[203] He claimed that the abortive Rising was of minor significance, Fenianism 'having for its object *the organization of the political, financial, and military resources of the Irish nation in America for the purpose of overthrowing British domination in Ireland, using the United States as its base of operations*'.[204] Fenianism would 'keep alive in the American mind a burning hatred of Great Britain' and induce US politicians to oppose the British Empire, whose press had become alert to 'grave dangers'... from the continuance of Fenian propagandism'. After O'Donovan Rossa's release in 1871, for instance, the *Irish People* scooped his earliest recollections.[205]

O'Mahony supported the Irish language through a poetry column with translations by Michael Cavanagh and Michael Heffernan, asserting the value of Gaelic culture. O'Mahony pursued a long-term strategy of reversing British policy as the mission of his Brotherhood:[206] 'We work to renationalise our people – England works to destroy their nationality.'[207] It was essential to reverse the pervasive anglicization, arising from Irish lack of national self-confidence, otherwise even a military success against the British, which was unlikely after centuries of oppression, would remain pointless:

> We, therefore, work not so much for a bloody insurrection as for a thorough revolution of the Irish people – intellectual, moral, political, and national. This

revolution is now going forward. It is changing the slavish disposition of the people. It is ransacking musty archives for the long hidden glorious pages of our annals. It raises its flag. It heals divisions. It bands the people together in the holy cause of freedom and nationality.[208]

This made O'Mahony a precursor of the Irish cultural revival of the 1890s. Such ideas, without the Gaelic language, were also disseminated by John O'Leary on his return to Dublin in 1885. Ultimately, O'Mahony, Luby and O'Leary shared the conviction that 'human liberty goes before Irish patriotism', that is, if an independent Irish government acted tyrannically, any Fenian would be duty-bound to oppose it. The *Irish People* expressed concern for 'other oppressed peoples', mentioning the Cretan struggle against the Turks and the sufferings of the poor in the East End of London, but excluded black Americans because 'we are no advocates for negro supremacy or even for negro equality'.[209]

O'Mahony was assisted by Peter McCorry, ex-editor of the *Glasgow Free Press*, who had emigrated after failing to concoct an alibi for Michael Barrett. McCorry deplored how the Irish tolerated being caricatured in the British press instead of supporting the chain of radical publications linking the diaspora to develop 'self-respect' and gain freedom via Fenianism. He regretted that an alliance between Irish and British workers was not possible at present. In reality, the *Irish People* and the *American Gael*, O'Mahony's final newspaper venture in 1873–4, as well as their counterparts in London and Dublin, struggled as minority papers.[210]

General Michael Corcoran of the
Fighting 69th Regiment (courtesy
Library of Congress Prints and Photo-
graphs Division, Washington DC).

CHAPTER 4

Arrests and Dissensions, 1864–6

Sir Robert Peel, Liberal chief secretary since 1861, Sir Thomas Larcom and the law officers consulted about the seditious press. On 13 February 1864 the *Irish People* had published 'The approaching crisis' in expectation of a European war, pointing to Hungary, Venice and Poland as revolutionary role models. Solicitor General Lawson confirmed that treasonable articles appeared 'with impunity' in the Fenian papers, the *Nation* and the *Irishman*, while Dr David Bell, a former Presbyterian clergyman associated with the *Irish Liberator*, travelled the country as an organizer, as did Edward Coyne of Callan. Dublin Castle decided that prosecutions should only be brought if there was a likelihood of success. Sir George Grey, the Home Secretary, concurred in ignoring the issue at present, given that these papers were competing with each other acrimoniously. British freedom of the press, a cornerstone of the liberal state and much admired by fellow Europeans, meant that most radical newspapers escaped prosecution between 1863–8.[1]

Pierce Nagle, a teacher and the President of the NBSP in Clonmel, had been associating with the IRB since the McManus funeral. This resulted in his dismissal from Powerstown National School. He approached Dublin Castle to inform, while working as a paper-folder for the *Irish People* in 1864.[2] The Dublin Metropolitan Police began watching the newspaper and its personnel, although convinced that the IRB was perfectly 'contemptible'.[3] Disquieting incidents occurred during 1864–5, including men drilling, a parish priest being burnt in effigy for 'felon-setting' in Skibbereen and a crowd of 500 protesting at the arrest of Fenians in Carlow.[4]

In May 1865 Stephens visited Glasgow and Edinburgh, accompanied by Matt MacLaughlin from Kiltimagh, Co. Mayo, chief organizer for Scotland. Stephens told members to fill 'up the ranks of the soldiers of Ireland', for 'on no consideration would the struggle for our country's independence be postponed'. On 25 July Pierce Nagle warned of 'an uprising this year'.[5] In August, at Dangan fair near Midleton, the constabulary refused to release a drunken labourer from custody, when a bystander protested: 'We are all belonging to the Fenian Brotherhood, and the time is coming at which we must strike the blow.'[6] A riot erupted and the 200-strong crowd chased the police, who barricaded themselves into their makeshift barracks. When the door was smashed open, the constabulary fired on the attackers, fatally wounding Laurence Kelly, an IRB member. Subsequently, Margaret Walsh 'was hunted by a mob, and had to run for her life', having testified about the assault on the temporary police station in her home.[7]

John Warner, a former militia sergeant who drilled the Fenians in Cork, changed sides and informed a magistrate that the Rising was imminent. He claimed that the IRB would attack barracks, murder the constables to seize their weapons and kill the Catholic Bishop of Cork, burning his corpse in tar for having opposed Fenianism. Warner pointed to J.J. Geary's pub on North Main Street as the headquarters of sedition in Cork, where John O'Donovan gave 'lectures on engineering and military training'.[8] Brian Dillon, a local leader, struggled to restrain his men, who demanded action. By early September there were reports of drilling and infiltration of the military from Limerick, Mallow, Emly, Co. Tipperary, Kerry, Kilkenny, Sligo, Belfast and Newtownards, Co. Down. The *Cork Constitution* did not interpret this as a recreational activity, but pointed to parallels with the start of the Rising in 1798:[9] 'It was then, just as now, common to drill in large companies, and on being observed there was always a football ready, so that the spy came apparently upon a number of young peasants engaged in sport.'[10]

On 1 September, Lord Wodehouse reassured Lord John Russell at the Foreign Office that he was evaluating intelligence reports and would act if sufficient evidence became available: 'But they are very *wary*, and the difficulty is considerable of obtaining tangible proofs, tho' I am quite prepared to run the risk of exceeding the law, if necessary.'[11] It would not surprise him if 'some Irish desperadoes who have been trained to arms in the American Civil War should not run over in steamers with arms to some places like Skibbereen, and raise an insurrection in Cork and Kerry where the people are quite disposed for evil'.[12]

While confident that a Fenian outbreak would prove 'contemptible', Wodehouse urged the Duke of Somerset, First Lord of the Admiralty, to take every precaution, requesting gunboats to patrol the south and southwest coasts. The duke agreed that vigorous measures now would prove ultimately merciful in restoring order and sent the frigate *Liverpool*, paddle steamer *Gladiator* and gunboats *Nightingale* and *Hyena* to Queenstown, where Admiral Charles Frederick, in charge of the Irish coastline, was to be guided by Wodehouse.[13]

The viceroy confided in the home secretary, that, despite a lack of Fenian arms, the British intelligence network predicted 'an outbreak early this autumn' in Munster, where 'the movement is spreading and in Cork county the feeling in favour of it amongst the small shopkeepers and the young farmers is strong. Parts of Kerry, Tipperary and Kilkenny are also affected with a very disloyal spirit.'[14]

From 5 to 12 September Lord Wodehouse received letters from aristocrats, including Lord Shannon, who worried that the Rising would wreak revenge on 'Protestants and landlords', simultaneously suspecting the professed loyalty of the Catholic clergy. He pointed to Killeagh, Midleton, Castlemartyr, Youghal and Clogheen as centres of sedition. Lord Lismore, Lord Lieutenant for Tipperary, requested a company of infantry to be stationed in Clogheen, while Lord Fermoy, who occupied this ceremonial post in Co. Cork, announced an imminent meeting of 150 magistrates. He informed Lord Wodehouse of the 'great alarm' in his county, where farmers were withdrawing their money in gold to hide at home. The attorney general forwarded a letter from John Fitzhenry Townsend, QC and deputy grand master of Irish freemasons, whose recommendation to provide troops for Skibbereen was supported by his cousin Thomas Somerville of Drishane, a deputy lieutenant for Co. Cork.[15]

On 8 September Pierce Nagle purloined a letter from Stephens to the Clonmel IRB, when Patrick Power, the designated courier, became intoxicated and fell asleep in the *Irish People* office. Nagle travelled to Tipperary and read to the assembled officers:[16]

> There is no time to be lost. This year – and let there be no mistake about it – must be the year of action. I speak with a knowledge and an authority to which no other man could pretend, and I repeat, the flag of Ireland – of the Irish Republic – must this year be raised. As I am much pressed for time, I shall merely add that it shall be raised in flow of hope such as never beamed around it before. Be, then, of firm faith and best cheer; all goes bravely on.[17]

Instead of burning the letter, Nagle handed it to Superintendent Daniel Ryan afterwards.[18]

Lord Wodehouse had heard reports that Munster gentlemen were sending their valuables away for safekeeping. He contemplated decisive action, but

moved cautiously. Consulting Sir George Grey, Sir Robert Peel and Lord Strathnairn, he regretted that the constabulary was 1500 men below par; only salary
increases could remedy this and at present the military would have to substitute
for the police. He supported Lord Strathnairn's plan of an anti-Fenian cordon
by Royal Navy ships signalling any hostile approach to the coastguards and
police, who would relay information inland to the troops, which was adopted.
By October British vessels had extended patrols to the Shannon estuary and
Lough Swilly.[19]

On 12 September Lord Wodehouse informed the home secretary that the
attorney general was 'anxiously' seeking 'tangible evidence' to seize the Fenian
leaders and the *Irish People*: 'The articles are openly treasonable and the newspaper is distributed broadcast through the country and eagerly read by the
shopkeepers and peasantry. It is cleverly written (I always read it every week)
and does infinite mischief … The office is the headquarters of the conspirators.'[20]

He hesitated, as 'press prosecutions are always odious' and juries did not
invariably support Dublin Castle, but in the disturbed state of the country it was
'monstrous' that the *Irish People* could propagate revolution – Dublin Castle
would be expected to act. His analysis was confirmed by an open letter in the
Cork Constitution, where an anonymous gentleman denounced the viceroy
for tolerating this conspiracy, while the *Irish Times*, hitherto contemptuous of
Fenianism, repeated the southern paper's message that the government must
put down disorder, caused 'by a pack of rebellious mechanics and labourers and
shopboys'. This was followed by an unanimous petition for military protection from the magistrates, whom Lord Fermoy had convened, providing a final
impetus for arrest.[21]

Lord Palmerston's cabinet relied on their Irish representative's judgement
and on 14 September, Lord Wodehouse and James Anthony Lawson, in the
presence of Sir Thomas Larcom and Lord Strathnairn as military adviser, agreed
'to arrest the Fenians in Cork and Dublin simultaneously tomorrow night'.[22] On
15 September detectives broke into the *Irish People* office and detained everyone
in the vicinity, smashed the newspaper type and seized documents. Others were
arrested at home, but Stephens, Kickham and Edward Duffy evaded capture
and hid in Sandymount. The police restricted access to the telegraph offices to
prevent sympathizers warning Fenians elsewhere.[23]

In Cork city the police force was stealthily augmented to 150 constables,
who raided Geary's pub during the night. Although its proprietor managed to
escape, John Kenealy, John Lynch, Brian Dillon, Michael Francis Murphy, Mark
Adams and Patrick O'Shaughnessy were arrested. Co. Cork was proclaimed
and military reinforcements arrived from Ballincollig, Youghal and Fermoy.[24]

James Mountaine was among those detained in the second wave. Given the likelihood of raids, Geary had been careless in retaining seditious documents, but
John Sarsfield Casey, his apprentice, disposed of a list of 400 IRB members and
some rifles. John Lynch and his fiancée had naively preserved love letters, which
revealed their Republican beliefs and facilitated his conviction.[25]

Seizure of the Irish People, *Dublin (*Harper's Weekly*).*

After the *Irish People* seizure, the constabulary destroyed copies of its final
issue of 16 September in Cork, Cashel, Clonmel, Carrick-on-Suir, Ballyporeen
and Clogheen. The press welcomed the arrests for putting an end to this 'delusion'. The *Times* cautioned a minority, which still wanted to ignore 'so silly' a
movement to avoid raising its profile. Liberal principles, customary in England,
were inapplicable, given the chronically disturbed state of Ireland and its 'very
excitable' national character.[26] The *Times* reassured readers that the English
police were 'on the alert', minimizing rumours of Fenianism in Liverpool, while
pointing to the first arrests in Salford and Sheffield. The *Irish Times* found it
'almost incredible' how the conspiracy expected to succeed without arms or a
commissariat.[27]

Lord Strathnairn rejoiced with the Duke of Cambridge that the military
had not been required during the arrests. He reassured Lord Bandon, who
had supported Lord Fermoy's petition for protection, that part of the 1st
Royals would reach Cork on 18 September, while the remainder entrained for
Buttevant. Strathnairn expected assistance with billeting from Lord Bandon in
the eponymous town and from Thomas Townsend in Skibbereen. The soldiers
were 'perfectly ready to rough' it, but ought to be deployed effectively. The
commander-in-chief disapproved of accommodation 'in the scattered, struggling,

combustible houses of the very disaffected', which could result in attacks. A troop of dragoons and a company of infantry were about to occupy Bandon barracks, but further reinforcements depended on Lord Bandon making billets available.[28] Cork and Kerry remained unsettled. The *Freeman's Journal* warned that thousands, who appeared apathetic, were 'deeply sympathizing with the revolt' and would participate if the IRB went ahead.[29]

During a preliminary hearing on 30 September, Crown Prosecutor Charles Barry made the sensational claim that the Fenian movement was imbued with 'the character of socialism in its most pernicious and most wicked phase'; its plans were 'a combination of folly and wickedness not often paralleled in the annals of political fanaticism or crime'.[30] This attempt to destroy any middle-class sympathy for the leaders was based on the private letters of Christopher Manus O'Keeffe, an eccentric journalist and occasional contributor to the *Irish People*, who was not an IRB member:[31] 'The Irish aristocracy must be hounded down by the Liberal press, and slain afterwards by the hands of an aroused and infuriate people. This is the only way to liberate Ireland – everything else is nonsense.'[32]

The leaders never shared his sentiments, but the Crown prosecutor claimed that the Republic would begin with an 'indiscriminate massacre' of all but the working class, who were 'taught to believe that they might expect a redistribution of the property, real and personal, of the country'.[33] Lady Wilde, a former Young Ireland propagandist, had joined the literary establishment and disapproved of this 'decidedly … democratic movement': 'The gentry and aristocracy will suffer much from them. Their object is to form a republic – Heaven keep me from a Fenian Republic.'[34]

The arrests remained a hollow triumph while Stephens was at large. Fenian cadres on both sides of the Atlantic retained faith in him and public anxiety about an insurrection continued. At this juncture, Stephens contributed little leadership, blaming O'Mahony for the IRB's inability to resist arrest: 'scepticism, inquisitions, hesitation, etc., and *not* any imprudence on *our* part have brought us to this'.[35] He attributed the seizure of the *Irish People* to 'that damnable blunder' of P.J. Meehan, who had lost documents and a money draft on 22 July, which facilitated the authorities in tracking Fenian funding.[36] Stephens needed money, but advised O'Mahony that, in case of his arrest, he should procure weapons and gather 'all the fighting men … and then sail for Ireland. The heads here may be in the hands of the enemy, and much confusion may prevail; but, with a Fenian force to rally them, be sure that overwhelming numbers shall be with you. *But this must be done before next Christmas*, after which date I would have no man risk his life or his money.'[37]

The constabulary continued a 'most energetic vigilance' when investigating transatlantic steamers. The *City of Dublin* from New York, for instance, was searched in vain off Fastnet. This made the second, 'very imposing' boarding party of the HMS *Liverpool* awaiting her near Spike Island unnecessary. When the captain of the *Helvetia* hesitated disembarking his American passengers in Cobh in rough weather, the authorities threatened to send 'a man of war after him' unless he let them access potential suspects. In Skibbereen, an American expedition continued to be rumoured, great excitement prevailed and people withdrew their money from the banks. The police repeatedly examined travellers on the Bandon to Skibbereen road, particularly those with American 'slouch hats'. The latter town was now guarded by 120 soldiers.[38]

Ellen O'Leary arrived from Tipperary to assist the IRB. She was unique among the conspirators in possessing a private income. Her opinion of Stephens was published posthumously: 'For myself, believing him at this time to be the right man in the right place, I felt an ardent admiration, had unbounded trust in him, and was willing, under his direction, to do anything for the cause.'[39] Stephens asked Ellen to access her brother's bank account, where funds transmitted by the Fenian Brotherhood were accumulating, but it had been frozen by Dublin Castle.[40] Stephens remained in hiding until Dublin Castle learned that somebody resembling him was keeping a low profile since the seizure of the *Irish People*. On 11 November Stephens and companions were surprised and arrested. Refusing to recognize the court, he caused a sensation. Stephens treated Dublin Castle as the usurper by conducting himself as the legitimate head of the Irish Republic, who needed to enter no defence:[41]

> I have employed no attorney or lawyer in this case, and that I mean to employ none, because, in making a plea of any kind, or filing any defence … I should be recognizing British law in Ireland. Now, I deliberately and conscientiously repudiate the existence of that law in Ireland – its right, or even its existence. I repudiate the right of its existence in Ireland. I defy and despise any punishment it can inflict on me. I have spoken.[42]

The London *Times* described Stephens as

> rather below the middle stature, with smooth cheeks, a fair complexion, a fine, large auburn beard, and hair of light brown colour, curling around the back of the head, the front and top being entirely bald … The eyes are small, lively, and restless. The temperament is evidently sanguine and nervous, indicating quickness and perception, energy, and determination … His manners are gentlemanly, saving a certain abruptness and impatience. He was, however, apparently very much at ease during the day, not at all like a prisoner charged with a great crime, but rather like an attorney watching a case, with a full consciousness of

his own superior ability and the goodness of his cause, with sovereign contempt for 'the other side'.[43]

Pierce Nagle identified Charles Kickham as a prominent Fenian who was present during meetings in Tipperary. Kickham found it difficult following proceedings in the police court, despite his hearing trumpet. Ostensibly to assist his colleague, Stephens gave a loud commentary, which reduced the proceedings to a farce. Kickham's indignation centred on charges that the IRB planned wholesale assassinations, partly based on a letter found among his papers, which suggested the burning of hayricks and hocking of cattle as revolutionary tactics. Kickham had always rejected such schemes.[44]

Kickham had published his first novel, *Sally Cavanagh or the Untenanted Graves*, as a serial in the *Hibernian Magazine* during 1864. A tenant farmer, unjustly evicted, is compelled to emigrate in search of funds, while his landlord attempts to seduce Sally Cavanagh, the virtuous wife. Forced to enter the workhouse through a series of misfortunes, the heroine is separated from her children, who die and are buried as paupers. Her husband returns with money, but is too late – the tragedy has driven Sally insane. The novel ends with a nationalist call to arms.

In court, Charles Kickham came in for this unflattering portrait: 'A tall, spare man of anything but prepossessing appearance, deeply pock-marked, deaf (having to use a tube) and very short-sighted, and from his restless and uneasy deportment one would suppose that he was of an undecided and irresolute character.'[45] The *Times*, on the other hand, alluding to his disabilities with sympathy, commented 'he is an educated, gentlemanly person, apparently earnest and truthful'.[46] Even A.M. Sullivan, who portrayed the prisoners as nationalist martyrs, considered Kickham's appearance 'somewhat peculiar. He was a tall, strong, rough-bearded man, with that strained expression of face which is often worn by people of dim sight.'[47]

Lord Wodehouse rejoiced with Lord Clarendon, the foreign secretary, that Stephens's arrest on 11 November was 'the heaviest blow we have yet struck against this seditious faction', while the documents seized in the *Irish People* office provided 'ample evidence'. As Stephens had blocked the creation of a command structure in favour of retaining absolute power, his arrest caused disruption. F.F. Millen and then Colonel Kelly took over, but a rescue was soon mooted, for Stephens's presence was deemed essential.[48] Messengers travelled between Dublin and Paris, where Edmund O'Leary, a Fenian paymaster, wrote to O'Mahony that Mrs O'Donovan Rossa had arrived, stating that 'the men are not in the least discouraged, knowing that they can get all the prisoners out absolutely whenever they like'.[49]

Stephens's detention proved brief: on 24 November he escaped from Richmond bridewell. Ellen O'Leary had raised £200 on her property in Tipperary to obtain the necessary funds. The 'chief executive of the Irish Republic' was released with the help of duplicate keys and hidden in safe houses, including those of Mrs Boland and Mrs Butler, a fashionable dressmaker, in an operation planned by Colonel Kelly and John Devoy, assisted by Fenians among the prison staff.[50] Lord Wodehouse learned of this 'most disastrous' escape during an official visit to Waterford: '*Dies nefastus*,' he lamented, before returning 'sorely crestfallen to Dublin'.[51] The viceroy regretted 'the outburst of exultation of the disloyal all over Ireland' and the dismay of the propertied classes, believing that disaffection was now worse than in 1848. He informed Lord Clarendon that[52] 'the whole mass of the peasantry are sullen or actively disloyal, so are the small tradesmen, the artisans, and the railway and telegraph clerks, porters, engineers etc'.[53] Despite his description and a reward of £1000, placarded in Dublin, Stephens was not recaptured.[54]

Preparing for the trials by special commission, Dublin Castle discovered the 'executive document', which Luby had failed to hide. It appointed O'Leary, Luby and Kickham as an IRB council during Stephens's absence in America in 1864 to cover an emergency, but had never come into force. Kickham was not even aware of its existence. This alerted the authorities to his leadership role, while the originals of editorials carelessly retained in the newspaper office underlined the significance of these three writers. Dublin Castle gossiped that when Crown Solicitor Anderson and Prosecutor Barry realized what a treasure trove of seditious material had been seized, they danced with joy.[55]

Correspondence, which the Fenian staff had foolishly preserved, identified key supporters. The administration discovered that both John Sarsfield Casey and his brother Daniel had written to the *Irish People* as 'the Galtee boy' and 'the Galtee boy's brother' respectively. The former, still winding up J.J. Geary's business, was arrested. 'Honest' Thomas Hayes, a wheelwright in Bloomsbury, was similarly convicted. He had financed the *Irish Liberator*, the newspaper of the NBSP in England, later becoming an IRB 'centre' in London. Disagreements with Dr Bell, its editor, led Hayes to correspond with the *Irish People*, which retained his letters.[56]

Luby, the nominal proprietor of the *Irish People*, sued Dublin's chief police magistrate for breaking into the premises, protesting that in 1848 the stridently seditious *United Irishman* was not seized until John Mitchel, its editor, had been convicted. He portrayed the raid as unconstitutional, but the law concluded that the newspaper formed the headquarters of a conspiracy and the safety of the state was paramount.[57] The Fenian leaders took an action for libel against the

Freeman's Journal for publishing Archbishop Cullen's pastoral, 'Fenianism and Orangeism', likely to prejudice the public against the prisoners by describing their organization as 'a compound of folly and wickedness wearing the mask of patriotism'. Dr Cullen abhorred uprisings as liable to end in massacre; on a more rational level, he criticized the IRB leaders for lacking common sense and secrecy.[58] On 14 November the London *Times* editorialized that, 'as treason is a serious thing, and as these people are undoubtedly guilty of it, we say not a word to anticipate the justice that will be rendered them in due time', which further compromised a fair trial.[59] One of the few public figures supporting the Fenians was John Martin, the veteran Young Irelander, who praised the characters of John O'Leary and John O'Mahony, the 'Irish Garibaldi', but considered their chances of success as 'hopeless'.[60] Peter Gill, the radical editor of the *Tipperary Advocate*, queried sensationalist claims emanating from Dublin Castle that the Fenians had planned assassinations. He predicted that these were intended to blacken their names and would prove untrue. (They were rejected by the foreman of the jury at Luby's trial.)[61]

The trials

On 27 November the trials began in Dublin. The leaders were accused of conspiring to overthrow the state to establish a Republic, aided by foreign auxiliaries, while publishing seditious material.[62] They were charged with treason-felony, which had been introduced in 1848. As it did not carry the death penalty, the evidence for conviction was less stringent than for high treason. The judges were John David Fitzgerald and William Keogh, both of whom had had contact with the IRB and should have been disqualified.

Crown Prosecutor Barry used a common tactic of denigration by contrasting the IRB leaders, mere rabble rousers, with the 'respectable' nationalists of 1848 of a 'far higher calibre and station'.[63] Admitting that the Fenians were more extensively organized, Barry decried the folly of those who presumed that 'England, with her power, with her inexhaustible resources' would tolerate a republic nearby.[64] Dublin Castle had obtained the secret resolutions of the Chicago congress, when the Fenian Brotherhood addressed the people of Ireland:

> We are solemnly pledged to labour earnestly and continuously for the regeneration of our beloved Ireland. That pledge, with the blessing of providence, we shall redeem, and when the wished for time will have arrived, we shall be prepared with you to meet the implacable persecutors of our race in battle array; to put an end forever to the accursed system under which our unhappy people have suffered such cruel tortures, or die like men in the attempt.[65]

The Crown prosecutor interpreted this as a declaration of intent from the Fenian Brotherhood to the IRB. It referred to thousands of American soldiers sworn to serve the cause as well as to the Irish at home, 'partially disciplined soldiers of liberty, silently enrolled'.[66]

In the absence of Stephens, his second-in-command was tried first. Luby was an ineffective conspirator in the final analysis: his failure to hide the 'executive document' constituted a major blunder, copper-fastening his and his two colleagues' conviction through evidence of a revolutionary directory. Likewise, treating the wild outpourings of Christopher Manus O'Keeffe as amusing eccentricities rather than burning them, betrayed lack of judgment.[67] Defendants could not give evidence on their own behalf, but were allowed to speak before sentencing. An unwritten convention decreed that rebels ignore flawed testimony, which could be expected from British 'justice'. The 'speech from the dock' had been a propaganda weapon since 1798, but Luby proceeded cautiously for fear of prejudicing the court against his comrades:[68]

> But, with regard to the entire course of my life, and whether it be a mistaken course or not will be for every man's individual judgment to decide – this I know, that no man ever loved Ireland more than I have done – no man has ever given up his whole being to Ireland to the extent I have done. From the time I came to what has been called the years of discretion, my entire thought has been devoted to Ireland. I believe the course I pursued was right; others may take a different view. I believe the majority of my countrymen this minute, if, instead of my being tried before a petty jury, who, I suppose, are bound to find according to British law – if my guilt or innocence was to be tried by the higher standard of eternal right, and the case was put to all my countrymen – I believe this moment the majority of my countrymen would pronounce that I am not a criminal, but that I have deserved well of my country.[69]

The idealists in charge of the *Irish People* had overlooked inappropriate activities in the building, allowing 'Pagan' O'Leary to cast bullets and store his weapons. Luby and Kickham, when reinstating Pierce Nagle after a quarrel, demonstrated that they lacked a 'sixth sense' necessary for successful conspirators.[70] Nevertheless, Luby redeemed himself in the dock by his idealism: 'The cause of Ireland is not to be despaired of, that Ireland is not yet a lost country – that as long as there are men in any country prepared to expose themselves to every difficulty and danger, in its service, prepared to brave captivity, even death itself, if need be, that country cannot be lost. With those words I conclude.'[71]

In political trials Dublin Castle tended to engineer juries of Anglo-Irish Protestants, a minority likely to support the authorities. O'Leary (and some weeks later, the Cork defendants) commented on this. He also repudiated the

4. ARRESTS AND DISSENSIONS, 1864–6

'foul charge' that the leaders were unprincipled and favoured assassination, pointing to Crown Prosecutor Charles Barry as a 'moral assassin'. O'Leary elaborated on the theme of loyalty and treason, alluding to the trial of Robert Emmet before the reactionary Lord Norbury:[72]

> I have been found guilty of treason or treason-felony. Treason is a foul crime. The poet Dante consigned traitors to, I believe, the ninth circle of hell ... Traitors against king, against country ... England is not my country; I have betrayed no friend, no benefactor. Sidney and Emmet were legal traitors, Jeffreys was a loyal man, and so was Norbury. I leave the matter there.[73]

Although John O'Leary was a hesitant speaker, averse to hyperbole, physically he was the most impressive of the prisoners:

> His features were sharply cut, his eyes dark and flashing, and his long hair and flowing beard black as the raven's wing, he generally had a look of stern resolution and haughty seriousness, which was admirably in keeping with the character of a man engaged in a dangerous enterprise. His figure was well knit and muscular, and altogether his was, in truth, a remarkable presence. He looked indeed the embodiment of a poet or painter's ideal of a desperate conspirator.[74]

Dr Webb, a fellow of TCD and later a county court judge, commented in verse on the irony of Judge Keogh trying the Fenians:

> *The felon's cell awaits O'Leary. Lo!*
> *The seat of judgment is the seat of Keogh,*
> *Thrice happy Keogh who, if you are not belied,*
> *Now try the crimes for which you were not tried.*
> *And seated on the bench can safely mock*
> *The nobler felon standing in the dock![75]*

By pleading 'guilty' in 1859, Rossa had accepted that should he be tried on this charge for a second time, he would be considered as convicted. Rather than conciliate Judge Keogh, Rossa conducted his own defence as a propaganda exercise, baiting him. He insisted on reading aloud from the *Irish People*, which had condemned Keogh's conduct. Rossa modelled himself on Robert Emmet, who had stood in the same Green Street court in 1803. Emmet's trial culminated after twelve hours, when he delivered his magnificent speech from the dock.[76] When Rossa's turn came, he merely cast doubt on the legality of the proceedings: 'The fact that the government seized papers connected with my defence and withheld them; the fact that the government stated that they would convict; the fact that they sent Judge Keogh, a second "Norbury" to try me. With these facts before me, it would be useless for me to say anything'.[77]

Passing sentence, Judge Keogh described Rossa as having 'entertained those criminal designs ... as far back as 1859', whereupon the prisoner declared himself 'an Irishman since I was born'.[78] Luby and O'Leary were sentenced to twenty years each, but Rossa received life. John Haltigan's role as foreman printer of the seditious paper meant seven years penal servitude.[79]

Behind the scenes, Lord Wodehouse alerted Lord Strathnairn to rumours that the Fenian Brotherhood planned to land an expedition in Kerry and Galway next St Patrick's Day and advised that under present conditions the demand for troops would continue. Two regiments had arrived and would be posted to the Curragh, Templemore and Birr respectively. Strathnairn believed that the army was generally loyal, but individual soldiers could be tempted by Fenian agents. Because of the 'mixed composition' of regiments, stationing the Irish at home was unavoidable, but they ought to be kept away from seditious districts.[80]

On 17 December 1865 the special commission transferred to Cork, where a higher percentage of the population than in Dublin had joined the IRB. The *Nation* compared precautions for transporting judges and informers to 'the headquarters of the Fenians in Munster' with those of Union generals travelling through Confederate territory during the Civil War.[81] Brian Dillon and John Lynch were among the first to be tried. Warner, the informer, identified them as present at drill and meetings in Geary's pub. The *Nation* commented that his character 'is such that his testimony should not ... warrant the hanging of a cat', but, here too, the authorities could rely on seditious documents to ensure a conviction.[82]

Neither of them could have constituted a military threat, for Dillon suffered from 'curvature of the spine', while Lynch had consumption. Dillon proclaimed his Republican convictions: 'My belief in the ultimate independence of Ireland is as fixed as my religious belief' and both were sentenced to ten years. John Kenealy and John Sarsfield Casey received ten and five years' penal servitude respectively, but James Mountaine was acquitted. Waiting to be sentenced, the men affirmed their nationalist faith by singing '*A chuisle geal mo chroidhe*', which Michael Doheny had composed on the run in 1848.[83]

As the special commission closed in Cork, news reached Ireland that O'Mahony had denounced William Roberts and the senators for 'perfidy and dishonesty'. They were 'to be kept out of the head-quarters lest they might rob the place'.[84] The *Nation* deplored such dissensions and, siding with the senators, concluded that one faction would have to withdraw: 'The strong probability is that the ten gentlemen referred to are right; their judgment is more likely than that of Mr O'Mahony to be wise and sound.'[85]

On 2 January 1866 the commission returned to Dublin for the trial of Charles Kickham, who, hoping for an acquittal, defended himself. Pierce Nagle claimed to have identified the accused's handwriting, but Kickham cast doubts. No overt acts of sedition could be proven, except his editorials. Kickham argued that one could write for a seditious paper without joining the conspiracy. Was his literary output not covered by the freedom of the press? He stressed that the *Irish People* advocated ideas regarding landlords, which were shared by the universally admired Thomas Davis. Considering the state of Ireland, Kickham questioned how any Irishman could not say 'give us our country to ourselves, and let us see what we can do with it'.[86]

He recalled the Parliament of 1782, which had obtained a measure of autonomy in domestic matters but consisted of government by an elite and was not revolutionary. Kickham defended physical force, commenting that 'concessions to Ireland had always been a result of Fenianism in one shape or another' and prophesied that 'the present manifestation of the national spirit' would yet prove his point.[87]

Judge Keogh facilitated the accused by permitting a friend to sit beside Kickham and provide a summary of the proceedings through his hearing trumpet.[88] The writer behaved courteously, while William Keogh sentenced him to fourteen years and paid tribute to this talented author. Although Kickham declared that he had been convicted for serving 'Ireland, and now I am prepared to suffer for Ireland', sympathetic onlookers must have wondered how he would cope. Impressed by his courage, the *Kilkenny Journal* reflected that 'there must be something rotten' in government, when 'such as him are in prison'.[89]

Only Martin O'Brennan, the proprietor of the *Connaught Patriot*, was arrested alongside the *Irish People* journalists in an overzealous mistake, not sanctioned by an absent Lord Wodehouse. O'Brennan had promoted the Irish language and covertly incited to insurrection by portraying a pre-colonial golden age in contrast to the miseries of British rule. Like Rossa and his peers in West Cork, he publicized the self-image of the peasantry as descended from Gaelic princes when Ireland was 'a lamp of enlightenment for the world' and England 'a nation of naked savages'. The exiled Irish would return, resembling the Israelites regaining their promised land. Having hailed a Fenian invasion as the 'redemption of Ireland from despotism and bad laws', O'Brennan's protestations of loyalty and his disagreements with the *Irish People* were ignored by Dublin Castle; he eventually pleaded guilty, was bailed and, after an unsuccessful interlude in London, fled to America.[90]

Forty-one men were tried, resulting in thirty-six convictions, three acquittals and one discharge on bail, while the jury disagreed in a further case. The *Irishman* illustrated its reports with handsome woodcuts. Popular interest also led to publishers selling photographs of Stephens, O'Mahony, Luby, O'Leary, their judges and senior counsel, Isaac Butt, as well as Ellen O'Mahony, 'head directress of the Fenian Sisterhood', and the informers Nagle and Schofield.[91]

Charles Gavan Duffy, now a statesman in Australia, commented privately on the futility of Fenianism, while admiring the character of the leaders: 'Poor fellows, God pity them! They had courage and devotion which rescues them from contempt ... Again, I have been dreaming constantly of the unfortunate Fenian prisoners. Fancy the condition of men of some culture like O'Leary, Kickham, and O'Keefe, utterly without books, and without pen and ink.'[92] John Mitchel, however, prophesied: 'The Fenians are going through the mill the British government keeps to grind us. But the thing is not over.'[93]

Dublin Castle took decisive action to break up the conspiracy: between 15 September and 6 October 1865 the constabulary arrested 179 men in eighteen counties and a further eight in England. When the initial panic had subsided, approximately fifty suspects were released and forty-one tried. In cases of insufficient evidence, regional organizers like James Cody and Michael O'Neill Fogarty of Kilfeacle were remanded in custody.[94] In contrast to 1848, incarceration did not herald the collapse of the IRB. In Dublin, Ellen O'Leary, Letitia Luby and Mary Jane O'Donovan Rossa rallied the rank and file.[95]

Veterans of the American Civil War arrived in Queenstown (Cobh) and between late 1865 and the following February approximately 500 were 'visiting' Ireland. Carrying arms was considered the right of a free citizen in the US, but restricted to the propertied classes in Ireland. Flaunting their new status, Fenian officers brought their weapons. They were 'coming over to drive the British army into the sea with the help of the locals', the press announced. The 'ignorant and excitable lower orders' interpreted their presence as evidence that an insurrection was imminent.[96]

Some failed to destroy incriminating documents and were arrested, including Captain Charles Underwood O'Connell, Captain John McCafferty, who carried a small arsenal, and William Mackey Lomasney, the son of emigrants from Fermoy. It took two constables to wrest Mackey's concealed revolver from him. General John Gleeson, 'a fine young man', was related to 'the most respectable farmers' in Borrisoleigh and attracted attention with his gold-mounted gun.[97]

Colonel William Halpin, who had resigned as city engineer of Cincinnati to assist in planning the insurrection, warned O'Mahony on 6 October that his officers ought to avoid Queenstown and land in Britain with only a brief note of introduction. He reported the arrests of Colonel John W. Byron, formerly a leading organizer in the Army of the Potomac, and Colonel Patrick Leonard. Halpin urged that an Irish paymaster should settle their accounts at intervals, rather than issuing advance payments, which led to reckless expenditure. He regretted that men, who were not yet needed, had been sent.[98]

Table 3. *Fenian arrests from 15 September to 6 October 1865*

	City/County	No. of arrests
1.	Dublin	41
2.	Cork city & county	33
3.	Mayo	32
4.	Galway	18
5.	Kerry	14
6.	Tipperary	12
7.	Kilkenny	5
8.	Waterford	4
9.	Clare	3
10.	Fermanagh	3
11.	Tyrone	3
12.	Down	2
13.	Kildare	2
14.	Limerick	2
15.	Wexford	2
16.	Belfast	1
17.	King's County (Offaly)	1
18.	Longford	1
	Total	179

(Source: *Irishman*, 7 October 1865)

According to the constabulary, there had been no sedition in Borrisoleigh until the Gleeson brothers returned from New York. They and other American officers were observed near Thurles in company with Colonel Michael Kerwin, a leading Fenian Brotherhood strategist. Captain Gleeson lodged in the public house of his cousin, Edward Finn, which was the IRB rendezvous for Borrisoleigh. He attended fairs and races as an organizer while the general made a military survey of Nenagh. Resuming their activities between their two arrests, they ranged as far as Limerick.[99]

Developments in the USA

Amidst tensions, the Brotherhood prepared for its third congress on 16 October 1865 in Philadelphia. Edward Archibald had engaged a nominal Fenian and veteran of the Irish Brigade as his spy. On disbandment this overwhelmingly Fenian unit consisted of up to 1300 effective men, many of whom intended to travel to Ireland. Archibald heard of O'Mahony hiring twenty ships, which he disbelieved, although the US government was selling off surplus war stock.[100]

British officials observed American politicians courting the Fenians vote during Reconstruction. While most Irish-Americans desired independence, middle-class men 'perceive[d] the improbability of the final success of the movement', but realized that open criticism would be considered 'treachery' and lead to financial losses and ostracism. In St Louis, for example, well-off Irishmen were coerced into contributing to the Fenian funds. This split within Irish America explains many difficulties faced by O'Mahony and, later, Roberts. Reluctant members, loath to oppose their more impetuous, underprivileged compatriots, quietly hampered the Brotherhood by keeping the British informed. Others oscillated between the two sides in search of an income, 'a truly Irish proceeding', as Sir Frederick Bruce, the British minister in Washington, commented.[101]

In Philadelphia, Consul Kortright characterized the congress as 'declamatory speeches' against Britain with 'vainglorious boasting' about the imminent Irish Republic. Every effort was to be made to involve the US government and people in this enterprise, using the precedent of Britain's support for the Confederacy. Kortright's informer was intimate with the Fenian inner circle, which counted 681,000 members on its American muster roll, while the IRB claimed to have 400,000 men with a further 8000 in Scotland, 7000 in England and 3000 in Wales. These figures were gross overestimates; even Stephens never pretended to more than 200,000 followers at home. Some were supposedly sworn for 'special service', for instance, the burning down of cities and docks throughout Britain to create a diversion during the Rising. The Brotherhood was considering whether to vote to annexe Ireland to the US after liberation. Michael Murphy, the Toronto Fenian chief, boasted that he could raise 125,000 Irish-Canadians for action, unwittingly strengthening the Senate (or Roberts) faction.[102]

The American Fenians tried to downplay the *Irish People* arrests by highlighting IRB prevalence in Liverpool and claiming infiltration of the military, the police and coastguard in Ireland. The newly established American Fenian Sisterhood was supposedly conveying messages and money, disguised as emigrants.[103] Sir John Michel, commander of British forces in Canada, informed Sir Frederick Bruce of Fenian 'raids on the Canadian frontier' rumoured for late 1865 and urged that Washington be reminded to enforce the neutrality laws. Bruce consistently outflanked the Fenians, who tried to gain sympathy for oppressed Ireland and revenge on Britain, which had tolerated Confederate agents in Canada and enabled the southern states to terrorize US shipping during the war. Aware that the president needed to maintain 'the support of the Irish vote at this critical moment' to achieve swift re-integration of the south into the Union, Bruce blocked official British censure of the Johnson administration to prevent a further deterioration of Anglo-American relations. Instead, he employed low-key discussions and considerable forbearance as the US government could not be seen to back down before Britain.[104] **X**

During the Philadelphia congress, the central council controlled vital sub-committees, remodelling the Brotherhood to resemble the administration of the United States under 'president' O'Mahony. It assumed the role of an Irish government in exile, while the position of 'head centre' was abolished. The 'circles' were to elect a 'house of representatives', which failed to materialize, however. A new executive of fifteen senators replaced the central council, choosing the deputy president of the Brotherhood, who was simultaneously chairman of the senate. O'Mahony had little influence over this body. He could nominate his cabinet, which consisted of secretaries of war, the navy, the treasury and civilian affairs, but needed senatorial endorsement. The president might be overruled by a majority of two-thirds of the senate and, in certain circumstances, replaced by his deputy. O'Mahony feared that, reduced to a mere figurehead, he would serve as a scapegoat in case of failure. The senate also appointed an agent for the sale of Fenian bonds, a major source of income, as well as an 'agent for the Irish Republic', whose only function was to sign said bonds. The new officials were well paid and had a salaried staff, while lavishly remunerated Brotherhood organizers were active throughout the US.[105]

While the congress was in progress, Bernard Doran Killian, the shrewd treasurer of the Brotherhood, met President Andrew Johnson and William Henry Seward, Secretary of State in Washington. He requested the release of John Mitchel, detained as a Confederate propagandist. The Brotherhood hoped to benefit from Mitchel's status by appointing him its financial agent in Paris. During discussions with Johnson and Seward, Killian tried to ascertain their likely response to an insurrection, accompanied by a diversionary attack on Canada, where some Fenians considered seizing territory to launch their invasion. The Brotherhood doubted whether Washington intended to enforce the neutrality laws in retaliation for British actions during the Civil War, a suspicion that also crossed the mind of Sir Frederick Bruce. The politicians, careful not to alienate the Irish vote, replied that they 'would acknowledge accomplished facts'.[106]

Table 4. *Fenian Brotherhood leadership, 1863–September 1865*

Head Centre	John O'Mahony, New York
Central Treasurer	Patrick O'Rourke, New York
Assistant Central Treasurer	Capt. W.F. Meehan
Military Department	Col Patrick Downing
Central Corresponding Secretary	M.F. Heffernan, New York
Private Secretary of Head Centre	Michael Cavanagh, New York
Assistant Private Secretary to Head Centre	'Red Jim' McDermott
Central Council	
James Gibbons	Philadelphia
Brig. General Michael Corcoran	Army of the Potomac
Col Matthew Murphy	69th Rgt. NYVNA Corcoran's Irish Legion, Army of the Potomac
Richard Doherty	Lafayette, Indiana
Michael Scanlan	Chicago

(Source: *Proceedings of the First National Convention of the Fenian Brotherhood, held in Chicago, Illinois, November 1863*)

Table 5. *Cabinet of the Fenian Brotherhood, post-October 1865*

President	John O'Mahony
Vice President and President of the Senate	William R. Roberts
Secretary of Civilian Affairs (provisional)	Col Patrick Downing
Secretary of Military & Naval Affairs	General Thomas Sweeny
Secretary of the Treasury	Bernard Doran Killian
Treasurer	Patrick O'Rourke
Agent of the Irish Republic	Patrick Keenan
Bond Agent	P.A. Collins
Correspondence Secretary	M.J. Heffernan

(Source: *Irishman*)

Bernard Doran Killian (courtesy Dublin City Archive).

Johnson agreed to release Mitchel, a celebrated journalist in poor health, to boost his profile with Irish America for the congressional elections that autumn. As these would dictate the course of Reconstruction in the southern states, the president appeared to collude with the Fenians to the extent of ignoring their purchases of US weapons. On Killian's return to Philadelphia, the congress delegated him and Senators William Roberts and Stephen Joseph Meany to make a formal approach to the American government on the Canadian question, when the president repeated his ambiguous reply. This was strictly confidential, but Roberts, according to O'Mahony, announced 'with his usual blatant emptiness, that he had some other glorious, glorious news' from the White House, which could not be publicly revealed. Most Fenians accepted this at face value. Killian was said to be skilled at outwitting opponents and it is possible that Johnson half-assented to something, which he hoped would never happen.[107]

O'Mahony claimed that General Thomas Sweeny made his debut in Fenian affairs at the Philadelphia convention. He had met Stephens in Brooklyn in 1858, warning him that an invasion of Ireland during peacetime would be difficult.[108] Sweeny had emigrated from Dunmanway as a child and joined the US army. He was chosen by the senators as Fenian secretary of war. O'Mahony derided him as 'their pet and pliant general', although delighted that the US government allowed a regular army officer to assist them. The senators had to act before the network of Fenian-infiltrated army units disintegrated after

demobilization.[109] Sweeny advised Roberts in October 1865 that he believed the
IRB 'totally unprepared' for insurrection, but considered the Canadian frontier
of more than 1300 miles vulnerable to attack.[110]

Colonel Halpin had assured O'Mahony that the IRB remained unbowed but
was in urgent need of money and weapons. The convention endorsed Stephens's
actions, voting that available moneys be transferred to Ireland by Captain James
Murphy as IRB representative. Arguments, especially over the 'lost documents'
of P.J. Meehan, disrupted the deliberations. Delays resulted in the premature
departure of many of O'Mahony's supporters, who had exhausted their funds.
The senators, 'smart business men', felt that the Irish government in exile needed
a 'Fenian capitol'. Roberts, Killian and Sweeny spent $24,000 to rent 'the capa-
cious and elegant brownstone building known as the Moffat Mansion' in New
York for eighteen months. Even after accommodating various Fenian depart-
ments, including the Sisterhood, it proved too large. O'Mahony was powerless
to veto an arrangement, which he considered imprudent and extravagant:[111]
'A presentiment of coming evil came upon me when I first entered the new
building, and I even remarked to one of my friends, who accompanied me, that
I feared it might prove the "tomb of the Fenian movement".'[112]

Moffat Mansion, Fenian headquarters
(Illustrated London News, *courtesy Mike Ruddy).*

The senate refused to send funds to Ireland immediately. In Dublin, Stephens and his military council declared that the uprising would take place during the last week of December 1865 to allow the Fenian Brotherhood time to prepare. When Mitchel was ready to depart for Paris on 10 November the senators raised further difficulties and O'Mahony threatened them with public exposure unless the $60,000 allocated were forthcoming.[113]

O'Mahony lamented that by 1865, General Michael Corcoran, General Thomas Smyth and Colonel Matthew Murphy, his military experts, and Michael Doheny and Fr Edward O'Flaherty of Indiana, his political advisers, were dead and replaced by intriguers and mediocrities. Unknown to him, many senators were pursuing the alternative strategy of an assault on British North America. Sweeny envisaged a winter attack on the Canadian frontier. This idea had been mooted as far back as 1812 and 1848 and presupposed support from French-Canadian sympathizers, as the Brotherhood had only 3000 members in Canada. The senators assigned $56,000 to Sweeny for this scheme, which O'Mahony and Killian blocked on discovering the plot.[114]

The Brotherhood intended to raise large sums by selling 'Fenian bonds', which patriotic investors could redeem six months after the establishment of the Irish Republic. When the bond issue was ready, Patrick Keenan, the agent authorized to sign it, withdrew his name; O'Mahony suspected that the Senate clique had manipulated him into stopping support for the IRB in favour of the Canadian scheme. Michael Scanlan, one O'Mahony's most determined opponents, supervised the burning of bonds already printed. O'Mahony commented: 'It was an hour of exceeding sadness and despair for me.'[115] Almost simultaneously, they learned of the arrest of Stephens, which confirmed the senators in their Canadian plans. But General Millen and Colonel Kelly were determined that a Rising would go ahead. O'Mahony signed the bonds without authority to provide immediate support; on 9 December the senators impeached him 'for perfidy and malfeasance in office' and replaced him with Roberts.[116]

O'Mahony and Killian retained the remaining $10,000 and locked the Senate party out of the Moffat Mansion, while the senators had managed to seize $9000. On 14 December Roberts portrayed himself as the champion of Stephens and the 'men in the gap', for whom he was holding the Brotherhood together. Millen, briefly in charge of the IRB, had been sent back to New York by Stephens, then in Richmond bridewell. Arriving on 15 December 1865, he was welcomed by a beleaguered O'Mahony, who appointed this 'sterling patriot' his secretary of war, while the senators retained Sweeny. Shortly afterwards, however, Stephens expressed distrust of Millen, whom O'Mahony dismissed. Colonel Halpin returned to New York, tasked by Stephens to heal the split, and remained to support O'Mahony.[117]

Three months later, Millen contacted the British consul to provide him with a comprehensive report on the transatlantic movement. By May 1866 he had moved to Texas and sold his information to the Foreign Office for £250, rationalizing this treachery as due to disappointment with the leadership. He considered O'Mahony 'anything but impressive in appearance as a revolutionary chieftain', while his secretary, Michael Cavanagh, was 'a very ignorant and very ill bred labouring man'; nor did Millen care for the ambitious department store owner, 'now known as Colonel Roberts'.[118]

The split deprived the IRB of support at a critical juncture. The *New York Times* heaped ridicule on Irish America, relating how the Fenian leaders had duped their supporters, those 'frugal and industrious Irish servant girls', into sacrificing their savings.[119] One wonders whether American politicians and British diplomats encouraged the portrayal of 'Fenianism as farce' as part of the sidelining of these ineffectual 'Celtic' conspirators, which culminated in an Anglo-American entente after the 1871 Treaty of Washington.[120] The *New York Times* derided how 'the two Irish Republics in New York have been wrangling', mockingly re-interpreting the initials 'FB' as the 'Fenian burlesque':

> The principal characters are the 'CEIR' [chief executive of the Irish Republic] (invisible thus far) and the 'HC' [head centre]. The scene of action is supposed to be in Ireland, but it is in reality in Union Square, New York; the object was originally said to be to establish a Republican government in Ireland, doubtless on the plan of Sir Thomas More's *Utopia*, crossed with Swift's *Laputa*; but that object was very soon modified into the capture of Canada and all the other colonies of Great Britain; and of late it has been modified still further, so that the end and aim of the 'Fenian Brotherhood' now is to see which faction can call the other the hardest names.[121]

News of the split added to Stephens's troubles during the *Irish People* trials. On 12 December, Peter Quirke, 'centre' of Carrick-on-Suir, Rody Kickham, Mullinahone, Michael Kelly, Kilkenny city and delegates from Dublin, Limerick, Cork, West Cork and Leitrim met in Carrick-on-Suir. They expressed support for O'Mahony, which was publicized in Ireland and America.[122]

O'Mahony asked to become Stephens's agent to sell Fenian bonds in America, where 'subscriptions had almost ceased'. The Senate wing ostensibly supported Stephens, while hoping to exploit the existing tensions. On 22 December 1865 Stephens endorsed O'Mahony, apologizing that his '*drag chain* policy' had kept him 'in a state of pain and irritation', when his outbursts 'must have hurt you most keenly'. Their disagreement was now over. Stephens rejoiced that his sensational escape facilitated him 'to hold our forces together' and denounced the senate. Stephens miscalculated his tactics when advising O'Mahony about the senators: 'I would lash them from me like so many dogs.' This widened the breach. The senate now hinted that Stephens was a double agent whose jail-break had been engineered by the British.[123]

He had impressed upon O'Mahony that even a small American expedition was essential and sent pilots to New York to guide its ships to the secluded harbours of Munster. The harassed Fenian chief lacked funds, but was forced to support ten pilots and many suspects who had fled Ireland since September 1865. By August 1866 this would cost the Fenian exchequer $10,000, for the men, intending to sail with the invasion force, did not seek employment. On arrival in New York there were frequent recriminations, as Stephens had invariably blamed their difficulties on O'Mahony. Some recently returned Irish-American officers, disgruntled with the lack of preparedness in Ireland, joined the seceding senators; others believed that an insurrection would end in abysmal failure.[124]

Stephens in a dilemma

In late 1865 Head Constable Thomas Talbot warned that there were 120,000 Fenians in Ireland. William Meagher, 'centre' for Carrick-on-Suir, made similarly inflated claims during an IRB meeting in November: as well as 1000 sworn members in the town, 'he could turn out 60,000 men in the counties of Tipperary, Waterford, and Kilkenny' for the Rising. Devoy's estimates are equally suspect and it is only possible to guess at IRB numbers.[125] At the zenith of Stephens's power, there may have been 20,000 IRB men in Ireland and Britain. His organization enjoyed great popular sympathy, however, which would become active support, should he obtain modern weapons. Stephens's insistence that 1865 would be the 'year of action' galvanized the Dublin IRB, while the Fenians in Cork City jail expected an outbreak during the winter of 1865–6.[126]

Lord Wodehouse disbelieved rumours of imminent insurrection in November 1865, but after the rescue of Stephens from Richmond jail, 'the people went wild with delight' and envisaged a Rising. Resident Magistrate Hanna, Carrick-on-Suir, suspected that the local blacksmiths were about to manufacture pikes. Head Constable Talbot reported that William Meagher had returned from Dublin to prepare for action by dividing Carrick into districts, listing owners of weapons and their attitude towards Fenianism. James Hetherington of Mullinavat acted as a Fenian courier, but Talbot failed to find his documents while he slept. Nor could he locate the concealed arms depot.[127]

In mid December the military council confirmed to Matt MacLaughlin, who had travelled to Dublin, that members of the Scottish IRB who could support themselves until 1 January should proceed to Ireland immediately. MacLaughlin spread the word in the Glasgow and Dumbarton area, Edinburgh, Dalkeith, Dunfermline, Perth, Dundee and Blairgowrie. Colonel Kelly, Stephens's chief of staff, expected guns to be shipped from France. In Dublin, Kelly kept the 'circles' on alert until late December, when Stephens pressurized his officers for a postponement as he was badly handicapped by the split.[128]

Colonels Kerwin and Halpin, leaders of the 'military council of the Irish Republican Army', disagreed, because conditions were unlikely to improve. They urged an immediate uprising as the Fenian-infiltrated regiments and 150 Irish-American officers remained available. These included Colonel Byron, active in Tipperary and Limerick, Major John Augustine Comerford and the Gleesons.[129] Colonel Kelly was in daily contact with the men in Dublin, but Stephens hesitated and risked the disintegration of the IRB. The home organization lacked firearms. Stephens had promised that they would be supplied from America, but sceptical IRB members had imported rifles piecemeal since 1863. Eventually, Stephens permitted the manufacture of pikes in Dublin and Cork, but these were obsolete against a modern army. The efforts of the O'Donovan brothers to teach cartridge-making and military engineering were equally doomed, given the few guns available. Devoy believed that the Dublin IRB possessed 800 rifles and 1000 other weapons, including pikes, for its 8000 members, but this may have been an overestimate and the overall situation was hardly better.[130]

In December 1865 the IRB sent Colonel Ricard O'Sullivan Burke, who had served in an engineer corps during the American Civil War, to Birmingham to purchase arms. By January 1866 he had bought 2000 rifles and ammunition for £2000, assisted by Harry Shaw Mulleda and Joseph Theobald Casey.[131] Some were sent to Cobh, hidden in bolts of fabric addressed to John Daly, a prominent merchant and alderman of Cork Corporation, and collected by Fenian sympathizers.[132]

Lord Wodehouse informed Sir George Grey of 'a panic amongst the gentlemen in a few places in the south of Ireland', but declined further military reinforcements for hitherto quiet locations such as Waterford. The constabulary continued to lack recruits and Wodehouse urged Gladstone as Chancellor of the Exchequer to raise their pay, as an effective force was required. Threats of rebellion over Christmas saw Dublin Castle beset with applications for troops, but the viceroy was convinced that they were unnecessary.[133]

Armed police and military patrolled the streets in Dublin and Cork. In Clonmel, bank managers were warned of an intended attack and 150 men of the 73rd Highlanders rushed from Christmas worship in Limerick to Clonmel amidst mistaken reports that the prison had been attacked. Panic continued elsewhere in early 1866, 'some well-founded', according to Lord Wodehouse, who proclaimed Dublin city and county, as well as Tipperary and Waterford. Constantly beset by rumoured outbreaks, he consulted with Chichester Fortescue, the Chief Secretary, and tactfully nudged Lord Strathnairn into accepting two more infantry regiments. Wodehouse, alluding to contingency plans made in 1848, directed the commander-in-chief to follow suit.[134]

With hindsight, O'Mahony believed that Stephens should have informed the IRB that no Rising was possible during the Brotherhood split and departed for New York to confront the senators. O'Mahony also considered that, if some courageous attempt at insurrection had been made, in spite of all difficulties, this might have united the American movement. Stephens, however, continued to prevaricate.[135]

CHAPTER 5

Fenian Infiltration of the Armed Forces, 1864–78

Although Ireland accounted for only a third of the population of the United Kingdom in 1840, almost 40 per cent of British soldiers were Irish born. After the Famine, poverty compelled thousands of labourers and tradesmen, of whom 20 per cent were illiterate, to join police and army. Soldiers' pay and conditions were poor, diet and clothing inferior, barracks insanitary and very few obtained permission to marry. Enlistment from Ireland declined in tandem with its population in the second half of the nineteenth century. Commissions were purchased by gentlemen of means, as salaries were inadequate. The officer corps proved itself of dubious value during the Crimean War, however, and the sale of commissions was abolished in 1871. The day-to-day management of units depended on non-commissioned officers, whose promotion was based on merit.[1]

Contrary to the consensus of the liberal state in Britain, Ireland was held by the military, organized in the Dublin and Cork divisions. On 1 December 1866 detachments in the Dublin division were stationed in the Irish capital, the Curragh, Newbridge, Carlow, Athlone, Longford, Mullingar, Birr, Castlebar, Boyle, Sligo, Galway, Belfast, Armagh, Newtownards, Newry, Dundalk, Belturbet, Londonderry, Carrickfergus, Enniskillen, on Lough Swilly and Lough Foyle and by the Shannon. A total of 21,730 men, which included the troops of the Cork division, were stationed in the eponymous city and its harbour, Ballincollig, Bandon, Kinsale, Skibbereen, Bantry, Duncannon, Tralee, Limerick, Clonmel, Cahir,

Fermoy, Doneraile, Lismore, Mitchelstown, Clogheen, Carrick-on-Suir, Kilkenny, Waterford, Youghal, Templemore, Buttevant, Charles Fort, Kinsale and Nenagh.[2]

Since 1856 the Curragh formed the largest training centre of the British army, capable of accommodating 10,000 men. Highly visible detachments demonstrated British power and deterred rebels. Soldiers benefited the local economy, while the officer class reinforced an Anglo-Irish mindset.[3]

Table 6. *Number and percentage of Irish soldiers in the British army, 1840–73*

Year	No. of Irish NCOs and other ranks	Irish proportion of British army in per cent
1840	39,193	37.2
1868	55,583	30.8
1873	42,284	23.7

(Source: Spiers, 'Army organization and society', 337)

The Young Irelanders mistakenly believed that many privates sympathized and would join their insurrection. The Fenian leaders also hoped to subvert the army, as successful infiltration would compensate for their lack of experienced officers and arms, demoralize soldiers loyal to the Crown and reduce the need for a large American expedition with its challenge of evading the Royal Navy. But Stephens hesitated, afraid that Dublin Castle would realize what was afoot before his followers were ready for action.[4]

Driscoll and Sullivan, two young IRB members from Skibbereen, had enlisted after abandoning an agricultural training course in Glasnevin, Dublin. They enrolled several soldiers without authorization from the leadership and assured Devoy that the majority of Irishmen could be suborned. In garrison towns, civilian Fenians had pre-empted Stephens by swearing in soldiers, while in Lancashire, in particular, IRB members accessed training and rifles through volunteer regiments.[5]

Stephens was forced to withdraw his objections by the 'Pagan' O'Leary, who threatened to inform the American Fenians that the 'chief executive of the Irish Republic' was 'opposed to demoralising' the military. Patrick or 'Pagan' O'Leary, alias John Murphy, had suffered a head wound in the American-Mexican War. A fanatical separatist, O'Leary argued that national self-reliance was fatally undermined by Christianity, which facilitated the Norman and subsequent invasions.

He detested both the Catholic Church and the British Empire.[6] His recruitment technique was simple, but effective: IRB men in the army introduced their friends to minimize the risk of betrayal. O'Leary, an old soldier, reminded his audience that England would use 'young and healthy' Irishmen to abandon them when crippled 'to beg on the streets or die in the poorhouse'. Few survived to gain the military pension after twenty-one years' service.[7]

He proved most effective when recalling the Famine, especially evictions carried out by soldiers, as well as the Irish exodus, which he had witnessed. Many of his hearers were themselves victims of the clearances and O'Leary encouraged them to reveal their often tragic reasons for enlisting. Using their loss and anger, he described Irishmen firing on their own 'for England's shilling a day as worse than a dog', but insisted that they 'could smash the English army and give Ireland a sweet revenge for 700 years of robbery, persecution and slavery'. Devoy conceded, however, that O'Leary's efforts were haphazard and 'mainly propagandist'.[8]

An alert Superintendent Daniel Ryan of the DMP had O'Leary shadowed. Leaving Dublin for Athlone he attempted to recruit but was arrested in November 1864 and sentenced to seven years' penal servitude. A letter from Stephens was found on him, which urged caution when contacting IRB men in the Cork and Ballincollig barracks and to subvert the military in Fermoy only if authorized by the local 'centre'.[9]

William Francis Roantree of Leixlip, O'Leary's successor as organizer, had returned from an attempt by William Walker, the American freebooter, to establish a colony in Nicaragua, a rather inconsistent venture for a separatist. Roantree consolidated IRB groups by visiting garrisons in Dublin, the Curragh, Cork, Fermoy, Buttevant, Waterford and Limerick, appointing a soldier Fenian as the 'centre' of each infiltrated regiment. Detectives followed him and he was arrested with the staff of the *Irish People*.[10]

Finally, Stephens put John Devoy in charge of the military Fenians. He and Colonel Kelly concentrated on the Dublin regiments, which they hoped to deploy for the Rising. During the four months Devoy remained at large, he improved command structures by selecting IRB soldiers to take charge of squads and companies under their regimental 'centres'. Captain John McCafferty was to command the Fenian cavalry and Devoy arranged a meeting with his best men among the 5th Dragoons and the 10th Hussars. McCafferty favoured revolvers and guerrilla tactics, as used by Confederate irregulars during the Civil War, to the disappointment of the trained swordsmen. Meetings in bars were unavoidable in order to communicate with the soldiers, but little drink was consumed while the organizer and his contacts withdrew to consult.[11]

W.F. Roantree (courtesy NLI).

Devoy, writing from memory, claimed that 8000 soldiers had taken the IRB oath in Ireland, in addition to 7000 serving abroad. His figures are undoubtedly an overestimate. Army strength in Ireland rose from 19,403 to 22,899 men from 1865–7. Organizers enrolled large numbers from 1864 on, but their separatist convictions were never tested in action. Many may have accepted offers of free beer without taking their oath to a visionary Irish Republic seriously, an opinion shared by Lord Strathnairn, who could not determine the level of IRB penetration.[12]

Devoy believed that seven Dublin-based regiments harboured 'crack' units of the IRB, including the 10th Hussars, whose 'centre' was the young John Boyle O'Reilly, and the 61st Regiment under Thomas Chambers. The latter, a native of Thomastown, Co. Kilkenny, had deserted on 25 May 1865 to recruit for the Fenians in London, Aldershot and Shorncliffe Camp, Kent.[13] When Chambers resumed contact with the 61st in Dublin, Fenian comrades concealed his presence. Patrick Keating, a native of Clare, served as 'centre' of the 5th Dragoons, where his comrade Martin Hogan was among the cream of swordsmen. Devoy also referred to Fenians in the 8th, the 24th and the 73rd Foot, the 9th Lancers and the first battalion of the 60th Rifles.[14]

John Devoy (courtesy NLI).

In Cork J.J. Geary's pub was used to swear soldiers into the movement. The informer Warner stated that 200 of the 4th Dragoons in Cahir, Fermoy, Ballincollig and Cork, 200 men of the Cork militia rifles and some of the 2nd Queen's Regiment had joined the IRB by September 1865. The Cork Fenians planned that, once the Rising began, these soldiers would induce their comrades to fraternize with the insurgents to facilitate overthrowing the government, as had happened when the troops of King Francis II of the Two Sicilies refused to fight Garibaldi in 1860. The Bourbon king was isolated, however, unlike the British Empire.[15]

Anticipating an insurrection, Fenian agents were most active between October and December 1865: Edward Pilsworth St Clair and Peter Maughan, both members of the diaspora in London, approached soldiers in Aldershot and Woolwich Arsenal. When candidates agreed to join the proposed Rising, civilian clothes and transport to Dublin were arranged. Devoy directed this well-organized underground network, paying deserters 1s. and 6d. per day, two pence more than the British army rate, as an incentive. These experienced fighters would direct insurgents or assist in seizing their barracks. They stayed in lodgings, working as drill masters and attending seditious meetings, where money was collected to purchase arms.[16]

Devoy surmised that 12,000 militiamen, of whom half had taken the Fenian oath, were training in Ireland during 1865, but their actual figure stood at 22,000. William O'Brien observed how the North Cork Rifles in Mallow demonstrated unusual military fervour and betrayed their allegiance by singing Fenian songs. An official return of untrustworthy members of April 1866 pointed to one hundred militia men in Carlow. Military skills were shared with fellow conspirators. The authorities removed weapons to central depots by 1865 and decided against holding annual training camps for the following two years.[17]

From 1865–8 rumours that military, navy and police had been infiltrated kept the middle classes and Loyalists on edge, simultaneously encouraging donations from American sympathizers. Consul Kortright of Philadelphia had acquired the quarterly report of the Fenian Brotherhood of September 1865. It stressed the importance of subversion to claim that every company of the British army contained eight Fenians, while five were embedded in each volunteer company throughout England. Two-fifth of the Irish police could not be trusted, awaiting an opportune moment to set their barracks on fire, before withdrawing in concert with the rebels. Many coastguards had apparently joined the IRB to facilitate the landing of the American expedition. After Stephens' jailbreak it was whispered in New York that he would not be recaptured, the detectives having been 'liberally bribed'. In February 1866 Mitchel was said to disburse Fenian funds to suborn the Irish police and military from Paris. Such stories would prove hyperbolic.[18]

According to Devoy, the 87th Regiment, although stationed in Portsmouth, contained 200 Fenians. William Curry, the 'centre', planned to seize a steamer to sail to Ireland when the insurrection broke out. Following the *Irish People* arrests on 15 September 1865, twenty of its most impatient members, among them Corporal Patrick Tierney, reached Dublin on furlough as a Fenian vanguard. They expected immediate action.[19]

The Fenian NCOs

In April 1865 Colonel Somerset Calthorpe of the 5th Dragoons briefed Sir George Brown, Commander-in-Chief in Ireland, on Fenian penetration of several regiments. His information derived from the confession of Patrick Foley, who had been inducted into the IRB by 'Pagan' O'Leary and James Montague, a fellow dragoon. The terminally ill Sir George Brown, a veteran of the Peninsular and Crimean Wars, considered Fenianism a minor issue. On 11 July Sir Hugh Rose, soon to become Lord Strathnairn, arrived in Dublin to replace him. Strathnairn

had received his military education in Prussia. The Fenians highlighted his 'ruthless sternness' in suppressing the Indian Mutiny by blowing Sepoys 'from the
cannon's mouth'.[20]

Unlike Sir Edward Blakeney, one of his predecessors, who had decided to
ignore disaffection among the soldiery in 1848, Strathnairn felt that if 'instances
of disaffection' had been dealt with promptly, 'so many cases of Fenianism as
now present themselves would not have occurred'.[21] Strathnairn advised the
Duke of Cambridge, his commander-in-chief, that, while the lower classes exaggerated the threat, Dublin Castle had provided him with a map, 'marking the
counties and localities in which Fenanism, as well as those in which Ribbonism
exist' in August 1865. Agrarian combinations were spread over fourteen counties, while the IRB predominated in Kilkenny, Cork and Limerick with a partial
presence in a further eight. The Irish had become formidable fighters since
participating in the Civil War, but without an American expedition, Strathnairn
dreaded that the IRB might attempt guerrilla warfare in Munster by seizing
small police stations and disrupting railway lines.[22]

Although subordinates dragged their feet, he persisted to uncover Fenianism
'of a very bad description' and deplored a 'false *esprit de corps*' (more likely a
feeling of superiority), reminding him of the British before the Indian Mutiny,
unable to credit the plotting of native soldiers until it was almost too late.
Strathnairn coerced commanding officers to support junior ranks in their investigations, which paid dividends.[23] Colonel Percy Feilding, Coldstream Guards,
responsible for army discipline, initiated an intelligence operation, assisted by
Captain William Whelan. Patrick Foley became their first double agent. He was
joined by James Maher of the 8th Regiment in March 1866; within weeks, the
latter had survived an assassination attempt. Feilding agreed that loyal subjects
were anxious about 'unpleasant rumours' regarding a 'vast amount of disaffection and Fenianism' in the army, announcing his intention to punish the few
genuine culprits.[24]

Lacking time to visit the Munster garrisons, Devoy delegated responsibility
for regiments in Kilkenny, Cahir, Fermoy, Buttevant, Templemore, Limerick,
Waterford and Cork to local leaders, who reported directly to Colonel Kelly
in Dublin. These civilians were to maintain communication with designated
Fenians representing their regiments, but did not recruit. 'Other places were
wholly unattended to,' including most units stationed in England. Devoy's
strategy meant that these unsupervised soldier Fenians attracted attention
through their lack of caution, for instance in south Tipperary.[25]

Charles McCarthy, who was born in Effin parish near Kilmallock in 1834,
joined the 53rd Regiment in 1853 to embark for India, where he fought on

numerous occasions and was rewarded for his bravery during the Indian Mutiny. Returning to Ireland, McCarthy won prizes as an athlete.[26] 'Esteemed by his officers,' he was promoted to colour sergeant and, finally, acting sergeant major. For a working man, McCarthy had reached the pinnacle of an army career. Before his posting to Clonmel, he established an NCOs' dramatic society, which performed for local charities in Kilkenny.[27]

Col Sergeant Charles McCarthy (Irishman).

In contrast to the US army, it was exceptional for a British private to achieve officer status. Sergeant Major Thomas Darragh, born in 1834 as the son of a Protestant farmer in Wicklow, had been a member of an Orange Lodge before joining the 2nd Queen's Regiment in 1852. He embarked for South Africa, was transferred to China in 1859 and decorated for bravery. Highly recommended by his commander, Darragh had been suggested for an officer's commission, but would have encountered a great deal of snobbery if promoted, for he was not a gentleman by birth. When sworn into the IRB by the informer Warner, Darragh sacrificed a successful career, probably frustrated by the lack of structures to promote outstanding men in an age of great change. A British comrade of John Boyle O'Reilly, destined to become a public figure in America, predicted that he could be promoted to sergeant major and 'that would have been the end of him', Devoy tartly concluded.[28] Fenian agents, 'of a superior and very intelligent class', like Colonel Byron suborned the military by holding out inducements to non-commissioned officers: 'Commissions in the Irish Republican Army were promised them in some instances, but in all, promotion was to reward their treason.'[29] Byron travelled through Munster with his Federal commission and uniform, visible evidence of his rapid rise through the ranks, which 'might be gained in Ireland under a Republican government'. The *Nation* as well as Lord Strathnairn concluded that soldiers 'even of steady habits were momentarily deluded' by such career prospects.[30]

Thomas Darragh's meetings with Brian Dillon and J.J. Geary, whose premises were under observation during the summer of 1865, aroused suspicion. Claiming Geary as his cousin, Darragh had introduced him to the non-commissioned officers' mess. Arrests began following the seizure of the *Irish People*. Darragh was detained on 22 September at the Fleetwood School of Musketry in Lancashire.[31]

In November 1865 an anonymous letter alerted the authorities that a Sergeant McCarthy had given James Stephens a tour of the Clonmel barracks, which could be handed over to the insurgents at will. Dublin Castle, suspecting the Clonmel and Carrick-on-Suir region as 'the very hotbed of Fenianism', dispatched Head Constable Talbot, an outstanding plain-clothes detective, experienced in investigating agrarian murders in Co. Westmeath.[32] Talbot posed as 'John Kelly', a returned Yank and member of the Fenian Brotherhood. Local conspirators failed to check his credentials, thereby facilitating their entrapment. During 1865–6, Talbot associated with the separatists of south Tipperary and Waterford. A Protestant, he duped his associates by attending Mass in a devout manner, while gratifying their Fenian convictions when denouncing priests in politics. He socialized in Tom Burke's pub in Clonmel, singing 'Bold Fenian Men', a ballad by Michael Scanlan, the poet of American Fenianism:[33]

> *See who comes over the red-blossomed heather*
> *Their green banners kissing the pure mountain air*
> *Heads erect, eyes in front, stepping proudly together*
> *Freedom sits throned on each proud spirit there*
> *Down the hill twining, their blessed steel shining*
> *Like rivers of beauty that flow from each glen*
> *From mountain and valley,*
> *'tis Liberty's rally –*
> *Out and make way for the bold Fenian men!*

Local 'centres' compounded their folly by allowing 'John Kelly' to recruit his own 'circle', which enabled him to become an *agent provocateur* and flush out subversives. On 1 January 1866 Philip Morrissey and John Daniel, leaders of the Carrick IRB, introduced Talbot to Colour Sergeant Charles McCarthy and Private James Keilley of the 53rd Regiment. McCarthy lamented his removal from Clonmel as 'a great loss to the cause', for he had intended to hand over the magazine with its arms, Keilley having copied the keys.[34] Talbot testified that Colour Sergeant McCarthy had said 'there was too much talking; to keep quiet and to keep silent, and victory was at our doors; that we would not have much fighting, as they would do most of the work for us, and that if he remained in Carrick he would soon have it in as good order as Clonmel'.[35] In Carrick-on-Suir, arms, which should have been in his care, were now guarded by a corporal, whom McCarthy considered tasked to spy on him. McCarthy would put 'a pistol to his head and blow the b-s out' to obtain weapons for the Rising.[36]

The friendship between Colour Sergeant McCarthy and Keilley attracted attention because of the considerable social gulf between non-commissioned officers and soldiers. A nervous McCarthy tried to find out when the steamers departed for America. He told Corporal Michael Brennan, his orderly room clerk, whom he had sworn into the IRB, that he lived in constant fear of arrest.[37] Talbot also learned that Bombardier Lowe had enrolled forty-four artillery men in Clonmel as Fenians. He covertly reported to Dublin Castle and went about armed with two pistols.[38]

The Rising postponed

Although the trials of the *Irish People* staff continued into early 1866, much of the IRB structure remained intact. Stephens's letter to the Clonmel leaders, declaring 1865 'the year of action', was widely disseminated through newspaper reports and Fenians were encouraged to come over from Britain. Devoy and Lord Strathnairn both estimated that 'perhaps about 300 or 400' of these had arrived and loitered at street corners.[39]

Stephens, after his rescue from Richmond jail, 'kept it up to the very end of the year. Then, when the men were keyed up to the highest pitch of enthusiasm and expectancy there came a sudden change. The fight was postponed.'[40] The Fenian Brotherhood split scuppered effective help for the IRB. The Irish-American colonels Kelly, Halpin and Kerwin of the IRB military council pleaded in vain for an immediate insurrection, as circumstances were unlikely to improve. They doubted that Stephens could heal the dissensions in the US.[41]

The situation of the soldier Fenians became very precarious. Patrick Keating, the 'centre' of the 5th Dragoons, had first enlisted as a youth. In 1848, he was dismayed to guard John Mitchel on his way to Spike Island. Bought out by his family, Keating subsequently re-enlisted and took the IRB oath. When he had to escort Thomas Clarke Luby to Mountjoy Prison after sentencing, the dragoon burst into tears, making 'him a marked man'.[42]

Lord Strathnairn was unaware that Dublin Castle had sent undercover agents to various garrisons until Colour Sergeant McCarthy and others were identified and Talbot, who had advised McCarthy on likely IRB recruits, revealed himself as a police spy. Strathnairn learned of Fenian incidents at Shorncliffe Camp, Kent, and with the battalion depots of the 11th and 10th Regiments in Newry and Belfast respectively.[43] On 17 February Robert Cranston of the 61st Regiment told co-conspirator John Abraham that the Rising was imminent. Cranston was to select Fenians in Richmond barracks to render the rifles of loyal soldiers ineffective. Revolutionaries among the military would join the civilian attack on the barracks, while loyal troops could not fire their weapons. In the confusion, the Fenians would seize the building.[44]

That very day, the government suspended habeas corpus and the large number of arrests included nearly all the American officers. IRB men were dissatisfied with 'Stephens's inaction ... almost open mutiny was growing fast'.[45] An anxious Abraham revealed that 'all the Irish in the 61st' were Fenians, but Colonel Redmond disagreed, describing him as 'thoroughly frightened' of both his officers and the IRB, which would kill him, should his betrayal become known. Colonel Redmond mistakenly insisted to Strathnairn that Robert Cranston was the only Fenian in his regiment.[46]

On 20 February, an all-night conference involving Stephens, colonels Kelly and Halpin, John Nolan of Carlow, chief organizer for Ulster, Edmond O'Donovan, representing Clare, David Murphy of Limerick, Mortimer Moynahan of Skibbereen and Devoy took place. Their lack of arms was a major difficulty, for the organization possessed a mere 2000 rifles. A further 2000 had been purchased by Colonel O'Sullivan Burke, but could not be smuggled to Ireland at present.[47]

Devoy and others insisted that Stephens take action or witness the destruction of the IRB, but the latter continued to prevaricate. When the meeting reconvened on 21 February, Devoy clamoured for insurrection. IRB men and subversives in the 61st and 60th Regiments, the former being the Fenian flagship, would take the initiative by seizing Richmond barracks late in the evening. Thomas Chambers was to lead his comrades; it was hoped that the rebellion would spread in Dublin and further afield. If successful, the IRB could seize large quantities of arms; but nobody knew how many rebels might turn out, as the Fenians lacked a majority in any barracks. Devoy argued that the infiltrated regiments were capable of spearheading a revolution, but with few American officers still at large and Halpin and Kelly insisting that the rifles hidden in Liverpool should be brought over first, this plan was abandoned: 'Thus, the last chance for a Rising in that year was thrown away,' lamented Devoy.[48]

Lord Strathnairn, whose hobby was hunting, shared his delight at the habeas corpus arrests with Wodehouse: 'I congratulate you, very sincerely, on the capital bag of Irish American Fenians which you have caused to be made; and I hope that the arrests in the country may be equally numerous.'[49] He supported the Duke of Cambridge in demanding a joint operation with the police to round up the deserters. Double agents Foley and Abraham alerted Colonel Feilding to a Fenian rendezvous and on 22 February the DMP surrounded Pilsworth's pub, arresting twelve soldiers and seven civilians. They included Devoy and his assistants, Thomas Chambers and Edward Pilsworth St Clair, as well as Stephen O'Kelly, the London-based organizer. A nationalist crowd assembled outside and the police summoned military support. Comparing the Fenians to the United Irishmen, the *Times* commented triumphantly:[50]

> The police had an encounter with a body of armed men last night, which reminds one of the scenes of 1798, and reveals the fact that the Fenians have corrupted the military to a greater extent than had been imagined. The conduct of the police deserves the highest praise. They acted at the imminent risk of their lives, and did their work well.[51]

Lord Strathnairn declared the 61st Regiment greatly improved afterwards, given its previous lack of respect towards the officers. Next to the Buffs, he considered the 61st the most suspect unit.[52]

Inexorably, the remaining Fenian deserters were seized and detained on inadequate rations. Captain Whelan urged the dejected men to save themselves by giving information, claiming that Boyle O'Reilly and Devoy had turned Crown witness. Most soldiers only said enough to minimize their sentences.[53]

An incensed Lord Strathnairn characterized his officer corps as aristocratic amateurs, unaware of Fenians sauntering in and out of the Royal Barracks in Dublin or recruiting in various canteens. The 'smart' American Colonel Byron, 'son of a broken-down farmer, a tenant of Lord Lismore', spent a great deal of money on the soldiers and non-commissioned officers of the 73rd Regiment. He gained access to the Castle barracks in Limerick, suborning a militia sergeant. Having been stationed in that town years ago, Strathnairn recalled its 'avidity' for gossip, wondering how the officers of the 73rd could claim ignorance of Byron's intentions. He deplored Sergeant Major Darragh's pivotal position in the 2nd Queen's with his unsuspecting superiors mooting to send him to infiltrate the Cork IRB, of which he was a leading member. The commander-in-chief dreaded what mischief might have ensued, had the 2nd Queen's not been 'a very good, very English regiment' with a competent and popular commander.[54]

Lord Strathnairn cancelled civilian access to all barracks to implement strict security and pointedly informed officers of their duties. He even considered sidelining inadequate ones. Strathnairn realized that Fenian agents succeeded because Irish soldiers entertained 'ideas of aggrieved nationality, imbibed from their earliest youth', but some had 'repented when it came to the point of breaking into open treason or mutiny'.[55]

Strathnairn decided against altering the customary rotation of regiments in and out of Ireland to exclude the suspect ones – this would only amplify rumours of untrustworthiness. Many units contained Irishmen, making adjustments impractical, but Fenian clusters were surrounded by a majority of loyal comrades, whose example they would ultimately follow. It was feasible to relocate the five depot battalions in Ireland, however, including some of the 11th Regiment in Templemore. Largely composed of Tipperary men, whose Fenian displays had featured in the press, this unit was neutralized and sent to Ulster in December 1865.[56]

Strathnairn knew that the Irish working class, the backbone of the British army, was also the mainstay of Fenianism, and sought an understanding with the Catholic hierarchy, whose opposition would help to suppress the IRB. Strathnairn considered the majority of the clergy loyal, except for a few 'young and ill-conditioned' priests like Fr Lavelle. As a publicity exercise on St Patrick's Day 1866 during this volatile period, he claimed the military was sound, leaving aside a minority, which had succumbed to 'treacherous temptations' for 'a reign of terror and spoliation'.[57]

Lord Strathnairn intended to make examples by having some Fenians tried for high treason, but evidence was first vetted by Thomas Emerson Headlam, Judge Advocate General at Horse Guards in London. This barrister and politician firmly upheld the liberal state and Strathnairn complained to the Duke of Cambridge, another strict disciplinarian, that his powers had been restricted since the Indian Mutiny. Ultimately, soldier Fenians were court-martialled for mutiny, which facilitated convictions and had 'a more exemplary effect', as evidence of high treason remained doubtful.[58]

Sergeant Major Darragh stood accused of 'mutinous conduct in Cork, in not reporting an intended mutiny of her majesty's forces ... and for having ... joined a treasonable and seditious conspiracy'.[59] Darragh had been introduced to J.J. Geary by Warner to provide military leadership in Cork during the insurrection. His relationship with the recently convicted Brian Dillon also counted against him. Darragh protested that he had endured five months in solitary confinement, when non-commissioned officers on a charge usually suffered only house arrest. He queried the uncorroborated testimony of the informer, for Warner had a poor military record.[60]

Darragh, on the other hand, had enlisted as a teenager and retained an unblemished reputation. He explained his relationship with Geary as due to the publican tendering for a drinks contract for the sergeants' mess. Darragh expostulated that had he really joined the IRB he would be more fit 'for a lunatic asylum than a prison', but was convicted. A general lack of caution among the Cork IRB had allowed Warner to gain access and Geary, instead of supporting Darragh's statements, fled abroad.[61]

As legal adviser to the British army, Thomas Emerson Headlam insisted that convictions rested on the evidence of two witnesses, but Lord Strathnairn urged the Duke of Cambridge to press for one being acceptable, as long as he possessed credibility. Both commanders were concerned about discipline. An irate Strathnairn argued that soldiers could get off scot-free if they committed treason in front of a single witness. Headlam's legal niceties might prove disastrous, as 'cases of Fenianism are now so numerous and they are of so much delicacy and importance'.[62]

Colour Sergeant McCarthy protested in vain that a military court had no jurisdiction over him in peacetime and that the proceedings amounted to a covert trial for high treason. He felt entitled to a civil court. The *Times* supported severe measures, for 'a man who solemnly takes service under any government, and then proves false to his flag and his uniform, has forfeited all claims to mercy'.[63] Lord Strathnairn thundered that British subjects were not conscripted, but seemed unaware that Irishmen volunteered from economic necessity. Corporal Brennan, guilty of treason, was promised legal immunity by Colonel Feilding to corroborate Head Constable Talbot, the leading Crown witness. McCarthy was convicted.[64]

The government and the Duke of Cambridge agreed to commute Sergeant Major Darragh's death sentence to transportation for life, 'as the most important part of the informer's evidence is not confirmed'.[65] The evidence regarding McCarthy was clearer and Strathnairn and Wodehouse agreed that such 'deeply planned treason' by 'a non-commissioned officer of a high grade ... who conspires to overthrow his sovereign's government and the public order, of which the army is the aid and support, is as grave as it is dangerous'.[66] Colonel Feilding argued that McCarthy's intention to seize the Clonmel magazine deserved the death penalty, which would restore discipline, provide more informers and destroy confidence in the IRB. It would refute rumours that Dublin Castle feared the consequences of killing these soldiers, as Fenianism remained powerful. Strathnairn quietly anticipated McCarthy's execution, but was once again stymied by Headlam.[67]

The trial of William Foley for mutiny was not without embarrassment for Lord Strathnairn. In 1853 Foley had enlisted in the East India Company and served during the Indian Mutiny. Returning to Europe six years later, he joined the

5th Dragoons and, in 1864, the IRB. Given his excellent character, Foley became Strathnairn's orderly and spied on his commander until arrested two years later. Devoy considered him 'one of our best and most faithful men' among the military.[68]

Although the military authorities were steadily eradicating the Fenian threat, the populace continued to sympathize. In Kilkenny in December 1865, Daniel Darcy, a cabinetmaker and associate of the Callan IRB, tried to swear in Gunner Lyons of the Royal Artillery with the promise of 'a "burst" before New Year's Day'.[69] Lyons cooperated with the authorities but locals detested him as an informer, which culminated in a riot. Patrick Manning of the 14th Regiment, home on leave from Aldershot, shouted: 'Although I wear the bloody queen's uniform, I am a Fenian,' before joining a crowd, including two prostitutes, which chased two artillery men and administered a vicious beating.[70]

By May 1866 Colonel Feilding believed that the IRB had started a new organization for subverting the military. After Devoy's detention, Dr Edmund Power, a Dublin 'centre', successfully infiltrated the 85th Regiment, aided by William Moore Stack, a law clerk. The latter, a native of Knockanure near Listowel, was an energetic and intelligent captain in Power's circle, but also 'credulous, very fond of drink' and indiscreet. During 1865–6 associates questioned his revolutionary commitment. Arrested in December 1866 and sentenced to ten years, Moore Stack failed to gain from informing, as Dublin Castle considered his news out of date. Isolated cases of military subversion recurred, while the New York *Irish People* claimed, perhaps from motives of propaganda, that disaffection continued 'to prevail to an alarming degree in some Irish regiments'.[71]

Dr Edmund Power, CSO/ICR /16
(courtesy NAI).

Fenian tradition relates that John Patrick O'Brien enlisted to remain in Ireland, when the Rising was postponed. Colonel Feilding, however, considered him a very intelligent medical student, who infiltrated the 8th Regiment in May 1866, subsequently deserting from Newry to subvert the 85th as 'Thomas Simpson'.[72] An informer alerted the authorities and O'Brien was sentenced to fifteen years, when he responded defiantly with 'three cheers for the Irish Republic'. Nevertheless, these suspects were fortunate that the authorities did not realize that infiltrated regiments had Fenian commanders or 'centres'.[73]

Police infiltration

Devoy's narrative of DMP infiltration is anecdotal, naming Michael Breslin and Michael O'Clohessy, both brothers of IRB 'centres'. John J. Breslin was one of two warders facilitating Stephens's rescue from Richmond jail. Superintendent Mallon also realized that the 'Fenians have a friend in Thom's printing office' who supplied confidential information. Michael Graham, a former letter carrier, memorized the faces of the G-men and helped the IRB keep watch on DMP activities. Some constables had Fenian sympathies and assisted on occasion, motivated by family and local loyalties. Michael Breslin felt that the majority of the Dublin police force would have deserted to the IRB, had it 'gained an initial success'. They upheld the state from pragmatic rather than ideological considerations.[74]

Colonel Feilding doubted the trustworthiness of the DMP, as information of two forthcoming raids had 'leaked', but an element of professional rivalry also existed. Lord Strathnairn, for instance, reacted defensively when Superintendent Ryan claimed in January 1866 that three regiments were almost Fenian to a man. When Devoy's *Recollections* appeared in 1928, revolutionary relatives were celebrated as heroes and diplomatic reticence was no longer necessary. Given the lack of concrete information, police infiltration by the IRB was limited.[75]

Infiltration of the Royal Navy

Since the 1840s the Royal Navy had been employed to encourage loyal subjects, while overawing potential rebels. The Irish administration increasingly depended on the navy to guarantee internal security by providing logistical support, blockading foreign invasions and containing uprisings. The rear admiral commanding in Irish waters was based in Haulbowline near Cork, one of the most disaffected counties during the 1860s, but simultaneously a very successful recruiting ground for the navy. Lord Strathnairn considered that nothing was as likely to prevent an Irish-American expedition to Ireland as an alert Royal Navy. The Channel Squadron of seven large ironclads and a gunboat with more than 240 guns arrived as a deterrent in the summer of 1865. The speed with which troops could be sent from Britain to Ireland was an important consideration, although discussions in November 1866 revealed that only one regular troop ship was immediately available and no more than 1500 men could be transported to Ireland at short notice. By 1867 mostly gunboats were patrolling Irish waters. The *Erin's Hope* managed to cruise the west coast and narrowly evaded arrest, nevertheless, her mission failed due to coastguard vigilance. When communication by train was interrupted during the Rising, Admiral Frederick despatched HMS *Helicon* from Cork to Dublin with the mailbags and important reports for Lord Strathnairn.[76]

Incidents were kept out of the press, for example, near Bantry, where some navy ratings on HMS *Liverpool* were arrested in December 1866 for uttering disloyal sentiments. A sailor who managed to burn seditious documents and pictures of Emmet, Stephens and Luby, belonging to a comrade, was sentenced to fourteen lashes, but still avowed himself a Fenian. The commander of the *Liverpool* feared that at least thirty of the eighty Irishmen aboard were IRB members; the constabulary, on the other hand, suspected all.[77] During an undercover operation in January 1867 police agents socialized with these sailors and soldiers from the 13th Regiment, to probe Fenian links. The crew of the *Liverpool* named 'Long and Sullivan, both petty officers' as sympathizers, who had been demoted and transferred. Local Fenianism was moribund, due to the number of arrests. Organizers in the Royal Navy made little headway, although John Flood of the Royal Artillery, Portsmouth, informed the *Irish People* in Dublin that when he obtained this paper, 'dozens' of military personnel were 'coming to me for a loan of it'.[78]

Beginning in late 1865, military intelligence dealt Fenianism decisive blows. Subversive secrecy was lacking and probably unobtainable anyway. One hundred and eighty soldiers, who had taken the IRB oath, were imprisoned. Charles McCarthy, John Boyle O'Reilly, Thomas Chambers, Michael Harrington, Thomas Henry Hassett, Patrick Keating, Martin Hogan, Robert Cranston and James Keilley were among the fifteen receiving the death penalty, invariably commuted to life, with the exception of Boyle O'Reilly, who got twenty years. This avoided the creation of Republican martyrs, which would revive the faltering separatist movement. By transporting almost all soldier Fenians to a penal settlement in the Antipodes the following year, the authorities hoped to criminalize and remove them from the Irish consciousness.[79]

In the eyes of the establishment, these soldiers had committed double treason and retribution would follow:

> Exemplary punishment of Fenian soldiers who have violated their oaths of allegiance and have committed a double crime of treason, that is as civil subjects and as soldiers, is necessary. This is the more necessary because there cannot be the slightest doubt that the Fenian conspirators have not lost sight of the so obvious policy of causing their agents to enlist into regiments where, provided with plenty of money, they have a more favourable opportunity of tampering with soldiers and gaining information useful to their employers, than if they were out of the Army.[80]

Towards the end of his life, McCarthy justified himself by stating, that despite having 'sworn allegiance to the English queen no man was justified in throwing off the allegiance he owed to his country'.[81] Richard Pigott considered him, Thomas Darragh and John Boyle O'Reilly the most intelligent among the military Fenians. 'Trooper Reilly' earned a literary career after absconding from penal servitude in Australia.[82]

Lord Strathnairn regretted 'extremely' that soldiers, about to be tried for treasonable conduct, could only be court-martialled to two years in prison, which he believed 'quite insufficient' and a poor deterrent. He recommended that the Mutiny Act should be amended.[83] Minor participants like William Curry, a deserter from the 87th Regiment, who had smuggled Devoy's instructions into the barracks, were punished with two years and fifty lashes, which he endured unflinchingly by biting on a sixpence. Verbal 'complicity with the Fenian conspiracy' earned Gunner Flood two years and being tattooed with '"B.C." (bad character)'. Ignominiously drummed out of the army, he 'cheered lustily for the Fenian Brotherhood and for the Irish Republic', whereupon Strathnairn demanded a second court martial. It was standard practice in peace time to brand deserters, as described in an illicit letter from John Boyle O'Reilly:[84]

> I send you a note I got from Tom Chambers. Poor fellow, he's the truest-hearted Irishman I ever met. What a wanton cruelty it was to brand him with the letter D, and be doomed a felon for life. Just imagine the torture of stabbing a man over the heart with an awl, and forming a D two inches long and half an inch thick, and then rubbing in Indian ink. He was ordered that for deserting. His brother was nearly mad, and no wonder.[85]

Aftermath 1866–78

By June 1867 Lord Strathnairn's confidential report reassured the cabinet that there was no longer any cause for apprehension. Despite individual cases of Fenianism, collective treason among Irish-Catholic soldiers had failed to materialize and orders to suppress the Rising were carried out, even by apparently infiltrated regiments. However, had an insurrection broken out in 1865, before Strathnairn eradicated Fenianism, 'something disagreeable might and would probably have occurred'. This confirmed Devoy's assessment that Stephens had hesitated too long. Strathnairn had always concealed his mistrust of the Irish soldiers, but reiterated that redress of grievances was necessary, as only the aristocracy was pro-British, while the Catholic middle class and senior clergy detested Fenianism 'because it is opposed to their respective interests', although they remained ambivalent about English rule. He urged the disestablishment of the Church of Ireland to conciliate Catholics and their hierarchy, the latter having recently proved 'very advantageous' to the government.[86]

The Rising had failed to impress, but the commander-in-chief counselled vigilance regarding Fenianism: 'However much they may be weakened morally and physically by their late utter break down, and by the flight of their leaders, they are only lying on their oars, but quite ready to profit by any of the political contingencies, which I have shadowed out, to embark on a fresh treasonable crusade.'[87]

The convicted soldier Fenians were transferred to British prisons, where Thomas Chambers became convinced that they suffered greater hardships than the criminals:

> The whole object of the prison officials was to break our spirits. This is no fancy, we could plainly see it. I was told by Governor Morris and by Director Gambier that the then secretary of state had given orders that I was to be treated worse than ordinary prisoners. I believe the same instructions were given regarding McCarthy ... The deputy governor in Millbank told me on 3 November 1866 that ... I would be lead [sic] the life of a dog.[88]

John Boyle O'Reilly corroborated that the years spent in Dartmoor, the Siberia of the British prison system, fatally undermined the health of McCarthy and Chambers:

> Here they were set to work on the marsh, digging deep drains, and carrying the wet peat in their arms, stacking it near the roadways for removal. For months they toiled in the drains, which were only two feet wide, and sunk ten feet in the morass. It was a labour too hard for brutes, the half-starved men, weakened by long confinement, standing in water from a foot to two feet deep, and spading the heavy peat out of the narrow cutting over their heads. Here it was that

Chambers and McCarthy contracted the rheumatic and heart diseases which followed them to the end.[89]

Protest was pointless, as complaints had to be made to prison staff, who might retaliate. Chambers recalled that 'McCarthy bore his sufferings with the dignity of a soldier and patriot, and with the most perfect Christian patience. He was not a man to complain.'[90] His constitution began to break down around 1869, according to John Patrick O'Brien: 'It was in Millbank Prison ... that I first saw the late Charles McCarthy, he then appeared to be enjoying very good health ... I had frequent opportunities of seeing him exhibiting his strength; I mean in reference to his lifting heavy weights ... After being with me for some time he began to suffer from indigestion and from diarrhoea.'[91]

McCarthy developed heart problems, but the warders continued to make him carry substantial loads. Although Woking Invalid Convict Prison in Surrey had been designated for such convicts, no military Fenian was transferred there. Medical officers disagreed about McCarthy's diagnosis and his complaint was neglected. Heart disease was followed by depression, occasionally lessened by the company of Thomas Chambers:[92]

> McCarthy's health was quite broken, and he had sunk into a melancholy that was something hopeless; but while he was chained to Chambers he used to laugh all the time like a boy. The English Government at that time thought it was a salutary exhibition to parade the Irish rebels in chains in the streets. I remember one day when we were marched through the streets of London, all abreast on one chain (we were going from Pentonville to Millbank), with the crowds staring at us, Chambers made McCarthy laugh so heartily that it brought on a fit of coughing, and we had to halt till the poor fellow got his breath.[93]

Harsh treatment was worsened by security concerns, as the authorities rotated the soldier Fenians between Chatham, Portsmouth and Dartmoor. In the last named prison the convicts were so hungry that they ate mud cake with weed roots from the drainage ditches and swallowed their tallow candle stumps. When officialdom decided to transport the majority of IRB prisoners to Australia in 1867, McCarthy, Chambers and John Patrick O'Brien were the only military rebels left in England, presumably because two had been non-commissioned officers, while Lord Strathnairn believed that O'Brien had intended 'to poison the food of his comrades, and to shoot them, assisted by other Fenians, with revolvers as they came down the stairs to turn out, on the alarm being sounded'.[94] The soldier Fenians were excluded from the amnesty of 1871 on the grounds that convicted mutineers did not qualify as political prisoners. The Duke of Cambridge as commander-in-chief felt that freeing them would undermine discipline. With the passage of time, public interest in them declined.[95]

Occasionally a court martial claimed that the Fenians intended to perpetrate atrocities when seizing a barracks, but this seems unlikely as the IRB leadership under Stephens aspired to conventional warfare. Planning to create an underground army to take the field with American support, rather than develop guerrilla tactics consigned the IRB to failure in 1865–6. When Sergeant O'Brien of the engineers, a member of the Dublin IRB, volunteered to blow up Woolwich Arsenal during the insurrection, a 'somewhat frightened' Stephens declined his offer, for 'it would shock the civilised world'. The battle-hardened Colonel Kelly disagreed. O'Brien predicted that the 'tender-hearted' Fenian leaders were 'unfit to fight the English, who stopped at nothing' and abandoned the movement.[96]

No case of a higher British officer joining the IRB has been discovered, although 'Colonel C.H. O'Riordan' claimed to have served in the 10th Hussars. In 1864 Charles Holmes O'Riordan made a seditious speech before his old regiment in Macroom and was tried and acquitted of Fenianism. It emerged that he had been a sergeant during the Crimean War. Non-commissioned officers formed the highest ranks in the Fenian conspiracy.[97]

In conclusion, an estimated 7000 soldiers had taken the IRB oath in Ireland and Britain. Their potential remained unrealized, however, due to difficulties of effective organization and limited funds, while the reckless conduct of many Fenian privates endangered their movement. Irrespective of the dedication of organizers, regiments were despatched overseas at intervals, removing revolutionaries. Although some infiltrated troops remained in Ireland, none protested against the arrest of their Fenian comrades. The indecisiveness of Stephens, combined with the habeas corpus detentions and courts martial, destroyed any chance of a formidable insurrection.[98]

CHAPTER 6

Two Attempted Invasions and a
Prelude to Insurrection, 1866

Early in 1866 the rival wings held conventions to legitimize themselves. The fourth congress opened on 3 January in New York, reverting to the Chicago constitution of 1863 with O'Mahony as 'head centre', Bernard Doran Killian treasurer and Patrick Downing secretary of civilian affairs, while F.F. Millen represented the IRB. O'Mahony affirmed that his mission consisted of 'Ireland first; Canada after, if the Canadians wish it'.[1] Mitchel congratulated O'Mahony on having shed the restrictive Philadelphia constitution. He warned that an invasion force was essential for their insurrection, but the US, being at peace with Britain, 'would never allow' its departure. Although the funds Mitchel dispensed in Paris were soon exhausted, he still dreamed of 'a decisive movement' by Stephens. The latter sent Captain John McCafferty across the Atlantic to appeal for money.[2]

Colonel Roberts, President of the Senate faction, held his congress in Pittsburgh on 19 February. Their policy consisted of seizing British territory in North America as a bridgehead for an Irish invasion. He and General Sweeny, 'the man of action', called for subscriptions. The split had a catastrophic transatlantic impact, diminishing Fenian influence in the US while depriving the IRB of vital support. Mitchel commented that many sensible nationalists withdrew in dismay.[3]

Suspension of habeas corpus

On 1 January 1866 Colonel John Stewart Wood, Inspector General of Constabulary, issued secret instructions to county inspectors in Munster, Leinster and parts of Connacht, excluding Ulster but for Co. Monaghan, to prepare for an outbreak by stockpiling ammunition. Confidential consultations would decide if some outposts should be withdrawn and merge with larger barracks. Towns, which were suitable for defence, having access to provisions and communications, were to be earmarked for loyal subjects as centres of resistance, while awaiting the arrival of troops. The county inspectors should remain silent till further notice, but 'sealed copies' for subordinate officers were being sent as a precaution. These instructions remained in force until 13 March 1867. Informal contacts in the Kildare Street Club, Dublin led to a meeting of the nobility, gentry and merchants of all parties and denominations in the Rotundo on 1 February, chaired by Lords Downshire and Charlemont. Reminiscent of the Cork conference in September 1865, they demanded that the executive take action, urged military reinforcements and pledged support for 'extraordinary' measures.[4]

Simultaneously, Lord Wodehouse informed Lord Strathnairn that he had received requests for troops, largely from Munster, including Killarney, Macroom, Clonakilty, Dungarvan, Fethard, Clogheen, Roscrea, Nenagh and Charleville. Bishop Moriarty surreptitiously informed Chief Secretary Fortescue that Killarney did not require soldiers. Wodehouse decided to prioritize Galway, Ballina, either Wexford or Enniscorthy, and Dungarvan or Lismore as key points, followed by Boyle, Longford and Clarecastle and either Macroom or Millstreet.[5]

Henry Arthur Herbert, Muckross House, Killarney, a former chief secretary for Ireland and present Lord Lieutenant of Kerry, resented that Dr Moriarty's conclusions were preferred to his own, although supported by Lord Castlerosse and Sub-Inspector Colomb of the constabulary: 'The successful interference of the bishop is looked upon as a kind of triumph of the Fenian sympathizers over the magisterial authority.'[6] Herbert doubted that Dr Moriarty and his parish priests were well informed, considering 'the young clergy... disloyal to a man'. He believed that the hierarchy detested Fenianism as 'an indication of the waning of an influence they have hitherto found omnipotent'. Priests could not admit to themselves an active conspiracy among Catholics 'for the first time directed against his own order, as well as against the parson and law lord'.[7]

Individual aristocrats pressurized Wodehouse to suspend habeas corpus, proclaim their districts or cancel militia training.[8] On 8 February Lord Powerscourt, who had attended the Rotundo meeting, reiterated its recommendations to rescue Ireland from economic stagnation, caused by the 'demoralisation and confusion consequent on the socialistic schemes of the Fenians'. He urged the suspension of habeas corpus. Within days, the authorities proclaimed Roscommon, Wicklow, Armagh, Wexford and the rest of Longford and Cavan, while Stephens continued to prevaricate.[9]

Chichester Fortescue and Wodehouse consulted with Gladstone, identifying three principal grievances: land tenure, the established church and denominational education. The Lord Lieutenant wanted a land bill brought in this season and disagreed with politicians, who callously considered that the issue would resolve itself 'naturally as the result of emigration and general improvement'. Lord Wodehouse concluded that the government could gain immensely if the law became the tenants' protector against harsh landlords. Aware that Irish people trusted Gladstone, he detested being 'daily and hourly engaged in the repugnant task of repression and punishment, I am sensible that if we wish this country to become loyal and prosperous, we must deal with some of the questions to which I have alluded'.[10]

Wodehouse believed that Fenianism 'continues quite undiminished' and anticipated 'an outbreak'. In spite of the proposed legislation, he remained pessimistic: 'The old hatred of English rule fomented by the Irish in America burns too strongly for any measures to cure under a long time. It can only die out slowly, and will I fear survive the present century whatever we may do.'[11] Gladstone assented, promising progress along these lines, which would benefit Ireland after the suppression of Fenianism.[12]

Lord Strathnairn realized that agents were 'taking sketches of the forts and barracks in Ireland'. He feared that Fenian veterans might copy the guerrilla tactics of the Confederates during the Civil War, for instance, by using landmines to counteract the lack of an American expedition: 'The intercepted plans of the Fenians show this. They are quite right in planning the capture of Athlone, the strategical part of Ireland; the Magazine Fort which commands that part of the Dublin position.'[13]

Initially, he opposed the suspension of habeas corpus, citing unease among English Liberals at such a measure, which could prove counterproductive and stimulate support for those detained: 'The persons arrested have an ostensible right of complaint, and excite a certain amount of sympathy, because their conduct, however suspicious, has not been tried or proved according to any form of law usual in England.'[14]

But Strathnairn's proposed legislation to deport such agents was rejected by Wodehouse. Speed was of the essence, as 'the conspirators, undeterred' by the trial and conviction of their leaders were organizing 'an outbreak'. Both were aware that 340 American officers remained at large in the country, with a further 160 in Dublin. The most dangerous and reckless of these were General John

Gleeson, his brother Joseph and Colonel Byron. The authorities worried that panic would ensue, should a few battle-hardened individuals attack a country house, for instance. Wodehouse estimated that '300 or 400' Fenians had arrived from Britain and loitered in Dublin, awaiting the Rising. The police had seized 'three regular manufactories of pikes and bullets' in Dublin and believed that more existed. They failed to find any rifles, which Lord Wodehouse presumed hidden. Disaffection was spreading.[15]

Table 7. *Sample of Fenian Brotherhood officers arrested in Ireland, 1865–8*

Name	Birthplace & date	Occupation	Residence in America	American Military Service	Place/Date of Arrest
Laurence O'Brien	Cahir, 1842	Bricklayer	New Haven, Connecticut	Capt. 9th Connecticut Volunteers, 1861–4	Clonmel Prison, 1867
Joseph H. Lawlor	Ireland		Norwich, Connecticut	Lieut 9th Connecticut Volunteers, 1861–5	Limerick, 1867
William Mackey Lomasney	1841. Parents from Castlelyons, Co. Cork		Detroit	Federal Army	Cork, 1865 and 1868
John McClure, brother-in-law of Patrick Joseph Condon	New York, mother from Tipperary	Clerk	New York	11th NY Cavalry	Kilclooney Wood, March 1867
Charles Underwood O'Connell	Co. Cork	Farmer's son	New York	Federal Army	On arrival in Cork, 1865
Charles H. O'Riordan				Capt. Federal Army, ex-NCO in 10th Hussars, British army	On landing in Cork, 1865
John Warren	Clonakilty	Builder, journalist	Boston	Capt. 63rd NY, Irish Brigade	On landing from *Erin's Hope* near Dungarvan, June 1867

Name	Birthplace & date	Occupation	Residence in America	American Military Service	Place/Date of Arrest
William J. Nagle	New York		New York	Officer, Federal Army	On landing with *Erin's Hope* expedition, 1867
Michael O'Regan	Ardagh, Rosscarbery, 1826			Federal Army	Castletown-send, Nov. 1865
Cornelius O'Leary	Cork, 1840	Hosiery trade in Carrick-on-Suir	Washington	Sgt. 88th Regt, Federal Army	Carrick-on-Suir, Mar. 1866
Daniel C. Moynihan	Killarney			164th NY Regt, 1862, acting ordnance officer, 2nd division, 2nd corps, Army of the Potomac	Dublin, Feb. 1866 with Col Michael Kerwin and Lieut B. McDermott
Col Denis F. Burke	Limerick, 1841			69th NY National Guard in 1861, later 88th NY, Irish Brigade, commanded his regiment 1863–4	1867
Patrick Joseph Condon	Cahirmoyle, Co. Limerick, 1831			Capt. 63rd NY State Volunteers	Dublin, Feb. 1866; Cork, 2 Mar. 1867
John Augustine Comerford	Native of Massachus-setts? Family in Kells, Co. Kilkenny	Grocer, farming background		3rd Massachusetts Cavalry, 1862, promoted to major 1865	Dublin, Feb. 1866
James Joseph Bible	Lismore, 1840	Shop assistant		Capt., Federal Army, 1861	Dublin, Feb. 1866; near Carrick-on-Suir, Mar. 1867
Joseph O'Carroll	Tipperary			Lieut 4th NY Cavalry, 1863	Dublin, 1866

(Source: various newspapers; Fenian files, NAI)

On 14 February he informed Sir George Grey that the suspension of habeas corpus was 'indispensable for the safety of this country'. Fortescue, Strathnairn, Sir Thomas Larcom and other advisers were in agreement. Wodehouse requested to be telegraphed about the progress of the bill to facilitate arrests. On 16 February the government alerted him that the suspension would come before Parliament the following day. Detentions began that morning, even before it became law.[16]

General John Gleeson and his brother, Joseph, were arrested in Borrisoleigh, although the latter had just been released due to lack of evidence. Colonel Byron was another of the 703 suspects seized between February and July.[17] A flight of Yankee officers in their square-toed boots ensued. Colonel John James O'Connor had arrived on the Iveragh peninsula in 1865, when drilling began 'at night, generally on remote strands at low water' on Valentia and the adjoining mainland. The day before the habeas corpus suspension the police failed to find anything incriminating in O'Connor's lodgings, but when they returned with a warrant he was gone.[18] In Kilmallock the constabulary kept O'Sullivan's hotel, the Fenian headquarters, under observation. Patrick Walsh had returned from consultations with the Brotherhood in America, accompanied by John Dunne, a Civil War veteran. They were organizing this neighbourhood as well as Bruff and Kilfinane. Both fled before the arrival of the constabulary, although Dunne was eventually detained in Charleville. Numerous suspects stealthily prepared for emigration to evade arrest. The administration also failed to prevent some of the American officers from relocating to Britain, in spite of Sir George Grey's instructions.[19]

Disgruntled Fenians demanded action, but Stephens and Colonel Kelly rejected Devoy's proposal to strike, as the necessary 2000 rifles remained inaccessible due to police vigilance and the American officers, selected as leaders, were under arrest. Although the IRB had not imploded after the *Irish People* trials, it was badly disrupted by the habeas corpus detentions. Stephens decided to reunite the American movement and was smuggled on board a collier in Dublin port, accompanied by Colonel Kelly. Lord Wodehouse discounted renewed rumours that the Fenians would rise on St Patrick's Day, while the New York *Irish People* rejoiced at Dublin Castle's 'utter inability' to recapture Stephens.[20] On 24 March the viceroy

> heard that Stephens had arrived at Paris. I can't say much for our police. Stephens will come back again, and yet do harm. The Fenians however can never now really make a great coup. The complete unveiling of their whole scheme is fatal to them. No people but the Irish could be such egregious fools as to be led by such phantoms. On the whole I think there is no people on the face

of the earth more unworthy of respect. They have always been despised by the
Englishman and, as a nation, have always deserved his contempt.[21]

Wodehouse subsequently retracted, considering the Irish 'an unfortunate
people', whose faults the British had 'aggravated by evil treatment'. He believed
that 'perseverance in fair government' was needed to overcome 'this last folly'
and achieve 'slow but certain improvement' under English guidance. Suggestions
to investigate police collusion, given that Stephens had remained at large for
four months, were dropped as likely to prove embarrassing, while the trial of
Daniel Byrne, a warder implicated in his escape, collapsed. The *Irish People*
featured a letter from Colonel Kelly, which described Stephens's night in a luxurious hotel opposite Buckingham Palace on their way from Dublin to Paris.[22]

Meanwhile, Mitchel wrote to O'Mahony that the split in the Brotherhood
had reduced Fenian leverage over the US government to such an extent that
it only protested meekly against the detention of its citizens.[23] In an undated
fragment, Mitchel accused Stephens of grossly exaggerating the number of his
followers, correctly predicting that his influence with Irish-Americans would
vanish once 'the veil of distance' was removed.[24] He denounced Stephens's lack
of foresight as having provoked the habeas corpus suspension, given 'the multitudes of Americans he had brought over, as well as the many hundreds, perhaps
thousands, of men he had induced to come from England and Scotland, abandoning their business and appearing on the streets of Dublin as strangers having
nothing to do, which could not fail to attract the attention of the police'.[25]

Detained at the Lord Lieutenant's pleasure

The habeas corpus suspension facilitated the incarceration of suspects like
Edward Coyne, despite insufficient evidence for a prosecution.[26] Sometimes
habeas corpus prisoners were treated more severely than convicts: In March
1866 the *Waterford Citizen* reported that suspects in Waterford City jail were
locked up for twenty-two hours a day. An investigation by the grand jury
confirmed that they were not allowed to communicate with relatives and some
had become distressed. J.A. Blake and John Bagwell, MPs for Waterford city
and Clonmel respectively, protested to Attorney General Lawson, while J.F.
Maguire, MP for Cork, complained of similar hardships in Cork County jail.
Publicity led to better conditions.[27]

Six hundred and sixty-nine men were in custody by the second week of
April 1866. Hundreds were transferred to Mountjoy or Kilmainham, making
access for families difficult. Comrades still at large felt intimidated and many

abandoned Fenianism. Drilling ceased and the IRB became inactive by late May. Arrests of the rank and file were more extensive than during the Young Ireland period – early 1849 saw a total of 118 men detained, indicating that the Fenian conspiracy constituted a greater threat.[28]

*Marching Fenian prisoners into Cork County jail, April 1866 (*Harper's Weekly*).*

Held without trial, the detainees petitioned the government. Grounds for release were the prisoner's youth and inexperience, the danger that his health would break down or the suffering his innocent dependents endured due to his incarceration and loss of income. These 'memorials' to the Lord Lieutenant were supported by testimonials from authority figures such as local magistrates and clergy and families made strenuous efforts to obtain as many signatures as possible. Edward Kenny, a wealthy pig buyer, detained as IRB leader for Waterford city, had his successful petition endorsed by the R.C. bishop and the lord mayor of Waterford, for example.[29]

Richard Hoare, identified by Head Constable Talbot as among the inner circle of conspirators in Carrick-on-Suir, was taken to Kilmainham jail. Fr John Murphy of the Franciscan Convent in Carrick pleaded for the release of his perfect servant: 'Never out late, conduct exemplary … believes him not guilty, is greatly inconvenienced.'[30] Despite several appeals, Dublin Castle detained Hoare until he volunteered to emigrate; he sailed on 13 December 1867, having been held without trial for twenty-two months. Rossa, like Mitchel and Terence Bellew McManus, disapproved of petitioning, which required applicants to show deference and put themselves under obligations to British authority figures. The upper classes thought a Fenian could be identified by his fearless demeanour, signalling that he was the equal of anyone in an age, when gentlemen expected to be approached 'cap in hand'.[31]

Dublin Castle portrayed the Callan/south Tipperary Fenians as ignorant 'dupes' of their leaders, rather than acknowledging that they had repudiated the status quo since 1855. The authorities were reluctant to release Coyne and Cody, summarizing their careers: 'James Cody and Edmond Coyne – have both been remarkable for the active part they have taken in seditious movements for years and formed the deputation from Callan to the McManus funeral, besides being prominent at every Fenian meeting in the country.'[32]

Dublin Castle always consulted the respective sub-inspector of police and resident magistrate, whose objections vetoed release. William Hort, R.M., agreed that, Fenianism aside, Cody was 'a very well conducted young man and of the strictest integrity'. In Kilkenny and south Tipperary only John Haltigan had surpassed Cody and Coyne's zeal as IRB organizers, however. Cody's father pleaded that his son was in 'delicate' health, a euphemism for tuberculosis. James had attended specialists in Dublin and incarceration would be detrimental. The Codys had already lost their eldest son in the American Civil War.[33] Edward Coyne was concerned how his family coped. William Hort suggested both might be released 'on condition of their expressing contrition and taking the oath of allegiance, as whether they kept it or not it would destroy their influence among their dupes'.[34]

The authorities concluded 'that it would be imprudent to permit them to return to Callan, as their presence there – and that of Coyne in particular, would be sure to stir up the elements of sedition again. But as they must be discharged sooner or later, *I would recommend them to be so at any period that they may be prepared to embark for America with however the precaution that they should be escorted on board ship.*'[35]

The Callan leaders had to emigrate to be liberated. Philip Coyne assisted his relatives to join him in St Louis. A third brother, Michael, had already fled. It was standard procedure to free habeas corpus detainees only on board of the steamer. Cody's file concluded with instructions to his police escort to watch him sail, although 'handcuffs are not to be used in the performance of this duty'.[36]

Dublin Castle knew that Michael O'Neill Fogarty 'together with Charles J. Kickham was the head and front of the Fenian movement in the Co. Tipperary'.[37] By 18 May 1866 Fogarty was 'in delicate health, symptoms of pulmonary weakness, has an irritable cough, occasionally spits blood, strength failing, unable to take exercise' and the authorities discharged him after nine months on condition of departure for America.[38] These enforced departures could have unforeseen results. As Devoy recalled, organizers held in the Dublin prisons became acquainted with detainees from the provinces and these networks proved useful when conspiring in the US years later.

Michael O'Neill Fogarty, CSO/ICR/16
(courtesy NAI).

British diplomacy in North America

Diplomats had gained considerable information on Fenianism since December 1864. The Civil War made the Irish more acceptable as fellow citizens and many Americans shared their detestation of Britain, whose upper class had sympathized with the Confederacy, granting it belligerent status and condoning the construction of eighteen privateers in British dockyards, which had terrorized US shipping. Lord Palmerston, who had increased his majority at the general election in July 1865, feared American retaliation against Canada.[39]

Sir Frederick Bruce, the British minister in Washington, directed diplomatic efforts to neutralize the Fenian threat in North America from 1865 onwards.[40] In December, Bruce advised Lord Clarendon, the foreign secretary, to act in concert with the US administration concerning Irish transnational issues and not unwittingly re-animate Fenianism through contentious official protests. In a then acceptable, racist tone, Bruce added: 'It is to be recollected that Fenianism represents the lowest part of the Irish Roman Catholic population – the element that is antagonistic to the Protestant and the free Anglo-Saxon race,' which feared that its power as a voting block would vanish after the abolition of slavery.[41] Learning of Fenian schemes involving British North America, Bruce established effective communication with his consuls and the Canadian authorities. Informers found these officials eminently accessible and willing to pay. Edward Archibald, the New York consul, even tried to use transatlantic Fenian couriers and bodyguards to locate Stephens' hiding place in Dublin after his escape.[42]

President Andrew Johnson was facing congressional elections in 1866, as his relationship with this body deteriorated over Reconstruction. Sir Frederick Bruce hoped that the former Confederate states would soon be readmitted to the Union, given their British sympathies. He exercised forbearance, realizing that Johnson would become unpopular if seen to bow to British demands, while his Democrats were courting the Irish vote and humouring Fenian aspirations. In spite of Canadian pressure arising from rumours of Fenian incursions and British grievances that Washington had allowed the Brotherhood to recruit throughout its armies and tolerated an Irish government in exile in New York, Bruce persisted with his low-key approach. He cultivated Secretary of State Seward's companionship and remonstrated behind the scenes about the threat to Anglo-American relations, should the US let the Fenians commit hostile acts against a friendly power.[43]

Charles Francis Adams, the US Minister in London and a cultured scion of upper-class America, informed Seward about his fact-finding visit to Ireland, where depopulation had created a 'great and festering sore of discontent'. The 'disaffected class' was large, but 'poor, unarmed, and generally wanting in the elements of moral power', which rendered it unlikely to ignite a revolution.[44] Seward in turn warned Bruce that, although the US did not need conflict with Britain to consolidate the Union, should the Fenians make headway in the current political climate, they might gain American support. This was improbable, however, as few believed in their success or had any 'real sympathy' with their goals, given that the Republican ideals of Americans were much influenced by Protestant culture. Seward concluded that O'Mahony's invasion plan faced 'insurmountable' obstacles unless a great war broke out, hence the alternative but equally futile scheme of Roberts and Sweeny. General Grant, a future president, quietly advised Bruce that the Fenians would welcome suppression by the US to get them out of their current difficulties, deriding the idea of decisive action under Sweeny.[45]

'Indefeasible allegiance'

Since the first arrests of US citizens in September 1865, veterans demanded help from their consuls. This created a diplomatic minefield, as Britain insisted on the doctrine of 'indefeasible allegiance': a subject could not shed his obligations through naturalization elsewhere. George Archdeacon, the Fenian chief of Liverpool, argued that it made a mockery of the US citizenship oath. The large number of ex-officers detained under the habeas corpus suspension might generate American sympathy for Fenianism, given current Anglo-American tensions. In London, negotiations for compensation for the loss of US merchant shipping, sunk by the British-built *Alabama* and other Confederate raiders, continued. The arrests boosted the O'Mahony section of the Brotherhood, whose rally on 4 March 1866 in Jones' Wood, New York, was attended by 100,000 very sober sympathizers, in spite of Archbishop McCloskey's prohibition.[46]

George Archdeacon, Captain Patrick Joseph Condon and, in 1867, colonels John Warren and William Nagle publicized the willingness of US consuls to cooperate with Dublin Castle, rather than protest against the incarceration of their citizens, hoping to provoke an Anglo-American rupture. (The tone of correspondence between Sir Thomas Larcom and the consuls was usually cordial.) While Fenian foot soldiers agreed to emigrate under police escort after some months in prison, high-ranking former US officers, who were members of the IRB military council, resisted indignantly, given the lack of evidence. They demanded vigorous support from an ambivalent Consul West in Dublin.[47]

Kate, married to Colonel Denis F. Burke, the wife of General John Gleeson and other female relations pressurized US officials. Sympathisers, frozen out by Stephens, re-emerged to assist the women: James Cantwell in Dublin and Fr John Kenyon in Tipperary. There had been suspicions in 1865 that Mrs Gleeson was the conduit between her husband and O'Mahony in New York. When Colonel Michael Kerwin was released from a Dublin prison in July 1866, he consulted with Fr Kenyon and Mrs Gleeson in Templederry.[48]

In April the government agreed to abandon distinctions between naturalized and American-born US citizen, which Lord Clarendon and Adams, the US Minister, decided not to publicize. Lord Wodehouse in Ireland appreciated 'the importance of conciliating President Johnson', but warned Clarendon that releasing 'the whole batch' of Americans at once would dishearten loyal Irish subjects, while encouraging Fenianism. Many suspects had already been liberated by late June 1866 and he suggested discharging others gradually. Wodehouse wondered whether Adams realized that those remaining were 'really prominent men in the conspiracy'. If so, would he still lobby for their release? Clarendon forwarded this letter to Adams. By August the habeas corpus prisoners had been discharged on condition of returning to the US. Only Colonel Byron, insisting on his rights as an officer and a gentleman, remained incarcerated. Tensions led to a debate on citizenship and the Anglo-American naturalization treaty of 1870, sidelining Irish-Americans, an outcome not envisaged by the Fenians.[49]

Col John Byron (courtesy NAI).

Among those liberated was Captain William Mackey Lomasney, who had been re-arrested in Dublin. On arrival in Liverpool he consulted with Captain Timothy Deasy, a native of Clonakilty, and Captain Michael O'Brien. Mackey hoped to 'communicate with Colonel Kelly' on behalf of the Cork IRB; he refused to accept that there would be no insurrection.[50]

The Campobello 'fizzle'

In the US, any pretence of keeping Fenian plans secret had been abandoned. P.J. Meehan's *Irish-American* supported the Senate wing, while O'Mahony launched the *Irish People* to advocate his views.[51] He implied that Meehan had plotted to destroy the IRB with his ally A.M. Sullivan, Meehan having been expelled from the Brotherhood as a traitor in 1859. But O'Mahony's conduct was by no means as statesman-like as his memoirs would later claim.[52]

Bruce believed that mutual Fenian accusations of corruption had revived Protestant America's contempt for the Catholic Irish. This was amplified by the *New York Times*, which quoted Thomas D'Arcy McGee, former Young Irelander and minister for agriculture in Canada, who characterized O'Mahony as an apostate Catholic and spiritualist, probably directing his wing 'by the advice of the spirits' and the talented Killian as prostituting his talents for O'Mahony. The Roberts plan of 'a voluntary society making war' on the British Empire on the other hand was 'worthy of bedlam'.[53] Consul Archibald predicted the decline of Fenianism, but did not 'expect that the thousands of fanatics and zealots in the cause of a revolutionary movement in Ireland should entirely withdraw their pecuniary support', which they withheld from their church and its charities.[54]

Informers relayed that O'Mahony denounced the Senate wing's Canadian plans as *'un-Irish'*, while Roberts drew his chief support from the western states, which contained 'the most earnest and bellicose' members. Sweeny and Roberts were touring the Chicago region, denouncing O'Mahony. Fenians were drilling everywhere. O'Mahony emerged as the most successful fundraiser, while the senators believed that the US government tacitly supported their Canadian plans, having sold them their surplus war stock. American politicians were slow to move against the Brotherhood, hoping that the crisis would pass without the need to offend valuable voters. Many unemployed army officers remained available and an informer whispered of a three-point attack on British North America by the Senate wing: 'These fanatics are, I regret to say, in thorough earnest,' insisted Archibald to Lord Clarendon.[55]

O'Mahony's advisers clamoured to seize the initiative and retain their following. Killian promoted the capture of Campobello, an island off the coast of Maine, which belonged to New Brunswick, under the mistaken impression that Canada and the US disputed its possession. A Fenian occupation might provoke an international conflict, which would benefit Irish separatism. When the central council of the Brotherhood voted in favour of the Campobello raid on 17 March 1866, O'Mahony consented reluctantly. An absent William Halpin recorded his protest in writing. From Montreal, Fenian chief Francis Bernard McNamee warned Sweeny that the loyalty of his 1000 followers was split between the two wings and might fall to whoever was 'in the field first'. 'Red Jim' McDermott, who remained O'Mahony's confidant, although no longer employed by the Brotherhood, alerted the British consul in New York.[56]

Rumours of Fenian movements against Canada led Sir Frederick Bruce in Washington to obtain intelligence from local spies employed by Consul Henry John Murray in Portland and Vice Consul Robert Ker in Eastport,

Maine. They maintained contact with British naval and military reinforcements sent to New Brunswick and with the governors of New Brunswick and Nova Scotia; a Canadian secret service agent was also on standby. There was little Fenian enthusiasm in Maine. On 19 March 200 men attended a meeting in Portland, but disagreed about tactics and only thirty to forty joined the Senate wing. Informal contact between Vice Consul Ker and Washburne, the US Collector of Customs, spread the rumour that the Federal Army would arrive 'to prevent any breach of the neutrality laws'. Washburne was anxious to avoid an outbreak and ordered the patrolling US revenue cutter to call at Eastport on Saturdays, when the Montreal Steamship Company's vessels departed for England.[57]

Having made his arrangements, Killian left New York for Boston with ninety followers, armed in Fenian fashion with 'dirks' and revolvers, to meet 'centre' Patrick Sinnott, who had promised 10,000 volunteers from Massachusetts alone. The Fenian 'war vessel' was to land its rifles in Eastport prior to their arrival, but was delayed by red tape. In the meantime, O'Mahony experienced misgivings and 'countermanded ... the sailing', according to William H. Grace, one of the oldest Fenians in New England. O'Mahony despatched Colonel Patrick Downing to abort Killian's mission. When 150 Fenians arrived on the Portland to Eastport steamer on 13 April, Eleazer Clark, secret agent of the New Brunswick administration, shadowed them. He informed US customs that 129 cases of arms were leaving Portland on the Fenian schooner *E.H. Pray* and that Killian with 300 Fenians intended to invade New Brunswick and establish a Republican government to 'prevent confederation' in Canada.[58]

As the Fenians milled about Eastport for the next fortnight, Ker and Clark urged American officials to impound their weapons on arrival. The Vice Consul was advised that only the US commissioner and the marshal in Machias could confiscate the rifles and had both brought to Eastport at a cost of $220. After some wrangling, Captain Cooper of the USS *Winooski* held these arms until General George Meade's arrival on 19 April. Fenians raided Indian Island, seizing a British flag, stores and a bonding warehouse of the Canadian authorities to burn down the building, 'almost under the guns of HMS *Pylades*'.[59]

Arthur Gordon, Lieutenant-Governor of New Brunswick, called out the Canadian militia, volunteers and regular army. British officials spared no expense, hiring a boat crew to ensure swift communication with the six Royal Navy ships deployed. Murray's bill for this operation came to $1361, Clark receiving $546 plus $150 expenses. Minister Bruce in Washington was aware that Secretary Seward could not risk offending the Irish, but would 'do everything in his power secretly to thwart and embarrass the conspirators'. Relations between British and US officials were friendly; General Meade confided to Clark that he expected further Fenian movements between Buffalo and Lake Champlain and established a channel of communication.[60]

The checkmated Fenians fell to quarrelling among themselves and left Eastport between 26 and 30 April. Officialdom believed renewed raids 'extremely improbable', unwittingly facilitating the Senate wing. This episode depleted O'Mahony's funds by $40,000. He 'never ceased to lament' Killian's expedition, suspecting him, as did Consul Archibald, of being a secret ally of D'Arcy McGee.[61]

The hostile *New York Times* described the effect on the 'head centre' as 'perceptible and depressing. He never was remarkable for personal beauty or striking manliness, but there are times when fanaticism warmed his heart, and mounting to his eyes, illumined them with a bright and wildly beautiful light, such as enthusiasts and bigots have known since time began. Now he seems a whipped spaniel.'[62] The paper concluded that the worst enemies of Fenianism could not have hoped for a more disastrous outcome.[63] O'Mahony tried to excuse his lack of judgement as 'the consequence of the unreasoning pressure from Ireland which I had to meet, and of the malignant treachery of the seceders here, concurrent with a third pressure from my own faithful adherents underlying all'.[64] His attempt at reconciliation with the Senate wing also foundered.[65]

Although O'Mahony had requested Stephens's presence in December 1865, the latter only arrived in New York on 10 May to a welcome of ships sounding their horns and a Fenian artillery salute from the New Jersey shore. He addressed a huge crowd on Broadway, where the 9th Regiment was drawn up in his honour. Stephens hoped to convince his followers that an insurrection had to be abandoned, but they should preserve their organization for a future conflict. The Brotherhood might demand action, however. General Sweeny considered Stephens 'a British spy', while his opponent blamed the split on the dissident senators and O'Mahony for making the American Brotherhood independent in 1863. In public Stephens promised to 'fight in Ireland this year'.[66] Stephens censured the Campobello 'fizzle' and a humiliated O'Mahony resigned as 'head centre'.[67]

A British policeman, gathering intelligence in New York, reported that many Fenians were tired of donating money as this only resulted in arrests and ridicule. When Stephens commenced fundraising, his difficulties increased. Despite the goodwill of P.W. Dunne, he was unable to reunite the Brotherhood. In Ireland, Edward Duffy, in charge of the IRB, felt abandoned without funds or news.[68]

The Battle of Ridgeway

General Sweeny adapted his plan for a winter campaign along the exposed Canadian border with Fenians assembling in Milwaukee, Chicago and Detroit to invade western Ontario via the Great Lakes with a second column crossing from Ohio and Buffalo into Canada. They were to secure an area between Lake Erie and Lake Ontario and entrench themselves with a supply line to Buffalo, if possible to advance on Toronto. General Charles Carroll Tevis, a graduate of the US military academy at West Point, now adjutant general of the Irish Republican Army, and General William Lynch were to lead these wings. Sweeny hoped to lure Sir John Michel's British forces westward to clear the way for the third column to attack Quebec, assisted by Irish-Canadian and French sympathizers, and establish an Irish government in exile.[69]

But General Sweeny had never led a major campaign and, instead of the $450,000 envisaged, could only obtain $100,000 and 10,000 Enfield rifles. He expected 10,000 volunteers, which he hoped would be fed and accommodated by supporters in transit to the border. Initial success was essential, as Sweeny needed to boost his numbers by encouraging thousands of veterans to rally.[70] On 29 May 1866 the *New York Times* publicized that Sweeny's 'forces were already on the march and could not be stopped. Also, that he was opposed to the present movement, but that the Senate and their adherents were forcing him to move against his judgement. He anticipates another Campo Bello affair.'[71]

Colonel John O'Neill of Nashville, a Civil War veteran, was among those delayed by the need to raise money. At his destination, he discovered that fewer volunteers than expected had mustered, General Lynch could not be found and transport across the Great Lakes was lacking. US officials began impounding Fenian supplies. General Sweeny moved men available in the Midwest to Buffalo to be ferried across the Niagara river, but some turned back disgruntled and there was confusion among those moving towards the border. As the highest-ranking officer, Colonel O'Neill led the vanguard of 600, which crossed into Canada on 31 May to raise the Fenian flag at Fort Erie.[72]

Two columns of 2500 Canadian militia men under Colonel George Peacocke and local commander Colonel Alfred Booker advanced towards the Fenians from Toronto, when US officials blocked marine traffic between Buffalo and Canada. This cut off O'Neill, who intended to create a diversion before the bulk of the Fenian army invaded. Colonel Booker's troops stumbled across O'Neill's vanguard near the village of Ridgeway on 2 June 1866 and were routed by seasoned veterans led by a determined officer. A hundred of his men having deserted and lacking local support, Colonel O'Neill then retreated to Fort Erie, clashing with an eighty-man detachment sent to patrol the Niagara by Colonel Booker. The militia fled and their patrol boat came under Fenian fire. O'Neill learned that no other supporters had crossed the border while Canadian reinforcements were advancing. The US cutter *Michigan* arrested his followers in the process of being towed back to Buffalo on 3 June.[73]

Sweeny and General Samuel Spear, a distinguished US army veteran, were coordinating the invasion of Quebec, but their problems in Vermont mirrored those experienced by O'Neill. On 4 June, less than 1000 of the 8000 men initially required had arrived. Soon afterwards, Sweeny and his staff were arrested in St Albans. Nevertheless, Spear crossed into Canada on 7 June to seize Pigeon Hill and win a skirmish near Frelighsburg, but remained isolated.[74] Sir Frederick Bruce was mollified when President Johnson issued a proclamation, condemning the Fenians, whose 'unlawful expedition' Americans should shun. General Meade as well as civil officials were authorized to arrest them. Bruce warned that Ireland's 'chronic discontent' threatened Britain, as during a successful incursion the US might repay London for its Civil War interference by treating the Irish as belligerents, simultaneously winning their votes.[75] From Ottawa, D'Arcy McGee reassured Lord Wodehouse that Spear had surrendered, while 'the last of the Fenians on our eastern frontier have disappeared into the United States, yesterday [10 June]. They leave in our hands at that point, an officer and fifteen prisoners and on the western frontier about one hundred and thirty prisoners, and twenty-two killed on their side – with eight killed, and some fifty or sixty wounded, on ours.'[76]

Washington had allowed the Senate wing to buy 'war material at government sales' and tolerated an attempt at invasion, conduct 'unparalleled in the history of any civilised country', Bruce complained. The Fenian veterans, on the other hand, felt duped by the US government, expecting support when seizing British territory in return for their war service. James Gibbons, Vice President of the Brotherhood, denounced President Johnson as 'a dirty tool of the British' and General Sweeny blamed his failure on venal US officials, playing 'the role of British detectives' to abort his mission.[77] Bruce concluded: 'Americans, as a body, do not wish to be the instruments of the Irish, but they will be glad to use the Irish as their tools.'[78] D'Arcy McGee counselled that 'some examples must be made here, but our intention is to inflict only the *minimum* of capital punishment ... The whole affair, though costly ... has served Canada, politically, and in its *morale*.'[79] By uniting English and French Canadians against the common enemy, the invasion helped to create modern Canada.

O'Mahony in the dock

The Manhattan committee investigating the Moffat Mansion and Campobello episodes reported in August, blaming O'Mahony and his rapacious officials for squandering funds.[80] It had cost $104,401 to run the headquarters of the Brotherhood for three months, while O'Mahony received $2000 per annum and Killian and Patrick Downing $1500 each, compared to the modest $35,728 Mitchel had transferred to Ireland.[81]

In all likelihood, many salaried organizers of the Brotherhood were extravagant, even dishonest. P.H. Donegan, a native of Cork, had resigned as the (unpaid) 'centre' for the District of Columbia to run the Fenian organization's office in Washington at a salary of $100 a month. Convinced that the movement 'could not succeed', Donegan, a family man, wished 'to exchange so precarious a service' for 'more respectable and permanent' employment – as a spy. He shared recruitment and bond files with the British embassy, which learned that only the first of three classes of Fenian recruits were paid and sent to New York. These consisted of single veterans, as married men would be called upon later during the insurrection, while 'indigent men' enrolled in hope of active service and remuneration. In April 1866 Donegan considered revolutionary action 'imperatively necessary to revive the flagging zeal of subscribers and bond purchasers'.[82]

Although Donegan had sold $1523-worth of bonds during the first quarter of 1866, the subscriptions of US politicians remained nominal and were mere window dressing to gain votes. Only the Irish poor invested in Fenian bonds: 'Most of the bondholders are quite illiterate, and hardly able to sign their name on the coupons.' Money was also collected at public meetings, but when expenses, including the 'whisky expenditure account', had been deducted, Donegan had little left to forward to New York.[83]

O'Mahony, hitherto greatly trusted, was accused of 'betrayal' through 'incapacity or premeditation':[84] 'In fact, the Moffat Mansion was not only an almshouse for pauper officials and hungry adventurers, but a general telegraph office for the Canadian authorities and Sir Frederick Bruce, the British minister at Washington.'[85]

O'Mahony wondered subsequently why Patrick O'Rourke, their treasurer and his enemy, had not raised the alarm if their finances were descending into chaos. Bruce believed that the leaders of both wings used 'an expensive and corrupt body of agents to stimulate the zeal of the Irish', who 'consumed the contributions'. In old age, Devoy concluded that the animus of the Manhattan committee against O'Mahony had distorted its auditing techniques, while the disorganization of the Brotherhood had been exaggerated by a press, intent on ridiculing Fenianism.[86]

O'Mahony's indictment must be contextualized. In 1859 Richard O'Gorman had commented on the growing wealth of the US to William Smith O'Brien, but added that political morality was non-existent. He described the government as 'a filthy pool of shabbiness and corruption', especially in New York, where rising politicians learned 'the endless variety of means of cheating the public'.[87] Fenian officials may have succumbed to this.

O'Mahony exuded self-pity and snobbery, the latter not uncommon among gentlemen: 'For the sake of upholding the cause, I have been forced to endure the intercourse and even the intimacy of rough, uncultivated men, strangers to the manners or the sentiments of gentlemen – men that I verily believed hated me because I was not of their class.'[88] He denounced Roberts as a 'bosthoon' – a boor, who lacked credentials: '"President" Roberts is but a half-educated shopkeeper, of equivocal commercial antecedents, son of a shoneen baker from Mitchelstown and grandson of a former driver and proctor named Bishop. He can however get a speech by heart when 'tis composed for him and can declaim flatulent nothings with a certain theatrical aplomb.'[89]

O'Mahony characterized Thomas Sweeny as 'a man of low origin and no standing in the army'. Failing to analyse his contribution to the debacle, O'Mahony felt 'really so betrayed and deceived on all sides', considering Stephens 'sincere in his resolve, though selfishly arrogant and unscrupulous as to his means of success. He is a compound of fanaticism and vain-glory, nor will he make many mouths at a lie when he thinks it will help him along. To me personally he had been shamelessly ungrateful.'[90]

O'Mahony predicted that Stephens would, once again, create 'fevered excitement' by declaring the Rising imminent, resulting in 'another failure'. He continued to hope that an Anglo-American conflict might break out, while the Brotherhood retained 'a few thousand disciplined veterans' to spearhead action, but failed to grasp that this movement of the people, beset by disunity, had been outflanked by British diplomacy.[91]

The Fenian threat continued

Despite their breach of the neutrality laws, President Johnson's need for support in that autumn's elections meant that Roberts and Sweeny were soon released and their weapons returned. Roberts was much courted by both Democrats and Radicals, the latter opposing the president. Stephens suspected him of a pact with the former, but Fenians viewed Roberts with suspicion and in the fractured state of their movement, there was little hope of delivering a monolithic Irish vote. The Senate wing intended to renew its attack on Canada, while Michael Kerwin and Denis F. Burke led officers, returned from detention in Ireland, in declaring that an insurrection at home was viable.[92] Sir Frederick Bruce and the Foreign Office worked to control Canadian anger after the invasion by delaying the trials of Fenians and avoiding conflict with the US government. Martyrs might revive the warring Brotherhood, consequently all Canadian death sentences were commuted. When President Johnson lost the congressional elections in November, he could afford offending the Irish even less and the increasingly secretive Senate wing purchased weapons with impunity.[93]

Stephens had received $200,000 between September 1865 and May 1866, the remaining O'Mahony wing funds and the deteriorating schooner. He could no longer raise large sums, being distrusted for his previous lack of accountability.[94] Twenty years later Stephens wrote that after Campobello, that 'mad and most inglorious fiasco it was impossible for me – it would have been impossible for an archangel' to gain the support of Irish America.[95]

Although the Irish administration urged reform, nothing happened due to lack of interest at cabinet level. In June 1866 Gladstone's Reform Bill to extend the franchise brought down the government of Lord John Russell. Clarendon commented to Wodehouse, about to become the first Earl of Kimberley, that Russell and Gladstone had little to show for eight months in power, having lost their majority, offended the Liberals and failed to further 'the cause of moderate reform'. Clarendon concluded: 'you will not be sorry to come away from that odious country I guess'.[96]

The Conservatives returned to power under Lord Derby with Lord Abercorn as Lord Lieutenant and Lord Naas, soon to inherit the earldom of Mayo, as chief secretary. The following month, Mayo supervised the continuation of the habeas corpus suspension, which would remain in force until 1869, as Cork and Dublin remained disturbed.[97]

The IRB leaders improved security and based themselves in Britain, where habeas corpus arrests would not be tolerated. All but seventy-three of the suspects detained under the former administration had been released, when the Dublin IRB began to revive in September, directed from England. John Joseph Corridon, a transatlantic Fenian courier turned informer, warned that British and Irish Fenians were reorganizing energetically. In Cork, US Consul Eastman noted the arrival of 800 Americans, accompanied by growing confidence among the IRB. Magistrate Hort counselled that Kilkenny city contained 'too many disappointed characters', capable of joining any outbreak, if provided with leaders.[98]

Lord Mayo, as chief secretary, declared himself more discerning in his arrests than Lord Wodehouse, who had detained a total of 703 men. The

Abercorn-Mayo administration issued only 208 warrants up to 26 March 1867, all but seventy-eight of these between September and December 1866. This demonstrated that Dublin Castle possessed considerable intelligence, which created panic among the IRB. Urging a show of force, consecutive viceroys and Sir Thomas Larcom wanted to station numerous detachments throughout the country, as requested by influential figures, but faced persistent opposition from Lord Strathnairn, who wanted troops concentrated in major locations. The latter argued that Irish-American veterans could defeat a small unit under an inexperienced officer: nothing would benefit Fenianism more, while panicking loyal subjects. 23,000 soldiers were at present distributed among forty-four posts, in contrast to 32,000 located in 127 barracks in May 1848.[99]

The Irish police commissioners considered the situation 'critical'. Strathnairn revised previous plans to defend Dublin, but prophesied that 'there will be no Fenian Rising. There may be an attempt at "jacquerie",' but thought this unlikely, because of the reluctance of Roman Catholics to participate. Strathnairn was unimpressed with the enemy arsenal, although intrigued by phosphorus bombs or 'Fenian fire'. He believed that the insurgents were as yet unable to project 'it by an instrument like a fire engine', but would attempt to set buildings alight and throw it at advancing soldiers. Despite considering 'Fenian fire' a 'gimcrack', he feared any minor success would impact negatively on the government. Strathnairn requested engineers and artillery for the defence of Dublin and Cork, the more portable the better for city streets, unsuccessfully desiring a 'mountain battery', carried by mules, as used in India. The commander-in-chief was resolved to pulverize any buildings held by the rebels in Dublin, rather than storm them, anticipating British tactics in 1916.[100]

Other contingency plans included using workhouses as barracks. The Royal Navy searched incoming vessels for arms and gunboats patrolled the coast from Kingstown (Dun Laoghaire) to Cobh, Foynes, Galway and Belmullet by 1 December 1866 as a highly visible deterrent. Lord Strathnairn advised Lord Abercorn, the viceroy, not to neglect diplomacy to reduce sectarian tensions and further 'the *union* of good and loyal men of *all* beliefs, against the wickedest conspiracy'. He suggested the use of special constables, preferably headed by the Catholic mayor of Dublin and similar notabilities, despite mistrusting them: 'Special constables, the more Roman Catholics the better, might be *enrolled* without being called out as a precaution.' Rumours of insurrection persisted, amplified by the New York press. In his final speech before 100,000 people in Jones' Wood on 28 October, Stephens once again promised action 'before the New Year dawns'.[101]

General Millen, former President of the military council in Ireland, feared that Stephens had penetrated his double game and denounced him in an open letter as 'a political humbug, if not a cheat', who lacked military experience. Millen had been urged by his colleagues in New York to avoid controversy, but further undermined any sympathy with Ireland among the readers of the *New York Times*.[102]

This paper also commented that Ireland needed stability and industrial development, rather than the frenzied fundraising of the Stephens faction in Boston. Bruce learned from an informer that 'the captain' was less dangerous than Roberts, who had gathered $100,000, 'arms and 60,000 – 80,000 men' for a renewed Canadian assault. The diplomat longed for African Americans to gain the vote as a counterbalance to the Irish, whose grievances bedevilled Anglo-American relations. Carroll Tevis, the soldier of fortune, whom Sweeny had dismissed for disobeying orders, approached Bruce and obtained $100 per month to provide information. On 8 January 1867 the British minister reassured London that no immediate concerns existed about Canada, as the 'Fenian funds were falling off'.[103]

Military preparations

Addressing his lack of military expertise, Stephens hired General Gustave Cluseret, a French adventurer and radical politician who had served under Garibaldi, as commander-in-chief of the Irish Republican Army, assisted by Octave Fariola, an Italo-Belgian, and Victor Vifquain, a Belgian living in Nebraska. All were veterans of the Civil War.[104] Stephens told Fariola, his designated chief of staff, how 50,000 men would rise when the expeditionary force landed and that '150,000 more, belonging to the organization could be called to fill up the ranks. He said he had three fine steamers, and funds enough for a supply of 20,000 rifles ... he had torpedoes and Greek fire etc.'[105]

Stephens' dubious statements were supported by Colonel Kelly. These foreign officers, who did not join the Fenian Brotherhood, were reluctant to operate in British territory and would assume command only after the revolutionaries had established a *de facto* government in Ireland. Limerick was chosen as the 'centre of the insurrection', because its Atlantic location facilitated the arrival of an American expedition. Athlone would be isolated due to its central position, ideal for despatching British troops, and all means of communication disrupted. Colonel Fariola recalled that 'we considered the southern country as virtually ours'.[106]

The authorities would be lured into believing that Dublin was the main focus of attack, but the best Fenian weapons were to be shipped west, where bands of insurgents planned to harass the constabulary and disrupt lines of communication. As they gathered momentum, Fariola was to arrive with experienced officers selected from among the Polish, German and Italian political refugees in Paris to start the main insurrection. The IRB in England would ready itself to attack buildings with Fenian fire, including the London *Times*, if any captured insurgents were not granted prisoner-of-war status. The informer Corridon also claimed that destruction would be wreaked on the Liverpool docks to create a diversion.[107]

Fariola received £60 per month, the pay of an American general of brigade, with six months' salary in advance or a year's wages in compensation should there be no action. He was introduced to Edmond O'Donovan, the Fenian 'ordnance officer', and his brother William, alias Hamilton, their financial agent in Paris, before sailing to Europe in November. Fariola did some preliminary planning for an army of 50,000, attempted to recruit officers and win the sympathy of various European republicans for their cause. But as he failed to hear from Stephens and continued to lack money in Paris, little happened.[108]

Col John James O'Connor (Fenian Heroes and Martyrs).

Meetings of the Fenian war council in New York were attended by General John Gleeson, colonels Thomas Kelly, William Halpin, Patrick Condon, Thomas Francis Bourke and captains McCafferty and Doheny.[109] Condon, an illegitimate son of William Massey of Castleconnell, Co. Limerick, and Mary Condon, a servant, had already proved divisive: his claim of being a former colonel in the Confederate Army was rejected by the New Orleans Fenians, who wrote to O'Mahony, objecting to his appointment as a Fenian bond agent in 1865. He was described as 'a dangerous fellow', but O'Mahony made him a leading organizer. In late 1866 Condon began to call himself 'Godfrey Massey'.[110]

Stephens had managed to obtain less than one seventh of the 30,000 rifles, which he deemed essential for the Rising.[111] In late December he once again urged a postponement, but was deposed by his war council. Colonel Kelly stopped Captain McCafferty from shooting Stephens, though accusing him of trying to abscond with their funds. General Gleeson nominally replaced Stephens, while Kelly dominated the military council.[112] Having promised action since 1858, Fenianism faced an ignominious collapse unless an insurrection was attempted. On 9 January 1867 Kelly sold the Campobello ship for $14,000 to obtain funds. He provided Godfrey Massey with £550 to pay the officers in Britain and Ireland, who had been awaiting Stephens for months. Within a few days, Kelly, Halpin, Bourke and Massey sailed for England – action was imminent.[113]

Table 8. *Occupations of suspects arrested until late November 1866*[114]

Occupation of those arrested	No.
Tradesmen, artisans, millworkers	314
Shopkeepers	52
Publicans	25
Clerks and commercial assistants	45
Shop assistants and shopkeepers' sons	30
Farmers	35
Farmers' sons (a third of these are students)	20
National school teachers	20 (at least)
'Persons who had been in the American Army, labourers etc.'	211
Total	752

(Source: 'Habeas Corpus Suspension', *Irish Times*, 23 February 1867)

CHAPTER 7

The Rising – 'a counsel of despair', 1867–8

There, beside the singing river,
That dark mass of men was seen –
Far above their shining weapons
Hung their own beloved 'green'
'Death to ev'ry foe and traitor!
Forward! strike the marchin' tune,
And hurrah, my boys for freedom!
'Tis the Rising of the moon.
'The Rising of the Moon', John Keegan Casey[1]

On 6 December 1866 Lord Mayo sent Lord Strathnairn a memorandum that the lower class expected an imminent, 'desperate attempt' at insurrection. Aristocrats, merchants and farmers supported Dublin Castle, but the urban poor and, to a lesser extent, rural small holders, favoured the Fenians. The chief secretary intended to prevent an outbreak, which would revive 'old animosities of creed and race', while damaging the economy. Mayo considered the constabulary effective, but wanted to assess army strength and locations with Strathnairn, as 'all Irish experience has shown that the presence of a military force is the only means by which a sense of security can be given to an alarmed neighbourhood'.[2] In the six months before 1 March 1867 the number of soldiers in Ireland rose from 20,600 to approximately 24,000.[3]

Colonel Fariola reached Paris on 3 December 1866 to discover a shortage of funds. On 20 January 1867 he was summoned to London to reconcile the American officers, who were 'reduced almost to starvation' and dependent on the London IRB. Amidst much acrimony, Fariola failed to restrain a breakaway faction, headed by Captain McCafferty and John Flood, chief organizer for England since Stephens's departure in March 1866. They discounted assistance from the US and believed that less than 10,000 insurgents with 1000 muskets would mobilize in Ireland. Nor were they convinced that the military and constabulary had been successfully subverted. Many IRB members in Britain, having been sworn with assurances of an American expedition, refused to act without it. With hindsight, Colonel John James O'Connor commented that the movement in Ireland, 'drugged ... with so many doses of tall talk and bunkum', overestimated its strength and became restive. Colonel Kelly arrived in late January, determined to take the field as 'chief organizer of the Irish Republic' and expecting 'prompt submission' from McCafferty's 'self-constituted' directory.[4]

Colonels William Halpin, O'Sullivan Burke and John Healy, as well as Captain Michael O'Rourke, alias 'Beecher', a secretive paymaster active in England for the past year, and one Evans were among the Fenian Brotherhood officers of the directory. John Ryan of Liverpool ('Captain Doherty'), John Nolan, David Murphy and Daniel Liddy (the latter pair the old and new 'centres' of Limerick respectively) represented the Irish organization.[5] The directory summoned leading IRB organizers to endorse its plans: Michael O'Neill Fogarty of Tipperary, who had stealthily returned from America, 'undertook to speak for "four thousand men"' in Munster, supported by Dominick O'Mahony of Cork, Edward O'Beirne from Leinster and William Harbinson as 'head centre' for Belfast. Given the prevailing confusion, General Cluseret believed that O'Mahony, O'Beirne, Harbinson and Edward Duffy had been elected by the IRB to negotiate an alliance with the Fenian Brotherhood after Stephens's deposition.[6]

McCafferty's directory intended to capture 1500 rifles from an ill-guarded armoury, reminiscent of Terence Bellew McManus, who wanted to 'seize a couple of the largest Irish steamers at Liverpool and load them with arms' from the same depot in 1848. McCafferty proposed a guerrilla campaign:[7]

> They were ... to take Chester Castle by surprise, to disarm the soldiers, seize on all the arms, and carry them off; take possession of a train that was to go to Holyhead, cut the telegraph wires, and tear up the rails behind them ... they were to take possession of the mail steamer at Holyhead, and make a landing on such a part of Ireland as might be thought advisable. The daring of such a project made one almost pause before one could bring oneself to credit it.[8]

Their landing would launch the uprising. McCafferty wanted to redeem the Irish nation, whose failure to fight for survival during the Famine had earned it 'sneer[s] and contempt all over the world'. The directory considered Colonel Kelly's plans doomed, but, possessing a much-needed £2000, he was invited to join their discussions and participate in the Chester raid with Cluseret as overall commander. Kelly rejected McCafferty's scheme as 'perfectly mad' and likely to abort his own. The directory responded that their project 'was the better on account of its very madness'. Cluseret believed that many Irish-Americans lacked political awareness and simply demanded a battle for their money. He refused to immolate himself for Ireland, having been hired for an insurrection with a chance of success.[9]

Edward Duffy, who had resigned as Stephens's representative, travelled to London for consultations. He planned to 'spring' Luby, O'Leary and others from jail for £300 and one of his sisters was collecting the necessary funds. However, the American leaders insisted on insurrection. Duffy, Harbinson, O'Beirne, O'Mahony and O'Neill Fogarty declined to bestow IRB endorsement on the Chester scheme, when a single-minded Colonel Kelly enrolled them for his own directory.[10] Fariola considered these men patriotic and resolute, though 'rather poor specimens of the Irish democracy, intellectually speaking'. Co-opting Edmond O'Donovan as delegate for Limerick, on 10 February they constituted themselves the provisional government of Ireland, confirming Kelly as chairman and Fenian Brotherhood representative with Cluseret and Fariola as military leaders. Captain O'Rourke became the eighth member of the provisional government. The delegates returned to Ireland to prepare for insurrection.[11]

The following day McCafferty seized the initiative, when 1000–1500 Fenians from the north of England, including Michael Davitt, assembled for the Chester attack. But John Joseph Corridon, a Fenian Brotherhood officer, had turned informer. Troops suddenly appeared and the Fenians, sensing betrayal, aborted their raid. Up to 300 north-of-England members, having abandoned their jobs, sailed for Dublin, but were arrested on arrival, alongside McCafferty and Flood.[12] The *Irish Times* advised the authorities to 'disgrace' these 'disreputable-looking and effete' foot soldiers, rather than create martyrs. It believed that the 'Fenian flame is still flickering a little', before its final extinction. Corridon, however, informed Head Constable McHale in Liverpool that his dupes were determined to fight, notwithstanding the Chester fiasco.[13]

The Kerry Rising

It remains unclear whether Colonel O'Connor intended to act simultaneously with McCafferty's directory or was unaware that the Rising had been postponed. On 12 February Captain Mortimer Moriarty, who had returned from Canada, travelled from Cahirciveen to link up with Jeremiah Daniel Sheehan, the Killarney leader. The insurrection was scheduled to centre on this town, as it contained 1500 IRB members and sympathizers, the highest number in Kerry. In Fossa, Philip O'Rourke held his men in readiness. But an informer alerted the magistrates, who arrested Moriarty on the outskirts of Killarney, disrupting Fenian plans.[14]

In Cahirciveen, the sons and daughter of head constable O'Connell sympathized with the movement by quietly handing over police rifles to Colonel O'Connor. But the constabulary remained alert, forcing him to abandon the proposed attack and march his men towards Glenbeigh instead. (O'Connor was unaware that one of his followers had warned the authorities.) Only the thirty Irish-Americans among the one hundred 'respectable' insurgents carried modern arms. O'Connor, who intended to join Fenian detachments in Killorglin and Killarney, ordered the telegraph wires cut and raided Kells coastguard station for rifles. In the early hours of 13 February a policeman, sent to warn the Cahirciveen constables of the outbreak, refused to surrender to the rebels and was seriously wounded at Eisc an Chatha. He carried a warrant to arrest O'Connor and news of the detention of Captain Moriarty. The insurgents realized that nobody else had turned out and dispersed across the mountains.[15]

Panic reigned among the leading inhabitants of Killorglin, who sheltered in the police barracks. The magistrates feared an assault on Killarney, where the railway tracks were torn up. Gentlefolk raced into town, withdrew money from the bank and barricaded themselves into the luxurious Railway Hotel. The constabulary abandoned outlying stations and protected the gentry, who cowered in 'utmost terror' in the hotel, while Killarney's 6000 inhabitants were abandoned to their fate. Troops arrived to garrison the building, for nobody suspected that the insurgents had already disbanded.[16]

On 17 February Bishop Moriarty preached in Killarney Cathedral, castigating his congregation, which abhorred unrest, but would not defend the state. This led Lord Castlerosse to send his family to England. John Green, R.M., added that many locals, who condemned the IRB, would join up, if it appeared to succeed.[17] Dr Moriarty's family were comfortable farmers and shopkeepers in north Kerry. He supported British rule, while his brother Oliver, adept at obtaining intelligence, was resident magistrate for Limerick. They were political allies of the Earl of Kenmare, a powerful Munster landlord.[18]

In his Lenten pastoral of 1866, Dr Moriarty had pronounced rebels against 'lawful authority' destined for eternal damnation. The Kerry outbreak was 'an act of madness ... without parallel in the annals of lunacy', if the Fenians imagined that they could declare war on the British Empire. The bishop blamed Irish-American instigators:[19] 'If we must condemn the foolish youths who have joined in this conspiracy, how much must we not execrate the conduct of those designing villains who have been entrapping innocent youth, and organizing this work of crime.'[20] He evoked 'God's heaviest curse, His withering, blasting, blighting curse' on their leaders: 'But when we look down in the fathomless deep of this infamy of the heads of the Fenian conspiracy, we must acknowledge that eternity is not long enough, nor hell hot enough, to punish such miscreants.'[21]

William Monsell of Tervoe, Limerick, a Unionist landlord and convert to Catholicism who detested the Fenians as communist revolutionaries, Peter Fitzgerald, the Knight of Kerry, and Aubrey de Vere of Curragh Chase, Co. Limerick, applauded Dr Moriarty, who feared that political instability would erode religious tenets. He had his sermon printed and distributed. Dr Cullen, however, considered it provocative and likely to increase American support for Fenianism. His Lenten pastoral reiterated warnings against 'secret societies'.[22] Moving the second reading for the extension of the Habeas Corpus Suspension Act (Ireland) in February, Lord Mayo quoted Dr Moriarty, regretting that 'even in that congregation there were sufficient sympathizers with this movement to induce a certain number of young men to leave the church while the bishop was speaking'.[23]

Kerry remained uneasy. The telegraph wire, vital for communication with America, kept being cut. In early March the British army was withdrawn except for a detachment in Killarney, as Sir Thomas Larcom had information that action was imminent elsewhere, possibly in Tipperary. The Knight of Kerry objected. The military presence had proved 'most salutary' in Cahirciveen, given the many 'disaffected' people on his estate in Valentia. Lord Wodehouse, now Earl of Kimberley, wrongly predicted that 'the utter folly' in Kerry would abort any further 'ridiculous outbreaks', which prevented essential reform and investment.[24]

Talks with English radicals

Although Stephens had elicited the goodwill of Charles Bradlaugh for the Irish Republic in 1865, he instructed Colonel Fariola to avoid the English radicals, as he felt 'the greatest contempt' for John Bright and barely acknowledged Bradlaugh, Edmond Beales and William Randall Cremer. Colonel Kelly, a man of action, was unfamiliar with the European revolutionary underground, unlike

Fariola and Cluseret. Nevertheless, Kelly met Bradlaugh, Cremer and George Odger, the two latter members of the International Working Men's Association.[25] In an age of change and lower-class protest, the government dreaded a potential alliance of British radicals and Fenians, given the historic links between United Irishmen, Irish Confederates, English Chartists, trade unionists and reformers. Cluseret deplored how Fenianism focused on grievances, rather than cooperation with fellow democrats. Furthermore, contemporary sectarian agitation in northern England had led to a deepening of divisions, which restricted the likelihood of united action to London.[26]

Col Thomas J. Kelly (courtesy
Dublin City Archive).

Bradlaugh was radicalized by serving in the military in Ireland during 1851. In January 1867, he considered bringing 20,000 workers into the streets of London and 'shoulder[ing] a musket under Stephens'. Attributing socialist motives and a lack of anti-British animus to the Fenians, Bradlaugh urged Colonel Kelly to mobilize for a Reform League demonstration on 11 February to pressurize Disraeli and Prime Minister Derby to grant male suffrage, following the collapse of Lord John Russell's attempt to enlarge the franchise in 1866. Kelly was unable to oblige, however, as the London Fenians sided with McCafferty's directory. Cluseret and Fariola consulted privately with Bradlaugh and Giuseppe Mazzini. Liberal Britain provided exiled Europeans with an asylum, which they were reluctant to jeopardize, while doubting the revolutionary credentials of the Irish, who supported the reactionary papacy. Cluseret met with Odger, Cremer and John Bedford Leno to offer 2000 armed Fenians, should the government fail to concede electoral reform. Realizing that this proposal threatened civil war and was likely to be betrayed, the gathering dispersed.[27]

Bradlaugh drafted the proclamation of the Republic, although he considered the insurrection ill-advised, given Fenian disharmony and lack of preparation. It justified the Rising after centuries of misery inflicted by Britain, confirming all citizens as owners of Ireland rather than the parasitical aristocracy. Guaranteeing freedom of conscience, the proclamation demanded separation of church and state and appealed for solidarity between Irish and English workers in their common cause:[28]

> I. R. – Proclamation. – The Irish People to the World. – We have suffered centuries of outrage, enforced poverty, and bitter misery. Our rights and liberties have been trampled on by an alien aristocracy, who, treating us as foes, usurped our lands, and drew away from our unfortunate country all material riches. The real owners of the soil were removed to make room for cattle, and driven across the ocean to seek the means of living, and the political rights denied to them at home. While our men of thought and action were condemned to loss of life and liberty. But we never lost the memory and hope of a national existence. We appealed in vain to the reason and sense of justice of the dominant powers. Our mildest remonstrances were met with sneers and contempt. Our appeals to arms were always unsuccessful. Today having no honourable alternative left, we again appeal to force as our last resource.[29]

The provisional government concluded: 'Herewith we proclaim the Irish Republic'.

Condon, now calling himself Godfrey Massey, was designated brigadier general and sent on a fact-finding mission to Dublin, Cork, Tipperary and Castlebar. On 24 February he returned to London, informing the provisional government that Cork and Dublin, the main centres of Fenianism, could muster 18,000 men with 3000 pikes and 15,000 followers with 1500 weapons, but lacked modern rifles.[30]

Fariola and Cluseret's scheme initially proposed guerrilla warfare: numerous small bands were to harass the constabulary and disrupt communications by destroying roads and railways. Supported by sympathizers, they would keep Ireland in turmoil but avoid direct confrontation unless victory seemed certain. The insurgents would gather support and move towards the towns, seizing some along the west coast from Sligo to Kerry. As the British army pursued these irregulars 'at great fatigue and peril', the arrival of the foreign commanders would herald the second phase of the Rising.[31]

Given his difficulties, Colonel Kelly had to improvise. He promised his followers that Irish-American support would be forthcoming if they held out 'for three weeks'. In London, James J. O'Kelly, an early leader who had deserted the Foreign Legion in Mexico to participate in the Rising, now opposed it as ill-conceived. General Cluseret grudgingly consented to command 5000 insurgents, should these remain in the field for some time. He later recalled persistent tensions, but also some 'very noble young men' who participated from a sense of duty, disregarding the likelihood of failure.[32]

On the eve of Massey's return to Ireland to announce the date of the Rising, Cluseret discovered him 'completely drunk' and squandering money, but was unable to rescind his orders. Colonel Fariola, who would become chief of staff if the insurrection gathered pace, followed Massey to Cork to supervise him and to reassure the IRB that experienced foreign officers would lead it. But Vifquain, the third veteran officer hired, never appeared, while Cluseret withdrew to Paris. Ellen O'Leary bitterly criticized Fariola, who refused to replace Vifquain in Connacht. When Edward Duffy failed to obtain the arms promised by Colonel Kelly, he advised his followers not to participate in a useless sacrifice.[33]

Even worse, Fariola discovered that Massey had abandoned guerrilla tactics and repudiated any directive not originating from Colonel Kelly. Massey ordered an estimated 8000 insurgents, of whom one eighth might be armed, to converge on Limerick Junction. Fariola recalled that 'Massey's measures had been so utterly absurd, and in disregard of my instructions, that I requested him in the name of the provisional government to stop all future proceedings, and told him he had ruined the cause'.[34]

Fariola contacted Kelly in London, but the Rising 'could not be stopped'.[35] When Corridon, the Fenian officer assigned to Midleton, learned that Massey would reach Limerick Junction on 4 March while Captain Patrick Joseph Condon, alias George O'Dell, was to command in east Cork, he informed Dublin Castle, resulting in their arrest. In the ensuing confusion many districts failed to mobilize and action was restricted to Munster and parts of Leinster. Late on 5 March IRB contingents moved towards their assembly points, expecting to meet American officers with supplies of rifles.[36]

In early March Larcom briefed Lord Strathnairn that the Fenian 'military council' lacked funds, but was most active. Although their plans were difficult to pin down, the outbreak would probably occur on 5 March. Intelligence reports pointed to Limerick Junction, but Dublin was not a primary objective. Obtusely, the undersecretary belittled Fenian officers as 'bands of burglars and incendiaries' who had no ambition of 'conquering the country' but wanted 'plunder for themselves and noise enough to keep up the begging box in America'.[37]

Larcom postulated that should the administration succeed in short-circuiting the outbreak, Fenianism would collapse. Head Constable Thomas Talbot confirmed the Rising for 5 March, warning that the insurgents would assemble outside Dublin and that Colonel Halpin would direct the Fenian march on the city. After previous false alarms, Colonel Wood, inspector general of the constabulary, commented: 'I am quite tired of the whole thing.'[38]

Cork

In Cork city, James F.X. O'Brien had witnessed a woeful lack of preparation and voted against the Rising. Nevertheless, 1500 Fenians, half the Cork contingent, turned out at Prayer Hill. It was eventually decided to 'move towards Mallow' in the belief 'that there was a depot of arms thereabouts'.[39] Their weapons consisted of eight firearms and eighteen pikes. Eventually, O'Brien took charge, assisted by William Mackey Lomasney and Michael O'Brien, both veterans of the Civil War. They raided a mansion for arms, disrupted communications north of Cork and demanded that Ballyknockane constabulary barracks near Mallow surrender to the Irish Republic. When the police resisted, the building was set on fire, but Captain Mackey kept the child of a constable safe. Advised by Fr Neville, a local curate, the constabulary abandoned the barracks. Moving towards Bottle Hill, Burnfoot, the insurgents failed to meet other IRB groups and dispersed as the British army approached.[40]

Captain Timothy Deasy had been appointed to Millstreet and Colonel Moran to Mallow, but no action took place. In Midleton, Captain John McClure was to have assisted Captain Condon, his brother-in-law, but the latter and James O'Sullivan, the Midleton 'centre' and a clerk in Murphy's distillery, had been arrested.[41] Timothy Daly commanded the 400 Midleton Fenians, including contingents from Ballinacurra, Cloyne and Carrigtwohill. Among the insurgents was the idealistic, sixteen-year-old Patrick Neville Fitzgerald, who accompanied an older brother.[42]

Marching through Midleton, the Fenians challenged a police patrol, which refused to surrender. The IRB posse opened fire, killing a constable, before proceeding to Castlemartyr, where they attacked the barracks to seize its rifles. In the ensuing fire fight, Daly was shot dead, while his followers fled.[43]

Captain McClure, a 'cold and determined' young man, resided with Peter O'Neill Crowley of Ballymacoda before the Rising. This idealistic, successful farmer never forgot how Fr Peter O'Neill, his grand-uncle, had been tortured in 1798. O'Neill Crowley led a hundred well-disciplined Fenians, some of whom were equipped with 'sharpened rasps, fastened to rake handles with waxed hemp'. They seized the rifles of Knockadoon coastguard station, but marching towards Mogeely in expectation of larger detachments, realized that British troops were approaching. McClure and O'Neill Crowley dismissed their unarmed followers and went on the run in the direction of Mallow. John Edward Kelly, a native of Kinsale, who had returned from the US for the Rising, joined them.[44]

Awaiting an American expedition, O'Neill Crowley intended to link up with the Galtee Fenians. He failed to reach the Brazils of Cullane, Ballylanders, who hoped to shelter him. Mary Brazil, nee O'Brien, belonged to a family network, extending to James and William O'Brien of Mallow, which arranged safe houses. Scouts assisted O'Neill Crowley's men in Kilclooney Wood near Mitchelstown, while he visited Cork to learn that the insurrection had collapsed. These unusual activities alerted a local, who betrayed them. When the Waterford flying column searched Kilclooney Wood on 31 March 1867, O'Neill Crowley and McClure urged their companions to escape. Disdaining surrender, they fled, still firing, 'until a rifle bullet broke the lock of O'Neill Crowley's rifle, and also some of his fingers'. They dashed into the Ahaphuca river, where O'Neill Crowley received his final wound. British soldiers saved him from drowning. Dr Segrave, a military surgeon, rendered first aid and read aloud from the prayer book, which O'Neill Crowley always carried.[45]

Henry Edward Redmond, R.M., attempted to arrest McClure in mid-stream. The latter failed to shoot the magistrate as his pistol had become wet. Kelly was detained nearby, but a fourth, unidentified Fenian escaped.[46] Fr Timothy O'Connell, a curate in Kildorrery, anointed O'Neill Crowley. The military did not realize that his brother John O'Connell of Glantane, Lombardstown, Mallow, was an IRB leader on the run.[47] O'Neill Crowley said: 'I have two loves in my heart, Father … one for God, the other for my country. I am dying for my country; I would as willingly die for my God.'[48]

The priest subsequently publicized this 'most edifying' conduct. Dr Segrave tried to save O'Neill Crowley from bleeding to death, but a well-to-do farmer refused to let him rest in his home. While Lord Strathnairn rejoiced in the effectiveness of his flying columns, in Mitchelstown British officials were taken aback by the 'extraordinary spectacle' of O'Neill Crowley's funeral, which generated great sympathy for the IRB. As men feared arrest, females dominated the obsequies, led by his dignified sister, Kate:[49]

> First came a procession of women four deep, each woman carrying a large green bough; then followed a scattered group of women, next came the coffin, borne upon men's shoulders, although a hearse had been engaged and was actually in the procession. … His sister … walked after the coffin as chief mourner, her head covered with a dark hood.'[50]

The men followed silently behind this personification of a sorrowful 'Maid of Erin' and her female supporters. Shops closed as a mark of respect and a

Loyalist businessman commented that Lord Kingston, their landlord, would not receive such honours. In Fermoy the hearse was decorated with a 'harp without the crown', the symbol of Irish sovereignty.[51] Patrick Augustine Sheehan, then a student in the diocesan college, recalled:

> It was computed that at least 5000 men took part in the procession and shoul-dered the coffin of the dead patriot over mountain and valley and river ... I remember how a group of us, young lads, shivered in the cold March wind there on the College Terrace at Fermoy, and watched the dark masses of men swaying over the bridge, the yellow coffin conspicuous in their midst ... then we turned away with tears of sorrow and anger in our eyes.[52]

In *The Graves at Kilmorna*, Canon Sheehan transmuted his memory of ideal-ists, who ignored personal success, comparing them to the saints: '... the blood of the martyrs was the seed of saints, so the blood of the patriot is the sacred seed from which alone can spring new forces, and fresh life into a nation that is drifting into the putrescence of decay'.[53] Public support manifested itself in the relays of bearers, who carried the coffin thirty miles from Mitchelstown to Killeagh, employing the hearse only when darkness fell. Fr Maurice Power refused the use of his new parish church in Killeagh, fearing repercussions. A delegation from Kilmallock, travelling on one of William H. O'Sullivan's 'long cars', joined the crowds at the interment in Ballymacoda the following day.[54]

Limerick

The 'most desperate stand' of the insurgents occurred in Kilmallock. On 5 March William H. O'Sullivan, hotel owner and entrepreneur, whom the constabulary at Kilfinnane considered 'most dangerous', was arrested. Captain John Dunne, formerly the quartermaster of 164th New York Regiment, had returned from America for the second time to command the Kilmallock, Bruff and Charleville Fenians. The last two contingents were to disrupt communications and seize any available arms, moving towards Kilmallock, 'this dreary, poverty-stricken village', where they planned to take the constabulary barracks, one of the stron-gest in the south.[55]

The Bruree insurgents assembled at the railway bridge before trying to obtain weapons in the district and having their pikes assembled in the carpen-ter's workshop of the Walsh family in Tankardstown. They met Captain Dunne and other IRB groups outside Kilmallock, where the fifteen constables remained on duty throughout the night, hardly crediting rumours of impending attack. The assault commenced when they retired to bed at 6 am. Captain Dunne, in 'a green and gold uniform', carrying a Fenian sunburst banner, failed to burn out the barracks with Daniel Bradley, Patrick O'Riordan, Patrick Walsh and William O'Sullivan, a son of the imprisoned hotelier. For three hours they exchanged fire with the police, who were hampered by the twenty-six windows of their barracks. Captain Dunne had placed guards at the Kilmallock poorhouse to avoid being surprised by police reinforcements. When the day dawned, the likelihood of identification increased and Fenians without firearms slunk away, including the group at the workhouse.[56]

On the morning of 6 March the sound of gunfire convinced an anxious Sub-Inspector Milling to assemble ten constables before resuming his journey from Kilfinane to Kilmallock. They arrived after nine o'clock to open up a second front, opposed by ten or twelve determined riflemen, who made their last stand in the centre of the town.[57]

Alerted to the arrest of Godfrey Massey by the arrival of a courier, Captain Dunne declared further resistance useless. Suspects fled to the ports while these remained open. That afternoon, one hundred policemen searched Kilmallock. Two Fenians had fallen: Daniel Blake of Bruree, aged twenty-one, and the 'unknown Fenian'.[58] He was probably Patrick Hassett, the son of a publican, missing from nearby Bulgaden and never heard of again. Given that vintners with Fenian relatives in Kilmallock and elsewhere were deprived of their licences, the dead man's family may have opted to ignore his body rather than risk their livelihood. Dr Michael Clery, a likely sympathizer, whose family members were said to be among the combatants, became the third casualty. He was killed after attending bank manager C.H. Bourne, who had been wounded by Captain Dunne on refusing to surrender his gun to the Fenians.[59]

At the inquest, Fr Thomas Fitzgerald, a local curate, testified that Dr Clery was shot *'after the Fenian firing had ceased,* when the whole of them – who were a poor unfortunate crew – had run away'.[60] Fearing the constabulary, which was out of control, nobody approached the body until it was decided that *'a woman* [called Whelan] *should go, as women would be safe, and a woman in a blue cloak went out, two shots were fired by the police at her,* but struck a nearby house'.[61] Ned and Batt Raleigh, shoemakers in the Kilmallock workhouse, had been among the insurgents. Afterwards Ned returned to work, while his brother went on the run in Mitchelstown and the Glen of Aherlow. Due to a strong community spirit, some IRB men were released after a few months, as nobody would give evidence.[62]

In Limerick the constabulary had heard rumours of an imminent Rising. William Monsell as commander of the Limerick militia virtually lived in his club to organize the defence of the city in an energetic but tactful manner. He warned the House of Commons in July that unless reforms were introduced, the masses might yet succumb to the siren call of separatism. John Daly, a deter-mined young man, had been detained for administering the Fenian oath since November 1866. Discharged on bail, Daly refused to go to work, considering himself 'bound to free his country, and that all would be over in a few days'. The Limerick city contingent expected that the Dublin mail train would be stopped before reaching Cork, signalling the start of the insurrection. The Emly Fenians in Co. Tipperary were to take this news to Herbertstown.[63]

The Limerick IRB was delayed, waiting for their pikes until 2 am. Among forty Fenians only five had rifles and some broke into gun shops to arm them-selves. On reaching Herbertstown, they feared that the Rising was cancelled as the train had gone through. Half the Limerick contingent returned home, but Daly and the remainder reached Emly. They found the police barracks deserted and heard that Thomas Francis Bourke had taken the field. Michael H. Crowe, the Emly 'centre', had already mustered his men. Prominent were John Carroll of Cromhill and James, Pat and Michael Hogan, teachers in Kilteely, assisted by their colleagues, Anne Manahan and Margaret Gilhooly.[64]

Claims that 200 rebels stormed the Emly Barracks are mistaken, as clarified by official correspondence. The constables left for a neighbouring station, where they remained for a week, while the Fenians ransacked the empty building. A participant recalled:[65] 'We loitered around all that day, and we got plenty to eat. The men around there were drilling, and we slept very well that following night in a public house kept by Mrs Crooks.'[66]

Five hundred men assembled in this area, where, quite exceptionally, better-off farmers participated in the Rising. The Kilteely police barracks had also been evacuated. The Fenians demanded the arms of 'respectable' inhabi-tants, who thought it prudent to comply. John Daly admired the female rebels:[67] 'Some of the finest and the best Irish girls in that district marched with our body that day, giving us all the information possible.'[68]

The majority of the population fraternized with the insurgents, but those loyal to Dublin Castle felt transported to the American Wild West. The IRB recruitment drive in Kilteely included 'repeated threats to shoot anyone who refused to serve' and occasional gun fire 'intimidate[d] the villagers'. The rebels were 'drinking', according to a magistrate, and the inhabitants could now gain 'an opinion as to the relative merits of English and Fenian rule'. Oliver Moriarty, R.M., feared that this was a ruse to lure troops out from Limerick to attack the city.[69]

The insurgents expected to join 'General' Bourke when their female scouts brought word of his arrest at Ballyhurst – all was over. Handing their weapons to the Carroll brothers, who buried them under the altar of the Catholic church in Kilteely, the Fenians dispersed. The authorities concluded that the Limerick IRB did not lack men, but weapons.[70]

At Ardagh barracks near Cahirmoyle, the home of the late William Smith O'Brien, an IRB posse had broken down the door. But when an attacker charging upstairs was shot by the constabulary, his comrades abandoned the attempt. William Upton, a local cabinetmaker and leader, was among those who fled.[71]

Tipperary

Colonel Thomas Francis Bourke had been appointed for Tipperary town with Colonel O'Sullivan Burke in charge of the adjoining Waterford, where no insurrection was attempted due to poor turnout.[72] Bourke's family had emigrated from Fethard after the Famine. He fought for the Confederacy, was badly wounded at Gettysburg and suffered impaired health as a prisoner of war, but resigned as the Manhattan 'district centre' to fight in Ireland. Bourke claimed to have returned to recuperate, showing his withered leg. The constables noted that he looked frail and attributed the sores on his face to venereal disease. He went into hiding and consulted with John and Patrick Kenrick, who led the Fethard IRB, while family connections with Charles Kickham ensured assistance from Mullinahone.[73]

Patrick Kenrick. FP 250 (courtesy NAI).

On 2 March De Gernon, R.M., warned that the insurrection would begin in three days with an assault on Thomastown Castle, followed by raids on the banks in Tipperary. He urged that 'troops ... ought to be sent forthwith' to Limerick Junction, even if they had to sleep in tents. Lord Strathnairn and Lord Abercorn, the Lord Lieutenant, shared the magistrate's concern that Fenian bands would move from Tipperary towards Athlone, Limerick and Carrick-on-Suir.[74]

Local officials demanded additional military, fearing that Tipperary town and some gentry residences were unprotected. Thurles, the centre of a rich agricultural district and home of the Catholic Archbishop of Cashel, contained few policemen. The *Times* considered many of its inhabitants 'possessed by the Fenian folly'.[75] Gentlemen deposited arms with the police for safekeeping and some remained in town overnight. Considerable excitement prevailed among Fenian sympathizers, who stayed awake in anticipation of an attack on the constabulary.[76]

On the night of 5 March, the main force assembled at Bansha under Colonel Bourke, assisted by Michael O'Neill Fogarty with no more than '*one hundred and ten*' men, and Thomas Walsh, proprietor and editor of the *Cashel Sentinel*. Bourke was expecting reinforcements for a multidirectional attack on Tipperary town, supported by the inhabitants. De Gernon, reported a skirmish with rebels near Croghill on the Cashel road, when forty men with pikes were captured.[77] A 500-strong contingent gathered at Arlamon, Ballyglass, near Tipperary town, but units from Kilmallock, Bruff, Clonmel and Cahir had not yet arrived and Captain Jeremiah J. Finnan of Ardivillane remained behind to guide them. Formerly a national teacher in Bansha, he had been an organizer since 1865, in contact with Stephens and John and Ellen O'Leary. He went on the run after the habeas corpus suspension and enrolled men in Tipperary and Limerick for the Rising.[78] No reinforcements arrived, but Finnan reached Gortavoher constabulary barracks in time for the attack. Official reports establish that the insurgents departed after an unsuccessful fire fight.[79] Colonel Bourke, who had to ride a 'borrowed' carriage horse because of his disability, led the main contingent towards two ringforts at Ballyhurst as day dawned. Pikes were issued, but the insurgents lingered until noon, when a section of the 31st Regiment approached. The inexperienced rebels broke under fire, Bourke failed to rally them and was taken prisoner, while O'Neill Fogarty escaped. Young James Russell of Lattin, fighting with a pike, constituted the sole rebel casualty. His funeral through Tipperary town passed off quietly.[80]

On 14 March 1867 resident magistrate De Gernon rejoiced that his previous skirmish and Ballyhurst were the only disturbances in his district, which, although miserable from a Fenian point of view, 'saved Tipperary from being deluged with blood'.[81] The situation in the north riding was no different: large numbers of rebels marched through Borrisoleigh, but many of the insurgents, aware of their hopeless situation, dispersed. Returning from America for a second time, Captain Joseph Gleeson, 'who had a good fighting record in the Civil War, acted very badly' when assigned to the Thurles district.[82]

He was assisted by Thomas Mackey, a clerical student in St Patrick's College, Thurles, whose first cousin, Patrick Mackey, the IRB 'centre' of Templemore, had become inactive. The men were to assemble at Barnane Rock at the foot of the Devil's Bit and join Godfrey Massey at Limerick Junction via mountain roads. Gleeson had planned to destroy Aughall bridge near Templemore, which carried the main Dublin to Cork railway line, to prevent British troops being rushed to Munster. This had to be abandoned when the man bringing the incendiary material did not arrive. Captain Gleeson, aware of their untenable position, dismissed the men. An alternative account relates that he failed to appear for the insurrection to get drunk at a wedding. He went on the run, simultaneously hunted by the authorities and some embittered associates, eventually reaching New York, having been sheltered by 'so many true Fenian women'.[83]

It was claimed that 4000 rebels had assembled at the Devil's Bit, including 400 from Holycross.[84] Michael Sheehy, the Thurles 'centre', directed a well-drilled 'circle', armed with twenty antiquated muskets. Sheehy's widowed mother gave him her blessing and 'an elegant green sash', before he set out. The Fenians sometimes coerced farm labourers to join them, but this may have formed a plausible excuse upon arrest. Realizing the probability of defeat, some men went into hiding rather than fight. Sheehy's group assembled at the home of Captain Charles Burke, Kilcrue, Borrisoleigh. They continued together as far as Pallas Cross, when Burke proceeded to raid Gortkelly Castle for arms. They jointly attacked the evacuated Roskeen constabulary barracks and set it on fire before demanding the arms of an unpopular publican, who was a police pensioner and suspected as an informer. He refused, but in the confusion a shot hit his relative, young Patrick Treacy, who was tragically killed. As Sheehy and Burke 'had no knowledge of what was taking place elsewhere', they disbanded soon afterwards.[85]

A concerned Gore Jones, R.M., rode to Barnane Castle near Templemore, recently inherited by Captain Andrew Carden. His combative predecessor, 'Woodcock' Carden, had mounted a cannon on the roof after disagreements with his tenantry. Gore Jones found a team of constabulary and armed retainers holding 'Carden's wild domain', where all remained quiet. Resident magistrates, as representatives of the civil power, accompanied each flying column. They alone could authorize the military to open fire. Surprising 250 men near Drom village, Gore Jones ordered his police escort to shoot, but prevented a unit of the 31st Regiment from doing so. The insurgents scattered across the fields and were not pursued. Instead, Gore Jones hastened to Dovea House, home of John Trant, mistakenly expecting the main rebel army to approach from Holycross.[86]

The officer in charge of the 31st Regiment reported to an irritated Lord Strathnairn that they had surprised a group of Fenians, who could have been captured except for the resident magistrate's incompetent intervention. Strathnairn had to be circumspect, however, as the British public held a deep aversion to militarism. Anxious rumours about the Fenians continued in places like Nenagh for some time after the Rising, subsiding during searches by the Thurles flying column under their efficient colonel, Valentine Baker, 10th Hussars, throughout north Tipperary.[87]

Clare

John Clune, leader of the Quin district, had been re-arrested under habeas corpus in December 1866. The following February Colonel John Healy and Lieutenant Joseph Lawlor, two veterans of the 9th Connecticut Volunteers, were detained in Limerick, bound for the Clare Rising. The only collision with the authorities occurred at Kilbaha, where John Deloughery, a national teacher and clerk of Cross chapel, and Thomas McCarthy Fennell of Oughterard demanded the rifles of the coastguard. During the ensuing fracas McCarthy Fennell was wounded and subsequently captured, while the Kilbaha coastguards retreated to Carrigaholt.[88]

Insurgents also assembled in Miltown Malbay and near Ennis. Fr Patrick White recalled: 'They were led to believe that on the following day they would be massed at points of vantage, and provided with the arms supposed to be hidden and at the disposal of the leaders. They were deceived on every side.'[89]

A group of disappointed Ennis rebels marched towards Corofin in search of revolution. When raiding a herdsman's house, the woeful state of their arms was noted: a few guns, pitchforks, 'long wattles with spikes on the tops' and scythe blades with a bit of 'sugan around the lower part of them'. Here, too, the gentry panicked and sheltered in their club in Ennis, close to the constabulary barracks.[90]

Dublin

Dublin was to participate in the countrywide Rising with its main assembly point at Tallaght Hill, luring the British army into pursuit. Colonel Halpin would be in overall charge, with his force gathering in the Dublin Mountains at Killakee, while the Palmerston Fields, Rathmines, constituted a third rendezvous for a unit, tasked to move towards Wicklow. Once this first phase had succeeded, operations would begin in Dublin, where Denieffe awaited Halpin's signal, presumably to seize buildings. The 'centres' obeyed orders to withhold information from their men until twenty-four hours before the Rising. Only on 4 March did Superintendent Daniel Ryan feel certain that the Fenians would rise the following night, 'prompted to it by the American officers', many of whom were prepared to sacrifice themselves.[91]

Alerted to the threat to Dublin, Lord Strathnairn had principal points, for instance, the Four Courts, the Custom House and various railway termini placed under guard. He dispatched flying columns, one from Dublin, the other from Newbridge, in pursuit. An estimated 2000 to 7000 Fenians reached Tallaght during the night, where Sub-Inspector Burke lined up fifteen constables in front of the barracks, challenging the insurgents. An inadequately drilled 'circle' of 150 men under Stephen O'Donoghue disobeyed orders not to engage unless success was likely, fired on the police and was defeated. Takagami has pointed out that the 'disaster at Tallaght', described by Devoy, constituted a minor setback. Competent commanders could have regrouped the Fenians as guerrillas, facilitated by the inability of the military to advance in the rain and dark. This failure to improvise copper-fastened the Fenian defeat. At Killakee, Colonel Halpin's column never assembled. Altogether, some 200 men were arrested.[92]

The Dalkey Fenians were to move towards Wicklow, but failed to turn out, in contrast to approximately 600 men of John Kirwan's 'circle', who followed the Harcourt Street Line south from Palmerston Fields. A former sergeant in the Papal Brigade, Captain Kirwan had prepared his men well. When he was wounded, Captain Patrick Lennon, an ex-Civil War officer, took over. They imprisoned a police patrol, but aborted an ineffectual attack on Dundrum barracks before continuing to Stepaside police station.[93] Lennon demanded its surrender in the name of the Irish Republic, which occurred after an exchange of fire. Rifles were seized and the constables joined their captive colleagues. Halting at the Old Connaught, outside Bray, they consulted with local supporters, abandoning their original plan of taking Bray barracks and continuing to Arklow, as the police had been reinforced and no other Fenian groups were abroad. Lennon decided to march into the mountains, destroying any barracks in his path, but some 300 men went off to seek the main force at Tallaght. Lennon reached Glencullen early on the morning of 6 March to meet with dogged resistance from the local police. Only when the Stepaside constables warned that they might be placed in the firing line did their Glencullen colleagues surrender. Lennon must have grasped how isolated he was, disbanding soon afterwards.[94]

Louth

Colonel Patrick Leonard, a native of Louth who had fought with the 99th New York, and Harry Shaw Mulleda, assembled a thousand followers in the Potato Market in Drogheda. They faced immediate arrest, while the courier with their weapons failed to materialize. Devoy elided the chaotic end to this attempt: bayonets flashed, shots rang out and Luke Fullam, a shoemaker, fell among the three Fenians wounded, possibly by friendly fire. There were twenty-five arrests. 'Both in Meath and Louth hundreds of people took to the fields to hide' rather than join the insurgents, separating determined IRB members from their peers. They were to gather on the Hill of Slane with its associations with St Patrick and 1798, where arms would be issued. On arrival, the men found the venue changed to Mellifont Abbey, but all remained quiet.[95]

Kilkenny

No outbreak occurred in Co. Kilkenny, although abandoned pikes near Kilmacow suggested an attempt at assembly, but William Hort, R.M., and the Callan magistrates remained uneasy. They wanted troops to be stationed in this town, due to its 'immediate proximity to the most dangerous part of Tipperary coupled with the notoriously disaffected character of its populace'.[96] Hort portrayed Slievenamon as the holy mountain of separatists:

> The feeling in Callan has always been disloyal in the extreme, and though apparently crushed now in no part of the country was Fenianism more rampant than in it. Moreover it is in the immediate proximity to Tipperary and within a very short distance of Slievenamon the mountain which figures so prominently as refuge and fathering place for the disaffected.[97]

Few grasped that the insurrection had subsided. The military continued to be concentrated at Limerick Junction. It patrolled 'places from where the greatest danger is apprehended', including Bansha, Cahir, Clonmel, Carrick and Callan, but no Fenian forces materialized.[98]

The British army created seven flying columns for disaffected regions. The Thurles unit searched the eponymous town, Clogheen, Clonmel, Cashel and Fethard, sometimes in deep snow, while others concentrated on Carlow, Tipperary, Cork, Waterford, Clare and Mayo, each accompanied by an energetic resident magistrate. Officials were convinced that the visual impact of these units extinguished the rebellion in Tipperary, while the gentry in remote locations felt reassured by their swift arrival.[99]

Claims that blizzard-like conditions on the night of 5 March contributed to the failure cannot be substantiated, but by 9 March the *Irish Times* commented on 'the bitter severity of the weather', which would have hampered guerrilla tactics:[100] 'Outside the steppes of Tartary and the Polar regions it would be hard to find any colder bit of table land than this Limerick Junction Station. Just now the scene is wintry indeed. The snow is lying thick on the ground, a keen northeast wind sweeps the platform, and in the distance the mountains are frosted over.'[101]

Country people believed 'that the sky fights against the Fenians' with the harsh weather as nature's flying column. High prices for agricultural products convinced the farmers to prefer the British Empire to a 'Fenian Republic'. Approximately 7000 men turned out on 5 March, undermining claims of 'patriotism as a pastime', but their dedication was nullified by an inadequate leadership, which lacked funds and arms. These young men demonstrated that Irish problems needed attention, but the minority Tory administration under Lord Derby was too weak to act, leaving tenant farmers and the Catholic hierarchy unappeased.[102]

In St Louis, Missouri, Fenian sympathizers hoped to imitate the Confederate tactic of menacing US shipping during the Civil War by pledging money for the insurgents to buy privateers and demanding that Washington endorse the Irish Republic.[103] Colonel Kelly learned from the newspapers that a deputation, requesting belligerent rights had merely received expressions of sympathy from President Johnson. On a wet evening 10,000 people assembled in Union Square, New York, to express 'public sympathy with the Fenian insurgents'. From Virginia, Mitchel continued his love-hate relationship, repeating that an uprising would fail while Britain remained at peace, although admiring 'the patriotic eagerness' of his countrymen. In Dublin, Larcom considered that arresting as many leaders as possible shortly beforehand had proved successful, reducing the outbreak 'to a confused and disorganized scramble'.[104]

But Colonel Kelly refused to concede defeat, appealing for immediate aid from the Brotherhood in New York. He warned that independence depended on effective help or this struggle would drag on 'for twenty years longer': 'Two weeks more and we are lost. Aid before two weeks and Irish independence is a fixed fact.

Let the aid be, however, not in the shape of the paltry contributions which have hitherto only kept us in agony, but let every man deserving the name of Irishman give everything he is possessed of ...'[105] He admitted the Rising had been unimpressive to date, as 'all beginnings are more or less imperfect. Ours was a very small one. Just think we took the field on a little over a thousand pounds.'[106]

Godfrey Massey, Patrick Joseph Condon, Thomas Francis Bourke and Edward Duffy had been arrested, but William Halpin remained at large with sixty other officers and 'as soon as fine weather opens we will be hard at it again', Kelly promised. He pressed for an armed expedition to Sligo as 'of infinite service' and cautioned: 'Don't believe a tenth of the vile newspaper reports about complete suppression ... while we get a mouthful, the flag shall fly.'[107]

Four days later, Kelly reminded his supporters that no initial 'pitched battles' had been planned, but to hold out until recognized as belligerents or American aid arrived. The Fenian Brotherhood was not to cease its efforts unless he declared action in Ireland at an end, but he was badly hampered by lack of money and ready to try almost anything.[108]

Fariola supported Kelly by claiming that the Rising could have been resuscitated, given adequate funding. He apprised the Brotherhood of their 'greatest destitution', while in 'daily danger of being captured'. Surely, as champions of Irish independence, they were entitled to support? On arriving in New York from Kilmallock, Captain Dunne stated that 'the Irish rebellion is only slumbering' and not 'stamped out'. He claimed in the press that 'over one thousand drilled men' had been eager to join him, but due to police vigilance they were unable to access sufficient arms. Unaware that Massey had changed sides on arrest, Fariola and Kelly in London attempted to locate this emerging intelligence leak by writing to the home secretary, pretending willingness to inform.[109]

There were rumours that the Fenians might make a second attempt on St Patrick's Day by burning the shipping in Liverpool. The local force, assisted by Irish constables, observed the return of about forty participants from the Rising, while the American officers vanished. The inhabitants of Bradford, Sheffield, Shrewsbury and Glasgow remained on edge, but Colonel Kelly, although hinting at plans involving 'torpedo men' and 'chemical receipts' to his American allies, lacked the funds for action. Many IRB men had fled to Scotland and agents were seeking recruits and donations in Glasgow. In New York exiled IRB 'centres' held consultations with both wings of the Brotherhood, which failed to achieve unity and help for those insurgents who remained at large.[110]

Mrs Buckley, the wife of a printer who had since gone on the run and formerly the supportive landlady of John Edward Kelly, was detained in Cork in possession of seditious material. Superintendent Mallon concluded that in the aftermath of the Rising, women worked as Fenian couriers, 'doing infinitely more mischief in promoting it than men'. Victorians considered females unlikely to engage in conspiracy and the authorities had to handle them decorously.[111] Albina Mahony, a young dressmaker returned from the US, vowed to expose the police in the press when threatened with an intrusive body search during Captain Mackey's trial in 1868. Jointly with Mary O'Connell, Mackey's sister-in-law, Murphy sued Thomas Barry, RIC County Inspector for Cork, relating how they had been made to strip to their chemise in an overlooked room. The police claimed to have acted on information that they had carried 'revolvers about the city' and possessed Fenian papers. The girls won £50 in damages for 'assault and false imprisonment'. Women chaffed under the restrictions of Church and state and embraced opportunities to voice their opposition.[112]

After a month, the flying columns were disbanded. Lord Strathnairn believed that only three or four of them had experienced any meaningful action, but the overall effect was excellent. The long marches of the Thurles, Tipperary and Waterford columns, their sudden searches and arrests had driven many Fenians into hiding.[113] Protests against the reduction in police and military reached Dublin Castle from Lord Castlerosse in Killarney and W. E. Armstrong MacDonnell of Newhall, Ennis. The latter, Deputy Lord Lieutenant of Clare, considered Captain Peel of the flying column had been the only effective means of dealing with local insurgents. In late March 'armed parties' obtained 'money for the support and defence of the Fenian prisoners' from several houses. 'Major O'Brien', an otherwise unidentified Fenian leader and others were rumoured to shelter near Corofin; there were no arrests.[114]

Officialdom continued to find it difficult to source witnesses to prosecute.[115] Constable Joseph Murphy was among undercover agents on duty, but proved unsuccessful with the shopkeepers of Thurles, who feared being boycotted, should they cooperate with Dublin Castle. He lamented that this neighbourhood was infected with 'incurable Fenianism' and that its inhabitants consisted of 'a deep minded, cunning and conspiring pack', proud of not tolerating informers.[116]

The Erin's Hope

The Brotherhood of Manhattan bought and equipped a brigantine, advised by William Sweetman, one of the Irish pilots awaiting the departure of the Fenian expedition since November 1865. She left the North river on 15 April 1867 with 8000 rifles. On Easter Sunday the thirty-eight Fenians and nine sailors under the command of James Kerrigan, William Nagle and John Warren hoisted the Fenian sunburst, which had been made by the 'ladies of the Tara circle of Brooklyn' and christened her the *Erin's Hope*. When the coast of Mayo came into view after five weeks at sea, the Fenian contingent read an address of thanks to the naval personnel, presuming action imminent.[117]

John Warren, Erin's Hope, *CSO/ICR /16*
(courtesy NAI).

In the aftermath of the Rising, Colonel Kelly formed a new Irish directory to replace the provisional government, half of whose members had been arrested. This relationship swiftly deteriorated. As Kelly's pleas for help were answered by the *Erin's Hope* approaching Sligo, Michael O'Neill Fogarty and colleagues on the directory opposed her landing as too late. He accused Kelly of plotting another, unauthorized Rising by redirecting the ship to Cork, where Captain Mackey awaited her arms. The Colonel Kelly/O'Sullivan Burke faction later alleged O'Neill Fogarty and James J. O'Kelly had tried to sabotage their efforts by withholding the funds couriered from New York to prepare for her arrival. But rallying the IRB proved futile, as many leaders had fled and 'the men cannot be got out'. Due to the vigilance of the coastguards, West Cork could not be approached, but with few provisions left, a landing became imperative.[118]

As recalled by P.J. Kain, later an Episcopalian minister in New Jersey, the *Erin's Hope* narrowly avoided a collision with the Royal Navy when hailed by HMS *Black Prince*, which, however, failed to recognize her. The Fenians planned to let the British board, engaging in hand-to-hand combat as they retreated into the hold, while the *Erin's Hope* nudged closer to the superior warship. Then Colonel Tresilian, the Fenian chief engineer, would explode her powder magazine to inflict maximum damage on the *Black Prince*, ruthlessly sacrificing all present.[119]

On 1 June 1867 the *Erin's Hope* landed thirty-one Fenian volunteers at Helvick Head near Dungarvan, but twenty-eight were speedily arrested. They included Colonel William Nagle, Colonel John Warren and Captain Augustine Costello, whose trials revived Anglo-American tensions about British insistence on indefeasible allegiance. Nagle, being American-born, was released in May 1868, but Warren and Costello as naturalized citizens were sentenced to fifteen years, protesting vociferously. The controversy threatened to facilitate US politicians courting the Irish vote and Lord Clarendon, foreign secretary in Gladstone's first ministry, amnestied them in 1869.[120]

Rudolph Fitzpatrick, Fenian assistant secretary of war, was among those regularly warning British officials about another attack on Canada. Consul Edwards alerted Lord Stanley, the foreign secretary, to rumours of a new insurrection in Dublin on 31 May. The former O'Mahony wing doubted its feasibility, but would join the Senate section in acts of retaliation for imprisoned Fenian activists, he claimed.[121] An informer suggested that Roberts had urged him to kidnap and hold hostage judges Fitzgerald, Deasy and Whiteside, who had convicted numbers of Fenians, by using Orsini bombs, 'the size of apples, surrounded with points which, upon touching the ground or any other obstacle, would instantly explode with terrific force'.[122]

The Federal authorities had returned 30,000 confiscated weapons and the Fenian flag to the Senate wing. (The Buffalo Sisterhood embroidered 'Ridgeway and Fort Erie, June 2, 1866' on it; Maria Cruice, a leading member preserved it until her death in 1902.) In June Edwards learned that Roberts and James Gibbons of Philadelphia as president and vice president respectively had bought 1500 uniforms with a further 5000 ordered. Fenians would wear 'a green jacket trimmed with yellow braid, blue trousers with green stripe on side. Blue caps with green band. The buttons and belt plates which are of brass bear the initials 'I.R.A.' (Irish Republican Army) in relief'.[123]

'I am Captain Mac'[124]

One hundred and sixty-nine men were tried by special commission in Dublin, Cork and Limerick, resulting in fifty-two convictions and seven acquittals. A further 110 Fenians had pleaded guilty; twenty-five of them were sentenced to penal servitude and fifty to terms of imprisonment, but minor participants were released on guarantee of good behaviour. In August 1867 Ireland was proclaimed with the exception of Belfast and most of Ulster.[125]

But Mackey Lomasney, whom the IRB had tasked to procure arms, and his followers remained at large in Munster, conducting a limited form of guerrilla warfare. 'Captain Mac' travelled to London in August 1867 to collect 'a quantity of Greek fire, and a number of revolvers'. He raided two gun-makers in Cork, beginning shortly after the Manchester executions and culminating with a seizure of gunpowder from the Martello tower at Fota on 26 December. When he withdrew, the anxious gunners barricaded the door and fired their cannon to summon aid. The determined exploits of this David fighting the British Goliath created great sympathy for the IRB. T.D. Sullivan celebrated Mackey's daring in a song, 'The Cork Men and the New York Men' to the tune of 'The Groves of Blarney'. The constabulary depot in Dublin dispatched an undercover detective to follow up leads, rewards were promised and spies hired to arrest Mackey, who 'is in the habit of assuming all sort of disguise, even female attire to baffle the authorities'.[126]

Capt. William Mackey Lomasney
(courtesy Dublin City Archive).

Resident magistrate Franks wrote of Fenian agents being arrested in Knocklong and Kilteely and that the police attending the petty sessions in Hospital, Co. Limerick, complained that once again 'the people had become generally defiant and offensive to them'. The energetic De Gernon discounted pervasive rumours of insurrection, but recorded the despondent attitude of the propertied class and took precautions to forestall an attack on Bruff barracks with Fenian fire, commenting: 'The worst spot all around here is *Kilteely*, it gives tone to the disaffected elsewhere.' De Gernon requested more troops, which produced the 'happiest results' by[127] 'patrolling at all hours of the night, through the country on cars as with the flying column and it is with fear and trembling they hear cars rattle along the road'.[128]

Several magistrates believed that Captain Dunne, who had fought at Kilmallock, had returned to Munster. On 8 January 1868 the Dublin police captured Patrick Lennon, who led insurgents the previous March and had since directed a 'circle' to kill informers and seize arms. When Lord Mayo realized that the military wanted four cannons to protect Dublin Castle, he curtly vetoed an idea, which would cause panic among the law-abiding. Tensions ran high with Mayo informing Larcom from Lord Derby's estate of Knowsley Hall that Lady Mayo had learned he would be assassinated for having supplied information, which prevented O'Sullivan Burke's rescue from Clerkenwell. News from London was 'very menacing', including assassination plots 'in every direction'. Mayo blamed a fracas at fortifications in Co. Wexford on Captain Mackey's 'Cork gang' of guerillas, but a secret investigation by Oliver Moriarty, R.M., censured English troops, who had panicked in Duncannon and opened fire 'lavishly' without reason. Five guns were robbed from farmers in the Glen of Aherlow, as had happened prior to March 1867, but De Gernon could obtain no information. There were a further four, largely unsuccessful, attempts to seize arms in Cork until July 1868 and in Newport, Co. Mayo, gunpowder was stolen.[129]

On 7 February 1868 Mackey was surprised in a Cork pub, two men being paid at least £100 each for their vital information. In addition to the customary prize money for important arrests, Lord Mayo had offered £200 on behalf of Lord Abercorn, the viceroy, to whoever captured Mackey. This went to Head Constable Gale and his two subordinates. When 'Captain Mac' resisted arrest, a policeman knocked his pistol aside, which went off, fatally wounding another constable. Lord Mayo rejoiced at the capture, but 'riotous mobs' protested in the streets and had to be dispersed by force. Trouble continued while Mackey remained in Cork and Lord Mayo urged Colonel Wood of the constabulary to increase security in Cork jail, as 'we must not have another Clerkenwell'.[130]

In the dock, Mackey Lomasney explained his motivation as wishing 'to assist in the liberation of an enslaved nation; and I knew that the greatest sacrifices must be endured on our parts before the country could be raised to that proud position'.[131] The idealism of this 'poorly-dressed, sallow' youth with his faith in Ireland's 'glorious future', exposed the dilemma of constitutional nationalists like Charles Gavan Duffy, who admired Mackey's patriotism, while considering it 'wicked to foster a hopeless insurrection'. Gavan Duffy despised the calumnies of the press:[132] 'The stale and stupid lie that all these men of Irish blood and feeling who left a prosperous country which offers a career to everyone, for what was plainly a forlorn hope, are merely robbers in pursuit of plunder outraged common sense.'[133] Judge John O'Hagan wept and many were deeply moved by Mackey's speech, while the jury added a recommendation to mercy. Acquitted of murder, he was sentenced to twelve years for treason-felony.[134]

CHAPTER 8

Incarceration of the Leaders, 1865–8

With midnight always in one's heart,
And twilight in one's cell,
We turn the crank, or tear the rope,
Each in his separate Hell,
And the silence is more awful far
Than the sound of a brazen bell.
'The Ballad of Reading Gaol'[1]

The British penal system of the 1860s had evolved from the reform movement of the eighteenth century, sweeping away the filthy, overcrowded jails, which favoured wealthy prisoners. Jeremy Bentham, the utilitarian philosopher, had designed the panopticon to facilitate constant observation by warders, influencing nineteenth-century penal policy and inspiring the English national penitentiary in Millbank, London. Completed in 1821, it was not a success due to its location and administration.[2]

Administrators debated the merits of the separate versus the silent system. The former meant that the prisoners worked separately (and silently) in their cells, while the latter allowed inmates to associate mutely with each other. A mixture of both was adopted. The aim was to separate the convict from his criminal environment and to prevent 'old lags' corrupting first-time offenders. Inmates were deprived of human contact for lengthy periods, except for the exhortations of the chaplain to awaken their conscience to reflect on past crimes, leading to repentance and reform.[3]

Magistrates preferred the new system as better regulated, while appreciating the deterrent of solitary confinement, which terrified inmates by making them as lonely 'as the human mind could bear'.[4] A new style of architecture implemented these ideas and led to the erection of Pentonville Model Prison in 1842, which contemporaries admired as supremely modern.[5]

Pentonville became a blueprint for prisons elsewhere, the main Irish example being Mountjoy, which opened in 1850. Soon, however, the misgivings of the Spike Island chaplain that this system could inflict physical and psychological damage to prisoners were borne out.[6] Convicts deteriorated following periods in solitary confinement. Eventually, the concept of reform was abandoned for more traditional ideas of retribution. It was ironic that the new prisons, originating in a desire to regenerate the character of the criminals, proved more damaging than the old, loathsome jails. The harshest features of this system had been abolished, however, when the Fenians were sentenced in 1865.[7]

On conviction, any privileges previously enjoyed, such as appetizing meals sent in by relatives, ceased. Men's beards were shaved off and their hair cropped short. Ostensibly for reasons of hygiene, this was humiliating in an age when men wore long hair. After a medical examination, convicts received their uniform. James F.X. O'Brien recalled:[8] 'It looked to me like the Irish workhouse dress, but it was highly respectable when compared with the English convict dress I later wore of coarse drab tweed – with its large black stripes and branded all over with the *broad arrow* in black, which makes one look like a tiger on two feet.' They were photographed, then a new method of recording the identity of prisoners. This procedure soon became compulsory and photos of suspects were circulated within the prison administration. At least two officials, Sir Thomas Larcom and Samuel Lee Anderson, assembled collections.[9]

The Fenians had been convicted under statute 11 & 12 Vict c 12 & 13, making them liable to transportation of no less than seven years. In 1853, however, 16 & 17 Vict c 99 replaced transportation with penal servitude in any prison, as directed by the secretary of state. Serving one's sentence in the colonies had become less disagreeable than imprisonment at home with 'enlivening passages to Western Australia or Bermuda and back', when rules were relaxed. Charles Pennell Measor, deputy director of Chatham Prison, stressed that during the 1860s life sentences increased threefold in severity.[10] The Cork *Constitution* confirmed that the new rules had the desired effect of making the prisoners 'suffer for their crimes' by adding 'the pangs of hunger', while the *Times* denied that this was 'cruel, or cruelly administered'.[11]

The escape of Stephens from Richmond bridewell had demonstrated the difficulties of incarcerating the Fenians in Ireland, where the working class sympathized and some prison staff covertly supported them. After the habeas corpus suspension, the warders were 'anxiously and closely' watched by Captain Whitty, who, jointly with Lord Wodehouse, suggested gratuities to reward their loyalty. Dublin Castle and the Home Office discussed exchanging sections of the Irish and British prison populations or incarcerating the Fenians in Gibraltar. Finally it was decided that all, except short-term IRB prisoners, would be transferred to English jails. The viceroy considered this 'absolutely necessary', as 'their imprisonment here produces a dangerous excitement and requires extraordinary and expensive precautions diverting the police and military force from other urgent duties'.[12]

The prisoners included Colour Sergeant Charles McCarthy and James Keilley of the 53rd Regiment, John Boyle O'Reilly of the 10th Hussars, Sergeant Major Thomas Darragh of the 2nd Regiment, Thomas Chambers, Robert Cranston and Michael Harrington of the 61st, Martin Joseph Hogan, Patrick Keating, James Wilson of the 5th Dragoons and Thomas Henry Hassett of the 24th Foot. Colonel Percy Feilding of military intelligence was convinced that they remained in contact with the IRB, which had not lost heart by the summer of 1866. Feilding attributed his limited success in persuading soldiers to inform to their 'firm conviction' that they will be freed.[13]

In England, on the other hand, they could expect little support and, as an additional precaution, no Irish-born warders were allowed near them. On 23 December 1865 the first group, including John O'Leary, Thomas Clarke Luby, John Haltigan and Jeremiah O'Donovan Rossa, was transferred to London. Captain Whitty, director of Irish convict prisons and Colonel Henderson, chairman of the directors of British convict prisons, made the security arrangements after consultations with Sir George Grey.[14]

On arrival in Pentonville or later Millbank, the Fenians were strip-searched as a security measure. In British (but not in Irish) jails it was common to leave groups of naked prisoners waiting in the cold for medical inspection, which created lasting indignation. John Sarsfield Casey recalled 'such a scene of indecency that I fain would cast a dark over it. The most private parts, fore and after, were closely searched accompanied with such language as only the English utter.'[15] They exchanged their Mountjoy uniforms for those of Pentonville and were refused the accustomed warm underclothes, before attempting to sleep on low plank beds with laths nailed on for a pillow.[16] Rossa recalled that 'at night my ribs and hips felt the proximity of the hard board of my bed, so much that in time the skin on those parts of my body … became quite rough, and I learned to roll from side to side every fifteen minutes or so without waking'.[17]

Pentonville was supposedly designed to avoid extremes of temperature. In reality the prison became very cold in winter. Middle-class prisoners were not prepared for this. O'Leary and Rossa agreed that 'this is hell', while Charles Kickham missed fires and the company of women and children.[18] Oscar Wilde, although admitted to Pentonville thirty years later, recalled 'a fiendish nightmare'. Convicts were issued with a bucket for nightly toilet use, which became 'so full and overflowing' that staff felt ill on opening the cells next morning.[19]

Within weeks of the first Fenian prisoners arriving in London, the governor received an anonymous warning that suspicious individuals were gathering near the Tottenham Court Road, planning to explode 'the outer walls of Pentonville'.[20] The administration took precautions. This may have been the rescue attempt, led by Jerome Collins of Cork, then employed by a firm with a contract for Pentonville. Indiscreet talk meant that Collins had to flee abroad. From the beginning, the Irish state prisoners, as the IRB men described themselves, were treated as if they had already attempted to escape. Each evening their clothes were removed, while cell doors were opened noisily and lights flashed in their faces throughout the night.[21]

The initial period of incarceration was spent in solitary confinement under close observation to select the most appropriate second-stage prison. Michael Davitt described the suffering of those newly convicted:

> The first two years of penal servitude are the hardest to bear, and test mental endurance more than the whole of the remainder of an ordinary sentence. Liberty has only just been parted with. The picture of the outside world is still imprinted upon the memory, and home and friends ... are made to haunt the recollection whenever the association of ideas recalls some incident of happier days. Of these two years the heaviest portion is comprised within the nine or ten months which must be spent in what is termed 'probation' – solitary confinement in Millbank or Pentonville ... it is truly a terrible ordeal to undergo ... In Millbank this is especially so. The prison is but a few hundred yards west of Westminster Palace, from whence comes, every quarter of an hour, the voice of Big Ben, telling the listening inmates of the penitentiary that another fifteen minutes of their sentences have gone by! What horrible punishment has not that clock added to many an unfortunate wretch's fate, by counting for him *the minutes* during which stone walls and iron bars *will* a prison make ... until the terrible idea of suicide is forced across the mind as the only mode of release from the horrible mockery of the noisy, joyful world beyond the boundary walls. It is not surprising that many men have gone mad in Millbank.[22]

During the probationary period, inmates spent twenty-three hours a day on their own, when their work consisted of picking coir, a fibre extracted from coconuts, or sewing mail bags. Walking in the cold cells was forbidden and convicts were expected to sit on their toilet bucket seats. Silence was compulsory. Robert Anderson had himself locked into a cell in Kilmainham jail to interview a potential informer. He noticed that the cell window was high up and its glass painted over to prevent any view of the sky. Anderson became depressed: 'I seemed to be in a pit. There was no want of air, and yet I felt smothered.'[23] Prisoners depended on recalling pleasant memories or savouring minor pleasures. Kickham, for example, enjoyed observing 'a cat basking in the prison yard', remembered walks beside the Anner and his friend Denny Shea, the model for Phil Lahy in *Knocknagow*.[24]

A director of prisons visited the institution each week to supervise its administration. Director Gambier inspected the 'Irish state prisoners' for the first time on 26 December 1865.[25] Soon afterwards a minor Dublin Fenian volunteered information, hoping to obtain a pardon, as did William Moore Stack of Tralee in July 1867. Both were invited to make written depositions, but nothing was promised in return. The medical officer in Mountjoy had considered James Keilley too distressed for solitary confinement. In Millbank, however, he experienced its full rigours and made two statements. He was not rewarded for what was probably stale news. Keilley later attempted suicide.[26]

Convicts generally spent nine months in solitary confinement before being assigned to a public works prison. If well-behaved during their first year, they were promoted to third class. After two years a prisoner might merit promotion to second class, after a further year, first class, which meant food privileges and increased contact with relatives. The public works prisons, Portland (1848), Dartmoor (1850), Portsmouth (1850) and Chatham (1856) tried to recreate labour programmes, resembling the Australian convict experience. In Portland a great breakwater and fortifications were constructed and its famous limestone quarried. Granite was extracted in Dartmoor and in Chatham, the lives of many prisoners were sacrificed in extending its dockyard.[27]

In May 1866, within four months of their arrival in London, the bulk of the Fenians were transferred to Portland Prison in Dorset with the explanation 'that it was for the benefit of their health', which they considered a cruel joke.[28] The sick, for instance, John Lynch, Brian Dillon and Charles Kickham, were assigned to Woking Invalid Prison in Surrey. In selecting Portland Prison, security was paramount. Portsmouth contained '500 Roman Catholic prisoners, mostly Irish'; Dartmoor also had 200 Catholic inmates, who might conceivably fraternize with these separatists. It was standard practice to provide spiritual care, which meant hiring a Catholic chaplain at a cost of £120 p.a. and arranging a temporary chapel for the twenty-four IRB men.[29]

In the meantime, Denis Dowling Mulcahy read Sunday prayers in the same 'impassioned, vigorous and defiant' manner, which had characterized him during his trial, which cheered the Fenians, but provoked the warders.[30] His selections from scripture contained 'denunciations of tyrants and oppressors, and sympathy for their victims, with curses and punishments for the liars and perjurers, and blessings for all who had suffered persecution for justice's sake'.[31]

The IRB prisoners, mostly practising Catholics, were deeply offended when Captain Clifton, governor of Portland, 'sneeringly and insultingly' referred to their scapulars and *Agnus Dei* emblems as 'what is to be done with these charms, and amulets?'[32] Fenian propaganda also publicized that the governor 'was wont to tell us that *we* were worse than the criminals; that *we* were excommunicated by the church, and deserved to be punished, not only here, but hereafter – that is, in hell'.[33] They were accommodated in a hitherto unused section of Portland, where the cells received little natural light with stone floors adding to the pervasive cold. This block was prone to flooding and the men related incidents of huddling in wet cells; the governor, however, claimed nothing else was available.[34]

Victorian prison life was harsh. Portland had approximately 1500 inmates; in February 1867, for instance, the governor on his rounds persuaded two criminals to give up their hunger strike, which was attempted suicide and not yet a form of political protest. That same evening a convict set fire to his bedding and clothing.[35] Dense smoke led to evacuation, while the quick response of the warders saved the offender's life. Three convicts tried to kill themselves, another severed his main leg tendon with a razor, presumably to gain a respite from hard labour in the infirmary and there was a fatal accident in the quarries. A typical entry in the governor's journal read: 'Weather very cold with storms of snow. Wind N.E. Prisoners employed as usual. Suffering much from cold.'[36]

Diet, discipline and monotonous work were keystones of the prison administration. Food should suffice to maintain life, but consist of less than a labourer could earn. The editorial staff of the *Irish People* was unaccustomed to such hardships. John Sarsfield Casey praised the quality of the Mountjoy diet, where breakfast consisted of oatmeal stirabout with half a pint of milk. For dinner 12 oz white bread with a pint milk, and for supper 6 oz of bread and half a pint of milk were distributed. On two days during the week the main meal was two pints of soup with vegetables, meat and bread.[37]

While inmates in Millbank, Rossa, Thomas Francis Bourke and Denis Dowling Mulcahy breakfasted on 8 oz bread and three-quarters of a pint of cocoa and received 4 oz meat for dinner on four days, alternating with a pint soup or a pound of suet pudding. On Sundays, however, 12 oz bread, 4 oz cheese and a pint water were served, while supper consisted of 6 oz bread and a pint of gruel. Food allowances were slightly more generous in the public works prisons. The regular Portland diet was 16 oz bread with three-quarters of a pint of cocoa, 4 oz beef, a pint of gruel made with 2 oz oatmeal and a pound of potatoes, which were often rotten. Invalids in Woking Prison were given 20 oz bread, ¼ oz tea, 4 oz milk and 1 ½ oz sugar daily, to be divided between breakfast and supper. Their dinner consisted of soup with 8 oz of potatoes and bread. They were also entitled to 10 oz of meat per day, but this was not always received. The medical officer could prescribe sherry or rice pudding for those seriously ill.[38]

Many inmates felt half-starved. It was tacitly accepted that much of the food was barely edible for the newly incarcerated and caused digestive disorders. In Pentonville, Thomas Clarke Luby and Cornelius Dwyer Keane of Skibbereen suffered from violent diarrhoea, brought on by the gruel. Although entitled to an alternative, the medical officer considered 'they were malingering' and gave them only bread and water.[39] John Sarsfield Casey summarized the prison diet as 'rancid, tough, uneatable' beef, often swarming with maggots in summer. Only 'extreme hunger' forced him to approach this dinner.[40]

In 1870 Brian Dillon brought the permanently impaired digestion of Charles Kickham to the attention of the Devon Commission. Rossa, however, dreamed of 'platefuls of bread-and-butter' and exhibited the pragmatism of a survivor:[41] 'When eating my ration of bread I found a beetle or ciaróg cracking between my teeth, instead of spitting out in disgust what I had just chewed, I would grind away, telling myself that nature had provided for the excretion of anything that was foul and the retention of what was nutritious'.[42]

Meticulous rules and record-keeping were to demonstrate the success of the penal system, but served as window-dressing for an unsatisfactory reality. The Victorian administration did not respond to individual needs and victims sometimes reacted with despair or destructive protest. Leading prison staff had a military background, stressing efficiency while disregarding caring qualities. Warders, too, were harshly supervised and could be fined part of their wages for misdemeanours. Some took bribes to smuggle out letters, risking dismissal.[43] Attacks on prison staff, provoked by severe discipline and inadequate diet, were not unusual. In 1861, for instance, 1000 convicts rioted in Chatham and troops had to restore order. While Mulcahy and Bourke were inmates in Woking, an attempt was made to murder Governor Bramley.[44]

Official policy stated that Britain had no political prisoners, which was obviously untrue, for no criminals had to undergo daily strip-searching. John O'Leary concurred, bitterly referring to the 'system of treating political prisoners like pickpockets or murderers, first inaugurated by the government of

Lord Russell and Mr Gladstone'. At the very least the Fenians were victims of the Victorian prison administration with its passion for uniformity and repressive discipline.[45]

The authorities could grant favours, for example, permitting a convict to have family photographs, but when Mary Jane O'Donovan Rossa sent a photo of herself with their first child, born after Rossa's conviction to Portland, no exception was made. Her poem 'The Returned Picture' garnered publicity for the prisoners.[46] John O'Leary only received a bunch of shamrock, sent to him anonymously for St Patrick's Day 1866, on his release in 1871. Such pettiness embittered IRB men, aware that criminals obtained concessions.[47]

Shamrock sent to John O'Leary in jail, 1866 (courtesy National Graves Association).

The treatment experienced by the Fenians was harsher than that of their predecessors. Dr George Sigerson believed this was partly due to the greater vitality of Fenianism, which did not collapse after 1865 and continued to be supported by American allies, who 'threatened invasion'.[48] Having entered politics as Young Irelanders, the IRB leadership knew that William Smith O'Brien, Thomas Francis Meagher and Terence Bellew McManus had enjoyed comfortable cells and visitors while detained in Dublin.[49] Mitchel related in his *Jail Journal* that the authorities treated him as an educated gentleman, who wore a convict uniform only briefly. Smith O'Brien had been allowed to bring part of his library from Cahirmoyle and the Young Irelanders received preferential treatment on the transport to Van Diemen's Land. They benefited from the elevated social status of their chief, for Smith O'Brien was a brother of Sir Lucius O'Brien, the future Lord Inchiquin, who interceded for them with the colonial secretary.[50]

By the 1860s, however, an inflexible system had evolved. The IRB leaders did not compare favourably with Smith O'Brien's associates, who consisted of a minor landlord (John Martin), a successful shipping agent (Terence Bellew McManus) and John Mitchel and Charles Gavan Duffy, lawyers turned journalists. James Stephens was merely the son of an auctioneer's clerk from Kilkenny, while the intellectual elite of the early IRB hailed from the merchant class (O'Leary and Kickham).[51] Luby, although well connected, described himself as a law student, aged forty-three, in the Pentonville register. The Cork leaders consisted of Rossa, a shopkeeper, John Kenealy, a commercial traveller and several dismissed schoolteachers and law clerks. Among the insurgents of 1867, James F.X. O'Brien was socially the most elevated, with a business career, while the Irish-American officers had acquired status by rising from the ranks. In an age when class was paramount, the establishment was not impressed.[52]

Prisoners could earn 'marks', which translated into a remission of up to a quarter of their sentence. A maximum of eight marks might be obtained per day, six were considered a fair day's work, but any less made the convict liable for punishment. Warders assessed the performance of the inmates, who depended on their goodwill at all times, for marks could be subtracted for bad behaviour; invariably, the prison authorities believed the version of events recounted by their staff.[53]

Initially, Luby and O'Leary led the Fenians in stoic endurance, which the latter described:

> For more than three years I have borne, I trust not altogether unmanfully, much mental and physical suffering. How I have suffered I cannot tell; and even if I could, I would not. There was not a day or hour of all that time that might not bring forth its own peculiar pain, and perhaps the hardest thing of all to be borne was the constant fear lest something still worse remained to be borne.[54]

O'Leary considered himself fortunate, nevertheless, 'for some of my companions are dead and some are mad, and many are invalids for life ... but I still have the use of all my limbs and (I believe) of all my wits and for this, I say again, I thank God, and God alone'.[55]

Prisoners could petition the home secretary, but neither Luby nor O'Leary did. The latter explained: 'I was in the hands of my enemy, why should I complain?' The initial quarterly returns for Portland show that up to June 1866, Luby and O'Leary's conduct was 'exemplary', while Rossa was described as 'very good'.[56] The two intellectuals felt that one 'couldn't fight England in her own prisons' and that 'obedience and subordination' testified to 'the dignity of the national cause'.[57] When Luby cited Mitchel as his role model, Rossa riposted that the editor of the *United Irishman* had not been forced to clean latrines. His conviction 'that the dignity of liberty's cause required that men should suffer calmly and strongly for it' did not last.[58] Rossa disregarded his wife's advice to imitate the 'admirable dignity' of O'Leary and Luby and behave 'in a more rational manner'.[59] The younger generation, as typified by Denis Dowling Mulcahy and the Irish-Americans, was more outspoken and less influenced by the concept of gentlemanliness. Nevertheless, Captain McCafferty abandoned his plans to 'refuse to submit to the prison discipline' in late 1867 due to lack of support. James F.X. O'Brien, incarcerated for the attack on Ballyknockane barracks, considered Rossa's non-compliance feasible, if others had joined his protest.[60]

The Fenian leaders perceived themselves as victims of a hypocritical and petty British government, which was intent on criminalizing them, while simultaneously applauding the national aspirations of other Europeans. On arrival in Portland they were isolated and worked in the prison laundry, a potentially infectious task. Subsequently they laboured in the quarries by themselves, but in full view of the authorities.[61] The leaders objected vociferously to having to associate with criminals. Kickham was horrified, for fellow inmates in Woking included prisoner no. 2934, convicted of 'bestiality with a mare', no. 2935, 'indecent conduct towards three girls', no. 2936, 'sodomy', while no. 1006 had raped his daughters.[62]

Most Fenians failed to overcome their class prejudices: 'Of course we did not associate or scarcely speak to the unfortunates, altho [sic] I believe a portion of them had been *very respectable* & well educated – a good many of them had a great respect for our men ...'[63] Only Michael Davitt, John Boyle O'Reilly and Rossa, whom convicts helped to communicate with the outside world, openly acknowledged their common humanity. It must have been distressing for romantics with an idealized concept of the nation to realize that 'almost half of those men were of Irish parentage, and their crimes were substantially traceable to poverty or whiskey'.[64]

The *Times* deplored that

> the extreme difficulty of dealing with the Irish Fenians consists in the fact that they cannot be got to see the criminality of treason. Education has done little more for them than to enable them to read the literature of treason, with which their minds are saturated, and which colours everything connected with the history of this country. The worst rebels whose deeds and sufferings are recorded in that history they regard as martyrs to the holiest of causes, and they cannot think it morally wrong to imitate their 'glorious' example. They consider the present state prosecutions, like all such prosecutions in past times, as part of the old war between England and Ireland.[65]

Captain Edmund Du Cane, chairman of the directors of English convict prisons, agreed. The Fenians 'entertained such exaggerated notions of themselves and of the movement they had taken part in, as to persuade themselves that everybody was thinking about them and desirous of being revenged on them. And having this on their mind, shortly after they came to the prisons, a certain number of them began to make complaints.'[66]

Given an official desire to isolate and silence them, the Fenians grasped that arousing the sympathy of nationalists constituted their best court of appeal. Between 1865 and 1871, a veritable avalanche of smuggled-out news and propaganda appeared in the *Irishman* and the *Nation* and was copied in the US, where Irish-Americans approached politicians to intervene. Radical newspapers created the image of the cruelly tried, but indomitable Fenian, raising O'Donovan Rossa's profile, in particular. This subculture of defiant suffering, echoing Mitchel's *Jail Journal*, was to be continued in the prison memoirs of Rossa and Tom Clarke, appealing to national pride.

Rossa's correspondence was circumscribed by prison censorship, but he persisted with illicit messages.[67] Mass was no longer of solely religious significance, but offered opportunities for communication. The noisy liturgical responses of his comrades hid his quest for writing materials:

> 'I'll get you paper ...' intoned the voice.
> 'Have mercy on us.'
> '... and pen and ink.'
> 'Have mercy.'
> 'Our baker will send the letter.'[68]

The Fenian Sisterhood

Unlike the early Chartist movement, neither the IRB nor the Fenian Brotherhood facilitated women as political activists. Fenianism did not question the contemporary concept of the 'respectable' female's role being restricted to the home. Even the progressive John Boyle O'Reilly, who defended the rights of African Americans and First Nations as editor of the Boston *Pilot* after his escape from penal Australia in 1869, ignored this issue.[69] The *Irish People* depicted 'successful' women as ready to encourage and sacrifice husbands and sons. Luby wrote: 'Should the patriot's wife be unworthy of him then – should she be selfish, or even narrowly attached to her mere family – his human weakness will have a hair's-breath escape, if it do not yield to temptation.'[70]

A heroic spouse, Luby believed, would prove invaluable, preferring 'her husband in chains or dead than to see him abandon the cause of truth and justice'. John Lynch of Cork informed his fiancée that 'Irish women as well as Irish men' were needed, but outlined traditional roles like catering and nursing. Even Ellen Eliza Callanan, who had denounced the parish priest of Clonakilty for political dictation in the radical press, defined the 'holy duty' of Irishwomen as influencing their menfolk to be patriotic. Although the editors of the *Irish People* must have known of militant women in the Italian uprisings of 1848–9 and 1860, their example was ignored by these social conservatives. They followed in the footsteps of Charles Gavan Duffy, who had rejected the setting-up of a seditious 'Ladies Society' in 1848, when only adverse circumstances compelled him to let Margaret Callan and Jane Francesca Elgee publish the *Nation*.[71]

Sources reveal a shadowy network of female couriers, fundraisers, propagandists and organizers, who also ran safe houses and conveyed activists to the ports. Harriet Clarke, in a letter of 1868, described how she disguised herself as a Frenchwoman and tied her brother Joseph's bag underneath her crinoline hoops to mastermind his escape to France from London, despite six constables watching their home. Harriet gave nothing away when interviewed by her brother's civil service employers.[72]

Working-class women sometimes led violent protests. When young Michael McCarthy, the first to turn informer in Cork after the Rising, left with his body guards, such 'Amazonians' ambushed his carriage until restrained at gunpoint by the police. Subsequently, they assembled at his family home and assaulted his mother. A few females worked alongside the men as armourers: Catherine Tracy was brought up for remand for making 300 pikes and pike staves in Tracy's workshop in Dublin. In Tipperary, Peggy Lonergan of Moanure, a blacksmith, made pikes for the Lisronagh Fenians. Kate Devoy, a sister of John, and numerous others informally aided their detained relatives.[73]

Americans could join the Fenian Sisterhood, which had been established in 1864. The energetic Ellen O'Mahony, a high school principal in Quincy, Illinois, was appointed as 'head directress' by the leader of the Brotherhood and paid $1500 p.a. One of the earliest political organizations for women, the Sisterhood met with opposition from the Catholic hierarchy.[74] Bishop Timon of Buffalo, New York, for example, deplored the sisters as worse than the men and feared politics would corrupt them, 'should the women unsex themselves in meeting to speak with their Fenian brothers of politics, war, and blood, a sad change will soon be seen in the greatly famed purity of Irish women'.[75]

The constitution of the Fenian Sisterhood decreed that membership was restricted to 'ladies' of Irish birth or descent: 'I solemnly pledge my sacred word of honour that I become a member of this organization actuated by patriotic and honest motives, that I will faithfully fulfil my duties of membership, that I will foster and extend feelings of intense and intelligent love of country amongst Irishmen and women.'[76] They operated under male control, held bi-monthly meetings, collecting initiation fees of fifty cents and monthly dues of twenty-five cents per member. Those absent from four meetings without valid reason were fined fifty cents. Each branch elected a directress, secretary and treasurer. Contributions were regularly forwarded to the 'head centre', to whom Ellen O'Mahony reported on progress.[77]

The Sisterhood arranged social events to boost morale and funds, for instance, a ball in St Louis, Missouri, at which William Tecumseh Sherman and Thomas Sweeny, celebrated generals of the Civil War, were guests of honour. In Quincy, Illinois, they sewed and crocheted items for the Fenian fair in Chicago. In December 1865 Ellen O'Mahony supported the Brotherhood's 'final call' by urging members to emulate Polish women, who had sold their jewels for the cause and wore national mourning. Besides buying Fenian bonds, 'each sister should consider herself a bond agent'. Ellen brought communal pressure to bear by announcing that lists of contributors and non-contributors would be compiled.[78] The *New York Times* denounced her as a 'humbug', who preyed on 'poor, honest, hard-working, affectionate Bridget', indicating that the sisters were mostly servants. It suggested police intervention, marvelling how far 'this outrageous' organization would venture in equipping an expedition to Britain, 'with which we are at peace'.[79]

A representative of the sisterhood, 'a lady-like person', rumoured to be Ellen O'Mahony, travelled to Liverpool and Dublin to liaise with the IRB in January 1866.[80] As an auxiliary, the Sisterhood mirrored the split among the men, although the majority supported Colonel O'Mahony. By March a Miss O'Shea presided over the female part of the Senate wing. On 6 May 1866, reminiscent of aristocratic patronesses, their Buffalo branch presented the 'Buffalo, 7th Regiment, Irish Army of Liberation' with a Fenian sunburst on a green silk flag, which would fly at Ridgeway and Fort Erie.[81] In New York, Ellen O'Mahony's section held a ball in a room decorated with a portrait of James Stephens. A novel feature was 'an ancient Fenian war dance. Five couples, attired in the national dress of the old time, took their places in the centre of the hall, and, brandishing daggers in their hands, began to dance a lively Irish jig around four persons in the centre, representing captives.'[82]

Although the audience applauded enthusiastically, the *Irish Times* denigrated this reimagining of Gaelic culture as bearing 'a singular resemblance to the war dances of our aborigines'. Shortly afterwards the Sisterhood became defunct, Ellen O'Mahony having resigned.[83] In her memoirs, she praised the late Henry Clarence McCarthy, who had built up the organization and felt that 'the men out west were rather disappointed with Stephens', wanting a leader 'with a big patriotic record' rather than a minor 1848 rebel. O'Mahony also failed to impress: 'The face was wanting in firmness ... His dress was very carelessly arranged, and not at all elegant. He rambled from stall to stall, taking a throw here, buying a trifle there, but appearing throughout to have a pre-occupied air.'[84] Efforts to relaunch the Sisterhood in 1868 by 'tastefully dressed, intelligent-looking young ladies', some of whom made speeches in support of John Savage, the new leader of the O'Mahony wing, soon petered out.[85]

Ellen O'Leary and the Ladies' Committee

Ellen O'Leary resumed her unofficial role as executive officer of the IRB when Stephens left for Paris in March 1866. Dublin Castle released Edward Duffy, who was very ill with tuberculosis. Stephens appointed Duffy his representative, but failed to provide funds. Miss O'Leary became indispensable in holding the IRB together. Duffy also met Mary, John and Ellen's half-sister, 'a sweet, good girl'. They fell in love at first sight and became engaged.[86]

Ellen O'Leary and Mary Jane Irwin of Clonakilty, who had become the third Mrs O'Donovan Rossa the previous year, began to convey both money and information between Paris and Dublin in late 1865. Mitchel, based in the French capital, oversaw the distribution of 310,594 francs from December 1865 to April 1866.[87] Assisting him were Captain Laurence O'Brien, William O'Donovan and Edmund O'Leary, Ellen's half-brother. She also guarded the reputation of her imprisoned brother. When a judge suggested that John had invented correspondence to boost the impression that the *Irish People* directed Fenianism in Ireland and Britain, Ellen riposted that her brother, known 'as a man of honour and a gentleman', would hardly stoop to deceiving the public.[88]

She was the first relative to publish an account of visiting Portland prison with her half-sister Mary and Letitia Luby to inform the Irish people 'how the state prisoners are treated'. Ellen conversed with her brother through a grating with a warder seated between them, feeling 'almost speechless with rage'.[89] A devout Catholic, she was indignant how slow the authorities were to arrange Mass for the Fenians. She referred to the 'moral' tortures endured by the political prisoners, who had to stand to attention for warders, whom they considered among '*the lowest in creation*'.[90] As the ladies had a long journey, their visit was extended. Ellen did not 'sigh or weep – it was not a sight for tears. Little wonder if, in the bitterness of our hearts, we cursed those knaves and fools in America who, when we had cheerfully given up those we loved to a felon's doom, fell to quarrelling with each other.'[91]

Catherine Mulcahy (courtesy NLI).

The arrest of the *Irish People* staff was accompanied by the detention of prominent local activists during the winter of 1865–6. On 17 February 1866 the Habeas Corpus Act was suspended, leading to the incarceration of hundreds of suspects. Given the social composition of the Fenian movement, the dependants of artisans and clerks were in danger of becoming destitute. Abandoning them would have led to the collapse of the IRB. The relatives of the leaders formed a Ladies' Committee in Dublin with Letitia Luby and Mary Jane O'Donovan Rossa as treasurer and secretary respectively, and Ellen and Mary O'Leary, Catherine Mulcahy, Isabel Casey Roantree and Maria and Kate Shaw, sisters without Fenian connections, as committee members.[92] They ran an advertising campaign in the *Irishman* from 1866–9, appealing to the Christian charity of all women, irrespective of politics, as any dependants were innocent victims. The committee insisted that the leaders were inspired by patriotism, indignantly denying

> that they ever meditated anything immoral or irreligious. Their principles and aspirations were noble and unselfish. Many of them sacrificed their prospects in life to work for freedom. Some may think them mistaken, but none can call them base. The newspapers that so vilely calumniate them do not believe their own utterances; neither does the crown prosecutor believe that the ravings of one man are the sentiments of a party.[93]

The Ladies' Committee supplied appetizing meals and visits for those awaiting trial. It paid for lawyers, while providing funds for dependants who had lost their breadwinner. From the beginning, support was almost exclusively working class and remained inadequate; a total of £825 had been subscribed by 23 June 1866. The ladies regretted that the Irish unlike the Polish middle class shunned patriotism, preferring to embrace all things English.[94]

The committee operated in a businesslike manner, acknowledging donations weekly in the *Irishman*. The Fenian Sisterhood of New York and Brooklyn was its greatest single contributor, having organized a special bazaar in April 1866 and provided £448 by June. Local committees were set up in Salford and Pendleton, Blackburn, Barnsley, Birmingham, Warrington, Oldham and Dundee. There were contributions from Graig, Co. Kilkenny, Mullinahone, Drogheda, Derry, Edinburgh and New South Wales.[95] Some donors gave their names, but bearing in mind the danger of displaying Fenian sympathies, many adopted pseudonyms. After March 1866 the ladies became disillusioned with Stephens, who showed little concern for his followers. The committee learned that a large sum had been collected at his final meeting in New York in October, but failed to reach Dublin. The women did not realize that Richard Pigott, whose financial difficulties led him to embezzle and inform, was siphoning off donations.[96]

In February 1867 the committee explained its rules: wives and mothers of prisoners, who had been employed as tradesmen or mechanics, were paid 6s. plus 2s. 6d. for the first child and 1s. 6d. for all subsequent ones per week; dependants of those, who had been in 'higher employment' received more. Until August 1866 when their private means ran out, Mrs Luby and Mrs O'Donovan Rossa acted as volunteers. They subsequently received £2 per week each, but whenever funds were insufficient payments were reduced to dependants and employees alike. On several occasions committee members were forced to advance money, which they could ill afford. By February 1867 the ladies were supporting eighty families, but subscriptions remained inadequate. During the winter any surplus was taken up by the need for warm clothing, while the release of detainees during 1866 meant financing their emigration. After the Rising, the imprisoned insurgents were aided. Mary Jane O'Donovan Rossa lobbied for funds on emigrating to the US, when the Senate wing of the Fenian Brotherhood sent £200 in September 1867, members having been requested to contribute one dollar each.[97]

High-profile figures contributed, including Fr Patrick Lavelle of Partry, Co. Mayo, John Mitchel, and Archbishop MacHale of Tuam. The last named had transmitted donations of £1000 in 1867 and £400 from the Antipodes the following year, but Cardinal Cullen disapproved.[98] Given the charitable aspect of this project, Dr Cullen's opposition appears almost obsessive. By 1868 some branches of the Ladies' Committee had ceased to function. A rival committee supporting the prisoners' dependants was active in Cork and appeals for individual Fenians competed for subscriptions.[99]

The London *Times*, rather patronizingly, described Irishwomen as fighting alongside the men with a stone in their stocking, but took the Ladies' Committee with its 'ingenious' prospectus seriously. When the authorities prohibited their fundraising bazaar and concert of 1866 in Dublin, the New York *Irish People* seized upon this as indicative of British fear, not just of Irishmen, but also their wives and mothers. Mrs Luby and Mrs O'Donovan Rossa became semi-public figures and Dublin Castle considered arresting them in February 1866. Lord Wodehouse blocked this 'ticklish' meddling with females, even when searched by 'polite' policemen.[100]

These women displayed considerable persistence in difficult circumstances. While controversy regarding the misappropriation of nationalist funds was common in nineteenth-century Ireland, the probity of the Ladies' Committee was never in doubt. They worked successfully for charitable and political purposes, distributing approximately £10,000 from 1865 to 1872 and may have been a model for the Ladies Land League. Unlike some early Chartists, the Fenian women made no public speeches, nor did they question the contemporary status of females, withdrawing into private life once their husbands were released.[101]

In May 1867 Mary Jane O'Donovan Rossa, secretary of the Ladies' Committee, who had only been allowed to visit her imprisoned husband twice, emigrated to America. A poet, she gave dramatic recitations to earn her living and generate publicity for the prisoners. At her debut in New York she was supported by Horace Greeley, the influential editor of the *New York Tribune*, Susan B. Anthony and Fenians like colonels Denis F. Burke, William Nagle and John W. Byron, as well as Stephen Joseph Meany and Charles G. Halpine, better known as the poet 'Miles O'Reilly'. The 'remarkably handsome' Mrs O'Donovan Rossa was stylishly dressed in black to signify mourning with emerald sash, ribbons and a green wreath in her hair. This impersonation of a sorrowful Erin successfully toured the US and Canada for fourteen months, aiding the prisoners' fund and providing a forum for the estranged factions to meet.[102]

Women who worked for Fenianism have left only fleeting traces and even their names remain mostly unknown, although Devoy acknowledged that they 'were the chief agents in keeping the organization alive in Ireland from the time that Stephens left for America in early 1866 until the Rising of March 5, 1867'.[103]

The International Working Men's Association

John Pope-Hennessy's letter regarding the Fenian prisoners in the *Pall Mall Gazette* attracted the attention of the central council of the International Working Men's Association, which petitioned the home secretary on 24 February 1866.[104] The IWMA requested that Sir George Grey receive a delegation of British workers to show 'the suffering Irish people' that English labourers were concerned for these prisoners. This, the earliest petition in the Home Office file, was signed by William Randall Cremer, the association's secretary, a carpenter who later became the driving force of the peace through arbitration movement.[105] The home secretary refused to receive them. The IWMA publicized this without comment, but decided to support the appeal of the Ladies' Committee through its paper, the *Workman's Advocate*.[106] The IWMA had close links with the Reform League, which campaigned for one man one vote and the secret ballot, then a revolutionary concept. Some of the 400 branches of the league in Britain could be galvanized to support the prisoners. When the franchise was broadened in 1868, however, many working-class voters turned conservative.

The leaders of the embryonic communist movement, Karl Marx and Friedrich Engels, took considerable interest in Irish affairs. Engels was influenced by his links with the Lancashire-Irish family of Mary Burns, a social radical, who introduced him to the 'Little Ireland' slums of Manchester. After her death, Engels took her sister Lydia ('Lizzie') as his common-law wife. Lizzie sheltered Fenians on the run and transmitted her revolutionary enthusiasm to the young Eleanor Marx.[107] Marx and Engels saw Irish-English tensions as part of a capitalist policy to split and dominate the working class, convinced that Irish independence would be a step in the right direction. English radicals were generally critical of Fenian methods, but justified them as the result of British 'injustice and misrule'.[108]

Sympathetic newspaper coverage was essential in keeping the issue of those incarcerated before the public. The demise of the *Irish People* had increased the readership of Pigott's *Irishman*, which became strongly pro-Fenian. It praised Charles Kickham as the author of popular ballads and proceeded to reprint his tales.[109] The Victorian press featured original poetry, an important propaganda weapon. In 'Evening Twilight on a Tipperary Hillside', the young John Locke celebrated Kickham's pastoral locale, at the same time commemorating his sister Anna, whose death, it was claimed, had been hastened by the shock of the poet's conviction:

> *And thou, sweet Anner, how canst thou dance*
> *And leap through the winding wold,*
> *When he who sang of thy sparkling stream*

Lies bound in the Saxon's hold?
Ah! How did they banish for long, long years
The hope and prop of a sister's heart
And the light of a brother's eyes?

Locke concluded by lauding Kickham's talent and patriotic devotion, combining motifs familiar from Moore's *Melodies* with the reality of suffering and sacrifice.[110]

Death in prison

In the nineteenth century, dying in prison was not uncommon. Victorians subscribed to the concept of a 'good death': the dying acted in an edifying manner, attended by a clergyman and family members. They demonstrated their faith and envisaged a grave visited by relatives, who would erect a monument, testifying to their worth. A 'bad death', on the other hand, was the destiny of people on the margins of society, who died far from home. Particular dread clung to the idea of capital punishment, for its victims were buried in quicklime in an unmarked grave – the final ignominy.[111]

Although the separatist ethos of the IRB had failed to triumph, its elite believed in the importance of bearing witness and a tradition of Christ-like sacrifice for an idealized Ireland emerged. Reporting the reburial of Daniele Manin in Venice, the *Irishman* related how he had endured 'the scant and bitter bread of exile' after the abortive uprising against the Austrian Empire in 1848, dying in 1857. It concluded that somebody once deemed a traitor could become a celebrated patriot: 'The martyrs of a cause are not seldom its evangels, they bring the good tidings of its coming triumph.' Nevertheless, the patriot's fate might be tragic before his vision was realized, like Lord Byron, who died before the liberation of Greece. These ideas appealed to IRB members, who saw themselves in the line of Republican succession.[112]

John McGeough was the first habeas corpus prisoner to die in Crumlin Road jail, Belfast, on 23 March 1866, followed by the death of treason-felony convict John Lynch on 2 June.[113] John Pope-Hennessy attempted to visit the dying man, but the Home Office held Lynch incommunicado. A rigid interpretation of the prison rules also barred his fiancée, who had promised to bury him in Cork. Brian Dillon, on becoming a patient in the infirmary, alerted the governor to this last wish of his friend, but the home secretary objected and Lynch became the 'forgotten Fenian' in the paupers' plot of Brookwood Cemetery, Surrey. The movement was badly disrupted during the summer of 1866 and an appeal to rebury him evoked little response.[114]

Relatives blamed the death of John Fottrell, a former habeas corpus prisoner, on 1 November on ill treatment in Mountjoy. On 23 December William Meagher, the Carrick-on-Suir 'centre', who had been detained for eleven months, died in the same prison, apparently of 'Asiatic cholera'. The demise of Daniel Kane, also of Carrick, was attributed to his sufferings in Kilmainham. The prison governor failed to inform Meagher's family of his death for a fortnight. He and Kane were only saved from the paupers' plot by the intervention of an unnamed young lady, who successfully remonstrated with the authorities and 'followed the remains from the prison to Glasnevin and remained there during the interment'.[115]

These suspects were kept in greater isolation than convicts. The penal authorities succeeded in covering up a 'terrible state of things within the prison', of which both the public and the chief secretary remained in ignorance until the medical officer began to leak details to the press, culminating in questions in Parliament. One hundred and forty Fenians were detained in an overcrowded Mountjoy Prison, where four deaths occurred. Dr Robert McDonnell considered it unprecedented that thirteen untried political prisoners had endured solitary confinement for eight months and more, while their health continued to deteriorate.[116]

Such deaths failed to capture the popular imagination. Activists prioritized plans for an insurrection, but there were manifestations of sympathy, notably at the funeral of Captain John Delahunt, whose family had emigrated from Fethard after the Famine. In 1861 he had joined the Fenian Brotherhood in Milwaukee and enrolled in the 17th Wisconsin Regiment.[117] Seriously ill with tuberculosis, he returned for the Rising, accompanied by Colonel Thomas Francis Bourke and Captain Laurence O'Brien. On his deathbed, Delahunt was cared for by John and Patrick Kenrick, the leading conspirators in Fethard, who also maintained contact with Colonel Bourke in hiding. When Captain Delahunt died on 1 March 1867 without relatives, he was honoured by the largest funeral procession Fethard had seen in fifty years.[118]

CHAPTER 9

'Suffering in a great and noble cause', 1867–75

'The consciousness of suffering in a great and noble cause – the same cause for which Tone worked and Emmet could but die – will console all true Irishmen in the hour of trial.'[1]

John Lynch to his fiancée Bridget Noonan, c. 1865

Although the insurrection, the climax of Fenian preparations since 1858, had failed, William Mackey Lomasney and other leaders justified it from the dock by asserting Ireland's right to independence:

England will most miserably fail if she expects by force and oppression to crush out – to stamp out, as the *Times* exclaimed – this glorious longing for national life and independence ... I know in my soul that the motives which prompted me were pure, patriotic, and unselfish. I know the motives that actuate the most active members of the Fenian organization; and I know that very few persons, except such contemptible wretches as Corydon, have profited by their connection with Fenianism. My best friends lost all they ever possessed by it.[2]

The collapse of the Rising reassured those who had feared that its success might herald the return of Famine exiles, clamouring for a redistribution of property. It became feasible to show compassion for the imprisoned, portrayed as misguided and suffering idealists. They captured the imagination of the Catholic public and inspired an effective amnesty campaign from 1868 onwards. Short-sighted decisions by the British authorities, in particular the execution of the Manchester Martyrs, fuelled anti-English sentiment and increased IRB support.

In April 1867 a report from Dr McDonnell of Mountjoy to the inspector of convict prisons in Ireland was leaked to the press. It highlighted the deterioration of the untried political detainees, many of whom had been reduced to 'sickly and emaciated invalids' due to the harsh conditions.[3] On 16 May Richard Joseph Stowell died, nine hours after his discharge from Naas jail. In poor health, Stowell had been convicted of a minor offence, but bureaucratic red tape delayed his release.[4] His death became a turning point and sympathy for the victims of British injustice manifested itself when 1000 men followed his coffin: 'The concourse of mourners at his funeral was so large as to be a demonstration.'[5] Virtually unknown when alive, Stowell's 'name was enrolled on [sic] the political martyrology of Ireland'. Subscriptions led to the erection of a Celtic cross in Glasnevin for his first anniversary.[6]

The Conservative minority government with Lord Derby as prime minister and Gathorne-Hardy as home secretary responded with a commission of inquiry into prison conditions. The habeas corpus detainees remained outside its remit, however. The inquiry was conducted by Alexander Knox and George Pollock – hardly an impartial choice, for both were embedded in the British establishment, the former as a stipendiary magistrate and the latter as a surgeon from a military and judicial background. Fenian complaints included inadequate and disgusting food, being accommodated in dark cells, which stank from their proximity to the latrines, frequent strip-searching and neglect of medical concerns. The IRB men considered themselves not only deprived of the privileges of political prisoners, but treated worse than criminals.[7]

Charles Kickham had been transferred from Portland to Woking Invalid Prison in July 1866, as his disabilities rendered him unsuitable for work in the Dorset quarries. He suffered from scrofulous, oozing sores, a form of tuberculosis. In Woking he missed the comradeship of the Fenian elite and objected bitterly to the regular strip-searches, which meant waiting naked for an indefinite period in a cold cell with outstretched arms and open mouth. This security measure also served to humiliate.[8] Despite his determination to endure 'unflinchingly all that man can inflict upon me', Kickham broke down on at least one occasion and 'burst into tears'.[9] A Victorian gentleman, he abhorred the moral degradation of having to associate with criminals.[10]

Knox and Pollock interviewed Kickham on 14 May 1867 and rejected his charges, suggesting that he had endured worse scrofula sores as a free man. They claimed he was benefiting from imprisonment in salubrious Surrey, healthier than any London charity hospital. This was spurious, as none of the Fenian leaders belonged to the working class, which patronized such institutions. Knox and Pollock conceded that the writer had been made to associate with two criminals, 'carefully selected by the governor as the most harmless and inoffensive old men' available. The commissioners concluded that he 'had nothing to complain of beyond the fact of his being a convict'.[11]

Charles Kickham in prison uniform, 1866
(courtesy Sheila Foley, Mullinahone).

The sudden death of John Lynch of Cork on 2 June 1866 had evoked little public response, but loyal comrades continued to highlight his fate. Knox and Pollock stressed that Lynch, although apparently healthy on admission to Pentonville, had been spitting blood during the 1860s. The medical officer in Woking believed that men afflicted with tuberculosis rarely survived imprisonment.[12]

In Seán McConville's memorable phrase, O'Donovan Rossa transformed his imprisonment into a 'theatre of war', resisting British rule by defying the prison regulations.[13] Frequently sentenced to bread and water, Rossa recalled: 'I kept myself a free man in prison; while they had my body bound in chains, I felt that I owed them no allegiance, that I held my mind unfettered – that I was *not* their slave.'[14] Governor Clifton enforced a tomb-like silence in the punishment cells, but a manacled Rossa protested by imitating the dances of his youth in West Cork. He composed 'Jillen Andy', a poem describing the Famine burial of Julia ('Jillen') Hayes of Chapel Lane, Rosscarbery, which he linked to his own sufferings, shared by thousands of Irish people:[15]

How oft in dreams that burial scene appears,
Through deaths, evictions, prison, exile, home;
Through all the suns and moons of twenty years.
And oh! how short these years, compared with ones to come.

Rossa believed that Fenian endurance would succeed, but Knox and Pollock characterized him as 'thoroughly unmanageable' and apt to misapply his talents. Squirrelling away scraps of paper and hiding ink bottles by hanging them outside his cell window, Rossa communicated with the press, having concocted, according to the commissioners, 'a letter stuffed full of the most absurd and unfounded accusations against everybody, and contrived, no one knows how, to convey it to another convict who was about to be removed. The letter was to be dropped on the railway, and was addressed to the editors of any of three or four papers. It contained this story of his wrongs, and was to set the country in a blaze.'[16]

Had Rossa been an ordinary convict, the commissioners argued, he would have been flogged for 'open defiance'.[17] This was certain to create sympathy among the Irish diaspora and could unite constitutional and physical force nationalists. Given his bad example, he had been transferred from Portland to Millbank for a second period of solitary confinement instead and since then 'comparative peace has reigned at Portland'.[18] The commissioners rejected any charges against the administration and pitied the prison governor of Portland, for the Fenians had 'caused him more trouble and anxiety than all the other convicts put together'.[19] Their report of June 1867 concluded that the newspaper stories had been contrived by the more aggrieved prisoners, for 'penal servitude, we repeat it, is a terrible punishment; it is intended to be so, and so it is. The convict authorities, however, must do their duty to all alike. The only true cause of complaint the treason-felony convicts have against them is that they can't get out.'[20] Knox and Pollock had 'been strongly impressed ... with the admirable arrangements of our convict establishments', which Irish nationalists rejected as a whitewash. Thomas Duggan, an imprisoned Fenian and former teacher, commented that the commissioners couldn't have compiled 'a more favourable report', if the warders had been invited to join them. Duggan longed for Charles Dickens to depict 'the annoyances and cruelties perpetrated' in prisons.[21]

The *Irishman* reported Lord Mayo's statement in the House of Commons, that the mental deterioration of two of the habeas corpus detainees in Mountjoy required admission to a lunatic asylum. Dr McDonnell and the Catholic prison chaplain had protested in vain that some men became insane through prolonged solitary confinement.[22] On 9 September William Harbinson, the 'centre' for the Belfast district, was found dead in his cell in Crumlin Road jail, Belfast, apparently of heart disease.[23] Twelve thousand participated in his funeral procession, as 'the deceased was regarded as a martyr to the Fenian cause'. The following month John Kelly died from the rigours of incarceration in Limerick. It was claimed that 10,000 people attended his obsequies.[24]

The Manchester Rescue

Romantic nationalism re-interpreted a series of disastrous events as vignettes of heroic defiance in the chain of apostolic succession. Kickham regarded the continuance of the IRB, despite its failure in the field, as evidence of 'the warm and generous nature of a people, who reject with loathing the cold hearted suggestion that honour should be only accorded to the successful and the victorious'.[25]

After the *Erin's Hope* arrests, Colonel Kelly had become persona non grata for the remaining activists in Dublin. Exiled IRB 'centres' in New York, including J.J. Geary of Cork and James Cooke and Maurice O'Donoghue of Dublin, endorsed President Roberts. His emissaries arranged the election of IRB representatives supporting the Senate wing in London and Ireland. Kelly and O'Sullivan Burke, struggling to revive the London IRB, were violently opposed by James J. O'Kelly, now allied to Roberts. The latter travelled to Paris, but gained only partial control over the home organization at his conference in July. He planned renewed outbreaks in Ireland and Canada, unaware that Rudolph Fitzpatrick kept the British informed.[26]

A courier from the former O'Mahony wing became suspicious on reaching Southampton and opened a despatch for Colonel Kelly, instructing him to destroy 'a few yards of railroad' occasionally to keep up the excitement, 'no matter at what risk' to ensure the flow of Irish-American donations. On return to New York, the messenger joined the Roberts (formerly the Senate) wing, which publicized this on both sides of the Atlantic.[27]

On 18 August Kelly held his IRB convention in Manchester, attended by fifty-eight delegates and not the 'three hundred ... from Ireland, Scotland, Wales and England', claimed years later by O'Sullivan Burke. Kelly remained chief executive, with Captain James Murphy commanding in Scotland, Captain William Mackey Lomasney in Munster and Edmond O'Donovan in Ulster. Captain Edward O'Meagher Condon, a native of Mitchelstown, took charge in Manchester and Captain Timothy Deasy in Liverpool. O'Sullivan Burke, an experienced gun runner, would be generally responsible for England. They based themselves in Britain, where the Habeas Corpus Act precluded arbitrary arrests, but with the 'circles' disrupted, the collapse of the IRB seemed probable.[28]

The convention denounced Roberts's attempt at a takeover in Ireland and Britain. It opted for a 'military' provisional government with Kelly as 'chief executive of the Republic'. Lawrence Farley, envoy of the Fenian Brotherhood, conveyed these resolutions to John Savage, its new chief executive. To add to the confusion, IRB members, on whose behalf John O'Connor Power was negotiating in New York with both wings in late 1867, decried both the Manchester and the Paris conferences as unrepresentative. He maintained that from May 1867 until the first Supreme Council elections in January 1868, the IRB lacked a 'legally constituted governing body'.[29]

On 11 September, the authorities scored a major success by arresting Kelly and Timothy Deasy under the vagrancy act in Manchester. Local members decided on a rescue, led by O'Meagher Condon, who had planned to free Canadian Fenians arrested near Campobello in 1866. He requested assistance from O'Sullivan Burke in London. William Hogan, a businessman and IRB leader in Birmingham, and Daniel Darragh alias William Pherson Thompson, formerly a school teacher in Ballycastle, Co. Antrim, purchased forty revolvers.[30]

O'Sullivan Burke supervised operations on 18 September, when a party of approximately forty Irishmen held up the prison van with Kelly and Deasy on their way from court to Belle Vue Prison. Bungling officials ignored telegrams, which warned them to tighten security. Brandishing their revolvers, the Fenians attacked, while the unarmed police escort fled. But the rescuers were hampered, as Sergeant Charles Brett, travelling inside the vehicle, refused to hand over his keys to unlock it. During frenzied attempts to open the van before police reinforcements arrived, a shot was fired, which killed the policeman. Deasy and Kelly escaped, but sixty Irishmen were arrested, including Michael O'Brien of Ballymacoda, William Philip Allen of Bandon, Michael Larkin of Lusmagh, Co. Offaly, Edward O'Meagher Condon and Thomas Maguire, a marine. Amidst English panic, members of the Irish community were roughly handled. In Co. Cork, however, the rescue was celebrated with bonfires.[31]

The trial of the rescuers was conducted in an oppressive manner and Ernest Jones, veteran Chartist and barrister, returned his brief in protest. All five accused were convicted of the murder of Sergeant Brett, for by the law of association, anyone involved in a killing was considered guilty. O'Meagher Condon concluded his speech from the dock with the phrase 'God save Ireland', the rallying cry of nationalists until 1916. Appeals for mercy by Charles Bradlaugh, John Stuart Mill, John Bright and George Odger failed. The courageous defiance of the accused in hostile surroundings won the admiration of Irish people all over the world, while the press corps drew attention to the dubious quality of the evidence, particularly in the case of Thomas Maguire, who was pardoned.[32]

In the dock William Philip Allen declared that he had neither killed Sergeant Brett nor received a fair trial. He begged pardon for all his sins and admitted participating in the rescue. Explaining that his generation was marked by Famine suffering and exile, Allen concluded: 'It is well known to the whole world what my poor country has to suffer and how her sons are exiles the world over; then tell me where is the Irishman who could look unmoved and see his countrymen taken prisoner and treated like murderers and robbers in British dungeons? May the Lord have mercy on our souls and deliver Ireland from her sufferings!'[33] Michael Larkin, too, denied having fired a weapon. Michael O'Brien, who had covered the retreat of the rescue party, questioned the probity of the prosecution witnesses, stating he had not shot anybody. In a last letter to his brother in Ballymacoda, O'Brien associated himself with the death of their neighbour, Peter O'Neill Crowley, and the martyrdom of the Irish people:

> I must say, though much I like to live, I cannot regret dying in the cause of liberty and Ireland. It has been made more dear to me by the sufferings of its people – by the martyrdom and exile of its best and noblest sons – the saint, the bishop, the priest, the scholar, and the soldier have suffered and died proudly, nobly, and why should I shrink from death, in a cause made holy and glorious by the numbers of its martyrs and the heroism of its supporters as well as by its justice.[34]

O'Brien was motivated by 'centuries of misery' under British rule, placing himself in line with Tone, Emmet, Bellew McManus and Mitchel. He predicted that his execution would encourage his countrymen during 'the inevitable struggle'. This fusion of Christian and patriotic precepts appealed to an Irish public, shocked by rumours of atheism among the IRB in 1865.[35] O'Brien pleaded for unity, but the rift in the transatlantic movement remained so bitter that the *Irish-American* and the *Nation* publicized that Colonel Kelly was not popular with his followers, could barely raise contributions and had made little progress organizing. Kelly had been threatened and apparently resigned in Dublin, where the IRB did not want him. He was advised to return to America and retire.[36]

The US government instructed its minister in Britain to intervene on behalf of O'Meagher Condon and O'Brien as naturalized citizens. Charles Francis Adams, the Anglophile son and grandson of former presidents, interceding solely for O'Meagher Condon, whose sentence was commuted to penal servitude for life. Adams had warned O'Brien, whom he assisted as a suspected gun runner in 1866, that no further help would be forthcoming. After the Canadian and Irish outbreaks the British had been careful to commute capital sentences to avoid creating martyrs, although this only happened after intercessions by both archbishops of Dublin and fifty-nine parliamentarians in the case of Thomas Francis Bourke. In Washington Secretary of State Seward told Sir Frederick

Bruce that Bourke's speech from the dock 'had produced considerable excitement' and the president would have to take 'some action', given the importance of the Irish vote.[37]

Col Thomas Francis Bourke
(courtesy NLI).

But Manchester highlighted the threat of armed Irish-American 'rowdies' in Britain, succoured by their ethnic communities. Panic erased any liberal reluctance and the executions went ahead on 23 November. Lord Kimberley approved of the government's 'firmness', regretting the 'enormous error' of not having hanged Thomas Francis Bourke and the Fenians in Canada to deter their followers. Hitherto, the British, although not loved by the Irish people, had kept 'some sort of order' through fear. They could neither jeopardize the safety of Northern Protestants nor the security of the British state by allowing an independent republic to spring up next door:[38]

> To give up Ireland is in my mind utterly out of the question. It would be base and wicked to abandon the Northern Irish and the other Protestants & to leave the island a prey to civil war … Moreover an independent Ireland would be hostile to us in time of war. We should be compelled to reconquer the island. We must keep our hold on her, cost what it may, and the cost will be, as it has ever been, heavy.[39]

Irish communities expressed revulsion at the vindictiveness of the executions. The *Irishman* appeared with mourning borders, warning that England had committed 'a deed of blood' likely to 'overshadow its name before the whole world'. Allen, Larkin and O'Brien joined the Republican pantheon as the 'Manchester Martyrs'.[40] Using O'Meagher Condon's slogan 'God save

Ireland', T.D. Sullivan composed a rousing ballad, which remained the unofficial national anthem until 1916. Holding the trial in the hostile environment of Manchester rather than transferring it elsewhere constituted a misjudgment, which impacted on Anglo-Irish relations into the twentieth century. Repatriation of their remains, averting an ignoble interment in quicklime, was also refused.

Focusing attention on the courage of its members, the executions gained the faltering Fenian movement thousands of sympathizers. Dr Sigerson predicted, 'in death they will be more powerful than in life', which could 'have been averted by a humane policy'.[41] The executions united Ireland's Catholic population and erased distinctions between 'Fenian and anti-Fenian journals' in their shared grief and indignation. The English press was, however, 'astonished that anybody should look upon the men hanged otherwise than as common murderers', deepening the gulf between the two nations.[42]

In New York the *Irish People* declared the arrest of Kelly and Deasy illegal, which justified their rescue, while considering the tragic killing of Sergeant Brett an 'act of war'. Kelly threatened in the radical press that, unless those Fenians arrested were treated as 'prisoners of war', government ministers might become the targets of 'deplorable' reprisals. He disclaimed any ill feeling towards the British working class, but his English branch of Fenianism, headquartered near Buckingham Palace, might attack 'the vast commerce' of London, Liverpool or Manchester. This would create economic chaos and could end in revolution. In reality Kelly lacked the necessary resources, but such pronouncements, coupled with his continuing freedom, caused alarm.[43]

There had been a previous outburst in the *Irish People*, claiming that 'desperate acts in a desperate (and just cause)' might be necessary for national survival. Using Lord Strathnairn's brutal suppression of the Indian mutiny as justification of how to deal with the British Empire, the writer suggested a repetition of the historic burning of Moscow in 1812 for 'London, the Sodom and Gomorrah of the sinful world'. These arguments foreshadowed O'Donovan Rossa's dynamite propaganda from 1874.[44]

Colonel Kelly kept up psychological pressure through letters, which circulated in the transatlantic press. An IRB officer wrote that the chief executive remained in London 'and will not run from his post', despite a major manhunt. Kelly appealed to John Savage, newly elected president of the former O'Mahony wing, to develop a secure line of communication, concluding, 'our sacrifices are nothing compared with the objects in view'. He agreed with the *Irish People* that Britain's often misguided policies and even economic progress in Ireland were irrelevant, as long as the Fenian spirit persisted. They would only settle for 'complete independence'. Colonel Kelly was to remain in England until April 1868.[45]

THE ILLUSTRATED LONDON NEWS.

REGISTERED AT THE GENERAL POST-OFFICE FOR TRANSMISSION ABROAD.

No. 1454.—VOL. LI.   SATURDAY, NOVEMBER 9, 1867.   WITH A SUPPLEMENT, FIVEPENCE

MR. LOWE ON UNIVERSITY EDUCATION.

ANY thoughts on education which Mr. Lowe deems it worth his while to submit to the public it will be sure to receive with profound respect; but when, as in his address to the Edinburgh Philosophical Institution, the right hon. gentleman enters on a discussion of that question in its relation to the national Universities, one hardly knows whether the pre-eminent qualification of the speaker or the importance of the subject presents to cultivated minds the more powerful attraction. Certain it is, however, that neither the one nor the other will suffer in the reader's estimation from a careful study of Mr. Lowe's recent speech.

THE FENIAN TRIALS AT MANCHESTER: THE PRISONERS LEAVING THE NEW BAILEY FOR THE ASSIZE COURT.—SEE PAGE 517.

*The Manchester Martyrs leaving Salford jail (*Illustrated London News*).*

He took George Jacob Holyoake, the secularist, to task for having pronounced him a 'perfect political vacuity', exclaiming 'what I may lack in statesmanship I hope to make up in persistence'. Holyoake suspected that Fenianism was not friendly towards England or electoral reform. Kelly responded that latent Fenian support for the Reform League demonstrations had saved them from suppression like the Chartists. His section of the Fenian Brotherhood was aligned to the IRB in England and the English democracy: '[We] now confine our hostility to the few thousand aristocratic vampires, and their minions, who live in luxury and debauchery on the sweat of millions of producers, English as well as Irish ...'[46]

Manchester Martyrs processions

In Manchester, two processions of 5000 and 1500 people honoured the men the day after their execution in spontaneous manifestations of 'indignation and anger'. A third, 'much larger and more carefully prepared' demonstration took place a week later, which also happened in Cork city and Bandon.[47] Although Allen may have been a native of Tipperary town, he grew up in Bandon, where, despite its Orange affiliations, large crowds walked 'in inclement wintry conditions, bearing a coffin symbolising that of William Philip Allen. It halted for prayers outside the Bridewell, where Allen's family lived and again outside the convent, where the nuns turned out to pray for the souls of Allen, Larkin and O'Brien. The coffin was then interred in the grave of Allen's young sister.'[48]

An impressive mock funeral was held in Dublin, where John Martin addressed those assembled outside Glasnevin Cemetery, before the procession visited the tomb of McManus. A.M. Sullivan, an advocate of constitutional means, responding to demand, radicalized his *Weekly News*, which greatly outsold the rival *Irishman* in south Kilkenny, for instance. In February 1868 Sullivan and Pigott were sentenced to six and twelve months in prison for seditious libel relating to the Manchester executions, but Lord Mayo ameliorated conditions to prevent claims of martyrdom, given the freedom of the press in a liberal state. The Sullivan brothers continued to profit from sales of their bestselling *Speeches from the Dock*. Kept informed by Larcom, Lord Kimberley misjudged the public mood to describe A.M. Sullivan and Sir John Gray, MP, proprietor of the *Freeman's Journal*, as 'wretched agitators'. Kimberley disbelieved in a speedy 'remedy for Irish calamities', but urged abolition of the unjustifiable established church to deprive separatists of support.[49]

British army reinforcements were sent to Cork, where immense crowds assembled. Fifteen hundred men in military formation and 1400 girls, wearing green, accompanied temperance bands playing funeral music. The attendance wore green and black ribbons, the Fenian colours. A week later a similar event took place in Midleton. Observers noticed 400 well-dressed young women, and not just poor people, among the throng. Irishwomen at home and abroad embraced such opportunities to declare their political views, reminiscent of female participation in early Chartism.[50]

The families of Michael O'Brien and Peter O'Neill Crowley lent their support. Further demonstrations occurred in Kanturk and Skibbereen.[51] In Mitchelstown shopkeepers and farmers participated. At the Requiem Mass in Youghal, an empty coffin draped in black took centre stage in the church and the congregation wept openly.[52]

Although the initial impetus in Cork and Limerick came from the trades' guilds, these demonstrations were managed by a small cadre of Fenians. Oliver Moriarty, R.M., recorded that many of the 12,000 participants belonged to 'a better class than I was prepared to see taking part'. The event culminated with fervent prayers and an impromptu address by the charismatic Fr Patrick Quaid, parish priest of O'Callaghan's Mills, Co. Clare, in Mount St Lawrence Cemetery, Limerick.[53]

When Bishop Moriarty prohibited priests in his diocese from saying Mass for the Manchester Martyrs, although he believed that their conduct had been 'Christ-like', the *Times* lauded, but the *Nation* condemned him for praying for them privately. A committee of IRB sympathizers was planning a Manchester Martyrs procession for Killarney with Daniel O'Donoghue, MP, giving the oration in ancient Aghadoe Cemetery. As local magistrates feared a revival of Fenianism, Dublin Castle prohibited it, sending troops and police to Killarney. Lord Castlerosse pressurized the O'Donoghue to avoid a collision. He was reminded of how Daniel O'Connell, his grand-uncle, abandoned the mass meeting at Clontarf in similar circumstances and withdrew from 'his Fenian friends', aborting their plans.[54]

Kerry folklore records that a child answered 'Allen, Larkin and O'Brien', when Bishop Moriarty asked confirmation candidates, 'who were the martyrs?' During the summer of 1868 a placard with the inscription 'pray for your martyred countrymen' was displayed during the traditional pilgrimage to Mount Brandon near Dingle, whenever Dr Moriarty, who led 6000 people, was out of sight.[55]

The Clerkenwell explosion

The executions of the Manchester martyrs galvanized radical support in Britain, where Marx believed that 'Fenianism has entered a new phase ... baptised in blood by the English government'; but any advantage was swiftly dissipated. On 27 November Colonel O'Sullivan Burke and Joseph Theobald Casey were arrested in London. O'Sullivan Burke, a former military engineer, arranged to be 'sprung' from the Clerkenwell House of Detention, but fatally miscalculated the quantity of gunpowder for blowing up the prison wall. The explosion killed twelve working-class people and injured a hundred more on 13 December. Dublin Castle knew of the plot through an informer and had alerted the London Metropolitan Police, whose reaction was inadequate and muddled.[56]

The *Times* warned that 'these public enemies' apparently contemplated 'terror throughout the United Kingdom', which cancelled any further 'clemency and forbearance' for the Fenian conspiracy.[57] The *Irish Times* traced the roots of the Clerkenwell outrage to the American Civil War: 'The barbarous character which Fenianism has assumed in England is of foreign importation, and the discovery that there are living in the world of London, moving about in the darkness, men, who ... could plan a deed such as that at Clerkenwell has created indescribable alarm.'[58]

The conservative press feared that American desperadoes had utilized desperate men of the British underclass for recent, large Reform League demonstrations in London, which threatened the status quo. The *Irish People* agreed that English criminals might imitate Fenian methods. Irish communities, deeply suspected, hastily repudiated the separatist minority and protested loyalty to Queen Victoria. Amidst universal condemnation, the London committee of the pro-Roberts IRB denounced the Clerkenwell 'atrocity'. This wing concluded, however, that 'the explosion was the work of very few and very ignorant persons', intending a prison rescue rather than a terror campaign. The deaths 'were purely accidental and entirely undesigned'. While Charles Bradlaugh, campaigning for the Reform League, had pointed to unjust land laws and mass emigration as motivating the Manchester martyrs during his lecture in nearby Stalybridge on the day of their executions, the governing body of the league now distanced itself from Colonel Kelly.[59]

Friedrich Engels and Karl Marx considered 'this last escapade' very stupid. Londoners sympathetic to Ireland would hardly 'allow themselves to be blown up' for the Fenian agents, warning that 'such secret, melodramatic, and conspiratorial methods generally end in failure'.[60] Responding to the Clerkenwell explosion, Colonel Kelly restrained his 'resentment', pointing to 'the horrible outrage perpetrated against the whole Irish race by the Manchester executions', as well as the affront to democracy. He accused the authorities of exacerbating ethno-sectarian tensions on the *divide et impera* principle and believed them capable of burning a few houses in populous districts to increase anti-Irish feeling. Nevertheless, the IRB should act only in self-defence.[61]

The *Irish People* in New York, representing Colonel Kelly and the Savage (formerly O'Mahony) wing, argued that there was no justice for political prisoners in England, which legitimized any jailbreak. Having failed to absorb the Irish, Britain plotted their *'extermination'*. It was opposed by Fenianism, dedicated to save 'Ireland or to ruin the British empire'. Given this desperate struggle against 'the gigantic might and malignity of England', moral constraints could be abandoned.[62] The paper vowed to rescue 'all prisoners', execute informers and seize 'arms and ammunition' when practicable. Rather than questioning Fenian methods after the recent fatalities and recall an earlier, idealistic motivation, it threatened, 'we shall not handle them with kid gloves on, and that every successive stroke which we shall henceforth deliver will be more "violent" than the last. We are strong in the consciousness of the lawfulness of our means, as well as the holiness of our end. We shall not be diverted from our purpose by the casuistic tirades of aristocratic journals, nor by the hangman's rope.'[63]

Other voices within the Savage wing, which portrayed itself as the Irish government in exile, urged a settlement, consisting of a local Irish Parliament with representatives in the Imperial one. Foreshadowing the Home Rule issue, the press pointed to the Austrian Empire, which had resolved long-running conflict by granting Hungary partial self-government.[64] Should this compromise be rejected, the Brotherhood would continue its crusade, culminating in 'the complete disruption of the United Kingdom, involving – as it surely must do – the destruction of the British empire'.[65]

The *Irish People* accused Britain of hypocrisy, recalling how it had greeted the torpedo disasters of the Civil War 'with infinite gusto' and had proclaimed that people struggling for independence 'cannot be over nice'. A French citizen in Dublin wrote to the *Nation*, recalling how Felice Orsini had plotted to assassinate Napoleon III in Paris, helped by Englishmen, and was excused by the British press.[66]

Orsini's escape from an Austrian dungeon had been celebrated in Britain, where he found asylum, before attempting to assassinate Napoleon III in 1858 with bombs, which killed eight people and injured 156. An accomplice was tried and acquitted in London. The *Irish People* appeared unaware that Thomas Allsop, a former supporter of Feargus O'Connor, had ordered Orsini's bombs in Birmingham. Years later George Jacob Holyoake revealed how he had transported this live ordnance on a train for testing. He, as well as Mazzini, considered such weapons justified against a tyrant. Allsop escaped prosecution by fleeing to New York, communicating with his wife through Michael Doheny. But in 1867 Holyoake condemned what he perceived as murder and assassination in liberal England.[67]

Throughout 1868–9 the *Irish People* propagandized that Fenianism had gained from the Manchester and Clerkenwell events, as well as Captain Mackey's guerrilla exploits, which forced an anxious Britain to maintain expensive security measures. The movement, supported by 'the Irish nation in America' sought to restore 'Ireland to the Irish' and reverse emigration, portrayed in Mitchelite terms as the systematic 'eradication of our race'.[68]

Influential British voices warned that 'if Fenianism is not uprooted Fenianism will uproot the government'. The *Times* counselled against further coercion. The *Chronicle* feared that Irish people no longer believed in vague promises of redress at some future date; this needed to be addressed. Archbishop Manning of Westminster published a letter to Earl Grey, a proponent of Irish reform, to counteract the threat to the Union. A cessation of the 'cynical, sarcastic disdain' of the press towards the Ireland should precede equality of the churches and equitable land laws. Recent separatist violence was not just 'the folly of a few apprentices and shop boys', but sustained by the 'just discontent of almost a whole people', whose American relatives had experienced democracy. Dr Manning underlined the social control exercised by Catholicism to Gladstone, who tried to obtain support for reform.[69]

Wrangling between the transatlantic Fenian branches continued. Meanwhile, the attempted assassination of a younger son of Queen Victoria by an unbalanced Irishman in Sydney and the killing of Thomas D'Arcy McGee in Ottawa by a Fenian sympathizer increased public alarm.[70]

Temporary Secret Service Department

Lord Mayo had lobbied to intensify surveillance of subversives in Britain since becoming chief secretary in July 1866, but was stymied by Sir Richard Mayne, the elderly commissioner of the London Metropolitan Police. Colonel Feilding, tasked to ferret out Fenian infiltrators in the British army, had covertly transferred his spies to England since 1865 and organized the infiltration of the IRB in Liverpool and London. Detectives now scrutinized Irish communities in Manchester, Glasgow and Liverpool.[71]

Home Secretary Gathorne-Hardy was horrified how police incompetence had facilitated the Manchester rescue. He dreaded public unrest from trade union outrages in Sheffield, the Reform League's occasional defiance of government and a potential alliance between old Chartists, English radicals and Fenians. The IRB was gun-running from Birmingham and there were rumours that subversives would seize arms from volunteer regiments. After the Clerkenwell explosion, an 'attempt to blow up Millbank Prison' was feared and its warders armed. Sappers and police searched the sewers beneath Buckingham Palace, Somerset House and the prisons, in case the Fenians utilized them. The Home Office planned emergency lamps, should they sabotage the gas lighting, unaware that Colonel Kelly's supporters could barely organize the Clerkenwell attempt.[72]

In Ireland, unrest continued. Packages of liquid phosphorous ignited in a Dublin letter box, followed by Mackey Lomasney's raids for weapons and gunpowder. As in 1866, there were rumours of activism and night-time drilling at Vinegar Hill. From the Tipperary/east Limerick region resident magistrate De Gernon reported the continuing hostility of the populace, which hoped for an Anglo-American war and talked of attacking police barracks with Fenian fire.[73]

Lord Mayo and Prime Minister Derby happened to set up the Secret Service Department a few days before the Clerkenwell explosion, despatching Colonel Feilding to the Home Office. As the panic subsided, the SSD was disbanded in March 1868 and only Robert Anderson remained with the Home Office to investigate Fenian activity in English cities in conjunction with his brother, Samuel Lee.[74]

Michael Barrett, an IRB man and stevedore working in Glasgow, was tried and convicted of the Clerkenwell outrage on the testimony of informers, while Captain James Murphy, in overall charge, and Jeremiah O'Sullivan, who claimed to have ignited the gunpowder barrel, escaped.[75] Barrett condemned the legal proceedings as biased and refused to 'ask for mercy' in the separatist tradition, which won him Irish admirers. On 26 May 1868 he became the last man to be publicly executed in England. With the passage of time the memory of the numerous victims faded and 'manly' Barrett's courage was eulogized and his name inscribed on the Manchester Martyrs' cenotaph in Glasnevin.[76]

The death of Edward Duffy

Convicts could be released on medical grounds, provided they expressed contrition. Andrew Kennedy, a minor organizer in Nenagh, had almost become an informer. Serving a sentence of five years, he was diagnosed with chronic bronchitis. Humbly regretting his Fenianism, Kennedy petitioned the home secretary and was discharged. The death of William Harbinson some days earlier may have influenced the authorities, for his funeral became a major demonstration.

Few IRB men would consider this option, however, as it meant repudiating nationalist convictions.[77]

Edward Duffy, the IRB organizer for Connacht, was rearrested in March 1867, convicted in August and died in Millbank Prison, London, on 17 January 1868. Press coverage was extensive. Duffy transformed his demise into a 'good death' par excellence. According to the *Nation*, his patriotism 'was only equalled by his devotion to religion, and his death was like that of a saint'.[78] He was engaged to Mary O'Leary and wrote to her half-sister Ellen to prepare her for his death. Duffy also longed to talk to Rossa, whose ingenuity in subverting prison rules failed on this occasion. The episode led to great bitterness and one of Rossa's best poems, 'A lament for Edward Duffy', which depicts the tragedy of imprisonment. The suffering rebel's path is, however, illuminated by a vision of freedom and the loving approval of relatives and comrades:[79]

> *The news of death is saddening, even in the festive hall;*
> *But when 'tis heard through prison bars 'tis saddest then of all.*
> *Where there's none to share the sorrow in the solitary cell,*
> *In the prison within prison – a blacker hell than hell.*
> *That whisper through the grating has thrilled through all my veins –*
> *'Duffy is dead!' a noble soul had slipped the tyrant's chains,*
> *And whatever wounds they gave him, their lying books will show*
> *How they very kindly treated him, more like a friend that foe.*

The poem appeared in the *Nation*, which praised this 'most remarkable literary effort'.[80] Duffy's death became a deeply moving episode of Rossa's prison memoirs, forming a powerful vignette of Fenian propaganda. Duffy was transformed into a martyr and immortalized by at least four Fenian poets.[81] While Mary Jane O'Donovan Rossa's lines are saccharine, Ellen O'Leary commemorated him memorably in 'The felon's last wish' and 'To God and Ireland true':[82]

> *I sat beside my darling's grave,*
> *Who in the prison died,*
> *And though my tears fall thick and fast,*
> *I think of him with pride:*
> *Ay, softly fall my tears like dew,*
> *For one to God and Ireland true.*[83]

The *Times* blamed Duffy's death on those who had stimulated 'the wretched delusion to which he has fallen a victim'. When relatives claimed his remains, the authorities wisely allowed a private funeral to Glasnevin Cemetery.[84]

In May 1868, on Richard Stowell's first anniversary, his own, as well as the graves of Anne Devlin, Robert Emmet's assistant, Terence Bellew McManus and Edward Duffy were decorated with wreaths and black and green ribbons. The following month a major demonstration took place. James Wexted Stenson, a militia sergeant and formerly a newspaper compositor and publican in Thomondgate, had been detained under the Habeas Corpus Suspension Act for letting Colonel Byron access the Castle Barracks in Limerick. Stenson's health never recovered on release from jail. His funeral was modelled on the Manchester Martyrs' demonstrations of the preceding winter and 2000 people followed the remains to Mount St Lawrence Cemetery. Only terrible weather prevented the participation of 500 women.[85]

Such events were not always organized by IRB sympathizers, however. James Mountaine, a veteran Republican, had been re-arrested under the Habeas Corpus Suspension Act in 1866. His health deteriorated after release and he died on 6 November 1868. Canon Maguire of St Peter and Paul's in Cork, a brother of the founder of the *Cork Examiner*, directed his dignified funeral.[86]

Ostensibly, attending a funeral was an act of Christian charity. From 1869 on the amnesty movement benefited from these often carefully choreographed events. When Daniel Darragh was dying in Portland, the *Nation* urged the authorities to conciliate nationalists. But the home secretary renegaded on a promise to release the body. Fearing 'a Fenian demonstration' organized by John 'Amnesty' Nolan, officials buried Darragh in the prison and an unseemly wrangle ensued until William Hogan of Birmingham was allowed to reinter the remains in Ballycastle, Co. Antrim.[87]

The Amnesty Movement

Gladstone had been aware since 1845 that endemic landlord-tenant tensions and the privileged position of a Protestant state church were poisoning the body politic.[88] Manchester and Clerkenwell formed tragic catalysts. An American Fenian commented how the storming of Hyde Park during a Reform League demonstration in July 1866 resulted in a speedy enlargement of the franchise, as likewise, the 'lamentable catastrophe' of Clerkenwell 'aroused the English public to the … immediate amelioration' of conditions in Ireland. Gladstone believed that a just solution meant that Europeans would cease their 'most painful commentaries' on Britain's policy towards Ireland. With hindsight, Robert Anderson deplored that Gladstone had 'proclaimed' how the explosion brought Irish grievances 'within the sphere of practical politics', unwittingly encouraging outrages.[89]

The separatist movement opined that such concessions indicated 'the way forward' and that 'the firing of Fenian revolvers' on English streets rather than humble petitioning caused the disestablishment of the Church of Ireland. The *Irish People* reflected whether landlordism might also end, 'after the blowing up of the next arsenal'.[90] The *Irishman* hailed the 'Fenian project' of James Stephens, which had exposed the unconstitutional government of Ireland, depending on troops and the habeas corpus suspension, measures alien to the liberal state.[91] In all likelihood the majority in Ireland would have been concili-ated by the speedy introduction of equitable land laws and greater educational and economic advancement for Catholics.[92]

An era of reconciliation seemed imminent as the Prince and Princess of Wales arrived for a rare royal visit to gratify Loyalists and conciliate Catholics. The Liberals enjoyed considerable Irish support and expectations ran high that, once Gladstone had replaced Disraeli and the Tories after the general election in November 1868, the prisoners would be amnestied. Peter Gill, the radical jour-nalist, dissented when the town commissioners of Nenagh expressed confidence in Gladstone. Gill suggested they should thank the Fenians, who had guided the Liberal leader to Irish issues. In August 1868 Cork Corporation became the first civic body to plead for a general pardon. During a later debate, the councillors exculpated the Fenians by maintaining that their incarceration was 'a disgrace to England', given their 'unselfishness, the amazing self-sacrifice and … patrio-tism'. Other municipal authorities were invited to join the appeal.[93]

In January 1869 a petition containing 250,000 signatures informed Queen Victoria that the convictions had been obtained through jury-packing. Most Irish people believed that 'the political prisoners have already suffered suffi-ciently to vindicate the power of British law', which was contrary to 'the prac-tice of all civilised countries in relation to political offenders'. Representatives of Clonmel, Limerick, Dublin, Cobh, Dungarvan, Skibbereen, Roscommon, Galway, Waterford, New Ross, Tramore, Thurles and Listowel added their pleas for clemency.[94]

Widespread interest in the prisoners in late 1868 resulted in the formation of a central amnesty committee.[95] A deputation bearing 700 signatures solicited the support of Isaac Butt, who had defended both the Young Irelanders and the staff of the *Irish People*. The idealism of the IRB elite impressed him, although their plans were 'utterly devoid of all chances of success'.[96] Urging the British to conciliate, rather than issue 'a declaration of war against Irish nationalism', Butt became pres-ident of the new movement, ably assisted by its secretary, John 'Amnesty' Nolan. Branches were established in Ireland and Britain; in London, for instance, it had the support of the central trade union council under George Odger.[97]

James Stephens presenting Erin's case to Europe and America, Irishman
(courtesy Dublin City Archive).

Denis Dowling Mulcahy told Dr Sigerson that the prison administration
had become more lenient after the general election and political status of sorts
was ultimately conceded. The soldier Fenians, those suspected of assassination
or involved in the Manchester rescue continued to be treated harshly, however.
Under the direction of Nolan, the Amnesty Association held weekly meetings in

Dublin, publicizing its work by recording financial contributions and letters of support. Preparing for the Dublin demonstration in October 1869, he even reassured ladies of arrangements for them 'to assist and take part'. The changing political climate was illustrated by the many middle-class supporters.[98]

On 24 February 1868 Rossa was transferred to Chatham, a public works prison in the Kent marshes, described by Charles Dickens as 'a most beastly place. Mudbank, mist, swamp and work; work, swamp, mist and mudbank'.[99] Coerced to labour with thieves and obliged to salute the governor in military fashion, Rossa went on strike, informing him 'that it was not to him I meant disrespect, but to the government'. Being punished, he refused to leave his cell and was dragged to the office by warders who attempted to push his reluctant limbs into the required salute.[100]

Rossa burned 'to be avenged' and, on 17 June 1868, 'saluted' the governor with the contents of his water pail. The latter ordered the Fenian's arms to be handcuffed behind his back and went on immediate leave. Captain Edmund Du Cane and Colonel Henderson, the chairman of prison directors, decided against flogging Rossa. Henderson declared himself 'unwilling, except as a last resort, to employ corporal punishment' and characterized Rossa's conduct as indicating imbecility, but was probably deterred by the likely public outcry.[101]

Rossa's manacling continued for thirty-five consecutive days, the handcuffs being changed to his front during meals and taken off at night. Not only was his treatment inhumane, it was in breach of regulations. Afterwards the demeanour of the autocratic Captain Du Cane softened and Rossa was permitted to associate with Colonel Halpin, Augustine Costello and John Warren of the *Erin's Hope* expedition. When treated with consideration, Rossa responded favourably.[102]

Being requested to form a government by Queen Victoria in December 1868, Gladstone proclaimed his mission to 'pacify Ireland'.[103] He began with disestablishing the Church of Ireland and preparing a very moderate land bill, but liberated only forty-nine of the eighty-one Fenian prisoners in March 1869. The amnesty excluded the leaders, military Fenians and participants in the Manchester rescue. There were exceptions, however: James F.X. O'Brien, who had led the attack on Ballyknockane constabulary barracks, John Haltigan and James O'Connor, printer and clerk of the *Irish People* respectively, and Charles Kickham, whose poor sight and hearing had deteriorated in prison, were among those released.[104]

In Dublin, the central amnesty committee appealed for funds for the released men to enable them to make a fresh start in life and to defray its own expenses and those of the Ladies' Committee. This 'national tribute', centred on church gate collections on St Patrick's Day, was prohibited in the Dublin archdiocese, due to the unwavering opposition of Dr Cullen, but permitted in Limerick by Bishop George Butler. By April 1869 more than £2000 had been contributed.[105] The amnesty was unconditional, which meant the men could return home. James F.X. O'Brien was enthusiastically received in his birthplace, Dungarvan, while Kickham and Haltigan were greeted by up to 4000 people in Kilkenny, which had been illuminated in their honour. Haltigan joined Pigott's *Irishman* until 1873, when he emigrated to America, where two of his sons had become newspaper publishers. Kickham returned to his beloved Mullinahone to write *Knocknagow*, encouraged by O'Mahony, who arranged its publication in the New York *Emerald* from March to September 1870.[106]

John Kenealy (courtesy Dublin City Archive).

The thirty-four convicts freed on 15 May 1869 in Western Australia included Denis Cashman, Thomas Duggan, John Kenealy and John Sarsfield Casey. As their pardons did not include a passage home, collections among the Irish-Australian working class raised more than £3000. This also enabled fifteen of the Fenians to emigrate to San Francisco. John Boyle O'Reilly, who had escaped from Australia in February and became editor of the Boston *Pilot*, cabled Denis Cashman a welcome invitation to join his staff. John Kenealy established a business career and resumed his revolutionary involvement with Clan na Gael in Los Angeles. John Sarsfield Casey and nine companions returned to a triumphant welcome home to Cork in the spring of 1870.[107]

A few Fenians chose to remain behind. Thomas Duggan, who at forty-seven was the oldest, opted to spend the rest of his long life in Western Australia, where he resumed his teaching career. Having 'entered an old men's refuge as a pauper' in 1904, an appeal for funds provided him and James Keilley with a comfortable old age, occasionally honoured for their Fenian past. John Golden, a native of Kells and a participant in the abortive Rising in Kerry, worked for a Fenian sympathizer, an emigrant from Cashel, whose daughter he married, but died of lung disease in 1883.[108]

Many supporters were disappointed by the limited releases and denounced the 'sham amnesty'. On the hills above Cork and in its streets, bonfires burned nightly, while crowds cheered for 'Captain Mackey and all the Fenians' in the mistaken belief that he, too, would be liberated.[109] When colonels Warren and Costello, two naturalized American citizens included in the amnesty, attended a farewell banquet in Cork, the lord mayor eulogized the Manchester Martyrs, Michael Barrett and the mentally unbalanced Henry James O'Farrell, who had attacked a son of Queen Victoria, as heroes. The ensuing uproar proved counterproductive for those still imprisoned, but Dublin Castle realized that Fenian sympathies ran deep.[110]

In May the amnesty movement split into the pro-Gladstone moderates, in favour of tact, and John Nolan's followers, who urged vigorous action. Nolan's new organization enjoyed the support of Isaac Butt, G.H. Moore, A.M. Sullivan and John Martin, while attracting the goodwill of progressive British politicians, including Bright and Bradlaugh, who contended that the rulers of Ireland must accept some responsibility for her problems.[111]

'He frequently had to eat his meals on his belly like a dog'[112]

On 17 May 1869 Richard Pigott was allowed access to Rossa to facilitate his defence in a law case. Subsequently the *Irishman* published a highly sensationalized account of Rossa's handcuffing, claiming that he was forced to lap his stirabout 'on all fours as an animal does' or starve.[113] This insult was passionately resented by the Irish people, often depicted as lesser beings in the British press. The Home Secretary, Henry A. Bruce, denied the allegations in Parliament, claiming there was 'nothing vindictive or unusual in the punishment inflicted in this case'. Bruce also revealed that on 16 June 1868, Rossa had doused Captain Powell, the governor of Chatham, with the contents of his chamber pot rather than with water, as Rossa later claimed.[114]

Richard Pigott used this incident to increase the circulation of his *Irishman*. Timothy McCarthy Downing, MP for Cork, Rossa's solicitor during the Phoenix trials, visited him to learn the truth, leading to Pigott's exaggerations being exposed in the *Nation*. Rossa's manacles had been changed to the front during meals, which he ate with a spoon. But in an open letter to the home secretary, McCarthy Downing also revealed the stonewalling and lack of truthfulness he had experienced from prison officials.[115]

'Amnesty' Nolan ran a series of fifty-four mass meetings during 1869, modelled on O'Connell's Repeal rallies. In Cork, 4000 people supported resolutions demanding the 'unconditional release of the Fenian convicts'.[116] At the same time gatherings took place in Limerick, Duhallow, Ennis and Mullingar. Others were organized for Kilkenny, Clonmel, Cashel, Newport, Kilfinane, Thurles and Limerick, culminating in an attendance of 200,000 at Cabra, near Dublin. The constabulary reported that at the Emly amnesty meeting in September, the locals marched with military precision, 'causing considerable terror to the loyal and well disposed'. The chief organizer was Malachy O'Donovan, who had led the occupation of Emly police barracks in March 1867.[117]

Dominick O'Mahony, FP 292 (courtesy NAI).

At the meeting in Millstreet in November Dominick O'Mahony proposed the first resolution, calling for the liberation of the political prisoners and a demand to resolve tenant farmers' grievances. He had been detained as the 'head centre' for Cork for more than a year and was only released in May 1868, but campaigned vigorously until 1874. The police feared that old Fenians controlled the amnesty movement, eagerly awaiting a new opportunity to strike.[118]

Since these protests began the magistrates had noticed that 'the people have become much more defiant and confident'. They deplored the forthcoming event in Tipperary town on 24 October 1869, which would encourage the disaffected. 'Thoroughly Fenian in its character', it united priests, businessmen and local suspects. Careful planning had coordinated the arrival of the various contingents. In Kilfeacle the police recorded during Mass that Fr O'Connell advised his congregation to stay sober, for there 'will be paid spies and hirelings amongst you, your enemies and mine'.[119] After the final blessing, the priest led his flock in procession, accompanied by the Golden band. The Kilfeacle flag, bearing the motto 'death before dishonour', was carried by Cornelius Fogarty, a brother of Michael O'Neill Fogarty. And, in a scene that could have been from *Knocknagow*, the little village marched to the Tipperary amnesty meeting. The constabulary lamented that Kilfeacle remained 'the great seat of Fenianism'.[120]

The constabulary reported from Galbally that the congregation approved of Fr John Hackett's sermon, which stated that the prisoners might have erred, but had 'committed no crime'. He concluded by condemning the government: 'their sceptre was the sword, their diadem the black cap, their throne the gallows'. Also in October, the General Council of the International participated in an international amnesty demonstration in London, attended by 100,000 people, demanding 'justice for Ireland'.[121]

Mitchelstown's Catholic population contributed £50 to decorate the town for its amnesty meeting with 'an immense and gorgeously painted emblematic banner' of 'Erin mourning her captive sons'. The pupils of the Christian Brothers, each carrying a small flag with 'amnesty' written in gold, surmounted by a cross, led the way, followed by five priests and 1200 well-dressed locals. This was an amazing transformation when one recalled that John Sarsfield Casey had been denounced and banned from these schools for Fenianism. Kilfinane, Cullen, Kilmallock, Kilbeheny, Clogheen and Ballylanders sent impressive contingents, but the main focus was on 'a bright, intelligent boy' among the Fermoy men, the only son of Colour Sergeant McCarthy, who carried a placard, 'Release my father'. The *Nation* depicted a citizens' army on the move rather than a gathering of humble petitioners. It considered the Mitchelstown demonstration the most impressive to date.[122]

In November 1869 during a gathering in Kilclooney Wood, the tree near which Peter O'Neill Crowley had been fatally wounded was destroyed by nationalist souvenir collectors. Rev. W. Fitzgerald addressed the crowd, refuting the 'slander' that the Fenians were atheistic socialists, as 'poor Crowley' had worn a crucifix and a holy medal. He had lived long enough to receive the last rites, which the priest considered a sign of divine approval. Gladstone was 'groaned' for not keeping his promises and the inconsistency of his attitude to Irish and Italian nationalists highlighted. One thousand priests in Ireland and Britain favoured amnesty, including the influential Dean Richard O'Brien of Limerick, founder of the Catholic Young Men's Society. Isaac Butt claimed that during August 1869 alone, more than a million people had attended forty-three amnesty demonstrations.[123]

The Rossa and Kickham election campaigns

During the summer of 1869 James F.X. O'Brien heard about the Tipperary by-election from Denis Caulfield Heron, the Liberal candidate. This eminent Catholic barrister enjoyed the support of the clergy and was on good terms with the Fenians, having defended O'Brien and others. The *Nation* considered him much the best candidate, who would also promote tenant right. In Nenagh Peter Gill of the *Tipperary Advocate* 'suggested that O'Donovan Rossa ought to be put forward', which struck James F.X. O'Brien as 'a very good idea'.[124] Mitchel had previously urged the running of abstentionist candidates in the *Irish Citizen*, but Rossa was nominated rather late. O'Brien believed that the Fenian ethos, so prevalent in Tipperary, could provide a spectacular demonstration in favour of amnesty.[125]

Peter Gill advised that Daniel O'Connell, an enthusiastic IRB member who farmed 120 acres near Toomevara, should be asked to help. O'Brien and O'Connell contributed £6 to start a fund for election expenses in the *Irishman* and O'Connell toured the county to rally supporters. Rossa needed to be nominated immediately, so O'Brien did not consult Kickham, the senior leader in Tipperary, who disapproved of such tactics. Fr Patrick Lavelle of Partry, acting as Heron's go-between, offered to donate £500 to the Ladies' Committee on condition that Rossa would withdraw, but O'Brien refused.[126]

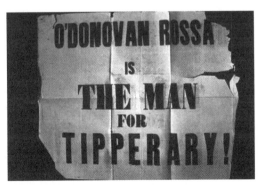

O'Donovan Rossa election poster (courtesy NAI).

Patrick Mackey, the first IRB 'centre' of Templemore, was an agent for Power's Distillery. Detained during the habeas corpus suspension until June 1866, when Sir James Power provided bail for him, Mackey was ill, but supported Rossa's candidature.[127] Thomas Condon of Clonmel, another influential Fenian, canvassed eagerly. Kendal and Patrick O'Brien, affluent natives of Cullen, Co. Tipperary, became guarantors for the election expenses, which forced them to sell some of their land. The barony of Clanwilliam, with the town of Tipperary at its centre, favoured Rossa decisively.[128]

Thomas Ryan, a tea dealer and 'prominent member of the Dublin amnesty committee', provided striking placards, which were 'posted throughout the county recommending O'Donovan Rossa as the man for Tipperary'. The constabulary considered Ryan 'very mischievous', but a magistrate advised that worse posters would be put up, if these were removed. The DMP stated that Ryan was 'an enthusiast in politics', who mixed patriotism with business, facilitating him to sell three times more tea than before.[129]

Violence was common during open balloting and 'farmers were taken out of their beds in Templemore and Borrisoleigh and forced to swear that they would vote for O'Donovan Rossa'.[130] Some voters were intimidated, others hesitated between Heron and the political prisoner. The turnout was low and only 2000 of the 12,000 men entitled to vote did so. Rossa won by 103 votes on a memorable occasion when the people, rather than the landlords or the Catholic clergy, dictated the outcome. Addressing Rossa's supporters, Peter Gill pronounced Tipperary 'the foremost county of Ireland', which had asserted the rights of the common man. He stressed the need for reform and intimated that a revolution might follow if their demand was refused. Gladstone could demonstrate that his desire for reconciliation was genuine by liberating Rossa.[131] If the Fenians were not freed, Gill promised

> that we will go from county to county, and from borough to borough, wherever there is a vacancy, and wherever they want to give promotion to a barrister or aspirant, we will meet them there, and we will have Luby in – we'll have O'Leary too, and we'll have Denis Dowling Mulcahy (enthusiastic cheering); and before we have done we will have the materials of a real Irish Parliament.[132]

John Martin compared this victory to the historic Clare election of 1828, which had resulted in Catholic Emancipation. He stressed that it was futile to expect 'security of tenure and fair rents' from an English Parliament. The *Nation* believed that the electors of Tipperary had focused international attention on Ireland.[133] In England a young Eleanor Marx 'went quite wild' with joy, but Friedrich Engels urged the Fenians to learn from their amnesty and election campaigns and 'abandon their conspiratorial tactics and the staging of minor coups in favour of practical activities which, though seemingly legal, are far more revolutionary than anything they have done since their unsuccessful insurrection'.[134]

The Home Office vainly attempted to keep Rossa in ignorance of his candidature amidst rumours of a rescue attempt. In Chatham Rossa's companions debated his tactics, if brought before the House of Commons. Some urged that he should assert his nationality by speaking in Irish. Rossa, like Mitchel, interpreted his election as a momentous rejection of 'foreign rule'. There were exuberant celebrations, involving bands and blazing tar barrels, although the windows of some opponents were also broken.[135]

Lord Kimberley, the former viceroy, remained unimpressed, believing that Irish unhappiness was the result of the national character, as illustrated by this by-election: 'The Tipperary ruffians have elected as their member, the rowdy felon O'Donovan Rossa, a most fit and proper representative of them.' Lamenting 'what a descent from Grattan and O'Connell, or even Wolfe Tone and Emmet', he predicted that the British would now witness the power of the IRB, as it marshalled the nationalist community. Kimberley feared Gladstone was deluded if he believed in a speedy reconciliation between Ireland and England.[136]

An undischarged felon was presumed dead in law, which disqualified Rossa from taking his seat. Following T.P. Gill's advice, T.P. O'Connor of Laffana and Thomas Mackey of Templemore, a clerical student, nominated Charles Kickham for the next round, without obtaining the consent of the IRB leadership, which considered their point made.[137] William Hurley, a wealthy butterbuyer who had been elected chairman of the Tipperary town commissioners on several occasions, was an IRB sympathizer and participated in both elections. In February 1870 these commissioners, 'led by the chairman', proceeded to vote for Kickham.[138] Anticipating success, supporters lit bonfires on Slievenamon, but Kickham lost by four votes, having abstained from electioneering because of his distaste for parliamentary politics. Elections were expensive and the Fenian activists needed American help to settle their debts.[139]

Dublin Castle was reluctant to agree to a further amnesty, as the IRB had not disbanded. Its membership was greatly reduced, but better organized. In December 1869 spymaster Samuel Lee Anderson wrote to Sir Thomas Larcom that the IRB had been 'wonderfully stimulated by the release of the prisoners' and Rossa's victory. The leaders, learning from past mistakes, had become 'very determined' and exercised 'amazing secrecy'.[140] Members were thoroughly vetted and feared retribution, if indiscreet. Although Dublin Castle had recruited two informers, they could learn very little. Anderson did not anticipate an immediate insurrection, but the tenant right agitation had revived Ribbonism and 'sedition has become, one might almost say, the religion of the people'.[141]

The Devon Commission

Gladstone appointed another inquiry on 10 May 1870, chaired by William Reginald Courtney, Earl of Devon and a popular landlord in west Limerick. Other members of the Devon Commission included Dr Robert Lyons and Dr Edward Greenhow, both physicians with considerable experience in the field of public health, G.C. Broderick, a barrister and journalist, and Stephen de Vere, the respected Anglo-Irish philanthropist and convert to Catholicism. This unsworn inquiry was to ascertain if the health of the Fenian prisoners had been neglected and whether they had been treated with 'unnecessary severity or harshness' or 'subjected to any exceptional treatment in any way' beyond that customary during penal servitude.[142]

John Nolan, secretary of the Amnesty Association, suggested that a representative of the prisoners should question witnesses, while reassuring the home secretary that the person selected 'will be perfectly unobjectionable', merely desirous 'of soliciting the whole truth'. This elicited the response: 'Most certainly not I should say. The enquiry would be endless and impossible to control.'[143] Isaac Butt, President of the Amnesty Association, enhanced his profile as the nationalist champion by stating in an open letter that the families of the prisoners required his presence to ensure that the issue would 'be fully and openly investigated, and that the investigation should be so conducted as to satisfy the public opinion not only of Ireland, but of the civilised world'.[144]

Butt offered to relay the testimony of those Fenians already released, but the Home Office declined, as the complaints of those discharged or deceased were outside the parameters of the commission. The prisoners were given time to write down their grievances and could, theoretically, request consultations with friends, but when Denis Dowling Mulcahy and Brian Dillon applied for visits from fellow prisoners, the Home Office responded 'most decidedly not'.[145] O'Leary, Luby and Mulcahy declined to testify, as this unsworn inquiry failed to guarantee 'that their testimony would be published ungarbled', but Rossa participated 'in order to expose the delusive character of the former inquiry'.[146] The leaders in Portland indicated that they might air their charges in a forum of their choice at a later date. O'Leary commented that they would have 'to be an extraordinary humble-minded class of men' not to complain. In spite of such criticism, Lord Devon was greatly concerned to facilitate the prisoners.[147]

The IRB captives reiterated the longstanding issue of medical neglect. Charles Underwood O'Connell had developed heart disease. He exhibited an 'excessive and unceasing nervous tremor', but still had to undergo 'bread and water punishment'. The Devon Commission described Brian Dillon as a 'very weak and deformed man'.[148] Nevertheless, during the winter of 1867 he had cleaned snow-covered bricks, while the following summer, Dillon hoisted blocks with rope and wheel, although ill with dysentery. The commissioners considered him barely able to walk and concluded that some tasks assigned to him were unsuitable.[149]

The Devon report, while tactful towards the prison administration, conceded that the Fenians had grounds for complaint concerning diet and medical treatment and that disciplinary guidelines were jettisoned during in the summer of 1868, when the governor of Chatham had Rossa manacled: 'Both the governor and the visiting director exceeded the power and authority entrusted to them.'[150]

The Amnesty Campaign after 1871

Popular support for the prisoners resulted in the 'conditional' amnesty of January 1871, which meant exclusion from Britain and Ireland for the remainder of their sentence. Rossa, Devoy, Thomas Francis Bourke, William Mackey Lomasney, John McCafferty and Denis Dowling Mulcahy were among those exiled. Waiting to welcome them to New York were Colonel Thomas Kelly and Captain O'Rourke on behalf of the IRB abroad, John Savage and John O'Mahony, representing the Fenian Brotherhood, and the United Irishmen, formerly the Senate wing, under William J. Nicholson, Patrick Downing and Mortimer Moynahan. Forcing the emigration of these men to the US proved short-sighted, as many became 'dedicated agents' of revolution. The Home Office excluded all participants in the Manchester rescue and the military Fenians from this amnesty, but Rossa publicized rumours of their ill-treatment.[151]

Amnesty campaigners stated that Thomas Chambers, a leading soldier Fenian, had been without a visit for nine years. Access eventually became possible for those who could prove kinship. But officialdom intimidated visitors, who feared their employers might dismiss them, when detectives began watching their homes. Thomas Chambers believed that it was easier for a murderer to keep in touch with his family. He petitioned the home secretary in 1868, 1869, 1870, 1871, 1873 and 1876 without result and came to believe that his appeals were ignored.[152] By 1873 Chambers had grown cynical:

> When I consider the trial or rather the burlesque by which I was condemned and the ill treatment I have been receiving this last seven years, I can't help thinking that by asking for mercy I acknowledge that I have received justice. It is gross injustice and unworthy of the government of a civilised nation to treat me as a felon and force me to associate with felons even if guilty of the crime of love of country.'[153]

Under pressure to respond, the prison administration pronounced Chambers, popular for his caring qualities, to be 'a man of an irritable, resentful disposition, and discovers an insult in everything', which was a standard response when dealing with articulate Fenians whose patience had run out.[154]

After 1871 the Amnesty Association lost momentum, though it and the concept of electing prisoners to Parliament in protest entered the political repertoire of separatists. John O'Connor Power, then a leading spokesman of the Irish Party, persisted in raising this issue in the Commons.[155] In 1872 an illicit letter from the imprisoned Michael Davitt, who protested against the brutal treatment experienced by him and Thomas Chambers, heralded a new spokesman. O'Connor Power and Davitt as men of the people realized that since the Famine, thousands of Irishmen had joined the British army from economic necessity, including O'Connor Power's brother and Tom Clarke's father.[156] Charles Stewart Parnell also publicized this subject. When he rejected the establishment attitude that the Fenian rescuers of Kelly and Deasy had committed murder, declaring in Parliament: 'I wish to say as publicly and directly as I can that I do not believe, and never shall believe, that any murder was committed at Manchester,' Irish nationalists applauded their new champion.[157]

During the O'Connell centenary commemoration in 1875, a violent clash occurred between the organizers and the Amnesty Association, which felt that the political prisoners were being forgotten. This resulted in John Nolan, a leading participant, losing his job and leaving for New York, where he died in 1887. In Cork an active committee led by Michael Francis Murphy, a Fenian veteran, supported the families of the prisoners by soliciting contributions from the Irish in the north of England and campaigning for an amnesty after 1874.[158]

Dion Boucicault, the popular playwright, returned to London to stage *The Shaughraun*. Conscious of his Irish origins and the triumph of his play with its Fenian hero, Boucicault wrote to Prime Minister Disraeli on 1 January 1876 that thousands supported Home Rule while an amnesty for the political prisoners was overdue. Disraeli ignored this as a 'publicity stunt', but in April Boucicault distributed posters in London, pleading for Michael Davitt, Colour Sergeant McCarthy and their comrades in Fremantle. He emphasized that the former soldiers had been imprisoned for almost ten years.[159]

The conservative Duke of Cambridge, Commander-in-Chief and cousin of Queen Victoria, persistently blocked the release of the military Fenians on grounds of army discipline. Such treatment smacked of revenge, for the authorities perceived them as having committed double treason: as subjects and as soldiers. By the 1870s nineteen military Fenians remained, with only McCarthy, Thomas Chambers and John Patrick O'Brien incarcerated in England. The group of ex-soldiers detained in Fremantle smuggled out several letters appealing to Clan na Gael for help:[160] 'It is most certain that the British government will never release one of the soldiers. This is as true Holy Writ; most of us are beginning to show symptoms of disease, in fact, we are all ailing to a greater or less extent, and cannot expect to hold out much longer, and one of our number, the finest man amongst us named Patrick Keating, is dead.'[161]

Col Patrick Downing, 42nd NY Infantry (courtesy Library of Congress Prints and Photographs Division, Washington DC).

CHAPTER 10

Resurgence and Decline, 1868–78

Efforts since October 1867 to revive the IRB led to the creation of the Supreme Council early the following year. This body asserted its autonomy from both wings of the Fenian Brotherhood. The Supreme Council claimed to represent the army and people of the Republic in Ireland and Britain and appealed for unity in its first message of 24 April 1868. The declared membership of 200,000 was, however, a gross exaggeration.[1]

The Supreme Council deplored the 'disastrous' Rising, which originated in the desire of 'some individuals in the United States' to retain their influence, but also acknowledged the participation of 'very brave' men. It insisted on long-term preparation while awaiting the moment to strike. Captain Mackey had conducted gun raids till 7 February 1868, when a policeman was fatally wounded during his arrest.[2] The new leadership rejected guerrilla tactics as 'unmanly', dreading disastrous incidents, which would diminish their movement. Its Cork directory posted a proclamation on 12 April 1868, forbidding the seizure of arms. Henceforth, anyone who committed such 'mean and cowardly acts' was threatened with punishment. Occasional attempts continued, nevertheless. In August, for instance, Pierce Drew, Protestant rector of Youghal, and his daughter repulsed a Fenian attack. The following June a similar raid resulted in the death of former suspect Andrew Campbell. It was condemned for keeping Ireland unsettled and delaying its economic development.[3]

The supreme councillors reaffirmed the 'inherent and undying' opposition of the Irish people to the British government, the cause of the 'sorrowful exile' and death of millions, without hating the English people. The IRB justified the Manchester rescue, while regretting the tragic death of Sergeant Brett. The unauthorized Clerkenwell explosion, however, was 'outside the pale of civilisation and humanity' and should the councillors apprehend the perpetrators, 'their punishment would be commensurate with our sense of justice'.[4]

The Supreme Council established formal command structures and the first constitution in 1869, which, revised in 1873, continued in force until 1917. There were eleven supreme councillors: seven elective ones represented the four Irish provinces, Scotland, Northern and Southern England and a further four could be co-opted. The constitution proclaimed them to be 'the sole government of the Irish Republic'; the president of the IRB was also 'the president of the Irish Republic'. The executive consisted of president, secretary and treasurer and the vote of any two of these officers was binding. Meetings took place biannually. A majority of two-thirds was required to expel a member of the Supreme Council.[5]

IRB 'centres' were supervised by their 'county centres', who chose a sub-committee, which elected the respective supreme councillors for their two years in office. The 'county centres' also selected civil and military secretaries for their regions. 'County centres' were required to forward monthly reports to their civil secretary, while weekly membership fees of 3d. for arms and an additional 1d. per month for civil expenses were levied on the membership by 1870, as American funding had ceased. The cities of Dublin, Cork, Belfast and Limerick had additional governing bodies, chosen locally. The constitution prohibited any IRB officer from receiving wages. This counteracted the disrepute inflicted by the large salaries paid to Fenian Brotherhood officials during 1865–6. Funds remained modest for the remainder of the nineteenth century and volunteering was the norm.[6]

John O'Connor Power, John 'Amnesty' Nolan, James ('Jem') Fox of Leeds and Edmond O'Donovan were among those reviving the IRB, joined in 1869 by Charles Kickham, James O'Connor and James F.X. O'Brien, while James J. O'Kelly ('Fitz') and Michael Davitt specialized in obtaining arms.[7] John Daly, 'gifted intellectually, a good speaker, and ... most resolute and outspoken', had fled after the Rising to return to Limerick in 1869. G.H. Moore, who had refrained from involvement because of Stephens, became a trusted adviser and amnesty supporter until his death in 1870. The new leaders rejected a return to the dictatorship of Stephens, which success alone could have justified. He continued to retain a personal following and the 'Stephenites' opposed the authority of the Supreme Council until 1878.[8]

Charles Kickham served as president of the Supreme Council. In 1870 with the serialized publication of *Knocknagow or the Homes of Tipperary*, he became the most popular Irish novelist. He was, however, severely handicapped and had to leave the management of the IRB to its secretary, John 'Amnesty' Nolan, and subsequently Charles Guilfoyle Doran. The latter had organized in Co. Tipperary in 1866, before being appointed clerk of works for St Colman's Cathedral, Cobh. His cultural interests endeared him to the IRB elite. As Kickham's health declined, John O'Leary, who continued to comment from his Parisian exile, was co-opted, becoming leader of the Supreme Council after 1882. Generally speaking, the IRB secretary was the most influential member of the executive with its president as a figurehead. [9]

The Supreme Council invited William O'Brien of Mallow, the young brother of James, a veteran of the Rising, to assist in overcoming the 'sad state of dilapidation and mutual recriminations'. O'Brien served as secretary for Munster for two years, but found that the 'personal bitterness' in Cork was such that nationalist politics stagnated until the advent of Parnell. [10] James F.X. O'Brien, a peripheral member prior to 1867, became the *bona fide* commercial traveller for a Cork firm as a cover for re-organizing the movement. From 1869 to 1873 he toured mainly in Munster and Connacht, frequently tailed by policemen. O'Brien believed that the majority of the people were 'strongly in sympathy with the IRB – that is: in favour of an Irish Republic'. [11]

IRB members, after vetting for 'sobriety, truth, valour and obedience to authority', pledged: 'In the presence of God [name] do solemnly swear that I will do my utmost to establish the national independence of Ireland, and that I will bear true allegiance to the Supreme Council of the Irish Republic, and the constitution thereof, and implicitly obey the orders of the officers of the Supreme Council of the Irish Republic, so help me God.' [12] The constitution upheld the ideal of a non-sectarian state and permitted members to participate in parliamentary elections, if authorized by the Supreme Council. Having proclaimed the fatuity of constitutional methods in the past, the IRB now ordered that 'persistent efforts should be made to obtain control of all local [government] bodies' to increase its power. [13]

In 1871 Patrick Neville Fitzgerald left his native Midleton to work in Cork. Aged seventeen, he transferred from the Stephenites to the Supreme Council IRB. Claiming he had retained some of their funds, the former attacked a meeting chaired by Fitzgerald in Bowling Green Street. Although the Supreme Council group fled for their lives, they eventually constituted the majority in Cork with Fitzgerald as the 'centre' and organizer for the south and west of Ireland. Dublin Castle heard from an informer: 'The two chief traits in his character are his love of Fenianism and gambling. He is quick tempered and impulsive and at horse racing is supposed to have lost considerable sums of money and to have recouped himself from any funds which he may have had on hands as a Fenian organizer.'[14] Fitzgerald's chief lieutenant, 'Long John' O'Connor of Cork, described as 'six feet six of treason felony', also joined the IRB at an early age and displayed similar tenacity.[15]

Table 9. *Membership of the Supreme Council in 1875–6*

President	Charles Kickham	Mullinahone & Dublin
Secretary & Munster Representative	Charles G. Doran	Cobh
Treasurer	Patrick Egan	Dublin
Leinster	John Leavy	Dublin
Connacht	John O'Connor Power	MP, London
Ulster	Robert Johnston	Belfast
South of England	John Ryan	London
North of England	John Walsh & William McGuinness	Middlesbrough & Preston
Scotland	John Torley	Duntocher
Co-opted	Joseph G. Biggar	MP, Belfast & London
Co-opted	John Barry	North of England

(Source: Moody & Ó Broin, 'The IRB Supreme Council, 1868–78', 292)

Butt and Home Rule

Sympathizers campaigning for Rossa and Kickham had found participating in such a popular movement satisfying. This sparked a coalition, which promoted John Martin, a moral force constitutionalist, as parliamentary candidate for Longford. His supporters included Stephen Joseph Meany, Edmond O'Donovan, James J. O'Kelly and John 'Amnesty' Nolan, as well as John and William Dillon and the moderate A.M. Sullivan, detested as a felon-setter until recently.[16] Martin was defeated by the aristocratic Reginald Greville-Nugent, who received 1478 votes against Martin's 411. However, his victory was declared void due to bribery and intimidation by the Catholic clergy. The new generation of IRB leaders organized itself for electioneering, which formed dress rehearsals for the Home Rule victories of 1871 (Limerick) and 1872 (Kerry). Orthodox Fenians lacked an alternative programme.[17]

Land tenure, the political prisoners and the Catholic hierarchy's demand for denominational university education remained key issues, straining the alliance between the Irish electorate and the Liberal Party. Gladstone's Landlord and Tenant Act (Ireland) 1870, although an indicator of future developments, proved ineffective. Less than 1000 tenants availed themselves of the 'John Bright clauses' to borrow two-thirds of the cost of buying out their landlord, if he consented to sell, at 5 per cent interest over thirty-five years. These terms were beyond the means of most tenants, while substantial farmers with leases of thirty-one years or more remained excluded.[18]

The majority of the Catholic community wished to prioritize the land over the amnesty issue, while IRB policy insisted that this should be settled after independence. In November 1869 the Munster Farmers' Club arranged a major tenant right meeting in Limerick. John Daly, fearing the amnesty question would be marginalized, created havoc with his working-class followers until the proceedings were abandoned.[19] Daly interpreted the 'battle of the markets' as a moral victory for the prisoners, while moderate nationalists realized that an agreement with the IRB was imperative.[20]

William Henry O'Sullivan, FP 422 (courtesy NAI).

Disestablishment of the Church of Ireland and the changes in land tenure created Protestant dissatisfaction with Gladstone. Isaac Butt conceived a 'federalist' solution, whereby Ireland, Scotland and England would control their domestic affairs, but remain united through the sovereign and the Imperial Parliament in London. Butt hoped to lead nationalists and disgruntled Anglo-Irish landlords to highlight Ireland's case for redress, but needed guarantees that the IRB would not strangle his initiative at birth.[21]

In September 1871 Butt stood for Limerick with the enthusiastic support of its lower-middle class, assisted by William Henry O'Sullivan of Kilmallock. Simultaneously Butt assured the clergy that he favoured a Catholic university scheme.[22] Although the celebrated champion of imprisoned Fenians, Butt's policies were strictly constitutional. Charles Barry, the attorney general, who was without a seat in Parliament, opposed him. As Crown prosecutor, Barry had falsely accused the Fenian elite of socialism and assassination in 1865.[23] The *Irishman* revived John O'Leary's riposte, declaring Barry a 'moral assassin', when he stood for election in Dungarvan in 1868. Shopkeepers demonstrated their contempt by silently showing him photographs of the incarcerated Fenians; his candidature failed. The burghers of Dungarvan did not support revolution, but respected 'sincere patriots'.[24] When seeking election in 1871, the attorney general dreaded a 'Fenian welcome' from John Daly and his cohorts so much that he arrived secretly in Limerick, his birthplace, where Dr Butler, the Catholic bishop, kept aloof, realizing that ordinary people would bring about Butt's return.[25]

Hitherto, Lord Kenmare had been pivotal in deciding the parliamentary representation for Kerry. For the 1872 by-election, he proposed his cousin, James Arthur Dease, who could afford an expensive contest on behalf of the Liberals. The latter was opposed by Rowland Ponsonby Blennerhassett, a minor landlord, championed by Home Rulers and IRB sympathizers. The *Nation* denounced Dease's supporters, particularly the O'Donoghue of the Glens, MP for Tralee, who had abandoned nationalism in favour of reviving his finances, to become 'among Irish politicians what a Cyprian is among virtuous women' – employing a Victorian euphemism for a prostitute.[26]

Although Dr Moriarty regarded Butt's movement as Fenianism in a new guise and prohibited his priests from supporting Blennnerhassett, the junior clergy ignored him. Fr Denis O'Donoghue, Parish Priest of Ardfert, openly defied his bishop and the political clique centred on Lord Kenmare, the 'Muckross House caucus, the Tammany ring of Kerry electioneering'.[27] Fr Michael O'Sullivan of Ballylongford also supported the Home Rule candidate, demanding an amnesty for the Fenian prisoners. Both priests led their flock to Listowel to vote for Blennerhassett, whose victory marked a turning point, as the will of the people overcame the traditional domination of the landlord class in politics, even when supported by a bishop.[28] Lord Kenmare perceived Home Rule as a loss of power for his class and 'a severance of the British connection', attributing Blennerhassett's victory to 'a vast amount of intimidation ... guided from Dublin' by a combination of Fenians, the nationalist press and some priests.[29] The outcome in Kerry was more significant than Butt's victory in Limerick, for Blennerhassett was an unknown, unlike the 'father of Home Rule'. The introduction of the secret ballot in 1872 facilitated democratization, as tenants could now follow their conscience without having to run the gauntlet of landlord retribution.[30]

In 1873 the Supreme Council granted Isaac Butt three years of benevolent neutrality to appeal to the whole political spectrum. Charles G. Doran, its secretary, was assured that, should Butt fail, he would cede the field to the physical force men.[31] In the meantime the IRB constitution allowed activists to engage in constitutional politics: 'The IRB shall await the decision of the Irish nation, as expressed by a majority of the Irish people, as to the fit hour of inaugurating a war against England, and shall, pending such an emergency, lend its support to every movement calculated to advance the cause of Irish independence consistently with the preservation of its own integrity.'[32]

In theory the IRB would be guided by the opinion of the Irish people when planning another Rising. At a Home Rule conference in November, Charles G. Doran and John O'Connor Power indicated that the organization should play a greater role in future.[33] Fenian electioneering in the 1874 general election, when Gladstone and the Liberals were defeated, culminated in John O'Connor Power, a supreme councillor, and William Henry O'Sullivan being elected to Parliament. The choice of these men signalled a more democratic access to power, for O'Connor Power, born in 1846, had spent part of his childhood in the Ballinasloe workhouse and was largely self-taught, while O'Sullivan, a successful entrepreneur, had a strong social conscience. Both were former habeas corpus suspension detainees.[34]

O'Connor Power, who possessed little income in an age when politicians were expected to pay their election expenses and support themselves in London, was suspected of using Fenian funds to facilitate his parliamentary career. He seems to have been egocentric, antagonizing both the Fenians and the Irish Parliamentary Party. To his credit he pursued the issue of the political prisoners in Parliament, which few dared to broach. Subsequently, Joseph G. Biggar, an Ulster MP, was co-opted to the Supreme Council. He hoped to convert the Fenians to constitutional nationalism, but the issue of IRB leaders swearing two mutually exclusive oaths – to forcibly establish a Republic, while pledging allegiance to the British state as MPs – soon became divisive on both sides of the Atlantic.[35]

Mitchel predictably disapproved of 'that helpless, driftless concern called "Home Rule"', declaring he would publicize separatism by non-attendance at Westminster, if elected. He was defeated as a candidate for Cork city in the general election of 1874, but would return if another opportunity arose. Devoy perceived an abstentionist campaign as discrediting English rule, while alerting her enemies 'that Ireland was a possible ally in case of war'.[36]

Dublin Castle was warned that 'extreme nationalists' were using Home Rule to promote separatism, but in case of failure, would revert to revolutionary methods. During the Co. Tipperary by-election of 1875 Mitchel enjoyed widespread support, which was led by Charles G. Doran, John Daly and Charles Kickham, as well as the young John Dillon.[37] The election of an undischarged felon was invalid, when Mitchel announced that he would stand as often as he was declared ineligible. Re-elected on 11 March 1875, he stated that 'the chief fact about my past life which recommended me to the people of Tipperary was that I had made no peace with England'.[38] He died shortly afterwards while visiting his childhood home near Newry. Nine days later, John Martin, his lifelong friend and a great promoter of nationalist unity, followed him in death.[39]

Arms smuggling

The IRB continued to prepare for an uprising, but an international conflict involving the British Empire failed to materialize. Gun-running created rural support for Fenianism and rifles were occasionally used for agrarian intimidation. In the US citizens exercised their right to bear arms, in line with the Victorian concept of 'manliness', demonstrating self-reliance and courage. In Ireland the state restricted access to weapons to the propertied classes.[40]

From 1869 onwards Dublin Castle recorded visits to Tipperary by William Hogan, an important IRB leader in Liverpool and Birmingham, whose brother, John, worked as a tailor in Borrisokane. Hogan was resourceful and calm, engineering his acquittal on a charge of having supplied the revolvers for the Manchester rescue. Suspected of distributing arms and sending out agents, he travelled to Borrisokane in December 1869 and to Parsonstown [Birr], Clara, Tullamore, Roscrea and Nenagh during 1871. The constabulary in Liverpool continued to shadow him. Another gun-running operation from Birmingham to the west of Ireland was directed by Michael Davitt, ending with his arrest and trial in 1870 and a sentence of fifteen years' imprisonment.[41]

On 16 June 1871 an armed IRB posse crossed the railway viaduct near Mallow and broke into an armoury of the North Cork Rifles. They removed one hundred rifles, loading them onto carts until surprised by a militia sergeant, who raised the alarm. The Fenian party, including James O'Brien of Mallow and David Sheehy, future MP and father of Hanna Sheehy-Skeffington, exchanged fire with the North Cork soldiers as they retreated. Two men were later convicted and sentenced to two years, but thirty-seven weapons remained in IRB hands.[42]

The leadership, in spite of the difficulties in training a secret army, failed to explore innovative methods, such as guerrilla fighting. Kickham, O'Leary and their followers remained fixated on the unrealistic idea of a voluntary organization defeating the British army. Contemporaries considered open warfare worthy of an emerging nation, but it must have become increasingly difficult to keep enthusiastic men in a state of silent readiness.

James F.X. O'Brien and William O'Brien, a leader and journalist in Cork, questioned the value of activities, which exhausted IRB funds but remained of 'almost ludicrous inadequacy'. Arms had to be kept hidden from the constabulary and were often poorly maintained or lost when personnel changed after disagreements. James F.X. O'Brien welcomed Butt's Home Government Association as an alternative, convinced that its proponents would be radicalized as they began to grasp 'the shocking misgovernment' of Ireland.[43]

O'Brien believed that the decline of the IRB began after 1871: the reluctance of members to pay dues and the dearth of safe venues, which meant meeting in taverns with their risk of loose talk, constituted major difficulties. In 1873 he resigned as travelling organizer, but continued his involvement in Cork. The IRB deteriorated alarmingly. O'Brien considered one high-ranking Fenian untrustworthy, while several others had embezzled funds. When denouncing robberies 'planned by some daring men who gave out that their object was to get money for the organization', he 'was threatened'.[44]

In March 1875, for instance, Robert Sullivan and William Mulcahy, Cork Fenians, who had robbed a messenger of £380, were sentenced to twenty years' penal servitude. This may be the incident recalled by William O'Brien in his *Recollections* when, starting a literary club to revive the IRB, a businessman and ex-member assisted him enthusiastically. The latter, who faced bankruptcy, then participated in a theft, ostensibly to support the movement, but was arrested. When Supreme Council officers condemned these criminals, they were opposed by their apologists. Although innocent, William O'Brien considered himself lucky to escape arrest, given the infiltrated state of the IRB. T.H. Ronayne, the 'centre' for Midleton, experienced an immediate, suspicious police search on return from Cork with rifles for his 'circle'. An IRB inquiry to identify the informer proved futile and William O'Brien resigned in 1875.[45]

Convinced that the IRB had outlived its usefulness, James F.X. O'Brien proposed to stand it down, while retaining a skeleton committee in case of future developments, as had happened with the EMA. Contemporaries believed that the Irish yearning for nationhood was ineradicable. After O'Brien's suggestion failed to be adopted, he resigned in December 1874. These difficulties, including opposition from the small Stephenite IRB, induced the Supreme Council to consider an Irish-American alliance, which could provide funding, and it turned to a new organization – the Clan na Gael.[46]

Continuing decline of the Fenian Brotherhood

In June 1867 Jerome Collins and other Fenians in New York reacted to the fragmentation of the Brotherhood by founding the Napper Tandy Club, a discussion forum, open to all. Vetting of members, an initiation oath and strict secrecy were observed, in contrast to the easygoing organization of the past. In time Napper Tandy was joined by other clubs, which evolved into the Clan na Gael Association.[47]

In January 1868 Colonel John O'Neill, 'hero of Ridgeway', succeeded Colonel Roberts as president of the Senate wing, but negotiations to merge with the Savage section collapsed and a 'campaign of mutual vituperation' resumed.[48]

Thomas Beach of Colchester, England, had fought under the French alias of 'Henri Le Caron' in the Civil War alongside Colonel O'Neill. This friendship, combined with Fenian carelessness, enabled him to spy for the Home Office from 1868. Le Caron accompanied the politically unsophisticated O'Neill on a visit to the White House, where the beleaguered President Johnson declared that 'my sympathies are entirely with you, and anything which lies in my power I am willing to do to assist you', recalling that two years ago he had only issued a proclamation against Fenian infringement of the neutrality laws five days after their invasion had failed.[49]

Le Caron witnessed '6000 armed and uniformed' Fenians parading through Philadelphia during their annual convention in December 1868. The delegates unanimously voted in favour of invading Canada, although the vital element of surprise had been replaced by greater Canadian preparedness. O'Neill pressed ahead, hampered by his senate, which refused to move unless victory seemed certain, but talked of action to retain their following. Le Caron oversaw the distribution of arms along the Canadian border, simultaneously communicating with Judge J.G. McMicken, Chief Commissioner of police in Ottawa.[50]

Consul Archibald wrote reassuringly from New York that O'Neill's ability to raise funds was reduced. By late 1868 the vaunted union between the Senate wing and the IRB had come to nothing. Although John O'Mahony enjoyed the support of Colonel Kelly, Captain James Murphy and Captain Michael O'Rourke, activists returned from Ireland, a British detective described him as 'shabbily and scantily attired – the funds' of the Savage (formerly O'Mahony) wing 'are running low'.[51]

According to Devoy, John O'Connor Power returned to New York in 1869 to link the IRB and Clan na Gael, whose clubs were quietly absorbing the best members of the Senate wing. Although the IRB consisted of just a few hundred men, O'Connor Power insisted that it would direct the transatlantic movement and the Clan should merely provide funding. In 1924 Devoy recalled him as 'a haughty person, very egoistical and arrogant in manner, and his terms for union were impossible. They were a foretaste of de Valera's.'

Discussions with William J. Nicholson and John McCarthy as secretary and treasurer of Clan na Gael broke down. Having failed in his attempt to set up a rival organization, O'Connor Power was warned to leave New York.[52] The ninth convention of the Fenian Brotherhood under John Savage reported a similar conflict with two unnamed IRB representatives, whose divisive mission terminated on 1 December 1869.[53]

In April 1870 Sir John Young, Governor General of Canada, called out 6000 militia men and two gunboats in anticipation of an invasion. Colonel O'Neill was re-elected as president and demanded 10,000 men and $50,000. The governor general was aware that bitter infighting between O'Neill and his senate, formerly opponents of O'Mahony, continued to weaken the Brotherhood.[54] The invasion of 25 May 1870 proved another failure, undermined by Le Caron and Rudolph Fitzpatrick and also repudiated by the rival Savage leadership. Young expressed regret over the hesitant US response to the Colonial Secretary, Lord Granville, although the Canadian troops performed well. Within three days the remaining Fenians had given up. The Senate wing now split: on 23 August, the majority changed their name to United Irishmen at the Cincinnati convention, but a reconciliation with the 'almost defunct' Savage faction failed, due to the latter's intransigence.[55]

O'Neill, imprisoned in the US for infringement of the neutrality laws, denounced his senators, James Gibbons, P.J. Meehan and P.W. Dunne. He criticized their extravagant, paid organizers and those Irish-American politicians, whose patriotism constituted a path to remunerative work. Dunne and James W. Fitzgerald had hoped for posts as whiskey inspectors, which O'Neill was to obtain through President Johnson. His remnant of the Brotherhood now joined the Savage section.[56]

*James W. Fitzgerald, an early Fenian
of Cincinnati, Ohio, Fenian senator
and Clan na Gael member (*Irish-
American, *courtesy Mike Ruddy).*

The amnestied Fenians arrived in New York in January 1871 to great acclaim. They founded the Irish Confederation, a name redolent of 1848, as an umbrella organization, in spite of warnings from John Boyle O'Reilly and John O'Mahony that the factions were unlikely to reconcile.[57] On receiving the funds of the defunct Canadian Brotherhood, the exiled leaders donated them to James O'Connor of the IRB to establish an alliance with the home organization. O'Connor, a journalist with the *Irishman*, transferred this $3500 via his employer, Richard Pigott, who embezzled it, conscious that a secret society could not involve the police.[58]

In February 1871 James W. Fitzgerald and William J. Nicholson, significant figures in the secretive, shadowy Clan na Gael, and simultaneously chairman and secretary of the United Irishmen (ex-Senate wing), transferred their authority to the political exiles. A narrative emerged that Stephens, not the senators, had caused the split of 1865. But O'Mahony, returning to prominence after the resignation of John Savage, blocked any merger during the tenth general convention of his Brotherhood:[59] 'I think we would be unworthy of the holy cause in which we are engaged were we to consent to have the brand of infamy affixed upon the glorious name of Fenianism, which, however reviled by enemies to-day, will be revered by future generations of Irishmen.'[60] The delegates rejected disbanding in March 1871 as a 'surrender … to a self-constituted directory', which would be 'cowardly and unconstitutional'.

O'Neill's final attempt to invade Canada occurred on 5 October 1871, when he hoped in vain to link up with Louis Riel and the Red River Métis. Lacking

Brotherhood support, he trustingly asked Henri Le Caron to procure weapons. O'Neill's forty followers captured Fort Pembina in Manitoba before the arrival of American troops, when their raid collapsed. He withdrew from Fenianism, spending the remainder of his life working for Irish settlers in Nebraska.[61]

In 1872 Michael Scanlan and John O'Mahony were reconciled. The former admitted that the Chicago faction had been over-eager to push ahead, while O'Mahony 'was as advanced as were the Irish people and moved as fast as it was safe to travel' and 'above reproach' in financial matters.[62] But mistrust prevailed and the Irish Confederation collapsed in the spring of 1873. The rival Brotherhood recalled O'Mahony as leader, hoping that he could revive it. Although the constitution stressed that it 'shall never be dissolved ... until the object of Fenianism' was obtained, only a shadow remained. Clan na Gael, known to insiders as the United Brotherhood, emerged as the forceful promoter of separatism, aware of the poor state of the IRB.[63]

In Cork, Clan members, returning home, formed the United Brotherhood of Ireland as a breakaway group, but when 'Long John' O'Connor, its representative, travelled to New York to gain recognition in 1874, Devoy discouraged opposition to the IRB and 'the new organization dissolved'. The following year, Fr Eugene Sheehy, a priest in Kilmallock, who openly associated with Fenianism, became so dissatisfied with the membership in Co. Limerick that he set up a new body, which was, however, blocked by IRB hostility.[64]

The alliance of IRB and Clan na Gael

In July 1875 the home organization ratified a 'compact of agreement' to receive funding from the Clan; the latter insisted on policy changes. Devoy organized the setting up of a Revolutionary Directory of seven delegates, which began work in 1877. Originally intended to consist of three members from Clan na Gael, three from the IRB and one representative of the Australian Fenians, difficulties of communication caused the last to be omitted. A quorum consisted of three delegates from either side, plus one man from the sister organization.[65]

John O'Connor Power travelled to New York as the revolutionary envoy from Ireland, but failed to gain endorsement for sitting simultaneously in Westminster and on the Supreme Council. O'Mahony, Luby and Rossa denounced him.[66] Dr William Carroll, chairman of Clan na Gael, and John Devoy feared that the present Supreme Council was being outmanoeuvred by Isaac Butt and A.M. Sullivan of the Nation. They persisted with their IRB alliance to avoid another split, although very dissatisfied with O'Connor Power and worked for 'a more radically revolutionary' Supreme Council.[67] As Dr Carroll expected the demise of the Home Rule movement and the rise of the physical force party, active opposition was deemed unnecessary. Devoy concluded that the Revolutionary Directory would facilitate neutralizing opportunists like O'Connor Power.[68]

By March 1876 the Fenian Brotherhood was in terminal decline, not least because of the Clan–IRB alliance. O'Mahony remained at the helm, while the past conduct of Stephens was excused as due to the schismatic senators of 1865. The fourteenth convention invited Stephens to return as 'chief organizer', claiming the movement had deteriorated without him.[69] This increased the difficulties of the Supreme Council. Devoy counterattacked, accusing the autocratic Stephens of 'cowardice and deception', while Dr Carroll questioned O'Mahony's political judgement, recalling how the 'Moffat Mansion revolutionist' had lost control of his senate and frittered away money needed in Ireland.[70]

According to Devoy, the Republican cause was

> above personal friendship, and I would not hesitate to sacrifice the friendship of those even with whom I shared the hardships of a British prison, if there is a question of taking back the man who brought ruin and disgrace – ay, the worst disgrace of all, a bloodless defeat – on a movement that commanded the devotion and unquestioning obedience of the best spirit and manhood of the land.[71]

Only in 1924 did Devoy concede that, while the Fenian Brotherhood had been guilty of waste and disorganization, lacking the disciplined structure of the Clan, O'Mahony was scapegoated by rivals and a hostile press.

Devoy insisted that Kickham and Doran end their toleration of supreme councillors serving as MPs.[72] Denis Dowling Mulcahy, having qualified as a medical doctor, went on a lecture tour in Ireland and England to advocate physical force. His supporters found it impossible to hire a venue in Cork, while in Dublin a 'free fight' broke out among the 'sparse' attendance. Dr Mulcahy had a hasty temper and was unlikely to conciliate anybody.[73] In Tipperary town he arrived for his lecture accompanied by Charles Kickham, James O'Connor and Charles G. Doran to be welcomed by 7000 people. Mulcahy regretted that parliamentary candidates failed to emulate abstentionists like Rossa and propagated Mitchel's definition of Home Rule as 'a delusion, a snare and a fraud'. Doran concluded that Home Rule had proved unsuccessful.[74]

'Mr John O'Connor Power, M.P., and Mr John Daly'[75]

John Daly had become so dissatisfied with the Home Rule agitation as to attempt disrupting a procession to honour Isaac Butt, MP for Limerick, in April 1876.

Supported by the Catholic clergy and influential farmers, this city was 'en fête', which 'was marred to some extent by an outrageous though of course unsuccessful attempt on the part of some forty or fifty persons to put, by sheer violence, an abrupt end to the day's proceedings'.[76]

The *Nation* derided Daly and his working-class 'bludgeon-men' for presuming to represent the 10,000 Home Rulers assembled.[77] Michael MacDonagh, one of those present, snobbishly described John McInerney, a cousin of the Dalys, as a 'carpenter', assisted by Tom Ryan, the 'bill sticker' and Ned Hartney, the 'pig jobber'. Daly was arrested, while others required treatment in Barrington's Hospital.[78]

On 28 May 1876 the Supreme Council discussed terminating its cooperation with Butt's movement. The controversy continued until 20 August, when the supreme councillors voted to cease their support, giving the Fenian MPs six months to withdraw from Westminster; O'Connor Power, Joseph Biggar, John Barry and Patrick Egan had left the IRB by August 1877. Henceforth Charles Kickham insisted on all councillors abstaining from constitutional politics, although the Home Rule agitation continued to be tolerated.[79]

Daly supported Kickham, while feeling aggrieved by O'Connor Power, a talented orator from an impoverished background. During a visit to America, this supreme councillor had openly renounced his IRB allegiance. Fenians recalled the betrayal of Sadleir and Keogh.[80] Daly orchestrated a confrontation in the Free Trade Hall in Manchester, where O'Connor Power was to lecture on 'Irish wit and humour'. A member of the audience asked whether the speaker was an adherent of Wolfe Tone and Emmet (signifying a Fenian) or a follower of Isaac Butt. Both Joseph Biggar, who chaired, and O'Connor Power declined to answer, given the non-political nature of the evening. This acted as the signal for the IRB men, who stormed the platform: 'It was very plain that many had come there not to hear a lecture on Irish wit and humour, but to fight the battle of "Repeal versus Home Rule".'[81] The *Manchester Guardian* described how chairs were turned into weapons: 'Some of the missiles struck the organ, and injured it, and when the audience had dispersed the floor of the hall looked like a field the morning after a battle.'[82]

An anonymous Irish Catholic, as well as William O'Neill Daunt wrote to the *Nation*, feeling 'shame and indignation' regarding 'the Sunday recreations the O'Connor Power [sic] is providing for the Irish', as English goodwill was essential to regain their rights. Reports of how the 'ungodly Irish' spent the Sabbath gave Catholics a bad name and played into the hands of opponents. John O'Leary, although supporting physical force, proceeded to censure 'such attempts to stifle freedom of thought'.[83]

The harassment of O'Connor Power continued. In September 1877 Parnell was addressing a Home Rule meeting in Dumbarton, when 'a great uproar took place at the door of the hall. All rose to their feet and stood upon the seats.' A hostile mob forced its way in and 'hundreds in the hall became wild with excitement, and shouted as if eager for a fray with the intruders'.[84] John Daly and his followers arrived by special train from Glasgow to hunt O'Connor Power, who had absented himself. Daly vowed to 'pursue with unrelenting hatred the man who betrayed their principles, and starve him into submission or wipe him out'.[85]

Daly, declaring himself 'willing to endure any vicissitudes in Ireland's cause', stood beside Parnell amidst applause. A Fenian voice reassured Parnell 'we have no objections to you; we object to O'Connor Power' and the gathering concluded by 'approving of the active policy of Messrs. Parnell and Biggar'.[86] Moderate nationalists condemned Daly's attacks on 'peaceable meetings'.[87] But when O'Connor Power retaliated in print, a ferocious newspaper controversy erupted.[88]

John Torley, the Scottish representative on the Supreme Council, denied charges of rowdiness during a public meeting, when Daly announced that 'Mr Butt had no right to the leadership of the Irish people; that it was not the custom with the Irish to accept a played-out Tory to lead them; and although he admired and respected Mr Butt in his private capacity as a gentleman, he was here tonight to refute and denounce his political programme.'[89]

In 1880 Michael Davitt concluded that O'Connor Power was unscrupulous and ambitious – a 'renegade to former nationalist principles'.[90] Daly and Devoy believed that the constitutional movement had failed, as Butt proved incapable of dominating his disparate MPs, while his respect for Parliament prevented him from acting forcefully. He won no concessions, but Parnell and other dissidents gained publicity for their cause by disrupting the proceedings.[91]

The Catalpa *Mission*

Three events, a rescue and two funerals, demonstrated the emergence of Clan na Gael as the leading revolutionary body. Some military Fenians had already died in Fremantle, where seven of them continued to serve life sentences.[92] All appeals for clemency having failed, Devoy initiated a rescue. He received advice concerning Western Australia from John Boyle O'Reilly and Denis Cashman in Boston, Thomas McCarthy Fennell in Elmira, New York, and John Kenealy in Los Angeles. Other released Fenians helped with fundraising, including Thomas Francis Bourke, Ricard O'Sullivan Burke and Captain Laurence O'Brien. Devoy hired Captain George Smith Anthony of New Bedford to command a whale-hunting ship bought by the Clan. Whaling was in decline, many vessels having been destroyed by Confederate raiders during the Civil War and bitterness about British complicity lingered in New England. The *Catalpa*'s route led to Western Australia, where John J. Breslin had established contact with the prisoners.[93]

The popular William Foley had been released and acted as go-between, although suffering from heart disease. After ten years of incarceration Thomas Henry Hassett, Michael Harrington, Martin Joseph Hogan, Thomas Darragh, Robert Cranston and James Wilson enjoyed some freedom of movement outside Fremantle Prison. The rescuers excluded James Keilley, whose betrayal of information to the authorities in 1866 had become known, while Thomas Delaney, a drunkard, remained in close confinement. The American team was surprised to discover two IRB men in Fremantle, intent on the same mission.[94]

In 1875 Martin Hogan had smuggled a plea for help to Michael Francis Murphy, Secretary of the Amnesty Association in Cork and a relation of Charles G. Doran of the Supreme Council. Members raised £1000, which included £400 collected by John Barry, IRB representative for the north of England. Denis Florence McCarthy and John Stephen Walsh ('John Walsh of Middlesbrough'), an organizer for the north of England, were despatched to Fremantle. The men, both natives of Munster, put themselves at Breslin's disposal. British intelligence had become aware of the IRB mission, but its ineffectual warning to the Australian authorities compounded their lax security.[95]

On 17 April 1876 six Fenian prisoners evaded observation to reach a waiting boat. When their escape was discovered, a dramatic pursuit by armed steamship ensued. Captain Anthony refused to surrender them to the colonial authorities, who threatened to open fire. The commander of the *Catalpa* replied that in international waters any hostile act against his ship attacked the US and would provoke an international incident – the *Catalpa* was allowed to depart.[96]

Unaware of developments in the Antipodes, 140 members of Parliament including such outstanding Liberals as John Bright, Anthony Mundella and Henry Fawcett, used the occasion of Queen Victoria assuming the title of empress of India to petition for the liberation of the Fenians on humanitarian grounds.[97] Two weeks after Prime Minister Disraeli had rebuffed them, news of the rescue reached Westminster. Dublin celebrated with a torchlight procession. On 19 August a triumphant *Catalpa* sailed into New York harbour in a major publicity coup for the Clan, based on meticulous planning and sustained secrecy; it formed a redeeming contrast to Fenian operations of the 1860s.[98]

On completing his task William Foley visited Tipperary to see his last surviving relative. In New York he participated in the public welcome for those rescued, before dying of heart disease on 1 November 1876. Devoy stressed that this 'humble' man was honoured as a political prisoner and loyal Fenian. Clan na Gael acted as Foley's next of kin and 6000 members marched behind his coffin.[99] On arrival at the East River ferry, military honours were rendered before the cortège continued to Calvary Cemetery, where 'three volleys were fired over a soldier's grave'.[100]

British secret service reports confirmed how the Fenian Brotherhood, 'formerly so numerous and so wealthy', had 'steadily declined', despite multitudes of sympathizers throughout North America. The Brotherhood had been destroyed 'by never-ending feuds and dissensions'; active revolutionaries joined the Clan, which conducted its affairs 'with vastly more efficiency', so that it took Consul Archibald ten years to obtain information concerning its structure and cipher.[101]

The O'Mahony funeral

During the 1870s O'Mahony experienced hardship and lost an inheritance invested in a newspaper. By December 1875 the 'head centre' received treatment for 'Morbus Brights Disease', incurable kidney failure.[102] According to the *Irish World*, 'little is known of O'Mahony's private life, as he was always very secretive', though with 'plenty of friends willing and eager to help him in the day of adversity, but the man was too proud and sensitive to appeal to them, and shrank from obtruding his real condition on public notice'.[103]

He accepted some aid from John Savage and Richard O'Gorman, nevertheless. The *Irishman* considered O'Mahony 'a strange being … all his life a bookworm', who was known for his 'wonderful philological research and accuracy' and greatly admired by the 'German Celtic scholars'.[104] When O'Mahony resigned as 'head centre', the fifteenth general convention of the Fenian Brotherhood saluted him as 'the father of Fenianism'. He died on 6 February 1877 from oedema 'of the lungs causing suffocation and he suffered terrible agony'.[105] As the Brotherhood consisted of less than 500 members in New York, Rossa, his successor, involved various Irish societies in organizing the funeral, modelled on that of Terence Bellew McManus sixteen years previously.[106]

The *New York Times*, which disapproved of Fenianism, used O'Mahony as an object lesson for the futility of its plots:

> He died like all Irish patriots of the sword – alone, friendless, wretched, and forgotten. I do not say this in any unsympathetic spirit. John O'Mahony was a man of rare parts. He was a good scholar, a good writer, an industrious, sober

man, and, I believe, an honest man, according to his lights. But politically he was a fool, and he paid even with his life the penalty of his folly ... He relied on that which he knew to be a reed shaken with the wind – the voice of the men ready to fight the battalions of England.[107]

The paper conceded his 'great efforts' were partly successful, but 'that he lamentably failed as a leader of men, to say nothing of his childlike incapacity to read character and to judge under-bred plotters with whom he was surrounded, the fiasco of "the Moffat House" and the miserable life he led for ten years, ending in death accelerated by poverty, amply testify'.[108]

Rossa had called for donations to a 'Skirmishing Fund' to commence terrorist operations in England in 1876. The *New York Times* denounced this as a 'dodge' to extract money from Irish-Americans, contrasting Rossa, a hotel-keeper in the Five Points slum, with O'Mahony, whom it had derided in the past. His death deprived 'the once noisy and not to be despised' Brotherhood of the one scholarly gentleman to lend it respectability.[109] This was a common British tactic of denigration, which described revolutionary predecessors as greatly superior to present protagonists.

Assertions that the 'head centre' died neglected by his peers are exaggerations, originating with Dr Mulcahy, who declared 'that O'Mahony "died in a garret, a pauper"'. The Fenian chief lacked any interest in personal comfort. Dr Mulcahy wished to vindicate him, but tended to overreact, as apparent from his several law cases.[110]

The trustees of the Skirmishing Fund loaned Rossa $2030 for the obsequies, when he convinced himself that 'the Clan na Gael and the [almost insolvent] Fenian Brotherhood have promised to refund the money'. Dr Carroll agreed that the Clan would contribute, given its prominent role in the funeral, but repudiated Rossa's misconception.[111]

O'Mahony reposed in the armoury of the 69th Regiment, where 10,000 people filed past before Requiem Mass in St Francis Xavier's Church, Sixteenth Street. The pall-bearers included Richard O'Gorman, John Savage, Thomas Francis Bourke, Devoy, Luby, John J. Breslin, Rossa, Patrick Ford, Denis Cashman, John Warren, Augustine Costello, James, second son of John Mitchel, and a son of the late James Mountaine of Cork. Colonel Roberts, O'Mahony's former rival, also attended. Dr Mulcahy, William Francis Roantree and Stephen, a brother of James J. O'Kelly, were among the American delegates who accompanied the remains to Cobh. This deputation warned the Cork Fenians that the spy 'Red Jim' McDermott was shadowing them.[112]

On 9 February 1877 Charles Kickham, on behalf of the IRB, appealed for a committee to organize the public funeral. O'Mahony having been a Young

Irelander as well as a Fenian founder, the *Irishman* and the *Nation* suspended their rivalry, allowing James O'Connor and Thomas Sexton to cooperate as joint secretaries, while John Leavy served as treasurer. The latter and O'Connor were high-ranking Fenians, but Sexton, a member of the *Nation* staff, supported constitutional nationalism.[113]

The secretaries 'with all due filial reverence' requested the use of the pro-cathedral from Cardinal Cullen, who refused with a pompous lecture. Dr Cullen lauded O'Connell, the Liberator from penal laws and condemned O'Mahony as the head of an organization proscribed by the pope:

> I am not aware that Mr O'Mahony has contributed any great or signal service to his country, but that rather he provoked hostile legislation against us, and by word and example brought unsuspecting young men into breaches of the law, and serious troubles. I have not been able to learn that he has been a great bene-factor to the Catholic Church; on the contrary, he is said to have been a very lukewarm Christian, to have been careless about the practices of religion, and to have written papers from time to time in a hostile spirit against the Church or her ministers.[114]

Dr Cullen intended to repudiate a Fenian event, but his message was singu-larly devoid of charity. The *New York Times* believed Fenianism in decline and deplored the cardinal's attempt to advance 'his educational and ecclesiastical schemes' through the Home Rule Members of Parliament, while unwittingly facil-itating IRB propagandists to portray themselves as 'persecuted patriots'.[115] Alfred Webb, the veteran Quaker nationalist, also dissented. He had 'great respect' for O'Mahony, 'a man devoted to his country, and he was willing to undergo exile for a cause he believed right. He was a scholar whose translation of Keating must ever be esteemed a solid and valuable contribution to the study of Irish history.'[116]

Nevertheless, Webb, a committed Home Ruler, felt that participation in this funeral would send the wrong signal, for the deceased believed to the last in 'settling the differences between England and Ireland by the sword'. The remains were received in the pro-cathedral of Cloyne in Cobh. In Cork, where no church was available, 'hundreds came in from the country districts'.[117]

The Fenian elan of the past was absent in Cork and the funeral seemed smaller than that of Brian Dillon in 1872. It resembled a commemoration of separatism, as Jeremiah O'Donovan of Tower, a former political prisoner, John McInerney, Michael Power of Tralee, John Sarsfield Casey, Patrick O'Keeffe, 'centre' of Kanturk in 1865 and James O'Connor of Dublin shouldered the coffin. The Mandeville brothers, nephews of the deceased, and Thomas O'Mahony of Mitchelstown, a cousin, were chief mourners, while green and black, the Fenian colours, were universally worn.[118]

'At all the Munster stations a crowd, large or small, was waiting on the platform' when the train passed, with the largest contingents at Charleville and Limerick Junction, near O'Mahony's old home. On arrival at the Junction,

> though it was the middle of a working day, some 600 persons flocked out of Tipperary ... As the train drew up at the Junction platform, every head was uncovered and the band broke into the 'Dead March'. This part of the proceedings was very decorous and impressive, especially remembering the almost riotous enthusiasm with which Tipperary rushed to the same spot to hug John Mitchel.[119]

The organizers wished to take the coffin out at Thurles, but Dr Croke vetoed a lying-in-state in the cathedral. In Dublin, the cortège waited until evening to allow working men to participate, when they proceeded to the Mechanics Institute in Abbey Street. Although impressive, the final procession to Glasnevin lacked the size and impact of the McManus obsequies.[120] The attendance resembled a subversive roll call, including John Daly, P.N. Fitzgerald, William Moore Stack of Tralee, Michael Cusack of Drangan, Michael Halley of Tramore, C.J. O'Farrell of Enniscorthy, Denis Florence McCarthy, John Leavy of Dublin, John Hickey of Kingstown, Robert Johnston of Belfast and several IRB leaders from Britain.[121] Respecting Dr Cullen's veto, Charles Kickham spoke outside Glasnevin Cemetery on the theme of national resurrection, asserting that the Fenian movement, begun 'by Doheny, O'Mahony and Stephens ... is an existing thing'.[122] Inside, 'Mr Doran, of Queenstown, a layman, having said the prayers for the dead, the clay was cast upon the coffin, and all was over'.[123]

In Fethard 10,000 sympathizers followed an empty coffin with bands playing the 'Dead March' from *Saul* to Captain Delahunt's grave in Rathcool Cemetery, where this 'patriot soldier' of 1867 and O'Mahony were commemorated. Astonishing sobriety prevailed. Another funeral procession in Carrick-on-Suir, an area central to O'Mahony's efforts in 1848, was attended by 12,000 people and presided over by John Francis Meagher, a former habeas corpus detainee. His brother William, the local IRB 'centre', had died in Mountjoy in 1866.[124]

The funeral had an unseemly aftermath, for Dr Mulcahy insisted that Rossa had promised him $1000 in expenses and compensation for abandoning his medical practice to travel to Ireland. He received only half that sum and, as the Fenian Brotherhood was insolvent, Mulcahy initiated legal proceedings against the trustees of the Skirmishing Fund, which continued until 1884.[125] Devoy characterized the conflict with Dr Mulcahy and Rossa as 'a lunatic on one side threatening us with a lawsuit and on the other a drunken man bringing us into disgrace by raving in the papers'.[126]

The last Fenian prisoners

The *Catalpa* rescue had tightened security for those imprisoned in England, including the ailing Colour Sergeant Charles McCarthy. In 1877 he smuggled out a letter, stating that 'nothing less than our lives are aimed at, and that too in a cowardly assassin-like manner'.[127] When finally released in January 1878 Charles McCarthy, John Patrick O'Brien, Thomas Chambers and Michael Davitt were feted in Dublin. Thanking O'Connor Power, MP, for his support, Charles McCarthy 'sobbed rather than spoke'.[128] Chambers recalled how twelve years in prison had broken his comrade:

> He was straight, broad-shouldered, and moved about with a smart military pace. He was in every respect a perfect model of a soldier. When we met in London, after our release last month, he looked old and haggard – like a man that has gone through much suffering. His jaws and eyes were sunken in, his shoulders drooping down, and inclining to the front. His chest was sunk, his back round, his head inclined forward, and he tottered when walking like an old man of seventy.[129]

The ex-prisoners were invited to meet Parnell and the press on 15 January, when McCarthy suddenly collapsed and died. At his inquest the jury stated that ill treatment in prison had 'hastened his death'.[130] As a Fenian, McCarthy's remains were barred from any Catholic church, but the Clarendon Street Carmelites placed him in a sodality room, outside Cardinal Cullen's jurisdiction. (To the public, he appeared to repose in a side chapel.)[131]

The *Irish Times* reported that on one day alone 15,000 people paid their respects, pronouncing McCarthy misled 'by a false enthusiasm, and honest but fatally mistaken notions of patriotism and duty'.[132] His funeral to Glasnevin Cemetery developed into a nationalist demonstration, with a 'team of four Belgian horses of spotless black' drawing the 'magnificent glass carriage of Messrs Fanagan of Aungier Street'.[133] When subscriptions for a fund to aid the political prisoners were being sought, Archbishop Croke defied Dr Cullen by stating that McCarthy's fate had evoked general sympathy: 'They suffered long, and much for the political faith that was in them; and the country for which they forfeited ten years of freedom is not likely to be unmindful of their protracted captivity and privations. Poor McCarthy's death presents one of the most tragic incidents in all this sad and sickening episode of our history.'[134]

When rebuked, Dr Croke reminded Cardinal Cullen of the political change wrought by the IRB:

> I could never bring myself to rank Fenians as a body with Freemasons, for instance, or to make the great bulk of our Irish Catholic people, ninety percent

of whom are Fenian in heart and sympathy, answerable for the freaks and infi-
delity of a few amongst them ... I cannot at all agree with your eminence that
the Fenians have effected no good. They have given us a tolerable land bill and
disestablished the Protestant church.[135]

A government inquiry into allegations of ill-treatment followed in February
1878. Nationalists believed that London hoped to 'whitewash the Chatham screws'
through an unsworn investigation. O'Connor Power stated that McCarthy could
not have criticized his jailers without risking retribution, but 'he complained
bitterly to his friends'.[136]

John Patrick O'Brien returned to his birthplace, Nenagh, where Peter
Gill addressed a 'Fenian demonstration', consisting of the sons of respectable
tradesmen and farmers. O'Brien retired from politics to superintendent the
public baths in Tara Street, Dublin. Thomas Chambers visited his old home
in Thomastown, Co. Kilkenny, which was illuminated in his honour, before
accompanying Michael Davitt on a speaking tour of Britain. Chambers reaffirmed his Fenian convictions and participated in discussions between the IRB,
Davitt and Parnell, when a policy of mutual toleration was agreed.[137]

In the wake of McCarthy's death, efforts to liberate the remaining eight
Fenians redoubled. The visiting committee reported that Thomas Ahearn, who
had been sentenced for shooting at a policeman in 1866, was beginning to
lose his reason in Dartmoor. The US government continued to urge the release
of Edward O'Meagher Condon.[138] The British responded by discharging him
and Patrick Melody, both convicted of involvement in the Manchester rescue,
despite the latter's persistent declarations of innocence, on condition of exile
abroad. By February 1879 Thomas Ahearn, James Clancy, Patrick Tierney and
Edward O'Kelly, the final prisoner, had been freed.[139]

Thomas Chambers emigrated to the US, but his health never recovered.
John Boyle O'Reilly, whom he had supported during bouts of depression in
prison, arranged his hospitalization, 'his body a mass of aches and diseases
that agonised every moment'. The doctors were unable to help and Chambers
commented: 'They never saw a man before who was suffering from the drains
of Dartmoor.'[140] Boyle O'Reilly recalled: 'He was wasted to a skeleton. He had
suffered horribly for nearly twenty years. When he went to prison he was the
happiest and merriest fellow I ever knew.'[141]

Thomas Chambers died on 2 December 1888. His friend concluded that, 'in
his case, at least, England's vengeance was complete'.

Dynamiters, Land Leaguers and the Rise of Parnell, 1878–84

By 1871 Rossa was a Fenian celebrity. Suffering from post-traumatic stress, however, he developed a drink problem. Separatism was stagnating; dissensions continued and the final attempts to invade Canada proved farcical.[1]

In the autumn of 1874 Patrick and Augustine Ford of the *Irish World* called for bands of skirmishers to conduct raids on Britain, that 'desolating curse of Ireland', to break the state of paralysis. The empire was weaker than imagined and determined revolutionaries could force it to its knees within a quarter of a century. Conferring with Rossa and McCafferty the following year, Patrick Ford insisted on dropping plots of prison breaks and royal kidnappings in favour of skirmishing, a war of attrition against Britain, as an insurrection was not feasible. On 4 March 1876 Rossa appealed for a 'Skirmishing Fund' of $5000 in the *Irish World* to attack England, while the revolutionary organizations continued long-term preparations. This initiated the first urban bombing campaign in the world.[2]

The American Civil War had introduced highly destructive methods of warfare. In an age of technological progress, 'infernal machines' were experimented with and used in disputes in the US. During the second half of the nineteenth century, wars were invariably inhuman, but the appliance of science might deliver decisive blows instead of traditional, protracted campaigns. States that refused to adapt would lose out. European revolutionaries deployed the 'propaganda of the deed', including assassination and bombing. Irish-American activists embraced dynamite as levelling the odds, allowing them to carry grievances into the heart of the empire to spread terror, before vanishing abroad. Rossa followed Mitchel in welcoming any weapon against England:[3] 'I say very plainly and emphatically that, if the destruction of London is to be the price of Irish freedom, the Irish people should pay that price for it. Let justice be done, though the heavens should fall.'[4]

Rossa envisaged dedicated teams of bombers. Should any activists be sentenced to death, he favoured reprisals, including the burning of towns. He ignored A.M. Sullivan's warning of the likely consequences for two million Irish people in Britain.[5] Revolutionary violence was justifiable against reactionary regimes, but not the liberal state. During the nineteenth century and especially the land war, Ireland was held by troops and coercion, which undermined respect for the law. Patrick Ford and the proponents of skirmishing exculpated themselves by pointing to the violence perpetrated by Dublin Castle.[6] Ford provided Rossa with his popular 'skirmishing column' in his *Irish World*. When a correspondent enquired how much dynamite would 'blow up Fermoy barracks', Rossa explained that this psychological warfare also forced Britain into expensive security measures. From San Francisco an approving Captain McCafferty inquired: 'Have you any design on Canada?'[7]

The majority of his transatlantic peers considered Rossa a loose cannon, unwittingly jeopardizing operations like the *Catalpa* mission. John O'Leary rejected the 'active policy' with horror, 'somewhat relieved by an almost equally strong element of the grotesque'. Privately, he wondered 'what kind of idiots are the people that mind such a man?' In 1883 Davitt warned the Glasgow Young Ireland Society that a bombing campaign would cost their 'just' cause the support of 'the English democracy', while driving Irishmen out of politics. The dynamitards were 'worthy of incarceration in a political bedlam'. He also warned Britain to remember that ill-treated and exiled political prisoners had relations abroad who might avenge them. Davitt urged Westminster to address the mainsprings of Irish discontent – Dublin Castle and Irish landlordism, rather than ignoring Ireland when quiet.[8] Rossa riposted to those who persisted with chivalrous conduct: 'You want "honourable warfare". Well, wait till England will let you have it, and you'll wait till you'll lie down and die.'[9]

The Clan agreed on the desirability of a fund for special projects, but felt that the term 'skirmishing' suggested disastrous exploits.[10] Until 1876 Stephens's prison break constituted the only successful Fenian operation, the Manchester rescue having caused one accidental death and three executions.

Any further disaster would confirm the Irish as incapable of effective action. Rossa's personal problems escalated and the Clan gained control of the fund by threatening to expose his financial transgressions.[11]

Expelled from the Clan, Rossa held a convention in Philadelphia in June 1880 to found the United Irishmen and his eponymous newspaper. He attracted disgruntled men of little standing and 'Red Jim' McDermott, now a journalist in Brooklyn, who praised the motto of the extremists, 'not a cent for blatherskite, but every dollar for dynamite'. The United Irishmen demanded to inspect the accounts of the Skirmishing Fund, now renamed the National Fund. Its trustees refused, leading to further in-fighting with Devoy.[12]

Parnell, Davitt and the New Departure

Charles Stewart Parnell, a Wicklow landlord, succeeded the recently deceased John Martin as MP for Meath in 1875. His obstructionist politics attracted attention. James J. O'Kelly alerted Devoy in August 1877 to 'the creation of a political link between the conservative and radical nationalists'. O'Kelly believed that Parnell 'could render really important services' with adequate support.[13] Parnell's speeches stressed his reliance on 'the people' and his refusal to petition for favours, while, like O'Connell, hinting at physical force. His uncompromising tone appealed to Fenians. Butt, on the other hand, had achieved little in Parliament. Parnell considered 'the position of the Irish members painfully humiliating'.[14]

In January 1878 Dr William Carroll, Chairman of Clan na Gael, met Parnell and became convinced that he favoured independence, if supported by the people. Davitt and Devoy urged that British rule would become 'more difficult or impossible', if the nationalist spectrum cooperated.[15] On 7 November 1878 Devoy offered his support, provided Parnell declare in favour of self-government, campaign vigorously on the land question, avoid sectarian issues and support oppressed nationalities in Parliament. But this telegram, encapsulating the conditions for the 'new departure', was ignored by Parnell and repudiated by a disapproving Charles Kickham, President of the IRB, whose acquiescence Devoy had assumed. Querying 'the policy of isolation from the public life', initiated by Stephens, Devoy concluded that public representation was essential: 'A mere conspiracy will never free Ireland.'[16]

By October 1878 Alfred Webb, one of Butt's earliest supporters, considered their efforts a failure, his leader having been consistently 'rebuffed'. Webb questioned 'continuing a moribund agitation'. The middle classes failed to support Home Rule, for conditions in Ireland had improved steadily since 1870.

Rather than shunning the British Empire, young men joined its administration. They benefited from access to the civil service, increasingly based on educational merit, and began encroaching on the political power of the gentry. Webb believed that the majority was disinclined to make sacrifices to change the relationship between Ireland and Britain. Parnell visited Webb, declaring he wanted 'to bring about a different state of affairs ... we shall see the outcome'.[17]

Conferring with the Supreme Council in January 1879, Davitt and Devoy failed to gain majority support for their 'new departure'. IRB members could continue electioneering, but were barred from entering Parliament. Devoy recalled that when the Land League was founded, Fenian followers 'interpreted the permission rather freely and became the backbone and driving force'.[18] In March, Devoy met Parnell in Boulogne and found him eager to cooperate. The revolutionaries remained convinced of the ultimate failure of the constitutional movement and anticipated their return to prominence. Parnell became the chairman of the Parliamentary Party in May 1880, the ailing Butt having been deposed.[19]

The IRB in difficulties

By 1876 members felt dissatisfaction with Charles G. Doran, Secretary of the Supreme Council. Depending on American subsidies, the IRB was in the power of the Clan. The ousting of O'Connor Power, Patrick Egan and Joseph Biggar deprived it of energetic leaders. In 1878 Dr Carroll, inspecting envoy of the Clan, found it in bad shape. In Munster the membership had declined alarmingly, due to inefficiency and local disagreements. Doran recorded that the IRB in this province consisted of only 1742 men in possession of 286 rifles, sixty-two revolvers, 500 rounds of ammunition and £259. Rumours of Stephens making a comeback, in opposition to the Supreme Council, persisted.[20]

In March 1878 Charles G. Doran resigned as secretary. John O'Connor had helped to hold the IRB together after the 1865–6 arrests, subsequently emigrating to the US.[21] Returning as a Clan envoy, O'Connor remained as secretary, 'the most efficient one it [Supreme Council] ever had. He became a Royal Arch Mason for the purpose of covering his tracks, and it enabled him to travel at will in England and Scotland for many years without arousing suspicion.'[22] Dr Carroll believed that without O'Connor's admirable tact only 'organized factions would now exist' in Ireland and Britain. From his secret address in Paris, O'Connor screened conspirators, who awaited instructions to contact him at the Musée des Thermes et de l'Hôtel de Cluny or by checking the poste restante at Charing Cross, London.[23]

Table 10. *The Munster IRB on 28 January 1877*

County	No. of men	No. of weapons long	short	Ammunition	Cash
Kerry					
Tralee	75	12	4		£9
Ballyduff	30	2			£1–15
Ardfert	20	2			
Causeway	15	2			
Firies	20	3			2–10–0
Total for Kerry	160	18	7	500	13–5–0
Cork City:					
North	100				
South	150				24–0–0
Backstream	40				
Blackpool	50				94–0–0
Douglas	40				
Total for Cork City	380				118–0–0
Co. Cork					
Buttevant	25	1			
Cullen	81				4–0–0
Clonakilty	12	12			15–0–0
Castlemagner	50	3			
Carrigtuohill	22	3			
Dunmanway	0	15			
Grange	70	9			
Watergrasshill	30	9			
Mallow	20	7	5		
Macroom	60	6	12		
Midleton	50	20	12		
Little Island	40	9	3		
Passage	65				
Total for Co. Cork	525				
Tipperary	57	15	5		30–0–0
Limerick	60	24			79–10–0
Waterford	300	70			
	200	60	12		
Clare	60				
Total	1,742	286	62	500	£259-15-0

(Source: Ó Broin, 'The IRB Supreme Council, 1868–78', *Irish Historical Studies* vol. 19, no. 75, 322–3)

The 1876 alliance between the two societies entitled the Clan to inspect the IRB and Dr Carroll and Devoy did so in 1877 and 1879. Devoy conceded that the IRB had suffered greatly, not as a result of British action, but through internal quarrels. In the US, Rossa led his faction amidst copious publicity, denouncing the Clan as inactive and proclaiming Stephens the true head of the movement. According to Devoy, a 'propaganda of disorder and sometimes slander was carried on from America' and, reminiscent of O'Mahony's difficulties during the 1860s, 'assertions of dishonesty' about the IRB leadership were credited and culminated in resignations. This kept Fenian officers 'in constant hot water' with little time to conspire.[24]

The revolutionary organization only survived in parts of Ireland and Devoy noticed that rural districts suffered from haphazard arrangements: 'The people are naturally easy going and careless themselves while rather exacting with regard to their leaders. They expect too much from the S.C. and do not stop to enquire where the resources are to come from.'[25] Nevertheless, the present membership of 25,000, even if exaggerated, could form a core for rebuilding the IRB. His findings were discreetly circulated among Clan na Gael officers, which enabled Le Caron to copy them for Robert Anderson in London.[26] In this secret service report, the section about Fenian infighting is underlined, indicative of future British strategy. The Clan remained unaware that F.F. Millen, who was the military organizer of the Revolutionary Directory, had spied for the Foreign Office during the 1860s. When re-organizing the IRB 'centres' in early 1879, Millen grasped the opportunity to discover their identities, as well as the firearms at their disposal.[27]

O'Connor Power, the expelled member for Connacht, had 'commenced a war to the knife on the S.C.', reducing its membership in the north of England and attempting to win over followers in Ireland until counteracted by John Daly. The Clan chiefs lamented that the British hardly needed detectives, given the lack of secrecy among IRB officers: 'God help us with such revolutionists as the leading conspirators.'[28]

During the late 1870s, a shift in membership occurred: of 25,000 men enrolled, 10,000 resided in Ulster and 7000 in Connacht. Economic distress was felt in the northwest, where the IRB flourished. Munster and south Leinster had ceased to dominate and could only mustered 5000 and 2000 adherents respectively. Devoy reported that the majority of members in Ulster, Connacht, Tipperary and Clare were small farmers and their sons, which he considered 'a much better representation than in '65'. These agrarian Fenians ensured the continuation of the Ribbon tradition.[29]

Many influential leaders hailed from Connacht and Ulster, including John O'Connor Power, Patrick Egan, Matt Harris of Ballinasloe, P.J. Sheridan of

Tubbercurry, the Sligo 'county centre', John O'Kane and Robert Johnston of Belfast.[30] Johnston, Harris and P.W. Nally of Mayo enjoyed the prosperous lifestyle of self-made men, previously unknown among the leadership. Unlike the *Irish People* intellectuals, they focused on the concerns of country people. The IRB depended for its appeal on the continuance of deep-rooted discontent, which the memory of the Famine and ongoing emigration provided.[31]

By the late 1870s falling prices and agricultural imports from the US resulted in hardship for small holders. The Mallow Farmers' Club protested that only 175,000 among 585,000 tenants were entitled to vote, excluding all but wealthy men from political decision-making.[32] In 1877 John Sarsfield Casey, returned to Mitchelstown since the 1869 amnesty, publicized the background to the attempted assassination of Patten Bridge, land agent of Nathaniel Buckley in the Galtees. Buckley had bought his estate as a speculation and 'stories of hardship, of unremitting toil' emerged. The agent sued for defamation of character, but 'such a feeling against the landlord system' had arisen that Casey was acquitted. William O'Brien, a talented journalist and former IRB officer, followed up with 'Christmas in the Galtees', a series of articles in the *Freeman's Journal*.[33] O'Brien argued that where the tenant's industry had been outstanding, reclaimed fields and 'decent housing were invariably a passport to harsher burdens'.[34] The issue was discussed in Parliament, with Timothy McCarthy Downing, MP for Cork, supporting O'Brien's exposé. Davitt referred to it during his speaking tour of the US.[35]

Potato blight recurred in the west of Ireland, threatening famine. Davitt responded by founding the Land League of Mayo, which became the Land League of Ireland on 21 October 1879. It went beyond the traditional demands of fair rent, fixity of tenure and compensation for improving tenants by seeking a permanent settlement of the land question. The league asserted the right of the people to their holdings, resolving to defend those evicted while ostracizing 'land grabbers' who betrayed their community. Davitt realized the league's revolutionary potential and persuaded Parnell to serve as president. The Clan provided Davitt with a donation from the Skirmishing Fund, while assisting Parnell and John Dillon during their American fundraising tour from December 1879 to March 1880, when Irish-Americans contributed generously.[36]

The Land League, with its promise of a redistribution of property, attracted great IRB support. In 1877 Brian Clune of Carrahan succeeded his brother John, who had been forced to flee to America in 1867, 'as "county centre" for Clare in which capacity he showed considerable energy and ability. He kept the barony and parish "centres" well in hand and looked carefully into the accounts and the disposal of the arms and ammunition.'[37]

The Clare IRB had close links with Ribbonism since the 1860s and when the land agitation began, Brian Clune organized 'outrages'.[38] Orthodox Fenians, who opposed the Land League, formed a minority, albeit including P.N. Fitzgerald and Charles G. Doran.[39] In Cork 'Long John' O'Connor heeded Devoy's lectures to participate in politics. O'Connor, impressed by Parnell's charisma and Davitt's arguments, left the IRB to found a Cork branch of the league. This caused violent tensions, as he tried to convince Fenians that the new venture 'was superior and more likely to be successful'.[40]

John O'Leary and the ailing Kickham, although sympathetic towards tenant farmers, insisted that the land issue should be dealt with after independence, as it would distract followers from separatism. These social conservatives enjoyed small incomes derived from fathers who had become minor landlords. Neither joined in the condemnation of landlords per se, arguing that large tenants could be quite as tyrannical.[41] According to Stephen Gwynn, a grandson of William Smith O'Brien and kinsman of T.W. Rolleston, this was a class issue: 'The men of the Fenian period, and still more the survivors from 1848, incline to regard the Land War as a vulgar quarrel about rents.'[42] The IRB leadership showed little social initiative. Kickham and O'Leary seemed content to assert their convictions through their writings and gentlemanly conduct, while postponing the realization of the Republic until they could field an army of citizens, suitably trained and equipped – an unlikely event.[43]

The Clan chiefs were convinced that Parnell and Biggar's parliamentary obstruction would fail, unless backed by the threat of physical force. Devoy brought $10,000 of the Skirmishing Fund across the Atlantic to revive the IRB. James J. O'Kelly, now a Francophile journalist and art dealer, was selected to re-establish the Fenian arms depot in London and ship weapons to Ireland, but the IRB leaders objected and the project was abandoned.[44]

O'Kelly accused O'Leary and Kickham of frustrating 'all progress because they have some private grief against their more active associates. Neither of the two men to whom I refer have any policy except the old *laisser-aller*, which may be resumed in talking big, denouncing every intelligent effort to make progress and do nothing.'[45] An exasperated O'Kelly joined Parnell to become MP for North Roscommon in the general election of 1880. O'Leary denounced him for defecting, while O'Kelly considered the former an 'old fossil'. William O'Brien had resigned from the IRB in 1875, but was drawn to the Home Rule movement to be elected MP for Mallow in 1883.[46]

In May 1880 Davitt was expelled from the IRB, followed by the departure of Matt Harris, John Barry and P.J. Sheridan. Patrick Egan, its deposed treasurer, now administered the Land League funds, assisted by William Henry

O'Sullivan. Harris and Sheridan also joined the league, while former political prisoners like William Moore Stack and John Sarsfield Casey organized in their districts. In Tralee 'violent and turbulent' Michael Power, an influential Fenian, came to the fore. In Fedamore Co. Limerick, Henry Casey, a weaver with IRB sympathies dating from 1867 and a close friend of John Daly, arranged meetings of the league. Even James O'Connor, Kickham's sympathetic host during his final years, deserted to agrarian agitation in 1881.[47]

Concessions for Ireland seemed likely when Gladstone and the Liberals returned to power in 1880. Parnell's star rose, not only with the 'new departure'-type Fenians, but, more importantly, among middle-class Catholics and their clergy. Agitation continued. Although its leaders advocated non-violent methods, the masses proved difficult to restrain. In December 1880 Dublin Castle initiated legal proceedings against Parnell and his lieutenants for conspiracy to prevent both the payment of rents and the leasing of the farms of evictees, but the case collapsed, unifying nationalists and increasing the flow of American donations. Chief Secretary Forster retaliated by introducing the Protection of Person and Property (Ireland) Bill, which was passed on 2 February 1881, authorizing the suspension of ordinary law in 'proclaimed' districts. Sir William Vernon Harcourt, the Home Secretary, had Davitt re-arrested, which sparked further unrest.[48]

The Dynamite War

The difficulties of small tenants in Connacht revived bitter memories of the Famine among an underclass that had failed to prosper in America. Other exiles, including the Ford brothers and Mackey Lomasney, Luke Dillon and Dr Thomas Gallagher, in spite of establishing lives abroad, empathized with Rossa and his fund reached $23,350 in 1876–7.[49] Many contributions originated with emigrants from the southwest of Ireland, where IRB recruitment ran high during the 1860s. Afterwards hundreds of these men fled to New York. The Clan leadership counselled restraint, stressing its traditional policy of awaiting England's involvement in a major war, but was ultimately forced to compete with Rossa to retain its foot soldiers.[50]

Edward O'Meagher Condon had joined the Clan after his release and favoured wild schemes to compete with the Land League, unlike Mackey Lomasney, his cautious friend.[51] The Canadian authorities paid Henri Le Caron to move to Detroit to covertly monitor Mackey, who ran a bookshop, giving no cause for concern until November 1880, when he began testing explosives. The Clan later recorded that the IRB had paid him $1000 'for experiments'. He did

not intend to injure ordinary Englishmen, but believed that a terror campaign
could rouse the fighting spirit of the Irish, focus international attention and win
concessions from Britain on the long walk to independence. Captain Mackey
had transitioned from idealistic insurgent to urban guerrilla.[52]

Alfred Webb, who believed that new technology at the disposal of governments would prevent subjects from initiating a revolution, urged the use of
'moral force'. Ford and Rossa concluded, however, that modern science facilitated terrorism, which was justified by the cruelty of colonial wars:[53]

> If Irishmen will wage a successful war against England, they will have to fight
> England with her own weapons. Two years ago England had a war in Kaffirland
> and Zululand, and to bring the natives to their knees – not alone to their knees,
> but to their graves – England, with dynamite and other destructive 'resources
> of her civilisation' as Gladstone calls them, blasted them in the very caves and
> caverns of the mountains in which they sought refuge.[54]

In 1879 questions were raised in Parliament whether dynamite had been used
against Basuto women and children hiding in caves, while Parnell and Joseph
Biggar protested against British troops murdering Zulus in cold blood.[55] Biggar
recommended that the military in South Africa should be instructed to treat
prisoners as 'customary amongst civilised nations'. When an internal inquiry
established that dynamite had been employed against 310 non-combatants,
the Duke of Cambridge could not grasp why this should draw criticism.[56]

Irish-Americans were familiar with Mitchel's works, which portrayed the
Famine as attempted genocide, the climax of British treachery. He explained
Irish poverty as originating in violent persecution, nowadays continued through
economic oppression:[57] 'While England lives and flourishes, Ireland must die a
daily death, and suffer an endless martyrdom ... if Irishmen are ever to enjoy the
rights of human beings, the British empire must first perish.'[58] Sharing a sense
of victimhood, Irish-Americans attempted to justify the civilian casualties of
dynamiting: 'England killed our people by starvation by the thousand, and they
merely laughed at us and said that we were lazy and indolent.'[59]

On 14 January 1881 Irish-American bombers struck for the first time at
Salford barracks, Manchester, when a child was killed. This was followed by
abortive attempts on the Mansion House in London and the main police station
and town hall of Liverpool. Several 'infernal machines' were seized at Liverpool
docks. Throughout the dynamite war, buildings of symbolic significance were
targeted, for the bombers feared that civilian casualties would provoke an anti-
Irish backlash. A furious Captain Mackey, assisted by John O'Connor of the
Supreme Council, attempted to drive Rossa's bombers out of Britain before they
could cause major damage:[60]

The amount of folly and bungling in connection with these attempts is simply disgraceful. They will have to clear out at once. Osborne [O'Connor] has men on their track and is determined to stop such nonsense. If allowed to go on confusion and anarchy would be the result. Some of them have been trying to inveigle our men into their crazy schemes, and if they are not compelled to leave here immediately, we might as well have no organization at all.

Mackey told Devoy that the home organization was not entitled to dictate policy. He complained that Rossa's methods of fighting the British Empire made 'our cause appear imbecile and farcical'. Captain Mackey meant to scare Britain into concessions to use as stepping stones to independence.[61] In July 1881 Stephens, a resident of Paris, denounced this 'wildest, lowest, and most wicked conception of the national movement', appealing for 'honourable warfare'.[62]

Robert Anderson informed the home secretary that Rossa had regained a level of sobriety, which made him dangerous, for until recently he had been unable to resist using donations for himself. Rossa's skirmishing concept proved 'so popular with the rowdy element' among the Clan, that its leaders were compelled to follow suit. By 1881 this fund had reached $91,453. It was being diverted from the American Land League to Fenian schemes, for since the arrest of Davitt, who linked the league and advanced nationalists, the Catholic clergy, a powerful segment of Parnellite support, attempted to destroy separatist influence. Anderson dreaded men like Rossa, who breathed revenge for Irish wrongs, seizing control of Clan na Gael.[63]

In 1881 during 'the great dynamite convention' of the Clan in Chicago, Captain O'Meagher Condon and others demanded action. Dr Thomas Gallagher, who was experimenting with explosives, volunteered to supervise their use in England. Le Caron recalled that dynamite was not mentioned in official reports, but remained 'in the air and in the speeches'.[64] He characterized Alexander ('Aleck') Sullivan of Chicago, the newly elected President of the Clan, whom he knew as state 'centre' of the Fenian Brotherhood for Michigan in 1868, as 'clever, unscrupulous, careful only of himself ... using Irish politics as a stepping-stone to advancement in American affairs, and reckless who or what suffered if but he did succeed'.[65]

Efficient organizing and networking established this associate of Parnell and Patrick Feehan, the Tipperary-born Archbishop of Chicago, in Irish and US politics, despite his unsavoury past. Due to changes in the constitution of Clan na Gael, which excluded the eleven regional representatives from the executive, Sullivan enjoyed greater power than any predecessor. In 1882, Philip Henry Cronin, newly arrived in Chicago, witnessed P.W. Dunne, the veteran Fenian, accuse Sullivan of misappropriating funds. The latter appointed Fr

Maurice Dorney, a popular local priest and his ally, as adjudicator and Dunne was expelled.[66]

Between 1876 and 1881 the Clan invested up to $60,000 of the Skirmishing Fund in the inventions of John Philip Holland, the brother of a Clare Fenian, who developed three prototypes of submarine. Rumours of war between England and Russia in late 1877 led General F.F. Millen of the military board of the Clan to hope that they might deploy this 'Fenian ram'. The *New York Times* described the 'Irish national torpedo-boat', which 'awaits a fitting opportunity' to decimate the Royal Navy. British consuls were reported to have inspected the vessel covertly.[67] In May 1881 it was undergoing tests in the Hudson river and London appealed to the Federal authorities to intervene. Although evidence of the Clan's commitment, the project lacked viability and petered out, strengthening the dynamite faction. Neither the 'Fenian Ram', nor the experimental 'Fenian Model' could be utilized, but the Japanese, American and British navies eventually adopted Holland's designs.[68]

The transmission of weapons to Ireland was directed by John O'Connor, assisted by Mackey Lomasney, P.N. Fitzgerald and John Daly. Between 1879 and 1882, 5000 rifles were purchased. A memorandum found during Daly's arrest in 1884 stated that from 1879 to 1881, 2844 rifles and 702 revolvers had been smuggled into Ireland. A further 4748 weapons, consisting of muzzle-loaders, revolvers and shotguns, were provided prior to 1879, placing a total of 8294 arms in IRB hands. Eventually Le Caron discovered that weaponry reached Ireland 'with regularity and precision'.[69]

Table 11. *Arms available to the IRB in 1881*

1879–81		
Revolvers smuggled	Rifles smuggled	Total of new weapons
2844	702	3546
Received before 1879		
Revolvers	Muzzle-loaders	Shotguns	Total of old weapons
1898	1194	1656	4748
Total of arms available: 8294		

(Source: CO 904/17/130, TNA)

In June 1882 Thomas Walsh, who had secreted 400 Snider rifles with bayonets, twenty-five large boxes containing six-chambered revolvers and quantities of ammunition in Clerkenwell, London, was arrested, having drawn attention to his depot through carelessness. The police ascertained that Walsh was using the railway network when dispatching consignments to Kilkenny, Clonmel, Castlegregory near Tralee and Kilrush, Co. Clare.[70]

A packing case arrived in Ennis, ostensibly addressed to the high sheriff of the county, who was a prominent Loyalist. His driver, an IRB man, secretly collected the weapons, delivering them to the East Clare 'centre'. The crate despatched to Kilrush, however, had attracted police attention. As the cargo boat left Limerick, a sympathizer warned Joseph Kett, the West Clare leader, to stay away. The box was supposedly intended for Michael Glynn, a loyal merchant and magistrate in this disturbed region. Questioned by officialdom, Glynn protested his innocence, but did not break an unwritten code that assisting Dublin Castle was little better than informing, given that some of his customers may have been sympathizers. Junior members of the Kett family were unaware that regular meetings in their home to 'read aloud' from the *Nation* were IRB gatherings. The trial of Thomas Walsh ended with a sentence of seven years' penal servitude, while increased police vigilance during the dynamite war stymied the importation of weapons.[71]

'A kind of guerrilla social warfare' raged against the land laws and the country was close to anarchy when Gladstone jettisoned his attempt to control Ireland by coercion. In April 1881 he introduced his second land act, which addressed the grievances of tenant farmers so thoroughly that it threatened to cut the ground from under the Land League. Violent speeches and confusion ensued, but Parnell lacked unanimous support and declined to withdraw from the House of Commons to form an independent Parliament in Dublin, for such a gesture could prove futile. Chief Secretary William Edward Forster continued to lobby for Parnell's arrest, which took place on 13 October 1881, on foot of the Protection of Person and Property Act.[72]

The 'no rent manifesto' followed on 18 October, whereupon Dublin Castle declared the league illegal and 'it was now war to the knife'. The Ladies' Land League deputized for the men and succeeded in making 'Ireland ungovernable by coercion', supported by financial contributions from abroad, which were funnelled via Patrick Egan in Paris. The utilization of women during this crisis was reminiscent of the IRB during 1865–7. In the absence of the leadership, agrarian outrages escalated.[73]

Parnell disapproved of the radical Ladies' Land League under his sister Anna's leadership. In April 1882 he and Gladstone agreed the Kilmainham

Treaty, which promised to inaugurate an age of reconciliation with Parnell abandoning violent agitation and Gladstone convincing the Liberals of the need for Home Rule. Lord Cowper, the viceroy, and Forster, who had championed repressive measures, were replaced by Lord Spencer with Lord Frederick Cavendish, the younger brother of the Duke of Devonshire and Gladstone's nephew-in-law, as chief secretary. On 6 May 1882 Cavendish and Thomas Henry Burke were stabbed to death in the Phoenix Park by the Irish National Invincibles, a secret society with fewer than fifty members.[74]

Horrified by the murders, Parnell volunteered his resignation to Gladstone, who rejected it as counterproductive. A shocked Davitt claimed he had left the movement and volunteered to assist the authorities during an interview with Howard Vincent, Director of Criminal Investigations, a dangerous proceeding if some of his Fenian critics should hear of this. Condemnation was almost universal, except in America, where Patrick Egan and Rossa dissented. In the aftermath, Parnell abandoned the semi-revolutionary Land League to form the Irish National League, a parliamentary body under central control.[75]

Spymaster General

George Trevelyan and Sir Robert Hamilton were appointed as new chief secretary and permanent undersecretary respectively. Reorganizing the police became an imperative task, given that Dublin Castle had run down its watch on the IRB since the 1860s. The commissioners of both the RIC and the DMP were forced to resign. On 25 May 1882 Lord Spencer appointed Colonel Henry Brackenbury, a gifted administrator with colonial police experience in Cyprus, as undersecretary for police and crime. A budget of £25,000 for two years was agreed with Gladstone.[76] Brackenbury proposed to infiltrate and destroy the IRB but left within weeks, hoping to serve in the Anglo-Egyptian War, and Edward George Jenkinson, a retired Indian administrator attached to Lord Spencer's staff, took over.[77]

Although Charles Kickham, who died on 22 August, was given a large, nationalist funeral, a rather disgruntled James J. O'Kelly, MP, warned that most provincial leaders had little confidence in the Supreme Council. Recent attempts to intimidate men into joining the IRB had backfired, for some informed the authorities, resulting in arrests.[78] O'Kelly regretted that the leadership still failed to grasp 'in what organization consists, and are managing very much on the old Stephens' plan which consists in a masterly inactivity – with the exception of getting in a small amount of arms from time to time'.[79] The stagnating IRB found it 'almost impossible' to appoint energetic officers. In a prophetic aside, O'Kelly deplored its lackadaisical management, as 'a secret police of a most dangerous character had been established'.[80]

The British felt that 'the new revived Fenianism' required 'more active' detectives, who shared the background of their suspects. This resembled the techniques of the French police, whose use of entrapment was officially rejected by Scotland Yard and the Home Office, but employed when necessary.[81]

The new Special Irish Branch of the CID under Howard Vincent met for the first time on 20 March 1883. Consisting of twelve officers, it was led by Chief Superintendent 'Dolly' Williamson and Chief Inspector Littlechild. Williamson maintained close contact with Robert Anderson and the Irish constables stationed in London, reporting directly to the Home Office. Home Secretary Harcourt requested the temporary assistance of Jenkinson, who was to gather and collate intelligence to increase efficiency. The Irish assistant undersecretary for police assembled his own team, in particular, Major Nicholas Gosselin, R.M., who 'understands these Irish scoundrels and can *talk* to them'. Gosselin arrived during the summer to set up networks of informers in northern England and Scotland, while Vincent and Williamson deplored this expensive rival operation.[82]

In America, dissensions intensified. Rossa, resentful at being ousted from the National Fund, continued to harass Devoy for an account of how it had been spent, in spite of having pocketed $1321. Amidst bitter exchanges, Devoy snarled that Rossa's drinking and 'bad business methods' were responsible for any short-fall, while the latter by 'his blowing and meddlesomeness had made it almost impossible to do anything' for Ireland through continually exposing any plans. Rossa drew attention to John Daly's intentions on arrival in New York in 1882 and continued to discredit the cause. The press ridiculed Rossa's followers as barely civilized and lacking reason and restraint, the basis for self-government.[83]

'Red Jim' returns

In March 1883 the Clan sent its first team to England. It was led by Dr Thomas Gallagher and included his brother Bernard, Tom Clarke, Albert 'Whitehead' Murphy (whose pseudonym derived from the Whitehead torpedo) and John Curtin Kent, a native of Fermoy.[84] Great secrecy prevailed, but unknown to Aleck Sullivan and the Revolutionary Directory, Dr Gallagher also received funding from Rossa. William Lynch ('Norman'), one of Rossa's men, accompanied him. They started to manufacture explosives in Birmingham, preparatory to attacking buildings in London. Due to carelessness rather than the work

of 'Red Jim' McDermott, arrests soon followed.[85] Dr Gallagher, Tom Clarke
and 'Whitehead' Murphy were sentenced to life imprisonment, while 'Norman'
turned Crown witness. In May Consul Edwards of New York counteracted the
dynamite propaganda by spreading distrust among Fenians when publicizing
that Irishmen had volunteered information to him.[86] By June Le Caron informed
Robert Anderson that although Clan na Gael was greatly disappointed that the
Gallagher mission had failed, its leaders would persevere. Anderson advised
Harcourt that they would experience 'new troubles' shortly.[87]

Dr Thomas Gallagher,
dynamiter (courtesy NLI).

Among the *agents provocateurs* recruited by Jenkinson in January 1883
was 'Red Jim' McDermott, who contributed to the dynamite fund of the *United
Irishman* as his *bona fides* and volunteered as a correspondent for Rossa's
paper. McDermott was assisted by Matthew O'Brien, another British agent,
who pretended to be his relative.[88] On arrival in Cork McDermott exaggerated his contacts with Rossa to win the confidence of Timothy Featherstone,
the *nom de guerre* of Edmund O'Brien Kennedy, a native of Ballyshonock,
Kildorrery, and participant in the Manchester rescue, who had returned to Cork
as Rossa's representative.[89] McDermott 'proposed a plan for the destruction of
the forts' at the entrance to Cobh. He succeeded in enlisting several members of
Featherstone's 'dynamite school', including Daniel O'Herlihy, a newsagent and
assistant in the grocery of John O'Leary's nephew, Denis Deasy, a former porter
of the Cork to Macroom railway, and Timothy Carmody, a slater. Some had
been Fenians since 1867.[90]

McDermott approached 'Long John' O'Connor in Cork. In hindsight, O'Connor believed that he, a Parnellite opposed to the dynamite war, was to be implicated in a plot to murder Judge Barry. McDermott ensnared another, unrelated John O'Connor, an Irish-American ostensibly visiting his parents in London.[91] This plot had links with Liverpool and Glasgow. McDermott travelled to Dublin, where he called on the imprisoned Michael Davitt, praising the Phoenix Park murders, 'whereupon the interview was terminated'. He also attempted to entrap James O'Connor, formerly of the *Irishman* and now a Parnellite journalist. Arrested in a drunken brawl, McDermott was released after appealing to Edward George Jenkinson, but a nationalist managed to copy documents found on McDermott, unmasking the spy.[92]

When Denis Deasy left Cork for Liverpool in March 1883, delivering explosives to a contact, arrests followed.[93] The authorities unsuccessfully pressurized him to turn informer. The men were convicted of attempting to overthrow Queen Victoria and manufacturing sixty pounds of dynamite in Cork. Four of them received life sentences and Deasy died in Chatham Prison the following May. O'Herlihy was acquitted on the treason-felony charge due to lack of evidence, but lost his business. 'Red Jim' wrote to Rossa, trying to blame his victims.[94] Davitt concluded in 1890 that McDermott had used the dynamite supplied by him to betray his dupes while in possession of the evidence of their guilt. Patrick McIntyre, a former Special Branch man, confirmed that it had been a case of entrapment.[95]

The Cork men stated that McDermott intended fomenting outrages in Castleisland, Co. Kerry, where 'turbulent, headstrong' Arthur Herbert, a magistrate who acted harshly, had been murdered for successfully opposing the Land League. With hindsight, McDermott's former associates suspected him of trying to orchestrate arrests for a large reward.[96] Lord Spencer concluded that the IRB, existing in Castleisland since 1863–4, continued to 'smoulder on' to merge with the Land League in October 1880.[97] Nobody dared oppose it and by 1883 Dublin Castle was fighting 'a complete state of lawlessness'. The authorities believed the local Fenians maintained contact with their counterparts in Tralee and Cork and communicated with O'Donovan Rossa. Regrettably, Samuel Hussey, a powerful land agent in Munster, had never conciliated the tenantry and was unable to restrain them now. In November 1884 Edenburn, his mansion near Castleisland, was damaged in an explosion, which the constabulary believed had links to Rossa. But William O'Brien, the editor of *United Ireland*, considered that the dynamite originated with 'Red Jim' McDermott, plotting to discredit Home Rule supporters by fabricating outrages.[98]

Capt. John McCafferty (courtesy NLI).

By October 1883 the secret service was aware of two Irish-American revolutionaries separately at large in England, Captain Mackey Lomasney of Clan na Gael and Captain McCafferty. The latter, now a silver- and gold-mining engineer, used his occupation as a legitimate front, but was intent on outrages. The police failed to arrest him before his return to the US.[99]

Journalists sensationalized Paris as the capital of the dynamite war, where McDermott socialized with suspects and dubious figures like the bibulous Joseph Theobald Casey and his brother Patrick.[100] In 1903 James Joyce, whose father recalled Fenian contacts from his youth, met Joseph Theobald Casey and included him in *Ulysses* as the bitter 'Kevin Egan':[101]

> Shattered glass and toppling masonry. In gay Paree he hides, Egan of Paris, unsought by any save me. Making his day's stations, the dingy printingcase, his three taverns, the Montmartre lair he sleeps short nights in, rue de la Goutte-d'Or, damascened with flyblown faces of the gone. Loveless, landless, wifeless ... *The boys of Kilkenny are stout roaring blades.* Know that old lay? I taught Patrice that. Old Kilkenny: saint Canice, Strongbow's castle on the Nore. Goes like this. O, O. He takes me, Napper Tandy, by the hand ... They have forgotten Kevin Egan, not he them. Remembering thee, O Sion.[102]

When McDermott returned to New York, he was almost assassinated after the arrests in Cork and Liverpool. He fled to England, where spymaster Jenkinson attempted to protect him through sham court proceedings, risking a political scandal if this became known. Well remunerated, he faded from view. Thus ended the dynamite campaign of O'Donovan Rossa, 'that wonderful fallen angel of patriotism', but bombings continued, courtesy of Clan na Gael.[103]

Aleck Sullivan as chairman of Clan na Gael manipulated the membership into cancelling their annual convention in 1883. He distrusted the IRB, considering the 'secret warfare... entirely in the hands of the Revolutionary Directory in America'. John Daly arrived in England in July 1883, consulting with IRB leaders in London, Liverpool, Glasgow and Belfast, before settling down in Birmingham with James Egan, an IRB comrade from Limerick. Under constant police surveillance, which included interception of his letters, Daly wrote that Clan na Gael failed to provide sufficient funds and suspected high-ranking IRB officers like John O'Connor and P.N. Fitzgerald of obstructing his mission.[104]

Jenkinson believed that 'very few' IRB members supported the bombing campaign. In March John O'Leary informed the public how 'utterly' he abhorred 'all these Invincible and dynamitic doings', which contradicted everything Thomas Davis had taught. But his approach was not always shared at grass-roots level, nor could the leadership enforce the necessary discipline.[105]

Daly was betrayed by 'Big' Dan O'Neill, an IRB member in Liverpool, and arrested on 11 April, in possession of [106]

> three love-apples [bombs] ready for use, with instructions how to use them. You can make a very good use of the cough medicine [nitro-glycerine] you say you have by getting a pocket-flask, one of those with a drinking-cup and screw top. Pour in the stuff, leaving sufficient room for the small brass tube I send for that purpose. When about to use, put a vial and lead in tube, put the tube in the flask, screw on the top, and all is ready ...[107]

Arrests and the disunity of the transatlantic movement heightened tensions. Simultaneously the IRB came under sustained attack from Dublin Castle. P.W. Nally, the Connacht leader, was detained for a lengthy period and convicted of attempted conspiracy to murder a land agent in March 1884.[108] Nally protested his innocence; nationalists suspected that he was victimized as a member of the Supreme Council, falling 'prey to one of the many sordid plots' hatched in Dublin Castle.[109]

That March P.N. Fitzgerald as chief travelling organizer collected the mandatory reports of the various IRB sections for transmission to John O'Connor in Paris. The authorities knew that Fitzgerald was smuggling arms to the west of Ireland and kept him under observation as he proceeded from Cork via Belfast to

London.[110] Suddenly, on 10 April, the police seized Fitzgerald on London Bridge. Patrick Sweeney, alias 'Skerrett', a bookkeeper and probably an American associate of the Supreme Council, was Fitzgerald's contact in London.[111] Sweeney had been shadowed by the police since 1883. He mailed the remaining documents to a hotel in Paris, although it was IRB practice to transport confidential items by courier. The Home Office claimed that the dead letter office in Paris had returned Sweeney's package, the 'Paris letters', which attracted attention by their seditious contents. In all likelihood, Jenkinson and Robert Anderson created this as a cover story for 'Skerrett', who had changed sides.[112]

Fitzgerald was removed to Sligo jail, accused of conspiracy to commit agrarian murders.[113] Simultaneously Daly and Egan were arrested in England, in a secret service operation to immobilize the IRB. The press suggested that Fitzgerald might inform like James Carey the previous year, but the *Glasgow Herald* exonerated him.[114]

Dublin Castle kept Fitzgerald incommunicado and delayed his trial, meanwhile urging his wife to save him through cooperation with the authorities. The *Irish Times* described Fitzgerald, Daly and Egan as men of humble origin, 'imperfectly educated', though 'exceptionally talented. In nationalist movements the most aspiring of them discern a field for their ambition.' Fitzgerald acted as 'a Fenian organizer … reserved in manner and mysterious in movement'. Daly was of 'a different stamp. He is self-assertive and excitable as the other is unassuming and self-contained.' Sligo people believed, correctly, that Fitzgerald was 'a Fenian of the old school', in favour of insurrection and abhorring assassination.[115]

Fitzgerald opposed Patrick Egan, Thomas Brennan and other land agitators, while P.J. Sheridan was his bitter enemy, having set up a cell of the Invincibles in Sligo. The authorities attempted to decode the 'Paris letters', which revealed the state of the IRB. In Co. Kilkenny, for instance, Fenian 'circles' survived in sixteen places, including Kilkenny city, Callan, Piltown, Newmarket and Bennettsbridge. In 1883 the 332 Fenians in this county possessed a pitiful ten rifles and eighteen revolvers, while Dublin and Co. Louth contained 650 and 503 IRB members respectively. Such revelations must have scared off members and potential recruits alike.[116]

John Moran, a Sligo informer, and Patrick Delaney, a convicted robber and former Invincible, testified against Fitzgerald. In 1883 Delaney's death sentence was commuted in return for information. He now hoped to be liberated. Fred Allan, the promising leader of the Dublin IRB, featured in the 'Paris letters' to be arrested on dubious evidence, apparently to intimidate the IRB.[117] Although Superintendent Mallon stated that Fitzgerald had managed to destroy one of these cryptic Fenian documents while in custody, the jury rejected the uncorrob-orated evidence of Crown witnesses and police and acquitted him.[118]

Edward George Jenkinson testified at Fred Allan's trial that he had received this material from Robert Anderson at the Home Office, when the court blocked Tim Healy, MP, from revealing that the Irish undersecretary for police directed covert operations in London. The *Nation* opined that the opposition of nationalist parliamentarians and press had forced Dublin Castle to end 'the gross scandal of arresting men on very shady evidence' to imprison them for months. P.N. Fitzgerald's welcome home in Cork was tinged with bitterness, for not only had his health suffered, but IRB morale continued to decline. Equally worrying was the cessation of communications between the Clan and the IRB by June 1884.[119]

Daniel O'Herlihy, almost a victim of 'Red Jim' McDermott in 1883, was pressurized to inculpate Egan, Daly and the Supreme Council the following year. District Inspector Starkie of the Cork detective branch suggested that, as half the IRB received funding from America while the remainder was in the pay of Dublin Castle, O'Herlihy might as well benefit, too. Should suspicion fall on him, Starkie could provide protection. 'As you gave Carey,' O'Herlihy riposted, referring to O'Donnell's killing of the informer in a major security lapse. The *Nation* believed that the authorities had tried 'not only to manufac-ture informers but to concoct criminal conspiracies', to continue 'the coercion code' and contain nationalists.[120]

Death of Captain Mackey

Captain Mackey Lomasney assembled explosives in his bookshop on the Harrow Road, London. On 13 December 1884 this 'resolute, daring, fearless man' rowed out to London Bridge with two assistants, when their bomb deto-nated prematurely.[121] Mackey's fate remained a mystery until his deserted store was discovered. The *Times* concluded that all three 'were blown to pieces by the explosion, that the mutilated bodies sank to the bottom, and that the fragments of the boat – it being a strong ebb tide at the time – floated here and there and were lost among the shipping'.[122] John O'Leary detested the dynamiters, but explained to W.B. Yeats that Mackey Lomasney 'was not a bad man', having been maddened into precipitate action by 'the spectacle of injustice'.[123]

CHAPTER 12

Lives of the Informers, 1859–1908

'No Irish insurrection would be complete without the inevitable government spy and informer, who is as essential to the plot as a chorus in a Greek play.'
Sir James A. Picton: a Biography, J.A. Picton (London 1891)

Daniel O'Sullivan, 'Goula', was the first Fenian informer to sit in the traditional chair on top of the witness table, visible throughout the court.[1] By 1858 the government informant had become a stock figure in Irish drama and the failure of the 1798 Rising was blamed on such duplicity. Padraic Kennedy has highlighted how this allowed the protagonists to rationalize divergent narratives of Irish identity: rebels could absolve themselves from addressing their shortcomings, while constitutionalists gained confirmation that conspiracy invariably ended in betrayal. British administrators considered informers evidence for inherent Irish 'treachery and lack of respect for the law', obliging them to persist with paternalistic government by unconstitutional means. Revolutionaries, on the other hand, perceived them as symptomatic of the illegality of English rule, which had to be resisted. All sides used this trope to divert blame to their opponents.[2]

The authorities received information about the Phoenix Society, but locals would not brave social ostracism to testify in court, while undercover agents, appearing all of a sudden in rural communities, were easily identified. Prosecution of secret societies in Ireland or elsewhere usually required the testimony of a spy, who needed corroboration as he had taken a seditious oath and received remuneration. Once one informer emerged, other suspects followed suit to gain immunity.[3]

Superintendent John Mallon of the DMP reasoned that the authorities were forced to use this method: 'It is the business of the police in Ireland to make use of such persons when occasion arises and when the objective cannot be fully attained by any less distasteful means...'[4] Working-class people sided with anyone defying law and order, but betrayal was also possible, for 'a good deal of that kind of patriotism can be bought for a five pound note in this poor country'. Informers were not an exclusively Irish phenomenon. Intelligence was frequently purchased in India. Asian aristocrats, observing the rise of the British Empire, cooperated to maintain their status. The Irish middle class at home and abroad wished to avoid open clashes with revolutionary compatriots, while similarly convinced that opposition to England was futile.[5]

Secret service networks

Both the constabulary and the DMP gathered information, which the law department of Dublin Castle collated by 1865, when Colonel Feilding established a military intelligence service. Since becoming chief secretary in July 1866, Lord Mayo expressed dissatisfaction with the quality of surveillance, as leading subversives relocated to Britain. On 18 September 1867 Home Secretary Gathorne-Hardy was stunned by the bungling of the Manchester police, despite warnings of an impending rescue emanating from Dublin.[6]

Lord Mayo failed to establish a dedicated police department, frustrated by Sir Richard Mayne, a founding commissioner of the London Metropolitan Police. Supported by Benjamin Disraeli, Chancellor of the Exchequer, Mayo despatched Colonel Feilding to the Home Office to run a temporary intelligence service. Feilding began investigating in the panicked aftermath of the Clerkenwell explosion, assisted by Robert Anderson, H.W. Hozier, Captain William Whelan and constables from Ireland to circumvent interference from Mayne. Dawning comprehension of Clerkenwell as a tragic blunder rather than an incipient terror campaign ended plans for 'a permanent centralised detective police force' in England and terminated Feilding's mission in March 1868. In late 1867 however, Thomas Beach, alias Henri Le Caron, visited England from the US, where he associated with Fenians. His father in Colchester had drawn official attention to his letters and Robert Anderson, who remained at the Home Office, became his handler.[7]

(Left) *Herrmann Schofield;* (right) *Pierce Nagle (courtesy NLI).*

Contemporaries criticized Fenian carelessness about security: Charles Gavan Duffy believed that 'the fatuity with which Stephens entrusted treasonable notices to ragged recruits who had joined him a few weeks does not, I think, exist in the history of conspiracies'.[8] Herrmann Schofield, an educated Pole who had fled Prussian military service to work for the *Irish Times*, was a case in point. Witnessing great sympathy with the Polish uprising of 1863, Schofield supplemented his income by lecturing on Poland. The IRB facilitated more than twenty speaking engagements in, for instance, Kingstown (Dun Laoghaire), Cork, Tipperary, Clonmel, Carrick-on-Suir and Waterford, urging him to stress parallels between the two nations. Leading Fenians mistakenly confided in Schofield as a fellow revolutionary. On emigrating to New York in November 1863, he approached E.M. Archibald to inform on Luby, J.J. Geary and John Kenealy.[9]

In order to prove a transatlantic conspiracy, Sir Thomas Larcom directed Consul Archibald to find a witness who could identify John O'Mahony's handwriting, linking him to the *Irish People* staff. Archibald summoned Schofield to masquerade as a sympathizer at Fenian headquarters, watching O'Mahony 'write by a lie and a trick'. Nationalists commented what an outcry the British press would raise, if any of Garibaldi's generals were similarly entrapped by the reactionary King of the Two Sicilies.[10]

Fenian photographs on sale included the informers Pierce Nagle, Patrick Power of Clonmel and Schofield. Having testified in Ireland, the last named hid in comfort in East London. Dublin Castle paid him half the sum demanded: £500 and his passage to New Zealand with an inclusive grant of land.[11] Schofield informed the authorities in October 1867 that he had been recognized and 'had much to suffer, much to endure. My name in Auckland was connected with everything that was base and degraded.' He departed for Australia, where 'threats of revenge were uttered, and one night I was even surrounded by an Irish mob, who swore to have my life'.[12]

Abandoning his business in Sydney, Schofield fled to San Francisco and begged the Home Office to remove him to a country without an Irish presence. The British authorities feared an attack on this notorious individual, which would reduce the flow of intelligence. Consular officials conveyed him to Prussia via New York, but Crown Solicitor Samuel Lee Anderson ignored Schofield when he pleaded for help from St Petersburg and, finally, Manchester. It transpired that this compositor was eminently employable, while also entitled to assistance from his trade union. Instead Schofield hoped to extract money to establish a German-language newspaper in Manchester. Dublin Castle terminated all contact in November 1870, as he had no 'claim whatever on the government'.[13]

In Killarney the IRB carelessly trusted John Dinneen, a native of Millstreet, who was friendly with a local leader but disapproved of Fenianism. Dinneen alerted a magistrate to the imminent arrival of Captain Moriarty, which aborted any attempt at insurrection in Killarney.[14] Inveigled to spy for the authorities, Dinneen eventually had to flee. He received a reward of £100, but protested that this was insufficient, given the loss of his good salary of £50 p.a. Nor could he obtain the desired British civil service post. Hiding in London, Dinneen fished for information among Fenian acquaintances after Kelly and Deasy's escape being assured of a reward of £600–1000 by Superintendent Williamson. By May 1868 he resented being exiled, estranged from his family, while suffering from consumption.[15]

Isolated and psychologically fragile informers continued to badger their handlers, as Edward George Jenkinson, a secret service chief of the 1880s, lamented: 'I have informants who have been sent away to different parts of the world who are a constant trouble to me ... and this must, I fear, continue until the Irish question is settled and the danger to these informants passes away.'[16]

Denis Dowling Mulcahy had made Pierce Nagle a captain in Clonmel without ascertaining whether he had taken the IRB oath. Briefly emigrating to New York, Nagle met Colonel O'Mahony, vouched for by his lifelong friend Mulcahy and was allowed to overhear the 'head centre's' deliberations. Returning to Dublin, Nagle became Stephens's confidential messenger, but volunteered to inform and revealed the latter's pivotal role. An unimpressed Superintendent Ryan dropped him the following January. In July Nagle warned that the Rising was imminent, demanding 'a civil service situation' in return. In September he provided Stephens's letter to the Clonmel leaders, confirming 1865 as the 'year of action',

which contributed to Dublin Castle's decision to arrest the leaders. Nagle testified in court, embarrassed to have his treachery revealed.[17]

Harry Shaw Mulleda, who had been detained without trial for twelve months
in Kilmainham jail, described how prisoners were encouraged to inform. Initially
he slept on straw on 'damp flagstones' in a dungeon lit by an unglazed opening,
though it was snowing outside. Mulleda complained, but was told to desist or
sleep on the bare floor. After five months on a diet of gruel, milk and bread,
Mulleda tasted soup and meat for the first time, on the recommendation of the
prison doctor. The warders alternated sending Fenians to the punishment cells
with urging them to inform in return for £50, a new identity and a civil service
appointment abroad.[18] Dublin Castle denied pressurizing the political prisoners
to inform, as claimed by John Warren, Augustine Costello and William Halpin,
who denounced 'the gorilla' Henry Price, Governor of Kilmainham:[19] 'Hell is a
very bad place, and the devil a very bad boy, but he could not hold a candle to
old Price.'[20] The *Times* perceived these accusations as ploys to gain American
support for the prisoners, but the unique, generous secret service pension for
the widow of Governor Price and Samuel Lee Anderson's confidential statement
confirm the Fenian version.[21]

Prince of informers

Fenian officers also changed sides if they realized that the movement was failing
or to avoid imprisonment. Between 1865–7 the Brotherhood hired high-ranking
officers to replace Civil War casualties for its Canadian and Irish expeditions,
mostly soldiers of fortune like Millen, Cluseret and Carroll Tevis, who became
double agents.

Opinions differed about the origins of John Joseph Corridon, 'that prince
of informers'.[22] John Denvir portrayed him as the son of a Liverpool prostitute,
while Fr O'Connell, superior of the Presentation Brothers in Kerry and former
teacher in the Listowel workhouse school, considered him his past pupil, the
son of a woman of loose morals. This seems likely, as the Ardfert church registers record the baptism of a 'John Corydon' in 1843 and one 'John Corrydon'
in 1845.[23] After the Great Famine his family emigrated to America, where he
enlisted in the 63rd New York Regiment, serving as a hospital steward during
the Civil War. In 1862 Corridon joined the Fenian Brotherhood and became the
leader of the General Thomas Smyth 'circle' in the Army of the Potomac, but
was demoted for drunkenness and reckless behaviour. He volunteered to serve
in Ireland, establishing himself as a Fenian courier.[24]

After the habeas corpus suspension in February 1866, American Fenian officers and some Dublin leaders relocated to Liverpool, Manchester and other English cities to avoid arrest. Corridon attended meetings in the Liverpool pubs, where money to sustain the movement was collected. He grew disillusioned, not least because Stephens failed to repay his loan of £130. According to Superintendent Mallon, Corridon was arrested in circumstances suggestive of sexual misdemeanour, and pleading to escape exposure, 'he commenced to betray, and went on betraying his associates out of a sense of gratitude to the police'.[25]

Corridon admitted leading 'an immoral life' with an Irish woman in a Liverpool brothel. He informed from September 1866, which forced the Fenians to abandon their Chester Castle attack. He justified himself as 'break[ing] up a swindle', which 'was not worth shedding one drop of blood for', while expecting '£2,000 from the Crown, and that he would take all he could get'.[26] John Denvir thought Corridon resembled a flashy provincial actor, while the *Nation* depicted a sociopath, with 'red hair curled like that of a negro, a large head, fleshless, lanthorn [lantern] jaws, a cold blue eye, and a pinched expression, [whose] manner, though cool, was utterly destitute of the tinge of remorse and shame which humanised that of Massey'.[27] Corridon remained unaware how disreputable his unhesitating betrayal appeared. Shielded by his bodyguard, he enjoyed taunting nationalists; for instance, when threatened by a London-Irish crowd outside Bow Street police court, Corridon drew his loaded revolver, 'retreating backwards'.[28]

Godfrey Massey

Godfrey Massey was brought up in Doonass, Co. Clare, as Patrick Condon, the illegitimate son of a gentleman whose surname he assumed on returning to Ireland. Massey claimed to have served in the 2nd Texas Cavalry of the Confederate Army and subsequently became a commercial traveller, joining the Fenian Brotherhood. O'Mahony appointed him 'central organizer' for Louisiana and Texas in December 1865. Educated and with a plausible manner, Massey ingratiated himself with Colonel Kelly.[29]

Soon afterwards a 'Southern Fenian informant' warned Stephens that the Brotherhood in New Orleans believed Massey, recently married to a wealthy local, to be a British spy. They had alerted O'Mahony and felt insulted by his reply, suspecting him 'either drunk or crazy when he wrote it'.[30] But Massey retained the confidence of the leadership. During the split, he assured Patrick Downing, one of O'Mahony's closest friends, that he would never forget 'who stood sponsor for the Fenian Brotherhood at the font at its birth', describing

O'Mahony as 'an Irish patriot in the fullest sense of the word', which must have been balm to the beleaguered 'head centre'.[31]

In January 1867 Massey arrived for the Rising and, as liaison officer for Munster, learned the identities of the leaders. Corridon alerted the authorities to his role, which resulted in Massey's arrest on the eve of the Rising, when he fainted at Limerick Junction 'like a delicate female'. Dublin Castle threatened to try him for high treason, culminating in the death penalty, while his wife, a Southern belle, urged him to turn Crown witness. Massey claimed to have abandoned his revolutionary principles only on being betrayed.[32]

Matthew Anderson, Crown Solicitor for Dublin, and his son and assistant Samuel Lee Anderson were key figures in the Dublin Castle law department. Robert, the younger son and also a lawyer, was hired to collate confidential information for Lord Mayo. He began his career as a spymaster, befriending detainees who traded snippets of information for release. Anderson claimed to have entered Kilmainham jail and 'turned' Massey.[33]

Robert's reminiscences are contradicted by Samuel Lee. The latter, applying for a permanent post after the Fenian trials, recounted his services as outside the remit of the liberal state: 'It is no part of the duty of a Crown solicitor to go to the gaols and induce prisoners to become informers. Had it not been for me Massey would never have given evidence, and without him the prosecutions not only in Dublin but in the provinces, and that of [Ricard O'Sullivan] Burke in London would have presented a very different aspect.'[34]

Samuel Lee persuaded participants in the *Erin's Hope* expedition to become prosecution witnesses and, although the police refused to assist him, suborned prisoners in Kilmainham to convict Colonel Halpin. He 'did all this without ... compromising the government', while helping Lord Mayo to deny 'accusations of illicit practices' in Parliament, which the *Irishman* had raised. Samuel Lee Anderson was made a Crown Solicitor, 'well deserved – for faithful service'.[35]

Godfrey Massey's depression improved once he shared a comfortable cell with his wife and a payment of £86 enabled his relatives to leave for Australia. When he collapsed and needed a doctor after an early court appearance, the *Nation* diagnosed fear of Fenian retribution, combined with excessive alcohol consumption. It was customary to break down their inhibitions through 'plentiful use of stimulants' and dull the loathing, which informers encountered in public. They had to be kept in fortified police stations like Chancery Lane, Dublin.[36]

The *Times* considered Massey 'the most gentlemanly-looking person who has yet appeared in connexion with the recent Fenian movement. He was dressed in a suit of fine black cloth, with a smart frockcoat ... His complexion is rather sallow, his features regular and handsome. His voice is agreeable, but betrays a Limerick brogue, modified by the American accent.'[37] The *Nation* considered that Massey had been groomed for the occasion, but: 'His accent was essentially vulgar, with a lacquer of gentility which occasionally fell off,' revealing his true character.[38] With hindsight, T.P. O'Connor, journalist and constitutionalist, considered Massey's fate tragic, resembling one of Turgenev's characters, who had joined a conspiracy without realizing the trials ahead.[39]

Guarding the informers

Transferring prisoners and informants required considerable precautions, as ordinary people in Munster demonstrated their support of the Fenians raucously. When colonels William Nagle and John Warren of the *Erin's Hope* arrived under guard for identification by Corridon, rioting erupted in hitherto quiet Waterford. Denis Walsh, an innocent bystander, was killed, fifty people injured and mounted constables charged to clear the streets.[40] Corridon's brazen demeanour incensed the urban proletariat, who pursued him 'cursing and groaning, and calling down the malediction of heaven on him, they would have torn him to pieces could they but have laid their hands on him'.[41]

The detestation, in which informers were held, included their relatives: in Fethard, the father and brother of Pierce Nagle were pressurized into emigrating. John Walsh in Bruree was suspected of having alerted a magistrate to local plans for the Rising and had to spend months in police custody with his family. He testified at the Limerick Special Commission, before going abroad.[42]

Fishermen from Helvick Head were celebrated in verse for not giving evidence at the trial of the *Erin's Hope* officers. These native Irish speakers suddenly lost their knowledge of English or pretended deafness. Andrew Roche, a struggling farmer from Ring, who informed in return for having his rent of £10 paid, was reviled in Gaelic verse, however.[43]

Dublin Castle financed the emigration of even minor witnesses to London, Australia or North America. Increasing globalization through newspapers that connected Irish communities made this a challenge. The *Irishman* learned that Michael Hartnett, a respectable, middle-aged shop assistant who had betrayed Captain Mackey, left Liverpool for Melbourne on the *Explorer* in March 1868. This news was copied in New York.[44] Edward Brett, the van driver who had confirmed Thomas Francis Bourke's presence at Ballyhurst in court, was driven out of Richmond, Victoria: 'E – B – entering the house of God yesterday (Sunday) placed one shilling on the plate. One of the collectors flung the unholy coin into the street saying that "the blood of General Burke [sic] was upon it".

It is to be hoped that the meditations of the "informer" during Mass were of use to him. He started with a fresh name for another district this morning.'[45]

The early Fenian leadership consistently prohibited the killing of informers. John Warner, who had identified the conspirators in Cork, sometimes frequented pubs, where his boastfulness alerted the IRB. Denieffe was among those who demanded his execution as a warning to traitors. Thomas Clarke Luby immediately objected, but the rank-and-file disagreed. The arrest of the *Irish People* intellectuals removed this restraint and opportunistic, mostly unsuccessful, attacks on detectives and informers commenced.[46] Dublin Castle feared battle-hardened, ruthless Irish-Americans. Superintendent Daniel Ryan became convinced that Colonel Kelly had established a 'United Irish-American assassination company' or 'wheel within a wheel', hidden from more idealistic leaders, to remove spies, police and officials, while terrifying the membership into submission.[47]

In January 1866 Warner was deriding Fenianism in a bar when somebody grabbed his revolver and administered a beating. Afterwards he lived close to Howth constabulary barracks, guarded by an armed policeman. The ostracized Warner met an affable stranger in the ruins of St Mary's Abbey and took him home for a convivial evening. Corporal Patrick Tierney of the 87th Regiment, alias Edward O'Connor, stabbed Warner, who had a narrow escape, while Tierney received a life sentence for attempted murder.[48]

In September 'your loyal subject Crown witness John Warner' wrote to the inspector general of the constabulary requesting a revolver, clothing, ham, tea, sugar and £20 to pay his debts in Howth, for 'it is my principles to purtect my curactor [sic]'.[49] The Warner family was about to leave for an unspecified colony when the police authorities decided that 'bedding and other articles except the revolver applied for may be purchased in London by the constable who is to accompany him, at an expense not exceeding £10. It is not considered expedient to give Warner any arms.'[50] Warner concluded his illiterate letter with his 'blessing'; nothing more is known of him.

Disunited activists remained at large in Dublin and Britain during 1867, oscillating between the Kelly and Roberts factions. Some were particularly eager to assassinate Talbot and Corridon. In Dublin Robert Atkinson was badly wounded on 12 September, being mistaken for Head Constable Talbot.[51] The Bloomsbury district of London was a Fenian haunt, where police officers and informers hunted suspects nightly. On 28 September Fenians mistook a military bandsman for Corridon and killed him. By November he, Massey and Nagle were being guarded by the London Metropolitan Police. Corridon received a weekly allowance of £3, while Massey got £6. (This meant that the former earned £156 p.a., compared to Dinneen's salary of £50 as a shop assistant.)[52]

Superintendent Ryan believed that Roberts had supplied the new Dublin directory with twenty revolvers. John Walsh, a pawnbroker's clerk and veteran of the
Rising, was its guiding spirit alongside John Murphy and Michael Feely in association with James Cooke, a Dublin IRB stalwart, now representing the Roberts's
wing of the Fenian Brotherhood in London.[53] The 'United Irish-American assassination company' wanted to assert the continuity of Fenianism in spite of a frag-
menting leadership and heightened tension, as the trial of the Manchester rescuers
drew to a close. The mysterious shooting dead of Constable Patrick Keena and
the wounding of Sergeant Stephen Kelly on 31 October 1867 may have been a
failed attempt to kill Corridon and Devany in the Chancery Lane Crown witness
depot, where they awaited the call to testify. It is improbable, however, that the
'shooting circle' under Patrick Lennon, on the run since the Rising, intended to
assassinate Lord Mayo, given contemporary respect for public figures.[54]

There is anecdotal evidence that women also became informers. Fanny, the
widow of Henry Rowles, a minor Invincible, was left to provide for their large
family when he died unexpectedly on 18 March 1883. She relayed background
information about the wives of Invincibles about to go on trial.[55]

Rewards

There were rumours of generous rewards after the successful prosecutions of
1867, facilitated by Corridon and Talbot. The *Nation* gave a rather fanciful
description of celebrations in Dublin Castle, involving lawyers, G-men and
prison staff. Among the toasts, Samuel Lee Anderson was saluted with a parody
of 'John Anderson, my jo' by Robert Burns, which alluded to his Scottish
descent, aligned to an eagerness to 'clutch the cash':

> *Sam Anderson, my jo, Sam,*
> *A precious youth are you;*
> *'Tis many a trick you know, Sam,*
> *That others never knew;*
> *All speak aloud your praise, Sam,*
> *From Larcom to Judge Keogh,*
> *And all the Gs they swear by you*
> *Sam Anderson, my jo.*[56]

A list of minor informers fell into the hands of the *Irishman*, which repeated the
nationalist moral that informing was counterproductive, as the Crown witnesses
were 'altogether dissatisfied' and 'never for a moment imagined the government

would pay them so badly'. Rewards varied from five to fifty pounds, in addition to a choice of free tickets and suitable clothing for North America, Australia or South Africa, often for whole families. While waiting to testify in court, informants were maintained in custody. Any family members who remained at large in the community received an allowance.[57]

Fenian sympathizers longed to punish informers, which occasionally led to victimization. The prosperous Hennessy family of Kilclooney Wood, who had locked the door as Peter O'Neill Crowley and his men approached, was mistakenly suspected of betraying him to the authorities. They suffered twelve years of ostracism and their good name continued to be blackened until the 1960s. The next generation, having grown up in the shadow of social exclusion, lobbied to see the relevant official files to clear themselves.[58]

The Anderson brothers insisted on special precautions after Robert's 'first Fenian informant was shot like a dog on returning to New York'. This was William Millen (or Million) of the *Erin's Hope*, killed by a son of Michael Doheny. Anderson had confided Millen's name to the chief secretary, who told the Lord Lieutenant over dinner in the Viceregal Lodge, when they were overheard by a servant. Henceforth Robert Anderson avoided giving details to cabinet members. Samuel Lee urged precautions concerning confidential correspondence, as busybodies among the Dublin Castle staff read anything marked 'secret' and it was unknown with whom they shared their research.[59]

The fate of Nagle and Talbot

On 24 July 1866 Nagle wrote to Sir Thomas Larcom to declare himself 'pennyless [*sic*] and need I add friendless'.[60] He pleaded that his reward should be speedily determined, as his notoriety precluded him from working. According to Superintendent Daniel Ryan, Nagle received 'a very reasonable allowance' of £2 per week. In November Matthew Anderson gave him £250 severance pay, while Lord Mayo authorized a pension of £100 per annum, which would pass to his widow, indicating she had supported his duplicity.[61] By 1871 he called himself 'Thomas P. Kennedy' and was living in Hornsey, London, with his wife Margaret and three children. In 1873 the press queried a report that he had been shot in a quarrel over a woman, but was spirited away before the IRB could act. Richard Pigott rightly considered such accounts apocryphal. In 1874 Nagle's sister-in-law reported his death in Islington to Robert Anderson. His widow continued to enjoy the pension until her demise in 1908. Accounts that he was discovered in Camden, London, stabbed through the heart, are erroneous.[62]

Table 12. *Informers from Munster discharged in 1868*

Name	Place of origin	Maintenance in Ireland	Reward	Free passage
Daniel & Henry Holmes	Kilmallock	£25 for relatives	£50 & outfits	With family to Canada
Patrick Nelian	Kilmallock	Frequent sums of £10 & £5; wife had £1 & 4s. weekly for a year	£40 & outfits	With family to Melbourne
John Walsh	Bruree	Maintained in custody	£40	With family to New York
James Healy	Kilmallock		£25 & outfit	Queensland
Thomas Dixon	Co. Limerick		£25 & outfit	Melbourne
Edward Brett	Tipperary	Mother got 12s. weekly while he informed	£20	Melbourne
John Gleason	Killarney		£20 & outfit	With family to Cape of Good Hope
Edmund Dowdall			£15 & outfit	Queensland
James Joyce	Kilmallock	Wife got £25 while he informed	£15 & outfits	With family to America
Patrick Daly	Ardagh, Co. Limerick		£10 & outfit	Queensland, Australia
James Naughton	Ardagh, Co. Limerick		£10 & outfit	Queensland, Australia
John Ward[63]	Ardagh, Co. Limerick	His father got 6s. weekly while he informed	£10 & outfit	Queensland, Australia
John Farrell	Tipperary, had been among the Ballyhurst insurgents		£10	Destination of his choice
Michael Ryan			£10	America
Thomas Ryan	Tipperary		£10	
James Louchnam	Tipperary		£10	Destination of his choice
? Latchford			£10	Destination of his choice
J. Cashel	Co. Limerick	Maintained in police custody	£5	New York

(Source: *Irishman*, 20 June 1868; 25 April 1868; Mary Kury, Ardagh Heritage Group)

The IRB constitution of 1869, which proclaimed the Supreme Council 'the sole government of the Irish Republic', warned adherents that betrayal could result in execution. In 1873 capital punishment was reserved for when the organization was 'at war'.[64] The only important individual to suffer this fate prior to 1883 was Head Constable Talbot, who had infiltrated the IRB in south Tipperary in 1865–6, resulting in approximately twenty arrests and the conviction of Colour Sergeant Charles McCarthy. Tall, 'with a decidedly handsome, manly countenance', Talbot was the son of a Protestant farmer in County Westmeath. 'A consummate dissembler', he retired on double pension, but soon tired of hotel-keeping in Ulster.[65]

Intent on becoming a rate collector, Talbot returned to Dublin. The authorities, aware of his recklessness acerbated by a drink problem, urged him to emigrate. Shot, he still pursued his attacker. Recovery appeared likely until haemorrhaging occurred. When Talbot died on 16 July 1871 the crowd outside the hospital cheered, convinced that the fires of hell awaited him. The *Nation* believed Talbot responsible for his fate, having 'studiously courted' public notice by 'swaggering, defiant and provocative' through Dublin.[66]

Isaac Butt defended Robert Kelly, who had been caught red-handed, in a sensational trial. Counsel revealed that the doctors had subjected Talbot to two unsuccessful operations to remove the bullet, inadvertently inflicting further damage, before attempting a cover-up. Kelly was acquitted of murder but sentenced to fifteen years for shooting at the police and found fame as a Fenian avenger. In 1874 Dion Boucicault modelled the informer in *The Shaughraun*, his highly successful melodrama, on Thomas Talbot.[67]

Secret service accounts reveal that annuities paid to the major informers depended on their 'good behaviour'. The Irish authorities notified the Home Office that Robert Anderson, in London since 1868, was already using his Notting Hill address to covertly pay 'secret service pensioners' hiding in the metropolis. This arrangement was to continue for forty years. Circumspect ex-informants escaped detection, as Robert and Samuel Lee Anderson ensured secrecy by corresponding outside the official channels.[68]

The death of John Devany, an Irish-American clerk, who earned almost £400 for informing during 1867–8 to retire with a pension of £78, illustrates the modus operandi. Mrs Devany telegraphed Robert Anderson for immediate help when her husband was dying. Anderson instructed Chief Superintendent 'Dolly' Williamson of Scotland Yard to arrange for a 'most economical' funeral, to be paid from secret service funds. Devany, aged thirty-three, was buried in the paupers' plot in St Mary's Catholic Cemetery, Kensal Green, in February 1875. A few months later Anderson informed Thomas Henry Burke, permanent undersecretary in

Dublin Castle, that Devany's child was dying of fever. His widow had already been helped with £15 of secret service money, but might need more.[69] ✗

In June 1868 Dublin Castle and the Home Office agreed to discontinue police protection for Godfrey Massey, whose departure from London was imminent. He received a lump sum of £300 and an annuity of £200.[70] Considering the appropriate reward for Corridon, Samuel Lee Anderson reflected that two pensions of £1000 each and one of £500 had been paid to the leading informers in 1798. Corridon had risked his life when betraying the Fenians. He was more important than Massey, whose arrest he had initiated.[71] As 'the "Fenian informer" *par excellence*, it would be very inexpedient to have him coming before the public in any way which would show an inadequate settlement of his claim'.[72] But Corridon was also 'a man of very loose habits and indifferent character who never can earn his bread at any honest occupation. He dares not appear much in public in any part of the world. He had a wife and children to support.'[73] Anderson decided on £200 per annum as appropriate, half of which would be paid from the Irish secret service fund and the remainder by the Home Office. More money 'would only lead him into danger'.[74]

Corridon had moved his family from Kingston, Surrey, to Whitton. On 11 October 1869 Louis Kyezor, a Jewish philanthropist, prepared to evict Thomas Hydon Green, an elderly drunk, but was shot dead by his tenant, who committed suicide. In 1820 the Cato Street gang had plotted to murder the British cabinet in London in protest at widespread social problems, before being betrayed by George Edwards, an *agent provocateur*, and Thomas Hidon, a local milkman. It emerged, after the Kyezor murder, that Thomas Hydon Green was probably one of these individuals who had been rewarded with a post in Somerset House. The *Times* mentioned that Hydon Green claimed that Kyezor had made remarks calculated to damage a fellow tenant, a certain Mr Johnson.[75]

John Joseph Corridon now called himself 'Henry Johnson', a native of Scotland, aged twenty-eight; in an amazing coincidence the two informers became neighbours.[76] Although a quarrel described during the inquest took place outside Corridon's door, his identity remained hidden. By 1875 he had become dissatisfied with his pension and demanded more. Corridon was the father of a growing family, which had suffered its share of illness. He feared being unmasked and wrote that 'not a knock comes to the door but I think it is my last moment on earth'.[77]

Robert Anderson worried that Corridon might be sued for debt, being unmasked in the process. Thomas Henry Burke declared £200 sufficient 'for this fellow' and advised that Corridon should lead an upright life, for if he compromised the government, his pension would cease. Anderson pontificated that such individuals were not supported to reward villainy, but had been necessary to convict the Fenians and appropriate annuities allowed them to disappear from view.[78]

In Whitton 'Henry Johnson' paid an annual rent of £14 for his cottage, designed for 'the poorer working classes'. In 1879 he was identified in London, bursting into a meeting, armed with two revolvers, but spirited away by his police guard. 'Constantly drunk,' Corridon recklessly frequented dangerous localities; the police feared 'he will meet a violent death'. By 1881 he had moved with his five children to a lodging house in Egham, Surrey.[79] He was in danger of discovery in December 1884, when Edward George Jenkinson, chief of the Irish secret service, intervened and relocated him. Corridon received a new identity and only his death in February 1888 has been uncovered to date.[80]

Patrick Foley of Waterford, the leading military double agent, had been instrumental in tracking suspects in Dublin. Colonel Feilding transferred him to Liverpool to ferret out conspirators. By December 1866 Foley had abandoned plans to join the English civil service as too dangerous. Feilding urged that he 'should be dealt with *speedily* and most liberally. I would recommend that such provision should be made by government as to preclude the possibility of this man or his wife ever being in want.'[81]

Feilding reminded Dublin Castle that Foley had been the first soldier to inform voluntarily and others would notice his generous reward. Foley received a free passage abroad, a lump sum and an annuity. Finding himself penniless in Boston, he 'was befriended by John Boyle O'Reilly years later. But he died in misery soon after.' His widow Ellen, alias Mrs Wood, continued to receive a secret service pension of £24 p.a. through Robert Anderson; she died in New Zealand in 1908.[82]

Godfrey Massey, now 'Mr Stanley', spent the remainder of his life in France. Although the *Pall Mall Gazette* described him 'promenading in disguise' in Paris, he escaped retribution to rear a family. In 1908 his daughter Gertrude telegraphed Anderson in London that her father had died in Marseille. As had been agreed with Lord Spencer in 1868, half of Massey's pension went to his widow, who returned to New Orleans, where she still lived in 1920.[83]

The Phoenix Park murders

By the mid 1870s the authorities had downgraded Fenian intelligence gathering. A contemptuous Superintendent Mallon monitored the squabbling factions in Dublin, but was blindsided when a splinter group assassinated Lord Frederick Cavendish and Thomas Henry Burke. The Irish National Invincibles, founded in late 1881 by

Frank Byrne, Patrick Egan, P.J. Sheridan and John Stephen Walsh of Middlesbrough, all eminent Land League leaders, were assisted by Captain McCafferty, who may have contributed his profits from American mining speculations.[84]

During a period of violent conflict, they enrolled politically unsophisticated, urban Fenians with little interest in the land issue. James Carey, their most prominent recruit, was a builder who had participated in the 1867 Rising before being elected to the Dublin directory of the IRB. In 1880 he served on a committee to 'remove' informers. The self-important Carey was active in his Catholic parish and aspired to a role in politics. Infuriated by the arrest of Parnell in October 1881, these men repudiated the Kilmainham treaty as a betrayal. The Invincibles set out to 'make history' on 6 May 1882 by stabbing to death Thomas Henry Burke and his companion, the new chief secretary.[85]

While the police hunted for the perpetrators, John Kenny, an informer, was killed and Invincible attempts at assassination continued in Dublin. On 17 August five members of a family perished in an agrarian murder in Maamtrasna, Co. Galway. In November a constable died after a shoot-out between rival Fenian gangs in central Dublin. The country seemed about to descend into anarchy. James Mullett, a publican who had previously joined the Invincibles, became uneasy and informed to shorten his sentence. Detaining James Carey on suspicion produced further incriminating evidence. On 4 December 1882 John Adye Curran began directing a star chamber inquiry, which allowed him to question suspects under oath.[86]

Curran and Mallon harassed this revolutionary underworld until Robert Farrell, a minor conspirator, made a statement, leading to seventeen arrests. Superintendent Mallon tricked Carey, now a town councillor, into 'turning' by staging clues that a fellow activist had testified. Nine Invincibles informed and five were executed in Kilmainham jail, including Joe Brady, Tim Kelly and Daniel Curley. Their handlers, who had supplied weapons and money, escaped.[87]

Carey informed to save his life. The Phoenix Park murders were universally condemned in Ireland, but so was this apostate, who had betrayed his recruits. Dublin Castle used the evidence of such an upwardly mobile conspirator to create disillusionment. It also needed to relocate him and eight family members and decided on Natal, which contained few Irish inhabitants.

Sailing to Cape Town, 'Mr Power' made friends with Patrick O'Donnell, a Donegal-born miner on his way to South Africa. Carey's noisy behaviour attracted attention and an illustration in the *Weekly Freeman* confirmed his identity. The apolitical O'Donnell shared the general detestation of informants and killed Carey on board the steamer to Natal. He was condemned to death and hanged in London in December 1883, 'the latest martyr of British law'. Dublin Castle

suffered a major security failure and the myth of the relentless Fenian organization, which had sent O'Donnell across continents to punish Carey, took root.[88]

Other informers were recognized on their way to Australia and had to be
returned to Europe by the Royal Navy. Michael Kavanagh, an Invincible driver,
and Joseph Hanlon, whose evidence had convicted Tim Kelly at his third trial,
settled in Cyprus supervised by the British authorities. Kavanagh, an alcoholic,
predeceased Hanlon ('J. O'Loughlin'), who died in 1892, aged thirty-two. James
Smith, who had identified Undersecretary Burke for his assassins to inform
afterwards, was dead by 1885, but Peter Carey and Robert Farrell prospered in
a colony, the *Flag of Ireland* averred. Few of the informers met violent ends, but
most led miserable, brief lives, cut off from their Irish past.[89]

Was Patrick Hoctor an informer?

In the aftermath of the Phoenix Park murders, Edward George Jenkinson
recruited agents to destroy the Fenian movement from within. The most
important informer of the southwestern police division had joined in June 1887,
codenamed 'Nero'. His handlers considered him so valuable as to pay him an
exceptional £205 for 1889. Owen McGee identified him as Patrick Cogan, a
journalist and longstanding member of the 'Stephenite' IRB in Cork, but queried
the veracity of his information.[90]

P.N. Fitzgerald, FP 159 (courtesy NAI).

In November 1887 Major Gosselin, R.M., plotted to disrupt the GAA to
create conflict. Patrick Hoctor, P.N. Fitzgerald and John C. Forde attempted to
seize control of the association during its annual convention in Thurles, culminating in a fracas. A second congress followed and was dominated by moderate

nationalists. According to McGee, Hoctor had turned double agent and intensified this controversy. The IRB blamed him for the debacle, barring him from senior positions. Hoctor went abroad, working with John O'Connor and Dr John McInerney in the US. Returning down-at-heel to Limerick in February 1890, Hoctor failed 'to reorganize the IRB' and was suspected of having embezzled £300 from it and the GAA, although Fitzgerald continued to trust him.[91] McGee believes that during 1889–90 British intelligence directed Hoctor 'to stay close to and subtly counteract every action of Fitzgerald, the principal travelling organizer of the IRB, who in turn had rumours of being either an informer or embezzler thrown against him'.[92] This theory implies that Hoctor was 'Nero' or his close associate, but fails to consider Hoctor's absence abroad. He continued to retain a power base in Limerick and north Tipperary and was instrumental in erecting the first monument to a Gaelic athlete, William Real of Pallas, who held the world record for 'shoving from the shoulder'. Nor would the redoubtable Daly family have permitted Hoctor to give the funeral oration for Edward, father of Kathleen and Ned, if he had been demoted.[93] John C. Forde, 'county centre' and a member of the GAA board for Cork, was another candidate for prime informer. In 1889 Fr O'Connor of Cork publicized his conviction that the governing body of the local GAA contained informants. Forde was one of two suspects and had to resign. By 1892 he was accused of embezzling funds and had lost his IRB position.[94]

That year, Hoctor married Maggie, a daughter of the prosperous Clery family of Gibbinstown House, Bulgaden, Co. Limerick. She was probably related to those Clerys who had participated in the attack on the Kilmallock constabulary in 1867. Hoctor became a successful agent in the whiskey trade, but his dictatorial manner continued to cause conflict, for instance, when he threatened a servant of his in-laws with a revolver. The public collapse of the marriage followed in 1900 after he assaulted his wife, who had refused a separation on his terms while accusing him of an affair. Hoctor was among those who temporarily deserted the IRB for the Irish National Alliance, but his failure to retain a senior position was probably due to his abrasive character.[95]

Being accused of informing had almost become a rite of passage – the register of suspects compiled in the 1890s notes that Robert Johnston, a prime mover in Ulster for a quarter of a century, who had begun life as a labourer and was 'now very well to do', apparently as a result of embezzling IRB funds.[96] Such suspicions, especially endemic in Cork, undermined the movement and were fostered by Jenkinson and Gosselin. The latter described his tactics: 'A certain amount of fiction is inevitable and when more peaceful days come I shall I hope be able to formulate a better system, meantime we must go on as we are.'[97] In the absence of definitive evidence, the case against Hoctor remains unproven.

CHAPTER 13

Towards an Alternative Reality,
1884–1908

'So long as the Irish Republican Brotherhood exists, so long will there be a faction in Ireland who will fight for a Republic.'

Ormonde Winter, Director of Intelligence, 1920[1]

The Reform Act of 1884 increased the Irish electorate from 200,000 to 700,000 men, greatly augmenting Parnell's following. Gladstone, serving as prime minister for the second time, was beset by imperial problems, which, culminating in the death of General Gordon and the fall of Khartoum in January 1885, led to his resignation in June. Parnell's party won 86 out of 104 Irish seats in the subsequent general election.[2]

Behind the scenes, Charles Gavan Duffy and Lord Carnavon, a leading Conservative, were discussing Home Rule. Some high-ranking Dublin Castle officials favoured self-government. Prodded by Lord Spencer, the administration began to promote Catholic professionals, albeit without relinquishing coercion. Edward George Jenkinson urged Spencer and his successor, Lord Carnavon, to reach a settlement with moderate nationalists to isolate Fenianism. Parnell, holding the balance of power, negotiated with Lord Salisbury, but failed to gain concessions. In January 1886 the Conservatives withdrew from government and Gladstone formed his third administration with Parnell's support. Coercion and land legislation having failed, the prime minister chose the revolutionary solution of a limited form of Home Rule. His crusade split the Liberal Party, giving rise to militant Unionism in Ireland. Lord Randolph Churchill became the spokesman of this ally of the British Conservative Party.[3]

By 1887 the RIC estimated that a quarter of Parnell's MPs shared an IRB past, opting for his obtainable objectives without abandoning separatist aspirations. Thomas Condon of Clonmel, for instance, a second-generation Fenian, was elected for Tipperary East in 1885, declaring that he would revert to rebellion, should constitutionalism fail.[4]

Such men were upwardly mobile to an extent that would have been unthinkable twenty years earlier. Condon, a butcher, served nine terms as mayor of Clonmel from 1889 onwards. Parnellite MPs adopted the gentry pattern of utilizing local government to dispense patronage. Irish Unionists mistrusted them as opportunistic, but respected the statesman-like Parnell. William Monsell of Tervoe feared Home Rule as socialism, portraying southern Unionism as cultured bastions of wealth, whom the government should support to maintain control.[5]

'Long John' O'Connor, P.N. Fitzgerald's chief assistant, admired Parnell's election victory of 1880 in Cork, where the IRB had failed with Mitchel's candidature six years earlier. When Parnell selected 'Long John' for Tipperary South in 1885, he was duly elected, but the *volte face* of such a high-ranking IRB officer caused resentment.[6] In 1890 Charles G. Doran declared him 'a traitor' for having sworn allegiance to Queen Victoria to join Parnell and Gladstone, 'misleaders of the people'. The Fenian audience was motivated by envy of this former publican, who fled 'amid hisses and shouts of "tis bottlewashing you should be as you were before, instead of sitting in Parliament"'.[7]

The Clan's relationship with the IRB

After 1882 the American representatives of the Revolutionary Directory unilaterally spent $128,000 and the unheralded arrival of dynamiters upset the IRB, which was entitled to veto operations in Britain. Since 1883 Aleck Sullivan and Michael Boland had falsely reassured the Supreme Council that these explosions would cease. Rumours circulated among the Clan that the IRB might betray the dynamitards to the authorities. John O'Connor, secretary of the Supreme Council, denied this, as the IRB objected to the bombings of 1883–4, 'but not to all kinds'.[8]

No Clan convention took place in 1883. The following year, its executive was reduced to three men, ostensibly to outwit spies. Power now rested with the 'Triangle' leadership under Sullivan, Boland and D.C. Feely. Nevertheless, Edward George Jenkinson could provide the British Cabinet with detailed information about the Revolutionary Directory for 1884. He knew that the IRB depended on a subsidy of $40,000 from the Clan; its leaders had been forced to tolerate the dynamite policy for the last two years to retain this lifeline.[9] Jenkinson realized that only when the British secret service rendered the Clan ineffective by cutting off transatlantic aid could the IRB be defeated. He concurred with Devoy that the American physical force leaders colluded with Parnell's movement so intently that it was 'very difficult indeed' to distinguish between their followers.[10]

While Sullivan became a power in US politics, John O'Connor as IRB envoy was excluded from the 1884 and 1886 Clan conventions and warned not to consult with Devoy and other critics of the 'Triangle'. Sullivan saw little reason to resume contact with the home organization, which objected to the dynamite war. He denigrated the IRB elite, opposed to Parnell but devoid of alternatives. O'Connor's requests for an audit of the Revolutionary Directory accounts were frustrated. This body collapsed and Clan funding for the home organization ceased.[11] Michael Hogan, 'county centre' for Tipperary from 1877–83, predicted that if the Clan abandoned the IRB, it would have to be rebuilt within twenty years.[12]

From 1886 Dr John McInerney, a close friend, acted as a covert channel of communication between the Devoy faction and O'Connor. Robust criticism by Dr Philip Henry Cronin and John Devoy split the Clan with the 'Triangle' retaining two thirds of members:[13] 'The violence of language and bitterness on both sides was intense and savage, more characteristic of a minor civil war than a political controversy.'[14] The Foreign Office knew that the remnant of the Fenian Brotherhood had also split, expelling O'Donovan Rossa for 'treason'.[15] Fenianism continued to be outmanoeuvred by the British secret service and simultaneously overshadowed by Parnell. The IRB never regained its mass membership of the 1860s and floundered, despite numerous, often local, attempts at revival. The movement colluded in its decline for the remainder of the nineteenth century, as convoluted clashes occurred with dreary regularity. The reduced pool of activists responded by infiltrating cultural and sporting bodies and participated in working-class politics.[16]

The Young Ireland Society

The Young Ireland Society had been founded in Dublin in 1881 as a literary club with an ethos inspired by Thomas Davis and the *Nation* circle. The YIS familiarized its members with Irish literature, music and art, demonstrating that there was more to life than agrarian and parliamentary struggles. Frederick J. Allan of Dublin, one of the new generation of IRB leaders, seized control of the

YIS. By 1883 he had joined the Supreme Council.[17] The YIS celebrated patriotic anniversaries, ran history classes for children and provided the guard of honour for the funeral of Charles Kickham in 1882. Two years later the society raised money for the dependants of John Daly and James Egan, recently arrested in England, despite the leadership's detestation of dynamiting.[18]

There are few mentions of Munster in the minutes of the YIS before 1884, symptomatic of the IRB's waning influence. Patrick Hoctor, the son of a publican at Islandbawn Mills near Newport, Co. Tipperary, and nephew of a member of the Papal Brigade, first featured in revolutionary circles in 1881, when proposing to lecture on Kickham for the YIS. Hoctor, the offspring of a mixed marriage and something of an outsider, established a branch in Newport, which functioned until 1891.[19] Twenty-two YIS branches, twelve of them in Munster, two in Co. Kilkenny and Scotland respectively and others in Connacht and Ulster were affiliated to the central committee in Dublin during the 1880s. Others were controlled by the Parliamentary Party.[20] The symbiotic relationship between the IRB and constitutional nationalists facilitated the latter to affirm patriotic credentials, while supplying charismatic speakers and sponsorship for YIS events, as the revolutionaries were unable to claim exclusively the Fenian heroes of the 1860s.[21]

The National Monuments Committee

The numbers honouring the Manchester Martyrs each November provided a barometer of nationalist support. By their first anniversary a limestone cross had been erected and was visited in Glasnevin Cemetery. In Cork 'kneeling thousands' recited the litany for the dead, using Fr Mathew's grave as their focal point. In 1883 Fred Allan responded to criticism that the graves of James Clarence Mangan, Terence Bellew McManus and John O'Mahony remained unmarked by setting up a National Monuments Committee under the YIS umbrella. Devoy promised financial help.[22] An appeal by John O'Leary and Michael Davitt elicited donations from Archbishop Croke, Charles Gavan Duffy and other prominent nationalists. Money was also raised through special GAA matches.[23]

Although the Risings of 1848 and 1867 had failed, the IRB promoted its alternative vision for Ireland through the erection of monuments, which opposed the triumphant British Empire with its sculptures of William of Orange and Queen Victoria. Statuary is usually erected by the victors, but the IRB sponsored a cult of remembrance, centred on its martyrs, heroic failures, who 'would not be forgotten'.[24] These projects could meet with opposition: in 1870 a cross, commissioned for the 'unknown Fenian' by the 'people of Kilmallock', was initially vetoed by a Protestant clergyman and the constabulary. Although a promise was extracted that there would be no inscription, some time later patriotic verses by Michael Hogan, the bard of Thomond, appeared on the monument.[25] The NMC triumped in 1885 with P.N. Fitzgerald unveiling Celtic crosses in Glasnevin to John Keegan Casey, who wrote 'The Rising of the Moon' and Stephen O'Donoghue, 'martyr for Irish liberty in 1867', when he fell during the Rising. The cemetery authorities had blocked a headstone for the latter in 1869.

After John Haltigan's death in 1884 a monument was raised in Kilkenny, paying tribute to his 'life long struggle for Irish freedom for which crime British law, aided by the informer, Nagle, consigned him to a living tomb ... but failed to subdue his noble spirit. May his unselfish patriotism be imitated until Ireland is once again a nation.'[26] This cross became the focal point of the Manchester Martyrs commemorations, often leading to unrest. P.J. O'Keeffe, an orphaned protégé of the Haltigan family, joined the IRB to become a locally important GAA and working-class leader, capable of summoning a gang of 'toughs'.[27]

The amnesty of 1871 allowed John O'Leary to return home in January 1885. An inspirational figure, he faced the uncongenial task of reviving an organization tarnished by the Phoenix Park murders and the dynamiters. Charles Gavan Duffy described him as 'a Fenian of a class which I had never seen before, and rarely afterwards; moderate in opinion, generally just to his opponents, and entirely without passion or enthusiasm except a devoted love of Ireland. He was a great reader of books, and, I fear, a great dreamer of dreams.'[28]

Publicly welcomed by the YIS, O'Leary declared 'he had come back from exile with the same opinions he carried with him into prison' and addressed gatherings in Ireland and Britain.[29] On the third anniversary of Kickham's death, O'Leary failed to unveil a political programme in Mullinahone, but acknowledged Parnell, then facing into a general election as 'the man on the horse', entitled to judge 'when and how he should take the fence'. O'Leary considered it 'the duty of all Irishmen' not to hamper Parnell, providing him with an endorsement by a member of the original IRB elite. The former would settled for a version of Grattan's Parliament, unlike P.N. Fitzgerald and other organizers.[30]

Luby recalled how he had helped Stephens crush anti-Fenian opposition during the 1860s, believing a Rising imminent. Luby concluded that the people had chosen Parnell: 'My old comrades and myself are out of the running. Hence, on my own principles, I should feel self-condemned if I tried by pen or act to obstruct him. On my own principles I should deserve to be crushed in turn.'[31]

Traditional Fenians hoped that Parnell would eventually opt for independence, but at present Luby and O'Leary withdrew from politics, a tactic endorsed by few activists. In his lectures O'Leary urged nationalists to sacrifice time and money for Ireland. Hatred of British rule was justified, unlike dyna-miting and assassination. O'Leary frequently quoted Davis to make his point that 'righteous men must make our land/ A nation once again.'[32]

For O'Leary (like O'Mahony), a revolution required a cultural revival in an era dominated by English popular entertainment.[33] He encouraged his audi-ence to study Irish history and folklore, reading Davis, Duffy and the 'trumpet-tongued' Mitchel. O'Leary recommended Irish poets, including James Clarence Mangan, Speranza and Eva of the *Nation*, and the novels of Carleton, Banim, Griffin and Kickham for their depiction of Irish character. He still hoped for the 'great gift' of an outstanding poet. O'Leary urged the 'localisation of patriotism' through commemorations and the erection of monuments, but did not consider the Gaelic language essential to nationality.[34]

He opposed a narrow focus on Ireland, recommending European writers, including Dante, Shakespeare and Goethe.[35] One wonders how the average Fenian responded to these erudite recommendations. After O'Leary became president of the YIS, its gatherings attracted W.B. Yeats, Charles Hubert Oldham, J.F. Taylor and T.W. Rolleston.[36] His lectures in Ireland and Britain rallied the IRB, but uproar ensued when O'Leary condemned 'recent dynamite outrages' by 'ignorant and unscrupulous fanatics'. Some listeners censured him for not employing every weapon against England and cheered for O'Donovan Rossa.[37]

O'Leary's disdain for *realpolitik* led him to denounce political compromise as eroding moral standards; 'expediency was only another name for lying and dishonesty'. He also refused to blame all Irish problems on 'perfidious Albion'.[38] His response was to disseminate cultural nationalism to a talented circle, including W.B. Yeats, Katharine Tynan, Rosa Mulholland, Rose Kavanagh and Dora and Hester Sigerson. Ellen O'Leary participated, writing poetry and advising a diffi-dent Yeats until her death from cancer in 1889.[39]

Maud Gonne

Gonne began her career as a separatist and social reformer by conforming to contemporary female standards, reciting patriotic poetry at charity events (albeit with royal patronage), reminiscent of Mary Jane O'Donovan Rossa. Irish women had lost any access to politics since the demise of the Ladies' Land League, nor did cultural bodies admit female members. Despite her beauty and wealth, Gonne was initially not welcome and occasionally suspected as a spy.[40] John O'Leary, a promoter of dialogue, perceived Gonne's potential as a bilin-gual propagandist in the French and American press and assisted her to become a popular public speaker. Her dramatic self-assurance portrayed a triumphant Erin, negating depictions of the distressed nation in need of guidance, so familiar from British cartoons. Fanny Parnell and later Maud Gonne utilized their femininity to appear less threatening to male colleagues, while benefitting from upper-class origins when exceeding accepted norms. The *Irish Times* only denounced Gonne after a decade as an activist, outraged by her anti-enlistment campaign during the Boer War.[41]

THE VETERANS OF THE I. R. B. OF '65 AND '67.

✻ DECORATION ✤ DAY ✤ CEREMONIES. ✻

MAY 30th, 1889.

HALCYON HALL, 537 THIRD AVENUE,
NEW YORK, *May 5th, 1889.*

> "Twice—thrice be they blessed for no common devotion,
> Was theirs to the Island that called them her own;
> The pulse of their hearts, like the tide of the ocean,
> Flowed true to the land of their fathers alone."

DEAR SIR:

The Veterans of the I. R. B. will assemble in the above hall at 10.30 A. M., on Decoration Day, and proceed in a body to Calvary Cemetery to decorate the graves of their dead brothers who lie buried there; a detachment will be sent to decorate the graves of our brothers in Flatbush. Since last performing this sacred duty some of those who were with us then have departed from our midst; of those, two were, by a life-long devotion to Ireland, deservedly dear to all who participated in the last attempt to redeem our Mother-land, namely, JEREMIAH O'FARRELL and Corporal THOMAS CHAMBERS, nor must we forget our gifted brother JOHN LOCKE, the Poet.

As it is our intention to make this celebration as elaborate as possible, and in every way worthy of our dead brothers, and the great sacrifices they made in behalf of our Country's Freedom, we appeal to our brothers and friends for funds to enable us to do so. We cannot touch our own funds for any but benevolent purposes, and the necessary expenses must be contributed voluntarily for flowers, music and other requisites for our ceremonies.

The graves of the following deceased Patriots have already been located and marked out for decoration:

Col. Michael Doheny............Tipperary	Edward Walsh................Tipperary	Capt. John F. Cavanagh..........Tipperary
John Breslin ....Dublin	Peter and Mary Curran...........Meath	William Donoyan................Dublin
John Delany............Borris-in-Ossory	Michael Harrington....Australian Prisoner	John Walsh....................Kildare
Denis Cronien............Kingstown	John J. Geary....................Cork	Jas. H. Casserly................Dublin
Thos. Farrell...............Liverpool	O'Neal Fogarty................Tipperary	John Egan....................Birmingham
John Kearney...............Mill Street	Jeremiah O'Farrell..............Kilkenny	Jeremiah O'Meare..............Skibbereen
John Hughes ....Tipperary	Thos. Costello..................Limerick	Jeremiah Welstead.............Limerick
Denis Corbett ....Charleville	John Rooney...Columbkille, "Erin's Hope"	Thos Plunkett.................Dublin
Henry Davis ....Dublin	Edward O Keefe...............Galway	Jos. Fagan................Roscommon
William Mellville..........Manchester	Ephraim Breslin..............Dublin	Daniel R. Lyddy...............Limerick
Charles Spillane ....Skibbereen	Lawrence Walsh.............Waterford	Arthur Anderson............Liverpool
Thos. Cromien..............Wicklow	Edw'd J Byrne............Dublin	Patrick Lynch..............Meath
Harry Mullady.................Dublin	Patrick Walsh..............Limerick	John Locke................Kilkenny
William Foley........Australian Prisoner	Andrew Lalor..............Queen's Co.	Thos. Ford................Dublin
Capt. M. O'Rourke, "Beecher"	John Howe..............Waterford	Charles Clarke...............London
Irish American Officer	Lawrence Cunningham...........	

The Oration will be delivered at the grave of JEREMIAH O'FARRELL, of Kilkenny.

> "On the National Banner in letters of glory,
> Inscribe them to serve as the Watchwords for men,
> Who roused from despair by their Patriot story,
> Shall dare all the deeds of those Heroes again."

In addition to the above list of names we shall be glad to receive those of any others of our Comrades who are buried in Calvary or Flatbush, and their friends will oblige us by forwarding the number of plot, section and grave.

Subscriptions and flowers may be sent to any of the Officers of the Committee, whose addresses are appended.

In the list above presented appears the names of many who have played prominent parts in our movement. All of them have been true to our principles, and their whole lives have been devoted to our common cause. It is, therefore, only meet and just that we should honor their memory and do justice to the noble aspirations which actuated them. In doing so we will reflect credit on ourselves and keep alive the old feeling of Patriotism which, in the end, must make our native land Free and Independent.

SAMUEL CAVANAGH, *Chairman Committee,* 527 E. 13th Street.
J. P. KEELY, *Vice-Chairman,* 363 Bowery.
E. PILSWORTH ST. CLAIR, *Secretary,* 30 New Bowery.
P. J. HAYBURNE, *Fin. Secretary,* 20 Rutgers Place.
EDWIN WHELAN, *Treasurer,* 112 E. 108th Street.

Communications regarding graves of deceased brothers must be sent in at the earliest moment to the Secretary, as above.

Programme of the IRB Veterans' Association, New York 1889
(courtesy Jeanne Ahearn Mogayzel).

By 1889 the central committee of the YIS retained little control over its branches, although the NMC remained active. After twelve years of planning, the McManus monument neared completion. The NMC had paid Sir Thomas Farrell £600 for sculpting the figures of Erin, fidelity and patriotism with £100 outstanding. The Dublin Cemeteries Committee consulted the attorney general regarding the proposed inscription, which lauded McManus and O'Mahony:[42] 'All outlaws and felons according to English law, but true soldiers of Irish liberty; representatives of successive movements for Irish independence. Their lives thus prove that every generation produces patriots who were willing to face the gibbet, the cell, and exile to procure the liberty of their nation and afford perpetual proof that in the Irish heart faith in Irish nationality is indestructible.'[43]

Dublin Castle banned this as 'seditious', but the NMC refused to back down and stalemate ensued until 1933, when the National Graves Association as its successor erected the monument.[44]

Thomas Francis Bourke Monument, Calvary Cemetery, NY
(author's collection).

The Gaelic Athletic Association

Michael Cusack had been encouraged by P.W. Nally, an outstanding athlete and member of the Supreme Council for Connacht, to form 'a society for the preservation and cultivation of our national pastimes'. Traditional sport, as celebrated by Kickham in the figure of Matt the Thrasher in *Knocknagow*, was in decline. Nally organised such an event in Mayo with Parnell as patron, supplanting landlord control and initiating a democratization of athletics. In 1884 an IRB gathering in Co. Dublin, which included P.N. Fitzgerald, Patrick Hoctor and James Boland, discussed creating a national athletics association.[45]

When Cusack called the historic Thurles meeting of 1 November 1884, Nally and Fitzgerald were in prison. Nevertheless, at least two Fenians were among the seven founders of the Gaelic Athletic Association: John Wyse Power, a journalist and native of Waterford, and J.K. Bracken, the monumental sculptor from Templemore, Co. Tipperary.[46] Dublin Castle credited Patrick Hoctor with being the first to exploit the GAA as an IRB recruiting ground in 1886, when he achieved 'considerable success' in Clare. The following year P.N. Fitzgerald introduced the GAA to Kerry in the public house of Thomas Slattery of Tralee, where it was enthusiastically taken up.[47]

The activities of leaders like Fred Allan, P.N. Fitzgerald, Patrick Hoctor and Maurice Moynihan linked the GAA, the YIS and the NMC in Dublin.[48] Moynihan of Tralee used his travels as a butter-buyer's clerk in Kerry to organize. William Moore Stack, the former 'centre' of the Tralee Fenians, supported the local YIS, while pointing his son Austin in this direction. Likewise, Patrick McInerney of Ennis, an IRB stalwart, served on the county board of the GAA. He was the custodian of the Fenian arms fund in Clare, where Dublin Castle considered him 'an authority and referee on all matters connected with outrage'.[49] Brian Clune of Carrahan, and later Tullyrohan near Ennis, 'county centre' for Clare from 1877, sat on the Clare county board of the GAA and, according to the constabulary, was feared by any neighbour loyal to Dublin Castle.[50]

By 1886 the three vice presidents of the GAA were IRB men from Tipperary: J.K. Bracken, F.R. Moloney and Patrick Hoctor.[51] The latter's intransigent management style led to a public rebuke by Archbishop Croke to avoid personality clashes. In November 1887 the power struggle between the Fenians under Hoctor, Fitzgerald and John C. Forde, the 'county centre' for Cork, and the constitutional nationalists allied to the clergy, culminated in the IRB seizing control during the Thurles convention. Edward Bennett, a '67 Fenian, was elected president. Archbishop Croke intervened, assisted by Michael Davitt, and a new GAA convention took place in January 1888, which a chastened Fitzgerald attended.[52]

By 1890, in spite of reports that both organizations were in the doldrums in Munster, Dublin Castle believed that the IRB had regained 'supreme control' in Clare and Kerry, while dominating almost one hundred clubs in Cork and Limerick.[53] The constabulary considered the GAA strongest in Cork, Cavan and Galway. In Munster it provided a power base for Fitzgerald and Hoctor. The authorities observed 'almost military scenes before some sporting events, when the players marched around the field, their hurleys on their shoulders as if they were rifles' in a vision of the Fenian army to come, which impressed onlookers.[54]

Clan na Gael tensions and murder

Clan members as well as the IRB Supreme Council were enthusiastic about Gladstone's Home Rule Bill, considering it a stepping stone to 'complete separation'.[55] But Conservatives opposed any transfer of local government for threatening the integrity of the empire. The Liberal Party split over this issue. In June 1886 the First Home Rule Bill was defeated by thirty votes and the Conservatives won the ensuing general election. Parnell emerged with enhanced status, intent on eventual victory.[56]

Clan na Gael divisions continued to fester. The Sullivanite majority began to use the name 'Irish National Brotherhood' to distinguish itself from the Devoy wing. In January 1887 the Supreme Council considered it held the balance of power between the warring factions and contacted both. John O'Connor favoured Devoy, who advocated a 'wait and see' policy regarding insurrection. Major Gosselin believed that the Sullivan section made 'use of dynamite and the knife occasionally, just to keep the dollars flowing and help the parliamentary men'.[57]

In 1888 the convention of both wings conceded Dr Cronin's demand for an investigation. The 'trial' committee held the 'Triangle' accountable for a shortfall of $87,000, although $128,000 had been wasted between 1881–4 without authorization. Michael Boland was convicted of embezzlement, while Aleck Sullivan and D.C. Feely, in spite of censure for slovenly business methods, won acquittals.[58]

'Trial' notes were to be destroyed, but Dr Cronin denounced Sullivan, utilizing his summary for a pamphlet, which revealed how the 'Triangle' abandoned the destitute family of Captain Mackey Lomasney. The doctor further predicted his murder, while bringing the Clan into disrepute and destroying Sullivan's influence. The 'Triangle' denounced Devoy, Dr Cronin's ally, as a British agent, but nobody realized that Sullivan had unwittingly facilitated Le Caron's spying for years. Nor did the leaders suspect that F.F. Millen's latest offer to inform had been rebuffed by the Foreign Office.[59]

The *Times* Commission was established in response to articles on 'Parnellism and Crime', some written by Robert Anderson. It sat from September 1888 to November 1889. On 5 February Le Caron testified in his 'true colours, as an Englishman', damaging Parnell and revolutionary associates like Aleck Sullivan and Patrick Egan. He claimed that other British agents were embedded in the Clan, which misled Sullivanites into believing Dr Cronin was among them.[60] On 4 May 1889 the doctor was kidnapped and murdered in Chicago. The 'trial of the century' dropped the charges against Sullivan from insufficient evidence, but exposed rampant Irish-American police corruption and the inner workings of the Clan to a horrified public. Sullivan withdrew from Irish affairs, while members with middle-class aspirations resigned.[61]

To connect Parnell with outrages, the government gave representatives of the *Times* unprecedented access to P.W. Nally, John Daly and Tom Clarke to pressurize them into testifying against him, but the prisoners rejected this opportunity to shorten their sentences.[62] Daly and Clarke must have reflected how the Conservatives could use the Special Branch to undermine the legitimate actions of Irish parliamentarians, confirming their Fenian convictions. Parnell was sensationally cleared of having endorsed the Phoenix Park murders and increased his support.[63]

The dynamite war, petering out in 1885, had killed one civilian and caused numerous injuries in Britain. Faith in this 'scientific' weapon proved unfounded. It and the endemic infighting distressed Thomas Clarke Luby greatly. He summarized their political credo to O'Leary: 'I would feel myself justified in refusing to obey – aye even in resisting and denouncing – representative leaders, if they were dynamiters of the Rossa or "Invincibles" stamp, and that even if they were backed by the voice of our whole Irish nation. Why this? Simply because I would regard them as utterly immoral; outlaws alike of true society and God!'[64]

After the Cronin murder, Luby commented how nothing 'would now astonish me; that is, *any abomination turning up in Irish-American patriotic affairs*'. He regretted the loss of the moral standards handed down by the Young Irelanders: 'But the great slaughterer of my illusions – and, by God, they have been, of late years, most unmercifully hacked and butchered – is your modern Irish patriot politician, with his new-fangled methods of patriotism.'[65]

Secret service developments

By 1886 Edward George Jenkinson, although assistant undersecretary of police for Ireland, worked from the Home Office, spending unprecedented sums of money. Not only did he refuse to share intelligence with Chief Superintendent

Williamson of Scotland Yard, but should his unofficial position in London become known, an outcry was likely. Jenkinson was probably the source of a *Times* article, which claimed that Rossa had run agents in Munster and Britain with an explosives factory in Cork. In reality, much of this could be traced to an agent provocateur hired by Jenkinson. The latter, whose position had never been regularized, alienated most of his peers and various home secretaries failed to effect cooperation between the intelligence chiefs.[66] This became public knowledge and Jenkinson was dismissed in December 1886. Major Nicholas Gosselin, his eventual successor, succeeded in provoking further infighting among Irish revolutionaries.[67]

Jenkinson's great triumph, the conviction of John Daly and James Egan, began to look tainted by 1887, when Henry Manton, an alderman of Birmingham, asked the home secretary to review it, as Chief Constable Joseph Farndale of Birmingham had stated that the bombs were planted on Daly by a police agent. The Home Office commented this 'sounds incredible', though it had been informed by spymaster Jenkinson that 'plot is met by counterplot'.[68] Alderman Manton responded by publishing a pamphlet. The *Times* concurred with the Home Office that Daly, 'a desperado of the most unflinching type', constituted a serious threat and rejoiced at his capture, regardless of circumstances.[69]

In late 1889 Daly's friends established the Limerick Amnesty Association, which hoped to ease his imprisonment.[70] A visit from James Jones, Daly's adopted nephew and the secretary of the Association, led to the revelation that prison officials had poisoned Daly, apparently by mistake when dispensing medicine. Members of Parliament declined to attend the first public meeting of the Limerick Amnesty Association on 16 March 1890, which protested against the 'brutal punishment' of Irish political prisoners and demanded an independent inquiry into the poisoning episode.[71] The amnesty campaign was supported by Charles G. Doran, P.N. Fitzgerald, Patrick Hoctor, John Crowe and P.J. O'Keeffe of Kilkenny. Meetings were held in those Munster towns where the IRB retained support.[72]

Major Gosselin was aware that John O'Connor, Secretary of the Supreme Council, had not had been in contact with P.N. Fitzgerald for a long time, but was now urging the IRB to renewed efforts, while discouraging dynamiting. Although meetings were held in the north of England and Gosselin believed Irish people were tired of land agitation, which might revive Fenianism, he considered the IRB moribund, 'the body may be galvanised into movement but the spirit has fled'.[73] One of Gosselin's agents had infiltrated the Sullivanite Clan and reported its 'total disorganisation', while the RIC stated that this faction was so covered in opprobrium that nobody at home would affiliate with it.[74]

In 1890 Dublin Castle estimated that membership of the IRB stood at 50,000 men, with Connacht as its leading province, where it predominated in Galway and Mayo. In Leinster the organization was concentrated in the Dublin/Kildare region, while Cork and Limerick remained strongholds, though numbers had greatly declined throughout Munster. Given that its Irish membership was 36,000 in 1884 and following recent vicissitudes, these figures appear exaggerated.[75]

On 24 December 1889 Captain Willie O'Shea filed for divorce and a scandalized public learned that Katharine had been Parnell's mistress since 1880. Gladstone, in need of Nonconformist support, declined to campaign for Home Rule with the Irish leader, whose MPs faced a cruel choice between loyalty to their charismatic chief or continuing their alliance with Gladstone and the Liberals. The Irish Party split on 6 December 1890 and Parnell was forced to fall back on the IRB. While the Supreme Council did not formally permit its officers to join the Parnell leadership committee, John O'Leary, John Wyse Power and Fred Allan rallied to his defence.[76]

During the Kilkenny by-election in December 1890, a Fenian, probably P.N. Fitzgerald, acted as Parnell's assistant director of elections, supported by IRB men brought in from Dublin and Munster. Among them was John Kelly of Tralee, a close friend of John Stanislaus Joyce, father of the more famous James. Kelly was a 'propagandist for the Land League' and the Irish National League, celebrated for the 'O'Brien breeches episode'. He had smuggled a suit of Blarney tweed into Tullamore jail for William O'Brien, who had been forcibly stripped after refusing to wear prison uniform. Kelly was frequently detained and Dublin Castle 'took good care that his business' was ruined. This steadfast admirer of Parnell served as his channel of communication with the physical force men.[77]

Table 13. *Number of IRB members in Ireland in 1890*

Connacht	22,000
Leinster	12,000
Munster	10,000
Ulster	6000
Total	50,000

(Source: Nationalist Organisations, 1890–3, CO 904/16, TNA)

Table 14. *Membership of the Supreme Council 1887–90*

Office held	Name	Occupation & Location	Remarks
President	John O'Leary	Man of letters, Dublin	Police reports believed J. O'Connor was president, indicating O'Leary's inaction
Secretary	John O'Connor	Medical assistant, Paris	
Treasurer	Unknown		
Representatives of provinces:			
Munster	P.N. Fitzgerald	Commercial traveller & publican, Cork	
Leinster	C.J. O'Farrell	Clerk, Enniscorthy	
Connacht	Vacant, as P.W. Nally imprisoned, Dr J. Nally, brother or a sister may substitute for him	Children of a farmer & land agent, Balla, Co. Mayo	
Ulster	Michael O'Hanlon	Downpatrick	
North of England	William McGuinness	Publican, Preston, England	
South of England	John Ryan	Shoemaker, Acton, London	
Scotland	John Torley	Manager of chemical works, Duntocher,Glasgow	
Co-opted	John Sweeney, alias Skerrett		Probably the 'Skerrett' involved in Fitzgerald's arrest in 1884
Co-opted	Dr John McInerney	Physician, New York	
Paid organizers (1887)			
	Patrick Hoctor	Commercial traveller, active in Glasgow	
	John P. ('Jack') Boland[78]	To be based in Ulster	

(Source: September 1890, Nationalist Organisations, 1890–3, CO 904/16, TNA; Personnel of the Supreme Council, 1887–90, 533/S, CBS 1890, NAI)

Bishop Abraham Brownrigg of Ossory described the Parnellites as 'the lowest dregs of the people, the Fenian element' and was horrified by the brutality of a contest to which he contributed his share.[79] Some educated people in Kilkenny supported Parnell, as did the urban poor, who had no votes, but he was shunned by the farming class. James J. O'Kelly, a Parnellite, predicted correctly that clerical opposition would ensure repeated defeats at the hustings. In March 1891 Barry O'Brien acknowledged that without P.N. Fitzgerald the deposed chief would have had no effective organization.[80]

The Parnell split had a negative impact on every nationalist endeavour, including the IRB, the GAA, the remaining Young Ireland Societies and the amnesty issue. By 1893 Dublin Castle recorded that only fifteen branches of the YIS survived outside Dublin, with their 2500 members divided equally between the factions.[81] In Ennis Patrick McInerney, Fenian treasurer and armourer for Clare, had spearheaded support for Parnell. Brian Clune, the 'county centre', was also 'a prominent Parnellite'. But by 1892 his position was vacant 'due to the disorganisation of the IRB' in Clare; Clune was in 'very bad circumstances'. McInerney's influence was similarly diminished. A disappointed man, he was said to have 'taken to drink and his fidelity is questioned' by some of his revolutionary associates.[82]

An amnesty for the dynamiters

Having denigrated the IRB before the *Times* Commission, Parnell needed to re-establish Fenian support. After his defeat in the Kilkenny election, he focused on amnesty for the dynamiters as 'a bridge between Parnellism and Fenianism', which also facilitated his attacks on the Liberals. Initially, both factions of the Irish Party had supported amnesty, but as the split worsened, the anti-Parnellites withdrew.[83] This culminated in Parnell addressing a meeting in the Phoenix Park in April 1891. Patrick Hoctor heckled him about his failure to lobby Gladstone in 1884, when P.W. Nally had been convicted on dubious evidence. With supreme tactlessness, Hoctor pointed to his own, superior record as an amnesty campaigner. In the ensuing uproar, he was denounced as a 'Healyite', that is, anti-Parnell. Hoctor retorted that he attended 'as an Irish nationalist, having nothing to do with current politics at all'. P.N. Fitzgerald and others, seated on the platform beside Parnell, who was fighting for his political life, intervened to silence Hoctor. Dublin Castle believed that he had never fallen under the chief's spell; he may have felt that the IRB colluded in its fragmentation by supporting Parnell, rather than reforming itself.[84]

Parnell, assisted by John Redmond, raised the convictions of Egan and Daly during his last speeches in Parliament. A number of local government bodies came out in favour of amnesty. Public perception of James Stephens had also mellowed, a fund was collected and the authorities allowed him to return to Ireland in September 1891, on condition of abstaining from politics, but Stephens expressed support for the Amnesty Association.[85]

Following Parnell's death on 6 October, the Irish National Amnesty Association was founded. Fred Allan, Dr Mark Ryan, P.N. Fitzgerald and Thomas O'Gorman, a butter-buyer in Limerick, where he had chaired the local association, became honorary vice presidents. The *Times*, commenting on the bitter divisions among nationalists, mistakenly considered amnesty the one subject on which they were unanimous. Between 1892 and 1894, this movement failed to capture the public imagination and members of the Daly family remained its most consistent promoters.[86]

After the Second Home Rule Bill was defeated by the House of Lords in 1893, disillusionment with the warring factions of the Irish Parliamentary Party increased. Gladstone's efforts to solve the Irish question enjoyed little support among his cabinet. He was succeeded by Lord Rosebery as Liberal prime minister, who lost the general election of 1895, when the Conservatives under Lord Salisbury came to power for the following decade.[87]

The IRB declined to 29,792 men, of whom a mere 8120 paid their subscriptions and attended meetings. These figures were probably an overestimate. The constabulary reported that Connacht, once a Fenian stronghold, had become 'completely inactive', although 'circles' still existed.[88] By 1894 the movement in Dublin had split in four: the Supreme Council IRB, a clique of the adherents of James Stephens, a third group modelling itself on the Invincibles, led by James Boland, who in turn allied himself to local supporters of the Sullivanite Clan na Gael. Assistant Commissioner Mallon of the DMP could not remember a time when both parliamentarians and secret society men had been 'so much divided'.[89]

In July 1894 Fred Allan chaired a meeting to revive the Supreme Council with funds from the US. A coalition of the IRB and Irish supporters of the Sullivanite Clan briefly held sway, but details remain sketchy. James Boland, Denis P. Seery and Patrick Hoctor, all of Dublin, P.N. Fitzgerald of Cork, Thomas O'Gorman and John Crowe, both of Limerick, and one of the Nallys of Balla were said to be involved. P.J. O'Keeffe, Kilkenny, C.J. O'Farrell, Enniscorthy and Robert Johnston and H. Dobbyn of Belfast also joined, but within a year this executive had collapsed, 'chiefly through the action of P.N. Fitzgerald'. A strong promoter of the Devoy Clan, he may have become dissatisfied with this compromise.[90]

The IRB sent P.N. Fitzgerald and John O'Connor to the 1894 convention of the Devoy Clan in Philadelphia. Their consultations with both wings failed to heal the split. Claims that the IRB was experiencing a revival met with disbelief. O'Connor was seen 'evidently having a good time' and not acting like the representative of 'a great military organisation', the *New York Times* reported. Nicholas Gosselin and John Mallon admitted that 'O'Connor and his objects are a great mystery' and even his home in Paris remained unknown.[91]

The Clan feud between Devoy and the 'Triangle', which lasted fifteen years, disrupted the movement on both sides of the Atlantic. By 1895 William Lyman, a New York building contractor and former protégé of Aleck Sullivan, had assumed leadership of the Sullivanite Clan, which called itself the 'Irish National Brotherhood' or 'Irish National Alliance' for some years. These names were also used for supporters in Britain and Ireland. Lyman attempted to control what remained of the IRB, challenging its leaders and the Devoy faction of the Clan.[92]

The INA attracted physical force men on the fringes of the Home Rule movement, who had hoped to influence events should the parliamentarians succeed, as well as some constitutional nationalists, 'in despair' since the defeat of the Home Rule Bill. It entrusted Lyman with unprecedented powers and $55,000 from its treasury. Although British spies had successfully infiltrated the INA, Major Gosselin could not discover if and when Lyman sent men on bombing missions, as he 'is rich, sober, determined, and a fanatic in his hatred of England'.[93] Gosselin feared that the INA would attract 'every man who is mad enough to believe in a policy of force' in Ireland, while denunciations by the rival Devoy Clan remained ineffectual: 'The old IRB and its Supreme Council stick to the Clan na Gael but they are old fossils,' as Lyman attracted young activists.[94]

Dr Mark Ryan, a former supreme councillor, became the main representative of the INA in Britain, assisted by Dr Anthony MacBride in London, his brother John, the future Boer War leader, in Dublin, and Robert Johnston, until recently a member of the Supreme Council, in Belfast. W.B. Yeats also joined the 'new movement'. James Egan, released in 1893, his conviction as a dynamiter being deemed unsafe, became their agent. This indicated great dissatisfaction with the old organization.[95]

Discussions about reuniting the movement among the remaining IRB leaders, who had little money, petered out. After Patrick Hoctor, too, went over the INA, the Special Branch in Munster realized that the conflict would intensify into a power struggle between Fitzgerald and Hoctor's supporters in the Amnesty Association. Considerable disorganization ensued.[96] J.K. Bracken, 'a cool, cautious man', who had been inactive for some years, joined the INA. Despite a 'stiff and constrained manner', which made him unpopular, Bracken retained great influence in north

Tipperary, where he proceeded to denounce P.N. Fitzgerald. It was also rumoured that Bracken's attacks were due to his not having been paid for the headstone for Michael Seery, a prominent Dublin Fenian.[97] ✗

In Limerick the Amnesty Association fell under INA control in January 1896, when John Crowe, a long-serving IRB 'centre', was deposed as vice president of the city branch. Two organizations, the 'Amnesty Association of Great Britain, London', controlled by the INA, and the 'Irish National Amnesty Association, Dublin', affiliated to the IRB, competed with each other.[98]

During 1895 the populist *Reynolds's Newspaper* ran a series of articles, written by Patrick McIntyre, a disgruntled former Special Branch detective, whose revelations that Rossa and most of the dynamiters were the victims of *agents provocateur* revived the amnesty issue.[99]

In his prison memoir, Tom Clarke recalled that Governor Harris of Chatham had invented 'a scientific system of perpetual and persistent harassing' of the Irish prisoners, which was 'specially devised to destroy us mentally and physically'.[100] Clarke witnessed seven dynamiters suffering psychological distress. When he and John Daly drew attention to their mental deterioration, they were 'laughed at' by the staff.[101] Official documentation confirms that letters mentioning disturbed prisoners were confiscated. Parnellite MPs and Irish-Americans lobbied for a number of years.[102] The Home Office stonewalled until shortly before the discharge of 'Whitehead' Murphy, when it conceded 'some weakness of mind'. On release in 1896, both he and Dr Gallagher were diagnosed as insane, while the latter also bore marks of physical abuse.[103] 'Whitehead' Murphy, sent home to his mother in Skibbereen, vanished, was found roaming Cork and had to be escorted to New York; both he and Dr Gallagher were admitted to a psychiatric institution.[104]

John Daly was among four dynamiters liberated in 1896. The previous year, the local Amnesty Association ran him as parliamentary candidate for Limerick with the assistance of Maud Gonne, when he was elected in the abstentionist tradition. English criminals occasionally went on hunger strike, driven by despair. Daly became the first Irish Republican to turn this into a political weapon.[105] Once discharged, he claimed that the prison regime had undermined his health, although he remained 'confident of the ultimate triumph of the Irish cause'.[106] The Home Office pronounced him 'not deteriorated', however.[107] Daly gave lectures for the Amnesty Association in Munster and the north of England, assisted by Patrick Hoctor, a leading INA organizer.[108]

Daly's American tour was to fund his new start in life. Kathleen Clarke claimed that her uncle had not been involved in the genesis of the Clan split and urged audiences to prepare for the 1798 centenary by uniting the movement. He was allied to INA figures in Ireland, however. When his liner approached New

York, two rival delegations waited to claim Daly, the INA (former Sullivanite Clan) with William Lyman and Maud Gonne, and the Devoy section. The latter outflanked his opponents by boarding the ship at the quarantine station with Jim Treacy of Kilmallock, who had been Daly's closest friend among the 1867 insurgents.[109]

Devoy offered his support and the total profit of his forthcoming speaking tour, which Daly accepted. Lyman, on the other hand, proposed the lectures should be under his patronage, with 25 per cent of the net profit going to Daly, who responded: 'Mr Lyman, at my age I don't want hard work, but I'd shovel coal before I'd accept an offer like that.' The tour realized £800, with which Daly founded his bakery in Limerick, but infighting continued, as Devoy's supporters vilified Gonne, who was touring America for Lyman's organization and to raise funds for the Wolfe Tone monument in Dublin.[110]

Demonstrating bitter fragmentation after Dr Cronin's murder, the Dublin 1798 committee had refused to authorize Gonne to collect money for the Wolfe Tone statue, although John O'Leary, its president, approved. She disliked Lyman's methods of spending money freely and inserting fictitious subscriptions to the amnesty fund in the American press to attract donations. When there was little left after expenses, Irish supporters experienced mistrust. Gonne was one of the few to resist Lyman's orders.[111]

Tom Clarke was the last of the prisoners to be liberated in 1898. In spite of patriotic sentiment during the 1798 centenary, the IRB failed to find employment for him on his engagement to Kathleen, John Daly's niece, and the couple emigrated to New York. Although Devoy had met his initial request for support with 'cold indifference', Clarke won the confidence of this notoriously prickly veteran.[112]

At the Buffalo Convention of his wing of the Clan in 1899, Lyman was deposed for embezzling funds. The Fenian movement began to unite, accompanied by the demise of the INA at home. In August, for instance, Patrick Hoctor travelled to Thurles with Patrick Tobin and John Menton of the IRB for discussions of how to amalgamate the factions. The following year, Hoctor and Dr Anthony MacBride represented the home organization at the annual conference of the Clan in Atlantic City, where unity was achieved.[113]

The 1798 centenary

The centenary of the 1798 insurrection was a major opportunity to publicize the separatist message, but the outbreak of the Spanish-American War aborted plans for the visit of numerous Irish-Americans, whose donations were needed to finance patriotic demonstrations. Initially, two rival 1798 associations in Dublin and a third in Cork were eager to run separate commemorative programmes. Their modus operandi consisted of establishing as many local committees as possible and affiliating them to the relevant central body.[114] In Munster John Daly, P.N. Fitzgerald, Michael Dalton of Tipperary, John Crowe, Charles G. Doran and Maurice Moynihan had been elected to control events for the IRB. One hundred and sixty local committees existed by March 1898, involving all shades of nationalism. The IRB continued to compete with INA supporters, as well as the Parliamentary Party, many of whose members revered the patriot dead. Although reconciliation featured in many speeches, the authorities believed that transatlantic 'disunion and distrust' impeded separatists.[115]

A compromise of sorts was reached and John O'Leary chaired the central committee in Dublin, but Maud Gonne considered him ineffectual: 'He was a noble figure-head but too old to grasp and make use of a situation.' Dublin Castle concurred and no longer shadowed O'Leary, who 'has not been for years an active IRB man'.[116] Torchlight processions were held in Dublin and Cork, while bonfires blazed at Ballyhurst, a scene of the 1867 Rising. This was followed by 'one of the most remarkable' commemorations in Munster, when William and Sophie Raffalovich O'Brien shared a platform with Charles G. Doran and P.N. Fitzgerald in Mallow.[117] In Limerick a torchlight procession of 5000 people greeted an energetic John Daly on return from his American lecture tour. Dublin Castle believed that he was forming 'a very dangerous gang of sympathizers amongst the worst class in the city', but that he made no impact among the middle classes.[118]

Peter O'Neill Crowley remained a popular hero whose relative, Fr Peter O'Neill, had been tortured in 1798. During the centenary a Celtic cross was erected where Crowley fell in Kilclooney Wood. Banners recalled Colonel John O'Mahony and his nephew, John Mandeville, who had died during the Plan of Campaign, and the victims of the Mitchelstown massacre of 1887. While the Munster IRB leaders attended, John Redmond, MP, sent his apologies, which may have been diplomatic given that his uncle, a resident magistrate, had accompanied the flying column that killed O'Neill Crowley. But only 6000 people attended in Kilclooney Wood, in contrast to the 20,000 who had witnessed the unveiling of his headstone in 1887.[119]

The RIC believed that efforts 'to excite enthusiasm over the centenary' met with 'very limited success', while nationalists displays, even in Cork, Clare, Kerry, Cavan and Sligo, where secret societies remained active, were remarkably weak and many committees struggled when fundraising. According to the police the people attended such events to enjoy the fine summer weather, but a prescient William O'Brien warned that 'a second Wolfe Tone has not turned up yet, but Ireland is a country of surprises'. He felt that only those 'living in a fool's paradise' failed to grasp that confidence in constitutional politics had been 'seriously shaken', not merely by British prejudice and opposition against Home Rule from within the Liberal Party, but also by the conduct of its Irish champions. A year of patriotic enthusiasm might foment a revolutionary threat if backed by Irish-American resources.[120]

Laying the foundation stone for the Wolfe Tone monument in Dublin formed the enthusiastic climax of the centenary in front of 30,000 people on 15 August. This had been organized by Fred Allan and, although the IRB excluded the INA, it was joined on the platform by the parliamentary leaders.[121] But this monument failed to attract donations and was never erected, becoming a separatist embarrassment.[122]

A total of thirty memorials were constructed, a considerable achievement for a poor country. While some committees fell under the control of parliamentary leaders, in Cork, Skibbereen and Kilrush the IRB remained in charge. Thomas McCarthy Fennell, now a successful businessman in America, acted as the main fundraiser for the Maid of Erin planned for Kilrush. The contract was awarded to J.K. Bracken, who declared it 'a labour of love', but there were delays as he was ill with cancer and his stoical spouse finished the work.[123]

Membership of the 1798 associations peaked at 31,000 men in 1898, but declined rapidly thereafter. The police became concerned about the veritable avalanche of nationalist propaganda targeting the younger generation, which depicted the United Irishmen and their successors as supremely heroic.[124] Bulmer Hobson and Patrick McCartan, schoolboys in Ulster, and Seán Moylan of Kilmallock were among those inspired by the centenary. Éamonn Ceannt, a school-leaver, felt similarly and rejected 'working for the British' civil service.[125] He joined the Gaelic League, which deepened his nationalism and provided him with like-minded friends, including Patrick Pearse.

Alice Milligan, an innovative propagandist and Ulster organizing secretary for the centenary, continued to spread the separatist message.[126] Her poetry celebrated legendary Celtic heroes and elevated Stephens, O'Mahony and O'Donovan Rossa to near-mythical status, while predicting that nationhood would be won by blood sacrifice.[127] A Northern Protestant, she pioneered the use of magic lantern slides with narration, traditional Irish music and audience participation, linking ethnic communities abroad through the Celtic Revival. William Rooney, Arthur Griffith's assistant, was another of this band of young nationalists; he edited pamphlets on the United Irishmen and ensured that the Irish language featured on all 1798 monuments.[128]

Rossa's rehabilitation

During the 1880s Rossa had become increasingly isolated. Luby and O'Leary scathingly referred to him as 'O'Botherum Bosha'. But after Home Rule was deferred *sine die*, Rossa successfully toured the south of Ireland in 1894, although William Redmond and other leading Parnellites were careful to disso-ciate themselves from the old Fenian, still animated by the desire of 'revenge for Skibbereen'.[129] Revisiting Cork after an absence of almost thirty years, Rossa stressed that Fenianism had forced British statesmen to address injustices, but lamented that physical force 'in Ireland seem[s] to be dead or sleeping'.[130]

His image underwent an astonishing transformation with physical force supporters hailing his steadfastness and sacrifices. In 1904 the *Times* noted the great enthusiasm that greeted him in Cork, in marked contrast to a lack of interest in the nationalist MPs.[131] Although the *Freeman's Journal* described parliamentary politics as more effective, depicting the Fenian past as 'a glorious insanity', latent sympathy and admiration for old rebels continued. These senti-ments were echoed by Jeremiah J. Finnan, who returned to Tipperary in old age, where he romanticized the IRB in verse, proclaiming 'the embers are alive' and awaiting an opportunity. The long decline of Fenianism was forgotten, as Finnan praised the sacrifices and persistence of its members.[132]

Table 15. *Return of political societies in late 1898*

	Number of circles/ branches	Members	Members in good standing
IRB	513	25,000	8500
INA	10	1270	470
Young Ireland Societies	9	1400	
Irish National League (Redmond)	6	615	160
Irish National Federation (Dillon)	221	27,400	900
1798 Societies		31,000	

(Source: Ó Broin, *Revolutionary Underground*, 92)

The fate of the early Fenians

Most IRB activists who had emigrated during the 1860s vanished into obscurity. Michael O'Neill Fogarty was among the exceptions, returning in 1870 and
giving bail for having fought at Ballyhurst. When he travelled to Lisdoonvarna,
Dublin Castle realised that he was ill with lung disease and ceased shadowing
him. O'Neill Fogarty died in New York in 1874. A descendant preserved the
programme of a Clan na Gael commemoration, which provides a veritable roll
call of the IRB in exile.[133] Many endured a similar fate, including James Cody,
one of the earliest Fenians. Suffering from consumption, he was allowed home
to die 'at Rogerstown, near Callan' in 1873, aged thirty-two.[134] Colonel John
James O'Connor, who had led the Fenians during the Kerry Rising in 1867,
managed to escape arrest. An officer of the Brotherhood, he appealed unsuccessfully to the Irishmen of Massachusetts, pleading for support to return to
Ireland as an organizer. O'Connor became sheriff of Shreveport, Louisiana, and
attempted to revive the movement in New Orleans, but died in 1870 from an
unhealed Civil War wound and exposure on the Kerry mountains.[135]

Dr Denis Dowling Mulcahy established himself as the first Irish physician
in Newark, New Jersey. A bibliophile, he collected material for a dictionary
of Irish biography, which was to denounce 'recreant patriots and repentant
rebels, who have acknowledged the right of England to rule Ireland', during the
1880s.[136] 'Combative for his own and the public's rights,' Dr Mulcahy turned
litigation into a way of life.[137] An unwavering supporter of physical force, he
blamed Devoy and Davitt for the rise of Parnell.[138]

Illustrating the close networks sustaining dedicated separatists, Mulcahy
stayed with Frank Mandeville in Ballydine, Clonmel, towards the end of the
former's life. Two generations of the Mulcahy and O'Mahony families had
conspired together since 1848. The doctor was consoled by another great friendship, dating from his years with the *Irish People*. He wrote to O'Leary: 'There are
three of us – you, Luby and myself, and mayhap no other three living Irishmen
have so strong an affection for each other.'[139] Mulcahy's life was clouded by
two misfortunes: he failed to become an outstanding physician due to his legal
preoccupations, and experienced a 'horrible romance', when Margaret Woods,
his housekeeper, claimed that after years of marriage, Mulcahy had committed
adultery with an unnamed party. The doctor denounced his domestic as 'a
blackmailer'.[140] Her daughter, a pugnacious girl, began to stalk him in Newark.
This 'ruined his practice'.[141] When Dr Mulcahy died on 11 September 1900,
Mrs Woods was denied access, but sent 'a pillow of roses' and legal proceedings
acknowledged the women as his widow and 'lawful daughter'.[142]

Thomas Clarke Luby died in Jersey City, New Jersey, in November 1901, his wife Letitia in 1903. Brief notices in the Irish-American papers showed that they had long since dropped out from revolutionary politics. In 1898 William Lyman revealed John O'Connor's modus operandi in his newspaper, the *Irish Republic*, which blocked him from moving secretly through Ireland and Britain henceforth. After decades of serving the IRB, O'Connor became depressed and 'withdrew in utter disgust' to Paris, where he died poor in 1908. Fenians who opposed the might of the British Empire often paid a high price for pursuing their alternative vision.[143]

The IRB after 1900

After 1900 IRB old-timers concerned themselves with local elections and Dublin Corporation appointments. Prior to Queen Victoria's visit in April, the Supreme Council discussed the dilemma facing Fred Allan, its secretary, who was personal assistant to the lord mayor of Dublin. Some stated that this prominent separatist would compromise the IRB by participating in the royal visit, but the majority sympathized with him, given his recent financial difficulties. Allan's duties included organizing the queen's party for loyal children in the Phoenix Park. Uproar ensued when James Connolly condemned 'secret Republicanism and public loyalty', while the Dublin crowd surrounded the mayor's coach after the official welcome, threatening to throw 'the lord mayor and his revolutionary secretary' into the Liffey.[144]

Maud Gonne protested by founding Inghinidhe na hÉireann, a political and social women's organization, which provided a 'patriotic children's treat' for the thousands who had shunned the royal fête. Anna Johnston ('Ethna Carbery'), a daughter of the Belfast Fenian, Annie, wife of James Egan, Jennie Wyse Power, ex-Ladies Land League, Bebe, a sister of the late P.W. Nally, and the wife of Dublin IRB veteran J.W. O'Beirne, became leading lights. Gonne sought help from Alice Milligan, having been impressed by her culturally inclusive, feminist *tableaux vivants* in 1898, to stage these with her women. Helena Molony, a prominent Inghinidhe organizer, recalled that during the 'quiet years' from 1900 to 1914 they seized the initiative rather than the IRB. Occasionally, they received support from Anna Parnell.[145]

Allan's choice was in contrast to James Egan, the city sword-bearer, whom Arthur Griffith cornered, recalling his imprisonment as a dynamiter. Egan wished to safeguard his job and claimed he would attend Queen Victoria in a private capacity, to which Griffith riposted: 'A man like you has no "private capacity".'[146] Reassuring Egan that Dublin Corporation would not dare dismissing him for patriotism, Griffith wrote a 'spirited' press release. Allan's lack of 'sincerity' split the Supreme Council. John O'Leary suggested he resign, but Allan's supporters disagreed and no meetings could be held until 1901. He was not re-elected as secretary, but his followers co-opted him. Dublin Castle learned that the Supreme Council, with P.T. Daly as the new secretary, could only rouse itself for properly constituted meetings on special occasions.[147]

When James Stephens died on 29 March 1901, the *Times* acknowledged him as a 'born conspirator' whose influence had been long eclipsed; disillusioned Fenians reinterpreted his grandiose title of COIR [chief organizer of the Irish Republic] as 'cowardly old Irish renegade'. The *Times* added that, although the physical force party 'still lurks in the holes and corners of Irish life', failing to be reconciled by reforms like the Local Government Act of 1898, the establishment did not fear the IRB, as long as Dublin Castle remained vigilant.[148]

John Redmond attempted to placate all shades of nationalism, for his party had only recently reunited and, before the Parliament Act of 1911, the House of Lords retained the right to veto any Home Rule Bill, which the Liberal Party and its Irish allies might conceivably pass. Tim Harrington, Lord Mayor of Dublin, J.J. Clancy and William Field represented the Irish Parliamentary Party. The attendance was 'invariably deeply respectful', which hinted at latent support for separatism.[149]

Michael Davitt, Charles G. Doran, Michael Lambert, the jeweller, who had made the keys to 'spring' Stephens from the Richmond bridewell in 1865, and other Dublin Fenians were pall-bearers. The tricolour, conceived by the Young Irelanders in 1848, draped his coffin. John O'Leary, P.N. Fitzgerald, Patrick Hoctor and James Egan led a cortège consisting of 1000 members of the Dublin trades and GAA clubs. John Daly and John Purcell as mayors of Limerick and Kilkenny headed contingents. Alderman James Nowlan, the GAA President from Kilkenny, P.J. O'Keeffe, Edward Thomas Keane, Dr Mark Ryan, Frank B. Dineen and William Troy of Fermoy were among the IRB presence. Assistant Commissioner John Mallon, DMP, recorded that 'all was not harmony', as the 'Stephenite' Old Guard Union of IRB veterans disputed the honour of leading the procession with the National Foresters.[150]

In a brief speech, John O'Leary stated that Stephens had made Fenianism a power to be reckoned with. However, IRB discussions after the funeral led to several scenes. Dr Mark Ryan failed to impose his leadership, no decisions were taken and he 'and P.J. Hoctor got hopelessly drunk'. Mallon correctly surmised that Clan na Gael lacked confidence in this leadership.[151]

Dublin Castle had reduced the RIC from 14,343 officers in 1882 to 11,254 by 1901. Between 1903–5 no secret service money could be paid to any informant, who refused to disclose his name to higher government officials. Informers, always fearful of exposure, became scarce. The authorities did little to remedy this situation, unwittingly facilitating the IRB.[152] Agents throughout Ireland warned that the Boer War of 1899–1902 was undoubtedly reviving the IRB 'in very many localities, and has re-enlisted the active sympathy of old Fenians who had of late given up their hope of success by physical force'.[153]

Inspector General Andrew Reed of the RIC cautioned that 'antipathy to English rule' remained strong and was kept alive by the radical press. He considered 'a large class of young enthusiasts ... ripe for conspiracy under favourable circumstances', however improbable at present. The IRB faced three major obstacles to insurrection: cells of activists were 'small and isolated' and surrounded by a majority that paid lip service to their ideals; 'the great farming class ... have too large a stake in the country' since the land acts and blocked anything, which threatened 'their comfort'. Finally, the present IRB leaders were 'broken down impoverished men, looked upon with suspicion by their followers, and jealous of each other'. Reed advised the constabulary to remain vigilant for any future attempt to import arms, which would herald a Rising.[154]

With the British Empire at the zenith of its power, separatism appeared 'an extremely foolish enterprise without having the slightest chance of success'. In 1901 Denis McCullough, the son of the Belfast 'centre' and a third-generation Fenian, was sworn in. Appalled by the state of the movement, he began to remodel it. In 1904 McCullough and Bulmer Hobson, a Republican of Quaker origin, founded the Dungannon Clubs, a name recalling the Volunteers of 1782, as an IRB front. They were joined by Patrick McCartan, who had returned from America, supported by Joseph McGarrity of Philadelphia, a wealthy Clan leader. McGarrity had introduced his protégé to Devoy and Tom Clarke, who put him in touch with P.T. Daly, the new IRB organizer.[155]

In 1900 organizations working for the cultural and economic revival of Ireland united under the umbrella of Cumann na nGaedheal, led by Arthur Griffith, Maud Gonne and John O'Leary. In 1904 Griffith published *The Resurrection of Hungary: a parallel for Ireland*, arguing that the past thirty-three years of parliamentary agitation had been 'disastrous'. He favoured leaving Westminster for an Irish Parliament. Griffith believed that any progress had been made 'unconsciously' through 'the policy of Passive Resistance – with occasional excursions into the domain of Active Resistance at strategic points'.[156]

P.S. O'Hegarty joined the IRB in 1902 and served on its Supreme Council as South of England representative from early 1907. His section consisted of one hundred men in London. For a long time O'Hegarty was the only youngster among the leadership, which recruited cautiously by selecting earnest candidates, averse to alcohol and gossip. They were sourced from the Gaelic League, the GAA or Sinn Féin. Members paid subscriptions of one shilling per quarter and most of this was sent to Dublin, while leaders were expected to demonstrate commitment by bearing minor expenses themselves.[157] The leadership had to contend with an organization, which had deteriorated to 'a loose and nominal remnant of mostly individuals and, in a few places like Dublin, Belfast, Cork, Liverpool and Manchester, to very small groups without any real contact with each other but still maintaining IRB principles'.[158]

Diarmuid Lynch, a later Supreme Council representative for Munster, discovered that agrarian Fenianism survived in north Clare, where the elderly Tomás O'Loughlin, a Sinn Féiner and former Land Leaguer, ran an 'unofficial circle' of sixty men in the most secretive manner. (O'Loughlin's subsequent adherence to the Supreme Council was based on his friendship with Tom Clarke.) He consulted with unnamed members in Tipperary and east Galway.[159]

RIC records stated that Munster had long ceased to be a centre of Fenianism. Sometime before 1907, O'Hegarty requested Fitzgerald to tour Co. Cork to identify surviving members to revive the IRB, but neither O'Hegarty nor P.T. Daly could elicit a response. They were unaware that a disillusioned Fitzgerald had contracted heart disease. The Supreme Council authorized O'Hegarty to swear in his brother Seán, an employee of the Main Post Office in Cork, who established a new 'circle' with colleagues, as well as Tomás MacCurtain, a mainstay of the Blackpool branch of the Gaelic League, and Tom Barry. They ignored the old-timers, rightly suspecting that some had betrayed the IRB in the past, and the old cell gradually faded away.[160]

Merely 'ornamental' leaders had to be tolerated due to a lack of suitable candidates. In Kerry, for instance, Austin Stack presided over its only 'circle' as the nominal 'county centre', but organizers failed to spur him into action: 'his removal from office for laziness was many times mooted, but there was nobody else on offer'. After decades in the doldrums, the older leadership merely concentrated on 'keeping the spirit alive'.[161]

During the early stages of rebuilding the IRB military training was not desirable, but influence was exerted through nationalist activities. Dr Mark Ryan's section in London produced 'circulars', which members distributed among soldiers at 'shipping centres on the south coast' to dissuade them from fighting in South Africa. In Dublin Maud Gonne initiated a campaign with Inghinidhe, which portrayed Irishmen joining the British army as traitors to their country, while in Limerick the YIS printed pro-Boer pamphlets. There was frequent street fighting in both cities as a result.[162] Intermeshed cultural, sporting and political organizations were supported by older figureheads and acted as nurseries of future activists.[163]

Considering the grievances of Catholics and tenant farmers resolved, W.E.H. Lecky rejected Home Rule and mistrusted its promoters. In Unionist circles the Irish Parliamentary Party was discredited as that 'damnable gang of swindlers and murderers' posing as patriots.[164] These MPs depended on the donations of Irish-Americans and appealed to them in the language of revolution, simultaneously taking the oath of allegiance in Westminster to bargain for concessions. They lacked a consistent programme and were 'mere puppets' of the Roman Catholic bishops. The Sinn Féin leaders, however, embodied 'the rising force of resistance to clerical dictation' and possessed principles, attractive to educated young people, disgusted with political posturing.[165] In 1906 T.W. Rolleston, now combining cultural nationalism with unionist politics, analysed Sinn Féin:

> It is of course a relic from the old Fenianism, but in a way, it is worse than Fenianism. It does not, for the present at all events, contemplate serious action, as Fenianism did, but it throws itself all the more vigorously into the mission of influencing thought. With acute insight its leaders have perceived the use the Gaelic League can be to them in this direction, and they have accordingly ... practically gained control of its official organ, and have more or less terrorised the executive committee.[166]

In 1905 Undersecretary Sir Antony MacDonnell endorsed Sir Nicholas Gosselin's statement that he had not experienced 'the smallest apprehension' about Fenianism for years. Investigating secret societies constituted 'a waste of time', as the people were apathetic about politics and the IRB 'was very inactive'. The following year the Crime Branch Special concluded that no secret society continued 'at work, or even in existence, in Ireland'.[167] In 1906 Henry Campbell-Bannerman and the Liberals finally returned to power and Chief Secretary Augustine Birrell considered Ireland at its most peaceful in 600 years. But in Clonmel Thomas Condon, MP, warned that without the implementation of Home Rule, 'the old spirit will manifest itself, and violence will confront' England.[168]

When John O'Leary died on 16 March 1907, James Joyce in Trieste declared him '*l'ultimo Feniano*', the last of the Fenians, a venerable figure of stoic endurance: 'He had little reason to be happy: his plans had gone up in smoke, his friends were dead, and very few people in his country knew who he was or what he had done.'[169]

John B. Yeats, father of the poet, believed that in a materialistic age, O'Leary's devotion to the nation and his telling of unwelcome truths had been vital: 'Surely John O'Leary stands for Ireland of the past, heroic, unselfish suffering, nor was he unsuccessful as the unthinking would vainly imagine since but for him and his like the nation would have perished.'[170]

Table 16. *Membership of the Supreme Council, 1906–7*

President	Neal John O'Boyle	Farmer, Staffordstown, Antrim
Secretary	P.T. Daly	Printer, Dublin
Treasurer	James Geraghty	Tailor, Glasgow
	Representatives of IRB sections	
Leinster	Jack O'Hanlon	Corporation employee
Munster	Michael Crowe	GAA; railway employee
Connacht	Maj. John MacBride	
Ulster	Neal John O'Boyle	Farmer, Antrim
South of England	P.S. O'Hegarty	Post Office clerk, London
North of England	James Murphy	Shopkeeper, Liverpool
Scotland	James Geraghty	Tailor, Glasgow
	Co-opted members:	
	Fred Allan	Corporation employee, Dublin
	P.T. Daly	Printer, Dublin
	James Barrett	Manchester
	John Mulholland	Ironworker, Glasgow

(Source: statement by P.S. O'Hegarty, Bureau of Military History)

P.N. Fitzgerald died a few months later in October, still mistrusted by his fellow conspirators in Cork. P.T. Daly, 'a most dangerous man' according to the authorities, informed an IRB meeting in Glasgow that the movement was thriving in Munster since the death of an old leader, presumably Fitzgerald. Daly was falling out of favour with the 'extreme gang in Dublin', being suspected of siphoning off funds sent from America.[171]

By 1908 Daly had completed the foundations for the new IRB by visiting 'all Ireland' and reuniting 'what could be drawn together'. O'Hegarty considered the organization vigorous in centres such as Dublin, London and Glasgow. It had between 700 to 1000 members in the Irish capital and 100 and 150 men, respectively, in England and Scotland. Belfast, Cork, Limerick, Wexford, Liverpool and Manchester contained smaller groups. There was no representation in rural Leinster or Ulster and only two nominal 'circles' were left in Mayo and Galway, besides the one in Kerry. O'Hegarty cautiously estimated IRB strength at approximately 1200 men.[172]

'The spirit of Fenianism will respond at the right moment'[173]

On 5 December 1907 Crime Branch Special recorded the arrival of Tom and Kathleen Clarke in Cobh, where they were met by John Daly. Clarke intended to 'get things moving' and was an ideal intermediary after the long break between the Clan and the IRB. In the Republican tradition, Clarke, Daly and Devoy commanded great prestige, having suffered for their convictions, while conducting themselves as the torch-bearers of separatism. The Clarkes established a single-minded revolutionary network, which included Devoy, the Daly family, Patrick McCartan, Bulmer Hobson, P.S. O'Hegarty, Seán MacDiarmada and Diarmuid Lynch. This highly secretive inner circle abhorred the slipshod methods of the past and ruthlessly discarded anybody whose commitment appeared to waver.[174]

After decades of abortive attempts to revive the movement, Dublin Castle had been lulled into a false sense of security. Ultimately, the authorities underestimated the tenacity of figures like John Devoy and Tom Clarke, patiently awaiting 'Ireland's opportunity' with their male (and some female) supporters. Bulmer Hobson recalled that the emerging inner circle of the IRB, which for the first time contained no informers, remained hidden. Activists continued to swear in young men of Fenian antecedents – the countdown to 1916 had begun.[175]

Monument to John Keegan Casey,
Glasnevin (author's collection).

TO COMMEMORATE THE
LIVES, PRINCIPLES, AND SACRIFICES OF
TERENCE BELLEW McMANUS, YOUNG IRELANDER;
COLONEL JOHN O'MAHONY, YOUNG IRELANDER;
AND ONE OF THE FOUNDERS OF THE
FENIAN ORGANISATION;
CHARLES PATRICK McCARTHY,
DANIEL REDDIN,
PATRICK W. NALLY,
AND JAMES STRITCH,
MEMBERS OF THE IRISH REPUBLICAN BROTHERHOOD,
WHOSE REMAINS LIE BELOW.
ALL OUTLAWS AND FELONS ACCORDING TO ENGLISH LAW;
BUT TRUE SOLDIERS OF IRISH LIBERTY;
REPRESENTATIVES OF SUCCESSIVE MOVEMENTS FOR
IRISH INDEPENDENCE
THEIR LIVES THUS PROVE
THAT EVERY GENERATION PRODUCES PATRIOTS
WHO WERE WILLING TO FACE
THE GIBBET, THE CELL, AND EXILE
TO PROCURE THE LIBERTY OF THEIR NATION
AND AFFORD PERPETUAL PROOF THAT IN THE IRISH HEART
FAITH IN IRISH NATIONALITY IS INDESTRUCTIBLE.

Terence Bellew McManus monument,
Glasnevin (courtesy Patrick Cahir).

Biographies of Munster and Kilkenny Fenians[1]

A. Clare

1. Joseph Barrett, born in 1888 in Barna-geeha, Darragh, Ennis, helped on the family farm after finishing national school. He joined the IRB on 15 August 1908 with fifteen others, as it was the custom in the Ennis district to swear in the eldest sons of Fenians. His thirty-strong 'circle' acquired guns and agitated for the acquisition of estates by the Land Commission, trying to ensure that IRB members got preferential treatment when estates were broken up. Barrett became the captain of the Irish Volunteers in Ballyea, who were mostly IRB members. They assembled on Easter Sunday 1916, but were dismissed. Barrett retired as brigade operations officer for the mid-Clare brigade, IRA, to become an auctioneer in Kilrush.

2. Henry Broughton Sr, 50, Killaderry, Broadford, tenant farmer on forty-one acres, was recruited by the O'Donovan brothers (his nephews) and became the local IRB 'centre'. He was detained under the habeas corpus suspension from February to September 1866. Released on bail, Broughton abandoned Fenianism.

3. Henry Broughton Jr, 22, alias 'Wilson', Killaderry, son of the above, east Clare IRB man, who was detained in Dublin from January to October 1866; released on bail; FP 34.

Henry Broughton Jr, FP 34 (courtesy NAI).

4. Burke, Carey and Curtin, Kilrush, lads suspected of involvement in a robbery of gunpowder, which was discovered in Mrs Keating's cowshed in December 1867. After an inquiry in January 1868, their fathers were allowed to give bail for the boys.

5. John Burns, Ennis, shopkeeper, among those indicted in July 1867 for assembling for the Rising the previous March in Drumcliff, Ennis. Burns remained in custody until the next assizes, as an important witness had absconded.

6. John Connors, 24, Feakle, baker, committed to Kilmainham under habeas corpus suspension warrant in April 1866, discharged in August on condition of embarking for America; FP 83.

7. James Crowe, detained among the insurgents in Drumcliff, Ennis, in March 1867 and released on bail that May.

8. John Crowe, detained for having assembled with the insurgents in Drumcliff, Ennis, on 5 March 1867. He was released on bail the following May.

9. George Dixon, Ennis, arrested in March 1867 as a local insurgent. His trial was postponed until the next assizes, while he was allowed out on bail.

10. Martin Donnellan, Ballykelly, Kilseily, Broadford, herd for the O'Donovan holding, was sworn into the IRB by Edmond O'Donovan and acted as his agent until arrested in March 1866. Richard O'Donovan petitioned for his release, which took place in September. Dublin Castle warned Donnellan to leave the IRB or face re-arrest, which ended his revolutionary activities.

11. Stephen Donnelly, born in 1840 in Knockatooreen, Kilkishen, a Fenian from the age of eighteen. Imprisoned, he subsequently joined the Land League and the United Irish League and was again incarcerated. His funeral in Ennis was well supported by the United Irish League of east Clare in 1910.

12. James Dowdall, a discharged national teacher from Drummanneen, Crusheen, arrested in Nenagh in April 1867, suspected of Fenianism.

13. Fagan, Kilrush, painter, arrested there on 17 March 1867 on suspicion of involvement in the Fenian conspiracy.

14. Patrick Fitzpatrick, 17, pleaded guilty and was convicted of participating in the attack on the Kilbaha coastguard station in March 1867. Considered of good character, he was sentenced to eighteen months in July and was discharged from Ennis jail in June 1868.

15. Michael Flanagan, 'centre' of the Tullycrine/Kilmurry McMahon district, had to flee to America for Fenian activities. John Flanagan, Tullagower, Tullycrine, his nephew, born in 1888, became commandant, 2nd battalion, west Clare IRA, during the War of Independence.

16. Martin Fleming, Kilrush, shopkeeper and agent for the *Irish People* newspaper in Dublin, remarkably 'disloyal' in November 1866.[2]

17. Andrew Guthrie, Ennistymon, shoemaker, arrested in December 1867 for being drunk and 'declaring himself a Fenian', sentenced to either fourteen days in prison or giving bail.

18. Thomas Hanrahan, detained for having assembled with the insurgents in Drumcliff, Ennis, on 5 March 1867, was released on bail the following May.

19. Cornelius Hassett, about 21 years old, Ennis, had been reported on 6 March 1867 by the constabulary as constantly in the company of suspects John Maguire, Matthew McMahon and James O'Halloran. He was intelligent and active, often out all night and probably a Fenian agent. Hassett was arrested on 10 March. His widowed mother petitioned that she believed him innocent, although 'out' on the night of the Rising, while her business suffered during his detention. No evidence was forthcoming and W.E.A. MacDonnell of New Hall, the Deputy Lord Lieutenant for Clare, felt that others, since discharged, had been guiltier than Hassett, who was released on bail in August.

20. Thomas Healy, 32, a native of Clare, who had joined the Fenian Brotherhood in New Haven in 1864 and served in 9th Connecticut Volunteers for three years during the Civil War. Mentioned as 'an intelligent officer' on the Brotherhood's

roster of available personnel for the invasion of Ireland.[3]

21. Patrick Hegarty, detained for having assembled with the insurgents in Drumcliff, Ennis, on 5 March 1867, was released on bail the following May.

22. Stephen Hehir, detained for being among the insurgents in Drumcliff, Ennis on 5 March 1867, was released on bail the following May, his trial being postponed.

23. Thomas Hogan, Reanahumana, Co, Clare, a constable, who had resigned from the force in Limerick. He was strongly suspected of drilling the Fenians and was arrested in the Tulla district in February 1866. Hogan, a fine athlete, escaped from custody, resulting in an inquiry into police collusion. He surrendered in Ennis in July and his father petitioned that his resignation had been due to the strenuous demands of policing rather than Fenianism.

24. William J. Hynes was born in Kilkee in 1843. After the death of his father, the family emigrated to Springfield, Massachusetts, where he became a printer with the *Springfield Republican*. Hynes served as the 'centre' of the Springfield 'circle' of the Fenian Brotherhood around 1865. He studied law and was called to the bar in Little Rock and became a carpetbagger congressman for Arkansas for one term. During the 1880s, Hynes, then a successful lawyer in Chicago, supported Devoy's fight against the 'Triangle'.

25. James Keane, 70, was indicted for harbouring the wounded Thomas McCarthy Fennell after the attack on Kilbaha coast guard station in March 1867. Keane pleaded guilty and was discharged on bail, but would be brought up for sentencing should he fall foul of the law a second time.

26. Patrick Keating, born in 1826, a native of Clare, a labourer who served with 6th Carabineers and 5th Dragoons. He had fought in the Crimean War, was promoted (and subsequently demoted) to corporal with almost twenty years' military service. Keating became 'centre' of 5th Dragoons and was convicted and sentenced to death for mutiny in 1866, commuted to life imprisonment. Transported to Western Australia in 1867, Keating's health declined and he died while out on a ticket of leave in the care of Joseph Noonan in 1874.

27. McDonnell, Kilrush, alleged to be the tailor for the local Fenians, arrested on 17 March 1867 on suspicion.

28. Edward McInerney, detained for having assembled with the insurgents in Drumcliff, Ennis, intending to participate in the Rising of March 1867, as stated by the informer Nevin. He was released on bail in May.

29. Peter McInerney, Lisheen, Ballynacally, IRB organizer, who swore in Joseph Barrett among other young men in Drumquin as the IRB was being revived in 1908.

30. Michael McMahon, among those detained for assembling with the insurgents in Drumcliff, Ennis, on 5 March, was liberated on bail in May 1867.

31. John Maguire, Ennis, shopkeeper, indicted in July 1867 for assembling in Drumcliff, Ennis, for the Rising that March. He was remanded in custody until the next assizes as an important witness could not be found.

32. John Mahony, Kilrush, labourer, in whose home a seditious meeting took place, presided over by a Captain Lynch in November 1866.

33. Thomas Mahony, Kilrush, shopkeeper's son, communicated with the *Irish People* as secretary of the NBSP and was most active in promoting Fenianism in the

Kilrush district. Arrested in February 1866 under the habeas corpus suspension, several memorials petitioned for his release with the support of Fr Timothy Kelly, parish priest, and various businessmen vouched for by Sir Colman O'Loghlen, MP. Mahony was released in June.

34. Sgt Stephen Maloney, 35, a native of Tulla, served for five years on the frontier in the regular 8th US infantry and joined the Fenian Brotherhood in Utah in 1865; on the Brotherhood's roster of officers.

35. Richard Meade, 9th Regiment, indicted in July 1867 on suspicion of assembling in Drumcliff, Ennis for in the Rising in March. Meade was further remanded in custody as an important witness was no longer available.

36. Patrick Moran, detained for assembling with the insurgents in Drumcliff, Ennis, on 5 March 1867, was released on bail the following May.

37. Captain Michael O'Brien, 32, a native of Ennis, joined the Fenian Brotherhood in Chicago in 1859 and was one of its officers in 1863–4. A leader of the boot and shoemakers' union, he served briefly in 67th Illinois Volunteers during the Civil War and featured on the Fenian roster of available officers.

38. Edmond O'Donovan, born in 1844 in Dublin, was the second son of John O'Donovan and Mary Anne, née Broughton. O'Donovan Rossa swore the teenager and his brothers into the IRB. Edmond abandoned his medical studies in TCD to become a Fenian organizer in Broadford, O'Callaghans Mills, Scariff, Quin and Tulla. He also directed the TCD Fenian 'circle' and participated in the IRB school of military engineering in Dublin, experimenting with a phosphorus compound, 'Fenian fire'. Edmond was among the representatives of the Irish Republic preparing for the Rising. Repeatedly arrested, he benefited from the influence of Sir Thomas Larcom, his late father's friend. He continued to act for the IRB after the Rising and may have had links with the Clerkenwell explosion and the shooting of two constables in Dublin on 31 October 1867 before developing a career as a journalist and travel writer. In 1879 he reached central Asia to report on the conflict between the Tekke Turkmen and the Russian Empire. O'Donovan was one of the very few Europeans to survive exploring the inaccessible Merv Oasis. He published his famous account of life with the nomadic Turkmen, *The Merv Oasis: Travels and Adventures East of the Caspian* in 1882. Although retaining his Fenian associations he accompanied Hicks Pasha, the British commander of the Egyptian army fighting the Madhi in the Sudan, as a war correspondent, to be annihilated with this column in November 1883. O'Donovan is commemorated in St Paul's Cathedral, London.

39. John O'Donovan Jr, born in Dublin in 1842, the eldest of the O'Donovan brothers, studied medicine in TCD and was a protégé of Sir Thomas Larcom after his father's early death. Drawn into Fenianism, he founded an IRB 'circle' in TCD and acquired some knowledge of military science, which he taught as a travelling organizer in Munster. O'Donovan escaped arrest in Cork in September 1865 but was detained in Dublin from November until August 1866, afterwards leaving for New York. The remainder of his life proved an anticlimax: a good linguist, he reluctantly taught in Catholic schools in New York and St Louis, where he died in a swimming accident in 1873.

40. Richard O'Donovan, born in 1848 in Dublin, was the fourth of the brothers and shared their linguistic talents. Interested in

geography and statistics, Richard assisted Edmond in gun-running and recruiting for the IRB in Clare while living on their smallholding near Broadford. In 1875 he became an insurance translator in Liverpool and died in Prestatyn, Wales, in 1939.

41. William O'Donovan, third son of John O'Donovan, was born in Dublin in 1846 and had a talent for foreign languages. In 1865 Stephens sent him to Paris as an IRB paymaster alongside John Mitchel and Edmund O'Leary. He was involved in planning the Rising of 1867, but evaded arrest. During the 1870s O'Donovan became Paris correspondent of the *Irish Times* and worked as a Parnellite journalist in Dublin, before having to flee to New York. He assisted Devoy with the *Irish Nation* until its closure, developed health problems and died penniless in Manhattan in 1886. He is buried in Calvary Cemetery, New York.

42. Seamus Mór Ó Griofa, a native of Carrigaholt, founded a 'circle' in Crusheen while a post office linesman sometime before 1909. Sean O'Keeffe believed this to be the earliest Clare 'circle' after the reorganization of the IRB in preparation for the 1916 Rising.

43. James O'Halloran, Ennis, detained in the county jail for assembling in Drumcliff, Ennis, for the Rising on 5 March 1867, as stated by the informer Nevin. He was freed on substantial bail in May 1867.

44. Sean O'Keeffe, born in 1889 in Crusheen, left school early to help his widowed mother run the family farm; he also worked as a postman and builder. When young, O'Keeffe attended local 1798 commemorations and met old Fenians/Ribbonmen. In the early 1900s he joined Sinn Féin, Gaelic League, GAA and IRB meetings in Crusheen, being sworn into the latter in 1909. The IRB became instrumental in the formation of the Volunteers in

Crusheen, who were stood down on Easter Sunday 1916. O'Keeffe was also involved in the escape of Liam Mellow to America, disguised as a nun.

45. Thomas O'Leary, 'a man of great strength,' capable of holding any bull, belonged to an agrarian Fenian 'circle' with his brother Daniel, Michael and Peter Murphy, Michael Hehir, Andrew Lawlor and Murty Curtis. Ten years earlier Jeremiah Callinan had arrived from West Cork and refused to attend Mass in Ennistymon to avoid the police. The Murphys asked him if he was John Ryan, who had been involved in an assassination attempt on the notorious land agent Patten Bridge near Mitchelstown. Callinan answered in the affirmative and joined their secret society. They decided to attack Thomas Sexton of Ballygasteel, Lisdoonvarna, during the Plan of Campaign, due to a land dispute. Callinan had become Head Constable Gerard Whelehan's *agent provocateur* and led the moonlighters into an ambush on 11 September 1887. The RIC lay concealed in Sexton's farmhouse, when the Fenian posse gained entrance and a fierce struggle ensued during which Whelehan, who had only recently been transferred to Lisdoonvarna, was killed. Thomas O'Leary was sentenced to ten years' penal servitude and Daniel, Murty Curtis, Lawlor and Hehir to seven years each. The O'Learys' maternal cousin, Patrick Kerin of Miltown Malbay, who recalled the Ballygasteel incident to the Bureau of Military History, became a mid-Clare IRA activist during the War of Independence.[4]

46. Private Robert Quinn of 74th Regiment was suspected of having deserted to participate in the Rising in March 1867 in Drumcliff, Ennis, and continued to be detained in July.

47. Private Michael Redmond, 26, born in Ennis, a sapper and miner in the British

army who claimed to understand field fortifications, joined the Fenian Brotherhood in Alton, Illinois, to be listed on its roster of experienced military personnel.

48. James Rochford, detained for having assembled with the insurgents in Drumcliff, Ennis, on 5 March 1867, was released on bail the following May.

49. Patrick Tierney, alias Edward O'Connor, was born in Ennis in 1841. A leather worker and later a corporal in 87th Regiment, he attempted to kill the informer Warner in Howth in May 1866, but was arrested and sentenced to life. Isolated in Spike Island convict prison, Tierney tried to escape and was punished. His family remained unaware of his fate until his sister Bridget Cullen discovered his identity and lobbied for his release, helped by John O'Connor Power. Released in December 1878 on condition of permanent exile, Tierney's poor health precluded him from working. He received a Clan na Gael pension and was admitted to hospital in New Haven, Connecticut, where he died on 29 November 1882 from hip and spinal diseases contracted during imprisonment. A Celtic cross was erected in St Lawrence Cemetery, New Haven, in 1898; Captain Laurence O'Brien, who escaped from Clomel prison in 1867, served on the committee.

50. Richard Wall, detained for having assembled with the insurgents in Drumcliff, Ennis, on 5 March 1867, was released on bail the following May.

51. Thomas Walsh, Ennis, detained for having assembled with the insurgents in Drumcliff, Ennis, on 5 March 1867, as stated by the informer Nevin. Walsh was freed on substantial bail that May.

B. Cork

52. Mark Adams, 52, Cork, engineer with Beamish & Crawford, was arrested and identified as a Fenian by the informer Warner in September 1865. Eventually released on bail, Adams was dismissed by his employers alongside his eldest son (see below). He remained an IRB leader and was twice rearrested under the habeas corpus suspension in March 1866 and January 1868. He emigrated to the US with his family in 1870.

53. James Adams, 24, Cork, a mechanical engineer, had been a Fenian since 1865. In September 1870 thirty-nine rifles, a large amount of cartridges and some documents were seized in his lodgings in South Main Street, Cork, which had been proclaimed. Adams fled before he could be arrested and the constabulary suspected that his group was planning a raid on the Bank of Ireland in Cork and that he might have gone to London; FP 4.

54. Jeremiah Aher, 1843–1926, a native of Ballymacoda, was sentenced to seven years for participation in the Rising. Transported to Western Australia, he obtained a free pardon in 1869 and left for San Francisco in 1876.

55. Daniel Ahern, Ardnahinch, Killeagh, farm servant, arrested in March 1867 on suspicion of having participated in the attack on Castlemartyr constabulary barracks.

56. Annie Barrett, born 1888 in Killavullen, Cork, intelligence agent for the Mallow battalion, 2nd Cork brigade from 1918, told the Bureau of Military History in 1955 that her father, a Fenian, had escorted Peter O'Neill Crowley from his hiding place in Glenagare to Kilclooney Wood in March 1867.

57. David Barry, Cork, was charged as a member of Captain Mackey's group,

which had broken into Allports and made off with a number of weapons in late 1867. A search of the Barry home revealed a sword, items for pike-making and two military textbooks. John, David's eldest brother, was also taken into custody. David Barry was acquitted of robbery, but convicted of possessing arms in a proclaimed district.

58. John Barry, a native of Mallow, arrived in Dublin from Sheffield in suspicious circumstances and was swiftly arrested under the habeas corpus suspension in March 1866.

59. Richard Barry, Spa Walk, Mallow, carpenter, arrested and investigated as a participant in the Rising of 1867 at the local petty sessions.

60. Francis Bastable, a native of Kanturk, recently returned from America, arrested in December 1866 in Castleblakeney on suspicion of being a Fenian agent as he was constantly moving about the Ahascragh, Co. Galway district without obvious reason.

61. John Brennan, Castlemartyr, arrested under the habeas corpus suspension on 14 March 1866 as a suspect and taken to Cork jail.

62. James Brett, Leap, died in 1905, said to be aged 112. An early Fenian in this locality, which had been in contact with Skibbereen, Brett was visited by O'Donovan Rossa on his recent trip to Ireland.

63. Bartholomew Brien trained in a model school and taught in Cooscroneen National School near Union Hall until arrested on suspicion of Fenianism in March 1866.

64. Captain F.F. Buckley, 29, a native of Mallow, had ten years' service with the British army in India and the US forces and joined the Fenian Brotherhood in 1865 in Philadelphia, being named on its roster of officers.

65. John and Mrs Buckley, Cork city, Fenians, who shared their home with John Edward Kelly, the stealthy Irish-American organizer and drill master who was active in this region between 1861–7. John Buckley, a printer, had been suspected by the authorities before he went on the run after the Rising of March 1867, while his wife was arrested in possession of seditious documents. The Buckleys emigrated to Malden, Massachusetts, and were praised for their Fenian dedication in John Savage's *Fenian Heroes and Martyrs*.

66. Mary Jane Buckley, Cork, attended the trial of Captain Mackey Lomasney in company with Albina Mahony and Mary O'Connell. Capt. Mackey had frequented the Buckley household after his marriage in Cork and was much admired by the girls. The constabulary directed the female searcher from the bridewell to search the women for arms and documents without providing privacy. Miss Buckley possessed a 'Fenian alphabet' of anti-government verses. Unlike her friends, Albina refused to undress and all three were threatened with arrest. Buckley and O'Connell sued the RIC for indecent assault and were awarded £50 (see also Mary O'Connell). In 1869 the constabulary reported that Mary Jane Buckley was 'a noted Fenian in close communication with Mrs Capt. Mackey' and that her father and uncles were also IRB members. She was one of very few women featured in the Fenian index of names.[5]

67. Michael Buckley had returned to Cork from America about three months ago. Although young, he did not follow any reputable occupation, was suspected as a Fenian agent and detained in the city jail from March 1866.

68. Timothy Buckley, 23, blacksmith, was suspected of participation in the arms

raid on Mount Leader House under Bartholomew Moriarty, as well as trying to seize a gun from the railway station and tearing up the rails during the 1867 Rising. His companions James Lucey, Timothy Ring, both labourers, John Riordan, shoemaker, James Connell and Denis Dennehy, weavers, all from Millstreet, were also detained. The magistrates discharged all except Connell on bail, Henry Leader suddenly claiming that he had assisted Moriarty, who had hit him; FP 38.

69. John Bullen and Laurence Hynes, lads, charged with the robbery from Mr Hugo's, Sunday's Well, Cork, but found guilty of possessing arms in a proclaimed district. They were 'sentenced to be imprisoned for two years, and kept to hard labour'.[6]

70. Morgan Burke, 29, butcher, a native of Kinneigh, Dunmanway, a brother of Colonel Ricard O'Sullivan Burke. Morgan returned from the US around September 1866 to live in Coachford. He was detained in Mountjoy from March 1867 to April 1868 under the habeas corpus suspension and discharged on condition of leaving for America; FP 41.

Morgan Burke, FP 41 (courtesy NAI).

71. Thomas Burns, approximately 20–30 years old, Carrigrohan, law clerk, was detained for about two weeks in October 1865 on suspicion of belonging to a Fenian 'circle', according to the informer Warner. Burns was discharged on condition of appearing when called upon by the authorities, as no corroborative evidence could be found.

72. Edmund Butler, Killeagh, ex-national school teacher, had been detained under the habeas corpus suspension. He was arrested in March 1867 on suspicion of having participated in the attack on Castlemartyr constabulary barracks and sent for trial. Butler was bailed in June, on condition of appearing for judgement when called upon.

73. Richard Butler, Killeagh, carpenter, arrested at home with his brother Edmund in March 1867, accused of participation in the attack on Castlemartyr barracks by Daniel Doyle, who had turned informer. Butler pleaded guilty and was discharged on bail on condition of appearing for sentencing if called upon. 74. William Butler, Midleton, IRB organizer for this district during the 1860s and a personal friend of Peter O'Neill Crowley, died in September 1907, buried in Rosary Cemetery, Midleton.

75. James Callaghan and his brother John, carpenters, held in Cork jail as suspected participants in the 1867 Rising.

76. Thomas Callaghan, Kanturk, watchmaker, was suspected to be a Fenian agent and the 'centre' of Kanturk, facilitated by his itinerant occupation of repairing clocks and watches, which allowed him to spread sedition. Callaghan was detained from March to June 1866 and released after a memorial by his mother, who pointed out that he suffered from eye problems and might go blind if his incarceration

continued. Several priests and magistrates supported her.

77. Sgt Timothy Callaghan, 22, a native of Cork city, enlisted in 16th Massachusetts Volunteers and featured on the Fenian Brotherhood list of military personnel, preparing for the invasion of Ireland.[7]

78. Ellen Eliza Callanan, the Hill, Clonakilty, daughter of John Callanan, Young Irelander and merchant, wrote well-reasoned letters to the *Irish People*. She also corresponded with Charles Kickham and Cornelius Dwyer Keane in Kilmainham in late 1865. The Callanan family opposed the constitutional movement urged by Fr Leader, parish priest of Clonakilty, and objected to politics dominated by the gentry. Her father tried to sell his property in 1865 and appeared in poor financial circumstances. In February 1866 the family home, a visitor and her father were searched and arrested by the police, but nothing except her manuscripts found. The constabulary reported that John Callanan spoke of the Fenian expedition arriving to gain the rights of the Irish people. Ellen Eliza wrote to Dublin Castle in March, as her father continued to be detained in the county jail in Cork, that he intended to travel to America on business and could depart immediately if released. He sailed in May 1866. Ellen Eliza and her brother L.J. Callanan also emigrated to New York. She prospered as Mrs Madigan, returning to visit Clonakilty with her family. Her brother, a grocer, died in 1913 in New York.

79. William Callaway, a native of Passage West, ship carpenter, was arrested between his birthplace and Rochestown while drilling in March 1867 and detained in Cork county jail.

80. Patrick Canning, ex-British army, was arrested on suspicion on the Lower Glanmire Road, Cork, on 11 March 1867. He gave a confused account of his travels from Waterford via Midleton and appeared very tired. Canning was looking for work but could not name anybody who could confirm his statement. He was remanded and promised his discharge as soon as he could provide a character reference.

81. Charles Canty, 17, and Richard Keating, 19, were arrested on returning to Cork city in the early hours of 7 March 1867, having concealed empty haversacks under their coats. They were coming from the Blackpool direction, which also led to Ballyknockane constabulary barracks. The police suspected them of being insurgents and remanded them in custody for a week.

82. Timothy Canty, Cork, prominent IRB man in that city in 1879 when Devoy visited, later emigrating to Boston. He remained a Clan na Gael member in 1923.

83. John Carbery was held in Cork City jail as a suspect under the Habeas Corpus Suspension Act until June 1867, when he left for New York.

84. Lieut James Carey, 28, a native of Youghal, who served in 58th Illinois Volunteers for three years, was twice wounded and became a Fenian in 1864. He was 'capable of commanding a company ... and with a little practice an infantry regiment'.[8] Carey was listed among the military men of the Brotherhood in 1865, in preparation for the invasion of Ireland.

85. Timothy Carmody, born in 1840 in Mallow, a slater, was identified as a determined IRB officer and drill instructor in Cork city by the informer Warner and arrested in 1865 during the *Irish People* seizure. Discharged on bail by the special commission, he attracted the attention of the constabulary for a second time in November 1866 and was detained. Carmody protested his innocence – his petition for

release was supported by several magistrates – and he was discharged on 30 January 1867. The London police force reported that he was residing there and participated in gun-running to Munster, but had disappeared by July 1869.

86. John Sarsfield Casey, the son of a shopkeeper and small property owner, was born in Mitchelstown in 1846. He corresponded with the *Irish People* as 'the Galtee boy' and distributed this paper in Mitchelstown, leading to conflict with the parish priest. His father apprenticed him to J.J. Geary, a grocer in Cork, to detach him from the local Fenians, unaware that Geary was 'head centre' for Cork. Casey continued his IRB activities, leading to his arrest after the seizure of the *Irish People* in September 1865. He was tried and sentenced to five years. Transported to Western Australia, he kept a diary and assisted in producing a literary magazine on board the *Hougoumont*. Amnestied, Casey returned to Mitchelstown in 1870 and was employed by William Henry O'Sullivan of Kilmallock as a commercial traveller to sell their ale and porter. In 1875 he successfully challenged land agent Patten Bridge for rack-renting tenants. He lost a bitterly contested parliamentary election in 1876, but was chosen as coroner for east Limerick in 1878. Casey was a precursor of the Land League, which he joined. In 1887 during the Mitchelstown massacre, he risked his life to stop the constabulary firing into an unarmed crowd. Suffering ill health in later life, Casey died in 1896.

87. William Casey, 17, among a group of eleven men charged with illegal drilling with pikes at Aughadown, Skibbereen, during the night of 18 February 1866, according to the informer Michael Fitzgerald. Casey was refused bail and sent for trial at the assizes.

88. James Cashman, employee of Robinson's ship builders, Cork, was tried and acquitted for breaking into an armoury of the North Cork militia in Mallow with an IRB group to rob rifles in June 1871.

89. Maurice Cashman, ship carpenter, Slee's Lane, Cork, was arrested on 10 March 1867 on information that he had participated in the attack on Ballyknockane barracks. After an unsuccessful attempt to escape from the police, Cashman was remanded in custody.

90. John Clifford, Kanturk, was arrested on 13 March 1867 on suspicion of being a 'head centre' who had participated in the attack on Kilmallock constabulary barracks.

91. Private Patrick Clifford, 23, a native of Mitchelstown, served three years as a gunner. He had become a Fenian in New York in 1860 and gave the pledge of the Fenian Brotherhood to sixteen comrades in the 1st New York Artillery during the siege of Petersburg, Virginia, in 1865; on the roster of experienced officers.

92. Jerome Collins was born in Blackrock, Cork, in 1841. He trained as an engineer and worked on the North Gate Bridge in 1863 and was subsequently employed by a construction company in London, where he made an abortive bid to free the IRB leaders in Pentonville. Collins fled to the US, serving as the secretary of a company draining the New Jersey swamps. He provided employment for Fenians forced to leave Ireland from 1866 on, including John Daly, but the venture ended in bankruptcy. His talent for scientific experiments led to an innovative appointment as meteorologist to the *New York Herald*. Collins became the founder of Clan na Gael. His revolutionary involvement concluded in 1879, when he served as scientific officer of the US navy's North Pole expedition. The ship broke up, forcing the crew

to drag small boats towards the open sea. When they finally reached Siberia, Collins died with his camp in 1881. His remains were interred in Curraghkippane Cemetery in 1884.

93. Patrick Collins, arrested in Charleville on 15 March 1867, suspected of having participated in the attack on Kilmallock constabulary barracks. He was among those transferred to Cork jail.

94. William Connealy, 19, Co. Cork, served in 28th Massachusetts Volunteers for three years. When he added his name to the Fenian Brotherhood roster, having joined the organization in 1864, he was described as 'wounded in the leg, not fit for active service in the field'.[9]

95. James Connell, Millstreet, weaver, was arrested in March 1867 on suspicion of having been 'out' in the Rising, but acquitted and discharged in May.

96. Patrick Connolly, Gilabbey Street, Cork, drilled with IRB members in Brian Dillon's home in 1865, according to an informer.

97. Patrick Connolly, Denis Donovan and Timothy Sullivan, labourers, were charged with aiding and abetting organizer Cornelius Dwyer Keane during November 1864, when he was swearing men into the IRB in Rath, Skibbereen.

98. William Conway trained in a model school and employed in Passage West National School. He was arrested in January 1866, suspected of Fenianism.

99. Maurice Cotter, Midleton, shoemaker, arrested on 13 March 1867, suspected of having been with the Fenians who fired on the police in Midleton during the Rising.

100. Daniel Coughlan, Bridge Street, Skibbereen, an old resident, among the last survivors of the early Fenians in this town.

He was a close friend of O'Donovan Rossa and continued to believe in separatist principles until his death in 1911.

101. John Coughlan, Cork, sailmaker's apprentice, arrested on 10 March 1867 at Whitechurch with bullets and percussion caps in his possession, the latter bearing the imprint 'Irish Republic'. Coughlan, suspected of participation in the attack on Ballyknockane constabulary barracks, was committed for trial.

102. Denis Cramer, Cork, employed in shipbuilding, was remanded in custody in late March 1867 on suspicion of having been involved in the Ballyknockane attack.

103. Denis Creedon, Barrack Street, Cork, was arrested on 14 March 1867 on suspicion of involvement in the attack on the Ballyknockane police station.

104. Michael Cronin worked as a teacher without formal training in Rosnacahara National School and was arrested as a Fenian suspect in September 1865.

105. Jeremiah and Patrick Cullinane, Skibbereen, arrested as Phoenix conspirators in 1858 and remembered by Rossa as friends in 1898; their brother Henry was made a magistrate in the late nineteenth century.

106. Thomas 'the Bowler' Cullinane, born in Ballymacoda in 1844, a farm labourer who acted as Capt. McClure's messenger during the Rising. He was arrested while riding through Castlemartyr on 6 March 1867, sentenced to life and transported to Western Australia. Receiving a free pardon in 1869, Cullinane lived in the US until 1910 to return to Ballymacoda, where he died as a local celebrity in 1928.

107. David Cummins, born in Youghal in 1834, plasterer, was identified as among the Fenians taking Knockadoon coastguard station and seizing its rifles on 6

March 1867. He was sentenced to seven years and transported to Western Australia. During Prince Alfred's visit to the colony, Cummins was among those Fenians who felt humiliated and refused to work if separated to join teams of criminals. Cummins was pardoned in 1869 and left for San Francisco.

108. Lieut Owen Cunningham, a native of Skibbereen, who had enlisted in 23rd Illinois Volunteers for three years and was on the Fenian Brotherhood list of experienced officers for the invasion of Ireland, circa 1865.

109. James Joseph Curran, 96 Fairbane, Cork, had returned after fighting in the Civil War, but was unemployed and suspected as a Fenian agent. Arrested in March 1866, he petitioned for release on the grounds of visiting his father and family after three years in the US and intending to settle permanently in America; he was discharged in May 1866 and escorted on board ship by the police.

110. Young Curtin, draper's assistant in Great George's Street, Cork, and son of a publican in Carrignavar, was arrested in March 1867 on suspicion of involvement in the Rising.

111. Capt. William Cusack, born before 1835 in Cahir, had emigrated to Pennsylvania by 1860. He fought in the Civil War, including at Gettysburg, and was wounded and discharged in July 1864. He went to Ireland with several Americans and received a tumultuous welcome in Mitchelstown, where his family had a shop. There are suggestions that Cusack was related to J.S. Casey, the Galtee Boy. Returning to the US, he was a pall-bearer at O'Mahony's funeral in New York in 1877 and represented Philadelphia at that year's Clan na Gael convention, continuing as a Clan member until 1884, at least. Cusack died in 1895.

112. Timothy Daly, 34, Killeagh, carpenter at Coppinger's, father of eight children, led the Midleton Fenians, as their designated commander had been arrested before the Rising. Moving south, they came across a police patrol, whom Daly called upon to surrender to the Irish Republic. The police refused, the Fenians fired and Constable Sheedy was mortally wounded. The insurgents marched to Castlemartyr, where they planned to attack the barracks to gain arms, joined by the local contingent. Daly called on the police to surrender and in the exchange of fire, Daly was killed. A Celtic cross was erected over his grave in Killeagh.

113. Col William Davis, 33, born in Cork city, served three years in the Federal Army during the Civil War and was sworn into the Fenian Brotherhood in Virginia in 1862 by Capt. William O'Shea. He featured among the highest-ranking officers on the Fenian Brotherhood roster.

114. Denis Desmond, 27, Macroom, national school teacher, was observed drilling with several others in December 1865. Desmond also kept a pub, where one of his associates attempted to swear in Michael Connell, who informed the authorities. Desmond was indicted for treason felony and illegal drilling, but his trial at the special commission in Cork was abandoned. He was detained in the county jail and discharged on board the emigrant ship in May 1866.

115. John Dineen, a native of Passage West and a ship carpenter, arrested between Passage West and Rochestown while drilling in March 1867, detained in Cork jail.

116. Denis Donovan, Pouladuff, arrested at Cobh on 14 March 1867 on suspicion of having participated in the attack on the Ballyknockane constabulary barracks.

117. Charles Guilfoyle Doran, 1835–1909, with origins in Dunlavin, Co. Wicklow, began his revolutionary career as secretary of the NBSP in Dublin, coming to prominence in the IRB after the Rising. He served as secretary to its Supreme Council until superseded by John O'Connor, but remained a lifelong Fenian. Doran spent most of his life in Cobh as clerk of works during the building of the cathedral. A bibliophile, he researched and wrote about the history of Cork.

118. William Dorman, 19, among a group of eleven men charged with illegal drilling with pikes at Aughadown, Skibbereen, during the night of 18 February 1866, according to the informer Michael Fitzgerald; bail refused, to be tried at the assizes.

119. Simon Downey, born in 1845, a butcher in Cork city, was identified as participating in the attack on Ballyknockane barracks during the Rising. Sentenced to seven years and transported to Western Australia, he returned to Ireland after the amnesty of 1869.

120. Daniel Downing, one of four brothers from Skibbereen, relations of O'Donovan Rossa, who became members of the Phoenix Society and subsequently the IRB. He emigrated to the US, fought in the Civil War and died in 1876.

121. Capt. Denis J. Downing, Skibbereen, brother of Daniel and Patrick, who was employed as a draper's assistant and, aged nineteen, became the youngest Phoenix prisoner. He emigrated on release and joined the 42nd New York Tammany Regiment when the Civil War broke out, later becoming a sergeant-major of the 97th Regiment. He led the singing of 'Ireland Boys, Hurrah' after the battle of Fredericksburg in December 1862, which was sung by the Union Army and echoed along the Confederate lines. Denis fought in most of the battles of the Army of the Potomac until Gettysburg, where his leg had to be amputated. He was transferred to the veteran corps and chosen to assist at the execution of the assassins of President Lincoln in 1865. Suffering from TB, he returned to die in West Cork in May 1871.

122. Michael Downing, Cork, old clothesseller, whom an informer named as an IRB officer, often present in Geary's pub in 1865.

123. Col Patrick J. Downing, 24, a native of Skibbereen, had returned from the US in 1856 and was among those arrested for the Phoenix conspiracy but released on bail of £100 and two sureties of £50 each. He joined Stephens in Paris in 1859, afterwards travelling to America as his agent. He worked on the *Phoenix* newspaper and became a close friend of John O'Mahony. Downing, who had drilled in Ireland, gained a commission in the 42nd New York Volunteers during the Civil War and served with distinction in Meagher's Brigade, becoming lieutenant-colonel of the 99th New York National Guard. He was severely wounded several times, surviving some of the bloodiest battles, e.g. Antietam. Downing served as secretary for civil affairs of the Fenian Brotherhood in 1866. He died in Washington. His son, Rossa Downing, the Irish-American orator, was involved in the early days of the Friends of Irish Freedom.

124. Michael Doyle, Passage West, ploughman, suspected as an active Fenian, who swore men into the IRB in late 1866.

125. Timothy Doyle, Old Youghal Road, Cork, was among those arrested and investigated but not tried for the IRB raid on an armoury in the North Cork militia barracks in Mallow in June 1871.

126. William Draddy, from a farming background in Castlemartyr, had returned

from America to work in Fermoy. He claimed that he was about to leave for the US when arrested on 13 March 1867 on suspicion of participation in the Rising.

127. Patrick Drinan, labourer, arrested as a suspected participant in the 1867 Rising and held in Cork jail.

128. Jeremiah Driscoll, 21, clerk of Timothy McCarthy Downing, Skibbereen, was arrested as a Phoenix conspirator in 1858.

129. Peter Duggan, 19, among a group of eleven men charged with illegal drilling with pikes at Aughadown, Skibbereen, during the night of 18 February 1866, according to the informer Michael Fitzgerald. Duggan was refused bail and sent for trial at the assizes.

130. Thomas Duggan, 1822–1913, a native of Ballincollig from an Irish-speaking farming background, had been trained in a model school. He taught in Ballincollig National School. An early IRB 'centre', Duggan was dismissed from his job in 1862, emigrated to fight for the Confederacy in the American Civil War and returned to Ireland as a Fenian organizer. He was arrested in October 1865 and sentenced to ten years. Transported to Australia on the *Hougoumont*, Duggan gained a free pardon in 1869 to spend the rest of his life teaching in Australia.

131. Timothy Duggan, Skibbereen, 27, assistant in O'Donovan Rossa's shop, a member of the Phoenix Society, detained in Cork jail in 1858.

132. Capt. John Dunne, 27, a native of Charleville and a plasterer, became a Fenian in New York in 1859. He served for three years with 164th New York Volunteers during the Civil War as a lieutenant and enrolled himself on the Fenian Brotherhood list of officers. He returned to Ireland with Patrick Walsh in early 1866 and organized with the Kilmallock Fenians while living in Charleville. Dunne was briefly detained in Cork County jail during the early habeas corpus suspension. In 1867 he reappeared to lead the insurgents in Kilmallock, wearing a green uniform, and wounded the local bank manager, who refused to hand over his revolver. When a Fenian courier arrived with the news that the Rising at Ballyhurst had collapsed, Dunne discharged his followers, as further resistance would be pointless. On the run near Knocklong, he was described as with 'swaggering gait, but well set up like a military man, with bully look', who reached New York in April. There were at least three Fenians of this name, which makes identification difficult, but he is likely to have been the one who attempted to revive the Munster IRB in late 1867 and 1869. The authorities were concerned enough to have him traced at work in the US; in late 1870 he was reported to be in jail for bigamy.[10]

133. Patrick Dunne, Cork, carpenter, described as a leading IRB man in this city by the informer Warner and often present in Geary's pub in 1865.

134. Charles Egan, clerk to Mr Mullany of Cloyne, was the son of a pensioner in Killeagh. Egan had been previously sentenced to three months for possessing ammunition in a proclaimed district. He was re-arrested in March 1867 on suspicion of participation in the attack on Castlemartyr constabulary barracks and taken to Mideton bridewell.

135. James W. Fitzgerald, born in Cobh in 1838, emigrated to Quebec aged 15, settling in Cincinnati, Ohio, where he became manager of a marble and stone works before establishing his own business. During 1856 he was among those conspiring for Irish independence in Cincinnati and was arrested at the behest of the British consul.

In September 1857 Fitzgerald travelled to New York, invited by Michael Doheny to assist in founding the Fenian Brotherhood. In Cincinnati he became the 'centre' of the first 'circle' outside New York and later the 'state centre' for Ohio. As a Fenian senator he opposed Col O'Mahony, joined the Senate wing and led his men to Col O'Neill in Buffalo in May 1866. Considering O'Neill's 1870 attempt to invade Canada futile, Fitzgerald blocked it. He served among the directors of the *Irish Republic* newspaper, begun in Chicago in May 1867. An early, influential Clan na Gael leader, by 1865 Fitzgerald had become a lawyer and participated in American politics during the 1870s.

136. Michael Fitzgerald, a native of Dungourney and a labourer, had been commissioned a lieutenant in the Fenian Brotherhood for the *Erin's Hope* expedition. He was arrested near Dungarvan. Corridon said that he had been present at Brotherhood meetings in New York. Fitzgerald protested his loyalty to the British state and claimed to have landed in Ireland due to unforeseen circumstances. He referred the authorities to relatives in Clonmel. Scheduled for trial in October 1867, he was discharged for America in March 1868 after signing a paper in which expressed regret for his actions.

137. Michael Fitzgerald, schoolmaster, informed on eleven men known to him, with whom he drilled on 18 February 1866 in Aughadown, Skibbereen. He claimed that John Hurley was captain, had handed out pikes and given military commands to 200 altogether, probably an exaggeration. Hurley apparently said that all Protestant landlords would be killed. Fitzgerald was carefully guarded and taken to Bandon under cavalry escort.

138. Private Thomas Fitzgerald, 22, Youghal, had served seven months in the US artillery and joined the Fenian Brotherhood at the invitation of Patrick Clifford during the siege of Petersburg, Virginia, in 1865. He featured on the roster of officers available for action in Ireland.

139. Barry Fitzpatrick, Lavitt's Quay, Cork, printer, was arrested on 14 March 1867 on suspicion of having been among the Fenians who attacked Ballyknockane barracks.

140. Daniel Forde, Ballincollig, labourer, was detained for about two weeks in October 1865 on suspicion of belonging to a Fenian 'circle', according to the informer Warner. As no further evidence was forthcoming, Forde was discharged on condition of appearing before the authorities when called upon.

141. John Foster, 18, letter-carrier for Queenstown (Cobh) post office, was greatly suspected of being an IRB member, having been seen out at night with one Bourke, a post office clerk, presumably drilling. Loyal inhabitants were anxious and a magistrate confided that he wouldn't trust this post office with official correspondence. Foster was arrested and transferred to Mountjoy in April 1866 among the twenty-eight worst suspects of his district. His discharge was only contemplated in August, after he had begun to show symptoms of psychological distress.

142. William Francis, Cloyne, a former soldier, suspected by the constabulary of having drilled the Fenians in Cloyne and Midleton. He was an active agent, planning to further their aims by meeting in small groups. Arrested in February 1866, Francis petitioned for release on condition of emigrating with his wife and child. He left from Cobh on 15 June, having been allowed time to put his affairs in order.

143. Henry Galway, Skibbereen, attracted the attention of the constabulary by marching with a group of young men and using disloyal expressions in November 1869.

144. Eugene Geary, born in 1845 in Carrignavar, stealthily boarded the *Elizabeth Cann*, under repair in Cork harbour, in the aftermath of the Rising. She was bound for Halifax, Nova Scotia, but Geary was arrested on 23 April 1867 on information from a crew member. Sentenced to five years, he was transported to Western Australia and went to San Francisco after the 1869 amnesty.

145. Jeremiah Gleeson was trained in a model school and employed in Knocknagown National School, east Cork. He was arrested in January 1866, suspected of Fenianism.

146. David Golden, imprisoned as a Fenian for nine months in Cork. His grandson, David Thomas Golden, born in 1899 in Dublin, was aware of his Fenian antecedents and fought in the 1916 Rising in the GPO, escaping imprisonment to eventually settle in Chicago.

147. Patrick Gorman, arrested in Charleville in March 1867, suspected of having participated in the attack on Kilmallock constabulary barracks and transferred to Cork jail.

148. Patrick Greany, a native of Belfast, arrested in March 1867 as a suspected participant in the Rising in the Midleton district and held in Cork jail.

149. James Griffin, arrested at Turner's Cross, Cork, on 8 March 1867, suspected of having participated in the Rising. He refused to answer questions and had previously attracted the attention of the police by keeping pikes in a house in Francis Street.

150. Michael Harrington, 1825–86, a native of Goleen and apprentice boatbuilder, who served in the British army for twenty years. In 1856 he was decorated for bravery in India, fought during the Indian Mutiny and was wounded. He became a Fenian, deserted from 53rd Regiment and was arrested in 1866. Serving a life sentence in Western Australia, he was among those rescued by the *Catalpa* in 1876. Harrington joined Clan na Gael in New York and served as a member of the Central Park Police.

151. James H. Harrison, from Co. Cork, enlisted with 61st New York Volunteers for three years and joined the Brotherhood while in the army. He also signed on for the roster of available Fenian personnel.

152. Thomas Henry Hassett, 1841–93, born in Doneraile, a carpenter, who joined the Phoenix Society and fought in the Papal Brigade. In 1861 he enlisted in 24th Foot. He took the IRB oath in 1864 and became the 'centre' of his regiment and was said to have sworn 270 comrades into the IRB. He also developed a plan to capture the Pigeon House Fort. Hassett deserted, but was tried and convicted in 1866. Transported to Australia with a life sentence, he escaped in 1870 to remain at large for almost a year. After the *Catalpa* rescue in 1876, he became a saloon-keeper in Manhattan.

153. John Hawkes, Cork, porter in a bakery, arrested in September 1865 on suspicion of membership of the Fenian organization. This may be the Hawkes mentioned by an informer as an IRB officer and frequent visitor to Geary's pub.

154. J. Hegarty, born in Passage West, a ship carpenter, who was arrested between Passage West and Rochestown while drilling in March 1867; detained in Cork County jail.

155. Timothy Hegarty, near St Finbar's Cathedral, Cork, smith, who made some pikes for the local Fenians. He visited the home of IRB leader Brian Dillon, where members were drilling. Hegarty saw two rifles, which were raffle prizes ('flutes') to raise money for arms. Fearing arrest, he fled to London in September 1865, where 'head centre' Thomas Hayes refused to finance his emigration to America. On arrest, Hegarty was taken back to Cork and turned informer.

156. William Higgins, teacher and historian, was imprisoned for participating in the Rising of 1867. Afterwards, the only employment open to him was as a cooper in Ballincollig Powder Mills. His son, Joseph, became a teacher and sculptor, whose work can be seen in Cork.

157. Timothy Hinchin, a young man who lived on the north side of Cork, had been indicted for illegal drilling in Shandon Street, before being discharged at the assizes. In March 1866 he was detained under the habeas corpus suspension.

158. James Hourigan, Cork, captain of the corporation dredger around 1900 and an IRB member, whose Cork 'circle' had deteriorated badly. Hourigan was active in the Young Ireland Society by organizing commemorations and assisted in erecting the National Monument in Cork in 1906. He was one of the few old Cork Fenians mentioned in P.S. O'Hegarty's statement to the Bureau of Military History.

159. Thomas Huddy, weaver, arrested in Midleton in March 1867 as a suspected member of the Midleton Fenians 'out' during the Rising and detained in Cork jail.

160. James Irwin, born in 1846 in Clonakilty, a brother of Mary Jane O'Donovan Rossa, who shared her political convictions. He was arrested under the Habeas Corpus Suspension Act in March 1866.

Released in November, he returned to organize the IRB, was re-arrested and only discharged on condition of emigrating to America in May 1867.

161. Timothy Warren Irwin was born in 1849 in Clonakilty, a younger brother of James and Mary Jane, whose political views he shared. Irwin proposed the resolution for an amnesty of the Fenian prisoners at the Skibbereen amnesty meeting in September 1869, which was disapproved of by Michael O'Hea, Bishop of Ross, who considered the event promoted Fenianism. Timothy Warren Irwin died in California.

162. Cornelius Dwyer Keane (also Kane), 1839–92, Skibbereen, a national teacher turned law clerk, who became an early IRB 'centre'. A priest alerted the authorities to Keane's activities, while the informer Nagle described him as the 'head organiser' in Skibbereen. He was charged with administering the Fenian oath in Rath in November 1864 and was bailed until the next county assizes. His legal defence fund attracted subscriptions from Ireland, Britain and America. Re-arrested at the time of the *Irish People* seizure, Keane was sentenced to ten years and transported to Australia. Although amnestied, this did not permit him to return to his family in Ireland and he became a registrar of gold mines in Queensland.

163. James Kearney, 1846–1923, a shoemaker, sentenced to five years for assaulting a soldier in Macroom in May 1867 who was disrupting a Fenian meeting. Kearney was transported to Western Australia. Although a model prisoner, he only received his certificate of freedom in 1871 and became a shoemaker in Perth. Kearney married an Irish immigrant and settled at Macroon [sic, after his birthplace] Farm, Nannup, where he manufactured leather items, and his family prospered. His coffin was draped with the Irish tricolour.

164. John Francis Kearns, Coburg Street, Cork, printer, had been informed on by Michael McCarthy. The constabulary found a revolver and numerous files of the *Irish People* in his home. Accused of helping to tear up the rails of the Great Southern and Western Railway, destroying telegraph wires and storming the Ballyknockane barracks in March 1867, Kearns was sentenced to fifteen years. He became insane during imprisonment and was amnestied to die in the Cork Lunatic Asylum in 1873.

165. Daniel Keating, 26, among a group of eleven men charged with illegal drilling with pikes at Aughadown, Skibbereen, during the night of 18 February 1866, according to the informer Michael Fitzgerald. Keating was refused bail and sent for trial at the assizes.

166. Richard Keating was arrested as a suspected participant in the 1867 Rising and held in Cork jail.

167. John and Patrick Keeffe, sometimes O'Keeffe, sons of a prosperous farmer and publican near Killeagh, taken into custody on suspicion of involvement in the attack on Castlemartyr constabulary barracks in March 1867.

168. Patrick Kelleher, Killeagh, tradesman, arrested in March 1867 on suspicion of having participated in the attack on Castlemartyr Constabulary Barracks; held in Midleton Bridewell.

169. John Kelly, a native of Bantry, was suspected of gun-running with his brother Joseph after the discovery of arms in Cullinane's shop in 1871. John, apparently the 'head centre' of Bantry prior to 1870, relocated to Tralee, where he owned a drapery and became generally known as 'John Kelly of Tralee'. He retained his political commitment as a Land League and National League organizer but frequent arrests ruined his business, whereupon nationalists collected £500 from him. When Parnell left Dublin for Brighton for the last time in 1891, he asked Kelly, a staunch supporter, to escort him to the mail boat. As his health began to decline, John Stanislaus Joyce invited Kelly to recuperate in his home in Bray, Co. Wicklow. He features as 'Mr Casey' in the famous Christmas dinner scene in *A Portrait of the Artist as a Young Man*. Kelly died of tuberculosis in April 1896 and was buried in Glasnevin, where an imposing Celtic cross was erected by public subscription.

170. John Edward Kelly, 1841–84, a Protestant born in Kinsale, who emigrated to Canada with his family. He later lived in Boston and New York, trained as a printer and developed literary talent. Kelly joined the Fenian Brotherhood and the Phoenix Zouaves, an Irish militia unit. He became a drill instructor and was sent to Cork in 1861 to prepare for the insurrection. He organized stealthily for a number of years, ran a 'circle' and worked on the *Irish People* in Dublin. Undetected during the September 1865 arrests, Kelly escorted Thomas B. Hennessy and other newly arrived comrades from Boston around Cork to encourage the IRB. He was tempted to participate in the Kerry Rising in February 1867, but had no orders. Employed by the *Cork Herald* and lodging with John and Mrs Buckley, Kelly consulted with O'Neill Crowley and participated in the Kilclooney Wood skirmish in 1867, was tried and sentenced to death, which was commuted to life imprisonment. Transported to Australia, Kelly was freed in the conditional amnesty of 1871. He worked as a journalist and published *Illustrious exiles; or military memoirs of the Irish Race* (1875) in Sydney, which proved commercially unsuccessful. He advised the *Catalpa* rescue team on

arrival in Australia, eventually returning to Boston in poor health to join the *Boston Pilot*. John Boyle O'Reilly erected an imposing monument over his grave in Mount Hope Cemetery, Mattapan, Massachusetts.

171. David Kent had fought in the Civil War in the same regiment as William Mackey Lomasney, whom he joined in the attack on Ballyknockane Barracks in March 1867. He participated in the raid on the Martello Tower in Fota, was afterwards arrested, but freed on condition of emigrating. Thomas Kent of Castlelyons, who was court-martialled and executed for resisting arrest in arms in May 1916, supported by his family, was a cousin.

172. John Curtin Kent, 34, engineer, whose family had been evicted in Co. Cork and emigrated to the US, returned to join the earliest Clan na Gael dynamite attack, alongside Dr Thomas Gallagher and Tom Clarke. Before this bombing team was detected and sentenced to penal servitude for life, Curtin Kent revisited his cousin Thomas Kent of Castlelyons, who would be executed in 1916. Curtin Kent was released from Portland on 6 July 1895 and returned to the US.

173. James Leary was an assistant teacher in Carrigtwohill National School, east Cork, an active Fenian, supposedly drilling the men. He left his post and was arrested on suspicion in March 1866, but released on bail in May, after protesting his innocence.

174. James Lehane, 19, taught as an assistant teacher in Lisheen National School. He lodged with the Fitzgerald family and was collected by John Hurley, 23, for drill after dark. Lehane invited Michael, son of the house, to accompany them. Lehane and Hurley were among the young men identified by Fitzgerald and charged with illegal drilling with pikes on 18 February 1866 in Aughadown, Skibbereen. Bail was refused and they were sent for trial at the next assizes.

175. Sgt William Mackey Lomasney, 24, born near Fermoy in 1841, had taken the Fenian Brotherhood pledge in 1862 in Toronto from Edward O'Meagher Condon, his lifelong friend. Lomasney served in 179th New York Volunteers for a year and featured on the list of those available for the invasion of Ireland. (His activities are covered in the main text. He is usually regarded as the American son of emigrants from the Fermoy district, but contradicts this with his entry in the Fenian Brotherhood roster.)[11]

176. Eugene Lombard, a baker, was born in 1836 in Cork and convicted of involvement in the Ballyknockane attack during the 1867 Rising and sentenced to seven years. Transported to Western Australia, Lombard returned to Cork after the 1869 amnesty.

177. Edmund Lynch, Castlemartyr, arrested under the habeas corpus suspension on 14 March 1866 as a Fenian suspect and taken to Cork jail.

178. John Lynch, Bandon, born in 1842, sentenced to five years for Fenianism and transported to Australia, where he remained after receiving a conditional pardon in 1870.

179. John Lynch, 1831–66, widower, ran a pub in Cork city and later worked as a law clerk. Lynch was one of the earliest IRB members in Cork and became a leader. He attracted official attention when protesting against loyalist celebrations of the Prince of Wales' marriage in 1862. Arrested during the September 1865 sweep, he was sentenced to ten years on flimsy evidence, mostly his love letters. Although suffering from tuberculosis, Lynch was deprived of warm underclothing on arrival in Pentonville. His health deteriorated rapidly and

he died in Woking Invalid Prison on 2 June 1866. His fiancée was refused permission to repatriate his remains, which were interred in Brookwood Cemetery, Surrey. The National Graves Association erected a memorial tablet in this woodland cemetery in 2004.

180. Private Gerard Lyons, 27, a native of Macroom, served seven months in the Federal artillery and joined the Brotherhood in the trenches of Petersburg, Virginia, in 1865, shortly before the collapse of the Confederacy; on the Fenian roster of available personnel.

181. Timothy McAuliffe, an elderly man and engineer in the Cork Steamship Company's shipbuilding yard, arrested on suspicion of participation in the attack on Ballyknockane barracks. McAuliffe was discharged on bail when witnesses confirmed his alibi.

182. Capt. John McCafferty, born in Sandusky, Ohio, in 1838, claimed to have served in the Confederate Cavalry under Morgan in raids through Kentucky, Indiana and Ohio until taken prisoner, escaping repeatedly and finally reaching Canada. He joined the Brotherhood in Detroit and the clerk who entered him in the list of Fenian officers believed his tales of being an ingenious scout. His claim to military experience, which was essential to become a Fenian officer for the proposed expedition to Ireland, remains doubtful. McCafferty was a professional card-player and barman, whose Irish roots have not been traced. His flamboyant appearance attracted attention from the first arrest and discharge by the special commission in Cork in 1865. (His Fenian career features in the main text.) On being amnestied, McCafferty returned to the US. In late 1876 he left San Francisco, then the centre of western mining, for Arivaca,

Arizona, close to the Mexican border, where he became a mine owner with a talent for promotion. He served as a delegate of the territorial legislature, but resumed his revolutionary involvement in November 1881. McCafferty Canyon, Arivaca, is named after him. He remained a well-travelled mining speculator until his death in Colon, Panama, in 1909.[12]

183. Daniel McCarthy, Carrignavar, labourer, arrested on 15 March 1867, detained in the county jail, awaiting trial. He was discharged on bail in May.

184. Daniel McCarthy, Great George's Street, Cork, arrested in June 1871 near Blarney, suspected of breaking into an armoury of the North Cork militia in Mallow to steal rifles for the IRB.

185. Denis McCarthy, aged about 18, a porter in Great Georges Street, Cork, until recently, but now unemployed and suspected of participation in the attack on Ballyknockane constabulary barracks. He was arrested in Cork on 13 March 1867.

186. Eugene McCarthy, 30, clerk to McCarthy Downing, a leading solicitor in Skibbereen, arrested as a Phoenix conspirator in 1858.

187. Private James McCarthy, 38, a native of Glenagaura (Gleann Oirtheach in west Carbery?), served three years in the Federal artillery and joined the Brotherhood during the trench warfare around Petersburg, Virginia, in 1865, which led to the collapse of the Confederacy; on the Fenian roster of military personnel.

188. Jeremiah McCarthy, Clonakilty, 26, arrested in December 1866 under the habeas corpus suspension, suspected of Fenianism and detained in Cork. He had been imprisoned in Mountjoy in March 1866 and only recently freed on bail.

189. John McCarthy, Fermoy, had been among O'Neill Crowley's Fenian followers in Kilclooney Wood when the latter was arrested. McCarthy managed to escape and establish a business career in America. He was a relative of Thomas Kent, executed in May 1916 for resisting arrest with his family.

190. John McCarthy, Cork, sawyer, whom an informer observed drilling in Brian Dillon's home in 1865.

191. Michael McCarthy, about 18, Angel Lane, Cork, porter in a shop in North Main Street. On 5 March 1867 some young men asked him to participate in the Rising and McCarthy accompanied them to Bishop Street late that night. They marched to Prayer Hill, where he believed 2000 were present. Afterwards, McCarthy turned informer and provided the first narrative of what happened in Cork that Shrove Tuesday. He gave evidence calmly and had to be kept in police custody. It was said that his grandfather had also turned informer in 1848.

192. Timothy McCarthy, a native of the parish of Caheragh, residing in Bantry, who was the grandson of a man tortured in 1798. Sworn into the IRB by O'Donovan Rossa, McCarthy was imprisoned with him in Cork in 1858. He died in San Francisco in 1892.

193. Patrick McNamara was arrested in September 1865 in Castlemartyr on information that he had been with Rohan, a respectable farmer's son from Dungourney, in a public house. McNamara tried to swear Rohan into the IRB, who initially refused to confirm this when questioned by the resident magistrate in Youghal, before testifying. McNamara was detained in the county jail.

194. Morgan McSweeney, born in 1842, a baker in Cork, who participated in the attack on Ballyknockane barracks in March 1867. He was sentenced to seven years and transported to Australia until the unconditional amnesty of 1869 allowed him to return home.

195. Eugene McSwiney, Tomes, Macroom, an early IRB leader, who confirmed his support of O'Mahony and Stephens in writing when their leadership was challenged in 1864.

196. James McSwiney of Coolehane, Macroom, had been imprisoned for a year as a Fenian in 1867. When he died in May 1885, nationalists marched four deep to Clondrohid Cemetery, shouldering the coffin the whole way to demonstrate their respect.

197. John Mahony, 24 Nile Street, Cork, a publican, who had publicly celebrated the return of the amnestied Brian Dillon in the streets in 1871. His name was also found on James J. O'Kelly in connection with his scheme of sending weapons to Ireland the same year.

198. John Mahony, 31 Nile Street, Cork, compositor with the *Cork Examiner*, was also mentioned on James J. O'Kelly's list to facilitate the importation of arms for the IRB in 1871, see above.

199. Timothy Mahony, 60, and his son, Denis, 19, blacksmiths in Dwyer's Lane, Great George's Street, Cork, were arrested in February 1870 on suspicion of Fenianism, after a rifle was found hidden on their premises. Denis tried to escape but was captured by the police.

200. John Marrigan, 1820–1912, Donickmore, Dungourney, joined the IRB and was 'out' in Castlemartyr during the 1867 Rising. He later became a member of the Old Guard Benevolent Union for Fenian veterans and died an inmate of Midleton workhouse.

201. Garrett Mawe, arrested in Charleville on 15 March 1867, suspected of having participated in the attack on Kilmallock constabulary barracks. He was among those transferred to Cork jail.

202. Jeremiah Mescal, arrested in Kinsale and detained in Cork jail in March 1867 on suspicion of Fenian involvement.

203. William Meskill, Ballyheada, Ballinhassig, an old Fenian, who had hidden a barrel of gunpowder taken from the Martello Tower in Fota by Capt. Mackey in 1867. Meskill presented it to Ailbhe O Monachain during the War of Independence, when such supplies were scarce.

204. Declan Monsell had trained in a model school and taught in Schull National School until dismissed for drunkenness in October 1865. He was arrested on suspicion of Fenianism in February 1866.

205. Bartholomew Moriarty, Rathmore, Co. Kerry, stonemason and leader of the Millstreet 'circle', had been raiding for arms on the night of the Rising with his men. The elderly Henry Leader's mansion of Mount Leader was searched and he was struck over the head with a poker. He identified Moriarty as his attacker, who had been arrested in the meantime and volunteered information. Moriarty implicated twenty-three young men and arrests followed. Moriarty was sentenced to seven years at the Cork special commission, when the Leader family pleaded that this betrayal had decimated the Millstreet Fenians, many of whom fled abroad. He was transported to Western Australia, but liberated in September 1868 to seek obscurity.

206. Patrick Moroney, passenger on the *Helvetia*, was searched on arrival in Cobh in October 1865. A letter, advising him that his presence was not yet necessary, and a pamphlet about the Fenian Brotherhood were found, causing his arrest.

207. James Mountaine (also Mountain), 1819–68, had supported O'Connell's Repeal campaign and joined a Confederate Club in 1848. On meeting Stephens he became the first Fenian in Cork city in 1858. He owned a large shoe and leather business. His nationalist opinions were known, but he was acquitted of leading the Cork riots against the celebrations on the Prince of Wales's marriage. The case against him in 1865 was slight, but he was re-arrested in March 1866 under the habeas corpus suspension. Prison conditions and the death of his son undermined his health and he died in November 1868.

208. Michael Moynahan, an IRB member and brother of Mortimer, who left Skibbereen to work on the *Irish People*. He fled to America after the September 1865 arrests. In 1876 Moynahan made unsuccessful attempts to enrol the Irish workers of Portland, Oregon, in Clan na Gael.

209. Mortimer Moynahan, 21, Skibbereen, law clerk and an early member of the Phoenix Society, who became the most effective of the three IRB 'centres' in West Cork, according to Thomas Clarke Luby. Moynahan was forced to leave Skibbereen for Cork, following his detention during the Phoenix arrests of 1858–9. After the seizure of the *Irish People* in 1865, Mortimer acted as Stephens's link with the Cork region. He later fled to New York and joined the Fenian Brotherhood. His family endured destitution in the US; his wife had died by 1874 and three of their four children were in care. Moynahan remained active on behalf of Clan na Gael.

210. John Mulcahy, Cork city, tobacco twister, was among those who had participated in the Rising in March 1867.

211. John Mullens, 38, a native of Castletownsend, served in the Royal as well as the Confederate Navy as a petty officer with twenty-five years' experience. He became a Fenian in Chicago in 1864 and was recommended by Michael Scanlan for the Fenian Brotherhood's list of naval officers for their Irish invasion.

212. John Murphy, Sylvester Cotter and James Creed, draper's assistants in Bantry, were about to leave for America when they were arrested in February 1866 on suspicion of Fenianism.

213. Maurice Murphy, Killeagh, tradesman, arrested March 1867 for having participated in the attack on Castlemartyr Constabulary Barracks on the information of Daniel Doyle, 28, a blacksmith employed by him. Murphy was held in Midleton bridewell.

214. Michael Francis Murphy, 1831–76, hatter with a large shop in Great George's Street, Cork, arrested as a prominent Fenian in September 1865, but released on bail. A local leader, Murphy was detained twice more in March 1866 and February 1868. His wife, Catherine Barlow, also supported the IRB. He subsequently led the Cork Amnesty Association and was contacted by some soldier Fenians in Fremantle, Australia, seeking to be rescued, which resulted in two IRB officers being despatched at the time of the *Catalpa* mission. Murphy's adopted daughter, his wife's niece, married Charles G. Doran.

215. Patrick Murphy, Ballincollig, farmer, an active, influential man, whom the constabulary described as keeping 'bad company – identified with Cork and Ballincollig Fenians' in November 1866.[13]

216. Stephen Murphy, Barrack Stream, Cork, where he lived with his employer Cotter, a blacksmith, was arrested making

his way back to Cork in June 1871. He was among fifteen men questioned by magistrates during the preliminary inquiry. Murphy was tried and one of two men convicted of an IRB plot to rob rifles from the North Cork militia barracks in Mallow. He was sentenced to two years.

217. Alexander Nicholls Jr, born in 1844, Blarney, whose father owned woollen mills in Glanmire. An IRB 'centre', he was arrested and charged with high treason in October 1865. Nicholls failed to withstand pressure to plead guilty and was released on bail, but despised by his former comrades.

218. Sgt William James Nicholson, 20, a native of Mitchelstown, served with 175th Volunteers for three years and joined the Fenian Brotherhood in 1861 in Troy, New York. Nicholson's officers recommended him as 'intelligent and competent' on the Fenian Brotherhood roster of experienced fighters, prepared for the invasion of Ireland. In November 1866 Nicholson, 'centre' of a 'circle' in Troy, wrote to Col Thomas Kelly about fundraising. (This must be the W.J. Nicholson later described by Devoy as having been born in Cork as the son of an English sergeant, who was the Senate wing's 'head centre' for Troy in 1870, simultaneously serving as the first secretary of Clan na Gael.) Nicholson was involved in efforts to reunite the Fenian Brotherhood by offering control of the United Irishmen, the renamed Senate wing, to the amnestied Fenian leaders in February 1871. He was expelled from the Clan in 1874 for a shortfall of $3600, much of which he had lent to a man who failed to repay him.[14]

219. Cornelius Nolan, wood-turner, who provided 'bungs' for Sir John Arnott's brewery, was arrested in his father's house in Straw Hall, Peacock Lane, Cork, on suspicion of having been among the attackers

of Ballyknockane barracks in March 1867. A well-behaved young man, according to his employer, Nolan was released on bail of £20, as witnesses supported his alibi.

220. James Nolan, 27, a native of Cork, had gone to America as a teenager, joining the US navy in 1865, but deserted soon afterwards to work on cargo boats. In 1867 Nolan sailed as cook on the *Erin's Hope*, leaving his family in New York. He was shot in an altercation with Daniel J. Buckley in Sligo Bay. Fearing a long sentence after arrest, Samuel Lee Anderson persuaded him to give information, which included that Buckley had hidden some unpardonable conduct in an officer from the military authorities during the Civil War. Anderson blackmailed Buckley into turning chief Crown witness at the trial of John Warren and Augustine Costello, leaders of the *Erin's Hope* expedition. He and Nolan vanished into obscurity afterwards.

221. Batt O'Brien, national teacher, Leap, was arrested in March 1866 on suspicion of Fenianism and taken to Cork jail.

222. David O'Brien, Old Youghal Road, Cork, was among fifteen men arrested and investigated for the IRB raid on an armoury in the North Cork militia barracks in Mallow in June 1871.

223. Denis O'Brien, Cork, old-clothes seller, named as a leading IRB man by the informer Warner in 1865, having frequented Geary's pub, the Fenian headquarters in the city.

224. James O'Brien, Blarney Lane, Cork, was considered to be among the city's leading IRB men in 1865, a frequenter of Geary's pub.

225. James Nagle O'Brien, born 1848 in Mallow, son of well-to-do parents of Young Ireland antecedents and eldest brother of William. James abandoned studying for the priesthood and became a local IRB leader, who turned out for the Rising with his district. He also participated in Capt. Mackey's raids for arms and directed later episodes of gun-running, but suffered disillusionment from the general lack of organization in Munster. He died of tuberculosis in 1878, as did his youngest brother and sister.

226. 'Capt. P. O'Brien', alias Patrick Reidy, robbed a gun and solicited contributions for Capt. Mackey's wife in a threatening manner in the Millstreet district until October 1868. Arrested in Killarney, he escaped from Mallow jail by a ladder inadvertently left for repairs to repeat his exploits until re-arrested near Mushera Mountain and detained in Kanturk. Perhaps not a Fenian, but his activities kept rumours of political outrages alive in Mallow.

227. Patrick 'Rocky Mountain' O'Brien was born in Dromore, Caheragh, in 1851. He became a Fenian. In 1868 O'Brien watched the only cow of a poor family being driven away by bailiffs, when he and some locals 'rescued' the animal, routing the officials. O'Brien had to go on the run by leaving Bantry on a ship bound for Rio de Janeiro, followed by travels in North America. 'Rocky Mountain' participated in Col O'Neill's second attempt to invade Canada by briefly holding Pigeon Hill for the Irish Republic on 24 May 1870. He worked as a big-game hunter, suppling mining camps in Idaho and Wyoming. He also lived in New York and became a friend of O'Donovan Rossa, whose separatist views he shared and whom he helped financially. O'Brien wrote verses, lectured and returned on visits to West Cork. 'Rocky Mountain' died in 1919 in Long Island and was buried in Calvary Cemetery.

228. James Joseph O'Connell O'Callaghan, a native of Kanturk, was a draper's assistant in Arnott's, Henry Street, Dublin.

An early Fenian and leading recruiter, he swore John Devoy into the IRB in 1861. O'Callaghan's Dublin 'circle' was said to consist of 1000 men. Pierce Nagle had taken a Fenian letter to him and identified him to the police in September 1865, leading to his detention in the Richmond bridewell. O'Callaghan was not tried by the special commission due to lack of evidence and continued to be detained. His memorial for release pleaded deteriorating health and explained military items in his possession as belonging to his brother, an officer in the Federal Army. Superintendent Ryan objected to his discharge for some months, considering him 'deeply implicated'. In August 1866 the police escorted O'Callaghan on board a steamer to America.[15]

229. Capt. O'Connell O'Callaghan, 26, a native of Kanturk, who had served in 2nd New Jersey Volunteers for three years, was sworn into the IRB in Cork in 1865 by 'centre' Patrick O'Keeffe, according to the Fenian Brotherhood roster.

230. William O'Carroll, a well-educated baker in Cork, where he was among the members of the 'Davis Institute', founded in 1854–5 to further Irish independence along with James Mountaine and Brian Dillon. He refused to accept the defeat of 1848 and became one of the two earliest IRB 'centres' in that city, but grew critical of Stephens. Emigrating to Australia in 1862, he became a respected newspaper editor and citizen of Brisbane. Although he had relinquished Fenianism, O'Mahony offered to assist Rossa in 1884 if the necessary funds were available.

231. Capt. Charles Underwood O'Connell, 1838–1902, a native of Co. Cork, who joined the IRB in 1858. Stephens selected him as an organizer for Cork, Blarney, Cobh and Monkstown. He became one of the three early Cork 'centres'.

In 1862 O'Connell's father was evicted and the family emigrated. In New York, O'Connell organized a company to fight on the Federal side in the Civil War. He returned for the anticipated Rising in 1865, was arrested and sentenced to ten years, having incriminating documents on his person. Imprisonment shattered his health. Released in the 1871 amnesty, he returned to New York, where he worked in the city administration. O'Connell was killed in a fire at his Manhattan hotel in 1902 and buried in Calvary Cemetery, New York.

232. John O'Connell, Killeagh, tradesman, arrested in March 1867 on suspicion of having attacked the Castlemartyr constabulary barracks and held in Midleton bridewell.

233. John O'Connell, Glantane, Lombardstown, 'centre' of this district, fled after the 1867 Rising, assisted by his brother, Fr Timothy, curate of Kildorrery, to reach Cobh and America safely. The priest also attended O'Neill Crowley when mortally wounded and helped a woman in a hooded cloak, probably Kate Crowley, to remove incriminating documents belonging to her brother. Michael O'Connell, their grand-nephew, although the son of a Redmondite farmer, was to become quartermaster, Cork 4th brigade, 1st southern division, IRA.

234. John O'Connell, clerk in the drapery of Samuel Riordan, Skibbereen, was arrested as a suspect in March 1866 and taken to Cork jail.

235. Mary O'Connell, Cork, sister-in-law of Capt. Mackey, indignantly threatened the police after being searched in an overlooked room while attending his trial. She claimed falsely that she could shoot and knew where 500 revolvers were hidden. Mary said that after Mackey's arrest, her sister (his wife) Susan had foolishly gone

out several nights running to prevent Fenian retaliation against the police. Mary and Mary Jane Buckley were searched and sued the county inspector of the RIC for indecent assault and false imprisonment and were awarded £50 in July 1868.

236. Thomas O'Connor, 30, a native of Kinsale, was a member of the Fenian Brotherhood since 1860, having been enrolled by Michael Scanlan in Chicago. He was among the few without military experience to be included on the list of Fenian Brotherhood officers.

237. Daniel O'Donovan, Bantry, carpenter, was the local IRB treasurer in 1867 and retained some funds, which were used during O'Donovan Rossa's visits to Cork in the early twentieth century. Daniel remained a dedicated nationalist. He served on the local board of guardians for thirty years and in 1900 succeeded former Bantry IRB leader and MP James Gilhooly, 1847–1916, as chairman of the town commissioners. O'Donovan held important contracts during the building of Catholic churches and worked to erect housing for rural and urban labourers. He died in 1908.

238. Jeremiah O'Donovan, born in 1840, a farm labourer from Coolflugh, Tower, near Blarney and employed there at St Ann's Hill. He was charged with Thomas Duggan for administering the Fenian oath to a soldier in 1866. Sentenced to five years, O'Donovan was transported to Australia but received a pardon in 1869, which allowed him to return home, where he joined the amnesty movement. O'Donovan was a pall-bearer at the funeral of the amnestied Brian Dillon and continued working as a farm labourer in Blarney in later life.

239. Mary Jane O'Donovan Rossa, née Irwin, born in 1846 in Clonakilty, was the eldest child of Irwin Maxwell, town commissioner of Clonakilty in 1874–9. Her cousin and godfather was Timothy Warren Anglin, 1822–96, who emigrated to Canada, where he became a distinguished journalist and politician. Mary Jane was the third wife of O'Donovan Rossa. Her poems appeared in the Dublin *Irish People*. She served on the Ladies' Committee after the September 1865 arrests, subsequently emigrating to America to earn her living, while publicizing the plight of the Fenian prisoners. She trained in public speaking, reciting poetry at diaspora gatherings. Her collected poetry appeared in book form in the US. Mary Jane and Rossa lived in New York after his release. His controversies and their family of thirteen children occupied her henceforth, although she was not uncritical of his failings. She never fulfilled her early literary promise. The deeply religious Mary Jane participated in Rossa's funeral in 1915 and died suddenly in New York in August 1916.

240. William O'Donovan, Cappagh, Union Hall, had been greatly affected by Black '47, which he experienced as a child, and which inspired his interest in politics. A personal friend of O'Donovan Rossa, he was closely associated with the Fenian movement and narrowly escaped arrest. He later supported Home Rule.

241. Patrick O'Driscoll, farmer in Coolbawn near Bantry, arrested in March 1866 as a Fenian suspect and taken to Cork jail.

242. Patrick Sarsfield O'Hegarty, 1879–1955, the eldest son of John, a plasterer who had joined the Fenian movement in the US during the 1860s. O'Hegarty was born after his parents' return to Carrignavar and became a dedicated activist, intellectual and historian. An employee of the post office, Patrick Sarsfield took the IRB oath in London in 1902 and sat on the

Supreme Council from early 1907. Together with his brother Seán, 1881–1963, he did much to revive the IRB in the run-up to the Easter Rising.

243. Thade O'Herlihy, Berrings, Blarney, the last survivor of Capt. Mackey's Fenian band, had emigrated to Darjeeling, India. He returned home on a visit years later, claiming that Mackey's arms cache hidden in Berrings remained intact since 1868. In 1956 the farm of Jack Reilly was searched by the area commander of the FCA with a minesweeper, but no guns were located.

244. James O'Keeffe, Cork city, arrested in February 1866 under habeas corpus for associating with a number of suspected Fenians and buying drinks for sympathizers.

245. Capt. Patrick O'Keeffe, Rossline, Kanturk, born in 1839, returned from America in 1865 and corresponded with Thomas Clarke Luby in the *Irish People* office. He was arrested in Kanturk on information received in January 1866 and detained as the local 'head centre'. O'Keeffe appeared to be in New York during the Rising, when his home in Kanturk was searched. By 1868 he lived in Savannah, Georgia, but returned about five years later to become a commercial traveller and Land League activist. When arrest threatened again he returned to Savannah, where he died in 1899.

246. Lieut William O'Keeffe, born in Rathcormac in 1839, settled in New Haven, Connecticut in 1853. He enlisted in 9th Regiment in September 1861 and was promoted. After the Civil War, O'Keeffe travelled to Ireland, hoping to participate in the Rising. On his return, he married a sister of Capt. Laurence O'Brien of New Haven and became a police officer. He was still alive in 1891.

247. Alexander O'Leary, Cork, draper's assistant, arrested under the Habeas Corpus

Suspension Act and held in Cork jail in April 1866 as a suspected Fenian officer.

248. Daniel O'Leary, Clonakilty, journeyman baker, had told the crowd in March 1866 from John Callanan's window in this town that the American Fenians were coming to free them from tyranny and oppression. O'Leary was arrested and petitioned that he didn't have the money to emigrate or he would gladly do so and requested release on bail; he was discharged in May.

249. Denis O'Leary, Cork IRB, a tailor and participant in Capt. Mackey's 1867 exploits. A revolver, probably taken in the Allport raid, was found on him when arrested. Despite repeated imprisonment, he remained a Fenian. O'Leary died in the workhouse in 1905, when the Cork Young Ireland Society organized his funeral.

250. Jeremiah O'Leary, 1850–1910, Togher, Dunmanway, a wealthy shopkeeper, had been a Fenian in his youth but later became a constitutional nationalist.

251. Patrick O'Leary, 'the Pagan', real name John Murphy, born c. 1820 near Macroom, emigrated to the US, where he studied for the priesthood, but resigned in 1846 to fight in the Mexican-American War. A head wound left him unbalanced on the subjects of Christianity and Irish nationalism. He eventually returned to Ireland, where he became a rather eccentric IRB member and first chief recruiter in the British army. O'Leary was arrested in Mullingar and sentenced to seven years in July 1865 for attempting to swear in soldiers as Fenians. Amnestied in 1871, he returned to America, where he died in an army veterans' home.

252. Patrick O'Leary, Central Hotel, Bantry, was among Col O'Neill's advance guard on Fort Erie on 31 May 1866, when he was shot. O'Leary carried the bullet with

him to the grave and was remembered by O'Donovan Rossa on his deathbed in 1914, in spite of the latter's mental deterioration.

253. Edward O'Loughlin, hardware shop assistant in Midleton, joined local IRB suspects on the run after the 1867 Rising and was arrested near Youghal.

254. Cornelius (Con) O'Mahony, 1839–79, a former national schoolteacher from Macroom, who became James Stephens's secretary and a clerk in the *Irish People* office. He was arrested in September 1865, sentenced to five years for treason and transported to Australia, where he was amnestied and returned to teaching in Perth in 1869. He married and became principal of a Catholic school in Melbourne, where he died of typhoid in 1879. A large Celtic cross was erected over his grave through funds raised by Hugh Brophy, a fellow Fenian, who had been a 'centre' and building contractor in Dublin.

255. Dominick O'Mahony, a cooper, was the IRB chief for Cork in 1867. He travelled to London to consult with Col Kelly and became the Munster representative of the provisional government of the Irish Republic in February 1867. Betrayed by Corridon, O'Mahony was arrested and acquitted of participation in the Rising, but lost his business. He afterwards campaigned for amnesty and remained a Parnellite to the end. A fine public speaker, despite a drink problem, he died in 1899. In 1993 the O'Mahony clan erected a headstone in St Joseph's Cemetery, Cork.

256. James O'Mahony, Bandon, an Irish-language enthusiast and member of the Ossianic Society, became an early IRB facilitator and friend of O'Donovan Rossa. He met John O'Mahony during his visit to Ireland in 1860–61. Growing critical of Stephens and under financial pressure,

O'Mahony emigrated to Australia with William O'Carroll in 1862.

257. James O'Mahony, Millstreet, shoemaker, had been a courier for Edward O'Meagher Condon in Macroom in 1867 and assisted Capt. Timothy Deasy on the night of the Rising, according to his obituary. Magistrates believed that he had been among the Fenians who attacked Mount Leader House and its elderly owner to obtain arms, raided the railway station and tore up the rails in March 1867. O'Mahony was detained from April to July. His nationalist involvement continued, however, with membership of the Land League and its parliamentary successors. In September 1881 he found himself in Limerick jail under the Protection of Persons and Property Act. A member of the Old Guard Union of IRB veterans, O'Mahony died in April 1916, aged 75, as two of his sons fought in the British army.

258. Jerome O'Mahony, 1840–1914, Coolsnaugh, Dunmanway, a member of the rural district council, was involved at the start of the Fenian movement as an 'intrepid conveyer of rifles and equipment from Cork to the western portions of the county'. He had several narrow escapes from arrest. O'Mahony continued to believe in physical force, became a militant Land Leaguer and later a supporter of Sinn Féin. He was too unwell to support the Irish Volunteers, of whom he approved. As a member of the Dunmanway board of guardians, he inspired it to give preference to Irish goods for the workhouse – they were among the first to do so.[16]

259. John O'Mahony, Ballygorm, Midleton, went on the run after the 1867 Rising and was arrested with Edward O'Loughlin near Youghal.

260. John O'Mahony, Ballydehob, shoemaker, had been an active agent for the

Irish People in Dublin and was suspected of being an IRB officer. A copy of the Philadelphia convention of the Fenian Brotherhood was found at his arrest in March 1866. He pleaded that his aged parents depended on him and was discharged for America the following month.

261. Philip O'Neill, Killeagh, arrested in March 1867 on suspicion of having participated in the attack on Castlemartyr constabulary barracks.

262. Michael O'Regan, Ardagh, Rosscarbery, had joined the IRB with his two brothers early on, emigrated to America and served in the Civil War. He returned to Ireland with despatches from John O'Mahony and became a drill-master. O'Regan was arrested in September 1865 with drill books, cartridges for revolvers and seditious documents. He had attempted swearing in British naval personnel in Castletownsend, was convicted and sentenced to seven years. O'Regan was transferred to English prisons in late 1865 with Thomas Duggan, Brian Dillon and John Lynch. The *Skibbereen Eagle* reported in March 1869 that he had been amnestied and was visiting friends in West Cork.

263. Patrick O'Regan, a native of Ardagh, Rosscarbery, brother of Michael (above) and John, returned from New York, but found preparations for the Rising incomplete. He went back to the US and fell in the Civil War in 1863.

264. Denis O'Shanahan, Union Hall, shoemaker, suspected to be 'head centre' of that locality, was arrested in March 1866 and taken to Cork jail.

265. Thomas O'Shea, 24, clerk to a corn merchant, Skibbereen, arrested as a Phoenix conspirator in 1858.

266. Capt. William O'Shea, 28, a native of Bantry, was among those detained during the Phoenix conspiracy in 1858–9. Emigrating to the US on release, he continued his Fenian involvement and joined 42nd New York Volunteers at the outbreak of the Civil War. A close friend of O'Donovan Rossa, O'Shea was noted for his courage, participating in the great battles of the Army of the Potomac until killed at the Wilderness and Spotsylvania on 12 May 1863.

267. Cornelius O'Sullivan, Cork, cooper, was arrested in February 1868 on suspicion of having been among Capt. Mackey's team, which broke into Allports and made off with a quantity of weapons. He may be identical with Cornelius P. O'Sullivan, master cooper of the same name, who was tried and acquitted of robbing arms for the IRB from the militia barracks in Mallow in June 1871.

268. Cornelius O'Sullivan, an assistant teacher in the national school in Blarney, suspected of Fenianism and arrested in January 1866.

269. Capt. Eugene O'Sullivan, ex-US army, High Street, Skibbereen, the son of a blacksmith, was arrested on suspicion and taken to Cork jail in March 1866.

270. John Carey O'Sullivan, Mallow, a respectable young man, suspected of being the 'head centre' for Mallow, had fled to America after the September 1865 arrests. On return he was committed for trial as a member of the Fenian conspiracy in February 1866, based on the evidence of the informer Warner. O'Sullivan protested his loyalty to the state, had developed health problems and was released on bail in May. He was arrested for the second time in November and discharged on condition of emigrating to America in February 1867, where he served on the committee trying to reconcile the rival wings of the Fenian Brotherhood in March 1869.

271. Robert O'Sullivan, Sunday's Well, Cork, office boy for a merchant, was among fifteen men investigated on suspicion of breaking into an armoury of the North Cork militia in Mallow. He had previously attracted police attention when firing a revolver in Patrick Street. O'Sullivan was tried in August 1871 for conspiracy to rob arms for the IRB and was one of two men convicted and sentenced to two years.

272. John Patten was detained in Cork jail on suspicion of participation in the attack on Ballyknockane constabulary barracks in March 1867.

273. James Pomfret, Ballymacoda, farm labourer, arrested on suspicion of having participated in the Rising in March 1867.

274. John Potter, a native of Passage West and ship carpenter, arrested between Passage West and Rochestown while drilling in March 1867.

275. William Ramsell, Cork, arrested in Macroom in February 1868 on suspicion of a Fenian plot, possibly a gun raid on the local militia barracks.

276. Matthew Regan, employee of Beamish and Crawford, Cork, was absent from work during the Rising. An informer claimed that he had participated in the attack on Ballyknockane barracks, leading to Regan's arrest and the loss of his job.

277. James Ringrone, a young man, arrested at Turner's Cross, Cork, on 8 March 1867, along with James Griffin and John Fitzgerald, suspected of participation in the Rising. Ringrone was released within days, having produced two character witnesses and given bail of £20 to appear if called up for trial.

278. Daniel Riordan (Reardon), a Young Irelander, was involved in the IRB in 1865 and tried on the evidence of the informer Warner, but acquitted. He was imprisoned after the Rising of 1867 but remained a Fenian, dying in Cork in 1887.

279. Denis Riordan, Macroom, an early IRB member (Phoenix Society), arrested on suspicion in January 1859. He emigrated and died in America.

280. Michael Riordan, arrested on 15 March 1867, suspected of participation in the attack on Ballyknockane constabulary barracks and charged with high treason.

281. William Randall Roberts was born in Mitchelstown in 1830 and emigrated to New York in 1849. He worked for A.T. Stewart, the successful department store owner. Roberts opened his own 'Crystal Palace' store in the Bowery and retired, extremely rich, from business in 1869. He supported Fenianism, becoming the leader of the Senate wing, which promoted the invasion of Canada. This split the Brotherhood disastrously. After the unsuccessful attack on Canada in June 1866 Roberts was briefly detained by the US administration. His attempt to gain control of the IRB in the summer of 1867, in competition with the O'Mahony/Savage faction, failed. He retired from Fenianism on 1 January 1868 to become a US representative for New York and, having lost his fortune, was made ambassador to Chile. After years of declining health, he died in 1897, estranged from his wife, to be buried in Calvary Cemetery, New York.

282. Michael and William Roche, 20 and 23 respectively, among a group of eleven men charged with illegal drilling with pikes at Aughadown, Skibbereen during the night of 18 February 1866, according to the informer Fitzgerald. Both were kept in custody to await trial at the assizes.

283. Sgt Cornelius Russell, 25, Cork city, served with 19th Massachusetts during the

Civil War and entered on Fenian Brotherhood list of available officers.

284. Mark Shaughnessy, Cork, observed drilling by an informer in Brian Dillon's home in 1865.

285. Edward Sheehan, Fermoy, observed in Mitchelstown in company with Fenian suspects, notably John Sarsfield Casey, and soldiers of the 4th Dragoons stationed in Fermoy in 1865. Due to shadowing by the police, they had to abandon a proposed IRB meeting in the Galtee mountains.

286. Jeremiah Sheehan, 24, among a group of eleven men charged with illegal drilling at Aughadown, Skibbereen, during the night of 18 February 1866, according to the informer Fitzgerald; bail refused, to be tried at the assizes.

287. Singleton, labourer employed in the Midleton distillery, arrested as a suspected participant in the 1867 rising and held in the county jail.

288. Patrick Slattery, Blarney, arrested in June 1871 on the way home to Blarney on suspicion of breaking into an armoury of the North Cork militia in Mallow with other IRB members to obtain rifles.

289. Edward Smith, about 30, a native of Youghal, had emigrated to the US as a child but returned to Britain in 1862. He claimed to have been a dock labourer in Cardiff who had recently lost his job and arrived in Youghal on a collier in March 1867. Apparently looking for work, he could not provide the constabulary with any references from Cardiff and was remanded in custody as a suspected Fenian, pending inquiries.

290. Martin Smith, Watergrasshill, arrested in Cork city in February 1866 under the habeas corpus suspension as having been in recent contact with a number of suspects and 'standing "treats" to everyone of Fenian sympathies' in the pubs.[17]

291. David Spillar, 35, shoemaker, employed in North Main Street, Cork, was one of three men who accompanied Capt. Mackey to Cronin's pub. He tried to strangle Head Constable Gale rather than allow him to capture Mackey. Spillar fled afterwards, but was arrested on returning to Cork in the autumn of 1868.

292. Patrick Stack, 23, Fair Lane, Cork, was tried and acquitted of robbing rifles for the IRB from the North Cork militia barracks in Mallow in June 1871.

293. Patrick Sullivan, Blarney, arrested there in June 1871, was suspected of breaking into an armoury of the North Cork militia in Mallow to steal arms with the above.

294. John Swan, Cork, nailer, had been arrested on suspicion of having attacked Ballyknockane police barrack and tearing up the rails of the Great Southern and Western Railway. Swan was remanded in custody for a week while his family organized witnesses.

295. Sgt Cornelius Sweeney, 40, Aghinagh, Macroom, had served with the British army in India and was greatly experienced. He joined the Brotherhood in Cairo, Illinois, in 1864 and signed on for its roster of officers.

296. William Sweetman was a member of the Passage West IRB under 'centre' John O'Donoghue, who, together with John Callaghan, a Cork city 'centre', was assembling pilots to guide the projected Fenian expedition to Irish harbours. They sent Sweetman to New York in November 1865, but O'Mahony had no ships, due to the Fenian Brotherhood split. Sweetman awaited further orders from Jerry Creed, Fourth Ward, 'centre' of the Red

Hand 'circle' in New York until 1867. Creed asked him to assess and refurbish a brigantine in Greenpoint, New York, which the Brotherhood had purchased. Sweetman was commissioned as a lieutenant of 'the provisional navy of the Fenian Brotherhood' and organized the ship's departure from the North river for Sligo on 15 April with eight thousand rifles, six artillery guns, thirty-eight Fenians and nine crew. They christened her the *Erin's Hope* on Easter Sunday. On arrival they learnt that the Rising was over, were redirected to Cork, but could not land. They finally dropped the Fenians near Helvick Head to return safely to the US with the armaments. Sweetman settled in Poughkeepsie, New York State, recalling this episode in a letter to O'Donovan Rossa's *United Irishman* in 1901.

297. Michael Thompson, Castle Street, Cork, an ex-militia man, was arrested on 14 March 1867 on suspicion of involvement in the Ballyknockane attack.

298. James Treacy, employed for some years behind the counter of John Daly & Co., Grand Parade, Cork, had been suspected as a Fenian since the habeas corpus was suspended in February 1866. When two cases containing at least fifty hidden Enfield rifles and bayonets from Kynoch's of Birmingham were seized on arrival from England, Treacy was briefly detained.

299. Col S.R. Tresilian was born in Bandon in 1828 into a Protestant family. Originally an Orangeman and Freemason, he went into exile in 1848, having been involved with local Young Irelanders. His good education enabled him to qualify as a civil and military engineer in the US, where he fought in the Civil War. Tresilian was appointed chief engineer of 24th Army Corps under General Logan, who spoke highly of him. When the Fenian

Brotherhood prepared its Canadian invasion, Tresilian became chief engineer to General Sweeny. Likewise, when the Rising of March 1867 broke out, he sailed as engineer of the *Erin's Hope*, returning with her to New York. Afterwards he worked on the Hudson River Railroad. Tresilian died of tuberculosis contracted during the Civil War in 1869 and was buried with Masonic honours at Peimont, New York.

300. Sylvester Twomey, a native of Passage West and ship carpenter, was arrested in March 1867 while drilling between Passage West and Rochestown. He was detained in Cork jail.

301. Edward Walsh, Cork, smith, an IRB member, observed drilling with others in the home of Brian Dillon, a prominent Cork leader, in 1865.

302. Capt. Garret B. Walsh, 30, a native of Dunmanway, a Fenian since 1863, had served with 17th Wisconsin Volunteers for four years. He featured on the roster of Fenian Brotherhood officers available for active service.

303. James Walsh, arrested in Charleville on 15 March 1867, suspected of having participated in the attack on Kilmallock constabulary barracks and transferred to Cork.

304. James Mansfield Walsh, Ardnahinch, son of a respectable farmer, arrested at Cobh in March 1867, suspected of having participated in the attack on Knockadoon coastguard station during the Rising.

305. John Stephen Walsh, 1826–91, Milford (his funeral report states Tipperary, however), steel worker, a greatly trusted IRB organizer and member of the Supreme Council, known as 'John Walsh of Middlesbrough', where he was based for many years. Walsh and McCarthy were sent to Fremantle in an IRB rescue bid for the

military Fenians. Walsh was also a Land League organizer and associated with the Invincibles. After the Phoenix Park murders in May 1882 he fled to France and then New York, where he died poor. He is buried in Calvary Cemetery. British secret service records suggest that he may have 'talked' to get to America.

306. Michael Walsh, a brother of John Stephen, see above, was a foreman in Backhouse & Dixon's shipyard in Middlesbrough and a Fenian in 1870. Dublin Castle also suspected other employees of sedition.

307. Patrick Walsh, Cork, employed in the office of the *Cork Examiner*, was suspected of having ignited some Fenian fire in Patrick Street in January 1868.

308. Patrick James Walsh, born around 1842, was a brother of John Stephen Walsh, see above. An innkeeper in Middlesbrough and possibly an IRB member, he co-founded of the local amnesty association in 1891, but died the following year. A memorial cross in recognition of his nationalist commitment was erected in North Ormesby Cemetery in Yorkshire, England.

309. P.F. Walsh, 28, a native of Cork city, had joined the Brotherhood in Philadelphia in 1858 and served four years in the Federal forces during the Civil War. He featured on the Fenian Brotherhood roster and was recommended by his field officers.

310. Richard Walsh was suspected of having participated in the attack on Castlemartyr police barracks. Arrested in April 1867, he pleaded guilty and was discharged in June on condition of appearing if called up for sentencing.

311. Walter Walsh, Blair's Hill, Cork, and the elderly Timothy Mannix, both fishermen, accompanied Capt. Mackey when he

was arrested in February 1868 in Cronin's pub. They fought the police and tried to rescue him, while an unnamed woman acted as their lookout. Both were convicted in March 1868, sentenced to twelve months and released in February 1869.

312. William Walsh, Cork, labourer, was detained for about two weeks in October 1865 on suspicion. The informer Warner claimed that he belonged to a Fenian 'circle', but no further evidence emerged and he was discharged on condition of appearing before the authorities when called upon.

313. Col John Warren, born in Clonakilty in 1834, was a relative of Mary Jane O'Donovan Rossa and godfather of her sister Isabella. He emigrated to Boston around 1855, where he owned a liquor store and later became a journalist. He agitated to improve the conditions of the working classes and set up a company of the 63rd New York Regiment of Meagher's Irish Brigade, serving as its first captain. In 1864 Warren became the 'head centre' of the Fenian Brotherhood for New England. He was among the leaders of the *Erin's Hope* expedition. Arrested, he corresponded with Maxwell Irwin of Clonakilty and protested his rights as a naturalized US citizen, intent on increasing Anglo-American tensions. Sentenced to fifteen years, Warren was amnestied in 1871 to return to Boston. He died in an accident in 1895.[18]

314. Capt. Frank Welpley, 28, a native of Skibbereen, emigrated to New York, where he was among the founders of the Phoenix Brigade in 1858. A strong supporter of John O'Mahony, Welpley returned from Ireland after the McManus funeral to enlist in 69th New York Regiment and served with reckless bravery during the Civil War until killed at the

Siege of Petersburg in 1864. Annie O'Donovan, his widow, brought his remains back to Ireland, afterwards entering a convent.

315. Sgt Thomas J. Wise, 21, a native of Cork city, had served with the Federal Army's signal corps for two years and joined the Fenians in 1863 at the behest of Michael Cavanagh, Col O'Mahony's secretary. He featured on the Fenian Brotherhood roster.

C. Kerry

316. Peter Breen, 19, Killarney, assistant in the post office, was arrested on the word of John Sullivan, a baker in Tralee, in September 1865. The latter testified that Breen had sworn him into the IRB in Killarney to 'assist in forming a Republican government'. Breen was one of three suspects petitioning Dublin Castle that he had not been tried and asked to be discharged and leave the country on producing his ticket for America – he sailed on 7 May 1866.[19]

317. Lieut Francis F. Brennan, 21, a native of Kenmare and a Fenian since 1860. He joined the Tammany Regiment in June 1861 and subsequently 97th New York Volunteers. Brennan was severely wounded at Antietam, re-joined in the spring of 1864, but was killed in the Battle of the Wilderness. The Fenian Brotherhood roster recorded 'an able officer and a heroic man'.[20]

318. Daniel J. Buckley, 23, who left Kerry as a child for New York, was a jeweller and a member of the *Erin's Hope* contingent. Arrested shortly after arrival near Dungarvan, he was transferred from Waterford jail to Mountjoy in June 1867. His detention continued, despite the intercession of the US consul. Buckley had become a Crown witness by February 1868; FP 37.

Daniel J. Buckley, FP 37 (courtesy NAI).

319. Jeremiah Coffey, Killarney, shoemaker, was arrested as a Fenian on information received in late 1865.

320. William Collins, 20, a draper's assistant from Killarney, working in Dublin, was arrested as a Fenian suspect and detained in Kilmainham; FP 73.

321. Daniel Connell, Tralee, printer, to whose office the Fenian newspaper the *Irish People* (New York) was posted in 1866, thereby revealing his political affiliations.

322. Sgt Daniel Corcoran, 24, a native of Killarney, served in 99th New York Volunteers for four months and had been sworn into the IRB in 1865 by Mortimer Moynahan. He appeared on the roster of Fenian Brotherhood officers available for the Irish expedition.

323. John Cosgrove, Killorglin, was caught among a group marching and singing 'The Green Above the Red' near Killorglin by the constabulary in June 1868 and detained for a week.

324. Michael Cronin, Killarney, tourist guide, arrested as a Fenian in October 1865 on information received.

325. Paddy Daly, leader of the Dromad Fenians near Cahirciveen around 1866, enjoyed hunting, as did his friend Dr Barry, who warned him of an incipient police raid for guns, which Daly hid. They were never recovered and form part of the local folklore. Dr Barry's horse was 'borrowed' for Col O'Connor, the Fenian leader, during the Rising and duly returned.[21]

326. Sgt John C. Doran, 24, born in Kenmare, served with 1st Massachusetts Volunteers. He appeared on the roster of personnel available to the Fenian Brotherhood in preparation for their Irish expedition.

327. Jim Fitzpatrick, a member of an influential family who ran the hotel in Cahirciveen. He participated in the attack on Kells coastguard station in February 1867.

328. Private James Fleming, 22, a native of Kerry, served with 61st New York Volunteers for three years and joined the Brotherhood while in the army. He signed on for the roster of available Fenian personnel.

329. Robert Fleming, 18, Killarney, law clerk, was arrested in September 1865 with Peter Breen and Jeremiah Shaw on the statement of an informer and petitioned for release, promising to emigrate.

330. Patrick Foley, Tralee, marched with a pike in 1848, afterwards fleeing the country. He returned and in 1864 regularly attended the national reading room in Tralee, which was a Fenian meeting place. The authorities considered him an IRB member.

331. Capt. Patrick Foley, 24, a native of Killorglin, had been pledged as a Fenian by Michael Scanlon, one of the Chicago leaders, in 1859. He served with 23rd Illinois Volunteers for four years during the Civil War and was on the Fenian Brotherhood list of officers.

332. John Gallavin, Killarney, law clerk, arrested on 2 October 1865 on the word of an informer.

333. John Ginna, about 18, one of the young men marching in military style in Killorglin in June 1868; remanded in custody for a week.

334. John O'Neill Golden, son of Paddy Golden, farmer of Mount Foley, Kells, one of the Foilmore Fenians who participated in the Kerry Rising. He fled to Liverpool but told friends at home of his whereabouts to obtain character references in the name of 'John O'Neill' to enable his departure abroad. Arrested in Cobh on board of the ship taking him to America in July 1867, Golden was sentenced to five years, transported to Australia, but amnestied in 1869. Befriended by John Feehan of Gerringong, Sydney, a native of Cashel and a Fenian sympathizer, Golden worked on his farm from 1871 and married Feehan's daughter Ellen. He was employed as a carpenter in the construction of Jamberoo Catholic church, completed in 1879, but died of tuberculosis in 1883, requesting that 'God save Ireland' be put on his headstone. His name is spelt 'Goulding' in official records, but his relatives continue to use the original name on the Golden Mile near Kells.

335. Tom Griffin, Cahirciveen, dancing master, closed the last dance in the nationalist reading room before Lent early so that he and the men could participate in the Kerry Rising. Thirty Fenians assembled outside with pikes and rifles. Afterwards Griffin fled to Liverpool with John O'Neill Golden. They were arrested in Cobh on board the vessel for America on 19 July and tried in Tralee in August 1867.

336. Lieut Jeremiah J. Hanifin, 28, a native of Tralee, had served in the Confederate artillery during the Civil War and was listed among officers available to the Fenian Brotherhood in New York.

337. Patrick Hayes, born in Killarney in 1840, emigrated to with his family to New York around 1848. A member of the Fenian Brotherhood, Hayes joined 37th New York Irish Rifles in 1861, hoping that the Civil War would further Irish separatism. He was killed in action at Williamsburg in May 1862.

338. Capt. Cornelius Healy, born in Kenmare in 1836, emigrated to the US, served in 8th New Hampshire Volunteers for three years and became the 'head centre' of the Fenian Brotherhood in Manchester, New Hampshire. Discharged from the army in 1865, Healy travelled to Ireland in expectation of the Rising, but was arrested under the habeas corpus suspension in February 1866 and held in Tralee jail, where the US consul visited him and interceded for this naturalized citizen. Healy was liberated in March on condition he return to America.

339. John Healy, Tralee, harness-maker, a suspected Fenian, involved with Michael Power's group in the local Land League and National League and imprisoned under the Protection of Persons and Property Act, 1881.

340. John J. Healy, grocer in Henn Street, Killarney, prominent as secretary of the Manchester Martyrs procession planned for Killarney in 1867. Magistrates and police insisted on his detention in Tralee jail despite Healy's protestations of innocence in January 1868. Although female relatives depended on his support, he was not released until March on bail of £200 and two sureties of £100 each.

341. John Keane, a native of Listowel, had resided in Dublin for a month and was arrested as a Fenian suspect in Francis Street, Dublin, in March 1866.

342. Thade Keeffe, Killarney, cart-maker, was arrested on suspicion of Fenianism on information received in late 1865, but released on promise of appearing in court if called upon.

343. John Keegan, Tralee, noted as an IRB member by Dublin Castle in 1864.

344. Daniel Kelleher, Killarney National School assistant teacher, was arrested as a Fenian on information received in November 1865.

345. Kennedy, a native of Kerry, trained as a grocer's assistant in Cork before setting up his shop in a thatched house in Anascaul. He was briefly a deputy cess collector until sentenced to twelve months in Clonmel prison for an agrarian offence. His son Tagh Kennedy recalled that IRB meetings were held in their home and that of Peter Scannell, jarvey, who lived opposite him in Anascaul. The older Kennedy remained a Fenian until his death. Tagh, born in 1885, became the brigade intelligence officer, Kerry 1st brigade, IRA, under Austin Stack.

346. Joseph Looney, Killarney, gardener, arrested as a Fenian in October 1865 on information received.

347. William McCarthy, Kenmare, son of a hotel-keeper, was suspected as the companion of Fenians in 1864.

348. James Moriarty, Carrigeen, Brosna, Kerry, became an early IRB organizer, drilling recruits and keeping in touch with the 1865–7 leadership. He was connected to O'Donovan Rossa by marriage. Moriarty turned out for the 1867 Rising. In 1880 he founded a Land League branch in Brosna

and later a branch of the Labour League to improve the lives of agricultural labourers. He served as president of both and also on the local board of guardians. Moriarty acted as a successful arbitrator in agrarian and domestic disputes and died on 14 April 1919, when the local Volunteers fired shots over his grave, with the coffin draped with the tricolour. **X**

349. Michael Moriarty, a native of Cahirciveen, had emigrated to Toronto with his family as a result of the Famine. He became a Fenian, like his better-known brother Mortimer, and was arrested with Michael Murphy, the Canadian leader, on their way to join the Fenian attack on Campobello in April 1866. They later managed to escape to New York. Some authorities maintain, however, that Mortimer was the jail-breaker.

350. Capt. Mortimer Moriarty, alias O'Shea, was a native of Cahirciveen, whose memories of the Famine motivated him to join various Irish societies after his family emigrated to Toronto, where he became the first Fenian organizer. Moriarty sailed for Ireland in December 1866, when Col Kelly appointed him to Kerry, in the mistaken belief that Col O'Connor had been captured. Moriarty was informed on and seized on his way to Killarney to lead the local Fenians during the February Rising. A letter introducing him to Jeremiah Daniel Sheehan, the Killarney 'centre', was found on him, resulting in the latter's arrest and aborting any effective attempt at insurrection. At the Kerry assizes of August 1867, Moriarty was convicted and sentenced to ten years, but amnestied in 1871 on condition of exile for the remainder of his sentence.

351. Capt. Daniel C. Moynihan, 22, a native of Killarney, had taken the Fenian Brotherhood pledge in New York in 1859. He served with 164th New York Volunteers for three years, was wounded, captured and imprisoned in the notorious Libby prison of the Confederacy until paroled to become an acting ordnance officer in the Army of the Potomac. He travelled to Ireland, where he was detained under the habeas corpus suspension, eventually returning to New York to commence his career as a police officer.

352. Maurice Moynihan, Tralee, born 1864, was influenced to join the IRB by a teacher when attending St Michael's College, Listowel. A butter-merchant's clerk, he became a prominent IRB organizer and co-founder of the GAA in Tralee. By 1885 he was secretary of the GAA and rumoured to occupy the same position in the Kerry IRB. He also served on the committee of the local branch of the Young Ireland Society.

353. Cornelius Murphy, Killarney, labourer, arrested on suspicion of Fenianism in late 1865 on information received.

354. Patrick Nelligan, Tralee, stonemason, arrested for attempting to swear soldiers into the IRB in March 1869, discharged on bail.

355. M.J. Nolan, tinsman, Tralee, a Fenian suspect, who fled abroad after the Rising. On return he joined the radical element of the Tralee Land League under Michael Power and was imprisoned under the Protection of Persons and Property Act, 1881. He remained active in politics and was a founder member of the National League in Tralee; he died in October 1885.

356. Joseph Noonan (also Nunan), 1842–85, a native of Rathcormack, Co. Cork, and a successful building contractor throughout Kerry, joined the IRB in 1864 and participated in the Kerry Rising of February 1867 with some of his workmen. He had warned the authorities of what was afoot, probably

from concern for Head Constable O'Connell and family, his friends. Noonan afterwards escaped by boat to Muckross and fled to England, where he was identified and arrested in April. Although jumping from a moving train near Tamworth, Noonan was recaptured and taken to Ireland. In Killarney sympathizers attacked the police in expectation of his arrival at the railway station. Convicted and sentenced to seven years, Noonan was popular on the convict transport to Western Australia. Amnestied in 1869, he won a contract to build a bridge over the Swan river in association with fellow Fenian Hugh Brophy, giving employment to liberated comrades. By 1871 Noonan was an established architect, who married into a leading Catholic family in the colony. After the June 1870 escape of T.H. Hassett, Noonan and other trustees of a fund collected for the imprisoned Fenians were accused of failing to act, ending in Hassett's capture. Noonan was probably reluctant to implicate himself in a dangerous jailbreak, jeopardizing his new status. He contracted tuberculosis and died in Perth.

357. Tim O'Connell, 25, a boatman from Cahirciveen, was arrested in Cobh as a Fenian suspect, intending to depart for America; FP 78.

358. William O'Connell, a son of Head Constable O'Connell, Cahirciveen Barracks, whose family were sympathizers, participated in the Rising in Kerry in February 1867, was recognized during the raid on Kells coastguard station and sent for trial in August 1867. He spent the remainder of his life in the US, an acquaintance of John Devoy.

359. John James O'Connor was born in 1844 on Valentia and emigrated to Braintree, Massachusetts, as a child. He enlisted in 28th Massachusetts Volunteers in 1861,

distinguishing himself during the Civil War, and was twice severely wounded, the second time at the Siege of Petersburg in March 1865. This injury never healed properly. O'Connor had become a Fenian in the army and returned to Cahirciveen to organize for the Rising, well-spoken, discreet and in possession of funds. He had difficulty marching with the Fenians in February 1867 and a horse was 'borrowed' for him. They did not attack the constabulary barracks in Cahirciveen, which was protected by a gunboat in the harbour, but went to Kells coastguard station in search of weapons. On realizing that no other units had turned out, O'Connor went on the run, hiding in the house of Diarmaid na Bó in Glencar. He was betrayed and the military arrived to arrest him. When Diarmaid saw them he was so terrified that he would be hanged for sheltering O'Connor that he fainted. His wife saved the day by claiming that Diarmaid habitually suffered from fits and in the commotion, O'Connor managed to hide. He escaped from Cuan Trae to a ship bound for America, where he worked as a Fenian organizer in Michigan and around Lake Superior. O'Connor settled in Louisiana, married a sister of General Kenny, formerly of the Confederate Army, but died of his old wound in 1870.[22]

360. John Sarsfield O'Connor, a native of Kenmare, had been detained as a Phoenix suspect in 1858. He was the vice president of the Tralee Young Men's Society in 1863, when working in that town. This society was suspected of Fenianism, as it opposed its spiritual director and other priests by insisting on toasting the insurgents of 1798 and the exiled Young Irelanders at a St Patrick's Day banquet. The conflict led to the dismissal of O'Connor by his Catholic employers and the closure of the society by the clergy. Sympathizers presented him

with £61 to help him emigrate. Becoming a publican in Kenmare instead, O'Connor was prosecuted for selling the *Irishman* newspaper in 1865. He had also contributed items to the Chicago Fenian fair and was sympathetic towards the tenantry of the Lansdowne Estate. Dublin Castle continued to monitor his IRB involvement.

361. Lieut P.C. O'Connor, 26, a native of Tralee, fought in both the British and the Federal Army for nine years and had joined the Fenian Brotherhood in New York, being added to its roster of experienced officers.

362. William O'Connor, also William Henry O'Connor, 25, born near Tralee, where his relations continued to live, arrived in Dublin from Liverpool without valid reason. A printer, he refused to be photographed on arrest, 'before it was made compulsory'; FP 396.

363. Sgt D.O'C. O'Donoghue, 24, a native of Kerry, had served five years in the Engineer Corps of the US army, and was considered a capable, experienced officer, who joined the Brotherhood in Portland, Maine, and featured on its roster of officers.

364. Fr Edward O'Flaherty, Crawfordsville, Indiana, a native of Tralee, was an enthusiastic early Fenian and chief adviser of John O'Mahony. In 1863 he visited Ireland to meet the various 'centres' in the Dublin region, whose work he blessed, in opposition to Archbishop Cullen. O'Flaherty was the state 'centre' for Indiana. On return to the US his bishop censured him as an outspoken advocate of Fenianism. Fr O'Flaherty died suddenly in August 1863, aged about 40. He was buried in Lafayette.

365. John W. O'Neill, Cork, a native of Ahane, Brosna, appealed for donations for John Sarsfield O'Connor, who had been dismissed for his nationalist toasts on St Patrick's Day in Tralee in 1863 and

intended to emigrate. O'Neill, a well-known local Fenian, was arrested under the suspension of the habeas corpus in 1866 and also in 1872.

366. James O'Reilly, also known as Séamus Raol of Binn Bhán or 'Major Reilly', born in 1845, a shop assistant in Donoghue's Drapery, Cahirciveen, was considered a leading Fenian. Among the attackers of Kells coastguard station during the Kerry Rising of February 1867, he initially escaped and hid at home, but was spied on and reported to the authorities. O'Reilly was tried and sentenced to five years. Transported to Australia on the *Hougoumont*, he received a free pardon in 1869 and went to Melbourne in 1874 before returning to Cahirciveen. Locals recalled that he regretted not having remained 'down under'.

367. Robert O'Reilly, born in Scarriff, Caherdaniel, in 1844, was a fluent Irish speaker and clerk of the local petty sessions. He marched with the insurgents from Cahirciveen during the abortive Rising in February 1867. The only evidence against O'Reilly consisted of Col O'Connor, the Fenian commander, having stayed in his family home, which was also visited by strangers, conceivably Fenians. He was summarily dismissed from his government post. The 1901 census describes him as a farmer and rate collector. He remained a Republican and proponent of traditional culture and died in Kerry in 1923.

368. Philip O'Rourke, Fossa, Killarney, the local leader, whose 'circle' assembled in February 1867, awaiting the start of the Rising. Their activities were foiled by the arrests of Capts Moriarty and Sheehan.

369. Daniel O'Shea, Killarney, merchant, had been an early IRB member, but died in Brooklyn in 1899. His brother Eugene, a captain in the US army, had lived there

since 1856 and returned to Dublin in 1865, in constant communication with Stephens and one of his bodyguards. John, the third brother, had served in the US navy and was believed to have returned to Kerry. They hoped in vain to fight in the Rising.

370. Denis O'Shea, Kenmare, publican, was arrested as a Phoenix Society suspect in 1858. In late 1866 he was an IRB leader and organizer in this locality.

371. John O'Shea, Tralee, shipwright and Fenian, had returned from America and was in Liverpool in June 1864.

372. Daniel O'Sullivan, also Sullivan 'Agreem', to distinguish him from the informer of the same name, a national schoolteacher, 28, who was convicted of treason felony for the Phoenix conspiracy in March 1859 in Tralee and sentenced to ten years. He was discharged in April 1860 as part of a deal whereby Rossa and other members of the early IRB detained pleaded guilty. Sullivan emigrated to the US.

373. Florence O'Sullivan of Killabunane, Kenmare, was the son of Florence Roger O'Sullivan, middleman and head of one of the oldest families in the neighbourhood. Florence Jr was apprenticed to an apothecary in Killarney, where he was arrested in December 1858 as a Phoenix (early IRB) suspect. His father was also detained, although it is doubtful that he was ever a member. After his release, the son continued his medical training with a chemist in Dublin, but died young in 1862.

374. Jeremiah (or Patrick) O'Sullivan, 1845–1922, born near Cahirdaniel, the London IRB 'centre', who later claimed that he had positioned and fired the barrel that caused the Clerkenwell explosion on 13 December 1867. O'Sullivan, an athletic man, made a dramatic escape, spending the remainder of his life in New York, where he joined Clan na Gael and the IRB Veterans' Association.

375. Patsy O'Sullivan, 'Gabhan Ban', apprentice blacksmith, Anascaul, involved in agrarian agitation with Kennedy of Anascaul. Edward, brother of the notorious land agent Samuel Hussey and landlord of O'Sullivan's father, intervened to lighten their sentences when convicted. Patsy remained a lifelong Fenian, only supported by labourers and artisans on the Dingle peninsula, tenant farmers being too downtrodden for protest.

376. Dr Edmund Power, 1838–83, a native of Tralee, who studied medicine in Dublin, where he led an IRB 'circle' that infiltrated the British army. He was convicted and sentenced to fifteen years in Dublin in 1866. Serving his sentence in Millbank and Portland, Dr Power was amnestied in 1871 on condition of exiling himself. He established a practice in Oxford, New Jersey, US, distinguishing himself through his caring attitude towards the poor.

377. Capt. Michael ('Mick') Power, Tralee, was prosecuted in 1874 for burning Judge Keogh in effigy. His job as a pig-buyer served as a cover for his IRB activities. He agitated for land reform before the Land League existed. Power paid for guns, which he imported from Liverpool for distribution in Ardfert and Castleisland. He was among John O'Mahony's pall-bearers when his funeral passed through Cork in 1877. Power met Parnell in 1878 and supported him to the end. In 1880 the RIC considered Power the chief organizer of the annual Manchester Martyrs' demonstration in Tralee. He was a driving force in the Land League and the National League in this town and was imprisoned under the Protection of Persons and Property Act, 1881. An associate of William Moore Stack, John Kelly and Maurice Moynihan,

Power and his brother, Patrick, supported the early GAA in Tralee. In later life he resided in Cork, where Patrick H. Meade, a sometime mayor and IRB sympathizer, was a close friend. When he died in 1915 the Irish Volunteers provided a guard of honour. He is buried in Rath Cemetery, Tralee.

378. Col James Quirk, 34, a native of Castlegregory, and his brother, Capt. Daniel, had been officers in the Antebellum Shields Guards militia in Chicago, which had links to the Fenian Brotherhood. James had been given the Fenian pledge by Col O'Mahony in 1859. During the Civil War he served with 23rd Illinois Volunteers and was considered a most competent officer. He changed allegiance to the Senate wing during the split, drilling a reputed thousand Fenians in quarries near Chicago in preparation for the Canadian invasion of 1866. Quirk continued his commitment into the 1870s.

379. Michael Ryan, about 18, servant of Mr Butler of Waterville, had come into Killorglin with salmon and was arrested with others marching in Killorglin in June 1868. He felt his predicament and began to cry. Ryan was remanded in custody for a week.

380. John Sears, 35, born in Tralee, ensign, had been in the merchant navy for fifteen years as well as three years in the US navy. He became a Fenian in 1865 in New York and featured on the Fenian Brotherhood list of naval personnel for its invasion of Ireland.

381. Jeremiah Shaw, Killarney, manager of a tobacco department, arrested as a Fenian on information received in October 1865.

382. Jeremiah Daniel Sheehan, the son of a small farmer in Milltown, born around 1844, had served in the Papal Brigade and was subsequently a draper's assistant in Killarney. He became the local 'head centre' and was detained under the habeas corpus suspension in 1867 and eventually released on condition of exiling himself to America. Sheehan reappeared and in 1879 married Mary O'Sullivan, the widowed owner of the Innisfallen Hotel, Killarney, which they ran. In association with P.N. Fitzgerald, Sheehan revived the IRB in the Killarney district in 1878–9, but in 1885 became MP for Kerry East. He promoted land agitation, chaired the Killarney board of Poor Law guardians, was president of the local branch of the Young Ireland Society (prior to its dissolution in 1890) and also of the Killarney GAA. He retired as MP in 1895, also ran the International Hotel in Killarney, and died in 1929. His son, Dr Daniel Thomas Sheehan, born in 1883, attracted the attention of James Joyce by defending Synge's *Playboy of the Western World* during the 1907 riots.

383. John D. Sullivan, publican of William Street, Kenmare, in whose house Phoenix Society meetings were held, and where James Stephens stayed for several days in August 1858. He was described as an outwardly respectable man, when detained for some weeks as a Phoenix suspect that December. According to tradition, Sullivan had been evicted from his family's holding in Tuosist by Steuart Trench, the autocratic agent of the Lansdowne Estate. He supported Rowland Blennerhassett in the Kerry by-election of 1872 and also the Land League.

384. Capt. P.H. Sullivan, 29, a native of Kerry, served in 140th New York Volunteers for two years and is listed among Fenian Brotherhood members available for their Irish expedition.

385. Mike Tagney, Black Valley, Moll's Gap, an old Fenian, who accommodated an IRA ambush party led by Edward O'Sullivan, Beaufort, on 9 June 1921, under cover of hosting a dance. Next

morning the men moved to the tunnel on the N71 and attacked a Black and Tan convoy before escaping.

386. Sgt Patrick White, a native of Caherdaniel, had served in 9th Massachusetts Regiment for three years and featured on the Brotherhood's list of trained Fenian officers.

D. Kilkenny

387. Arthur Anderson, 28, born in Castlecomer, a silver-plate polisher employed in Newry and Liverpool. While 'head centre' of Liverpool after the arrest of George Archdeacon, Anderson appeared under the influence during the abortive Chester Castle raid and was replaced by James Chambers from Thomastown, Co. Kilkenny. Anderson was the bugle major of a volunteer corps. When the IRB tried to identify a major informer, he came under suspicion as he resembled Corridon. Anderson returned to Ireland on Fenian business and was detained in Kilmainham, which retrieved his Republican reputation; FP 6.

388. Walter Bishop, participant in some of the IRB demonstrations in Co. Kilkenny, turned informer during the arrests of 1865.

389. William Boyle, Kilkenny, a member of the Kilkenny Fenian Brotherhood committee in 1864.

390. Thomas Buskett, Kilkenny, a member of the Kilkenny IRB committee in 1864.

391. John Butler, Castlecomer, servant, suspected of being an IRB agent, active since 1864. Although unemployed and from a humble background, he was in funds and travelled about the district with George Walker, a carpenter from Coolbawn. They enlisted IRB members and collected money to purchase arms. Arrested in March 1866, Butler regretted his folly and promised to desist to be released on bail in September.

392. John Cahill, 17, grocer and agent for the *Irish People* in Ballyhale, was an active 'centre', arrested on Michael Keating's information in October 1865; he was discharged on bail in May 1866.

393. Patrick Callaghan, 25, clerk in the Callan office of Slieveardagh coal mines, had been sworn into the early IRB (Phoenix Society) by Martin Hawe during the summer of 1858, but turned informer when refused the sacraments by the parish priest of Callan. Callaghan had to be kept in Kilkenny jail to protect him from his former neighbours, but had little to relate, as he had been a lukewarm member.

394. Patrick Cantwell, arrested in Castlecomer in October 1866 for cursing the queen when tipsy.

395. Joseph Theobald Casey, 1846–c. 1907, a native of Kilkenny city and a cousin of James Stephens, whose Fenian movement he joined. Casey assisted Ricard O'Sullivan Burke's gun-running from Birmingham to Ireland and was arrested with him in London in November 1867. Their imprisonment in the Clerkenwell House of Detention triggered the disastrous rescue attempt of 13 December 1867. Acquitted but destitute, Casey appealed for donations to take him to the US during the summer of 1868. He settled in Paris with his brothers Patrick, Andrew and James, who were also Fenians. They volunteered for France during the Franco-Prussian war, when Andrew and James died of wounds after 1871. The surviving pair worked as printers on the Paris edition of the *New York Herald* and remained part of the revolutionary underground of the 1880s. Michael Davitt knew that their associates included British spies and suspected them of informing. He saw Joseph Theobald

Casey as a professional refugee, fond of dynamite and absinthe, while Joyce immortalized him in *Ulysses*.

396. Concerning his brother Patrick Casey, 1843–1908, also a Fenian on the revolutionary fringes, spymaster Robert Anderson suggested that he had assisted Richard Pigott in forging the Parnell letters for the *Times* Commission. Patrick returned to Dublin in old age, where John Stanislaus Joyce was among his drinking companions.

397. Michael Cloney, a native of Garryduff, arrived in Dublin from Manchester in December 1866. He was arrested at a Fenian meeting under the name of Thomas Simpson, 85th Regiment. This was an alias for John Patrick O'Brien, an IRB infiltrator. Cloney claimed that he wished to visit his brother William, serving with this unit, and his uncle Michael Nolan, farmer, in Garryduff. His father Patrick Cloney petitioned for his release, claiming Michael wanted to meet his family before emigrating to the US. He was discharged on condition of leaving Ireland in January 1867.

398. Major John Augustine Comerford, ex-US army, grocer, probably a native of Lowell, Massachusetts, with close family ties in Kells. Comerford travelled to Ireland and was staying with other American officers in Dublin. He was suspected of touring on Fenian business, but stated that he had accompanied Garrett, his elderly father, on a trip home. The constabulary was aware of Garrett's seditious views. Comerford was held under the habeas corpus suspension and released in April 1866 on condition of departing for America.

399. Patrick Comerford, Lady's Well, Kells, farmer and nephew of Garrett, who stayed with him on a visit home. Patrick Comerford was considered a Fenian by the constabulary and detained for three months in early 1866.

400. William Comerford, Kilkenny city, arrested in August 1866 for using seditious expressions and singing Fenian songs. He had previously escaped from the police and was remanded in custody.

401. John Connolly, 20, shoemaker from Kilshearon, Co. Tipperary, who had served in the Tipperary militia. He resided in Mullinavat, where he was arrested in October 1865 with treasonable documents in his possession. Michael Keating, a fellow Fenian, had informed on him. Connolly had sworn men into the IRB. Committed for trial in October 1865, he was detained until October 1866 and released on condition of leaving for Liverpool; FP 79.

402. James Connor, 26, Thomastown, sawyer, had attended IRB meetings and recruiting drives, sometimes accompanied by John Haltigan. Connor swore in Michael Keating, who turned informer, leading to his superior's detention in Kilkenny jail in October 1865. Connor volunteered information about himself and his associates to avoid trial, but withdrew it later. Committed for trial in November 1865, he was detained until August 1866 when he was discharged on condition of departing for America.

403. Edward (sometimes Edmund) Coyne, born in Callan in 1835, became one of the earliest EMA members in Ireland and the main IRB leader in Callan. Coyne attracted police attention on 22 February 1864 by his presence at a Fenian meeting on Slievenamon, which Charles Kickham chaired. A constable reported that a gathering in Callan town hall was jointly chaired by Coyne and James Cody and addressed by one Phelan, who stated that it was useless sending petitions to Parliament unless they were on the point of a pike. A search of the Coyne home on 16 September 1865 discovered eighteen copies of the *Irish*

People. When he was arrested in January 1866, the constables found a further box full of this paper. Coyne was only released on condition he join his brother Philip in St Louis during that summer, when his remaining family left Callan.

404. Michael Coyne, Callan, brother of Edmund and Capt. Philip Coyne of the Emmet Guards, St Louis, Missouri. Michael was detained under habeas corpus in early 1866 with other prominent local suspects and emigrated to St Louis on release, to be followed by his remaining family.

405. Patrick Culleton, 20, born in Kilbride, draper's assistant and suspected IRB man, who resided on the Quay, Waterford, where he was arrested in October 1867; FP 99.

406. Daniel Darcy, Kilkenny city, 26, cabinet maker, arrested for trying to swear in Thomas Lyons, a gunner of the Royal Artillery, in December 1865. Darcy promised him a commission and money and that the Rising would occur before the New Year. Lyons reported him to the authorities, his home was searched and patriotic decorations found. He was detained for seven months and only released on condition of going to America; FP 110.

407. John Delany, Callan, suspected of IRB membership since 1865 as an associate of Michael Heffernan Dunne.

408. Patrick Mansfield Delany, merchant and farmer, Kilkenny, after Haltigan the second local IRB 'centre' and a delegate at the McManus funeral. Delany was arrested when recruiting a militia man in 1862. Haltigan organized an IRB team under Roddy Kickham of Mullinahone to save Delany's harvest, modelled on 'The reaping of Mullough', when John O'Mahony's neighbours had done the same, while he was on the run in 1848. In September 1862 one thousand sympathizers, including 300 women, directed by artisans on jaunting cars, marched in military formation cheering loudly past Kilkenny jail, where Delany was held, to his farm. Other contingents came from Carrick-on-Suir, Ballingarry and Fethard. He was acquitted at trial but left for the US, where his fate remains unknown.

409. Peter De Loughry, 1882–1931, Kilkenny, son of Richard and a locksmith, inventor, cinema proprietor and activist, was sworn into the IRB in 1905. He attempted to revive the movement, but the Kilkenny city 'circle' was dormant by 1909. It was revived with De Loughry as 'centre' and Tom Hennessy as his deputy after a visit from Sean MacDiarmada in 1912. De Loughry followed in the footsteps of his Breslin cousins by making the key that liberated de Valera from Lincoln jail in 1919. After independence, De Loughry served as a TD and six times mayor of Kilkenny, but, outspoken like his mentor and fellow IRB man, Edward Thomas Keane of the *Kilkenny People*, his strong anti-clericalism damaged his political career.

410. Richard De Loughry, Kilkenny city, iron-founder and early IRB member, familiar with Stephens and the original leadership. He was a cousin of John J. Breslin, who sprang Stephens from Richmond bridewell. De Loughry emigrated to the US and became a member of Clan na Gael, but returned in 1872 and participated in fundraising events for the Manchester Martyrs, imprisoned Fenians and the exiled Stephens. A determined character, Richard was one of the GAA founders in Kilkenny, also associated with its working-men's club, which was a Fenian meeting place. Strongly anticlerical, he took the Parnellite side in the split. He died in 1895.

411. Patrick Devereux, Callan, small farmer, kept open house for Fenian drilling

until the suspension of the Habeas Corpus Act in February 1866. ✗

412. Patrick Doran, 21, a native of Kilkenny, employed in the Dowlais iron works in Methyr Tydfil, Wales. Arrested while drilling in December 1867, Doran was suspected of being an IRB 'centre', convicted and sentenced to seven years. He bore scrofula scars, a form of tuberculosis; FP 124.

413. Richard Dowling, Kilkenny, was acquitted of having shot at James Maher, 8th Regiment, who had informed on the military Fenians, in Hoey's pub in Dublin in April 1866. Dowling was subsequently rearrested under the habeas corpus suspension.

414. Patrick Downey, 32, miller and millwright in Goresbridge, who had been born in Australia but returned to Kilkenny, was suspected of being the Gowran 'head centre'. He consulted with John Haltigan, the chief organizer for Kilkenny. In March 1866 Downey absconded to avoid arrest. On return he associated with the disaffected in Goresbridge and Graigue and was imprisoned from April 1867 to March 1868. Although the magistrates were reluctant to release him, the prison doctor stated that Downey was spitting blood and suffering from tuberculosis. He was shadowed by the constabulary on discharge.

415. John Dunne, an unemployed grocer's assistant from Kilmoganny, was arrested at the lodgings of Thomas Dogherty Brohan in Dublin on 1 March 1866, but released in June on condition he emigrate to America.

416. Michael Heffernan Dunne, Callan, nail-maker, an early IRB member and recruiter. A democrat, described as the 'honest artisan', Heffernan Dunne pretended to stand for Parliament in a flamboyant campaign throughout Kilkenny in 1865. He mocked constitutional politics as benefitting only the rich and publicized physical force as an alternative. Arrested under the Habeas Corpus Suspension Act in February 1866, he was released on bail on health grounds in August. In 1872 he opposed Fr Robert O'Keeffe of Callan during his controversy with Cardinal Cullen about the control of local education. Heffernan Dunne informed the press that Fr O'Keeffe had 'virulently' denounced his democratic aspirations in 1865, preaching submission to authority, which the priest opposed when his own interests were concerned.[23]

417. Tobias Dunne, Callan, an IRB suspect associated with Michael Heffernan Dunne, held in Kilkenny jail in February 1866.

418. William Dunphy, Kilkenny, housepainter, suspected as a Fenian agent as he worked very little but spent his money freely, especially among soldiers. Dunphy was constantly in the company of suspected persons. When searched by the police, a new mould for casting bullets was found on him. Detained in Kilkenny jail from March to May 1866, when Fr Simon Fogarty successfully petitioned that, if released, sufficient funds would be found for the Dunphy family to emigrate.

419. John Fitzgerald, Knockbrack, Mullinavat, farmer, was suspected as an IRB agent, as American officers had stayed with him. Mr Moore, R.M., Rosbercon, had him imprisoned in March 1867, but locals were afraid to testify, despite tipping off the police. Loyal subjects breathed more freely since his arrest. Fitzgerald stated that returning from Waterford fair under the influence, he was coerced into accommodating a stranger, given the disturbed state of the country. He pleaded that his farm was suffering during his imprisonment and referred the authorities to Ambrose Cosgrave, J.P., his landlord. He was discharged on substantial bail in May.

420. John Fitzpatrick, Damerstown, Castlecomer, of good family, but an active IRB man since 1865. He fled in early 1866 after the habeas corpus suspension, returned and was arrested that December and held in Kilkenny. To resume work on the family farm, he offered to abandon Fenianism and was released on bail in January 1867.

421. James Grace, 16, son of a publican in Thomastown, was involved in Fenian drilling during the summer of 1865. A seditious letter was found during a police search of his home, resulting in his imprisonment from February to April 1866. Grace was freed through a petition signed by the principal inhabitants of Thomastown.

422. Henry Grady, baker and agent for the *Irish People* newspaper in Kells, was suspected of running a shebeen while supporting sedition. He was arrested in April 1866 and imprisoned for some months in Kilkenny jail.

423. James Haltigan, eldest son of John, was born in Kilkenny in 1847, worked on the *Irish People* and became a Fenian agent in Dublin and Kilkenny during 1866. The police believed him to be the 'centre' for Borris, Co. Carlow, and Arthur Kavanagh, MP, demanded his arrest. Haltigan emigrated to America, where he edited and published the *Sunday Citizen*, 1873–7, which was set up with an inheritance received by John O'Mahony and supported by the Fenian Brotherhood. James subsequently published the *Illustrated Celtic Monthly*, 1879–84, a mixture of nationalist articles, poetry and antiquarian and travel essays of Irish and American interest with attractive illustrations. James Haltigan spent the rest of his career working for the New York *Irish World* and died in 1917. Patrick, a younger brother, also worked as a printer on emigrating to New York, eventually receiving a law degree

from Georgetown University and becoming reading clerk of the House of Representatives in Washington.

424. John Haltigan, born in Kilkenny in 1819, was brought up on a small farm and apprenticed to the printing trade. By 1855 he owned a little land and was employed as the foreman printer of the *Kilkenny Journal*. Haltigan cherished the Young Ireland legacy and became a vital contact for the spread of the Fenian movement in Kilkenny. He remained an important leader before relocating to Dublin to work on the *Irish People*, where he set up another 'circle'. His wife, Catherine Keating, was also a nationalist whose sister had married Patrick Nowlan of Kilkenny, another dedicated, early IRB man. (Haltigan's activities are covered in the main text.) After the amnesty of 1869 he joined his son James in the US and acted as his foreman printer from 1873. On returning home in 1877, he worked for the *Cork Examiner* and died in 1884. He is buried under an imposing Celtic cross in St Patrick's graveyard, Kilkenny, erected by public subscription. His wife died in 1899. According to Kilkenny tradition, the IRB raised funds for his support, but this may have been for his widow.

425. Martin Hawe, 24, Kilkenny, leather merchant, an IRB (Phoenix Society) recruiter in Callan during the summer of 1858. Arrested on the word of Patrick Callaghan, he was the only Co. Kilkenny prisoner still detained in March 1859. The nationalist press protested at the postponement of his trial, given the lack of evidence. Hawe was eventually released and continued to recruit, a strong supporter of Stephens and O'Mahony. He was still residing in Kilkenny in 1894 when visited by O'Donovan Rossa.

426. Martin Hayes, Royal Artillery, was stationed in Kilkenny and arrested for

voicing Fenian sentiments, insubordination and desertion. Convicted at his court martial in December 1866, Hayes was flogged, drummed out of the army and branded with the letters 'BC' [bad character], as well as imprisoned for three months.

427. James Hetherington, baker in Mullinavat, was an active IRB leader during 1865 and in contact with Edward Coyne. He acted as the courier of the Carrick-on-Suir Fenians under William Meagher and was identified by Head Constable Talbot. Betrayed by Michael Keating, he absconded in November 1865 and was later arrested and discharged on bail in October 1866. Re-arrested in March 1867 in Ballybricken, Co. Waterford, Hetherington was detained until September, when the medical officer of Waterford jail feared for his sanity.

428. Patrick Hickey, who had treasonable documents in his possession and used seditious language, was arrested in Mullinavat in October 1865 and detained in Kilkenny jail until the next petty sessions.

429. James Holland, Kilkenny, mason and militia man, without ostensible means of support but consorting with suspected Fenians and spending money freely, especially on soldiers. The authorities were convinced that he was a paid Fenian agent and detained him in Kilkenny jail in March 1866. Holland petitioned that his brother was prepared to finance his emigration, which was agreed in June, although he remained in Kilkenny after release.

430. John Joyce, born in Kilkenny, a sailor with great experience, enrolled in the Fenian Brotherhood list for the invasion of Ireland by 1865.

431. John Kavanagh, relieving officer of the Kilkenny poor law union and a man of excellent character was among the IRB

leaders of this county in 1864. Later suspected of being the local 'head centre', Kavanagh led a working-class crowd in Kilkenny city to support Heffernan Dunne's mock candidature for Parliament. In December 1865 Kavanagh was observed consulting with Fenian Brotherhood agents from America. In March 1866 he was imprisoned for five months.

432. William Kavanagh, 30, Bridge Street, Callan, nailer, recently returned from America, arrested in January 1859 as a Phoenix Society member, informed on by Patrick Callaghan. Discharged from Kilkenny jail within a week because of insufficient evidence after a magistrates' inquiry.

433. John Kenna, Castlecomer, 'head centre', was in contact with John Kavanagh of Kilkenny, who asked him to bring 200 men into this city for an election demonstration for Heffernan Dunne in 1865. Kenna absconded abroad to avoid arrest.

434. Private Martin Kenny, 64th Regiment, observed at Fenian meetings in the house of Thomas Tobin, Castlecomer, prior to March 1866.

435. James Lalor, Friary Street, Kilkenny, was the son of a building contractor and became the vice commandant, 1st battalion, Kilkenny brigade, in 1917–8 and subsequently held the same rank in the Kilkenny brigade, IRA, 1918–21. Lalor was sworn into the IRB, aged seventeen, by Peter De Loughry, the local 'centre', in his home in Parliament Street in 1905. Meetings were held at irregular intervals, usually on Sundays in Tom Stallard's garden in Kilkenny. The twenty members of the 'circle' were occasionally visited by an IRB representative from Dublin and exhorted to keep the organization alive. The Irish Volunteers were established in this city after a meeting on 5 March 1915 addressed by Roger Casement and Thomas

McDonagh. Lalor joined and was involved in preparations for the Rising.

436. James Lawless, born in Kilkenny and employed in building the Augustinian Church, Thomas Street, Dublin, while involved in Fenian drilling. He later joined the Dublin militia to continue his military training with impunity.

437. John Lawless, 29, a native of Kilkenny, bricklayer, resided on Michael's Hill, Dublin; FP 265.

438. Patrick Lawlor, 20, a native of Graiguenamanna, nailer, resident in Dublin; FP 263.

439. John Locke, 1847–89, national teacher, Callan, tried to revive the IRB in 1867 after Coyne and Cody's departure for America. Locke was held in Kilkenny jail by April and was released for America in August, having lost his job. Fr Robert O'Keeffe of Callan, later notorious for the 'big chapel' controversy, championed him. He won fame with his somewhat sentimental poetry, especially 'Dawn on the Irish Coast' and published two novels in the US, but his private life was tragic – his only child died young. Locke is buried in Calvary Cemetery, New York, under a white marble Celtic cross, erected by the Kilkenny Men's Association.

440. Francis Lowe, Callan, suspected on foot of his association with Michael Heffernan Dunne since 1865.

441. David Lynch, Callan, miller's son, detained in Kilkenny jail in February 1866 as a persistent Fenian and associate of Michael Heffernan Dunne. He emigrated to America. For his brother, see below.

442. John Lynch, Callan, miller's son, held in Kilkenny jail in February 1866 as a suspected Fenian, copies of the *Irish People* having been found in the family home. He protested his innocence, supported by Fr Robert O'Keeffe, parish priest of Callan, and was discharged on bail in July 1866. Lynch fled to America.

443. Private John McEvoy, Kilkenny militia, was sworn into the IRB in Murphy's pub, Kilkenny city, in 1862 by Patrick Mansfield Delany, one of two local 'centres'. McEvoy had second thoughts and informed the authorities, which led to Delany's arrest and trial. IRB attempts to induce McEvoy to remove himself, a key witness, by emigrating, failed. However, his testimony proved insufficient for Delany's conviction.

444. Capt. Patrick McGrath, Chicago, 23rd Illinois Regiment, arrived in Ireland in July 1865 and was posted to Kilkenny, where he remained until it emerged that the Rising would not take place that year.

445. Michael Malone, born in Kilkenny, cousin of Stephens and an IRB member on the Kilkenny committee, later employed in building the Augustinian Church in Thomas Street, Dublin. He joined the Dublin militia with James Lawless to enable them to drill in safety.

446. Thomas Mangan, also Mannion, 29, Mill Lane, Callan, nailer, was arrested in January 1859 on the word of the informer Patrick Callaghan as a member of the early IRB (Phoenix Society). Mangan was released from Kilkenny jail soon after an official inquiry, which found no corroborative evidence.

447. Jack and Ned Marnell, Callan, members of the IRB, as recalled by painter Tony O'Malley, their grand-nephew.

448. Edward Martin, Kilkenny, transferred to Dublin with Haltigan in 1863 to work on the *Irish People*. He assisted with establishing Haltigan's IRB 'circle' in Dublin, but emigrated to London after the arrests of 1865, where he died in an accident in 1869. Initially misidentified as Col

Thomas Kelly, Martin was given a public funeral to St Patrick's RC Cemetery, Leytonstone, London. The author discovered a newspaper account, which led Charles McLauchlan of Manchester to his grave, where the National Graves Association erected a memorial tablet.

449. Lieut Albert E. Mathew, 31, a native of Kilkenny city, served three years in 1st Frontier Cavalry and had been a pledged member of the Fenian Brotherhood since 1864. He featured on its 1865 list of experienced officers as available for the Irish expedition.

450. Michael Milled, Callan, small farmer, suspected of swearing young men into the IRB in 1866.

451. John Moylan, 24, a native of Kilkenny, had served in the Irish constabulary and the British army before emigrating and joining the Fenian Brotherhood in 1865 in Massachusetts; on its roster of experienced officers.

452. James Nixon, 26, Thomastown, a carpenter held in Kilkenny jail in October 1865 on the evidence of Michael Keating, who identified him as an IRB member. John Haltigan had appointed Nixon, who had served in the militia, as drill sergeant, which activity took place at night near the Thomastown workhouse.

453. Edward Nowlan, Kilkenny, a representative at the funeral of Terence B. McManus in 1861.

454. Alderman James Nowlan, 1862–1924, son of Patrick, trained as a cooper, working in Kilkenny for Smithwick and in Dublin with Guinness. He became a long-serving, conciliatory IRB officer, joined the Confederation Hurling Club and was its secretary during the 1890s. This team lost the all-Ireland final against Cork in 1894. A strong supporter of the Irish language and member of the Gaelic League, Nowlan was elected to Kilkenny corporation from 1899–1910. He was president of the GAA from 1901–21. Police reports mention him attending the funeral of James Stephens in 1901. He joined Sinn Féin from the start and became one of the organizers of the Irish Volunteers in Kilkenny, after the departure of the Redmondite majority, alongside Peter De Loughry, Tom Stallard, Patrick Corcoran and Edward Comerford, all Kilkenny IRB stalwarts. Nowlan was arrested and interred after the 1916 Rising, in which he did not participate, and in 1919. He died in 1924 and was buried in an unmarked grave in Glasnevin Cemetery, a situation since rectified by the GAA.

455. Patrick Nowlan, cooper and early IRB man, left his native Kilkenny for employment in Cassidy's distillery in Monasterevin, Kildare, for some years. On his return Nowlan continued his involvement in all things Irish, assisting in the administration of a fund apparently meant for John Haltigan, formerly the city's first IRB 'centre', who had returned to spend his last years in Ireland. Nowlan was also a friend of James Stephens.

456. Thomas O'Bolger, originally Bolger, born in Kilkenny in 1846, a shoemaker whose family migrated to Dublin when he was a teenager. A determined IRB man, he went to England in late 1865, prepared to fight in the postponed Rising. Dublin Castle considered him addicted to drink. O'Bolger became a local leader and participated in the Manchester rescue in September 1867. His brother was also an IRB man and both later fled. By 1876 Thomas O'Bolger lived in Hoboken, New Jersey, and was a Clan na Gael leader. He may have travelled to Britain for the Clan. He was seriously injured in an accident in Rochester, New York, and died in 1911.

457. James O'Callaghan worked as an assistant teacher in Ballyhane National School, Kilkenny. A warrant for the arrest of this suspect was issued in November 1865, but he had fled.

458. Jeremiah O'Farrell, 21, Kilkenny, clerk and enthusiastic Fenian, who went to Dublin as caretaker of the *Irish People* office. Arrested in September 1865 but released on bail in poor health, O'Farrell was re-arrested in March 1866. He eventually emigrated to New York, where he died in 1889.

459. James O'Shea, member of the Fenian Brotherhood in Callan in 1864.

460. Denis O'Sullivan, 1837–1921, the Callan-born grand-nephew of the Gaelic diarist, Humphrey O'Sullivan, was a national schoolteacher in Ballydonnell, Co. Tipperary. Arrested as an early IRB member in January 1859, O'Sullivan continued his Fenian activities on release shortly afterwards and was shielded by the parish priest of Mullinahone. He fled to America when re-arrest threatened in 1865, gaining a doctorate in mathematics from Fordham University and going on to write mathematical textbooks.

461. Sgt Thomas Phelan, master tailor of the Kilkenny militia, whose father had fought at Waterloo, was suspected as a Fenian by the police. He was the first to be arrested in Kilkenny under the habeas corpus suspension of February 1866. Imprisoned in Dublin, the mayor and magistrates of Kilkenny intervened to declare him innocent, resulting in his release three weeks later.

462. Ryan, Kilkenny city, baker, arrested in December 1866 for using traitorous language, cursing the government and the police, but released on his own bail of £10 and that of two others of £5 as guarantees for his future good behaviour.

463. Michael Tallent, Gathabawn, Johnstown, had his home searched but nothing was discovered. However, he was arrested in February 1866 on information given to the constabulary.

464. Thomas Tobin, Castlecomer, butcher and prominent Fenian, whose house became an IRB meeting place and remained under police observation. After the arrests of Butler and Walker the constabulary hoped that this would disrupt Fenian communications with other places, but Tobin continued his activities. He was detained from March to May 1866.

465. Edward Toomey, 26, a native of Callan, storekeeper on a US navy vessel, had returned to stay with his father in October 1865. The constabulary considered him a Fenian. Toomey left for Liverpool but returned, claiming that he couldn't get a ship. He was detained from December 1866 to September 1867 and discharged on condition of working his passage from Liverpool to New York; FP 487.

466. James Walsh, Callan, among those suspected of IRB membership as associates of Michael Heffernan Dunne since 1865.

467. James Walsh, Hugginstown, son of a respectable farmer, was arrested under the habeas corpus suspension as a suspected Fenian in March 1866.

468. Joseph Walsh, Castlecomer, farmer, a Fenian captain who had recently returned and was still working for the movement in late 1866.

469. Patrick Walsh, farmer's son, brought to Kilkenny jail under the habeas corpus suspension in March 1866.

470. Capt. Richard C. Walsh, 28, Knocktopher, an artillery man, served four years in 1st Missouri battery and rose from private to captain. He had joined the Fenian

Brotherhood in St Louis, Missouri, and featured on the Fenian Brotherhood roster of officers.

471. Thomas Walsh, Callan, a suspect associating with Michael Heffernan Dunne since 1865.

472. Thomas Whelan, nailer and Kilkenny militia man, whom the police suspected in a general way. Arrested in February 1866, the mayor and magistrates of Kilkenny intervened and he was discharged three weeks later.

E. Limerick

473. Thomas Aherne, 22, was sentenced to one year's imprisonment for the attack on the Kilmallock constabulary barracks in March 1867.

474. Jonathan Allen, Boherboy, Limerick, 25, unemployed teacher, had attempted to entice soldiers into the early IRB, was unable to give bail and suffered imprisonment instead. This led to his small British army pension being discontinued. He was paralysed on his left side. Allen continued to have access to money and acted as secretary of the committee organizing the Manchester Martyrs' procession in Limerick on 8 December 1867. (Mrs Hogan, his respectably married sister, also participated.) He was detained for a second time from January to June 1868, having an appeal for funds for the families of the Manchester Martyrs in his pocket; FP 5.

475. Fr Robert Ambrose, born Dunganville, Ardagh, in 1851, a farmer's son who joined the IRB with his older brother Stephen. They participated in the attack on Ardagh constabulary barracks during the 1867 Rising, when Stephen was wounded. Robert got him to safety by travelling at night until they reached Ballysteen National School, whose master was married to Mary

Ambrose, the boys' aunt. Stephen escaped to the US. Robert was eventually arrested, but discharged, aged sixteen, in November 1867. Some years later he studied for the priesthood and was ordained in Maynooth. While serving in Ardagh during 1886–91 he organized the tenants to resist rack-renting. Fr Ambrose concluded his clerical career as parish priest of Glenroe to die in April 1926.

476. John Barrett, 25, born in Croom, a first-class fireman on shipboard for twelve months, who had become a Fenian in New York in 1863. Barrett was listed among the Fenian personnel for the invasion of Ireland.

477. Patrick Barrett, 28, Kilmallock insurgent, arrested after the attack on the local barracks in 1867.

478. Michael Barry, a young man in possession of £28 in gold and only a carpet bag, arrested in Cobh on 11 March 1867 while attempting to purchase a steamer ticket for America. The constabulary suspected him of having participated in the attack on the Kilmallock barracks.

479. Patrick Bayley, Francis Street, Limerick, ship carpenter, arrested under habeas corpus suspension in February 1866.

480. Thomas Begley, Bruree, 19, had been among the IRB men assembling at Bruree bridge, sentenced to one year for participating in the attack on the Kilmallock barracks.

481. Richard Bermingham, Tankardstown, led the Bruree insurgents towards Kilmallock for the attack on the constabulary barracks in March 1867.

482. Thomas Blackwell, a native of Cappamore, who returned from America and was very active with other suspects. Blackwell was arrested in early 1866. He

withstood attempts to turn him into an informer during an eighteen-month detention without trial.

483. Daniel Blake, Bruree, an insurgent, who was shot dead during the attack on Kilmallock RIC Barracks.

484. Daniel Bradley, born in 1847, draper's assistant in Kilfinane, engaged in swearing men into the IRB. He was among those planning the attack on Kilmallock barracks in March 1867. Bradley participated and was convicted and sentenced to ten years. Transported to Western Australia, he received a conditional pardon in 1871 and left the colony the following year.

485. Matthew Brazil, Kilfinane, land surveyor, whom the constabulary considered a committed Fenian, often accompanying Capt. Dunne, the chief agent in Charleville, and others in Kilmallock, driving about the country with suspects at night in early 1866.

486. John Brennan, Limerick city, last maker, among suspected Fenians arrested during a night raid in November 1866, when quantities of bullets and several pikes were seized in the Pennywell district.

487. Matthew Brennan, Patrick Street, Limerick, grocer, arrested in February 1866 as a suspect under the habeas corpus suspension and detained in the county jail.

488. Thomas Brown, Ballingarry, Limerick, schoolmaster, arrested in October 1865 and taken to Limerick jail as a suspected Fenian.

489. Edmund Burke, Kilteely, suspected of participation in the Rising of 1867 and detained in Limerick jail for some months.

490. Thomas Burke, Limerick city, tobacco spinner, an IRB member known to the constabulary, who participated in the Manchester Martyrs demonstration there on 8 December 1867.

491. Patrick Cagney, Rathkeale, formerly of the Federal Army, arrested in October 1865 and detained in Limerick jail as a suspected Fenian.

492. Edmond Cahill, 1841–95, Kilteely, farmer, was arrested for involvement in the Rising in Kilteely in March 1867. He had recently married and claimed to have been coerced into participating. Cahill was among the few from Kilteely discharged on bail. In 1890 he emigrated to the US and died in Brooklyn.

493. Richard Cahill, 21, farmer's son, observed among the Kilteely Fenians during the Rising in March 1867 and suspected as the 'centre' for this district. He fled, but was arrested in Cobh and sentenced to nine months.

494. Philip Cantillon, Bruree, was among local IRB members assembled at the railway bridge to participate in the attack on Kilmallock constabulary barracks.

495. Robert Cantillon, 23, was sentenced to one year's imprisonment for the attack on the Kilmallock barracks in March 1867.

496. John Carmody, Limerick, butter-merchant and leading organizer of the local Manchester Martyrs' procession on 8 December 1867. Dublin Castle detained him as an IRB man from January to March 1868. His release on health grounds was due to Sir James Spaight, a magistrate, who thought Carmody's Fenianism minor, although Oliver Moriarty, R.M. for Limerick, disagreed.

497. John Carroll, 20, Cromhill, tailor, a leader of the Kilteely Fenians, who had assembled his men at Nicker on 5 March 1867. They went through the district to get hold of arms before returning to Kilteely to occupy the constabulary barracks, which had been vacated. They were unable to join the Tipperary Rising via Emly, as

Col T.F. Bourke's force had been dispersed at Ballyhurst. Carroll and his brother hid the Fenian arsenal in Kilteely chapel, but the constabulary eventually seized these weapons. Carroll fled but was arrested in Cobh, accompanied by his sister, when attempting to buy a steamer ticket for America. He was sentenced to two years, but returned to participate in the Tipperary amnesty meeting of 1869.

498. Henry Casey, Fedamore, c. 1849–1914, weaver, joined the IRB when still a boy and served as local secretary of both the Land League and the Irish National League under Parnell and Davitt. Casey assisted in boycotting obnoxious individuals and was also active in the Irish Land and Labour Association, which championed the workers. He pressurized the local board of guardians to erect labourers' cottages to replace sub-standard housing. After the 1890 split he became an anti-Parnellite. A devout Catholic, Casey was a close friend of John Daly and William Lundon. He was instrumental in promoting the 1798 centenary in his district.

499. Robert Casey, master of Rathkeale workhouse, was taken to Limerick jail on suspicion of Fenianism in February 1866. He had been previously detained.

500. Thomas Childerhouse, Limerick, cork-cutter, walked in the Manchester Martyrs demonstration in this city in December 1867 and was probably a Fenian.

501. Timothy Cleary, a farmer's son from Bulgaden, had been charged for participating in the attack on Kilmallock barracks on 6 March 1867. In Limerick jail since April, the resident magistrate reported that it was impossible to obtain evidence to convict Cleary as the chief witness had vanished and another prisoner, who initially volunteered to testify, had withdrawn. Cleary declared himself in delicate health – a

euphemism for tuberculosis – and pleaded innocence. He promised 'never to have anything to do with Fenianism' again and requested release on bail. This was granted in late August.[24]

502. John Clery, 19, Kilmallock, the son of a respectable farmer and a cousin of Dr Clery killed during the Rising, was committed for trial at the Limerick special commission for participating in the attack on Kilmallock barracks.

503. Fr Edward Clifford, a native of Effin and curate of Loughill, on the Limerick side of the Shannon estuary, sheltered a number of Fenians escaping after the failure of the attack on Kilmallock barracks in 1867. He helped them to board ships at Foynes to reach America. Fr Clifford died in 1924.

504. John Coleman, alias John Hickie, Ballyloughnane, had fled the country from Kilmeedy to avoid arrest. In January 1867 the constabulary in Newcastle West received information that Coleman had returned and boasted that 150 American officers had arrived, determined to initiate the Rising.

505. Thomas Collins, Murroe, an elderly nationalist, died in June 1940. In his youth he had been an IRB member and on one occasion successfully delivered a consignment of arms from Limerick city to Ballyvara near Barrington's Bridge.

506. James Condon, publican in Killmalock, where the magistrates wanted to cancel the licences of anyone connected with the Rising. Fenian meetings were held in his pub, but Condon said he was unaware of them and any decision concerning him was postponed in October 1867.

507. Capt. Patrick Joseph Condon, born in Cahirmoyle in 1831, fought with 63rd New York State Volunteers and returned to

Ireland. He was detained under the habeas corpus suspension between March and July 1866. Protesting against his treatment as a naturalized US citizen, he tried to gain political capital for the movement. Condon returned for a second time, using the alias George O'Dell to command the Fenians in east Cork for the Rising, but was betrayed by the informer Corridon and arrested on 2 March 1867. Acquitted of high treason, which rested on the testimony of informers, Capt. Condon was discharged on condition of returning to the US in July 1867. He was married to a sister of Capt. John McClure. (Not to be confused with Patrick Condon alias Godfrey Massey.)

508. Willie Condon, 1840–1908, a native of the Mitchelstown district, who settled in Anglesboro. A follower of John O'Mahony, he joined the IRB. Condon was with the two O'Neills, John Lysaght, John Linehan and John McCarthy, armed supporters of Peter O'Neill Crowley in Kilclooney Wood, who escaped arrest. He had a green silk flag made for the first anniversary of the Rising, which featured prominently at Land League demonstrations, in which Condon played a leading role in Anglesboro, Ballylanders and Mitchelstown. Even Clifford Lloyd, a feared police officer favouring coercion, withdrew when Condon's supporters and the Fenian flag advanced on him. He was also present in Mitchelstown on 9 September 1887, protesting among 15,000 people, when the police opened fire, resulting in the Mitchelstown massacre. Towards the end of his life Condon served on the committee, which erected the statue of John Mandeville in the Square in Mitchelstown. His daughter, Hannah Condon Cleary, a Cumann na mBan leader, hid the flag inside a flour sack, which was buried in a milk can during the War of Independence. It survives to the present day.

509. James Connell, Kilteely, labourer, had been seen among the Kilteely insurgents and was arrested in June 1867, but evidence proved insufficient for a conviction. He was detained in Limerick jail until August. His memorial for release claimed that he had been forced to join the Rising and had committed no violence. Connell was discharged on bail.

510. Denis Connors, 19, Kilmallock, dealer, was convicted for the attack on the eponymous constabulary barracks in March 1867 on the lesser charge of Whiteboyism and sentenced to one year by the special commission in Limerick.

511. Joseph Connors, 27, Kilscannell, participated in the attack on Ardagh constabulary barracks and was afterwards arrested, remanded to the next assizes and eventually discharged on bail.

512. Capt. Michael Cook, 35, born in Co. Limerick, served three years with 72nd New York Volunteers and joined the Brotherhood in Buffalo in 1861; he was included on the Fenian roster for the projected invasion of Ireland.

513. Nicholas Corbett of Newtown Mahon, Limerick, clerk in the Chamber of Commerce, a very active IRB member, who attended all the important meetings and military lectures in O'Brien's pub, where cartridge-making was taught. He was detained from February to September 1866 as a dangerous individual. In early 1867 the constabulary considered him the acting 'centre' for Limerick city. Corbett solicited funds for the IRB after the Rising and was again detained from July 1867 until March 1868, despite a medical report that his life might be in danger. On discharge on substantial bail, he continued under police observation and was seen in the company of Edmond O'Donovan in July 1869, presumably on Fenian business.

514. Lieut Thomas M. Costelloe, 26, a native of Rathkeale, had been sworn into the IRB in Dublin in 1860. On emigrating he served two and a half years with 170th New York Volunteers and featured on the list of available Fenian Brotherhood officers.

515. Jeremiah Coughlan, Tipperary/east Limerick border, had participated in the occupation of Emly barracks and fled to America afterwards. He returned and acted as leader of the east Limerick crowd at the Tipperary amnesty demonstration on 24 October 1869. Coughlan warned his audience to stay sober, denying the constabulary any excuse to interfere.

516. Cornelius Cremin, 27, Garrynacoona, Effin, was among the attackers of the Ardagh constabulary barracks in March 1867. He was arrested, remanded to the assizes and eventually discharged on bail.

517. John Crowe, Limerick, treasurer of the IRB in that city and assistant to P.N. Fitzgerald from the 1880s on, kept a low profile, but was involved in erecting the Manchester Martyrs' monument in Mount St Lawrence Cemetery in 1887. He served as a leading member of the local amnesty committee during the 1890s and became the 'centre' for Limerick after the death of Richard Troy in 1892. His son, Michael, continued the family's IRB involvement into the early twentieth century.

518. Patrick Crowley, Bruree, assembled at the local railway bridge to attack the Kilmallock constabulary barracks. He was arrested and discharged on bail.

519. Daniel Curley, 18, Bruree, among those assembled at the railway bridge to participate in the attack on Kilmallock barracks, was arrested but later bailed.

520. Cornelius Daly, William Street, Limerick, clerk, arrested under the habeas corpus suspension in February 1866.

521. Edward Daly, 1848–90, Limerick, a brother of John, joined the IRB in his youth, was imprisoned in 1866 with the Pennywell suspects and participated in the Emly and Kilteely episodes during the Rising. His female relations were also energetic supporters. Edward joined the Limerick Amnesty Association. According to his daughter Kathleen, 'the delicacy resulting from his youthful imprisonment under the dreadful conditions prevailing' caused his early death.[25] Edward Daly's posthumous son of the same name was executed as one of the leaders of the 1916 rising.

522. John Daly, 1845–1916, Limerick, joined the IRB in 1863, was arrested for swearing in a man, but released in time to participate in the Rising. Afterwards he fled to America. He returned to work as an attendant in a mental home in England and became an IRB organizer during the 1870s. In 1884 he was sentenced to penal servitude for life as a dynamiter, having acted on behalf of Clan na Gael. Daly was released after a hunger strike in 1896, returned to Limerick and opened a successful bakery. He was elected mayor of Limerick three times from 1899 onwards. He introduced his fellow prisoner Tom Clarke to his late brother's family, leading to Clarke's marriage with his niece Kathleen, another committed revolutionary.

523. Thomas Daly, born in Kilmallock in 1846, had participated in the attack on Kilmallock barracks in March 1867. He escaped after the failure of the Rising, but was arrested in Cork and sentenced to five years. Transported to Western Australia, he returned to Ireland on receiving a free pardon in 1869.

524. Capt. Patrick Deveny, 27, Bruff, served four years in 10th Illinois Volunteers and joined the Fenian Brotherhood in 1865. He was listed among the officers of

the Brotherhood in 1865, in preparation for the invasion of Ireland.

525. John Thomas Dixon, Nicker, shoemaker, arrested after the Rising. The authorities considered him a leading participant in Kilteely, but found it difficult to obtain evidence or arrest other important suspects. Dixon volunteered to inform in Limerick jail, pointing to Michael Grogan, a farmer's son from Kilteely, as the leader. The resident magistrate considered the informer 'the most abject cowardly creature', who was transferred to Ballybough Crown witness depot near Dublin for his safety. He was mentioned in the 1868 list of informers in the *Irishman* as Thomas Dixon, in receipt of a reward of £25 with outfit and free ticket to Melbourne.[26]

526. Owen Donegan, car-driver for Sullivan's hotel and transport business in Kilmallock, was arrested on 5 March 1867 together with 'centre' Daniel Liddy in Limerick city. Donegan was in possession of £55 and Oliver Moriarty, R.M., considered him one of Liddy's messengers, just as the Rising was to break out. Donegan petitioned Dublin Castle in May that the main charge against him was the money found on him and that he suffered from eye disease, having been operated on by Sir William Wilde. He feared that prolonged imprisonment would render him totally blind and was discharged on bail in July 1867, when Kilmallock welcomed him home with a triumphal arch of green branches and houses specially decorated in his honour.

527. Francis Donnellan, Thomondgate, Limerick, publican and mechanic for Messrs Russell, arrested under habeas corpus suspension in February 1866 as a Fenian 'centre', in whose house meetings had been held, attended by Col Byron and other leading agents. The authorities in Limerick decreed him to be one of thirteen 'dangerous' men, who were to remain in prison for 'the welfare of the country'. Donnellan memorialized Dublin Castle, pleading that his business and family would be ruined. He offered substantial bail to be released in August 1866.[27]

528. Patrick Downes, Limerick, labourer and IRB suspect, arrested in this city in a night raid during November 1866, alongside John and Edward Daly, when quantities of bullets and several pikes were seized in the Pennywell district, probably on foot of information received.

529. John Duane, Newcastle West, arrested under the habeas corpus suspension, held in Limerick jail in April 1866 until bailed.

530. Michael Dunne, a young man, was arrested at Cobh on 11 March 1867 with only a carpet bag while attempting to purchase a steamer ticket for America. The constabulary suspected him of participation in the attack on the Kilmallock barracks.

531. Myles Egan, Limerick, hatter, a known IRB man who participated in the Manchester Martyrs demonstration in this city on 8 December 1867.

532. Cornelius Enright, Ballyrobin, publican, participated in the attack on Ardagh constabulary barracks in March 1867, but escaped arrest. He subsequently served as treasurer of a committee to erect a monument to the Fenian Joseph Kennedy of Glin. In 1882 he was detained in Clonmel prison as secretary of the local Land League and was arrested a second time for making a seditious speech.

533. Maurice Fitzgibbon, born in Kilmallock in 1848, was convicted and sentenced to five years for his part in the attack on the local constabulary barracks in March 1867 and transported to Western Australia on the *Hougoumont*. After a free pardon in 1869 Fitzgibbon left for San Francisco.

534. Michael Foley, 25, sentenced to one year for participating in the Rising in Kilmallock in 1867.

535. Nicholas Gaffney, Kilmallock, born in 1840, a plasterer and prominent, early IRB member, whose political education began with reading old files of the *Nation* as a child. The local IRB derived from the NBSP, but was under police observation after the McManus funeral and could no longer use the nationalist reading room in Kilmallock. They met through hurling; trusted members cut ash for pike handles at night and some smiths made pikes. By 1864 Gaffney felt neglected by Stephens, as no weapons or funds were sent down and they could only cast bullets. Learning that the Rising would take place in 1865, they hoped to seize the arms of Kilmallock constabulary barracks. Some men, who were friendly with the police, borrowed a rifle to go hunting and gain experience. After the suspension of habeas corpus in February 1866, Gaffney fled to Glasgow. Falling in with some American Fenian officers there, he travelled to the US, where he attempted to participate in the Canadian invasion, not returning to Kilmallock until 1868. By 1881 Gaffney was the right-hand man of James W. Joyce, building contractor and secretary of the Kilmallock Land League, whom he supported during his imprisonment in 1881. His son Joe, a teacher in Ballinasloe, was most concerned that Kilmallock should set up a company of Irish Volunteers and obtain rifles, as the IRB revived in the early twentieth century.

536. Capt. John Ambrose Geary (sometimes Guiry), born in Shanrath in 1837. His family was evicted and emigrated to the US, where he fought in the Confederate Army. He joined the Fenian Brotherhood in 1863 and became its representative in Louisville, Kentucky. In 1866 Geary returned to Co. Limerick, staying with relatives in Shanrath, while organizing the Castlemahon district. When visiting Newcastle West in February 1866, after the suspension of habeas corpus, he was oppressively shadowed by Head Constable Sullivan. This was a common tactic to get a suspect to give up his plans. Geary warned him to desist, before firing at the policeman's legs. He went on the run, hidden in Hartnett's of Glenduff, where Mrs Hartnett's presence of mind saved him during a police search. She got him to Fr Walsh of Glantine, who transferred him to Fr Nolan of Ardagh while sympathizers planned a safe route from Co. Limerick to the US. Geary also participated in the Fenian attack on Canada under Col John O'Neill, was captured and bailed to return to the US. He revisited Ireland after independence and died in Kentucky in 1926.

537. Patrick Geary, 21, arrested in Cork on his way to America. The police suspected him of involvement in the attack on Kilmallock barracks, but Geary's father claimed that he had been forced to serve in the Fenian ranks by Capt. Dunne. He was transferred to Kilmallock pending inquiries and ultimately brought before the special commission in Limerick.

538. Michael Grogan, 26, Kilteely, farmer, one of the Fenian leaders of this district who had just been married and turned out for the Rising on horseback. He fled, but was arrested and sentenced to two years for high treason in Limerick jail.

539. Alice Harris, one of the two girls who accompanied the Fenians on their march from Bruree via Tankardstown to Kilmallock to participate in the Rising. She carried bread as a primitive form of commissariat.

540. George Harris, Bruree, among the men assembled at Bruree bridge to participate in the attack on Kilmallock barracks in March 1867.

541. Michael Hartnett, 20, born in Abbey-feale, a seaman in the US service for three years, sworn as a Fenian in 1864. He featured on the list of Fenian naval personnel of the Brotherhood.

542. Michael Hassett, Bridge Street, Limerick, publican, arrested under the habeas corpus suspension in February 1866.

543. Christopher Hawthorne, among those attacking the Kilmallock Barracks during the Rising of 1867, arrested and discharged on bail.

544. Private Healy, Royal Artillery, was drummed out of his corps in the New Barracks, Limerick, for desertion and disloyal language in June 1867, according to his court martial, and handed over to the civil authorities for imprisonment. He had been in the army for eleven years and was suspected of Fenianism.

545. Daniel Hennessy, a strong young man, detained in Cork on 12 March 1867 and positively identified as having participated in the attack on the Kilmallock barracks.

546. Denis Hennessy, 20, a participant in the Rising in Kilmallock, fled, but was arrested in Cobh on his way to America. He was sentenced to seven years, transported to Western Australia, pardoned in 1869 and left for San Francisco.

547. Thomas Hickey, Limerick city, carpenter employed by Messrs Russell, had been in custody since 20 February 1866. The prisoner's position in the Fenian movement was not known, but he had spoken of revenge against Judge Keogh at the time of the special commission and threatened that the owners of carriages would be killed and replaced by Fenians. Hickey protested that he was not an IRB member, had committed no crime and had a family to support. His wife Ellen added that he suffered from consumption and

prolonged incarceration would endanger his health. She requested an investigation, while her petition received considerable community support.

548. James Hogan, national school teacher in Kilteely, was known to the authorities for several years as a determined Fenian. He and William Lundon had carefully avoided detection, unlike the lesser lights, who were arrested after the 'Kilteely Rising'. Detained from May 1867, Hogan protested that his character had been excellent for twenty-eight years, he was attending to his school during the Rising and needed to provide for his family. Several memorials for release proved unsuccessful, although the people of Kilteely supported him. Hogan was transferred from Limerick jail to Mountjoy. In July the board of education investigated his conduct and Hogan lost his job. The medical officer of Mountjoy reported that his health continued to deteriorate, endangering his life. Hogan was discharged in March 1868 on condition of providing bail.

549. John Hogan, Kilteely, was among the local insurgents in March 1867 but not arrested until February 1869. He was released that April.

550. Martin Hogan, 24, led the Bruff Fenians towards Kilmallock for the attack on the constabulary barracks during the Rising.

551. Martin Joseph Hogan, 1833–1900, had worked as a coach-painter in Limerick City before enlisting in the 5th Dragoons. Celebrated among British soldiers for having cut an iron bar in two with one slash of his sword, he joined the IRB in 1864; Hogan was convicted of desertion and mutiny in August 1866 and transported to Western Australia on the *Hougoumont*. He was among those rescued by the *Catalpa*, eventually settling in Chicago.

552. Patrick Hogan, George's Street, Limerick, draper's assistant, had lost his previous job in a large shop in this city around December 1865 because he was an active Fenian 'centre'. He attended all important IRB meetings in Limerick. Hogan had also worked in a drapery in Ennis, where he swore in a number of young men. He was arrested under the habeas corpus suspension in February 1866. The authorities decided, during local discussions in April, that Hogan was one of thirteen dangerous individuals who should be transferred to Mountjoy Prison. The authorities pressurized Hogan to accept emigration rather than discharge on bail, but he persisted and was freed from Mountjoy in July.

553. Thomas Hogan, Henry Street, Limerick, baker and Fenian sympathizer, was very active in preparing and marshalling the Manchester Martyrs demonstration in this city in December 1867.

554. Edmund Houlihan, born in Darnstown in 1839, was a native speaker of Irish and a good musician who lost his sight in an explosion of gunpowder during the Fenian attack on the barracks in Kilmallock. Houlihan took to the roads as a travelling musician for more than fifty years. Known as 'Rambling Jack', he performed rebel songs and traditional airs in tune with his separatist convictions. Houlihan died in Darnstown in 1931.

555. James Jones, baby son of a ship's engineer who had smuggled John Daly out of Ireland after the Rising, was adopted by the Daly family after his father's early death. Jones, a small timber merchant in Limerick, became a separatist and served as the secretary of the Limerick Amnesty Association. Suffering from poor health, he died in 1894.

556. Patrick Keane, Bruree, assembled to march to Kilmallock for the attack on the barracks on 6 March 1867.

557. Joseph Kearney, Limerick, clerk, a suspect who associated with leading local IRB members in 1892. He was also president of the Limerick Young Ireland Society. Dublin Castle knew that Kearney had attended a subversive meeting on 31 July 1892, at which P.N. Fitzgerald was present, and a 'mission' to America was arranged. Kearney left for the US the following month.

558. Thade Keeffe, Bruree, assembled at the local railway bridge to participate in the attack on Kilmallock constabulary barracks in March 1867.

559. John (in some accounts William) Kelly, Pennywell, Limerick, gas fitter, was arrested on suspicion in November 1865 or '66 and held until the spring assizes. He was released due to lack of evidence, but had become ill and died in October 1867. Sympathizers organized his funeral to Kileedy graveyard, which was attended by an estimated 10,000 people. IRB men desisted from firing three volleys over his grave due to a strong police presence.

560. Joseph Kennedy, 31, Ballinloughnane, Ardagh, was among the Old Mill Fenians, who included his cousins Michael and Con Kennedy and his father-in-law John Coleman, Drominacrine, who joined in the attack on Ardagh barracks. Kennedy was arrested on 2 April 1867 and sentenced to ten years. Released in poor health in 1877, he died on 15 September, aged 42. William C. Upton began collecting for a monument in Ardagh graveyard.

561. Patrick Kennedy, Bruree, farmer's son, assembled to march to Kilmallock for the attack on the barracks on 6 March 1867. He subsequently fled to Cork, where he was arrested.

562. Thomas Laffan, 23, Tankardstown, participated in the attack on Kilmallock barracks on 6 March 1867.

563. Lieut Joseph H. Lawler, a native of Ireland, who enlisted in 9th Regiment in Connecticut in September 1861 and was promoted several times during the Civil War. After demobbing in August 1865, Lawler went to Ireland as a Fenian but was arrested in Limerick. He returned to the US where he became a police captain in New Orleans, where he died in 1893.

564. James Leahy had participated in the attack on Kilmallock constabulary barracks and fled afterwards, but was arrested and identified in Cork.

565. Michael Liston, 19, of Coolybrown and a native of Coolcappa, was among those who attacked Ardagh constabulary barracks in March 1867. He reached Cobh, where an Ardagh policeman on the lookout recognized and arrested him. Liston was remanded to the assizes and eventually discharged on bail.

William Lundon, FP 279
(courtesy NAI).

566. William Lundon, 1839–1909, a native of Kilteely, where he ran a school teaching boys aspiring to the priesthood. Lundon became a prominent IRB organizer for Limerick and Tipperary and went to the US, also participating in the invasion of Canada before returning for the Rising. He was considered a prime mover in the Kilteely district alongside James Hogan, NT, and detained under the Habeas Corpus Suspension Act from May 1867 until the summer of 1868. Lundon subsequently supported agrarian agitation. Around 1890 he was presented with £202 collected by nationalists in honour of his patriotic sacrifices. He became an MP in 1900, making his maiden speech in Irish. A splendid Maid of Erin monument marks his grave.

567. Daniel Liddy, butcher, had been suspected of being the 'centre' for Limerick city, before going to America. On his return he was arrested on 5 March 1867 and detained for a year. Liddy was liberated on condition of leaving for New York, where he reassured John Savage concerning the state of the IRB in April 1868. He also served on a committee set up to assist Irish political refugees, who landed in the US without contacts to rebuild their lives abroad.

568. James Lyons, Bruree, marched to Kilmallock for the attack on the constabulary barracks on 6 March 1867.

569. Thomas Lyons, Killmalock, a publican, whose licence was not renewed in October 1867 because he had allowed Fenian meetings to take place on his premises.

570. Private James McCann, 28, from Rathkeale, served seven months in the Federal artillery and joined the Brotherhood during the trench warfare around Petersburg, Virginia, in 1865, which led to the collapse of the Confederacy; on the Fenian roster of available military personnel.

571. John McCarthy was among the Kilmallock insurgents who attempted to flee, presumably hoping to depart on a ship in the Shannon estuary. He was arrested in Cahirconlish in possession of a revolver,

ammunition, money and his prayer book, the latter object identifying him as an IRB organizer, equipped to swear in members.

572. James McDonnell, Limerick, a young porter and known Fenian, who marched in the Manchester Martyrs demonstration in this city in December 1867.

573. John McDonnell, assistant clerk of Rathkeale workhouse, arrested in October 1865 and taken to Limerick jail on suspicion of Fenianism.

574. Thomas McDonnell, Ballingarry, slater, detained in Limerick jail in March 1866 as a suspected Fenian.

575. John Magner, 22, Cahermoyle, a participant in the attack on Ardagh constabulary barracks in March 1867. He was arrested, charged and remanded to the next assizes.

576. John Maguire, 15, participated in the attack on Kilmallock barracks in March 1867 and was sentenced to one year's imprisonment.

577. Patrick Maguire, 60, arrested after the attack on the Kilmallock barracks in March 1867.

578. William Manahan, Windmill Road, Limerick, solicitor's clerk, arrested under the habeas corpus suspension in February 1866.

579. George Mannix, Military Road, Limerick, solicitor's clerk, arrested under habeas corpus suspension in February 1866.

580. Patrick Mannix, fought in the Rising in Kilmallock in 1867, involved in the attempted Fenian invasion of Canada in 1870 and later a subscriber to the Skirmishing Fund.

581. Richard Marwin, Killmallock, a publican, whose licence was cancelled because he had opened up for the insurgents at 6 am on 6 March 1867 and a shot was fired from his house.

582. Tom Meaney, Bruff, an IRB commander who led the local Fenians towards Kilmallock on 5 March 1867 but died in his late twenties in June 1868. His edifying death, praying for his country's liberation, resulted in a patriotic funeral demonstration to Clogheen Cemetery near Elton, 'the quiet, even march of hundreds of the glorious peasantry of our country bearing branches of green over their heads through the heart of a splendid country'.[28]

583. Thomas Meehan, 22, Kilmallock insurgent, participated in the attack on the local barracks and was subsequently arrested.

584. Capt. Minahan, 42, a native of Co. Limerick, had served in the Crimean War as a lieutenant in the British army and a captain of Volunteers in the fortification of Washington DC and in railroad construction in Pennsylvania during the Civil War. He joined the Fenian Brotherhood in Pittsburgh in 1865 and appeared on the Fenian Brotherhood roster of officers.

585. James Moloney (or Maloney), 18, Rathkeale, baker, participated in the attack on Ardagh constabulary barracks in March 1867 and was arrested. Remanded to the assizes, Moloney was finally discharged on bail. He emigrated to Worcester, Massachusetts, to join family members.

586. James Molony, Limerick city, cabinetmaker, among those arrested during a surprise raid late at night in November 1866, when quantities of bullets and several pikes were seized in the Pennywell district.

587. Michael Moroney, 21, Bruree, among IRB men assembled at the local railway bridge to participate in the attack on Kilmallock constabulary barracks.

588. Thomas Morony, William Street, Limerick, clerk, arrested under the habeas corpus suspension in February 1866.

589. Patrick Murnane, Bruree, assembled at the local railway bridge for the attack on Kilmallock constabulary barracks.

590. Daniel Murphy was detained near Kilmallock within days after the 1867 Rising, convicted and sentenced to nine months for possessing ammunition, although there was no evidence that he had participated in the attack on the barracks.

591. David Murphy, 35, had been incarcerated as a prominent Limerick Fenian before working as a cashier on the *Irishman* in Dublin. He realized that Richard Pigott, the owner, was siphoning off funds from nationalist causes. In September 1868 Pigott dismissed Murphy for embezzlement. Murphy was out on bail when shot on 4 October 1872 by Edward O'Kelly, an IRB member, who believed he was executing an informer. Murphy survived, but the accusation of dishonesty was left hanging over him until April 1873, when Pigott dropped the charge. Murphy strenuously demanded 'a searching investigation'. O'Kelly remained silent on arrest and was convicted and sentenced to life at his third trial in June 1873. Amnestied in 1879, he died that July.[29]

592. James Murphy, William Street, Limerick, leather-cutter, was soliciting funds in aid of the Fenian movement, together with Nicholas Corbett, in July 1867. Both were then considered IRB leaders, as many activists had been arrested or fled. Murphy also participated in the Manchester Martyrs commemoration in Limerick on 8 December 1867.

593. Martin Murphy, Limerick, sawyer, an IRB member who participated in the Manchester Martyrs demonstration in this city in December 1867.

594. Michael P. Murphy, shoemaker, 'head centre' of Limerick during 1865, returned from the US, where he had been a clerk in the Fenian Brotherhood's Moffat Mansion in 1866. Murphy organized in conjunction with Col Byron, but vanished after the habeas corpus suspension. Superintendent Ryan received intelligence that he was in London planning a Rising for 17 March 1866, which would be accompanied by mayhem in London, Liverpool and Manchester. Murphy had returned to Limerick by early 1867 with Col John Healy and Lieut Joseph Lawlor, veterans of the 9th Connecticut Volunteers. Murphy was also observed planning with Edmond O'Donovan in Limerick. In February his hiding place was traced from Kilrush to lodgings in Limerick. When the police stormed upstairs, Mrs Brown, his landlady, delayed them to allow Murphy and the American officers to burn documents and maps intended for the insurrection. He was not discharged until January 1868 and emigrated to the US.

595. Patrick Murphy, 40, Ardagh, participated in the attack on the local constabulary barracks and was arrested, remanded to the next assizes and then discharged on bail.

596. Capt. John Murray, 33, led forty men in the attack on Ardagh barracks on 5 March 1867. After its failure he fled, but was arrested in Adare. He was released after a court appearance in June 1867.

597. Michael Noonan, 1844–1923, Kilmallock, was sentenced to five years for the attack on the local constabulary barracks and transported to Western Australia. He returned home, being included in the free pardon of 1869. Towards the end of his life Noonan was among the last survivors of the 1867 Rising in Kilmallock, still publicizing the names of his comrades.

598. John O'Brien, Limerick, baker, a known Fenian, who marched in the

Manchester Martyrs demonstration in this city in December 1867.

599. Sgt David O'Cloghessy of either Ballintober or Ballintubber, both Co. Limerick, was a gunner with six months' experience in 3rd Connecticut Battery of artillery, when he volunteered for the Fenian Brotherhood roster.

600. Capt. Thomas O'Connell, Abbeyfeale, a Civil War veteran, detained in Limerick jail in February 1866 on suspicion of Fenianism. His friends protested that he was neither an officer nor an intimate friend of Capt. Geary, the Fenian who recently shot a policeman in Newcastle West.

601. Charles O'Connor, Sandmall, Limerick, pig buyer, observed by the police as participating in the Manchester Martyrs' procession on 8 December 1867.

602. Martin O'Connor, Limerick, dealer, among those rounded up by the constabulary in November 1866 during a night raid, when quantities of bullets and several pikes were seized in the Pennywell district.

603. Mary Josephine O'Connor, daughter of David O'Connor of Bruff, was born in 1869 and emigrated to Manchester. She assisted James (Seumas) Barrett, a leading Fenian in northern England, who cared for the Manchester Martyrs' monument in St Joseph's Cemetery, Moston. A lifelong Republican, she was still involved in gun-running in the 1940s.

604. Lieut Patrick O'Connor, a native of Bruff who had been a clerk in the US, landed from the Erin's Hope but was arrested near Dungarvan on 5 June 1867. Incarcerated in Waterford and Dublin, he was not discharged until April 1868 on condition of returning to America.

605. John Francis O'Donnell, 1837–74, a native of Limerick, journalist, and editor of the Tipperary Examiner and a leading contributor of poetry to the Dublin Irish People under the pennames 'Caviare', 'Monckton West' and 'P. Monks'. As London correspondent of the Irishman, O'Donnell tried to visit the IRB prisoners in English jails. Although talented, O'Donnell did not realize his potential. He died in London and was buried in St Mary's RC Cemetery, Kensal Green.

606. Michael O'Donnell, clerk at O'Sullivan's Hotel, Kilmallock, was held in Bruff bridewell as a suspected Fenian. He had previously been a police constable and was believed to have written to co-conspirators in Limerick, advising that Kilmallock and Charleville had money and arms for an insurrection. O'Donnell was transferred to Limerick jail to be tried in January 1867.

607. Thomas O'Donnell, nineteen, was arrested as a participant in the attack on Kilmallock barracks.

608. Thomas O'Callaghan O'Donnell, born in 1847 in Kilmallock, became a teacher, contributing poetry to the Irishman and acting as the Kilmallock correspondent of the Irish People. He emigrated to New York in 1866, where he wrote for various papers. O'Callaghan O'Donnell claimed descent from seventeenth-century Seán O Duibhir a Ghleanna and was a cousin of Patrick W. and Robert Dwyer Joyce.

609. Jeremiah O'Leary, Croom, national schoolteacher, was detained in Limerick County jail in April 1866 as a suspected Fenian with his colleague Daniel Murphy of Manister, Croom, and Henry Thornhill, a relative of the local postmaster. Dublin Castle had received a letter from Limerick city that O'Leary was a 'centre', while his sister ran a female 'circle'. Protestant and Catholic clergy, however, petitioned for their liberation. In May Fr McCormick, the parish priest, requested Murphy's release on bail as a good teacher, especially

as his fellow accused had been discharged.

610. William O'Sullivan, 18, Kilmallock, eldest son of William Henry O'Sullivan, hotel proprietor and businessman. He participated in the Rising of 1867 in Kilmallock after his father's arrest and was tried and sentenced to five years. O'Sullivan was amnestied and returned to Kilmallock. He remained committed to Fenianism, but imprisonment had damaged his health and he died in 1881, aged 31.

611. Patrick Pickett, in official records Pigott, 22, Kilmallock, an IRB member tasked with capturing the mounted police constable, who carried the despatches between Kilmallock and Bruff. Pickett seized both horse and letters for Capt. Dunne. After the Rising he was sentenced to one year and learned that another Fenian was mistakenly enduring five years' transportation for this. According to Seán Moylan, his grand-nephew, he revealed the truth on release, but the 1869 amnesty was imminent and officialdom did not intervene. Pickett emigrated to Australia.

612. John Portley, born in 1832, agricultural labourer, had been a Fenian and was a fluent Irish speaker who handed on a wealth of Irish folklore and traditional history to his family. His son Morgan, who was born in Caherelly in 1897, other son Tom and nephew Tom Casey joined the Ballybricken company of the Volunteers in 1914. Casey was executed in May 1921. The Portleys lived in Kishikirk, Caherconlish, from 1921.

613. James Power, Denmark Street, Limerick, clerk, arrested under the habeas corpus suspension in February 1866.

614. Daniel Quinlivan, 20, a native of Ashgrove, participated in the attack on Ardagh constabulary barracks on 5 March 1867. The Quinlivans, being blacksmiths,

made pikes for the Fenians. He was subsequently arrested and charged, but appears to have been released by the autumn.

615. Batt (Bartholomew) Raleigh, 1843–1929, Kilmallock, a shoemaker in the local workhouse, was a committed IRB man before the Rising. He acted as dispatch rider for Capt. Dunne during the attack on the barracks in March 1867, but had to go on the run in Tankardstown, Mitchelstown and the Glen of Aherlow afterwards. He returned home eventually and participated in the annual commemorations of the Rising. Batt was one of the last of the Fenians when he died in Kilmallock after a 'long and honourable life'. He and his brother are buried in Ballingaddy churchyard.[30]

616. Ned (Edmund) Raleigh, born in 1837 in Kilmallock, a shoemaker in the local workhouse, who participated in the Rising, but avoided detection and returned to his job afterwards. Ned was only able to read, not write. He became the grandfather of Seán Moylan, IRA commandant and later Fianna Fail government minister who spent his childhood in Kilmallock and features in Seán Keating's painting, 'Men of the South'. In 1909 the constabulary still recorded Ned's attendance at the annual commemoration of the 1867 Rising in this town.

617. Pat Regan, Bruree, among insurgents marching to Kilmallock to attack the constabulary barracks in March 1867.

618. Patrick Riordan, born in Kilmallock in 1847, a car driver for O'Sullivan's Hotel, who participated in the attack on the barracks in 1867. He was speedily arrested and tried for treason felony, sentenced to seven years and transported to Western Australia. On receiving a free pardon, Riordan returned to Kilmallock in 1869, suffering from TB. He died in May

1870, when 5000 people attended his funeral, which was organized by John Sarsfield Casey, the 'Galtee Boy'. In 1911 Seán Mac Diarmada unveiled a monument over his grave.

619. Patrick Riordan, 20, Kilmallock, described in court documents as 'the smith' to distinguish him from the other insurgent of that name, was arrested and taken before the special commission.

620. Robert Riordan, 34, was charged with participation in the Kilmallock attack and sentenced to one year by the special commission.

621. Quartermaster Rowland, Limerick, 73th Regiment, was reduced in rank to sergeant, suspected of associating with Col Byron, a Fenian agent. Lord Strathnairn was very concerned that the military had been infiltrated in Limerick, in particular. Rowland's demotion was, however, rescinded in April 1866.

622. John Ryan, Kilteely, servant boy, was observed with a pike and green ribbon during the 1867 Rising in Kilteely.

623. Michael Scanlan, 1833–1917, a native of Castlemahon, who emigrated to Chicago with his family at the age of fifteen, where his brothers founded a successful confectionary business. Scanlan joined the Fenian Brotherhood, becoming a senator and leader of the Roberts faction. He wrote memorable ballads, notably 'The Bold Fenian Men' and 'The Jackets Green' and became the poet laureate of the movement. After the failure of both the Canadian invasion and the Rising, Scanlan was a co-founder and editor of the *Irish Republic*, a weekly newspaper, which preached physical force until 1873 and opposed the *Irish People* of the O'Mahony/Savage wing. Subsequently, Scanlan was employed by the state department

in Washington, becoming the innovative chief of the Bureau of Statistics. His wife, Ellen, also an immigrant, predeceased him in 1871. Her obituary, in the rival *Irish People*, praised her patriotic sacrifices.[31]

624. Jeremiah Scanlon, Bruree, assembled to march to Kilmallock with the local Fenians for the attack on the barracks on 6 March 1867.

625. Martin Sheahan, Mary Street, Limerick, tailor, arrested under habeas corpus suspension in February 1866.

626. John Sheehan, born 1837 in Kilmallock, was convicted and sentenced to seven years for his part in the attack on the constabulary barracks. Transported to Western Australia, Sheehan was included in the unconditional amnesty of 1869 and left for San Francisco.

627. John Sheehan, Newcastle West, publican, detained in Limerick jail in March 1866 as a Fenian, had been previously arrested and released on bail.

628. Roger Sheehy, Kilfinane, had attacked Head Constable Gleeson with a stone, wounding him. He was tried and acquitted when the chairman of Limerick sessions urged Sheehy to emigrate as an undesirable character. The police observed him drinking in Kilfinane and at Bruff fair with Capt. Dunne and arrested him as a Fenian. He was eventually released on bail of £50 and two sureties of £25 each on condition of good behaviour. Sheehy declared his intention to leave Ireland in April 1866.

629. John Shine, born in 1827, mason and farm labourer from Douglass, Limerick, who joined the 60th Rifles and was sentenced to ten years. Transported to Australia, he developed a drink problem and fell foul of the authorities. Freed in 1878, he left for Melbourne in 1882, probably bound for the US.

630. Richard Sloane, Newcastle West, weighmaster, detained in Limerick jail from March to April 1866 as a Fenian suspect. He was released on bail.

631. Thomas Southwell, Rathkeale, broguemaker, was taken to Limerick jail in October 1865 on suspicion of Fenianism.

632. James Sullivan, Bruree, assembled there for the attack on Kilmallock constabulary barracks in March 1867.

633. Capt. James S. Treacy, 1842–1902, Gibbinstown, was among the Fenians who took Ballyknockane barracks, Mallow, on 6 March 1867, led by Capt. Mackey Lomasney and James F.X. O'Brien. He also served in 8th New York Regiment and was a dedicated member of both IRB and Clan na Gael. Treacy sat on the Clan's executive board in the 1870s and 80s.

634. Richard Troy, a native of Fermoy, ran a bakery in Limerick. Dublin Castle considered him honest and likely to act cautiously to protect his business. Troy had been the 'centre' of Limerick city for some years when he died of lung disease on 5 July 1892 without the rites of the Catholic Church, indicating a determined separatist. The local IRB planned to erect a memorial cross over his grave.

635. Band Sgt Troy, Limerick, 73th Regiment, was detained in 1866 as a Fenian suspect for two months for his association with Col Byron before being released as innocent.

636. Thomas Turner, 23, participated in the attack on Kilmallock barracks, was arrested and brought before the Limerick special commission.

637. William Turner, 19, sentenced to one year for participating in the attack on the Kilmallock barracks in 1867.

638. Armourer Sgt Tyrrell, Limerick, 73th Regiment, was detained for two months as a Fenian suspect for associating with Col Byron and subsequently released as innocent.

639. William C. Upton, 1845–1925, a carpenter from Ardagh, was one of the leaders of the unsuccessful attack on the eponymous barracks in 1867. He attempted to set the building on fire after their first assault had failed. The insurgents dispersed when one of them was shot by the constables. Upton went on the run in Roscommon, using the alias 'Cleary', which he retained as his middle name. He escaped to America but returned to Ardagh in 1869 and became a builder. Upton was never tried, due to lack of witnesses. He remained a Fenian, supported the Land League and became a co-founder and key activist of the Munster Labour League in 1881. Upton also wrote a novel, *Uncle Pat's Cabin or, life among the agricultural labourers of Ireland* (1882), the first Irish social-realist novel written by a worker, which was praised by W.E.H. Lecky. Due to financial problems he returned to the US in the late 1880s, where his family prospered.

640. Daniel Vaughan, carpenter, arrested in his home, Thomondgate, Limerick, as a Fenian under the habeas corpus suspension in February 1866.

641. William Wall, 22, teacher in Kilmallock workhouse and the Kilmallock 'centre', was arrested in February 1866 for sedition and detained for six months before being allowed to emigrate. Wall left Kilmallock railway station under police escort in August 1866. He slipped a poem, declaring his intention of returning 'with vengeance on our lips' into his sister's hands, but joined the US army and died relatively young in Dakota; his brother Michael was also a Fenian.[32]

642. John Walsh, Kilfinane, painter, was identified by the constabulary as a Fenian

who associated with other suspects in November 1866. ✕

643. John Walsh, born in 1847 in Tankardstown, Kilmallock, a carpenter's apprentice, who joined the IRB and prepared for insurrection. On the night of the Rising, the Bruree Fenians met in his father's carpenter shop, where he had handles fitted to their pikes. They proceeded to Kilmallock to attack the barracks. Walsh was detained until his discharge on bail in June 1867, subsequently spending two years in America before returning to die in Athlacca in 1929.

644. Michael Stephen Walsh, Kilmallock, arrested in the aftermath of the attack for having sold paraffin to the Fenians to burn down the constabulary barracks.

645. Patrick Walsh, 25, Tankardstown, a farmer's son, was employed as a shop assistant by the O'Sullivans of Kilmallock. He was an important local organizer and had been under police observation since 1865. Walsh travelled to America on Fenian business and returned with Capt. John Dunne towards the end of that year. Walsh was busily swearing in new members in early 1866. He and Dunne fled to the US before they could be arrested under the habeas corpus suspension and continued their preparations for the Rising. Back in Kilmallock in late 1866, Walsh consulted with Richard Bermingham, the IRB leader of the Tankardstown district. On 5 March 1867 they commanded the Bruree and Tankardstown Fenians, raiding for arms as they proceeded to Kilmallock. Walsh was wounded during the attack on the barracks, but fought on. He was convicted, sentenced to fifteen years and amnestied in 1871, but excluded from Ireland for the remainder of his sentence. Being in poor health, Walsh returned in 1875, when he was arrested and made to serve his final six years.

646. Stephen Barry Walsh, 24, Kilmallock, son of a well-to-do woman, served as secretary of the NBSP in the town, which metamorphosed into an IRB 'circle'. Walsh was involved with the local Fenians, meeting in O'Sullivan's Hotel and Condon's pub, the two major IRB venues in Kilmallock. Walsh had just returned from Maynooth, when he was arrested in February 1866 and imprisoned in Mountjoy. Eventually released on condition of emigration, he returned to become a merchant. He participated in the local Land League and was arrested alongside Fr Eugene Sheehy in May 1881.

647. Patrick Ward, Bruree, 25, son of a farmer, distributed pikes among the Bruree IRB to participate in the Rising in Kilmallock. He was arrested in Cork city, convicted and sentenced to one year.

F. Tipperary

648. Peter Ahessy, Tinakilly near Mullinahone, carpenter and notorious Fenian, was among those suspected by the constabulary in early 1866.

649. William Philip Allen, 19, said to be a native of Tipperary town, although he spent his childhood in Bandon. Allen trained as a carpenter and emigrated to England, where he participated in the Manchester rescue. A police sergeant was fatally injured in this incident and Allen was convicted of murder and hanged on 23 November 1867 with Capt. Michael O'Brien and Michael Larkin. The flawed evidence and anti-Irish sentiment, which culminated in these executions, embittered Anglo-Irish relations, while the three entered the nationalist pantheon as the 'Manchester Martyrs'.

650. Robert Barry, Ballydine, Carrick-on-Suir, whom influential people considered

a dangerous organizer, travelling through the country and associating with soldiers. He was known to Head Constable Talbot. Barry was detained between March and September 1866 and discharged on substantial bail, after expressing regret for his Fenianism.

651. Daniel Boland, Cahir, had written and posted seditious placards in this town in December 1865.

652. Jeremiah Bourke, born in Glankeen in the 1840s, joined the IRB as a young man and raided for arms with his comrades in the Templederry district. The police had been alerted and opening fire, wounded Bourke and captured his companions. All were sentenced to imprisonment. During the War of Independence, Bourke's home in Templederry was a safe house, where Sean Treacy, Dan Breen, Seamus Robinson and Sean Hogan sheltered. He became a judge in the Sinn Féin courts, respected for his impartiality and intervened in cases, where he suspected sectarian motives behind IRA plans. Bourke died in 1933, the last survivor of the Tipperary Fenians of 1867.

653. Thomas Bourke, 26, grocer and cattle-dealer from Priesttown, Drangan, arrested in March 1866 and held for a year without trial; FP 42.

654. William Bracken, 25, a native of Roscrea, a mason who returned from Bradford, England, with money, though unemployed. An associate of General Gleeson, Bracken was detained between February and September 1866 and only released on condition of leaving for Liverpool; FP 27.

655. William Breen, porter, among young men arrested on suspicion in Tipperary town in late March 1867.

656. Corporal Michael Brennan, a native of Carrick-on-Suir, who had been sworn

into the IRB by Colour Sgt Charles McCarthy in October 1865. Brennan turned informer to gain immunity from prosecution. He was also promoted, but troops refused to serve under him and he committed suicide, according to John Francis Meagher, a leading Carrick Fenian whose pen name was 'Slievenamon'.

657. Thomas Brien, Mullinahone, tailor, a suspected IRB member in February 1866.

658. Timothy Brien, Five Alley, Nenagh, named by Andrew Kennedy as an IRB member in late 1865, eventually released from detention.

659. William Brien, Cahirvillahow, Kilfeacle, wearing a green cap and sash, was prominent among those travelling to the Tipperary amnesty meeting in October 1869.

660. Private William Broderick, 28, a native of Clonmel, had served three years in the Federal artillery and took the pledge from Col Patrick Downing in the Fenian headquarters in New York in 1865; on the roster of experienced personnel.

661. Thomas Dogherty Brohan, teacher, 'head centre' for Tipperary town, evaded arrest and fled to Dublin, where he was detained from March 1866 for eight months. Returning to Tipperary, Brohan was re-arrested near Bansha in early 1867, engaged in destroying railway tracks for the Rising. Bailed from the Tipperary bridewell, he left for the US, becoming a journalist in San Francisco.

662. Patrick Bryan, 23, draper's assistant, born Ballingarry, Co. Tipperary, resident in Dublin when arrested as a suspect in 1866. Bryan refused to be photographed, a procedure which subsequently became compulsory; FP 36.

663. Michael Buckley, Tipperary, was arrested on 5 March 1867 on suspicion of

having been involved in the Rising, but was discharged on bail in May.

664. Capt. Charles Burke, Kilcrue Watermill, organized pikes and raided houses for arms in the Borrisoleigh district during the Rising. He participated in the attack on Roskeen Barracks and Riordan's house with Michael Sheehy's section, when Treacy was killed. Burke went on the run near Templemore for four months, assisted by Thomas Mackey and John Walsh. He escaped to France and taunted the authorities with their failure to arrest him.

665. Edmund Burke, publican and meal-seller in Irishtown, Clonmel, whose premises were used for IRB meetings in 1864, was held under the Habeas Corpus Suspension Act from March until May 1866. The authorities released him as he might have been mistaken for Thomas Burke, a Fenian and fellow publican.

666. James Burke, 19, Kilcrue Watermill, labourer, brother of the notorious Capt. Charles, was arrested in April 1867 in the Borrisoleigh district near a dugout. Burke was suspected of having participated in the burning of Roskeen barracks and the shooting of the boy Treacy during the Rising. He pleaded guilty and was sentenced to nine months.

667. Patrick Burke, Kilcrue Watermill, supported the IRB with his whole family, including his sons, Charles and James. He provided a horse and cart for the insurgents and, although elderly, insisted on accompanying them for the Rising.

668. Patrick Burke of Mullinahone, Fenian and friend of Charles Kickham, assisted Thomas Francis Bourke when organizing the Rising in Tipperary. James Maher of Mullinahone, his grandson, collected valuable material about Charles Kickham and John O'Mahony, published in *The Valley*

Near Slievenamon (Kilkenny 1942), *Romantic Slievenamon* (Mullinahone 1954) and *Chief of the Comeraghs, a John O'Mahony Anthology* (Mullinahone 1957).

669. Thomas Burke, a publican of Main Guard and Dublin Street, Clonmel, where IRB men were sworn in. He was detained in Mountjoy for a year from March 1866 and only released when exhibiting symptoms of insanity.

670. Private Thomas Burke, stationed with 73rd Regiment in Clonmel, attempted to swear soldiers into the IRB during 1866, was detected by Head Constable Talbot and arrested.

671. William Burke, 22, Annfield, a labourer, was arrested in March 1867 on suspicion of having participated in the Rising. He was sentenced to twelve months in Nenagh jail, although it was admitted that he might have been misled into joining by his employer.

672. John and Morgan Burns, Drumbane, labourers, detained in Nenagh jail and committed for trial in April 1867, accused of participating in the Rising.

673. James Butler, Mount Catherine, Thurles, farmer, committed to Nenagh jail for participating in the Rising, but discharged on bail in July 1867.

674. Miss Butler, Thomastown, a national school teacher, who received clandestine letters for 'head centre' Michael O'Neill Fogarty. This was probably Ellen, a daughter of Thomas Butler, who married O'Neill Fogarty and emigrated with him to New York. Her sister married Edward Walsh, one of the leaders of the IRB in Tipperary town.

675. Patrick Butler, 30, Annfield, a labourer, who had participated in the burning of Roskeen constabulary barracks, was

arrested with James Burke of Kilcrue on the farm of Darby Quinane. They had hidden near a comfortable dugout with a platform for beds and seating, discovered by the police. Butler was tried in Nenagh in July 1867. His brother Charles, also a Fenian, had made a tremendous run from the constabulary in April 1867.

676. Col John Whitehead Byron, born in Clogheen in 1839, followed his family to New York in 1855, enlisted in 69th New York in 1861 and fought in the Civil War, briefly commanding the Irish Brigade. A high ranking Fenian, he became secretary of the Potomac 'circle' of the Brotherhood. He was wounded and incarcerated in the notorious Libby Prison, Virginia. Byron was an organizer in Ireland in the run up to the Rising and repeatedly arrested, but released each time due to lack of evidence. His insinuating manner and considerable daring made him highly effective. He was detained in Mountjoy from February 1866 until April 1867 during the habeas corpus suspension. Delia Parnell, mother of the future leader of the Irish Parliamentary Party, paid his fare to the US. In 1868 Byron acted as adjutant-general of the Fenian Brotherhood's war department. He held various civil service appointments and settled in Ohio, where he died in 1909.

677. Patrick Byron, among a group of young men arrested in Tipperary town in late March 1867, suspected of having participated in the Rising.

678. John Cahill of Caherbawn, Cashel, a Civil War veteran, had returned in November 1865 and was constantly travelling about this district and in possession of money from America. The constabulary surmised that he was a Fenian organizer, but Cahill did not incriminate himself. He was located in Cobh in February 1866, claiming he had failed to get a ship, but absconded when arrest threatened.

679. William Callaghan, servant, among young men arrested in Tipperary town in late March 1867 on suspicion of participation in the Rising.

680. Richard Carey, son of the late rector of Donoughmore, Lisronagh, had led a dissipated, reckless life in Fethard with low associates, who were suspected by the police. He was detained in Clonmel in February 1867. Mrs Carey denied her son's connection with Fenianism, supported by John Bagwell MP and several magistrates, and his discharge took place in May.

681. Michael Carroll, Borrisoleigh, publican, supported the candidature of O'Donovan Rossa as MP for Tipperary. He was believed to be an active IRB leader in January 1870 and also spoke at a meeting sympathizing with France in the Franco-Prussian War.

682. Michael Casey, Borrisoleigh, had returned from America to stay with his uncle on pretence of recovering his health. Suspected as a Fenian agent, he vanished to the US in January 1870.

683. Rody Cawley, a native of Nenagh, grocer, had returned from London to Dublin around Christmas 1865, where he was unemployed and took part in a street protest. Detained in Mountjoy in February 1866, Cawley's petition for release gathered strong support from the clergy and gentry of Nenagh, who highlighted his hitherto excellent character. He was discharged on bail in April.

684. Thomas Clarke, Nenagh, tailor, had been pointed out as one of the Fenian leaders by Andrew Kennedy, who later recanted his evidence. Clarke's character was good, except for his suspicious movements. He was in Nenagh jail in March

1866 and later transferred to Dublin. Numerous petitions for release proved futile. Clarke suffered from a serious head injury, for which a man had been sentenced to three years. He claimed that the aggressor's relatives had made up stories to gain revenge. The authorities refused to release Clarke on bail until his health had deteriorated by February 1867.

685. Francis Patrick Cleary, 18, medical student and assistant in Oldham's medical hall, Grafton Street, Dublin, was arrested in October 1865. A native of Tipperary, Cleary had lived in Nenagh, where he socialized with Andrew Kennedy, an IRB organizer. On Kennedy's arrest, a letter from Cleary was discovered, suggesting that the latter had spread Fenianism in Nenagh and hoped to send arms from Dublin. He pleaded guilty to the charges and was released on substantial bail.

686. James Cleary, Old Bridge Street, Clonmel, an illiterate rope-maker, was arrested in October 1865 on the word of the informer Power and detained in Richmond bridewell, Dublin, but subsequently released. In February 1866 a constable followed him and other suspected Fenians at night and thought they practised marching in Clonmel. Cleary was imprisoned from February to June 1866. He petitioned that he had six dependents, while his only crime consisted of giving the word of command to a few boys in the streets. Cleary was released on bail.

687. Michael Cleary taught as a monitor (an untrained assistant teacher) in Clerihan National School in south Tipperary until September 1865, when he was arrested on suspicion of Fenianism.

688. Thomas Cloghissey, an itinerant fiddler, was observed by the constabulary in Mullinahone. He had been bound to the peace in Fethard for illegal marching before 1866.

689. Owen Coffey, Rathfalla, Nenagh, named as a suspect by Andrew Kennedy in October 1865, eventually released.

690. Edward Comerford, Knockroe, Mullinahone, servant boy, who had been bound to the peace in Fethard for illegal marching prior to February 1866.

691. William Condon, Nenagh, named by Andrew Kennedy as an IRB man, eventually released.

692. Daniel Connell, Thurles, shoemaker, was strongly suspected as an IRB member, but nothing could be proved. He probably participated in the Rising and was not seen again afterwards. Connell fled to Liverpool with one Walsh. They lacked the money for two tickets to America, so Walsh emigrated and promised to send money for Connell to follow as soon as feasible. The latter became destitute like William Murphy, another Thurles Fenian, and both joined the same regiment. Lord Strathnairn was most concerned that this might constitute a new attempt to infiltrate the British army and forbade their discharge in May 1867, fearing they might subvert other units under false names.

693. Denis Connell, Crogue, was armed with a pike on the night of 5 March 1867 at a seditious assembly outside Tipperary town.

694. Michael Connell, a native of Aglish, Borrisokane, labourer, was arrested on arrival in Birr in March 1867, claiming he intended to visit his parents, who were unaware of his return from America. The authorities suspected him as a Fenian, as he carried a cheque, an unusual payment for a working man. He denied having served in the Federal Army.

695. Owen Considine, a native of Nenagh, brought O'Mahony and Doheny's offer of support to Stephens, leading to the founding of the IRB in 1858. Considine had been a member of a post-1848 group and became one of the earliest Fenians, but withdrew during a period of financial difficulty.

696. Patrick Cormack, Borrisoleigh, a labourer and itinerant former soldier, who was active as a Fenian organizer. He was twice arrested: in December 1865 for trying to swear a man into the IRB and in February 1866. His mother paid for his ticket to America to obtain his release that May.

697. David Coughlin, a native of Co. Tipperary, was working in the Dowlais Iron Works in Merthyr Tydfil, Wales, in December 1867 when arrested for drilling with Patrick Doran and others; he was convicted of treason felony.

698. John Cranly, Tipperary, a farmer's son, was held in Clonmel jail as a suspected insurgent from April to June 1867 until discharged on bail.

699. John Crean, Bansha, publican's son, no occupation, associated with Fenians in late 1866.

700. Edward Croke of Crohane, Mullinahone, was considered a 'bad character', whose companions were IRB men. He left for America in late 1865, but returned with Cornelius O'Leary and Edward O'Doherty, veterans of the Federal Army. Croke tried to swear men into the IRB and was detained in Clonmel jail until promising to return to the US.

701. James Croke, Kilfeacle, a farmer, who had fought at Ballyhurst in March 1867 and raced across country for two miles before the constabulary could arrest him. He spent six months in Clonmel jail.

702. James Crotty, Mullinahone, a slater suspected of being a leading IRB member in early 1866, as he was the constant companion of activist Rody Kickham.

703. Michael H. Crowe, 1842–1908, was a native of Breansha, Emly. The son of a small farmer, he joined the IRB in 1864 and was appointed 'head centre' of his district by James Stephens after enrolling 400 members. He participated in the Rising of 1867, then went on the run and eventually settled in Troy, Albany, where he continued his Fenian involvement.

704. Martin Cuddihy, 21, a native of Newport, Co. Tipperary, iron peddler, returned from New York and was detained as a suspect in Dublin in early 1867.

705. Patrick Cummins, Cashel, gardener, whom the constabulary suspected of being a Fenian sympathizer, only needing a leader to become actively disloyal. Cummins was arrested in early 1866, but eventually released on bail.

706. James Cunningham, Clonmel, mason, was among 'the chief promoters of Fenianism here' in 1865–6 and an associate of suspects Owen Sweeney, Thomas Burke, the publican, and Patrick Power, the future informer. He had fled to America by September 1866.[33]

707. John Cunningham, a warder in Nenagh jail, was suspected of being an IRB man and had been suspended, but reinstated, due to lack of evidence. In 1865 Cunningham persuaded Andrew Kennedy, a local IRB organizer, who had turned informer, to retract his testimony. Cunningham was arrested in March 1866, held without trial for three months and dismissed from his post.

708. Michael Cusack, Drangan, had come home from working in Cork and drilled eagerly with other Fenians in early 1866.

He fled to America after the Rising and probably trained in the 'dynamite school' in Greenpoint, Queen's, New York. In 1883 Cusack returned to Drangan and began smuggling arms to Tipperary; he was constantly shadowed by the police. A statue was erected to him in Drangan after 1910. He is not to be confused with Michael Cusack of Carron, Clare, the founder of the GAA.

709. John Dalton, Bansha, arrested for recruiting Fenians in June 1867, discharged on bail in August 1868.

710. Joseph Dalton, 27, Tankerstown, Bansha, a farmer's son, who was arrested on the information of Patrick Tyler, Toureen, Cahir, whom he had attempted to swear in at the back of a pub. Dalton had served nine months for attempting to rescue a prisoner from the police during Cashel races in 1865. He was detained in 1867 and only released on substantial bail in March 1868, when psychologically distressed; FP 108.

711. Michael Dalton, expected to return to Clonmel or Marlfield to visit his mother. He had been an overseer of government works near Adelaide, Australia, for four years. The constabulary was instructed to shadow him on information received when he landed in Dublin in June 1868 but he sailed for America from Cobh without visiting her.

712. John Daniel, Cloneen near Mullinahone, shoemaker, was observed marching with other suspects and said to be a 'centre' in February 1866.

713. John Darmody, Upperchurch district, labourer, arrested in early 1867 and charged with participating in the insurrection in north Tipperary. Exhorted by his sister, who threatened to commit suicide, he resisted pressure to inform at the trials in Nenagh during August 1867.

714. Dawson, Bansha, a teenage farmer, had just inherited from his father and organized a collection to assist the amnesty meeting on 24 October 1869 in Tipperary.

715. Hugh Delany, baker, Nenagh, a very active Fenian in late 1866.

716. John Delany, shopkeeper, Nenagh, much suspected as a Fenian during 1866.

717. Michael Delany, shopkeeper, Nenagh, returned emigrant, much suspected in late 1866.

718. Thomas Devane, Nenagh, a saddler and IRB member, among those identified when Andrew Kennedy temporarily turned informer. Devane was detained from February to August 1866, before being discharged on bail, although Kennedy had recanted in November 1865.

719. Henry Devine, baker, Clonmel, very disaffected in late 1866 and supporting the dependants of imprisoned Fenians.

720. Private James Dillon, 17th Regiment, acted as drillmaster of the Glenbane IRB at Ryan's farm near Cullen, Emly, on 17 February 1866. Surprised by the police, Dillon and his companions opened fire and wounded Constable Dunne. Sentenced to twenty years penal servitude, Dillon was among the last Fenians to be released in 1879.

721. William Dobbyn, Carrick-on-Suir, factory employee, arrested as an associate of William Meagher, Philip Morrissey and John Daniel, who discussed Fenian prospects in various pubs. Implicated as a member of Colour Sgt McCarthy's circle, Dobbyn was detained in early 1866 until his departure for America in October.

722. Capt. Michael Doheny, eldest son of Michael Doheny of Cashel, had emigrated to New York with his family after the Young Ireland Rising. He fought in the Civil War and returned to Cork as a

Fenian agent. Dublin Castle remained confused about his identity, mistakenly seizing Capt. James Doheny, a native of Callan, in February 1866. Michael attended IRB meetings in Dublin and moved to Liverpool after the habeas corpus was suspended. Arrested in Co. Dublin in March 1867, he declared himself 'disgusted with Fenianism and that [he] only came at the earnest solicitation of [his] mother, [his] father having been concerned in 1848'.[34] He was discharged in March 1868 and returned to America.

723. Capt. Morgan Doheny, 23, born in Cashel, second son of Michael Doheny Snr, served in 42nd New York Volunteers for three years. A member of the Potomac 'circle' and an organizer, he was described as an experienced officer on the Fenian Brotherhood roster for the projected expedition to Ireland. He died in America from an overdose of laudanum.

724. Thomas Donovan, about 13–16, a schoolboy from Emly, suspected of having been among the Fenians occupying Emly barracks during the Rising. The police detained him, considering him 'a pert lad'.[35] After an inquiry by magistrates Donovan was discharged on bail.

725. Michael McNamara Dooley, 25, a native of Waterford and a shopkeeper's son, had survived the Civil War with scars on his head, jaw and shoulder. He arrived in Carrick-on-Suir in February 1866. Arrested with other Fenian suspects, Dooley protested his innocence and was released on bail that November due to bad health.

726. Sgt Patrick Dooley, 34, a native of Roscrea, served in 3rd California Volunteers for three years under General Connor, a Kerryman born in 1820. Their mission was to protect civilians from the Mormons and to keep trade routes open against Native American resistance. Dooley joined the Fenians in Salt Lake City in 1863, according to the Brotherhood roster. It remains unclear whether he participated in the Bear River massacre of Shoshone Indians that January.

727. Michael Doughan, 26, Templemore, shoemaker and suspected IRB leader, in whose house meetings were held. He absconded in March 1866, after the suspension of habeas corpus. Returning in December, the constabulary continued to suspect him. Briefly arrested, he was bailed in January 1867; FP 128.

728. Daniel and Edward Droger, brought into Thurles and conveyed to Nenagh jail in April 1867 on suspicion of having been 'out' in the Rising.

729. Capt. John Dunne, 26, a native of Fethard, who had served in 23rd Illinois Volunteers for four years and was wounded in the Civil War. He joined the Fenian Brotherhood in Chicago in 1865 and returned to Dublin, where he was detained from March to May 1866. His release was conditional on his immediate return to America; FP 141. (Not to be confused with his namesake, who led the Kilmallock Fenians.)

730. John Dwyer taught in Tipperary National School until March 1866, when he was arrested on suspicion of Fenianism.

731. Laurence Dwyer, Clogheen, became a suspect when letters from him to Laurence Lonergan, blacksmith, were opened by police and treasonable references found. Dwyer was arrested and sent to Mountjoy in December 1866. He was released on bail in August 1867.

732. Michael and Nicholas Dwyer, Kilfeacle, were prominent among those travelling to the Tipperary amnesty meeting on 24 October 1869, wearing green caps and sashes.

733. Thomas Dwyer, Golden, was arrested after the Rising at Ballyhurst and sentenced to twelve months for treason felony in July 1867. He petitioned the Lord Lieutenant that he had never been in trouble with the law before, but was one of the last Fenians to be released from Clonmel jail in May 1868.

734. Thomas Dwyer, 25, a native of Thurles and an experienced seaman, who had served in the Royal as well as the US navy. He was enrolled in New York among Fenian naval personnel for their Irish expedition.

735. William Elliott, nailer, among young men arrested in Tipperary town in late March 1867 on suspicion of having participated in the Rising.

736. Richard Fahy, 26, Cappawhite, publican and road-contractor, was tried and acquitted for attacking a constable in February 1866. He was a close associate of Thomas Blackwell, the local Fenian organizer. Detained as a suspected IRB member, Fahy's wife petitioned for his release as the family was almost destitute, and he was discharged in July. By December 1866 the constabulary knew that he was involved in meetings in the Hollywood mines after dark. Fahy was imprisoned a second time until February 1867, when he agreed to emigrate.

737. John Farrell, Tipperary, labourer, among the insurgents at Ballyhurst in March 1867, became a Crown witness on arrest. He was rewarded with £10 and a ticket to a destination of his choice.

738. Timothy Farrell, miller, among young men arrested on suspicion in Tipperary town in late March 1867.

739. Fennessy, a native of Tipperary, had served in a local militia unit, which mutinied during the 1850s over outstanding payments on being stood down. He joined a line regiment to escape punishment, became a Fenian and was the 'centre' of the 3rd Buffs. Devoy described him as quiet, intelligent and sober. Fennessy returned from England, hoping for an insurrection, and carried IRB messages in Dublin.

740. Patrick Fennessy was employed in the Clashnasmut slate quarries near Carrick-on-Suir. A suspected Fenian agent, he visited the town and was arrested in March 1866. William Mercer, his employer, considered him innocent, but the authorities decided that the neighbourhood would benefit from his imprisonment in Clonmel. In declining health, Fennessy was discharged on bail in September.

741. Edward Finn, Borrisoleigh, publican and grocer, related to respectable farmers, a cousin of the Gleeson brothers and one of the first Fenians in this district. Finn was arrested on 26 February 1866 and released on bail in May.

742. William Finn, Tipperary, shoemaker, was arrested with a group of young men in Tipperary town in late March 1867, having participated in the Rising armed with a pike. Held in Clonmel jail on a charge of high treason, Finn was released in July, promising to be of good behaviour henceforth and to appear for sentencing if called upon.

743. Jeremiah J. Finnan, pen name 'Myles the Slasher', 1840–1913, from the Galtee region, a teacher, who joined the IRB at an early age and became acquainted with Stephens, John and Ellen O'Leary and Edward Duffy. Finnan went to America in 1866 to prepare for the Rising. He organized near Keeper Hill and in the Glen of Aherlow, 1865–7, and was present during the Rising. Having to flee to the US, he worked on the railroad, later obtaining teaching jobs and returning to Ireland on visits. Among his daring plans was a scheme to capture the Duke of Connaught on a visit to south Tipperary and hold him

hostage in a cave. During a similar attempt in the US with John Locke, the pair was arrested. This failure led to discussions and the founding of Clan na Gael under Jerome Collins. Finnan published nationalist poetry in the *Tipperary People*, keeping the flag flying for the next generation. He returned to Tipperary in old age and was buried in Mount Bruis, Ardvillane.

744. John Finnan, Shrough, Tipperary, 'head centre', who tore up railway tracks during the 1867 Rising and fled to America afterwards, but returned in the early 1870s.

745. John Finnan, Farnacliffe, Lattin, was an active Fenian during 1867 and subsequently agitated for land reform. He died in July 1915.

746. Lieut Maurice Fitzharris, a native of Ireland, had joined 42nd NY Tammany Regiment in 1861, aged 21. He rose through the ranks, fought at Gettysburg and was wounded four times. Having joined the Potomac 'circle' of the Fenian Brotherhood, Fitzharris travelled to Ireland in 1866, where he was detained as an organizer. As Capt. Fitzharris, he assisted T.F. Bourke during the Ballyhurst Rising and escaped after its failure to die before 1870 from old wounds.

747. John Fitzpatrick, Hollyford, gardener, moved to Tipperary town in the early 1860s, a Fenian who handed on his convictions to his family. Patrick, his son, participated in the Plan of Campaign and was imprisoned for some months. His grandson, Michael, born 1898, became quartermaster, 2nd southern division, IRA, during the War of Independence.

748. Patrick Fitzsimmons, Fethard, arrested in May 1866 with Patrick Gleeson, John Shea, William O'Brien and James Brennan, apparently drilling in the street; case dismissed.

749. Sgt William Flood, 28, a native of Donohill, served as a sergeant in 58th Illinois Volunteers for some months and joined the Fenian Brotherhood in 1865; on the list of officers of this organization available for action in Ireland.

750. James Flynn, Thurles, had left his employment without notice and was suspected of participating in the Rising, although no hard evidence was forthcoming. A warrant had been issued, but Flynn could not be found and had probably fled to America.

751. Cornelius Fogarty, Kilfeacle, a member of the notorious Fogarty family, held in Cashel jail after the Rising of 1867. He carried the Kilfeacle flag 'Death before dishonour' at the Tipperary amnesty meeting on 24 October 1869.

752. John Fogarty, 23, Kilfeacle, who lived with his brother Michael O'Neill Fogarty, was held during the suspension of habeas corpus from February to September 1866 and detained for a second time in 1867.

753. Johnny Fogarty, born in 1836, a son of Patrick Fogarty, The Moat, Kilfeacle, and a first cousin of Michael O'Neill Fogarty, returned from America to distribute subversive funds. An early Fenian who went on the run in Tipperary and Limerick during 1866, Fogarty was arrested in October and bailed in September 1867 on condition of abandoning Fenianism. After some years in the US he returned to Tipperary town, still retaining his convictions. His brother Patrick had been present at Ballyhurst in 1867 and was forced to emigrate. Johnny Fogarty's funeral Mass in May 1915 was that of a devout Catholic, while a '67 flag covered his coffin.

754. Thomas Fogarty, born in 1847 in Kilfadda, Borrisokane, was a labourer, who fought at Ballyhurst with a pike. Sentenced

to five years and transported to Western Australia, Fogarty was amnestied in 1869 and emigrated to San Francisco.

755. Daniel H. Gleason, Tipperary, ex-Tipperary militia, a bricklayer working on the Augustinian Church in Thomas Street, Dublin. An excellent IRB drill instructor, Gleason persuaded his men to join the Dublin militia, where they could drill in safety. He fled to Chicago after the Rising, became a successful politician and died in 1904.

756. John H. Gleason, born near Borrisoleigh in 1838, served in the constabulary and the Papal Brigade before emigrating to America, where he fought in the Civil War and was promoted to general in 1865. O'Mahony swore him into the Fenian Brotherhood in 1861; he became a leading organizer of the Potomac 'circle'. He returned home and was active in Borrisoleigh and Thurles in association with known Fenians, but arrested in February 1866 and held in Dublin until July. His wife, who had accompanied him, was in communication with New York. The US consul argued that this naturalized citizen should be released as he suffered from epileptic fits. It was rumoured that Gleeson returned to Ireland for the Rising, but this is unlikely. During the 1870 Fenian invasion of Canada, this rather boastful officer was again arrested. A younger brother, Patrick Jerome 'Battleaxe' Gleason [sic], 1844–1901, became mayor of Long Island City and owned the tram line to Calvary Cemetery, New York. Patrick enjoyed settling political disputes with his fists and became a byword for political corruption.

757. Capt. Joseph Gleeson, born in Fishmoyne, a brother of John H., who swore him into the Fenian Brotherhood in 1864. Gleeson served in 63rd New York Regiment during the Civil War and returned to Borrisoleigh in late 1865 in preparation

for the Rising, but was imprisoned between February and September 1866. He returned for a second time but failed to play a role in the Rising.

758. Timothy Gleeson, labourer, a brother of John and Joseph, was arrested as a Fenian in Ballymackey, Nenagh, in March 1867, as was their father, Michael, who had boasted of his seditious sons while drunk. There was no real evidence and he was discharged on substantial bail in June.

759. Joseph Gorman, formerly a porter at Bansha railway station, was dismissed for associating with Michael O'Neill Fogarty and his Fenian group. Gorman fled at the suspension of habeas corpus and was subsequently arrested in Freshford, Co. Kilkenny, using the alias 'James Murphy'. The authorities suspected him of having been among the Ballyhurst insurgents on 6 March 1867. Gorman suffered from heart disease, which the medical officer of the prison warned could prove fatal. He was kept in the infirmary until his discharge on bail in August.

760. Patrick Grady had been involved in an assassination attempt on Resident Magistrate Gore Jones, for which Hayes, his accomplice, had been sentenced to twenty years in 1863. Grady, an insurgent, turned informer at the treason felony trial of James Butler, Mount Catherine, Thurles, in August 1867.

761. John Greene, farmer, near Tipperary town, had gone to America briefly two years earlier. In early 1866 he was suspected of being a leader who drilled the IRB.

762. Michael Greene, a pensioner of 83rd Regiment, was arrested in February 1866 for attempting to swear a driver of the Royal Artillery into the IRB. He was committed for trial at the Clonmel spring assizes.

763. Patrick Greene, a native of Tramore, a classical tutor, had been staying in Tipperary with Jane Mandeville, the sister of John O'Mahony. The elderly Greene, an influential early Fenian in Carrick-on-Suir, was detained in Clonmel jail during 1866 until an appeal by John Blake Dillon, MP, proved successful.

764. John Halloran, Clonmel, hosted IRB meetings in his house in 1863, attended by Charles Kickham and Denis Dowling Mulcahy.

765. Thomas Hanly, 1845–87, Emly, participated in the attack on the abandoned local barracks in March 1867. When he died of consumption, locals organized a patriotic funeral.

766. Matt Hannon, Bansha, mason, among the most active in preparing the villagers for the amnesty meeting in Tipperary on 24 October 1869.

767. Pat Hannon, Bansha, carpenter, much occupied in organizing the locality for the amnesty meeting in Tipperary on 24 October 1869.

768. James O'Meara Harrington, 18, Templemore, was a son of Philip, military and merchant tailor of the same town. He himself worked as a tailor. Harrington was detained in Nenagh jail from July 1869 until 1870 for possession of treasonable documents. A soldier of 44th Regiment, arrested with letters incriminating Harrington, protested that they had been planted.

769. Thomas Harris, cooper, among young men arrested as suspected insurgents in Tipperary town in late March 1867.

770. John Hayes pleaded guilty to having participated in the sack of Roskeen Barracks in March 1867 under coercion and was allowed out on bail.

771. Patrick Hayes, carpenter, was among those arrested in Tipperary town in late March 1867 on suspicion of having been an insurgent.

772. Thomas Hayes, 15, IRB suspect transmitted from Thurles to Nenagh jail in April 1867, suspected of participation in the Rising, sentenced to two months.

773. 'Honest' Thomas Hayes, a native of Tipperary and successful blacksmith in Bloomsbury, London, supported the *Irish Liberator*, a radical newspaper in the metropolis. During a staff dispute Hayes wrote to the *Irish People* for advice, being friends with Thomas Clarke Luby. The *Irish People* failed to destroy this dangerous correspondence and its seizure in September 1865 compromised Hayes. When Hayes (the London 'head centre') refused to help Timothy Hegarty, who had fled Cork for New York as Stephens had ordered his men to remain for the Rising, Hegarty turned informer. Hayes was sentenced to ten years in 1866 but released in 1868, as Judge Keogh considered him a dupe of low intelligence. A rather eccentric character, he re-established his business on the Euston Road, London.

774. Michael Healy, 25, Borrisoleigh, was suspected of having been among those who attacked Roskeen Barracks near Thurles in March 1867, when the boy Treacy was shot dead. Healy petitioned to be freed from Nenagh jail on condition of emigrating, but was committed for trial. The authorities doubted that he had participated under coercion.

775. John Heeney, Cashel, shoemaker, considered among the most dangerous characters there, merely awaiting a leader or an insurrection to go into action in early 1866. The police kept him under close surveillance until he absconded to avoid arrest.

776. James Heffernan, 28, was born in Ballydruid Island near Cahir. He enjoyed a good education and as a Catholic felt called upon to serve in the Papal Brigade. A Fenian, he participated in one of the Canadian raids and when the amnestied leaders approached New York in January 1871, hastened to meet them, but caught his final illness and died that year in New Haven, Connecticut.

777. Rody Heffernan, Tipperary town, publican's son and a suspected leader, constantly in company with Fenian suspects in 1866.

778. Thomas Heffernan, Tipperary, draper's assistant, a prominent IRB man for the last three years, who went into the country for two or three days at intervals, suspected to be recruiting. The constabulary reported in November 1866 that Heffernan had left for America.

779. James Hegarty, Portroe near Nenagh, a respectable slater, briefly arrested in October 1865 with others on the information of Andrew Kennedy, who later retracted his statement. Hegarty and his companions were released on bail of £50 each.

780. Daniel Hennessy, farmer, a relative of Capt. Charles Burke of Kilcrue Watermill, hid the pikes belonging to the Devil's Bit Fenians on his land.

781. Daniel Hennessy, Tipperary town, tailor, who was observed at Ballyhurst fort armed with a pike on 6 March 1867.

782. James Hennessy had been arrested as an insurgent at Ballyhurst. Sentenced to twelve months in July 1867, he was released in April 1868.

783. James Heskins, IRB suspect transmitted from Thurles to Nenagh jail in April 1867, suspected of having participated in the Rising.

784. James Hickey was arrested shortly after the Ballyhurst Rising on suspicion of participation, sentenced to twelve months at the Tipperary assizes in July 1867 and released in April 1868.

785. Thomas Hickey, Coolnamuck, Carrickbeg, near Carrick-on-Suir, a farmer and one of O'Mahony's lieutenants, whose home sheltered the latter, Phil Gray and John Savage on the run, as described in the poem 'The Rebel Cot'. Hickey also participated in the attack on Portlaw constabulary barracks in September 1848. He became an early IRB leader and remained a strong supporter of Stephens and O'Mahony.

786. Timothy Hingerty, labourer, Nenagh, named by Andrew Kennedy as an IRB man in late 1865, eventually released.

787. Patrick or P.J. Hoctor, or Patrick Thorne Hoctor in later life, 1861–1933, was born near Newport. His mother, a Protestant, was one of the Thornes of Thornhill. (His career is covered in the main text.) In later life Hoctor was not trusted by the inner circle of the IRB or Devoy. He became a successful business man and judge at international trade exhibitions, moving from Kingstown (Dun Laoghaire) to London, trying to maintain his Republican contacts, but failed to be elected MP for North Tipperary in 1909, 1910 and 1915.[36]

788. Hugh Hogan, labourer, Nenagh, a suspected Fenian in 1866.

789. John Hogan, smith, Nenagh, an active IRB member in 1866.

790. Michael Hogan, 'county centre' for Tipperary, 1877 to 1883, was the first to receive a consignment of rifles when Clan na Gael began its scheme of smuggling arms into Ireland in 1879. Hogan assisted John O'Connor, the new Supreme Council

secretary, in reviving the IRB, but emigrated to Chicago in 1883. He died in Omaha in 1932.

791. William Hogan, also Horan, a native of Tipperary, was secretary of the St Patrick's Burial Society, an insurance company for Catholic emigrants in England. He was arrested in Birmingham in December 1867, accused of having obtained the revolvers for the Manchester rescue with Daniel Darragh, alias William McPherson Thompson. The authorities suspected Hogan of being the 'head centre' of Birmingham in 1867. He was acquitted on the arms charge, having created confusion and misidentification of the actual guns through a ruse. Hogan was actively organizing and gun-running in Birmingham, Liverpool and Nottingham, north Tipperary and the Irish midlands from 1869 to 1871. When his business declined, he emigrated to the US, abandoning his IRB links.

William Hogan (courtesy NLI).

792. Denis and John Horan, Rathfalla, Nenagh, both carpenters, who had been named by Andrew Kennedy as Fenians and were arrested in 1866.

793. John Horan, a native of Co. Tipperary, stayed in the Star and Garter Hotel, Dublin, for up to six months since arriving from America with little luggage and no ostensible business. He had a military air and was a naturalized US citizen. Detained under the habeas corpus suspension from 17 February until September 1866, Horan returned to America.

794. Thomas Hourigan, Nenagh, a mason, who was suspected as an active IRB member between 1866 and 1870.

795. John Johnston, baker, Roscrea, unemployed, but associating with William Bracken, lately returned from England. They had plenty of money, were in contact with Col Gleeson and suspected of being Fenian agents in 1866.

796. Edmund (or Edward) [O']Kavanagh, 25, Carrick-on-Suir, son of John Kavanagh, clerk in Malcomson's linen factory. A prominent Fenian and confidential IRB messenger, Edmund was dismissed by his employer. Arrested with his father in February 1866, Edmund's discharge from Mountjoy in January 1867 was conditional on his departure for America.

797. John [O']Kavanagh, Carrick-on-Suir, a shopkeeper, who had hidden John O'Mahony in 1848 and 'identified himself with every insurrectionary movement for the last twenty years'. The police stated that Kavanagh suffered from revolutionary 'mania'.[37] He was in the confidence of Stephens, sold the *Irish People*, served proudly as a local leader and received £1 a week from Fenian funds. Constantly surrounded by subversives, including Peter Quirke, Kavanagh met all agents arriving from Dublin and America. His daughter Kate also supported the IRB. Imprisoned without trial since February 1866, Kavanagh protested that, being seventy-seven years of age, after eighteen months in prison he

would not survive the coming winter. He was discharged in November 1867.

798. Martin Kearney, Fermoy, 23, publican's son, was arrested in Clonmel in suspicious circumstances in April 1867, having enlisted in 44th Regiment. He was discharged on bail a year later; FP 239.

799. Timothy Keeshan, Roscrea, miner, who had returned from California in 1864 and harboured Fenians in his home, also suspected to be acquainted with General Gleeson. By April 1866 Keeshan was imprisoned in Antrim jail. In the last stages of consumption, he was released shortly afterwards.

800. John Kelleher, 25, born in Ballymacarbry, Co. Waterford, employed as a merchant's clerk in Clonmel, where he was the chief IRB agent. Kelleher compiled a list of residences to be raided for guns. His year-long detention from March 1867 acted as a deterrent to local activists. Kelleher was discharged on health grounds.

801. James Kenna, shopman, Carrick-on-Suir, prominent IRB member in late 1866.

802. Andrew Kennedy, 35, Nenagh, an IRB organizer, who had been dismissed from the North Tipperary militia in 1865. He was arrested that May, when suspicious documents referring to 'rods' (pikes) were found on him. In October Kennedy attempted to swear in Jeremiah Corboy of Summerhill, Nenagh, an egg merchant, who informed the authorities. On arrest Kennedy volunteered to turn Crown witness and identified a number of Fenians. He revoked his evidence, however, and was tried and sentenced to five years for perjury. Suffering from chronic bronchitis, Kennedy was transferred to Woking Prison and twice petitioned for his release, expressing regret for his politics. Dangerously ill, he was released on licence in September 1867.

803. Edward Kennedy, Ballyrichard, was one of those accused of marching in military fashion through Carrick-on-Suir in October 1865, but was soon released.

804. Martin Kennedy, Nenagh, labourer, suspected as an IRB member in 1870.

805. Patrick Kennedy, Nenagh, miner, a prominent IRB member in November 1866.

806. Thomas Kennedy, Thurles, shoemaker, was in the confidence of well-known Fenians in late 1866. The constabulary considered him deeply implicated and a warrant for his arrest was issued in March 1867, although he seems to have fled the country.

807. John Kenrick, Fethard, tailor and IRB member, who assisted Thomas Francis Bourke in the run-up to the Rising and cared for Capt. Delahunt on his deathbed. Detained from March to June 1867, Kenrick's release on bail was due to poor health; he died soon afterwards.

808. Patrick Kenrick, Fethard, tailor and leading Fenian, in regular contact with T.F. Bourke before the Rising. A brother of John, Patrick was arrested in April 1867 and transferred to Mountjoy. Although he raised concerns regarding his health, Patrick was not discharged until 1868, when he emigrated to America.

809. John Kent, Ballylynch, Carrick-on-Suir, a clerk and constant associate of local Fenians, including Peter Quirke and the [O']Kavanaghs. Kent went to Mullinahone during the arrests in September 1865 to remove incriminating documents on Quirke's behalf. He was detained in Clonmel jail from February to May 1866.

810. Rody Kickham, Clonagoose, Mullinahone, 'an athletic man', who had returned from America to become an organizer in south Tipperary. He was arrested in Mullinahone in March 1864. A cousin of

Charles Kickham, Rody also drilled with the Liverpool Fenians, but retired to the US after the collapse of the movement and died in New York.

811. James Joseph Kirwan, 25, a native of Thurles, gunsmith, who had returned from the US and was arrested in Dublin among the insurgents in March 1867.

812. Michael Kirwan, Templemore, pawnbroker, suspected of being an IRB officer in late 1866.

813. Patrick Lahey (or Leahy), born in Thurles in 1847, labourer, participated in Capt. Charles Burke's raids for arms on 5 March 1867. Lahey helped to burn the house of a man who refused to join the insurgents, torched the Roskeen police barracks near Thurles and was involved in the incident in which the boy Treacy was killed. He was sentenced to five years and transported to Western Australia. Amnestied in 1869, he went to San Francisco.

814. Michael Lalor, butter-merchant, among young men arrested in Tipperary town in late March 1867.

815. William Landy, 20, shoemaker, born in Nenagh, but a resident of Dublin; FP 262.

816. Esmond Lawler, Tipperary, butter-merchant, was detained for two months as a suspect in Clonmel jail from March 1867.

817. Laurence Lonergan, 20, Ballylooby, a blacksmith and Fenian suspect, emigrated to America in November 1867, having been detained for a year.

818. Peggy Lonergan, Moanure, a female blacksmith, who made pikes for the Lisronagh Fenians in 1866.

819. Denis Long, transmitted from Thurles to Nenagh jail in April 1867, suspected of participation in the Rising. He pleaded guilty and was sentenced to ten months.

820. John Looby of Coolacussane, Dundrum, fled in March 1866, but returned in December 1867, apparently as an agent of Michael O'Neill Fogarty. Looby, the associate of IRB members, was imprisoned in Mountjoy as a warning to others. His mother petitioned for his release, for he was needed to run their 22-acre farm. Looby was discharged on bail in May 1868.

821. James Lynch, the Spittal, Tipperary town, painter, was observed with a gun at Ballyhurst on 6 March 1867.

822. Edward McCarthy, alias Davis, a native of Newport who had arrived in Dublin from America although he had no job or family there. McCarthy pawned four revolvers when he ran out of money. He was detained as a Fenian suspect from January to April 1867 and discharged on condition of returning to the US.

823. Sgt John McCarthy, 26, a native of Roscrea, served in 61st New York Volunteers as a drill sergeant and was twice wounded but not incapacitated. McCarthy appeared on the 1865 roster of military personnel of the Fenian Brotherhood, in preparation for their Irish expedition.

824. Pat McCarthy, Lisronagh, warder in Clonmel jail, facilitated the escape of Capt. Laurence O'Brien in 1867 in conjunction with the O'Neill family of Lisronagh. McCarthy was forced to resign and emigrated to America. His colleague, Pat Meehan, Scotch Road, remained undiscovered and continued to assist nationalist prisoners.

825. John McCormack or Cormack, Nenagh, carpenter, identified as one of the local leaders by Andrew Kennedy, was to be tried for treason felony until Kennedy recanted. His character was considered good, but the authorities continued to suspect McCormack and he was detained for five months and only released in August 1866.

826. Denis McCraith, 28, stationmaster in Bansha and a cousin and associate of Michael O'Neill Fogarty. McCraith turned the station into an IRB meeting point and was dismissed by the Waterford & Limerick Railway. Returning to Tipperary for the Rising, he was arrested and detained in Clonmel jail, where Corridon identified him in August 1867.

827. David McGrath, Carrick-on-Suir, arrested in late 1866 in possession of a letter from James Stephens, which appointed him 'head centre' of Carrick.

828. John McGrath, Crogue, Tipperary, shoemaker, was among one hundred men assembling in a field on the night of 5 March 1867; they dispersed under the impression that the military was coming. He claimed that he had met with armed rebels on the road towards Tipperary and was forced to join them. They went into fields near Garnacanty and then to Ballyhurst fort. On arrest, McGrath was eager to inform and the authorities removed him to a place of safety.

829. John McHenry, Nenagh, tailor, arrested in Francis Street, Dublin, as a suspected Fenian under the habeas corpus suspension in March 1866. He had been unemployed since arriving in the city.

830. Timothy Mackesey, Carrick-on-Suir (in some accounts Clonmel), cooper and firkin-maker, who was an associate of Colour Sgt Charles McCarthy. Inactive as a 'centre', Mackesey was accused of pilfering IRB funds while unemployed. Detained from February 1866 until August 1867 in Kilmainham on Head Constable Talbot's evidence, he was finally released on condition of leaving for America.

831. Patrick Mackey, Templemore, agent for Sir James Power's distillery, was the first 'head centre' of this district and consulted with the Gleeson brothers. According to the police, Mackey's family was respectable; he enjoyed an income of £200 p.a., but had a drink problem. He was detained from February until June 1866, when Sir James Power arranged his bail. In poor health, Mackey did not participate in the Rising, but was pivotal in selecting O'Donovan Rossa as the amnesty candidate for the by-election of 1869. He died young in 1873.

832. Thomas Mackey, Templemore, first cousin of Patrick, a clerical student in St Patrick's College, Thurles, and an IRB member, attended a planning meeting with Capt. Joseph Gleeson shortly before the Rising. (It is not known if he participated in the insurrection.) Mackey later became parish priest of Grand Rapids, Michigan, US.

833. Joseph McMahon, Nenagh, publican, on whose premises IRB members assembled in late 1865.

834. Thomas Madigan, Carrick-on-Suir, had returned twice from America since September 1865 and consorted with Edward O'Kavanagh and some soldiers in the pubs, where Madigan paid all bills. An officer of 53rd Regiment considered him a Fenian agent, intent on subverting the British army. Arrested in March 1866, Madigan was released in July and forced to emigrate to America.

835. Cornelius Maher, Upperchurch, farmer, one of the insurgents, testified concerning the role of Michael Sheehy and James Butler during the Rising at Roskeen Barracks. When the trial commenced, Maher revoked his statement, was tried for perjury and sentenced to six months in August 1867, but avoided the stigma of being an informer.

836. John Maher, Ballinure, labourer, suspected of participating in the Rising at Ballyhurst, held for some weeks in Clonmel jail before being discharged by May 1867.

837. Michael Maher, Thurles, butcher, an active Fenian agent who received funds from America and was rumoured to have been a captain of the Barnane Fenians during the Rising, but kept a low profile. He was discharged from detention on bail of £400 in August 1867.

838. Philip Maher, probably a brother of Michael, pleaded guilty to participating in the Rising in north Tipperary in August 1867 and was discharged on bail.

839. William Maher, the son of a very wealthy farmer near Mullinahone, was suspected of being a 'centre' in early 1866, as he had been drilling large crowds.

840. William Maher, house-painter, Clonmel, vanished in March 1867, probably to fight in the Rising. He was afterwards detained and discharged for America in April 1868.

841. Thomas Malony, Nenagh, identified as a Fenian leader in September 1865 by Andrew Kennedy, who later retracted his evidence.

842. Laurence Mangan, Catherine Street, Clonmel, labourer, was pointed out by Patrick Power, the informer, charged with Fenianism and sent to jail in Dublin in October 1865.

843. Robert Meagher, Kilbury, land steward, arrested on 10 March 1866, was suspected as a Fenian 'centre' by the police in Mullinahone. A great number of people met at his house, although he was socially above the usual IRB membership. Meagher protested his innocence and requested an investigation with reference to the Catholic clergy. He was manager of a farm belonging to minors, which would deteriorate if his imprisonment continued. Meagher and Patrick Greene jointly appealed to John Blake Dillon, MP, to be liberated.

844. William and John Francis Meagher were the sons of Denis Meagher of Lough Street, Carrick-on-Suir, and James Meagher, 'centre' of Carrick, whose Fenian funeral occurred in January 1865, was probably another relation. By late 1865 William had become the 'centre'. When pikes were discovered in their garden, Denis and William were detained in Clonmel jail, but released in January 1866. From February William and his teenage brother John Francis were detained in Clonmel and Dublin, where William died of cholera in December. John Francis headed a fund to erect headstones for the local Fenians. The sole survivor of the IRB leaders of Carrick, he wrote for the *Irishman* and the *Shamrock*, publishing *A Wreath of Prison Flowers*, a volume of poetry (1869), and the *Annals, Antiquities and Records of Carrick-on-Suir* (1881). In 1877 Meagher was instrumental in arranging the local funeral procession for John O'Mahony. Friends tried to collect a fund for him in 1890, as his health declined. Meagher died around 1900.[38]

John Francis Meagher (courtesy NLI).

845. Patrick Miller, Wexford militia, but residing in Portlaw for the past six years, was arrested for military marching with five other men in Carrick-on-Suir in October 1865. He was soon discharged on bail.

846. Andrew Milne (or Millen), 23, a Protestant tailor living in Clonmel, arrested in October 1865 as a suspected IRB leader. Initially committed for trial on the testimony of the informer Patrick Power, Milne was discharged on bail in March 1867.

847. Daniel Mockler, also referred to as 'J.D. Mockler', Mullinahone, a shoemaker and active IRB member, who represented Rody Kickham on occasion and whose home served as a Fenian rendezvous. He was imprisoned from March to May 1866.

848. Col Edmund Mockler alias Doheny, ex-US army, had emigrated in 1856 and bore the scars of his Civil War wounds. He returned to Ireland in 1867 and stayed with his uncles Maher of Lismolin and Nicholas and Michael Mockler in Beeverstown, near Mullinahone, before visiting his prosperous Doheny relatives in Dunmanway. It was rumoured that he participated in a meeting of mounted Fenians in this area. Mockler was arrested on 5 January 1868 and escorted to the county jail in Cork by twenty constables with fixed bayonets, as there were fears of a rescue. When it was confirmed that he was not the son but a nephew of 'the celebrated Doheny', who was indeed in poor health, his release followed. It also emerged that one of his successful uncles in West Cork dropped a hint to a magistrate to rid himself of this embarrassing guest.[39]

849. Michael Molony, Tipperary, a representative at the Terence Bellew McManus funeral in 1861.

850. Thomas Molony, Nenagh, named as an IRB leader by Andrew Kennedy in 1865, eventually released.

851. Philip Morrissey, second-in-command of the Carrick-on-Suir IRB, and an associate of Colour Sgt McCarthy, William Meagher and other suspects, often attended Fenian meetings in Clonmel. His brother, John, and his sister, who Thomas Talbot described as one of the strongest Fenian supporters in Carrick, were also involved. Among *agent provocateur* Talbot's victims, Philip Morrissey remained in Kilmainham from early 1866 until 1868, when he agreed to emigrate to America.

852. John Murphy, Cahir, telegraph clerk, suspected as a Fenian, constantly associating with what the authorities considered 'bad characters'. He was perceived as a danger in this garrison town because of his position and detained under the habeas corpus suspension from March to July 1866.

853. John Murphy, Carrick-on-Suir, among men marching in military formation in October 1865. Arrested by the constabulary, he was soon discharged on bail.

854. William Murphy, Thurles, carpenter, an IRB suspect, who was rumoured to have been 'out' in the Rising. He fled to England, where destitution forced him to join a cavalry regiment of the British army. On being identified, the Duke of Cambridge ordered that Murphy and Daniel Connell were not to be discharged, for fear they would re-enlist under false names and spread Fenianism undetected.

855. Timothy Nihill, Cullen, had formed an IRB 'circle' in 1865 and was considered to be the local 'centre'. He kept up contact with the Fenians in Oola, Co. Limerick. Nihill was present during drilling in Ryan's farmhouse near Glenbane, when a constable surprised the assembled Fenians, who shot him. Nihill was acquitted, however. In exile in France, he successfully taught English, due to his excellent education in Kilteely School under William Lundon.

856. Patrick Nolan, tailor, armed with a pike, was among the north Tipperary insurgents under Capt. Charles Burke and Michael Sheehy.

857. Matthew Noonan, Rathfalla, Nenagh, arrested in October 1865 on the evidence of Andrew Kennedy, later retracted. Probably identical with the coach-builder's assistant of the same name, who was detained in early 1866.

858. Thomas Norris, Irishtown, Clonmel, a chandler's assistant, who was constantly associating with local suspects. Detained for six months as a dangerous character, he was released on bail in September 1866. Norris was soon active again, in company with Andrew Milne and others, and imprisoned from November 1866 to February 1867.

859. Michael J. Nugent, 'a strolling character' and salesman without a permanent home, who occasionally visited Cahir. He was a close friend of John Murphy, the telegraph clerk, and an associate of Daniel Boland. When arrested in February 1866, Nugent was in possession of the *Irish People*, a Fenian newspaper from New York. He was suspected of being a IRB agent, his job facilitating him in disseminating separatism. Very frightened in detention, the authorities hoped he might give information and did not discharge him on bail until April.

860. Edward O'Brien, Cloneen near Mullinahone, had initially studied for the priesthood before becoming a law student. He was frequently observed among those drilling.

861. Henry O'Brien, 27, was born in Clonbeg, where his relatives remained. This suspect was formerly a police sub-constable and only in Dublin for about a month when arrested on suspicion; FP 376.

862. John O'Brien, Ballyporeen, was an agent for the *Irish People* and the reputed Ballyporeen 'head centre'.

863. John O'Brien, Cullen, Emly, freeholder, suspected of being a local IRB leader. O'Brien usually accompanied Timothy Nihill, who was charged with shooting a constable in February 1866. O'Brien also ran a 'dancing house' where the IRB met. He was arrested for drilling but released after four months. In 1869 O'Brien was the 'head centre' of Cullen. He and his brother were in possession of guns and pistols.

864. John Patrick O'Brien, a native of Nenagh, had emigrated with his family to London. A medical student, he used the alias 'Thomas Simpson' to enlist in 85th Regiment, awaiting the Rising, while infiltrating the British army. He was sentenced to life for desertion and Fenianism in Dublin in March 1867, responding with 'three cheers for the Irish Republic'. Ineligible for amnesty as a traitorous soldier, O'Brien was not released until 1878, when he witnessed the collapse and death of Colour Sgt McCarthy in Dublin. He settled down as the superintendent of the Public Baths in Tara Street, Dublin.[40]

865. Kendal Edmund O'Brien was born in 1849, a son of Richard O'Brien of Cullen, Golden, and brought up with a good education. He participated in the Rising aged 18. Subsequently O'Brien supported the IRB amnesty campaign to elect O'Donovan Rossa to Parliament. Rossa was disqualified as a felon and his supporters became responsible for the election debts. O'Brien and his brother Patrick, large farmers, sold some of their property to help out and Patrick was forced to emigrate. Nevertheless Kendal O'Brien continued his involvement in nationalist politics and assisted John Mitchel when standing for Parliament. He promoted the Land League, was evicted and elected to Parliament for Mid-Tipperary in 1900. In failing health, he continued to attend the House of Commons and died in London in 1909.

866. Laurence O'Brien, a tenant farmer on a hundred acres in Cloneen near Mullinahone, was suspected of being a 'centre', as suspicious persons held meetings in his home at night. Arrested in March 1866, he was soon released on substantial bail.

867. Capt. Laurence O'Brien, 1842–1923, born in Cahir, emigrated and fought in the American Civil War. He became the state 'centre' of the Fenian Brotherhood for Connecticut before returning to Europe. He was based in Paris as a Fenian paymaster, was active in England and went to Ireland for the Rising. Detained in Clonmel prison, he was rescued in November 1867 by Felix O'Neill and his sisters, who provided the necessary tools and could influence the prison staff. O'Brien filed through the bars of his window and used thread to deaden the noise, forming imitation bars from bootblack. Back in the US, he became a prosperous builder and one of the founders of Clan na in Gael in New Haven, Connecticut. He assisted Devoy with preparations for the *Catalpa* rescue.

868. Thomas O'Brien alias William Dwyer, 30, born in Tipperary town, farmer, arrested on arrival in Dublin as a potential Fenian and held in Mountjoy from March to September 1867. He was released on condition of going to America.

869. William O'Brien of the Spital, Tipperary, armed with a revolver while marching to Ballyhurst under T.F. Bourke on 6 March 1867, according to an informer.

870. William O'Brien, Tipperary, member of the committee of the IRB in Tipperary in 1864.

871. Capt. Joseph O'Carroll, alias Capt. Kearney, a native of Tipperary, who had a fine record in 5th New York Cavalry during the Civil War and travelled to Mullingar on Fenian business. According to Devoy, O'Carroll had become the 'centre' of an infiltrated British regiment there. He was arrested in Dublin sharing a bed with Maj. Comerford and Capt. Bible in March 1866 and detained in Mountjoy until November 1867, when he returned to America.

872. Daniel O'Connell or Connell, Grawn, Toomevara, a prosperous tenant farmer, was arrested while drilling on his land in September 1865. He was detained in Nenagh jail for four months, before being transferred for trial at the Dublin Special Commission, which sentenced him to two years in January 1866. O'Connell was released in December 1867 and returned home. An ardent promoter of Rossa's candidature for Tipperary in 1869, O'Connell was rejected as a member of the grand jury for 1892, because of his Fenian past.

873. Edward (or Edmund) O'Doherty, a native of Carrick-on-Suir, considered by the constabulary to be 'a determined, ill-conditioned fellow', who had returned from America, apparently 'capable of committing anything, no matter how revolting'.[41] He associated exclusively with Fenians, especially Edward Croke and Cornelius O'Leary, and was not short of money. O'Doherty was arrested in March 1866 and explained that the purpose of his visit was to escort his mother and brother to the US. Dublin Castle released him in January 1867, on condition of emigrating to America.

874. Brian O'Donnell, Victoria House, Clonmel, served on the provincial council of the IRB in 1864 and remained under police observation. He and Michael O'Neill Fogarty stood in for Denis Dowling Mulcahy, when the latter was absent.

875. Malachy O'Donovan, 1839–1921, IRB member involved in the occupation of Emly constabulary barracks in 1867.

After the collapse of the Rising, O'Donovan became a promoter of the amnesty movement. In November 1921, his coffin, draped with the tricolour, was carried to the grave by Irish Volunteers.

876. Capt. O'Dowd, one of the leaders present at Ballyhurst with T.F. Bourke on 6 March 1867, armed with a revolver and identified by John McGrath, an informer. O'Dowd was among the party of American officers seizing horses from Capt. Charles Massey of Grantstown at the start of the Rising – afterwards, Massey refused to identify the Fenians and retained his local popularity.

877. Edward O'Fogarty, Ballyrichard, arrested in February 1866 as an IRB suspect by the Carrick-on-Suir constabulary.

878. Arthur O'Leary, 1833 -61, born in Tipperary town, a tutor and minor poet and the brother of John and Ellen, who joined the IRB at an early stage, but died young of tuberculosis.

879. Cornelius O'Leary was born in Cork city in 1840, served in the Papal Brigade and settled in Carrick-on-Suir for some years. He fought in the American Civil War in 88th Regiment and was badly wounded, suffered a permanent disability and received a military pension. O'Leary returned to Carrick as a Fenian organizer with Edward O'Doherty and was detained in Clonmel jail from March until August 1866, when he agreed to permanent exile from Ireland. He died in 1926 and was buried in Holycross Cemetery, Flatbush, New York.

880. Felix Hugh O'Neill, 1810–1901, a gentleman farmer in Lisronagh, Clonmel, who had led the attack on Glenbower constabulary barracks in 1848 with Michael and Richard Comerford of Newtown, Carrick-on-Suir. As he had failed to post scouts, the rebels were surprised from the rear and fled. O'Neill spent some time in France to avoid arrest. He became a prominent IRB leader in Tipperary in conjunction with Denis Dowling Mulcahy and Michael O'Neill Fogarty. O'Neill trained the local Fenians for the Rising, but bad weather prevented them from turning out. He was involved in Capt. Laurence O'Brien's jailbreak in November 1867, hiding him in Lisronagh. Once again, O'Neill went abroad to evade arrest. The last native speaker among Irish scholars in his district, he supported land reform and was injured during the Mitchelstown Massacre in 1887.

881. Margaret O'Neill, sister of Felix, was a Fenian, who assisted Ricard O'Sullivan Burke with preparations for the Rising. She was also involved in the rescue of Laurence O'Brien from Clonmel jail, aided by her sister Jane and sister-in-law Catherine. O'Brien was hidden in a dug out in Lisronagh until Felix and Margaret could convey him to Waterford port, where he sailed for America. Her subsequent life was an anticlimax, her marriage to a sea captain in America collapsed due to his desertion or bigamy and she withdrew to Liverpool, where her elderly mother and married sister lived.

882. Michael O'Rourke, Ballyhane near Dundrum, blacksmith, in whose garden the constabulary found pike heads. Arrested in March 1866, O'Rourke was bailed from Nenagh jail in June, when plans for his trial were abandoned.

883. Thomas O'Rourke, Hollyford, miner, tried to set up an IRB 'circle' in Hollyford. He was detained in Nenagh jail from October 1865 to April 1866 and assembled with his followers on the night of the Rising in hopes of action. Arrested for a second time, O'Rourke was discharged for America in April 1868.

884. Patrick O'Shea, Tipperary, member of the Tipperary IRB committee in 1864.

885. Patrick O'Sheedy, Tipperary town, a grocer's assistant and reputedly its acting 'centre', who corresponded with the *Irish People* and was a constant companion of 'head centre' Thomas Dogherty Brohan and other suspects. Although the constabulary failed to obtain evidence for a prosecution, O'Sheedy was arrested in March 1866. He pleaded that his job necessitated contact with a variety of people, which led to his being mistaken for a Fenian. Nevertheless, he was only released on bail in February 1867.

886. James Phelan, Cloneen, Clonmel, member of the local IRB committee in 1864.

887. Michael Phelan, 25, draper's assistant, born Modeshill, Mullinahone, where his family still lived, but employed in Dublin, a suspected Fenian; FP 426.

888. Capt. Patrick Phelan, 40, a native of Tipperary, who served with 18th New York Cavalry for three years and commanded a light cavalry battalion, was included on the Fenian roster for the projected expedition to Ireland.

889. William Pope, Clonmel, according to the police a very bad, dangerous Fenian, who had returned from the US. He was also rumoured to have set several fires and was detained in Clonmel jail by March 1866, when his brother petitioned that stories had been spread by malicious persons and Pope would return to America if discharged. He was released in October 1866.

890. Patrick Power, Clonmel, one of Stephens's confidential couriers, had been sworn into the IRB in early 1865 by Owen Sweeney in Thomas Burke's pub. Power also distributed pikes in Clonmel. He became intoxicated in Dublin in September 1865, after collecting an important letter from Stephens for transmission to south

Tipperary. This document, stolen by the informer Nagle, helped to trigger the arrest of the Fenian leadership. In detention, Power turned informer.

891. Philip Power, 66, a native of Co. Waterford and an active sympathizer in 1848, had become a publican in Clonmel, where he was the only vendor of the *Irish People*. The police considered him deeply disloyal. Arrested in March 1866, Power protested his innocence as a personal friend of old Denis Mulcahy, while his daughter had sold the Fenian paper merely for profit. When his health declined in Clonmel jail, Power was released in June, but soon tried to swear soldiers into the IRB. He was again detained from December 1866 to June 1867, as the constabulary argued that he would participate in any potential outbreak.

892. Sgt J.J. Powers, 22, born in Nine Mile House, served in 50th Massachusetts Volunteers for a year and volunteered for the roster of Fenian Brotherhood officers.

893. William Purcell, servant of the Ryans of Gortkelly Castle, Thurles, had been forced to accompany the insurgents, who also obtained his employer's arms. He claimed during their trial in August 1867, that he had seen or heard little. The exasperated court threatened him with imprisonment unless he spoke up.

894. George Quin, Powerstown, Clonmel, sworn into the IRB by Pierce Nagle by 1865.

895. Michael Quinlan, Glassdrum, Cappawhite, a farmer, who was arrested in April 1867. According to Col Purefoy, Greenfields, Quinlan intended to attack the Cappawhite police barracks on 5 March, but had to abandon this due to disagreements among his followers. The informer Corridon identified him as a Fenian, but Quinlan was discharged on bail

in September 1867, after promising to abandon sedition.

896. Peter Quirke, Carrick-on-Suir, was very active during the 1865 Fenian demonstrations, which included a regatta and an IRB man's funeral procession. His elderly father was also a Fenian. Peter associated with local suspects, including Charles Kickham, Patrick Greene and the two O'Kavanaghs. Quirke was said to have collected rifles from the *Irish People* office in Dublin. The constabulary considered him the notorious 'head centre' of Carrick. He emigrated in early 1866.

897. James Rankins, farmer's son, among the insurgents at Ballyhurst, when he disobeyed a Fenian officer and tried to desert. He was shot and wounded. Visited by a resident magistrate at home, Rankins refused to inform. Witnesses disagreed whether Capt. O'Dowd or Harrison, another Irish-American, had fired at him.

898. Thomas Reddan, Nenagh, named as an IRB member by Andrew Kennedy in October 1865, eventually released.

899. John Renehan, draper's assistant, among young men arrested in Tipperary town in late March 1867 on suspicion of having participated in the Rising.

900. William Roche, Ballyhurst, armed with a pistol on 6 March 1867 at Ballyhurst fort during the Rising.

901. Richard Rogers, Borrisoleigh, detained for one month from April 1866 on the statement of Denis Buckley, 13th Regiment, that he was an agent, enlisting soldiers under the direction of General Gleeson, who would command the Fenians during the Rising. The general and Rogers were often present when the men drilled near Borrisoleigh. Among the arrangements for the insurrection was a plan to poison the rations of those British soldiers who had not turned Fenian and to tear down telegraph wires. Rogers protested that he was a victim of private spite and offered character references from R.C. clergy and magistrates; he finally volunteered bail and emigration, if released and was discharged in June on these conditions.

902. Thaddeus Ronayne or Roughan, Tipperary town, a shoemaker arrested in September 1865, after the police discovered his letter to the *Irish People*, in which he expressed the wish to follow Robert Emmet. Ronayne was released on bail in April 1866.

903. James Patrick Russell, Tipperary, insurgent, shot dead at Ballyhurst on 6 March 1867 and buried in Lattin graveyard, where his name is on the War of Independence monument. Jeremiah J. Finnan eulogized him in verse, to 'view with love the hallowed scene, and keep the grave of Russell green'.

904. William Rutherford, author of the booklet '*'67 Retrospection. A concise history of the Fenian Rising at Ballyhurst fort, Tipperary*' (1903), had been among the insurgents, as related by himself.

905. Denis Ryan, Ballyneety, Co. Limerick, a farmer's son, among young men arrested on suspicion of having been an insurgent in Tipperary town in late March 1867.

906. George Ryan, Five Alley, Nenagh, arrested on the word of Andrew Kennedy in late 1865.

907. James Ryan, Glenbane, Cullen, farmer, in whose home the Fenians drilled under Private James Dillon. Surprised by the police, James was involved in the shooting and wounding of Constable Dunne in February 1866. He was sentenced to fourteen years.

908. Sgt James Ryan, 30, a native of Carrick-on-Suir, had spent some months in the Federal artillery and belonged to the

Fenian Brotherhood's 'artillery circle' of the army of the Potomac; he featured on the roster of officers of the Brotherhood, available for action. ✗

909. James Ryan, Tipperary, had returned from America. After observation, the police issued a warrant for his arrest in 1870.

910. John Ryan, Glenbane, Cullen, farmer and brother of James, tried for aiding Private James Dillon, 17th Regiment, in shooting a constable in February 1866. After his acquittal in March 1867, Ryan continued to be detained on other charges.

911. John Ryan, Bawnmacshane townland, Mullinahone, a militiaman, who acted as drill instructor for the local IRB in early 1866. He was dismissed from the militia and imprisoned for five months.

912. John Ryan, farmer on eighty acres near Dundrum, was arrested on suspicion of having assembled for the Rising. He was held in Clonmel jail for three months. In October 1869 Ryan attracted renewed notice by attending a Fenian meeting in Tipperary.

913. John Ryan, Thurles, a grocer and publican, long suspected of encouraging Fenianism in his district. He sold the *Irish People* and, after its demise, the *Irishman*. His premises were a gathering place for the disaffected and General Gleeson was a constant visitor. On a market day in February 1866, Ryan displayed John O'Mahony's portrait (featured in the *Irishman*) in his shop window, which confirmed his Fenian allegiance in the eyes of the authorities.

914. John Ryan, Nenagh, a carpenter, who was released from Kilmainham in July 1868 after fourteen months in detention, which had damaged his health; he pleaded guilty to having tried to swear soldiers into the IRB.

915. Martin Ryan, farmer, Bohermore, near Tipperary town, suspected leader

in early 1866, meetings were held in his house and he was frequently in the company of the town's IRB leaders.

916. Martin and Simon Ryan, Rathcloheen, Kilfeacle, were observed by the constabulary as prominent among those attending the Tipperary amnesty meeting on 24 October 1869. They were wearing green sashes and hat bands.

917. Matthew Ryan, Dawsonsbog, Templederry, was among those members of the farming community who sheltered Capt. Charles Bourke of Kilcrue on the run, still recalled in folk memory in North Tipperary in 1938.

918. Michael Ryan, letter-carrier, Borrisoleigh, took an active part in Fenian displays in 1869.

919. Oliver Ryan had been among the 1867 insurgents and served a sentence in Clonmel jail, but was pardoned in early 1868.

920. Sgt Paddy Ryan, Tipperary town, was the best-known IRB member in Templemore and a NCO of the 11th depot battalion, which was transferred to Ulster before the Rising.

921. Patrick Ryan, Nenagh, shoemaker, very active in March 1870.

922. Patrick Ryan, the Spittal, Tipperary town, carried a gun at Ballyhurst on 6 March 1867.

923. Patrick Ryan, Clonmel, a nailer and a private in the south Tipperary militia in 1864, who had been sworn in by the informer Pierce Nagle. Ryan inducted militiamen into the IRB and served on its local committee. He was imprisoned in Clonmel for five months.

924. Thomas Ryan, a labourer employed by Mr Massey, Kilfeacle, and an insurgent in March 1867, who assisted in detaining

his employer during the Rising. Afterwards, Ryan turned Crown witness and was rewarded with £10.

925. Thomas Ryan, farmer, Emly, fled Tipperary for Killarney in the aftermath of the Rising. He became the lodger of a constable and told him that he had led the attack on Emly barracks after Harrison, an Irish-American leader, failed to arrive in time. He also stated that Capt. O'Dowd had shot Rankins for disobeying orders at Ballyhurst. Ryan complained that the IRB had never reimbursed him for money advanced. In May 1867 Ryan and two cousins were apparently sent to New Pallas barracks to shoot the sergeant, but did not succeed.

926. Thomas Ryan, Cappawhite, a publican, who constantly allowed Thomas Blackwell's IRB followers to meet on his premises in 1865–6. Ryan was liberated after three months in prison, as his wife pleaded that the family would otherwise have to enter the workhouse.

927. Timothy Ryan, Cappawhite, a schoolmaster and Fenian agent of Thomas Blackwell. Ryan emigrated to America, where he worked on road gangs in Brooklyn and New Jersey.

928. William Ryan, Carrick-on-Suir, a stonemason employed in Malcolmson's factory in Portlaw, was arrested as a Fenian associate of Colour Sgt McCarthy, William Meagher and Philip Morrissey. Ryan was held without trial for a year from February 1866.

929. William Sheedy, Nenagh, suspected as a companion of Fenians in late 1866.

930. Michael Sheehy, Thurles 'centre', a livestock dealer with a disciplined 'circle', which, however, lacked experienced officers. They turned out on 5 March 1867, raided residences for arms and burned Roskeen police barracks. Afterwards, he tried to flee but was arrested in Cobh on 21 March, disguised as 'Kate Ryan', a girl emigrating to America. Sheehy was sentenced to twenty years. Amnestied in 1871, Sheehy accompanied William Mackey Lomasney, whose sister he married, to Detroit, where he drowned in the Detroit river, probably a suicide.

931. David Slattery, Carrickbeg, a shoemaker, whom Dublin Castle considered 'an old revolutionary fanatic', constantly at public house meetings with local Fenians.[42] He attended the IRB gathering in William Meagher's house, when the Meaghers returned from Clonmel prison in January 1866. Slattery was arrested the following February and detained for five months.

932. John Slattery, insurgent, identified by the informer John McGrath at the Garnacarty fields near Tipperary, preparatory to the march to Ballyhurst on 6 March 1867.

933. Thomas Slattery, Knockballynoe, Kilfeacle, noticed by an informer as among those moving towards Ballyhurst from Garnacanty, Tipperary town, on 6 March 1867. He was prominent in the Kilfeacle procession to the Tipperary amnesty meeting on 24 October 1869, wearing a green cap and sash.

934. Charles Sloan, Tipperary, a baker, who was arrested on the evidence of an informer, having carried a pike at Ballyhurst on 6 March 1867.

935. Cornelius and Patrick Smith pleaded guilty to having been among the Fenians who sacked Roskeen barracks in March 1867. They were discharged on bail to appear for sentencing, if called upon.

936. Michael Stapleton had been among the insurgents leaving Thurles for the Rising to set the empty Roskeen constabulary barracks on fire. They moved to Riordan's

nearby house to demand arms, where young Tracy was fatally hit when a weapon went off. Stapleton was among twenty young men on the run, who surrendered in June 1867. Identified, he was the only one refused bail and sent for trial. Stapleton pleaded not guilty. His family testified that he had been dragged out of bed and forced to join Capt. Charles Burke's Fenian band. Mrs Ryan of Gortkelly Castle, which had also been raided for guns, testified to his excellent character. He was acquitted.

937. William Stokes, Knockroe, Mullinahone, suspected by the constabulary as an active, though cautious Fenian agent in February 1866.

938. John Sullivan, miller, held in Thurles jail in September 1865, as he had declared himself a Fenian under the influence of alcohol.

939. Michael Sullivan, Carrickbeg, was among a group of men arrested by the constabulary for marching in military fashion in Carrick-on-Suir in October 1865, but soon released on bail.

940. Patrick Sutton, Carrick-on-Suir, a head ganger on the Waterford to Limerick railway, had returned from the US in 1865 after a brief stay. An influential Fenian who believed in the forthcoming expedition from America, Sutton travelled to 'those notorious cricket matches', which were a cover for IRB meetings. He was in the confidence of leader Peter Quirke and frequently met Philip Morrissey, William Meagher and John Daniel. After his arrest in April 1866, his destitute family was forced to enter the workhouse. A petition for Sutton's release was supported by the local middle class and he was freed in October.[43]

941. Denis Sweeney, nicknamed 'the general', was among the north Tipperary insurgents under Capt. Burke and Michael Sheehy in March 1867.

942. Owen Sweeney, 42, Clonmel, a sawyer and member of the local IRB council, who was among Stephens's correspondents. He was arrested in April 1866 and detained until March 1867. The medical officer pressed for Sweeney's release, as solitary confinement was driving him insane.

943. Timothy Tobin, Bansha, constantly going about with the Fogarties and other Fenians, was detained between Febuary and August 1866. Tobin denied any wrongdoing, requested investigation of his case and was discharged on bail.

944. Stephen Tracey, 1837–64, a native of Tipperary, working as a shoemaker in Dublin, a 'B' in O'Callaghan's 'circle' in Dublin, who recruited 150 men to form his own unit. They drilled in an empty coach factory in Dorset Street, Dublin. Tracey died of TB in January 1864, his obituary appeared in the *Irish People* and more than 400 Fenians attended his funeral to Glasnevin.

945. John Vale, farmer's son, Carrick-on-Suir, was an early member and delegate at the McManus funeral, who identified himself openly with the IRB. He was prominent at the funeral procession of leader James Meagher in Carrick, the Fenian regatta and a large demonstration in this town during 1865. Vale was also in the confidence of 'centre' Peter Quirke. He was detained from March to August 1866 and released on condition of emigrating.

946. John Wall, Ballyrichard, arrested in February 1866 as an IRB suspect by the Carrick-on-Suir constabulary.

947. Edmund Walsh, Cloran, Mullinahone, tailor, was observed marching with suspects in early 1866.

948. Edward and John Walsh, Nenagh, both shop assistants and active Fenians in February 1870.

949. Edward Walsh, born in Tipperary town in 1840, inherited his father's coach-building business. He also worked as a steward for the Thomastown Castle Estate. Walsh joined the NBSP and the IRB in 1863. His home became a meeting place. He was one of the leaders of Thomas Dogherty Brohan's 'circle' and an associate of John O'Leary and James Stephens. In 1864 he married a Miss Butler of Thomastown, a sister-in-law of Michael O'Neill Fogarty of Kilfeacle. Walsh hid in a dugout inside his home to evade the constabulary. By May 1866 he remained at large in Tipperary, having been rescued from police custody. Eventually he fled to the US, but returned with his brothers Pat and Mike to fight in 1867. He was in charge of the Moat, Kilfeacle, where a branch of the Fogarty family lived. After the defeat at Ballyhurst, Walsh escaped to America for the second time. He retained his 'greatest aspiration' to fight for Irish freedom, but died in New York in 1877.[44]

950. James Walsh, born in Tipperary town, coach-builder and a brother of Edward (above). A committed Fenian and associate of the early IRB leaders, Walsh was arrested after shooting at the police in March 1866. He was convicted and sentenced to ten years.

951. James Walsh, Ballyhurst, was identified by an informer as moving through the fields of Garnacanty towards Ballyhurst on 6 March 1867.

952. John Walsh, Watergate, Clonmel, corn merchant, a member of the Fenian Brotherhood in Clonmel in 1864.

953. Joseph Warren, Nenagh, named by Andrew Kennedy as an IRB member in 1865, eventually released.

954. Sgt Bernard Waters, 26, Co. Tipperary, 58th Regiment (British army), joined the Fenian Brotherhood in Washington in 1864 and was enrolled on its roster of officers.

955. Thomas Whelan, Borrisoleigh, was suspected of having been among those, who attacked Roskeen Barracks in March 1867. He was a brother-in-law of Michael Healy. The authorities disbelieved that either was coerced into joining the rebels.

956. Patrick White, 20, Clogheen, suspected 'head centre' in that locality, who had committed no overt acts, but was detained in Clonmel prison from 22 February 1866 for six months. The prisoner's foster father pleaded for mercy, he and the prisoner promised to withdraw from Fenianism and the R.C. and Protestant clergy supported his petition for release, which Lord Lismore opposed, as he considered White a very dangerous character.

957. Patrick Woodlock pleaded guilty to having been among the Fenians who sacked Roskeen barracks in March 1867, claiming that he had been forced into joining the rebels. He was released on bail.

958. Henry Young, a native of Kerry, working as a blacksmith in Emly, where he made pikes and participated in the Rising. Although arrested, Young returned to Emly, but died of consumption in 1888.

959. John Young, Borrisoleigh, was arrested in possession of a Catholic prayer book to swear men into the IRB and a black veil to cover his face for night visits in early 1867.

G. Waterford

960. Capt. James Joseph Bible, born in Lismore in 1840, worked as a shop assistant before emigrating to the US, where he joined the Federal Army and fought in the Civil War from 1861. Bible was sworn into the Fenian Brotherhood by Col Patrick Downing and travelled to Dublin as an organizer,

but was arrested and detained from February to August 1866. He returned a second time and was apprehended in March 1867, walking to Waterford with Thomas Bourke (see below) and Terence Kent of Arthurstown, Co. Wexford, both Fenian suspects. Being freed in August, Bible departed for America for the final time; FP 20.

Capt. James Joseph Bible, FP 20 (courtesy NAI).

961. Thomas Bourke, Thurles, a coachbuilder and early IRB member in Waterford, who associated with General Gleeson in Templemore. Bourke was arrested with Kent and Bible on 7 March 1867, suspected of having participated in the Rising. A letter from Col Thomas Kelly, whose hopes for an insurrection persisted, was found in Bourke's bread and butter in Waterford jail. He was released in June 1867 because of incipient tuberculosis.

962. Walter Brennan, Waterford, aged about 17, arrested in September 1865, was among a small Fenian group drilling.

963. Jeremiah Buckley, listed as J.M. Buckley among the Fenians on the *Erin's Hope*, had previously commanded a company under Col O'Neill at Limestone Ridge. Following his arrest on landing in June 1867, Buckley was detained in Kilmainham for eleven months and only discharged on condition of not returning to Ireland. He died in the American Midwest in 1905.

964. John Cahill, Barrack Street, Ferrybank, chandler, was arrested with Thomas Byrne on 6 March 1867 on suspicion of being insurgents. They were returning to Waterford from Co. Kilkenny, where the constabulary had information of a large Fenian gathering the previous evening. Both were absent from home on the relevant night. Cahill was kept in jail for six months and discharged on bail, pleading that he had been led into the conspiracy and promised to desist in future.

965. Thomas Calton, aged about 56, Kilmurray, Ferrybank, Waterford, a publican and farmer, detained in Kilkenny jail for possession of a six-barrelled revolver with ammunition, a dagger and treasonable documents in April 1866.

966. Denis Cashman, 1842–97, a native of Dungarvan and a well-educated law clerk, became Waterford's first 'centre'. He subsequently worked in Dublin, where he was convicted and sentenced to seven years and transported to Western Australia, editing the *Wild Goose* magazine on board the prison ship *Hougoumont*. Amnestied in 1869, Cashman left for Boston to be reunited with his wife and surviving child, two sons having died during his imprisonment. He worked on the *Pilot* newspaper at the invitation of John Boyle O'Reilly and wrote the first biography of Michael Davitt.

967. Michael Cavanagh, 1822–1900, born in Cappoquin, a cooper, who learned Irish from his native-speaking mother, a fellow pupil of John O'Daly. Radicalized during the Great Famine, he joined a Confederate club, participating in the 1848 and 1849 Risings, including the attack on the Cappoquin constabulary barracks. Cavanagh escaped to

the US, where he became secretary to 'head centre' O'Mahony from 1858 to 1866. Cavanagh's best-known work is his biography of Thomas Francis Meagher. After O'Mahony's resignation as chief of the Fenian Brotherhood, Cavanagh joined the US army and settled in Washington. He had a deep interest in Irish history and folklore and was a brother-in-law of John Walsh of Cappoquin.

968. James Clancy, a native of Co. Waterford, born c. 1846, whose family emigrated to London, where he joined the NBSP and the IRB. Clancy was apparently scheduled to participate in a raid on the Bank of England, which had to be abandoned due to an informer. He enlisted in the British army for training purposes and to infiltrate it, but deserted for the Rising. He belonged to the London leadership under James J. O'Kelly, whom he aided in reviving the movement. Clancy wounded a policeman when resisting arrest in London in 1867 and was sentenced to life. Liberated in 1878, he became a journalist in the US and assisted Devoy with the *Gaelic American*. He died in New Jersey in 1911.

969. 'Old' Matt Coffey had been sworn into the IRB aged 18, was forced to flee to the US after the *Erin's Hope* fiasco in June 1867 and returned to Ireland late in life. By 1914 he was the only Fenian of that vintage in the Cappoquin area and joined Sinn Féin. Coffey could speak but not write Irish and determinedly promoted separatism.

970. Michael Cosgrave, 30, iron-moulder, born in Cork city, but employed in Waterford, had the reputation of a tough character. He was suspected of participation in the Rising, as he left his job on 5 March. Despite support for his release from magistrates and Catholic clergy, he was detained for six months until October 1867; FP 85.

971. Lieut James Daniel, 22, a native of Lismore, who had emigrated to the US aged 3, became a naturalized citizen and fought with 9th New York Militia in the Civil War. He returned to Cappoquin in January 1866, frequently visiting John Walsh, national teacher and a brother-in-law of Michael Cavanagh, supposedly in contact with the Fenians. When detained in Waterford jail Sir Richard Musgrave interceded for Daniel, as his late parents had emigrated with his help. He was released on condition of returning to America in April 1866.

972. Thomas Dermody (or Darmody), a publican and pig dealer in Ballybricken and a suspected Fenian whose house was used as a meeting place. He was arrested in February 1866 and protested that he had been a resident of Waterford for thirty years and sold the *Irish People* from commercial motives. He attracted suspicion for having collected subscriptions for the Ladies' Committee. After his discharge on bail in April 1866, two sergeants of the Royal Artillery accused Dermody of having used seditious language and he was jailed until September.

973. John Dillon, a successful wheelwright in Waterford, who was the city's 'centre' and managed the IRB in strict secrecy. He was arrested in early 1866 for having arms in a proclaimed district and detained until February 1867, when he was discharged on bail. Edward Kenny, his successor as 'centre', was also imprisoned.

974. Laurence Doyle, tailor, picked up near Dungarvan, suspected of being among the thirty-odd men who had arrived on the *Erin's Hope*. He was incarcerated in Waterford and Mountjoy. Committed for trial at the October special commission in Dublin, the US consul's intervention to have Doyle released on health grounds proved successful.

975. Stephen Farrell, 27, Ballytruckle, Waterford, tailor, was suspected as he had given up work since Christmas 1865 to frequent

pubs and swear in Fenians. Arrested in March 1866, he was soon released when it was pointed out that a cripple would be little use to the Fenians; his petition was supported by the mayor of Waterford and the parish priest. But Farrell was absent on the night of the Rising and suspected of subverting the military. Re-arrested in March 1867, he admitted in September of having being drawn into the conspiracy, but promised to give it up, volunteered to inform and was allowed to emigrate in February 1868. A year later, Farrell got permission to return to Waterford; FP 152.

976. William Foley, born in Co. Waterford in 1836, enlisted with the East India Company in 1853. Returning to Europe in 1859, he joined 5th Dragoons and, in 1864, the IRB. Foley possessed an excellent character and friendly personality, which saw him appointed as orderly to Lord Strathnairn. He spied on Strathnairn until his arrest in 1866. Court-martialled in August for mutinous conduct, Foley was sentenced to five years and transported to Australia. Sick from heart disease and unable to work after release, he conveyed messages between the *Catalpa* rescuers and the Fenian prisoners in Fremantle. Foley visited Ireland on his way to New York, where he died in November 1876. Devoy bought a grave for him in Calvary Cemetery.

977. Francis Foran, Waterford, a mercantile clerk, was arrested together with his friend Capt. Hyland on suspicion of Fenianism. Foran's employer intervened, stating that he had to support eight siblings and was blind in one eye, resulting in his release in April 1866.

978. Patrick Furlong, Waterford, a tailor and IRB suspect, was a close associate of John Dillon. Furlong was detained in Waterford jail from February to May 1866. His petition, claiming innocence, was supported by the mayor of Waterford and his employer. He was discharged on the grounds of ill health.

979. Lieut Michael J. Greene, painter, formerly of 9th Massachusetts Regiment, had been recognized as a Fenian at O'Mahony's New York headquarters by Corridon. Greene was arrested near Dungarvan as a Fenian captain from the *Erin's Hope* expedition. Detained in Waterford jail, he petitioned for release or trial in August, but was transferred to Mountjoy in December. An American citizen, Greene was released in February 1868.

980. James Haydon, a native of Waterford, had been dismissed from the constabulary and was arrested in Francis Street, Dublin, as a Fenian suspect under the habeas corpus suspension in March 1866.

981. Timothy Horan, a former US soldier, had returned to Tallow by 3 June 1867. He told the local head constable that he had sailed from New York to Liverpool in the *Orita* three months previously. In the latter city he had worked for a plasterer called Cassidy, but could not recall his address, nor would he name the captain or mate of the *Orita*. He stated that he was to escort his niece to America. The police suspected him to have been among the Fenian officers on the *Erin's Hope*. Before a warrant could be executed, Horan had vanished to America.

982. Michael Hughes, Mayor's Walk, Waterford, clerk, was arrested in March 1867 and pleaded that he was only seventeen and had to support his parents. His memorial received great local support and he was discharged on bail in September.

983. Matthew Hunt, a native of Cappoquin, who studied medicine in Dublin and was a member of the TCD 'circle' run by the O'Donovan brothers. He died of consumption in July 1865, aged 24.

984. Capt. Joseph Hyland, a native of Co. Waterford, who enlisted in 88th New York Regiment of the Irish Brigade and was badly wounded at the Battle of Spotsylvania in 1864. He returned to Waterford and was arrested under the Habeas Corpus Suspension Act, together with Francis Foran, but released in May 1866 on condition of leaving for America.

985. Lieut John Joyce, 21, a native of Waterford, served with 63rd New York Volunteers for two years during the Civil War and took the Fenain pledge from 'centre' Dr Reynolds in Petersburgh, Virginia, in 1864. He featured on the Fenian Brotherhood roster.

986. Rev. Dr P.J. Kain, a native of Ulster and an artillery officer on board the *Erin's Hope*, was arrested soon after landing at Helvick Head. Kain was sent for trial in October 1867, contracted TB in prison and was discharged on condition of returning to the US. He became an Episcopalian minister and succeeded his son Maurice as pastor of Sewaren, Woodbridge, New Jersey, where he remained until his death in 1913. In old age he recalled how the Fenians had prepared for the threatened confrontation between their brigantine and HMS *Black Prince*, an armoured warship, by mining the *Erin's Hope*. He retained great affection for the Fenian companions of his youth and was visited by Bulmer Hobson, who recalled a courteous, elderly man.

987. Capt. Joseph Kavanagh, a native of Passage East, had been in the US naval reserve during the Civil War, afterwards retiring to New York. He was appointed to captain the *Erin's Hope* by the Fenian Brotherhood. Kavanagh successfully steered her from New York to Sligo and Waterford with a Fenian group and arms, including cannon. Finding the Rising over on arrival at Helvick Head on 1 June 1867, Kavanagh dropped the men and returned to New York with the armaments.

988. William Kennedy, 22, a native of Glin, worked as a draper's assistant in Waterford city. He had taken the IRB oath, but claimed not to have attended any meetings. Kennedy was suspected of having been 'out' in the Rising and arrested in March 1867. Although his health deteriorated in Kilmainham and he was nearly blind in one eye, the local resident magistrate objected to his release until July 1868, on considerable bail.

989. James Larkin, Waterford, was suspected as an associate of John Dillon, the local IRB 'centre'. Larkin had boasted of hiding one hundred pikes. On arrest in March 1866, he denied having done anything except collect for the dependents of the Fenian prisoners, whom he considered deserving of charity. Larkin requested an official investigation and his release was supported by the mayor of Waterford and members of the gentry.

990. Thomas Lynch, Waterford, printer, had taken the IRB oath and vanished from home at the time of the Rising. He was subsequently arrested and detained for five months, before being released on bail.

991. Laurence Maher, publican, Waterford, whose house served as a meeting place, where the Fenian oath was administered. Maher, who was not an IRB member, denied this. Nevertheless, he was incarcerated in Waterford jail from March to September 1866.

992. Lieut Thomas H. O'Brien, 1840–1900, a native of Co. Waterford, who emigrated to New York as a child. He enlisted in 88th New York Regiment during the Civil War, was promoted to lieutenant and wounded at Antietam. At the Battle of Fredericksburg his jaw was shattered

and his windpipe partially severed. Col John W. Byron dragged him off Marye's Heights and saved his life. He rejoined the 88th for Gettysburg, but resigned afterwards. O'Brien became the leader of the Peeksville, New York, Fenian 'circle' in 1865. He was arrested in both Belfast and Dublin in early 1866 and held for over a year in Mountjoy. O'Brien returned to the US, where he died of throat cancer.

993. Private Edward Quirke, 33, born in Waterford city, who had served for three years in 69th New York during the Civil War. He joined the Fenian Brotherhood in 1864 and featured on its roster of available personnel.

994. Reddy, Waterford, a labourer, whom the police questioned in April 1868 after a bullet smashed into his knee. Reddy claimed this accident had happened while he was walking in Williamstown, but the authorities knew this location as a notorious IRB drill ground in 1866, where illicit military training had restarted.

995. Dr Laurence Reynolds, 1803–87, born in Waterford city, had been a Young Irelander at home and a Chartist in England. He subsequently became the surgeon of 63rd New York Regiment and, as the poet laureate of the Irish Brigade, composed its history in verse. He served throughout the Civil War, was the 'centre' of the Potomac 'circle' and an active organizer for the Fenian Brotherhood. At Fenian meetings in his hospital tent, Dr Reynolds served milk punch with lashings of whiskey. He featured on the Brotherhood's roster of available officers among the highest ranks.

996. James Sheedy, a native of Waterford, in whose New York home the Napper Tandy Club was founded in 1867 as a forum for discussions between the various Fenian factions, Jerome Collins being the prime mover. Initially very selective in its membership and with a low profile, it proliferated into the powerful Clan na Gael.

997. William H. Stephens, 26, born in Waterford city, had served three years in 193rd New York Volunteers and took the Fenian pledge from Col Patrick Downing in New York in 1865. He enrolled himself on the roster of officers available for an Irish expedition.

998. John Walsh of Cappoquin, 1835–81, a brother-in-law of Michael Cavanagh, contributed to the *Irish People* under the pen name 'Kilmartin', but withdrew from Fenianism after the seizure of the paper in September 1865. He became a national schoolteacher in Cashel and lies buried on the Rock, close to the round tower.

999. Maurice Walsh, Dunmore East, in whose pub IRB meetings took place and new members were sworn in, was arrested in February 1866. He protested his innocence, having been an old servant of Sir Robert Paul, who would provide bail. Walsh was released in May.

1000. Thomas Whittle, Tramore, a sailor whom the constabulary recommended for arrest as a suspected Fenian on his return from America. Whittle was held in Waterford jail from March to July 1866. He was to be liberated if 'leaving Ireland for Archangel whither Alderman Cox offers to take him'.[45]

Fenian Casualties, 1865–92

Name	Prison	Death, date	Cause of death, remarks
Laurence Kelly		7 Aug. 1865	IRB member, killed during an affray with the RIC in Dangan, Co. Cork
John McGeough	Belfast	23 Mar. 1866	Kidney disease; habeas corpus detainee
John Lynch	Woking, Surrey	2 June 1866	Tuberculosis; treason-felony convict
Patrick Buckley		2 June 1866	18th Regt., Cleveland, Ohio; died of wounds received at Ridgeway, Canada
Maj. John C. Canty, Fenian spy		2 June 1866	7th Regt., Buffalo, NY; fell at the battle of Ridgeway, Canada
Col-Sgt Michael Cochrane		2 June 1866	Terre Haute, Indiana, company; died of wounds received at Ridgeway, Canada
James John Geraghty		2 June 1866	18th Regt., Cleveland, Ohio; died in friendly fire, Ridgeway, Canada
Lieut Edward Lonergan		2 June 1866	7th Regt., Buffalo, NY; fell at Ridgeway, Canada on his 21st birthday
Thomas Rafferty		2 June 1866	18th Regt., Cleveland, Ohio; mortally wounded at Ridgeway, Canada
Maj. Bigelow		2 June 1866	Buffalo, NY; fell at Fort Erie, Canada

434

Name	Prison	Death, date	Cause of death, remarks
Capt. Donohoe		2 June 1866	Cincinnati, Ohio; fell at Fort Erie, Canada
S. Thompson		unknown	Memphis, Tennessee; a combatant at Fort Erie, Canada
Edward (Richard?) Scully		9 June 1866	18th Regt., Cleveland, Ohio; wounded at Ridgeway, died Buffalo 9 June 1866
Eugene Corcoran		10 June 1866	Brooklyn; fell at Malone
Sgt John Lynch		27 July 1867	18th Regt.; Buffalo, NY; died of wounds received at Ridgeway in Buffalo
John Lynch			18th Regt.; originally from Cincinatti, shot at Ridgeway, died Buffalo 11 June 1866
John Fottrell	Mountjoy	1 Nov. 1866	Habeas corpus detainee, died after release in Salford, England
William Meagher (or Maher)	Mountjoy	Dec. 1866	Suspected cholera; habeas corpus detainee
Daniel Kane	Mountjoy	Dec. 1866	Suspected cholera; habeas corpus detainee
William Kennedy	Richmond, Dublin	29 Jan. 1867	Hit a police officer who had attacked him with an iron bar and was sentenced to a year in jail, where he died aged twenty-eight
Stephen O'Donoghue		6 Mar. 1867	Insurgent, killed at Tallaght in the Rising
Thomas Farrell		6 Mar. 1867	Insurgent, died from wounds received at Tallaght during the Rising
Timothy Daly[1]		6 Mar. 1867	Insurgent leader, shot dead in the attack on Castlemartyr constabulary barracks

Name	Prison	Death, date	Cause of death, remarks
Daniel Blake		6 Mar. 1867	Insurgent from Bruree, shot dead during the siege of Kilmallock
Michael Clery		6 Mar. 1867	Medical student, killed at the siege of Kilmallock, a sympathizer
'The unknown Fenian', probably Patrick Hassett		6 Mar. 1867	Insurgent, found shot dead at the siege of Kilmallock
James Patrick Russell		6 Mar. 1867	Insurgent from Lattin, shot dead at Ballyhurst
Peter O'Neill Crowley		31 Mar. 1867	Insurgent leader from Ballymacoda, shot dead in Kilclooney Wood
Richard Joseph Stowell	Naas	16 May 1867	Convicted of possession of firearms; died of tuberculosis nine hours after release from prison
Denis Walsh		13 June 1867	Innocent bystander, killed when constabulary charged a crowd in Waterford city when in charge of *Erin's Hope* prisoners
William Harbinson	Crumlin Road jail, Belfast	Sept. 1867	Habeas corpus detainee, found dead in his cell
John (sometimes William) Kelly	Limerick	Oct. 1867	Habeas corpus detainee, released in a dying state
William Philip Allen	Salford, Manchester	23 Nov. 1867	Executed
Michael Larkin	Salford, Manchester	23 Nov. 1867	Executed
Michael O'Brien	Salford, Manchester	23 Nov. 1867	Executed
John Smith	Kilmainham, Dublin	Dec. 1867	Sailor on the *Erin's Hope* expedition, died from shotgun wound
Edward Duffy	Millbank, London	17 Jan. 1868	Tuberculosis; treason-felony convict

Name	Prison	Death, date	Cause of death, remarks
Lt-Col Michael Bailey		18 Jan. 1868	Buffalo, NY; died of wounds received at Fort Erie in 1866
Michael Barrett	Newgate, London	26 May 1868	Executed for the Clerkenwell explosion
James Wexted Stenson	Limerick	18 June 1868	Habeas corpus detainee; died after release
William Sheedy	Dublin	Oct. 1868	Detained under habeas corpus suspension; weak on release, collapsed in the street and died
James Mountaine	Cork	6 Nov. 1868	Acquitted in 1865, then habeas corpus detainee; health declined after release
John O'Donnell, also known as John Daniel	Dublin	After 1867	Habeas corpus detainee from Carrick-on-Suir during 1866; health undermined
William Ryan	Dublin	After 1867	Arrested in Carrick-on-Suir, habeas corpus detainee during 1866; health undermined
Andrew Campbell		17 June 1869	Fatally wounded while attacking a house to obtain arms at Ballinlough, Cork
Col William Nagle	Mountjoy	15 Aug. 1869	*Erin's Hope*, arrested in 1867 and detained until May 1868, returned to New York, where he committed suicide
David Callaghan		7 Nov. 1869	IRB gun-runner, assassinated by competing factions in Cork
Luke Fullam	Fremantle	Feb. 1870	Suffering from consumption, he died after release in Perth, Western Australia
Laurence Fullam	Fremantle	After 1871	Died from consumption in Perth

Name	Prison	Death, date	Cause of death, remarks
John Keegan Casey, the poet 'Leo'	Dublin	17 Mar. 1870	Habeas corpus detainee; died young, suffering from TB on release
Patrick Riordan	Fremantle	May 1870	Insurgent, returned to Kilmallock on release and died soon afterwards, his health shattered by imprisonment
John Rowe		25 May 1870	Shot dead during O'Neill's attempted Canadian invasion near Eccles Hill
M. O'Brien		25 May 1870	Shot dead during O'Neill's attempted Canadian invasion
Denis Duggan of Troy		May 1870	Shot dead during O'Neill's attempted Canadian invasion
Capt. Patrick Croman		May 1870	Died of wounds after attempted Canadian invasion
Daniel Darragh	Portland	28 June 1870	Family evicted during Famine, IRB organizer for North Antrim, bought revolvers for the Manchester rescue, died in prison
Patrick O'Shaughnessy	Cork	Dec. 1870	Held without trial in Sept. 1865, subsequently a habeas corpus detainee; died in poor health after release
Terence Byrne		24 May 1871	Treason-felony convict from Dublin; died after release. Monument states that imprisonment caused his death
John Kelly	Dublin	June 1871	Detained in Mountjoy after the Rising at Tallaght, his death attributed to his imprisonment

Name	Prison	Death, date	Cause of death, remarks
Michael Sheehy	Portland	After 1871	Treason-felony convict and leader in the Rising in Tipperary. Emigrated to Detroit after amnesty of 1871; suicide in Detroit river
Patrick Kearney	Naas	19 Apr. 1872	Struck a G-man when his forge was searched for arms in 1865, health ruined during imprisonment in Naas jail, returned from US to die in Dublin
Martin Hanley Carey	Portland	July 1872	Nervous breakdown in jail; badly beaten by police during an amnesty demonstration in 1871; committed suicide by jumping into the Liffey
Brian Dillon	Woking, Surrey	17 Aug. 1872	Treason-felony convict, amnestied in poor health in Feb. 1871
James Cody	Mountjoy	29 Jan. 1873	Former habeas corpus detainee, released for America in August 1866; returned in poor health in 1871
John Francis Kearns	Portland	27 May 1873	Treason-felony convict, went insane after two years, transferred during amnesty of 1869 to the Cork Lunatic Asylum, where he died
Michael Hassett	Limerick	27 Jan. 1874	Former detainee, headstone claims that 'cruel treatment … brought on the disease', leading to early death
Charles Moorehouse	Portland	Feb. 1874	Fought at Glencullen & Stepaside during the Rising. Served five years for participation in Manchester rescue, contracted frostbite in prison, had toes amputated; released suffering from tuberculosis

Name	Prison	Death, date	Cause of death, remarks
Harry Shaw Mulleda		1876	Assisted R. O'Sullivan Burke in gun-running, detained for a year before trial. Convicted of treason-felony in 1868, amnestied to America in 1871, among the 'Cuba Five'; suicide in New York after tragic death of wife and daughter
William Foley	Fremantle	1876	Spied on Lord Strathnairn, Commander-in-Chief of British army in Ireland, sentenced and sent to Western Australia, developed heart disease
Daniel Reddin	Chatham	1879	Participated in the Manchester rescue, became paralysed in prison, released in poor health; failed in legal proceedings against prison officials
Edward O'Kelly	Spike Island	July 1879	Released in failing health, died soon afterwards in New Jersey
Patrick Keating	Fremantle	1874	Released in failing health, died in Australia
William O'Sullivan Jr.	Fremantle	4 Nov. 1881	Returned to Kilmallock after amnesty and died aged 31
Daniel Bradley	Fremantle	After 1872	Died young after release
Col Patrick Leonard		Sept. 1874	Leader of the Drogheda insurgents, went on the run in March 1867, never arrested, but his health broke down and he died young
Sgt Charles H. McCarthy	Chatham	6 Jan. 1878	Died shortly after release
Cpl Patrick Tierney	Spike Island	29 Nov. 1882	Died of diseases contracted during imprisonment

Name	Prison	Death, date	Cause of death, remarks
Joseph Brady	Kilmainham	May 1883	Member of the Irish National Invincibles, hanged for the murder of Burke and Cavendish
Daniel Curley	Kilmainham	May 1883	Member of the Irish National Invincibles, hanged for the murder of Burke and Cavendish
Timothy Kelly	Kilmainham	1883	Member of the Irish National Invincibles, hanged for the murder of Burke and Cavendish
Michael Fagan	Kilmainham	1883	Member of the Irish National Invincibles, hanged for the murder of Burke and Cavendish
Thomas Caffrey	Kilmainham	1883	Member of the Irish National Invincibles, hanged for the murder of Burke and Cavendish
Joseph Poole	Richmond bridewell	18 Dec. 1883	Ostensibly hanged for killing John Kenny, an informer, in July 1882, but probably in revenge for the Abbey St affray, in which a policeman was killed
Denis Deasy	Chatham	May 1884	Dynamitard, died in jail, buried in Kilbrogan Graveyard, Bandon
William Mackey Lomasney		13 Dec. 1884	Dynamitard, killed by premature explosion of bomb under London Bridge; his fate was shared by the two men below
John Fleming		13 Dec. 1884	Assistant of Mackey Lomasney, killed by premature explosion of bomb under London Bridge
Peter Malon		13 Dec. 1884	Brother-in-law of Mackey Lomasney, died in the explosion under London Bridge

Name	Prison	Death, date	Cause of death, remarks
Edward Daly	Limerick	Sept. 1890	A brother of John, with whom he was detained in 1865. According to his daughter, Kathleen Clarke, thereafter his health was 'delicate', contributing to his death at 41
Robert Barton alias McGrath	England	Apr. 1891	Dynamiter, died of TB
P.W. Nally	Mountjoy	9 Nov. 1891	Convicted in dubious circumstances in 1884; his death was attributed to ill-treatment
Michael Harkins	Portland	July 1892	A resident of Philadelphia, participated in the Jubilee dynamite plot of 1887, orchestrated and betrayed by F.F. Millen on behalf of British intelligence; released in 1891 as very ill with TB
Christopher Dowling	Downpatrick	July 1896	Involved in a shooting in Dublin between rival Fenian factions, when a policeman was accidentally killed by colleagues. Dowling was sent to Downpatrick jail, where one eye was destroyed in an accident and his health deteriorated; served thirteen years of a life sentence and was only released shortly before his death
John Walsh	Kingston Penitentiary, Canada	1909	Tried to blow up the Welland Canal, Ontario, with Luke Dillon and John Nolan; died of liver disease in prison

(Source: various newspapers, *DIB*, Dublin Castle Fenian papers, National Archives of England and Wales files.)

Fenian-inspired Monuments in Ireland and Manchester, 1868–1908

Name	Location, type	Erected
1. Capt. John Delahunt	Rathcoole Graveyard, Fethard	After 1867
2. Richard Joseph Stowell	Glasnevin Cemetery, Dublin	1868
3. Allen, Larkin and O'Brien, the Manchester Martyrs	Cenotaph, Glasnevin Cemetery, Dublin, a bronze shield added in 1898	1868
4. The Manchester Martyrs	Celtic Cross, Kilbrogan Graveyard, Bandon, Co. Cork	1868
5. James W. Stenson	Mount St Lawrence Cemetery, Limerick	After 1868
6. Edward Duffy	Glasnevin Cemetery, Dublin	1869
7. The 'unknown Fenian', who fell in the attack on Kilmallock Barracks	Graveyard, Kilmallock	1870
8. Michael Hassett	Mount St Lawrence Cemetery, Limerick	After 1874
9. Col Patrick Leonard	Monknewtown, Slane, Co. Meath	1877
10. Joseph Kennedy	Ardagh, Co. Limerick	After 1877
11. The Manchester Martyrs	Cenotaph – a wooden cross, Kilpatrick Cemetery, Annacarty, Cappawhite, Co. Tipperary	Before 1878, replaced by a stone one in 1901

Name	Location, type	Erected
12. Fr John Murphy and 'his heroic followers'	Celtic cross near the site of Fr Murphy's chapel, Boulavogue, Co. Wexford	1878
13. Brian Dillon	Rathcooney, Co. Cork	Around 1880
14. The Manchester Martyrs	Cenotaph, a memorial cross, Listowel	1883
15. John Haltigan	St Patrick's Graveyard, Kilkenny	After 1884
16. Denis Deasy	Celtic cross, Kilbrogan Graveyard, Bandon, Co. Cork	After 1884
17. John Keegan Casey, 'Leo'	Glasnevin Cemetery, Dublin	1885
18. Stephen O'Donoghue and fellow participants in the 1867 Rising	Glasnevin Cemetery, Dublin	1885
19. The Manchester Martyrs	Rath Cemetery, Tralee	1886
20. The Manchester Martyrs and Michael Barrett	Emly, Co. Tipperary	1886
21. The Manchester Martyrs	Maid of Erin, Ennis	1886
22. John 'Amnesty' Nolan	Cenotaph, Glasnevin Cemetery, Dublin	1887, erected by Michael Davitt
23. Patrick O'Donnell	Cenotaph, Glasnevin Cemetery, Dublin	1887
24. Peter O'Neill Crowley	Ballymacoda, Co. Cork	Completed in 1887
25. The Manchester Martyrs	Mount St Lawrence Cemetery, Limerick	1887
26. The Manchester Martyrs	Memorial cross, Kilrush Graveyard	By 1888
27. Stephen Joseph Meany	Drumcliffe Graveyard, Ennis	After 1889
28. Michael Seery	Glasnevin Cemetery, Dublin	1890
29. Edward Boylan	St Joseph's Cemetery, Cork	1890
30. Matt Harris	Celtic cross, Creagh, Ballinasloe, Co. Galway	After 1890

Name	Location, type	Erected
31. Timothy Daly	Killeagh, Castlemartyr, Co. Cork	1891
32. The Manchester Martyrs	Birr, Co. Offaly	1894
33. William Real, Gaelic athlete	Pallas, Co. Limerick	1894
34. The Manchester Martyrs	Ladysbridge, Co. Cork	After 1894
35. John Kelly 'of Tralee'	Celtic cross, Glasnevin Cemetery	1897
36. The Fenian insurgents of 1867	Celtic cross, Kilmallock	1898
37. Charles Kickham	Statue in Tipperary Town	1898
38. Peter O'Neill Crowley	Kilclooney Wood, Mitchelstown, Co. Cork	1898
39. Wolfe Tone and the insurgents of 1798	Maid of Erin, Dundalk	1898
40. The insurgents of 1798	Celtic cross at their burial place in Graigue, Carlow	1898
41. Finnerty, a 1798 insurgent	An ornamental shield erected in Loughrea	1898
42. The Manchester Martyrs	Clonmel	1898
43. The insurgents of 1798	Celtic cross, Mountmellick, Co. Laois	1898
44. The insurgents of 1798	Celtic cross, Ballinakill, Co. Laois	1898
45. The insurgents of 1798	Lobinstown and Syddan in Slane district	1898
46. Wolfe Tone	St Stephen's Green, Dublin	Foundation stone laid in 1898, never erected; de Valera eventually unveiled a modern statue
47. French and Irish insurgents of 1798	French Hill, Castlebar	1898
48. The insurgents of 1798 and the Whiteboys, Askeaton, 1821	Tree planted on Croppy Hole, Rathkeale, Co. Limerick	1898

Name	Location, type	Erected
49. The Manchester Martyrs	A cross with Erin, Justice, Literature, Art, wolfhounds and the head of Christ. St Joseph's Cemetery, Moston, Manchester, England	Foundation stone laid by James Stephens in 1898
50. Bartholomew Teeling, Battle of Collooney in 1798	Collooney, Co. Sligo	1899
51. General Humbert, the French officers and the Irish insurgents of 1798	Maid of Erin, Ballina, Co. Mayo	1899
52. The insurgents of 1798	Maid of Erin, Sligo	1899
53. Peter Delaney, Fenian	Dunmore, Co. Galway	1899
54. The insurgents of 1798, 1803, 1848 and 1867	Billy Byrne of Ballymanus statue with Maid of Erin plaque, Market Square, Wicklow	1899
55. P.W. Nally	Maid of Erin, Balla, Co. Mayo	1900
56. The insurgents of 1798	Pikeman, Liberty Square, Thurles	1900
57. The insurgents of 1798	Clonakilty	1900
58. John Lavin, 'centre' of Roscommon IRB	Castlerea, Co. Roscommon	1901, unveiled by Maud Gonne
59. National monument to the men of 1798, 1848 and 1867	Maid of Erin, Bandon, Co. Cork	1901, thrown into the Bandon river by British troops and Loyalists in 1921; restored by 1925
60. The 1798 insurgents hanged in Claremorris	Celtic Cross on plinth, Knock, Co. Mayo	1902
61. The 'confessors of Irish liberty'	Maid of Erin with medallions of Lord Edward Fitzgerald and the Sheares brothers, site of Newgate jail, Dublin	1903
62. Fr Michael Murphy and the insurgents at the Battle of Arklow in 1798	Fr Murphy statue in front of RC church, Arklow, Co. Wicklow	1903

Name	Location, type	Erected
63. Edmond Power, hanged in Dungarvan, and the insurgents of 1798	Celtic cross with four marble columns, Town Park, Dungarvan, Co. Waterford	1903
64. John Boyle O'Reilly monument	Dowth, Co. Meath	1903
65. The insurgents of 1798	Statue of a '98 Rebel, Town Hall, Clonmel, Co. Tipperary	Work of J.K. Bracken, 1904
66. Sam McAllister, Michael Dwywer and the insurgents of 1798, 1803, 1848 and 1867.	Statue of Sam McAllister, Baltinglass, Co. Wicklow	1904
67. The Manchester Martyrs	Maid of Erin, Kilrush, Co. Clare	1904; this statue was pulled off its pedestal by Auxiliaries in May 1921, rescued by Republicans and restored during the 1930s
68. The insurgents of 1798, 1803, 1848 and 1867	Maid of Erin, Skibbereen, Co. Cork	1904
69. Fr John Murphy, executed in Tullow in 1798	Tullow, Co. Carlow	1905
70. The insurgents of 1798	Pikeman statue, Bullring, Wexford	1905
71. The insurgents of 1798, 1803, 1848 and 1867	Pikeman statue, Denny Street, Tralee	Unveiled in 1905 by C.G. Doran, destroyed by British forces in 1921, new sculpture erected in 1939
72. The insurgents of 1798, 1803, 1848 and 1867	The 'National Monument', Grand Parade, Cork, with statues of Dwyer, Tone, Davis and O'Neill Crowley	1906
73. John Mandeville, nephew of John O'Mahony	Bronze statue, The Square, Mitchelstown	1906
74. The Manchester Martyrs	Maid of Erin, Tipperary town	1907

Name	Location, type	Erected
75. Matthew Furlong, insurgent, killed in the Battle of New Ross	New Ross	1907
76. The insurgents of 1798	Sculptures of Fr Murphy and the Croppy Boy, Market Square, Enniscorthy	1908
77. McManus, O'Mahony and other Fenians	Maid of Erin, Glasnevin Cemetery, Dublin	Begun in 1885, not erected until 1933

(Source: various newspapers and Dublin Castle Fenian files)

Bibliography

PRIMARY SOURCES

I. Manuscripts
National Archives of Ireland:
>   Chief Secretary's Office registered papers; Habeas Corpus Suspension Act warrants and abstracts; Fenian F, R and A files; papers seized in *Irish People* raid; Fenian photographs; Fenianism, index of names; prison records; Crime Branch Special files.

National Library of Ireland:
>   Larcom, Mayo, Samuel Lee Anderson, Devoy, Luby, O'Leary and Henry Dixon Papers; Minute Books of the Young Ireland Society.

Bodleian Library: Kimberley papers.

British Library: Strathnairn papers.

National Archive of England and Wales:
>   Cabinet papers; Home Office files; Foreign Office: Fenian Brotherhood files; War Office files; Colonial Office: Fenians, Canada, files; Sir Robert Anderson papers, Balfour papers, Prison registers, Directors' order books, Governor's journals, Quarterly returns and convict files; Records of the Metropolitan Police.

Bureau of Military History 1913–1921 http://www.bureauofmilitaryhistory.ie/.

The Catholic University of America, Washington; American Catholic History Research Centre and University Archives; finding aids for WRLC special collections; finding aids for the Fenian Brotherhood Records and O'Donovan Rossa personal papers, http: aladin.wrlc.org/gsdl/collect/faids/import/CUfenian.shtml.

British Parliamentary papers:
>   Knox and Pollock inquiry: report of the commissioners on treatment of the treason-felony convicts in the English convict prisons, BPP, 1867 [3880], xxxv, 673, 1; Devon Commission, BPP 1871 [c. 319] [c. 319–1]; Inquiry as to the alleged ill-treatment of the convict Charles McCarthy in Chatham convict prison, [C. 1978] lxiii 769.

New York Public Library:
>   T.W. Sweeny papers.

St Mary's Cemetery, Kensal Green, London: burial registers.

Calvary Cemetery, Woodside, Queens, New York: burial registers.

II. Newspapers

Belfast News-Letter; Brooklyn Eagle; Cork Constitution; Cork Examiner; Daily Telegraph; Dundalk Democrat; Flag of Ireland; Freeman's Journal; Gaelic American; Glasgow Herald; Irish Freedom (Dublin); *Irish-American; Irish Independent; Irish Nation* (New York); *Irish People* (Dublin); *Irish People* (New York); *Irish Times; Irish Press; Irish World* (New York); *Irishman* (Dublin); *Kerry Evening Post; Kerryman; Kilkenny Journal; Kilkenny People; Limerick Leader, Nation; Nenagh Guardian; New York Tribune; New York Herald; Pall Mall Gazette; Reynolds's Newspaper; Skibbereen Eagle; Southern Star; Times; New York Times; Tipperary People; Tipperary Star; United Irishman* (New York).

III. Published Works of Contemporaries

Anonymous, *Proceedings of the First National Convention of the Fenian Brotherhood, held in Chicago, Illinois, November 1863* (Philadelphia 1863).

Anonymous, *Proceedings of the Second National Congress of the Fenian Brotherhood, held in Cincinnati, Ohio, January 1865* (Philadelphia 1865).

Anonymous, *To the Fenian Brotherhood of America. Official Report of the Investigating Committee of the Department of Manhattan, Fenian Brotherhood* (New York 1866).

Anderson, Sir Robert, *Sidelights on the Home Rule movement* (London 1906); *The lighter side of my official life* (London 1910).

Barry, Kevin, (ed.), James Joyce, *Occasional, Critical and Political Writings* (Oxford 2000).

Begbie, Harold, *The Lady Next Door* (Dublin 2006).

Bonner, Hypatia, *Charles Bradlaugh: a record of his life and work* (London 1894).

Bussy, F.M., *Irish Conspiracies: recollections of John Mallon, the great Irish detective, and other reminiscences* (London 1910).

Clarke, Joseph I.C., *My Life and Memories* (New York 1925).

Clarke, Kathleen, *Revolutionary Woman* (Dublin 1991).

Clarke, Thomas J., *Glimpses of an Irish Felon's Prison Life* (Cork 1970).

Colum, Padraic, *Arthur Griffith* (Dublin 1959).

Comyn, James, *Their Friends at Court* (Chichester & London 1973).

Davis, Richard (ed.), *'To solitude consigned': the Tasmanian Journal of William Smith O'Brien* (Sydney 1995).

Davitt, Michael, *The fall of feudalism in Ireland* (London & NY 1904); *Leaves from a prison diary* (New York 1885).

Denieffe, Joseph, *A Personal Narrative of the Irish Revolutionary Brotherhood* (Shannon 1969).

Denvir, John, *The Life Story of an Old Rebel* (Shannon 1972).

Devoy, John, *Recollections of an Irish Rebel* (Shannon 1969).

Duffy, Charles Gavan, *My life in two hemispheres* (London 1898); (ed.), *Literary and historical essays by Thomas Davis* (Dublin 1883).

Doheny, Michael, *The Felon's Track* (Dublin 1951).

Fennell, Philip, & King, Marie (eds), *John Devoy's Catalpa Expedition* (New York & London 2006).

Gonne MacBride, Maud, *A Servant of the Queen* (Dublin 1950).

Hawkins, Angus, & Powell, John (eds), *The Journal of John Wodehouse First Earl of Kimberley 1862–1902* (Cambridge 1997).

Healy, T.M., *Letters and leaders of my day* (London n.d.).

Hobson, Bulmer, *Ireland Yesterday and Tomorrow* (Tralee 1968).

Joyce, James, *A Portrait of the Artist as a Young Man* (London 1991); *Ulysses* (New York 1961).

Joyce, Stanislaus, *My Brother's Keeper* (London 1958).

Kickham, Charles J., *Knocknagow or the homes of Tipperary* (Dublin n. d.).

King, Carla (ed.), Michael Davitt, *Jottings in Solitary* (Dublin 2003).

King, Carla, & McCormack, W.J. (eds), John Devoy, *Michael Davitt: from the Gaelic American* (Dublin 2008).

Le Caron, Henri, *Twenty-five Years in the Secret Service: the Recollections of a Spy* (London 1892).

Legg, Marie-Louise (ed.), *Alfred Webb: the Autobiography of a Quaker Nationalist* (Cork 1999).

MacBride White, Anna & Jeffares, A. Norman (eds), *Always your friend. The Gonne–Yeats letters 1893–1938* (London 1993).

MacDonagh, Michael, *The Home Rule Movement* (Dublin 1920).

McGarry, Fearghal, & McConnel, James, (eds), *The Black Hand of Republicanism: Fenianism in Modern Ireland* (Dublin & Portland 2009).

Mangan, Henry (ed.), *Poems by Alice Milligan* (Dublin 1954).

Maume, Patrick (ed.), *Mitchel: The Last Conquest of Ireland (Perhaps)* by John Mitchel (Dublin 2005).

Maume, M., Maume, P., & Casey, M. (eds), John Sarsfield Casey, *The Galtee Boy* (Dublin 2005).

Mitchel, John, *Jail Journal* (Dublin 1921); *The History of Ireland from the treaty of Limerick to the present time* (Glasgow & London, n.d.).

Moran, Patrick Francis (ed.), *The pastoral letters of Cardinal Cullen* (Dublin 1882).

Moylan, Seán, *Seán Moylan: In His Own Words. His Memoir of the Irish War of Independence* (Aubane 2009).

O'Brien, R. Barry, *The Life of Charles Stewart Parnell* (London 1910).

O'Brien, William, *Recollections* (London & New York 1905); *Evening memories* (Dublin & London 1920); *Who fears to speak of ninety-eight?* (Dublin 1898).

O'Brien, W., & Ryan, D. (eds), *Devoy's Post Bag i & ii* (Dublin 1948 & 1953).

O'Connor, T.P., *Memoirs of an old parliamentarian* (London 1929).

O'Donoghue, Florence (ed.), Diarmuid Lynch, *The IRB and the 1916 Insurrection. A record of the preparations for the Rising, with comments on published works relating thereto, and a report on operations in the GPO garrison area during Easter Week, 1916* (Cork 1957).

O'Donovan Rossa, Jeremiah, *Irish rebels in English prisons* (New York 1882); *Irish Rebels in English prisons* (Dingle 1991); *Rossa's Recollections, 1838–1898* (Guilford, CT 2004).

O'Hegarty, P.S., *The Victory of Sinn Féin* (Dublin 1998).

O'Leary, Ellen, *Lays of Country, Home and Friends* (Dublin 1890).

O'Leary, John, *Recollections of Fenians and Fenianism* (Shannon 1969); *Young Ireland: the old and the new*, inaugural address to the Young Ireland Society (Dublin 1885); *What Irishmen should know. A lecture delivered at Cork, February 1886; How Irishmen should feel. Lecture delivered at Newcastle-on-Tyne, December 17th, 1886.*

Pigott, Richard, *Personal Recollections of an Irish National Journalist* (Cork 1979).

Ramon, Marta (ed.), *The Birth of the Fenian Movement. American Diary, Brooklyn 1859* (Dublin 2009).

Regan-Lefebvre, Jennifer (ed.), *For the Liberty of Ireland, at Home and Abroad: the Autobiography of J.F.X. O'Brien* (Dublin 2010).

Roche, James Jeffrey, *Life of John Boyle O'Reilly* (London 1891).

Rolleston, C.H., *Portrait of an Irishman* (London 1939).

Rutherford, John, *The secret history of the Fenian conspiracy: its origin, objects, and ramifications* (London 1877).

Rutherford, William, *'67 Retrospection* (Tipperary 1903).

Ryan, Mark, *Fenian Memories* (Dublin 1945).

Sheehan, Patrick Augustine, *The graves at Kilmorna* (New York 1915).

Sigerson, George, *Modern Ireland: its vital questions, secret societies and government* (London 1869); *Political prisoners at home and abroad* (London 1890).

Stephens, James, *'Reminiscences'* from *Weekly Freeman* (Dublin).

Sullivan, A.M., *New Ireland: political sketches and personal reminiscences of thirty years of Irish public life* (New York 1878).

Sullivan, C.W. (ed.), *Fenian Diary. Denis B. Cashman on board the* Hougoumont (Dublin 2001).

Sullivan, T.D., Sullivan, A.M., Sullivan, D.B., *Speeches from the dock or protests of Irish patriotism* (New York 1904).

Sullivan, T.D., *Recollections of Troubled Times in Irish politics* (Dublin 1905).

Tynan, Katharine, *Twenty-five years: reminiscences* (London 1913); *The middle years* (London 1916).

Yeats, W.B., *Autobiographies* (London 1980).

Wade, Allan, (ed.), *The letters of W. B. Yeats* (London 1954).

IV. Works of Reference

McGuire, James, & Quinn, James (eds), *Dictionary of Irish Biography* (Cambridge 2009).

Debrett's Illustrated Peerage and Baronetage (London 1864).

Matthew, H.C.G. & Harrison, Brian (eds), *Oxford Dictionary of National Biography* (Oxford 2004).

Vaughan, W.E., & Fitzpatrick, A.J. (eds), *Irish Historical Statistics* (Dublin 1978).

McMahon, Sean, *Irish Quotations* (Dublin 1999).

SECONDARY SOURCES

I. Books

Amos, Keith, *The Fenians in Australia 1865–1880* (Sydney 1988).

Ball, Stephen (ed.), *Dublin Castle and the First Home Rule Crisis: the Political Journal of Sir George Fottrell, 1884–1887* (London 2008).

Barnes, James J., *Private and Confidential: Letters from British Ministers in Washington to the Foreign Secretaries in London, 1844–67* (Selinsgrove 1993).

Barr, Colin, Finelli, Michele, & O'Connor, Anne (eds), *Nation/Nazione: Irish Nationalism and the Italian Risorgimento* (Dublin 2014).

Bartlett, Thomas, & Jeffery, Keith (eds), *A Military History of Ireland* (Cambridge 1996).

Belchem, John, *Irish, Catholic and Scouse: the History of the Liverpool Irish 1800–1939* (Liverpool 2007).

Bourke, Marcus, *John O'Leary: a Study in Irish Separatism* (Athens, Georgia 1967); *The GAA: a History* (Dublin 2000).

De Búrca, Marcus [Bourke, Marcus], *Michael Cusack and the GAA* (Dublin 1989).

Boyne, Patricia, *John O'Donovan (1806–1861): a Biography* (Kilkenny 1987).

Breen, Anthony M., *The Cappoquin Rebellion 1849* (Thurston 1998).

Buckley, David N., *James Fintan Lalor: Radical* (Cork 1990).

Callan Heritage Society, *The Callan Tenant League* (Callan c. 1988); *The Famine in the Kilkenny/Tipperary Region* (Callan 1998).

Callanan, Frank, *The Parnell Split, 1890–91* (Cork 1992).

Campbell, Christy, *Fenian Fire* (London 2002).

Carroll, Aideen, *Seán Moylan: Rebel Leader* (Cork 2010).

Clark, Samuel, *Social Origins of the Irish Land War* (Princeton 1979).

Cobb, Belton, *Critical Years at the Yard* (London 1956).

Comerford, R.V., *Charles J. Kickham (1828–82): a Study in Irish Nationalism and Literature* (Dublin 1979); *The Fenians in Context* (Dublin 1985); 'Ireland 1850–70: Post-Famine and Mid-Victorian', W.E. Vaughan (ed.), *A New History of Ireland V: Ireland under the Union, I* (Oxford 1989).

Cook, Andrew, *M: MI5's First Spymaster* (Stroud 2006).

Corfe, Tom, *The Phoenix Park Murders: Conflict, Compromise and Tragedy in Ireland, 1879–1882* (London 1968).

Corr, Michael J., & O'Donoghue, Anthony, *A History of the GAA in Midleton 1884–1986* (Midleton, n. d.).

Crew, Albert, *London Prisons of Today and Yesterday* (London 1933).

Cronin, Sean, *The McGarrity Papers* (Tralee 1972).

Cullen, Fintan, & Foster, R.F., *Conquering England: Ireland in Victorian London* (London 2005).

D'Arcy, William, *The Fenian Movement in the United States* (Washington DC 1947).

Davis, Richard, *The Young Ireland Movement* (Dublin 1987).

De Nie, Michael, *The Eternal Paddy: Irish Identity and the British Press, 1798–1882* (Madison 2004).

Donnelly, Mary (ed.), *The Last Post* (Dublin 1994).

Doyle, Eugene J., *Justin McCarthy* (Dublin 2012).

Dunne, Declan, *Peter's Key: Peter De Loughry and the Fight for Irish Independence* (Cork 2012).

Dwyer, Michael & Liam, *The Parish of Emly* (Emly 1987).

Ensor, Robert, *England 1870–1914. Oxford History of England* (Oxford 1992).

Evans, A.G., *Fanatic Heart: a Life of John Boyle O'Reilly* (Boston 1997).

Falvey, Jeremiah, *The Chronicles of Midleton 1700–1990* (Cloyne 1998).

Fleming, Lionel, *Head or Harp* (Gateshead 1965).

Frazier, Adrian, *The Adulterous Muse: Maud Gonne, Lucien Millevoye and W.B. Yeats* (Dublin 2016).

Gaughan, J. Anthony, *Austin Stack: Portrait of a Separatist* (Mount Merrion 1977).

Geary, Laurence M. (ed.), *Rebellion and Remembrance in Modern Ireland* (Dublin 2001).

Geoghegan, Patrick, *Robert Emmet: A Life* (Dublin 2004).

McGilloway, Ken, *George Sigerson* (Belfast 2011).

Gleeson, David T., *The Green and the Gray: The Irish in the Confederate States of America* (Chapel Hill 2013).

Glynn, Anthony, *High Upon the Gallows Tree* (Tralee n.d.)

Guarino, Eva, & Turnbull, Judith, *Collected Writings by and about James Fintan Lalor* (Rome n. d.).

Harmon, Maurice (ed.), *Fenians and Fenianism* (Dublin 1968).

Hearne, J.M., & Cornish, R.T., *Thomas Francis Meagher: the Making of an Irish-American* (Dublin 2006).

Henry, William, *Supreme Sacrifice* (Cork 2005).

Jenkins, Brian, *Fenians and Anglo-American Relations During Reconstruction* (Ithaca and London 1969); *The Fenian Problem: Insurgency and Terrorism in a Liberal State 1858–1874* (Montreal 2008).

Jenkins, Roy, *Gladstone* (London 1995).

Kelly, John (ed.), *The Collected Letters of W.B. Yeats* (Oxford 1997).

Keneally, Thomas, *The Great Shame* (London 1998).

Kenna, Shane, *War in the Shadows: the Irish-American Fenians who Bombed Victorian Britain* (Dublin 2014).

Kennerk, Barry, *Shadow of the Brotherhood: the Temple Bar Shootings* (Cork 2010).

Kenny, Kevin (ed.), *Ireland and the British Empire* (Oxford 2004).

Killeagh-Inch Historical Group, *Killeagh Parish Through the Ages* (Killeagh 2011).

King, Carla, *Michael Davitt after the Land League* (Dublin 2016).

Larkin, Emmet, *The Historical Dimensions of Irish Catholicism* (Dublin 1997).

Lee, David (ed.), *Remembering Limerick* (Limerick 1997).

Lee, James Melvin, *James Luby, Journalist* (Washington DC 1930).

Lehne, Sylke, 'Fenianism – a male business? A case study of Mary Jane O'Donovan Rossa (1845–1916)', MA thesis, Maynooth, 1995.

Loughlin, James, *The British Monarchy and Ireland* (Cambridge 2008).

Lucey, Donnacha Séan, *Land, Popular Politics and Agrarian Violence in Ireland: the Case of Co. Kerry, 1872–86* (Dublin 2011).

Lynch, Mary C., & O'Donoghue, Seamus, *O'Sullivan Burke, Fenian* (Cork 1999).

Lyne, Gerard J., *The Lansdowne Estate in Kerry under W.S. Trench 1849–72* (Dublin 2001).

Lyons, F.S.L., *Charles Stewart Parnell* (Dublin 2005).

Mac Atasney, Gerard, *Seán MacDiarmada* (Manorhamilton 2004); *Tom Clarke* (Sallins 2013).

McCracken, Donal P., *Inspector Mallon. Buying Irish Patriotism for a Five-Pound Note* (Dublin 2009).

MacDonagh, Oliver, The *Emancipist, Daniel O'Connell, 1830–47* (London 1989).

McConville, Seán, *Irish Political Prisoners, 1848–1922: Theatres of War* (Abingdon & New York 2005).

McGee, Owen, *The IRB: The Irish Republican Brotherhood from the Land League to Sinn Féin* (Dublin 2005).

McGrath, Walter, *A Cork Felon: the Life and Death of Brian Dillon* (Cork 1952).

McHugh, Roger, *Trial at Green Street Courthouse* (Dublin 1946).

Maher, James, *The Valley Near Slievenamon* (Kilkenny 1942); *Romantic Slievenamon* (Mullinahone 1954); *Chief of the Comeraghs: a John O'Mahony Anthology* (Mullinahone 1957); *Dawn on the Irish Coast* (Kilkenny 1985).

Miller, Kerby A., *Emigrants and Exiles: Ireland and the Irish Exodus to North America* (New York 1985); *Ireland and Irish America* (Dublin 2008).

Moody, T.W. (ed.), *The Fenian Movement* (Cork 1968); *Michael Davitt and Irish Revolution 1846–82* (Oxford 1990).

Morgan, Jack, *Through American and Irish Wars* (Dublin 2006).

Murphy, Nancy, 'Joseph K. Bracken, G.A.A. founder, fenian and politician' in Nolan, William, & McGrath, Thomas (eds), *Tipperary: History and Society* (Dublin 1985).

Newsinger, John, *Fenianism in Mid-Victorian Britain* (London & Boulder 1994).

O'Brien, Gillian, *Blood Runs Green: the Murder that Transfixed Gilded-Age Chicago* (Chicago 2015).

Ó Broin, Leon, *Fenian Fever: an Anglo-Irish Dilemma* (London 1971); *Revolutionary Underground: the story of the Irish Republican Brotherhood, 1858–1924* (Dublin 1976); *The Prime Informer* (London 1971).

Ó Catháin, Máirtín Seán, *Irish Republicanism in Scotland 1858–1916* (Dublin 2007).

O Cathaoir, Eva, & Mac Fheorais, Mathúin, 'The Irish Republican Brotherhood in Clare 1858–1871', Lynch, Matthew & Nugent, Patrick (eds), *Clare: History and Society* (Dublin 2008).

O'Connor, John, *The Workhouses of Ireland* (Dublin 1995).

O'Donoghue, Brendan, *In Search of Fame and Fortune* (Dublin 2006).

Ó Gráda, Cormac, *The Great Irish Famine* (Dublin 1989); *Ireland: a New Economic History 1780–1939* (Oxford 1995).

O Lochlainn, Colm, *Irish Street Ballads* (London 1984).

Ó Lúing, Sean, *Fremantle Mission* (Tralee 1965); *I Die in a Good Cause* (Tralee 1970).

Ó Néill, Eoghan, *The Golden Vale of Ivowen* (Dublin 2001).

Ó Ríordáin, Tomás, *Patrick Neville Fitzgerald: a forgotten Cork Fenian and GAA Pioneer* (n.p. 2004).

Ó Ruairc, Pádraig Óg, *Blood on the Banner* (Cork 2009).

O'Shea, James, *Priest, Politics and Society in Post-Famine Ireland: a Study of Co. Tipperary 1850–1891* (Dublin 1983); *Prince of Swindlers: John Sadleir MP 1813–1856* (Dublin 1999).

Steele, Karen (ed.), *Maud Gonne's Irish Nationalist Writings, 1895–1946* (Dublin 2004).

Pollard, H.B.C., *The Secret Societies of Ireland: their Rise and Progress* (London 1922).

Porter, Bernard, *Plots and Paranoia: a History of Political Espionage in Britain 1790–1988* (London 1992).

Potter, Matthew, *William Monsell of Tervoe, 1812–1894: Catholic Unionist, Anglo-Irishman* (Dublin 2009).

Priestley, Philip, *Victorian Prison Lives* (London 1999).

Quinlivan, Patrick, & Rose, Paul, *The Fenians in England 1865–1872* (London & New York 1982).

Quinn, James, *Young Ireland and the Writing of Irish History* (Dublin 2015); *John Mitchel* (Dublin 2008).

Rafferty, Oliver P., *The Church, the State and the Fenians* (Basingstoke 1999); *The Catholic Church and the Protestant State: Nineteeth-Century Irish Realities* (Dublin 2008).

Ramon, Marta, *A Provisional Dictator* (Dublin 2007).

Riall, Lucy, *Garibaldi: Invention of a Hero* (New Haven & London 2007).

Ryan, Desmond, *The Fenian Chief: a Biography of James Stephens* (Dublin 1967); *The Phoenix Flame: a Study of Fenianism and John Devoy* (London & Edinburgh 1937).

Senior, Hereward, *The Fenians and Canada* (Toronto 1978).

Seoighe, Mainchín, *Portrait of Limerick* (London 1982); *The Story of Kilmallock* (Kilmallock 1987).

Shiels, Damian, *The Irish in the American Civil War* (Dublin 2013).

Short, K.R.M., *The Dynamite War* (New Jersey 1979).

Sim, David, *A Union Forever: The Irish Question and US Foreign Relations in the Victorian Age* (Ithaca & London 2013).

Sloan, Robert, *William Smith O'Brien and the Young Ireland Rebellion of 1848* (Dublin 2000).

Stanford, Jane, *That Irishman: The Life and Times of John O'Connor Power* (Dublin 2011).

Stevens, Peter, *The Voyage of the* Catalpa (London 2003).

Steward, Patrick and McGovern, Bryan, *The Fenians: Irish Rebellion in the North Atlantic World, 1858–1876* (Knoxville 2013).

Thornley, David, *Isaac Butt and Home Rule* (London 1964).

Tierney, Mark, *Croke of Cashel* (Dublin 1976).

Whelehan, Niall, *The Dynamiters: Irish Nationalism and Political Violence in the Wider World, 1867–1900* (Cambridge 2012).

Woodward, Llewellyn, *The Oxford History of England: the Age of Reform 1815–1870* (London 1962).

Zamoyski, Adam, *Holy Madness: Romantics, Patriots and Revolutionaries 1776–1871* (London 1999).

II. Journals

Anonymous, 'The '67 Rising report from an American veteran' & 'The Fenian Rising in Kilteely', *Parish of Emly Journal*, 1990.

Amos, Keith, 'Clonmel's forgotten Fenian', *Tipperary Historical Journal*, 1989.

De Búrca, Marcus [Marcus Bourke], 'J.K. Bracken Centenary: a reflection', *THJ* 2004.

Cahir, Brendan [Ó Cathaoir], 'Isaac Butt and the Limerick by-election of 1871', *North Munster Antiquarian Journal* (1966), vol. x, no. 1; 'The Kerry "Home Rule" by-election, 1872', *JKAHS* no. 3 (1970).

Comerford, R.V., 'Patriotism as pastime: the appeal of Fenianism in the mid-1860s', *Irish Historical Studies*, vol. 22, no. 86, Sept. 1980.

Fitzgerald, Michael, 'Michael Doheny – the Cork connection', *THJ* 1993.

Geber, Jonny, 'Osteoarchaeological and archaeological insights into the deaths and intramural mass burials at the Kilkenny Union Workhouse between 1847–51 during the Great Famine', *Old Kilkenny Review*, 2011.

Griffin, Brian, 'Social aspects of Fenianism in Connacht and Leinster, 1858–1870', *Eire-Ireland* XXI, I (Spring 1986).

Kennedy, Padraic C., 'The Secret Service Department: A British Intelligence Bureau in Mid-Victorian London, September 1867 to April 1868', *Intelligence and National Security* 18, no. 3 (2003).

'Extracts from the papers of the late Dr Patrick McCartan', *Clogher Record*, vol. 5 no. 1 (1963).

McCarthy, Patrick, 'Conflicting loyalties – two Waterford Soldier-Fenians', *Decies, Journal of the Waterford Archaeological & Historical Society* no. 53 (1997).

McConnel, James, '"Fenians at Westminster": The Edwardian Irish Parliamentary Party and the Legacy of the New Departure', *Irish Historical Studies*, vol. 34, no. 133 (2004).

McCracken, J.L., 'The fate of an infamous informer', *History Ireland*, vol. 9 no. 2 (Summer 2001).

Mac Fheorais, Mathúin, 'J.K. Bracken – the Kilrush Connection', *Clare Association Yearbook 2011*.

McGee, Owen, 'Keeping the lid on an Irish Revolution: the Gosselin – Balfour correspondence', *History Ireland*, Nov./Dec. 2007 vol. 15 no. 6; 'Frederick James Allan (1861–1937), Fenian and civil servant', *History Ireland*, vol. 10, no. 1.

Mac Giolla Choille, Breandán, 'Mourning the martyrs: a study of a demonstration in Limerick city, 8. 12. 1867', *North Munster Antiquarian Journal* (1967), vol. x, no. 2; 'Fenians, Rice and Ribbonmen in County Monaghan, 1864–'69', *Clogher Record* vol. 6, no. 2 (1967).

'Fenian documents in the State Paper Office', *Irish Historical Studies*, vol. 16, no. 63, Mar. 1969.

McGrath, Walter, 'The Fenian Rising in Cork' in *The Irish Sword: The Journal of the Military History Society of Ireland*, vol. viii no. 33 (Winter 1968); articles on James Mountaine in *Evening Echo* (Cork) 30 & 31 Dec. 1968 and 1 Jan. 1969, Central Library, Cork.

Mandle, W.F., 'The IRB and the beginnings of the GAA', *Irish Historical Studies*, vol. 20, no. 80, Sept. 1977.

Marnane, Denis G., 'The Famine in South Tipperary', *THJ* 2000; 'Tipperary town one hundred years ago: issues of identity', *THJ* 2002; 'The war of independence in Tipperary town and district. Part II: the road to Soloheadbeg', *THJ* 2011.

Moran, Gerard, 'The Fenians and Tipperary politics, 1868–1880', *THJ* 1994.

Mulcahy, John, 'Jerome Collins and the quest for the north pole', *Old Blarney, Journal of the Blarney and District Society*, no. 7.

Murphy, Clare C., 'North Tipperary in the year of the Fenian Rising (part 1)', *THJ* 1995; 'North Tipperary in the year of the Fenian Rising (part 2)', *THJ* 1996.

Murphy, Nancy, 'Frank R. Maloney – Nenagh's GAA pioneer', *THJ* 1997.

Ó Broin, Leon, 'The Phoenix conspiracy', *The Irish Sword: The Journal of the Military History Society of Ireland*, vol. 14 (1980–1).

O Cathaoir, Eva, 'Edmond O'Donovan, Fenian and war correspondent, and his Circle', *Decies, Journal of the Waterford Archaelogical & Historical Society* no. 64 (2008).

O'Donnell, Michael, 'Thomas Francis Bourke (1840–1889)', part 1, *THJ* 1990; 'Thomas Francis Bourke (1840–1889)', part 2, *THJ* 1991.

Ò Duinnin, Nicholas, 'A boycotted family in lone Kilclooney Wood 1867', *The Avondhu*, 23 May 2002.

O'Halpin, Eunan, 'The Secret Service Vote and Ireland, 1868–1922', *Irish Historical Studies*, vol. 23, no. 92 (1983).

Ó Lúing, Sean, 'The Phoenix Society in Kerry, 1858–9', *Journal of the Kerry Archaeological and Historical Society* no. 2 (1969); 'Aspects of the Fenian Rising in Kerry, 1867: I. The Rising and its background', *JKAHS* no. 3 (1970); 'Aspects of the Fenian Rising in Kerry, 1867: II Aftermath', *JKAHS* no. 4 (1971); 'Aspects of the Fenian Rising in Kerry, 1867: III. Prelude to the trials', *JKAHS* no. 5 (1972); 'Aspects of the Fenian Rising in Kerry, 1867: IV. Kerry summer assizes, 1867', *JKAHS* no. 6 (1973); 'Aspects of the Fenian Rising in Kerry, 1867: V. Personalities and problems', *JKAHS* no. 7 (1974).

O'Mahony, Colman, 'Dominick O'Mahony', typescript of address to O'Mahony Society at unveiling of headstone in St Joseph's Cemetery, 21 June 1993, Cork Central Library.

Ó Sé, Liam, 'Gun-running in 1882', *The Other Clare*, vol. 29 (June 2005).

O'Shea, Kieran, 'David Moriarty (1814–77): III politics', *JKAHS* no. 5 (1972).

Ó Síothcháin, Tomás, 'The IRB raid on Mallow barracks', *Mallow Field Club Journal* no. 20 (2002).

Rice, George, 'Kerry's most exciting election – hard to keep voters in line in 1872', *Kerry Magazine*, published by the Kerry Archaeological and Historical Society, issue 19 (2009).

Ruddy, Bernardine, 'Denis Dowling Mulcahy', *THJ* 2008.

Sayers, Brian J., 'Attempted Rising – July 1848', *THJ* 2005; 'The insurrection of 1848', *THJ* 2006.

Semple, A.J., 'The Fenian Infiltration of the British Army', *Journal of the Society for Army Historical Research* (Autumn 1974).

Seoighe, Mainchín, 'The Fenian attack on Kilmallock Police Barracks' in *North Munster Antiquarian Journal* no. 10 (1967).

Takagami, Shin-Ichi, 'The Fenian Rising in Dublin, March 1867', *Irish Historical Studies*, vol. 29, no. 115 (May 1995).

Notes

1. W.E. Vaughan & A.J. Fitzpatrick (eds), *Irish Historical Statistics* (Dublin 1978), 3.
2. Niall Whelehan, *The Dynamiters. Irish Nationalism and Political Violence in the Wider World, 1867–1900* (Cambridge 2012), 196; Kerby Miller, *Ireland and Irish America* (Dublin 2008), 75.
3. Whelehan, *The Dynamiters*; Michael Davitt, *The fall of feudalism in Ireland* (London & NY 1904).
4. Donnacha Séan Lucey, *Land, popular politics and agrarian violence in Ireland. The Case of County Kerry, 1872–86* (Dublin 2011), 8.
5. Leon Ó Broin, *Fenian Fever: an Anglo-Irish Dilemma* (London 1971), 244.
6. R.V. Comerford, *The Fenians in Context* (Dublin 1985); 'Patriotism as pastime: the appeal of Fenianism in the mid-1860s', *Irish Historical Studies*, vol. 22, no. 86, Sept. 1980.
7. See John Borgonovo (ed.), *Florence and Josephine O'Donoghue's War of Independence* (Dublin 2006), 4. O'Donoghue was very aware of the hard lives of Kerry and West Cork farmers and wanted to create a better Ireland.
8. *Irish People*, 28 Nov. 1863; 5 Dec. 1863.
9. Ibid., 2 Jan. 1864; 7 Jan. 1865; 16 Jan. 1864; 19 Dec. 1863.
10. John O'Leary, *Recollections of Fenians and Fenianism* (Shannon 1969), vol. i, 78–9; *Irish People*, 5 Dec. 1863.
11. Adam Zamoyski, *Holy Madness: Romantics, Patriots and Revolutionaries 1776–1871* (London 1999), 85 & 291–3.
12. Marie-Louise Legg (ed.), *Alfred Webb: the Autobiography of a Quaker Nationalist* (Cork 1999), 38.
13. Ibid. Webb's views were echoed by Katharine Tynan, who exclaimed on meeting John O'Leary, returned home after imprisonment: 'Good God! What an indictment of our rulers!' Katharine Tynan, *The Middle Years* (London 1916), 12.
14. O'Hegarty, 'The Fenian movement', *The Voice of Freedom* (Dublin 1913), 23.
15. David Sim, *A Union Forever: The Irish Question and US Foreign Relations in the Victorian Age* (Ithaca & London 2013), 64.
16. Gosselin's report to Special Branch, Dublin Castle, 11 Apr. 1890, PRO 30/60/13/2, TNA.

459

17. 21 & 23 Dec. 1867, HO 45/7799, part II, TNA.

18. Diarmuid O'Donovan Rossa, *Rossa's Recollections, 1838–1898*; Joseph Denieffe, *A Personal Narrative of the Irish Revolutionary Brotherhood* (Shannon 1969).

19. William O'Brien & Desmond Ryan (eds), *Devoy's Post Bag i & ii* (Dublin 1948 & 1953); Breandán Mac Giolla Choille, 'Fenian documents in the State Paper Office', *IHS*, vol. 16, no. 63, Mar. 1969, 282; 'Fenians, Rice and Ribbonmen in County Monaghan, 1864–'69', *Clogher Record* vol. 6 no. 2 (1967). Also see Eva O Cathaoir, 'Fenianism in Co. Wicklow, 1858–99', *Bray Historical Record* no. 4 (1990).

20. Owen McGee, *The IRB: The Irish Republican Brotherhood from the Land League to Sinn Féin* (Dublin 2005); Máirtín Ó Catháin, *Irish Republicanism in Scotland, 1858–1916: Fenians in Exile* (Dublin 2007); Brian Jenkins, *Fenians and Anglo-American Relations during Reconstruction* (Ithaca, NY 1969); *The Fenian Problem: Insurgency and Terrorism in a Liberal State, 1858–1874* (Montreal 2008).

21. Marta Ramon, *A Provisional Dictator* (Dublin 2007); M.J. Kelly, *The Fenian Ideal and Irish Nationalism, 1882–1916* (Dublin 2007).

22. Patrick Downing of Skibbereen, Adjutant-General, Fenian Brotherhood, 13 July 1866, PRO HO 45/7799.

23. Borgonovo, *Florence and Josephine O'Donoghue's War of Independence*.

24. M. Maume, P. Maume & M. Casey (eds), *John Sarsfield Casey the Galtee Boy* (Dublin 2005), 61.

25. Declan Dunne, *Peter's Key: Peter De Loughry and the Fight for Irish Independence* (Cork 2012), 13, 18.

26. Denieffe, *A Personal Narrative*, 119–20; Maud Gonne MacBride, *A Servant of the Queen* (Dublin 1950), 300–01.

27. *Irishman*, 14 Mar. 1868.

1. IN THE SHADOW OF THE FAMINE: THE BIRTH OF FENIANISM, 1845–60

1. Diarmuid O'Donovan Rossa, *Rossa's Recollections, 1838–1898* (Guilford CT 2004), 108. Jeremiah O'Donovan Rossa, 1831–1915, derived his suffix from the ancestral lands of Rossmore, lost through eviction.

2. *Rossa's Recollections*, 72–3, 39, 117–8, 123; Kerby A. Miller, *Emigrants and Exiles: Ireland and the Irish Exodus to North America* (New York 1985), 291.

3. *Rossa's Recollections*, 123–4, 127–8.

4. Ibid., 126.

5. Ibid., 119–22, 130; John O'Connor, *The Workhouses of Ireland* (Dublin 1995), 177; Kinealy, *A Death-Dealing Famine* (London 1997), 125.

6. Ciarán Ó Murchadha, 'The years of the Great Famine' in Matthew Lynch & Patrick Nugent (eds), *Clare: History and Society* (Dublin 2008), 258–9; Kinealy, *A Death-Dealing Famine*, 127; T.W. Moody, *Davitt and Irish Revolution 1846–82* (Oxford 1990), 7–9; Mark Ryan, *DIB*, vol. 8, 697; Jane Stanford, *That Irishman: The Life and Times of John O'Connor Power* (Dublin 2011), 19–20.

7. Legg, *Webb*, 17; Vaughan & Fitzpatrick, *Irish Historical Statistics*, 260–1.

8. *Rossa's Recollections*, 141–2. When Rossa met his mother again in 1863, neither recognized the other.

9. Vaughan & Fitzpatrick, *Irish Historical Statistics*, 3; Miller, *Emigrants and Exiles*, 291.

10. Hickey, *The Famine in West Cork*, 148.

11. *Rossa's Recollections*, 110. John Denvir of Liverpool was also motivated by negative British press reaction to join the IRB.

12. *Rossa's Recollections*, 94–6. Dr Daniel Donovan, 1807–77, whose diary of a dispensary doctor appeared in the *Southern Reporter* during 1848, publicizing the suffering in Skibbereen.

13. Ibid., 130, 120. Gerard J. Lyne, *The Lansdowne Estate in Kerry under W.S. Trench 1849–72* (Dublin 2001), 76–7, confirms that traditional forbearance stopped with the Famine.

14. Cormac Ó Grada, *Black '47 and Beyond: The Great Irish Famine in History, Economy, and Memory* (Princeton 1999), 135–6; Hickey, *The Famine in West Cork*, 294, 305.

15. Jane Jordan, *Kitty O'Shea: An Irish Affair* (Stroud 2005), 6.

16. R.V. Comerford, 'Ireland 1850–70: Post-Famine and Mid-Victorian' in W.E. Vaughan (ed.), *A New History of Ireland V: Ireland Under the Union, I* (Oxford 1989), 380–1; L. Kennedy, P. Ell, M. Crawford & L. Clarkson (eds), *Mapping the Great Irish Famine* (Dublin 1999), 199; Donnacha Séan Lucey, *Land, Popular Politics and Agrarian Violence*, 8–9.

17. Comerford, 'Ireland 1850–70', 373–5, 382; Kinealy, *A Death-Dealing Famine*, 153–4; Caitriona Clear, *Social Change and Everyday Life in Ireland, 1850–1922* (Manchester 2007), 27.

18. Patrick Maume (ed.), *Mitchel: The Last Conquest of Ireland (Perhaps)* by John Mitchel (Dublin 2005), 209, 219, 214.

19. Jennifer Regan-Lefebvre (ed.), *For the Liberty of Ireland, at Home and Abroad: the Autobiography of J.F.X. O'Brien* (Dublin 2010), 23; Kinealy, *A Death-Dealing Famine*, 78.

20. John Mitchel, *Jail Journal* (Dublin 1921), xliv. Cheap editions were advertised even in the *Irish Times*, 8 Dec. 1876. W.E.H. Lecky complained in 1889 that Mitchel's works were widely disseminated and spread anti-British views: see Maume (ed.), *The Last Conquest*, xxiv–xxv; Tim Pat Coogan, *The Famine Plot: England's Role in Ireland's Greatest Tragedy* (New York 2012) repeats the genocide argument.

21. Sim, *A Union Forever*, 14–16; quoted Moody, *Michael Davitt and Irish Revolution*, 14.

22. James O'Shea, *Prince of Swindlers: John Sadleir MP 1813–1856* (Dublin 1999), 260.

23. *Rossa's Recollections*, 143.

24. Calvary Cemetery, New York, contains over three million dead and is the largest cemetery in the US – a veritable Irish-American necropolis.

25. R.V. Comerford, *Charles J. Kickham (1828–82): A Study in Irish Nationalism and Literature* (Dublin 1979), 24–7; Kickham's speech in Tipperary, *Irishman*, 20 May 1876.

26. Walter McGrath, *A Cork Felon* (Cork 1952), 11–2; James McGuire and James Quinn (eds), *Dictionary of Irish Biography*, vol. 2, 436–7; Maume, Maume & Casey, *The Galtee Boy*, 1, 3–4, 207; Tomás Ó Ríordáin, *Patrick Neville Fitzgerald: a Forgotten Cork Fenian and GAA Pioneer* (n. p. 2004), 7–9; *Irish Times*, 19 May

1913; Regan-Lefebvre, *Autobiography of J.F.X. O'Brien*, 21–3. See Appendix I.

27. John O'Mahony, introduction to Keating's history of Ireland, *Foras Feasa ar Eirinn* (New York 1857), 7.

28. *Irishman* (Dublin), 16 Aug. 1862; John Savage, *Fenian Heroes and Martyrs* (Boston 1868), 301–2; P.J. Leonard to *Irish World* (New York), 17 Mar. 1877. Here I am indebted to Dr Brian Sayers.

29. James Quinn, *John Mitchel* (Dublin 2008), 13–17; Richard Davis, *The Young Ireland Movement* (Dublin 1987), 127.

30. Davis, *The Young Ireland Movement*, 14, 143–5; Quinn, *John Mitchel*, 26–7.

31. Davis, *The Young Ireland Movement*, 145–7; Quinn, *John Mitchel*, 29–30; Gary Owens, 'Popular mobilization and the Rising of 1848: the clubs of the Irish Confederation' in Laurence M. Geary (ed.), *Rebellion and Remembrance in Modern Ireland* (Dublin 2001), 53, 55, 60, 62.

32. Quinn, *John Mitchel*, 36–7, 39; Michael Doheny, *The Felon's Track* (Dublin 1951), xiv–xvi, 163–8; Cecil Woodham-Smith, *The Great Hunger* (New York 1989), 350–1; Davis, *The Young Ireland movement*, 160.

33. Bourke, *John O'Leary*, 17–8; 'the rebellion, which actually commenced on that morning, had been decisively checked by fifty or sixty police', *Times*, 1 Aug. 1848.

34. Luby's personal reminiscences in *Irish World* (NY), 3 March 1877; Bourke, *John O'Leary*, 17.

35. Doheny, *The Felon's Track*, 237. Mangan's poem had been published in the *Nation* on 30 May 1846.

36. Doheny, *The Felon's Track*, 251–2; A.M. Sullivan, *New Ireland: political sketches and personal reminiscences of thirty years of Irish public life* (New York 1878), 128–9; Lyne, *The Lansdowne Estate*, 600–602, 627. 'Christabel': Mary McCarthy Downing, 1815–81; Timothy McCarthy Downing, 1814–79, later MP for Cork.

37. Doheny, *The felon's track*, 254, 269–70; Ramon, *A Provisional Dictator*, 47–8, 50; Savage, *Fenian Heroes and Martyrs*, 304.

38. Brian J. Sayers, 'The insurrection of 1848', *THJ* 2006, 107, 120–2, 129. Philip Gray, 1821–57, a native of Dublin, whose uncle was rumoured to have been hanged in 1798. He was inspired by the *Nation*, *DIB*, vol. 4, 226. Felix O'Neill, a member of the Catholic gentry, had volunteered his services to Doheny.

39. Sim, *A Union Forever:*, 14–6; John Belchem, 'Republican Spirit and Military Science: The "Irish Brigade" and Irish-American Nationalism in 1848', *Irish Historical Studies* 29, no. 113 (May 1994), 45–8, 52, 57–9, 62–3.

40. *Times*, 2 Aug. 1848;13 Mar. 1856.

41. Quinn, *John Mitchel*, 21; Michael Davitt, *Fall*, 47–8, 66; Miller, *Ireland and Irish America*, 71.

42. O'Leary, *Recollections*, vol. i, 26; Bourke, *John O'Leary*, 21–3; Ramon, *A Provisional Dictator*, 52–3.

43. O'Leary, *Recollections*, vol. i, 29, 35; Bourke, *John O'Leary*, 20–3; Luby papers, Ms. 331–3, NLI; John Devoy, *Recollections of an Irish Rebel* (Shannon 1969), 288. Joseph Brenan, 1828–57, *DIB*, vol. 1, 801.

44. Bourke, *John O'Leary*, 23–8; Brendan Kiely, *The Waterford Rebels of 1849* (Dublin 1999), 21–2; Anthony M. Breen, *The Cappoquin Rebellion 1849* (Thurston, Suffolk 1998), 41.

45. James Quinn, *Young Ireland and the Writing of Irish History* (Dublin 2015), 98–9; Doheny, *The Felon's Track*, xvii; Comerford, *Charles J. Kickham*, 32–3, 37.

46. Callan Heritage Society, *The Callan Tenant League* (Callan c. 1988), 18, 28–9, 32.

47. Ibid., 33–7; Davitt, *Fall of Feudalism*, 70–2; T.D. Sullivan, *Recollections of Troubled Times in Irish Politics*, (Dublin 1905), 12. Dr Cullen had been appointed Archbishop of Armagh in 1850 and was translated to the See of Dublin in 1852.

48. O'Shea, *Prince of Swindlers*, 402–5, 421–2, 417–9; Davitt, *Fall*, 71.

49. O'Leary, *Recollections*, vol. i, 57.

50. Sullivan, *New Ireland*, 240.

51. Mark Ryan, *Fenian Memories* (Dublin 1945), 2; Richard Pigott, *Personal Recollections of an Irish National Journalist* (Cork 1979), 91.

52. Denieffe, *A Personal Narrative*, v.

53. Dillon and O'Gorman to William Smith O'Brien, New York, 12 Dec. 1852, Ms. 445, NLI.

54. O'Mahony to Fr Lavelle, *Irishman*, 16 Aug. 1862.

55. Denieffe, *A Personal Narrative*, vii; Mitchel, *Jail Journal*, 356, 353–4. Mitchel's assistants were John Savage and John McClenahan.

56. Ibid., 377–9, 394–6; Quinn, *John Mitchel*, 54; John Hassard, *Life of the Most Reverend John Hughes, First Archbishop of New York* (New York 2008), 365. McClenahan succeeded Mitchel as editor.

57. Denieffe, *A Personal Narrative*, vii.

58. Patrick Geoghegan, *Robert Emmet: a Life* (Dublin 2004), 254.

59. Denieffe, *A Personal Narrative*, vii–viii; 1–3; Secret service account, 1872, HD 3/46, TNA.

60. Denieffe, *A Personal Narrative*, 7.

61. Jonny Geber, 'Osteoarchaeological and archaeological insights into the deaths and intramural mass burials at the Kilkenny Union Workhouse between 1847–51 during the Great Famine', *Old Kilkenny Review* 2011, 64–75.

62. Denieffe, *A Personal Narrative*, 7; Vaughan & Fitzpatrick, *Irish Historical Statistics*, 30; Walter Walsh, 'An exile remembers: Kilkenny city and environs around 1840', *Old Kilkenny Review* 2009, 110.

63. Denieffe, *A Personal Narrative*, 7–9.

64. Their families shared the then prevalent experience of emigration: Edward's sibling Philip, leaving in 1848, had set up in business in St Louis, Missouri; James's older brother, John, was also in America. Dunnamaggin parish, Croghtabeg townland, barony of Kells, baptisms: John, baptized 19 Jan. 1835 and James, baptized 17 Apr. 1838, sons of James Cody and Mary Walsh. Courtesy of the late Canon John Brennan, Callan. Fenian files, F 1182; F 1224, NAI.

65. Denieffe, *A Personal Narrative*, 10–13.

66. George Boate, 20 July 1855; Consul, NY, 24 July & 31 July 1855; Ex-constable John Walsh, 31 July 1855; Consul Rowcroft, 12 Nov. 1855 & 9 Jan. 1856; 14 Nov. 1855, Larcom papers Ms. 7,517, NLI.

67. Ibid., Vice-consul Schedel, 7 Dec. 1855; Denieffe, *A Personal Narrative*, i–x.

68. Ramon, *A Provisional Dictator*, 26–7; Stephens, 'Reminiscences', (articles from *Weekly Freeman*), 6 Oct. 1883, NLI.

69. 11 & 21 Feb. 1856, Larcom papers, Ms. 7,517; CSORP 1856/12589 & 14212, NAI.

70. Stephens, 'Reminiscences'.

71. Ibid.; Prionsias Ó Drisceoil, *Seán Ó Dálaigh: Éigse agus Iomarbhá* (Cork 2007), 151; Desmond Ryan, *The Fenian Chief* (Dublin 1967), 63–5.

72. Ryan, *The Fenian Chief*, 67, 69–72.

73. Stephens, 'Reminiscences'.

74. Ryan, *The Fenian Chief*, 80.

75. Ramon, *A Provisional Dictator*, 69; Denieffe, *A Personal Narrative*, 14–5; O'Leary, *Recollections*, vol. i, 71.

76. Denieffe, *A Personal Narrative*, 159.

77. Ibid., 160; O'Leary, *Recollections*, vol. ii, 237, vol. i, 71–2.

78. Denieffe, *A Personal Narrative*, 17–22; Ramon, *A Provisional Dictator*, 75. Corcoran, 1827–63, a native of Carrowkeel, Co. Sligo, a former Ribbonman, who had emigrated to New York in 1849 to become a tavern keeper. Kelly, 1833–1908, a printer from Mountbellew, Co. Galway; O'Rourke had been associated with the *New York Tribune* and became treasurer of the Fenian Brotherhood in 1863.

79. Denieffe, *A Personal Narrative*, 25.

80. O'Leary, *Recollections*, vol. i, 120.

81. Ibid.

82. Ibid., 123–4. Denieffe, O'Mahony, Rossa and Denvir refer to the 'Irish Revolutionary Brotherhood', as does the monument to the IRB veterans in Calvary Cemetery, New York: *New York Times*, 23 Sept. 1907.

83. Denieffe, *A Personal Narrative*, 25–6; McGrath, *A Cork Felon*, 12–3; Maume, Maume & Casey, *The Galtee Boy*, 213; *Irishman*, 14 Nov. 1868; ibid., 24 Aug. 1872; *Rossa's Recollections*, 8–9.

84. O'Leary, *Recollections*, vol. i, 180; *Rossa's Recollections*, 314; Denieffe, *A Personal Narrative*, 36.

85. Some authors suggest that D.D. Mulcahy had been involved in 1848–9, which is unlikely as he was born in 1840. Luby papers, Ms. 331–3, 78. O'Neill leased 262 acres in the townland of Lisronagh and a flour mill in Cregg, Griffith Valuation 1847–64. Comerford, *Charles J. Kickham*, 50, 55–6. ·

86. Denieffe, *A Personal Narrative*, 36; *Rossa's Recollections*, 150.

87. *Rossa's Recollections*, 149–150; *Irish Rebels in English Prisons* (Dingle 1991), 22.The phoenix rising from the ashes of Bombay Street, Belfast, was used as a symbol by the Provisional IRA, founded in 1969; Ed Moloney, *Voices From the Grave* (New York 2010), 14.

88. *Rossa's Recollections*, 144; O'Donovan Rossa, 'The Fenian Movement', *Brooklyn Eagle*, 28 June 1885; O'Donovan Rossa, *Irish Rebels in English Prisons*, 27–8. See Appendix I for the Downings.

89. *Rossa's Recollections*, 201, 204–5, 167.

90. Ibid., 235.

91. O'Donovan Rossa, *Brooklyn Eagle*, 7 June 1885; *Rossa's Recollections*, 200.

92. O'Donovan Rossa, *Irish Rebels in English Prisons*, 187–8; Eva O Cathaoir & Mathúin Mac Fheorais, 'The Irish Republican Brotherhood in Clare 1858–1871', Matthew Lynch & Patrick Nugent (eds) *Clare: History & Society* (Dublin 2008), 451–3.

93. *Rossa's Recollections*, 150; *Brooklyn Eagle*, 7 June 1885; Denieffe, *A Personal Narrative*, 33–4; Lyne, *The Lansdowne Estate*, 259– 62, 627–31.

94. O'Leary, *Recollections*, vol. i, 83–5; Denieffe, *A Personal Narrative*, 27–8. John Kenealy of Cork and James O'Mahony of Bandon gave financial support.

95. O'Leary, *Recollections*, vol. i, 70, 81.

96. Denieffe, *A Personal Narrative*, 29.

97. Devoy, *Recollections*, 27; O'Leary, *Recollections* vol. i, 84.

98. For example, *Irishman*, 14 Oct. 1865, where Andrew Kennedy was arrested in possession of a prayer book. Ibid., 11 Nov. 1865: in Mullinavat, Co. Kilkenny, Fenians sworn in an outhouse. The late Professor Brian Farrell told me that his father had been sworn in in a rainswept doorway in Manchester.

99. Devoy, *Recollections*, 27.

100. O'Leary, *Recollections*, vol. i, 240–1; Brian Griffin, 'Social aspects of Fenianism in Connacht and Leinster, 1858–1870', *Eire-Ireland* XXI, I (Spring 1986), 18–9, 23.

101. Devoy, *Recollections*, 50.

102. Eoin Kinsella, 'Riotous proceedings and the cricket of savages: football and hurling in early modern Ireland', Mike Cronin, William Murphy, Paul Rouse (eds), *The Gaelic Athletic Association 1884–2009* (Dublin 2009), 27–9; *Irish Times*, 7 Dec. 1865.

103. Fenian police reports, 1864–5, nos. 66 & 68, Box 2, NAI.

104. James Quinn, 'The IRB and Young Ireland: varieties of tension' in Fearghal McGarry & James McConnel (eds), *The Black Hand of Republicanism. Fenianism in Modern Ireland* (Dublin & Portland 2009), 5; *Nation*, 29 Aug. 1868.

105. Sullivan, *Troubled Times*, 37–8, 15; Frank Callanan, *T.M. Healy* (Cork 1996), 4.

106. A.M. Sullivan to Smith O'Brien, 25 Oct. 1858, Smith O'Brien papers, Ms. 446, NLI; Sullivan, *New Ireland*, 265; *Nation*, 30 Oct. 1858.

107. Davys to Larcom, 16 Sept. 1858, Larcom papers, Ms. 7,793, NLI; ibid., W.S. Trench to Larcom, 4 Oct. 1858; ibid., John Caulfield, 2 Oct. 1858.

108. Fr John O'Sullivan to Lord Mayo, 5 Oct. 1858, Mayo papers, Ms. 11,187/4, NLI. Lord Mayo inherited the title in 1867, and was, strictly speaking, Lord Naas until then.

109. Ibid.; 11 Dec. 1858; Lyne, *The Lansdowne Estate*, 628–9.

110. W.S. Trench to Larcom, 4 Oct. 1858, Larcom papers, Ms. 7,793; Fr O'Sullivan to Lord Mayo, 11 Dec. 1858, Mayo papers, Ms.11,187/4, NLI.

111. Sullivan, *New Ireland*, 265–6; A.M. Sullivan to Smith O'Brien, 25 Oct. 1858, Ms. 446, NLI; *Nation*, 30 Oct. 1858; ibid., 6 Nov. 1858.

112. 'For the cabinet', 10 Nov. 1858, Larcom papers, Ms. 7,793.

113. 11 Sept. 1858, Fenian police reports, Co. Kilkenny, 17 Sept. to 20 Jan. 1859, Box 1; ibid., 31 Oct. 1858, sub-inspector Cullen to Dublin Castle; 7 Nov. 1858, NAI.

114. 8 Nov. 1858, Constable Bourke to his superior, Fenian police reports, Co. Tipperary, S.R., Box 1.

115. *Times*, 13 Dec. 1858; 11 Dec. 1858.

116. Ibid., 11 Dec. 1858; Lyne, *The Lansdowne Estate*, 629–30. See Appendix I.

117. *Times*, 11 Dec. 1858; 4 Jan. 1859.

118. Ibid., 4 Jan. 1859.

119. Ibid.

120. Ibid.; 3 Jan. 1859, 'Confidential, secret societies', Fenian police reports, Co. Kilkenny, Box 1, NAI.

121. *Times*, 6 Jan. 1859; research of the late Canon John Brennan, Callan; *Irishman*, 8 Jan. 1859.

122. *Nation*, 15 Jan. 1859; *Times*, 13 Jan. 1859.

123. 12 Dec. 1858, Sub-inspector Cullen, Callan, Fenian police reports, Co. Kilkenny, Box 1; ibid., 15 Dec. 1858, Nenagh, Fenian police reports, Tipperary, N.R.; Fitzmaurice to Larcom, 16 Jan. 1859, Larcom papers, Ms. 7,793, NLI.

124. *Times*, 21 Feb. 1859.

125. *Rossa's Recollections*, 119–20.

126. *Times*, 9 Mar. 1859; ibid., 10 Mar. 1859; *Irish Times*, 14 May 1859; O'Donovan Rossa, *Brooklyn Eagle*, 21 June 1885.

127. Sullivan, *Troubled Times*, 42–3; *Irish Times*, 2 Apr. 1859; Kieran O'Shea, 'David Moriarty (1814–77) III Politics', *JKAHS* no. 5 (1972), 88; Seán Ó Lúing, 'The Phoenix Society in Kerry, 1858–9', *Journal of the Kerry Archaeological and Historical Society*, no. 2 (1969), 25–6.

128. *Irishman*, 16 Aug. 1862; Doheny to Smith O'Brien, 20 Aug. 1858, Ms. 446, NLI.

129. *Nation*, 16 Apr. 1859. See Appendix I.

130. Ibid.; O'Mahony (transl.), *Foras feasa ar Éirinn*, xxxv, which is the only reference by O'Mahony to the Famine, discovered by Dr Sayers.

131. Doheny to William Smith O'Brien, New York, 20 Aug. 1858, Ms. 446, NLI.

132. John Blake Dillon had been a member of this directory when resident in the US. Ramon, *A Provisional Dictator*, 84–6; Maume (ed.), *The Last Conquest*, xiv.

133. *Irishman*, 11 Jan. 1868.

134. Ibid.

135. O'Leary, *Recollections*, vol. i, 96.

136. Ibid., 135-6.

137. Maher, *Chief of the Comeraghs:a John O'Mahony anthology* (Mullinahone 1957), 100.

138. Ramon, *A Provisional Dictator*, 89.

139. Enclosure of Jan. 1859 in John O'Mahony to Charles Kickham, New York, 19 Oct. 1863, Fenian Brotherhood Collection, American Catholic History Research Center and University Archives.

140. The Ossianic Society was started in Ireland in 1853. O'Mahony became a co-founder of the American branch, which shared its accommodation with the Fenian Brotherhood at 6 Centre St, New York. Doheny and Michael Cavanagh were members. Ronald H. Bayor & Timothy J. Meagher (eds), *The New York Irish* (Baltimore 1997), 264.

141. *Irishman*, 16 Aug. 1862. 'Fenian' also became a pejorative term for Catholic dissidents.

142. *Proceedings of the First National Convention of the Fenian Brotherhood, held in Chicago, Illinois, November 1863* (Philadelphia 1863), 35. This pledge was not insisted upon when enrolling prominent recruits.

143. *Rossa's Recollections*, 301, 278–80.

144. British minister, Washington, to FO, 24 Dec. 1858, Mayo papers, Ms. 11,187(2).

145. Ibid., Archibald, 20 Dec. 1858; Archibald, 21 Mar. & 5 May 1859, HO 45/6877, TNA. From *an seabhac*, the hawk.

146. O'Leary, *Recollections*, vol. i, 95.

147. Ramon, *A Provisional Dictator*, 96–7.

148. Sullivan, *New Ireland*, 310.

149. O'Leary, *Recollections*, vol. i, 95, 119–21.

150. Ibid., 121.

151. *Rossa's Recollections*, 270–71.

152. Ibid., 272–3.

153. Ibid., 277–8.

154. Comerford, *The Fenians in Context*, 53; precis of information, Larcom papers, Ms. 7,697, NLI; O'Leary, *Recollections*, vol. i, 107–9.

155. *Irishman*, 16 Aug. 1862.

156. *Rossa's Recollections*, 227–9, 290–1; O'Leary, *Recollections*, vol. i, 128; Devoy, *Recollections*, 20; *Times*, 27 July 1859.

157. Sullivan, *New Ireland*, 305; Robert Anderson, *Sidelights on the Home Rule movement* (London 1907), 49, 54.

158. Hawe was still in contact with Rossa in 1894. Devoy, *Recollections*, 20. See Appendix I for O'Sullivan.

159. As Daniel O'Sullivan, the Phoenix defendant, and the informer shared the same name, the former was dubbed 'Agreem' and the latter 'Goula' to distinguish them. O'Leary, *Recollections*, vol. i, 129, 96.

160. Ibid., vol. ii, 240; *Rossa's Recollections*, 300–1, 303–4; *Irish People* (NY), 21 Nov. 1868; Precis of information, Larcom papers, Ms. 7,697, NLI.

161. Richard Davis, *Revolutionary Imperialist. William Smith O'Brien 1803–1864* (Dublin 1998), 271; Cantwell to O'Mahony, Paris, 27 Mar. 1860, Fenian Brotherhood Collection, CUA.

162. *Rossa's Recollections*, 292–6; Stephens to O'Mahony, Sept. 1860, Fenian Brotherhood Collection, CUA.

163. Cantwell to O'Mahony, 2 Nov. 1860, Fenian Brotherhood Collection, CUA. Conflict with Stephens led Cantwell to leave the IRB, settling in Dublin to support constitutional nationalism.

164. Precis of information, Larcom papers, Ms. 7,697.

165. Ibid.

166. Ibid.

167. *Times*, 27 Aug. 1859; 'The state of Italy' by Edward Law, Lord Ellenborough, 1790–1871, 9 Nov. 1859.

168. Lucy Riall, *Garibaldi: Invention of a Hero* (New Haven & London 2007), 337, 296 ff.; Sullivan, *New Ireland*, 277, 284–5. See Denis G. Marnane, 'Saving the Pope: Tipperary's Contribution to the "Irish Brigade" in 1860', *THJ* 2009.

169. Sullivan, *New Ireland*, 318–9; Devoy, *Recollections*, 20–1, 26, 30–1; Comerford, *The Fenians in Context*, 63; Thomas Kencally, *The Great Shame* (London 1999), 416–9. Daniel O'Donoghue, 1833–89, *DIB*, vol. 7, 405.

2. BOLD FENIAN MEN, 1861–5

1. O'Leary, *Recollections*, vol. i, 134–6; William D'Arcy, *The Fenian Movement in the United States* (Washington DC 1947), 17; Stephens (alias James Johnson) to O'Mahony, Sept. 1860, Fenian Brotherhood Collection, CUA.

2. O'Leary, *Recollections*, vol. i, 137; Precis of information, Larcom papers, Ms. 7,697; Fragment by John Mitchel, n.d., Fenian Brotherhood Collection, CUA.

3. O'Leary, *Recollections*, vol. i, 137–8, 131–2; Devoy, *Recollections*, 26.

4. *Rossa's Recollections*, 235; O'Leary, *Recollections*, vol. i, 138–9.

5. O'Leary, *Recollections*, vol. i, 138.

6. *Nation*, 19 Jan. 1861.

7. O'Leary, *Recollections*, vol. i, 139.

8. Denieffe, *A Personal Narrative*, 60.

9. Ibid., 60, 62.

10. D'Arcy, *The Fenian Movement*, 18; Sim, *A Union Forever*, 6.

11. D'Arcy, *The Fenian Movement*, 18; O'Leary, *Recollections*, vol. i, 136, 139.

12. Ramon (ed.), *James Stephens The Birth of the Fenian Movement*, 9.

13. Mitchel to O'Mahony, 8 May 1861, Fenian Brotherhood Collection, CUA.

14. Ibid.; O'Leary, *Recollections*, vol. i, 177; ibid., vol. ii, 8–9; Denieffe, *A Personal Narrative*, 74; Sullivan, *New Ireland*, 326–7.

15. Comerford, *The Fenians in Context*, 70–1; Mainchín Seoighe, 'The Fenian attack on Kilmallock police barracks', *North Munster Antiquarian Journal*, vol. x, no. 2 (1967), 157.

16. O'Leary, *Recollections*, vol. i, 145–7; Bourke, *John O'Leary*, 44.

17. James Loughlin, *The British Monarchy and Ireland* (Cambridge 2008), 97–8; Elizabeth Longford, *Victoria R.I.* (London 2000), 386, 390–1; Sullivan, *New Ireland*, 319.

18. Devoy, *Recollections*, 26. John Devoy, 1842–1928.

19. Comerford, 'Patriotism as pastime', 239–50; Donal P. McCracken, *Inspector Mallon. Buying Irish Patriotism for a Five-Pound Note* (Dublin 2009), 149.

20. Griffin, 'Social aspects of Fenianism', 17–9.

21. Damian Shiels, *The Irish in the American Civil War* (Dublin 2013), 27, 51–3; David T. Gleeson, *The Green and the Gray: The Irish in the Confederate States of America* (Chapel Hill 2013), 10, 15, 25, 39.

22. *Rossa's Recollections*, 289; McCracken, *Inspector Mallon*, 150.

23. Davis, *The Young Ireland Movement*, 120; *New York Times*,15 Sept. 1861; McManus entry, *DIB*, vol. 6, 99–100.

24. Ibid. Napoleon I had died in 1821, his body was transferred to Paris in 1840, but his tomb remained unfinished until 1861. *Times*, 6 Nov. 1852.

25. Official correspondence, 93, Larcom papers, Ms. 7,517; D'Arcy, *The Fenian Movement*, 18–9, 21; Luby papers, Ms. 331–3, 95, NLI; Michael Cavanagh, *Memoirs of General Thomas Francis Meagher* (Worcester, Mass. 1892), 417.

26. *New York Times*, 15 Sept. 1861.

27. Cavanagh, *Memoirs of General Thomas Francis Meagher*, 419–21; D'Arcy, *The Fenian Movement*, 19–20; *New York Times*, 19 Oct. 1861; Michael O'Donnell, 'Michael Doheny, Fenian leader', http://www.fethard.com/people/doheny.html. See Appendix I.

28. St Colman's Cathedral was not begun until 1868. *FJ*, 1 Nov. 1861. W.E.H. Lecky published similar sentiments in *The Leaders of Public Opinion in Ireland* (London 1861).

29. *New York Times*, 23 Nov. 1861.

30. Denieffe, *A Personal Narrative*, 166; Maura Murphy, 'Fenianism, Parnellism and the Cork Trades, 1860–1900', *Saothar*, vol. 5, May 1979; *Brooklyn Eagle*, 28 June 1885; *FJ*, 4 Nov. 1861.

31. William O'Carroll to O'Mahony, July 1861, Fenian Brotherhood Collection, CUA; *Irishman*, 16 June 1866. For Cavanagh, see Appendix I.

32. *Rossa's Recollections*, 237.

33. *Brooklyn Eagle*, 28 June 1885.

34. Mainchin Seoighe, *The Story of Kilmallock* (Kilmallock 1987), 204.

35. Luby papers, Ms. 331–3, 97, NLI; *Rossa's Recollections*, 237–8.

36. *Rossa's Recollections*, 238; *Brooklyn Eagle*, 28 June 1885; O'Leary, *Recollections*, vol. i, 168.

37. Denieffe, *A Personal Narrative*, 166; O'Mahony on Fenianism, *Irishman*, 8 Feb. 1868.

38. *FJ*, 5 Nov. 1861; O'Leary, *Recollections*, vol. i, 168.

39. Oliver P. Rafferty, *The Church, the State and the Fenians* (Basingstoke 1999), 27.

40. 'Cardinal Cullen, early Fenianism and the McManus funeral affair', Oliver P. Rafferty, *The Catholic Church and the Protestant State: Nineteenth-Century Irish Realities* (Dublin 2008), 156–7; John Belchem, *Irish, Catholic and Scouse: the History of the Liverpool Irish, 1800–1939* (Liverpool 2007), 163; *Irishman*, 10 May 1862.

41. *New York Times*, 22 Nov. 1861.

42. Ibid., 22 Nov. 1861.

43. *FJ*, 1,8, 9 Nov. 1861; .

44. *FJ*, 8 Nov. 1861; 1 Nov. 1861. President Lincoln's coffin was to be carried in a similar vehicle in 1865, which was later used for Henry Clarence McCarthy, the deputy head centre of the Fenian Brotherhood, in St Louis, US.

45. Ibid., 5 Nov. 1861.

46. Ibid.

47. Luby papers, Ms. 331–3, 100; Pigott, *Personal Recollections*, 114.

48. O'Leary, *Recollections*, vol. i, 167.

49. Ibid., 156–7.

50. Ibid., 158.

51. Denieffe, *A Personal Narrative*, 68–9, 170–3; O'Leary, *Recollections*, vol. i, 158–9. Quinn, 'The IRB and Young Ireland: varieties of tension', 7.

52. O'Leary, *Recollections*, vol. i, 160–1, quoting Luby papers, Ms. 331–3, NLI. This description is confirmed by a police report, CSORP 1877/3591, NAI.

53. *Irish Times*, 11 Nov. 1861.

54. Luby papers, Ms. 331–3, 16. Stephens, 'Reminiscences', NLI; Ryan, *The Fenian Chief*, 83; Sayers, 'The insurrection of 1848', *THJ* 2006, 121. Edward Hollywood, 1814–73.

55. Andrew Ryan was a member of the Ossianic Society, as were Smith O'Brien, Dr Sigerson and James O'Mahony of Bandon. Counsellor Crean assisted John Blake Dillon during his election campaign in Tipperary in 1865. Peter Gill's Nenagh home was known as 'the rebel's den', having harboured James Stephens in 1848. Gill's grandfather had been a close friend of Robert Emmet.

56. Only a selection of prominent delegates is given here; *FJ*, 9 & 11 Nov. 1861; *Cork Examiner*, 11 Nov. 1861. Duffy's family took the scarf he had worn as the Connacht representative to the US when they emigrated.

57. *Kilkenny Moderator*, 16 Nov. 1861.

58. *Cork Examiner*, 11 Nov. 1861; Ciarán O'Carroll, *Paul Cardinal Cullen: Portrait of a Practical Nationalist* (Dublin 2008), 154; Denieffe, *A Personal Narrative*, 70; O'Leary, *Recollections*, vol. i, 164.

59. *New York Times*, 27 Nov. 1861.

60. O'Leary, *Recollections*, vol. i, 164–5, 167–9.

61. Ibid., 163, 153. Estimates vary. Luby claimed that 200,000 witnessed the procession to Glasnevin. The *Irish Times* stated 20,000 marched, consisting of 'the lower orders' with a sprinkling of the respectably dressed, *Irish Times*, 11 Nov. 1861.

62. Sullivan, *New Ireland*, 323.

63. Luby papers, Ms. 331–3, 99.

64. Denieffe, *A Personal Narrative*, 71; Pigott, *Personal Recollections*, 115; *Rossa's Recollections*, 305–6.

65. Denieffe, *A Personal Narrative*, 74–5; O'Leary, *Recollections*, vol. i, 179–80, 194–6, 212–3, 217; D'Arcy, *The Fenian Movement*, 20–2.

66. O'Leary, *Recollections*, vol. i, 205, 207–9, 225–6; *Irishman*, 2 June 1866.

67. Cormac Ó Gráda, *Ireland: A New Economic History 1780–1939* (Oxford 1995), 250–1.

68. O'Leary, *Recollections*, vol. i, 192–3; HO 45/7799 part ii; *Times*, 3 Jan. 1866; Luby Papers, Ms. 331–3.

69. Belchem, Irish, *Catholic and Scouse*, 164.

70. Maume, Maume & Casey, *The Galtee Boy*, 9; *Rossa's Recollections*, 249–50, 247.

71. O Cathaoir & Mac Fheorais, 'The Irish Republican Brotherhood in Clare 1858–1871', 451–4; Devoy, *Recollections*, 32. See Appendix I.

72. Devoy, *Recollections*, 32; Seoighe, *The Story of Kilmallock*, 205. O'Sullivan, 1829–87.

73. Sullivan, *Troubled Times*, 47.

74. Ibid.; O'Leary, *Recollections*, vol. ii, 237–9.

75. Niamh O'Sullivan, *Aloysius O'Kelly. Art, Nation, Empire* (Dublin 2010), 6–8, 118–9. James J. O'Kelly, c. 1843–1916; Aloysius O'Kelly, 1853–1936. Other friends among the London IRB were Joseph I.C. Clarke, 1846–1925, journalist and playwright, and James Clancy. Merv is a Unesco World Heritage Site.

76. Denieffe, *A Personal Narrative*, 10. See Appendix I.

77. *Irish People*, 15 July 1865.

78. Denieffe, *A Personal Narrative*, 10; *Irishman*, 11 Nov. 1865.

79. *Irishman*, 11 Nov. 1865; *Irish People*, 8 July 1865.

80. Denieffe, *A Personal Narrative*, 34.

81. Ibid., 34–7, 46–50; *Rossa's Recollections*, 234.

82. O'Mahony to Kickham, 19 Oct. 1863, Fenian Brotherhood Collection, CUA.

83. Ibid., O'Mahony to Stephens (alias James Kelly), 19 Oct. 1863.

84. Ibid., O'Mahony to Kickham, 19 Oct. 1863.

85. On 10 May 1865 Kickham wrote to O'Mahony, regretting that 'these disagreeable reflections sway you so much ... O'Leary is your friend, though he disapproves of some of your public action'. Fenian Brotherhood Collection, CUA; ibid., O'Carroll to O'Mahony, July 1861.

86. *Proceedings of the first national convention*, 26–7.

87. *FJ*, 30 Oct. 1877; Ramon, *A Provisional Dictator*, 161–2.

88. *Proceedings of the first national convention*, 40–1.

89. Ibid., 33–4; O'Leary, *Recollections*, vol. ii, 12–13; David Wilson, *Thomas D'Arcy McGee* vol. ii: *The Extreme Moderate 1857–1868* (Montreal 2011), 222.

90. *Proceedings of first convention*, 17–18.

91. Ibid., 18; *Irishman*, 20 May 1871.

92. *Proceedings of first convention*, 31–2, 36–7, 9, 53.

93. O'Mahony on Fenianism, *Irishman*, 8 Feb. 1868; *Irish People*, 16 Jan. 1864; ibid., 13 Feb. 1864.

94. *Brooklyn Eagle*, 26 July 1885; John Rutherford, *The Secret History of the Fenian Conspiracy: its Origin, Objects, and Ramifications* (London 1877), vol. ii, 12, 2, 26; O'Leary, *Recollections*, vol. i, 219; Denieffe, *A Personal Narrative*, 87–8; Stephens to O'Mahony, 11 Dec. 1864, Fenian Brotherhood Collection, CUA; Peel to Larcom, 18 Feb. 1864, Larcom papers, Ms. 7,586, NLI.

95. Devoy, *Recollections*, 294–5; *Irish People*, 30 Apr. 1864.

96. *Irish People*, 23 Jan. & 13 Feb. 1864; 30 Apr. 1864; 16 Jan. 1864; *Irish-American*, 9 Apr. 1864; Ramon, *A Provisional Dictator*, 163.

97. Rutherford, *The Secret History*, vol. ii, 27; Stephens to O'Mahony, 11 Dec. 1864, Fenian Brotherhood Collection, CUA; O'Mahony on Fenianism, *Irishman*, 8 Feb. 1868.

98. Rutherford, *The Secret History*, vol. ii, 3–5, 28; Kickham to O'Mahony, 28 Sept. 1869, Fenian Brotherhood Collection, CUA; *Irishman*, 23 Feb. 1867; ibid., 2 June 1866.

99. *Irishman*, 2 June 1866; O'Mahony on Fenianism, 15 Feb. 1868; Devoy, *Recollections*, 58; Stephens to O'Mahony, 11 Dec. 1864, Fenian Brotherhood Collection, CUA.

100. O'Mahony on Fenianism, *Irishman*, 8 Feb. 1868; 15 Feb. 1868; Ramon, *A Provisional Dictator*, 164.

101. Rutherford, *The Secret History*, 28–9.

102. O'Mahony on Fenianism, *Irishman*, 8 Feb. 1868.

103. O'Mahony on Fenianism, *Irishman*, 7 Mar. 1868; 'Personal Recollections of John O'Mahony', 10 Mar. 1877.

104. O'Mahony on Fenianism, *Irishman*, 8 & 15 Feb. 1868; William Barnaby Flaherty, S.J., *The St Louis Irish* (St Louis 2001), 70; Gleeson, *The Green and the Gray*, 57–8; Stephens to Michael Corcoran, 4 Oct. 1863, Fenian Brotherhood Collection, CUA. Gen. Corcoran had been promoted by President Lincoln.

105. O'Mahony on Fenianism, *Irishman*, 15 Feb. 1868. For Scanlan see Appendix I.

106. Ibid.; *Proceedings of the Second National Congress of the Fenian Brotherhood, held in Cincinnati, Ohio, January 1865* (Philadelphia 1865), 14, 35–6.

107. *The Irish Vindicator*, 16 June 1877, Fenian Brotherhood Collection, CUA.

108. *Proceedings of the Second National Congress*, 6–7, 14; Rutherford, *The Secret History*, vol. ii, 51–2; O'Mahony on Fenianism, *Irishman*, 15 Feb. 1868.

109. *Irishman*, 15 Feb. 1868; Stephens (alias J. Hamilton) to O'Mahony, 11 Dec. 1864, Fenian Brotherhood Collection, CUA.

110. *Irishman*, 15 Feb. 1868; O'Leary, *Recollections*, vol. i, 107. See Appendix I for Roberts.

111. *Irishman*, 15 Feb. 1868.

112. *The Irish Vindicator*, 16 June 1877, Fenian Brotherhood Collection, CUA; O'Mahony to Jane Mandeville, 21 Mar. 1865, as quoted Maher, *Chief of the Comeraghs*, 95.
113. Patrick Downing to O'Mahony, 20 Apr. 1864, Fenian Brotherhood Collection, CUA; O'Mahony on Fenianism, *Irishman*, 14 Mar. 1868.
114. Stephens (alias J. Hamilton) to O'Mahony, 1 Mar. 1865, Fenian Brotherhood Collection, CUA.
115. Ibid.; ibid., 18 Mar. 1865. Stephens found somebody without known links to Fenianism to stand bail for this messenger, who returned to New York.
116. O'Mahony on Fenianism, *Irishman*, 15 Feb. 1868; Col Kelly to O'Mahony, 1 May 1865; Denieffe, *A Personal Narrative*, 191–2; Ó Broin, *Fenian Fever*, 47. Francis Frederick Millen, 1831–89.
117. Sim, *A Union Forever*, 93, 96, 129; *New York Times*, 14 Oct. 1865; Roy Jenkins, *Gladstone* (London 1995), 356–9; Jack Morgan, *Through American and Irish Wars* (Dublin 2006), 119; *The New Encyclopaedia Britannica*, vol. 29, *Macropaedia* (Chicago 1992), 236–7. Approximately 160,000 Irishmen fought for the Union and a further 20,000 for the Confederacy, see Lar Joye, 'Irishmen in the Confederate Army', *History Ireland* vol. 18 no. 1 (Jan. / Feb. 2010).
118. *Irishman*, 15 Feb. 1868; Stephens to Central Council of Fenian Brotherhood, 24 June 1865, Fenian Brotherhood Collection, CUA.
119. Ibid., Thomas Kelly to O'Mahony, 31 May 1865.
120. Ibid.; ibid., Thomas Kelly (alias Thomas O'Reilly) to O'Mahony, 21 June 1865.
121. Ibid., Thomas Kelly to O'Mahony, 21 June 1865.
122. Ibid., Stephens to Central Council of Fenian Brotherhood, 24 June 1865, Fenian Brotherhood Collection, CUA.
123. Ibid.
124. Ibid., Millen to O'Mahony, 24 June 1865.
125. *Irishman*, 15 Feb. 1868.
126. Ó Lúing, 'Aspects of the Fenian Rising in Kerry, 1867, I: The Rising and its background', *JKAHS* no. 3 (1970), 140–1.
127. Denieffe, *A Personal Narrative*, 95–6; Devoy, *Recollections*, 57–8; *Times*, 26 Sept. 1865.
128. 'John Daly's Recollections', *Irish Freedom*, Feb. 1912.
129. *Irishman*, 15 Feb. 1868; 22 Feb. 1868; Denieffe, *A Personal Narrative*, 102. Devoy's account that Dunne and Meehan were mainly money couriers is erroneous.
130. O'Mahony to Francis Mandeville, 4 Dec. 1866, Maher, *Chief of the Comeraghs*, 98.
131. 'O'Mahony on Fenianism', *Irishman*, 22 Feb. 1868; *Cork Constitution*, 9 Sept. 1865. The Fenian Brotherhood stage-managed McCarthy's funeral in St Louis.
132. Rutherford, *The Secret History*, vol. ii, 132–3; Maume, Maume & Casey, *The Galtee Boy*, 25–6.

3. THE IRISH PEOPLE, 1863–5

1. Davis, *The Young Ireland Movement*, 13; John N. Molony, *A Soul Came Into Ireland* (Dublin 1995), 101–3; Quinn, *Young Ireland*, 2, 129, 73.

2. Doheny, *The Felon's Track*, 19–20; O'Leary, *Recollections*, vol. i, 3.

3. James Maher, *The Valley Near Slievenamon* (Kilkenny 1942), 171–2; Mary Donnelly (ed.), *The Last Post* (Dublin 1994), 60; O'Leary, *Recollections*, vol. i, 3–4; Devoy, *Recollections*, 288–90; Molony, *A Soul*, 120–1. Letitia was a daughter of John Fraser, 'De Jean Fraser', a Young Ireland poet, who died in 1852. His poem 'Gathering of the Nation' is mentioned in Charles Gavan Duffy, *My Life in Two Hemispheres* (London 1898), vol. i, 64.

4. Quinn, *Young Ireland*, 123; Whelehan, *The Dynamiters*, 13–5; Anthony McNicholas, 'Co-operation, compromise and confrontation: the *Universal News*, 1860–9', *IHS*, xxxv, no. 139 (May 2007), 320, 322–4. Michael Davitt contributed poetry to the *Universal News*.

5. Precis of information, Larcom papers, Ms. 7,697.

6. Ibid.; Toby Joyce, 'The Galway American 1862–63: part 1: James Roche and the American Civil War', *Journal of the Galway Archaeological and Historical Society*, vol. 47 (1995), 108–9. Thomas O'Neill Russell, 1828–1908.

7. Joyce, 'The Galway American 1862–63: part 1, 110–1, 113, 117–8, 131; 'The Galway American 1862–63: Politics and Place in a Fenian Newspaper' (concluded), *JGAHS*, vol. 48 (1996), 104–5.

8. Joyce, 'The Galway American 1862–63: Politics and Place in a Fenian newspaper', 129–130.

9. Eva Guarino & Judith Turnbull, *Collected Writings by and about James Fintan Lalor* (Rome, n.d.), 68.

10. O'Leary, *Recollections*, vol. i, 227.

11. Devoy, *Recollections*, 140, 28, 41.

12. *Irishman*, 10 May 1862.

13. Comerford, *The Fenians in Context*, 97. Roche stated in the *Galway American*, 26 Apr. 1862, that Doheny had died of a broken heart, 'thrust aside by would-be dictators – intolerant and intolerable egotists', meaning Stephens.

14. *Brooklyn Eagle*, 12 July 1885.

15. O'Leary, *Recollections*, vol. i, 258; Davitt, *Fall*, 75–6; Pigott, *Personal Recollections*, 132.

16. *Times*, 29 Oct. 1865.

17. Ibid.; 'Fenianism photographed', *Irishman*, 19 Dec. 1874; O'Leary, *Recollections*, vol. ii, 1–2; *Irish Times*, 18 Mar. 1907.

18. Charles J. Kickham to John O'Mahony, 18 Jan. 1864, Fenian Brotherhood Collection, CUA.

19. Ibid.

20. Ibid.

21. Stephens to O'Mahony, 11 Dec. 1864, Fenian Brotherhood Collection, CUA.

22. Ibid.

23. Ibid.; Pigott, *Personal Recollections*, 127; 'Fenianism photographed', *Irishman*, 26 Dec. 1874; Bourke, *John O'Leary*, 71; Devoy, *Recollections*, 42.

24. *Irish Times*, 18 Mar. 1907; Comerford, *Charles J. Kickham*, 77; Bourke, *John O'Leary*, 49, 75–6.

25. O'Leary, *Recollections*, vol. i, 239–40; Devoy, *Recollections*, 293.

26. Luby papers, Ms. 331–3.

27. 'Fenianism photographed', *Irishman*, 19 Dec. 1874.

28. *Cork Examiner*, 9 Dec. 1865; Richard Pigott, *Personal Recollections*, 127–8; Bourke, *John O'Leary*, 51–2, 75, 121.

29. CSORP 1867/3398, NAI.

30. *Cork Examiner*, 9 Dec. 1865; Luby papers, Ms. 331–3, 11–2; Denieffe, *A Personal Narrative*, 82–3; Bourke, *John O'Leary*, 72–3; Comerford, *The Fenians in Context*, 98.

31. Denieffe, *A Personal Narrative*, 83–4; CSORP 1863/11941, NAI, quoted Seán McConville, *Irish Political Prisoners, 1848–1922: Theatres of War* (Abingdon & New York 2005), 119.

32. *Irish Times*, 25 Sept. 1865; Roland Sarti, 'Giuseppe Mazzini: father of European democracy?', Colin Barr, Michele Finelli & Anne O'Connor (eds), *Nation/Nazione: Irish Nationalism and the Italian Risorgimento* (Dublin 2014), 54.

33. *Irish People*, 28 Nov. 1863.

34. Ibid., 5 Dec. 1863.

35. Ibid.

36. Ibid.

37. *Irish People*, quoted Robert Anderson, *Sidelights on the Home Rule movement* (London 1906), 52.

38. *Irish People*, 5 Dec. 1863; 23 Jan. 1864.

39. Ibid., 2 Jan. 1864.

40. Ibid., 26 Dec. 1863.

41. Ibid., 2 Jan. 1864.

42. Ibid., 23 Jan. 1864.

43. Ibid., 12 Dec. 1863.

44. O'Leary, *Recollections*, vol. ii, 21–2.

45. *Irish People*, 13 Feb. 1864.

46. Ibid.

47. Ibid., 16 Apr. 1864; O'Leary, *Recollections*, vol. ii, 88–9.

48. O'Leary, *Recollections*, vol. ii, 66; *Irish People*, 16 Apr. 1864; *Nation*, 12 Dec. 1885; Dr Kain to O'Donovan Rossa, 20 Nov. 1909, Fenian Brotherhood Collection, CUA, see Appendix I.

49. *Irish People*, 7 Jan. 1865.

50. Ibid., 26 Dec. 1863.

51. Ibid.

52. Ibid.; 5 Dec. 1863.

53. Ibid., 26 Dec. 1863; 2 Jan. 1864.

54. Ibid., 16 Jan. 1864; 5 Dec. 1863.

55. Ibid., 23 Jan. 1864.

56. Ibid.

57. Robert Sloan, *William Smith O'Brien and the Young Ireland Rebellion of 1848* (Dublin 2000), 301.

58. *Irish People*, 2 Jan. 1864.

59. Ibid. In 1864, Kerry butter was selling at 'an extraordinary price' and landlords and tenants were enjoying splendid prospects: Lucey, *Land, Popular Politics and Agrarian Violence*, 9.

60. *Irish People*, 30 July 1864; O'Leary, *Recollections,* vol. ii, 43–4.

61. *Irish People*, 2 Jan. 1864.

62. Ibid.

63. Ibid., 19 Dec. 1863; 12 Dec. 1863.

64. Ibid., 28 Nov. 1863; 19 Dec. 1863; 12 Dec. 1863.

65. Rafferty, *The Church, the State and the Fenians*, 37; *Irish People*, 12 Dec. 1863.

66. *Irish People*, 16 Sept. 1865.

67. Ibid., 30 Jan. 1864; Vaughan & Fitzpatrick, *Irish Historical Statistics*, 34.

68. Thomas Hayes, the London IRB 'centre', refused to facilitate the escape of a Fenian suspect to the US, as 'they were ready to go to Ireland to fight at any moment': *Times*, 3 Jan. 1866; Charles U. O'Connell to O'Mahony, 1 May 1862, Fenian Brotherhood Collection, CUA.

69. *Irish People*, 6 Aug. 1864.

70. Michelle McGoff-McCann, *Melancholy Madness. A Coroner's Casebook* (Cork 2003), 80. In 1864 the number of illegitimate births in Ireland was approximately 4 per cent.

71. *FJ*, 17 May 1864; *Irish People*, 21 May 1864.

72. *Irish People*, 21 May 1864; O'Leary, *Recollections,* vol. ii, 31–2, 35.

73. *Irish People*, 21 May 1864.

74. Bishop John Lynch, 1 Feb. 1866, Archives of the RC Archdiocese of Toronto (ARCAT) LAE 0209.

75. *Irish People*, 12 Nov. 1864.

76. Besides the Fenians, Archbishop Roger Vaughan of Sydney also clashed with Dr Cullen. See Colin Barr, 'Imperium in Imperio': Irish Episcopal Imperialism in the Nineteenth Century, *English Historical Review* (2008) CXXIII (502) for how Cullen spread his devotional model trans-nationally.

77. *Irish People*, 12 Nov. 1864.

78. Ibid., Letter to editor, 26 Nov. 1864.

79. Ibid.; ibid., Letters to editor, 7 Jan. 1865.

80. Ibid., Letter to editor.

81. Ibid., 26 Dec. 1863; *Irish People* (NY), 25 July 1868.

82. James O'Shea, *Priest, Politics and Society in post-Famine Ireland: a Study of County Tipperary 1850–1891* (Dublin 1983), 147; *Irish People*, 23 July 1864.

83. Shiels, *The Irish in the American Civil War*, 27.

84. *Irish People*, 28 Nov. 1863.

85. Ibid., 26 Dec. 1863.

86. Morgan, *Through American,* 56; Gleeson, *The Green and the Gray*, 41; *New York Times*, 17 Nov. 1860; Susannah Ural Bruce, *The Harp and the Eagle* (New York 2006), 45; Kenneth H. Powers, 'The Fighting 69th: still going strong at 150', *Irish Sword: The Journal of the Military History of Ireland*, vol. xxiii no. 91, 3.

87. *Irish People*, 16 Jan. 1864.

88. *Brooklyn Eagle*, 12 July 1885; *Irish People*, 28 Nov. 1863; Quinn, *John Mitchel*, xvii. Two of Mitchel's sons fell, the third was wounded.

89. *Irish People*, 28 Nov. 1863; 2 Jan. 1864; *Brooklyn Eagle*, 12 July 1885. See Appendix I for Capt. Downing.

90. *Irish People*, 28 Nov. 1863.

91. Ibid., 12 Dec. 1863; 26 Dec. 1863; 14 May 1864.

92. Shiels, *The Irish in the American Civil War*, 74; Michael Corcoran, *DIB*, vol. 2, 847; *New York Times*, 23 Dec. 1863; *Proceedings of the Second National Congress*, 7–8, 66. Antietam constituted the bloodiest battle in US history in 1862 with 22,000 casualties, of whom 3500 died.

93. A. Wilson Green, 'History of Wilderness and Spotsylvania', Fredericksburg and Spotsylvania Co. battlefields memorials, http://www.nps.gov/frsp/wildspot.htm.

94. Fredericksburg National Cemetery, http://www.nps.gov/frsp/natcem.htm; . *Irishman*, 20 May 1871; *Irish People*, 2 Jan. 1864.

95. Stephens to O'Mahony, 1861, quoted in *Rossa's Recollections*, 286–7.

96. *Irish People*, 2 Jan. 1864; Davis, *The Young Ireland Movement*, 19. Mazzini, 1805–72, activist for a united Italy, spent long periods in exile in London.

97. *Irish People*, 2 Jan. 1864; 4 Feb. 1865.

98. Ibid., 26 Dec. 1863.

99. Ibid., 6 Feb. 1864.

100. Ibid., 17 Sept. 1864.

101. Anderson, *Sidelights*, 52.

102. *Irish People*, 19 Dec. 1863; 7 Jan. 1865; 2 Jan. 1864; 6 Aug. 1864; 13 Aug. 1864; 23 July 1864; 26 Aug. 1865. For Kickham on Poland, see Maher, *The Valley Near Slievenamon*, 205.

103. *Irish People*, 19 Dec. 1863; Charles Freeman, *The Horses of St Mark's. A story of Triumph in Byzantium, Paris and Venice* (London 2007), 242. Daniele Manin, 1805–57.

104. Peter Ackroyd, *Venice Pure City* (London 2010), 94–6; *Irishman*, 28 Mar. 1868; Ramon, *A Provisional Dictator*, 60. Manin's remains were reburied in the cathedral of San Marco in Venice in 1868.

105. Guarino & Turnbull, *Collected Writings*, 73–4.

106. *Irish People*, 28 Nov. 1863.

107. Ibid., 19 Dec. 1863; 28 Nov. 1863; W.B. Yeats, *Autobiographies* (London 1980), 358.

108. *Irish People*, 12 Dec. 1863; Lecky, *The Leaders of Public Opinion in Ireland*, 302–3.

109. *Irish People*, 12 Dec. 1863.

110. Ibid.

111. Ibid.

112. *Rossa's Recollections*, 104.

113. *Irish People*, 28 Nov. 1863.

114. Mill stated in 1846 that however convenient it might be for landlords that their despairing tenants emigrated in their thousands, Parliament should address this forced exodus or stand condemned for having made the country uninhabitable.

115. *Irish People*, 23 Jan. 1864.

116. See, for instance, *Irish People*, 14 Jan. 1865; 22 July 1865. Pigott, *Personal Recollections*, 98.

117. Marta Ramon, 'Irish nationalism and the demise of the papal states, 1848–71', Barr, Finelli & O'Connor (eds), *Nation/Nazione*, 182; ibid., Colin Barr, 'Paul Cullen, Italy and the Irish Catholic imagination, 1826–70' 149–50.

118. *Irish People*, 23 Jan. 1864.

119. Ibid., 16 Jan. 1864.

120. Ibid., 6 Feb. 1864.

121. Ibid.

122. O'Leary, *Recollections*, vol. ii, 53–4.

123. Ibid., 14.

124. Patrick Francis Moran (ed.), *The Pastoral Letters of Cardinal Cullen* (Dublin 1882), 395–7; Donal A. Kerr, 'Priests, pikes and patriots', Stewart J. Brown & David W. Miller (eds), *Piety and Power in Ireland 1760–1960* (Indiana 2000), 34.

125. Barr, 'Paul Cullen, Italy and the Irish Catholic imagination, 1826–70', Barr, Finelli & O'Connor (eds), *Nation/Nazione*, 149.

126. Moran, *Pastoral Letters*, 388; Comerford, *The Fenians in Context*, 31–2; George L. Bernstein, 'British Liberal politics and Irish Liberalism after O'Connell', *Piety and Power in Ireland 1760–1960*, 62–4; Kieran O'Shea, 'David Moriarty (1814–77): III politics', 91.

127. *Irish People*, 16 Sept. 1865.

128. Ibid.

129. O'Leary, *Recollections*, vol. ii, 113–14.

130. *Irish People*, 26 Dec. 1863

131. Ibid., 2 Jan. 1864; 23 Jan. 1864; 7 Jan. 1865; Matthew Porter, *William Monsell of Tervoe 1812–1894. Catholic Unionist, Anglo-Irishman* (Dublin 2009), 131.

132. For relations between the Catholic church and the IRB, see Rafferty, *The Church, the State and the Fenians*; Emmet Larkin, *The Historical Dimensions of Irish Catholicism* (Dublin 1997), 107–8; Sullivan, *Troubled Times*, 50.

133. Donnchadh Ó Corráin and Tomàs O'Riordan (eds), *Ireland 1815–1870. Emancipation, Famine and Religion* (Dublin 2011),50.

134. 'Pastoral letter on charity, education, and secret societies'; 'Letter to the clergy of Dublin, on Orangeism and Fenianism' in Moran, *Pastoral Letters*.

135. Christopher Hibbert, *The Royal Victorians* (Philadelphia & New York 1976), 88–9; Moran, *Pastoral Letters*, 395.

136. Moran, *Pastoral Letters*, 395–6.

137. *Irish People*, 7 Jan. 1865; 4 Feb. 1865.

138. Ibid., 4 Feb. 1865; 7 Jan. 1865.

139. Ibid., 8 July 1865.

140. Ibid., 15 July 1865.

141. *Nation*, 22 July 1865; Leon Ó Broin, *Charles Gavan Duffy* (Dublin 1967), 118.

142. *Irish People*, 4 Feb. 1865.

143. *Times*, 7 May 1863.

144. Eva O Cathaoir, 'The Poor Law in County Wicklow', *Wicklow: History and Society* (Dublin 1994), 529–30; *Irish People*, 19 Dec. 1863.

145. O'Leary, *Recollections*, vol. ii, 67, 179, 118–20.

146. Ibid., 173–4; Bourke, *John O'Leary*, 74.

147. McNicholas, 'Co-operation, compromise and confrontation', 311, 323–5.

148. Bernardine Ruddy, 'Denis Dowling Mulcahy', *THJ* 2008, 98.

149. This painting in the National Gallery of Ireland dates from 1883. Aloysius's work in Connemara created a new nationalist idiom of sturdy tenants, cottages, turf and donkeys.

150. Letter to the editor, *Irish People*, 7 Jan. 1865.

151. Ibid., 6 Feb. 1864; 30 Jan. 1864; 16 Jan. 1864.

152. O'Leary, *Recollections*, vol. ii, 3, 72, 91 ff.

153. Quinn, *Young Ireland,* 77; Richard Davis, *Revolutionary Imperialist William Smith O'Brien* (Dublin 1998), 338; *Kilkenny People*, 8 Apr. 1911. Rossa taught Irish in the Mechanics' Institute, Dublin.

154. *Irish People*, 23 Jan. 1864. 'Eva' was Mary Jane Kelly, 1826–1910, who married Kevin Izod Doherty, a fellow Young Irelander.

155. Ibid., 6 Feb. 1864.

156. Ibid.

157. O'Leary, *Recollections*, vol. i, 257–8. John Keegan Casey, 1846–70.

158. *Irish People*, 26 Dec. 1863.

159. Ibid.

160. *Irish People*, 26 Nov. 1864; reprinted in Comerford, *Charles J. Kickham*, 212–23.

161. O'Leary, *Recollections*, vol. ii, 142–3.

162. Ibid., 17–8.

163. Stephens, 'Reminiscences'.

164. *Irish People*, 16 Jan. 1865.

165. Ibid.

166. Ibid., 30 Jan. 1864.

167. Ibid. Others also doubted this trumpeted prosperity, see *Nation*, 18 Feb. 1865.

168. *Irish People*, 10 Sept. 1864. Ellen O'Leary's collected poems were published in 1890, but due to the rise of the Home Rule movement, which sought concessions from Britain, a conciliatory tone prevailed and her more outspoken verses were either omitted or toned down, turning her into a 'simple' singer. Her work was reassessed in Rose Novak, 'Ellen O'Leary: a bold Fenian poet', *Eire-Ireland* vol. 43:3 & 4, Fall/Winter 2008.

169. Bourke, *John O'Leary*, 198.

170. Jane McL. Côté, *Fanny and Anna Parnell: Ireland's Patriot Sisters* (Dublin 1991), 58–61.

171. *Irish People*, 1 Oct. 1864.

172. Danae O'Regan, 'Anna & Fanny Parnell', *History Ireland*, issue 1 (Spring 1999), vol. 7.

173. *Leinster Express*, 2 June 1882.

174. Sylke Lehne, 'Fenianism – a male business? A case study of Mary Jane O'Donovan Rossa (1845–1916)', MA thesis, Maynooth, 1995, 20–1. See Appendix I.

175. *Irish People*, 18 Mar. 1865.

176. Lehne, 'Fenianism', 21; O'Leary, *Recollections*, vol. ii, 107.

177. O'Leary, *Recollections*, vol. i, 262, vol. ii, 96–7; *Irish People*, 29 July 1865; Bourke, *John O'Leary*, 68. See Appendix I.

178. O'Leary, *Recollections*, vol. ii, 17. George Sigerson, 1839–1925, a polymath, had published *Poets and Poetry of Munster* in 1860; he was to play an important role in the Irish literary revival.

179. *Irish People*, 12 Dec. 1863.

180. Ibid.

181. Ibid., 19 Dec. 1863; quoted in Maher, *The Valley Near Slievenamon*, 204.

182. Ibid.

183. *Irish People*, 2 Jan. 1864.
184. Ibid., 9 Jan. 1864.
185. O'Brien turned pragmatist later. Portraying himself as a good Catholic nationalist in his memoirs, he omitted any reference to these contributions. After James Fenimore Cooper, *The Spy* (1821), where Harvey Birch suffers as a secret agent of the American revolution, but refuses any compensation for his patriotism.
186. *Irish People*, 16 Jan. 1864.
187. Ibid.
188. *Irish People*, 24 Sept. 1864.
189. Ibid., Letter from E.E.C., 15 July 1865; *Skibbereen Eagle*, 8 Nov. 1913; *Cork Examiner*, 24 July 1865; Lehne, 'Fenianism', 20. See Appendix I.
190. Joseph I.C. Clarke, *My Life and Memories* (New York 1925), 38; Devoy, *Recollections*, 44–5. Clancy, see Appendix I.
191. Devoy, *Recollections*, 293.
192. Bernadette Whelan, *American Government in Ireland, 1790–1913 – A History of the US Consular Service* (Manchester 2010), 164; Bourke, *John O'Leary*, 72; Matthew Kelly, 'The *Irish People* and the disciplining of dissent', Fearghal McGarry and James McConnel (eds), *The Black Hand of Republicanism*, 36, 51; Sullivan, *New Ireland*, 327; Roger Swift, 'The outcast Irish in the British Victorian City: problems and perspectives', *IHS*, vol. 25, no. 99 (1987), 264. *Irish Liberator*, begun Oct. 1863, second editor Dr David Bell with Maurice Sarsfield Walsh as sub-editor, both IRB.
193. Devoy, *Recollections*, 46.
194. James Joyce, *A Portrait of the Artist as a Young Man* (London 1991), 39. I am indebted to Michael Kelleher here.
195. Irish People (NY), 1 Feb. 1868; 8 Feb. 1868; 17 Mar. 1866; 4 Jan. 1868; 2 May 1868.
196. Ibid., 17 Mar. 1866.
197. Ibid.
198. Ibid.
199. Wodehouse to Sir George Grey, 4 Feb. 1866 & Grey to Wodehouse, 5 Feb. 1866, Ms. Eng. c.4,041, Kimberley papers, Bodleian. Col Kelly boasted that he had read it on the run in Ireland and England.
200. *Irish People* (NY), 24 Mar. 1866.
201. *Irish Times*, 23 Jan. 1868; *Irish People* (NY), 1 Feb. 1868; ibid., 8 Feb. 1868; ibid., 16 Jan. 1869.
202. *Irish People* (NY), 3 Feb. 1872. Margaret Anna Cusack, 1829–99, Anglican convert to Catholicism, writer and campaigner for social justice.
203. Ibid., 25 Jan. 1868; 18 July 1868; 12 Dec. 1868.
204. Ibid., 6 May 1871.
205. Ibid., 21 Nov. 1868; 9 Jan. 1869; 1 July 1871.
206. Ibid., 30 Jan. 1869; 13 Feb. 1869.
207. Ibid., 30 Jan. 1869.
208. Ibid.
209. Ibid., 8 July 1871; 8 May 1869; 13 June 1868; 7 Mar. 1868. Individual Fenians may also have participated in exterminating Native Americans, see Sgt Dooley, Appendix I.

210. Ibid., McCorry, *Irish People* (NY), 24 Apr. 1869. O'Mahony had inherited $500 from Michael Phelan, a Fenian supporter, which he invested in the *American Gael* and the *Sunday Citizen*.

4. ARRESTS AND DISSENSIONS, 1864–6

1. Peel to Larcom, 20 Feb. 1864, Larcom papers, Ms. 7,586, NLI. Lawson's opinion, 22 Feb. 1864.
2. O'Mahony on Fenianism, *Irishman*, 4 Apr. 1868; 7 Oct. 1865; *Irish Times*, 2 Oct. 1865; CSORP 1865/7556, NAI.
3. Devoy, *Recollections*, 69; *Irish Times*, 3 Mar. 1864. Lord Granville, the Liberal leader, quoted the police.
4. Jeremiah Falvey, *The Chronicles of Midleton, 1700–1990* (Cloyne 1998), 54–5; *Irish Times*, 20 Dec. 1864; 25 Jan. 1865.
5. Seán Ó Lúing, *Fremantle Mission* (Tralee 1965) 13; CSORP 1865/7556, NAI.
6. *Irishman*, 16 Sept. 1865; 12 Aug. 1865.
7. Ibid.; *Times*, 22 Aug. 1865; *Irish Times*, 11 Aug. 1865.
8. *Irish Times*, 20 Sept. 1865; *Nation*, 14 Oct. 1865.
9. McGrath, *A Cork Felon*, 16; *Cork Constitution*, 2 Sept. 1865; 5 Sept. 1865; *Times*, 9 Sept. 1865.
10. *Cork Constitution*, 2 Sept. 1865.
11. Wodehouse to Russell, 1 Sept. 1865, Ms. Eng. c. 4,031, Kimberley papers, Bodleian.
12. Ibid.
13. Ibid., Wodehouse to Somerset, 1 Sept. 1865; Somerset to Wodehouse, 2 & 4 Sept. 1865.
14. Ibid., Wodehouse to Sir George Grey, 3 Sept. 1865.
15. Ibid., Shannon to Wodehouse, 5 Sept. 1865; Sir Robert Peel to Wodehouse, 7 Sept. 1865; Fermoy to Wodehouse, 11 Sept. 1865; Lawson to Wodehouse, 12 Sept. 1865. Edmund Burke Roche, first Baron Fermoy, 1815–74, ancestor of Diana, Princess of Wales.
16. *Irish Times*, 2 Oct. 1865.
17. *Times*, 3 Oct. 1865.
18. *Irish Times*, 6 Dec. 1865.
19. *Cork Constitution*, 11 Sept. 1865; Wodehouse to Sir George Grey, 12 Sept. 1865, Kimberley papers, Ms. Eng. c. 4031; Wodehouse to Strathnairn, 11 Sept. 1865; Wodehouse to Fredrick, 13 Sept. 1865; Whelan, *American Government in Ireland*, 161. Sir Hugh Rose, Lord Strathnairn and Jansi, 1801–85, commander of the British army in Ireland.
20. Wodehouse to Sir George Grey, 12 Sept. 1865, Kimberley papers, Ms. Eng. c. 4,031.
21. Ibid.; ibid., Memorial of Cork magistrates, 14 Sept. 1865; *Cork Constitution*, 12 Sept. 1865; *Irish Times*, 12 Sept. 1865.
22. Angus Hawkins & John Powell (eds), *The Journal of John Wodehouse first Earl of Kimberley for 1862–1902* (Cambridge 1997), 174.
23. *Irish Times*, 16 Sept. 1865; Maume, Maume & Casey, *The Galtee Boy*, 30–1; Devoy, *Recollections*, 70.

24. *Irish Times*, 18 Sept. 1865; McGrath, *A Cork Felon*, 18. Geary managed to escape to the US, where he joined the Senate faction of the Brotherhood, but died in a horrific industrial accident.

25. Walter McGrath, *Evening Echo* (Cork), 1 Jan. 1969; Maume, Maume & Casey, *The Galtee Boy*, 19, 31–2; *Irishman*, 23 Dec. 1865.

26. *Irishman*, 23 Sept. 1865; 7 Oct. 1865; *FJ*, 22 Sept 1865; *Irish Times*, 19 Sept. 1865; *Times*, 5 Oct. 1865; 20 Sept. 1865.

27. *Times*, 22 Sept. 1865; 25 Sept. 1865; *Irish Times*, 16 Sept. 1865. Patrick Skelly, bookbinder, and John Fottrell, porter of the London and North Western Railway, both Salford, and James Quigley, silversmith, Sheffield, were arrested.

28. Strathnairn to Duke of Cambridge, 20 Sept. 1865, BL Add. Ms. 42,821; Strathnairn to Bandon, 17 Sept. 1865; Strathnairn to Bandon, 18 Sept. 1865.

29. *Irish Times*, 21 Sept. 1865; 5 Oct. 1865; *Irishman*, 14 Oct. 1865.

30. *Irishman*, 7 Oct. 1865. Barry was a brother-in-law of Judge John David Fitzgerald, who tried the Fenian leaders.

31. Pigott, *Personal Recollections*, 192. O'Keeffe had never joined the IRB, but was still sentenced to ten years.

32. *Irish Times*, 29 Nov. 1865.

33. *FJ*, 2 Oct. 1865.

34. Emer O'Sullivan, *The Fall of the House of Wilde. Oscar Wilde and his Family* (London 2016), 144. Jane Francesca Elgee, 'Speranza' of the *Nation*, 1821–96.

35. Stephens (alias J. Daly), 16 Sept., Fenian Brotherhood Collection, CUA.

36. Ibid.; Stephens to O'Mahony, 14 Oct. 1865, Denieffe, *A Personal Narrative*, 194. Devoy, *Recollections*, 59, states that Stephens stopped any threating of Meehan.

37. Stephens (alias J. Daly), 16 Sept., Fenian Brotherhood Collection, CUA.

38. Ms. 7,676, NLI; *Kerry Evening Post*, 11 Oct. 1865; *FJ*, 5 Oct. 1865.

39. Ellen O'Leary, *Lays of Country, Home and Friends* (Dublin 1890), 13.

40. Ibid., 16.

41. *Irish Times*, 13 Nov. 1865.

42. *FJ*, 16 Nov. 1865. Stephens's conduct foreshadowed Republican tradition.

43. *Times*, 16 Nov. 1865.

44. *Irishman*, 18 Nov. 1865.

45. *Irish Times*, 13 Nov. 1865.

46. *Times*, 16 Nov. 1865.

47. T.D. Sullivan, A.M. Sullivan, D.B. Sullivan, *Speeches From the Dock or Protests of Irish Patriotism* (Providence, RI 1878), 185.

48. Ó Broin, *Fenian Fever*, 18; Devoy, *Recollections*, 73–6, 78.

49. Edmund O'Leary, 1843–83, to O'Mahony, 16 Nov. 1865, Fenian Brotherhood Collection, CUA.

50. Ryan, *Fenian Memories*, 74; Devoy, *Recollections*, 77–86. Part of the rope with which Stephens escaped is in Kilmainham jail. Mrs Butler lived opposite the Kildare Street Club and had volunteered her home. After this became known, her customers deserted her and she died poor. Mrs Boland, sister of James and John O'Connor of the *Irish People*, was also a committed separatist.

51. Hawkins & Powell, *The Journal of John Wodehouse*, 179. Latin: 'unlucky day'.

52. Clarendon deposit, c. 99, 27 Nov. 1865, quoted in Ó Broin, *Fenian Fever*, 28.

53. Ibid., 5 Dec. 1865.
54. *Cork Examiner*, 4 Dec. 1866.
55. *Report of the proceedings at the first sitting of the Special Commission for the County of Dublin* (Dublin 1866); Devoy, *Recollections*, 294–5; Pigott, *Personal Recollections*, 159.
56. Maume, Maume & Casey, *The Galtee Boy*, 33–4, 200; *Times*, 3 Jan. 1866. See Appendix I.
57. Hawkins & Powell, *The Journal of John Wodehouse*, 174; *Irishman*, 11 Nov. 1865.
58. O'Leary, *Recollections*, vol. ii, 214; 'Letter to the clergy of Dublin on Orangeism and Fenianism', Moran, *Pastoral Letters*, 388–9, 394–5.
59. *Times*, 14 Nov. 1865.
60. *Irishman*, 7 Oct. 1865; Martin called O'Mahony 'the Irish Garibaldi', but without the Italian's love of England and his hatred of the pope.
61. Ibid., 14 Oct. 1865; Maro, pamphlet (n.p. 1866), 16, Larcom papers, Ms. 7,697, NLI.
62. *The special commission for the county of Dublin held at Green Street, Dublin, for the trial of Thomas Clarke Luby, and others, for treason-felony* (Dublin 1866).
63. *Times*, 30 Nov. 1865; Michael De Nie, *The Eternal Paddy: Irish Identity and the British Press, 1798–1882* (Madison 2004), 154. The *Times* rejoiced that disaffection had sunk from 'Smith O'Brien and his accomplices' to Fenian 'bricklayers and bagmen' and would soon die out altogether, *Irishman*, 14 Oct. 1865.
64. *Irishman*, 7 Oct. 1865.
65. *Irish Times*, 29 Nov. 1865.
66. Ibid.
67. O'Leary, *Recollections*, vol. ii, 216–7, 222; Devoy, *Recollections*, 294; Sullivan brothers, *Speeches from the dock, or protests of Irish patriotism* (New York 1904), 165–6.
68. O'Leary, *Recollections*, vol. ii, 223.
69. Devoy, *Recollections*, 302.
70. Denieffe, *A Personal Narrative*, 83–4; Luby papers, Ms. 331–3.
71. Devoy, *Recollections*, 302.
72. O'Leary, *Recollections*, vol. ii, 223–4. John Toler, first Earl of Norbury, 1741–1831, a judge and politician, opposed to Catholic Emancipation and supporting repression. Contemporaries considered him biased and lacking in knowledge.
73. Ibid., 224.
74. Pigott, *Personal Recollections*, 128.
75. James Comyn, *Their Friends at Court* (Chichester & London 1973), 20.
76. O'Donovan Rossa, *Irish Rebels in English Prisons* (Dingle 1991), 64 ff.; Patrick M. Geoghegan, *Robert Emmet*, 5: Emmet was regularly interrupted by Judge Norbury, but still presented his ideas.
77. O'Donovan Rossa, *Irish Rebels in English Prisons*, 78.
78. Ibid., 78–9.
79. Pentonville Prison, register, PCOM 2/71, TNA.
80. Wodehouse to Strathnairn, 4 & 16 Dec. 1865; Strathnairn to Duke of Cambridge, 3 Jan. 1866, BL Add. Ms. 42,824.
81. McGrath, *A Cork Felon*, 19–20.

82. *Nation*, 23 Dec. 1865.

83. Sullivan brothers, *Speeches from the dock*, 177, 179–80; *Nation*, 23 Dec. 1865; Maume, Maume & Casey, *The Galtee Boy*, 210, 117–8, 213, 99.

84. *Nation*, 23 Dec. 1865.

85. Ibid.

86. Comerford, *Charles J. Kickham*, 85–8; Sullivan brothers, *Speeches from the dock*, 186.

87. Sullivan brothers, *Speeches from the dock*, 186.

88. Comerford, *Charles J. Kickham*, 86–7.

89. Sullivan brothers, *Speeches from the dock*, 185, 186–7; *Irishman*, 25 Nov. 1865.

90. *Mail*, 6 Oct. 1865, 'News cutting re. arrest of Martin O'Brennan, Larcom papers, Ms. 7,676, NLI; Jenkins, *The Fenian Problem*, 37; Marie-Louise Legg, *Newspapers and Nationalism: the Irish Provincial Press, 1850–1892* (Dublin 1999), 94–5; *Irishman*, 7 Oct. 1865; 14 Oct. 1865; *Kilkenny Journal*, 20 June 1866. Martin A. Brennan, 1812–78.

91. Pigott, *Personal Recollections*, 201; *Irishman*, 30 Dec. 1865; 13 Jan. 1866; 14 Apr. 1866; 10 Mar. 1866.

92. Gavan Duffy, *My Life in Two Hemispheres*, vol. ii, 278.

93. Ryan, *The Phoenix Flame: a Study of Fenianism and John Devoy* (London & Edinburgh 1937), 134.

94. *Irishman*, 7 Oct. 1865; Pigott, *Personal Recollections*, 201; Habeas Corpus Suspension Act, 1866, (Abstracts) CSO/ICR/10, 165, 407; Index of names, CSO/ICR/15, NAI.

95. Devoy, *Recollections*, 112–3; O'Leary, *Lays of Country, Home and Friends*, 15–17, 23.

96. Wodehouse to Sir George Grey, 14 Feb. 1866, Ms. Eng. c. 4,042, Kimberley papers; *Irishman*, 16 Sept. 1865; *FJ*, 2 Oct. 1865.

97. *Irishman*, 14 Oct. 1865; *Irish Times*, 21 Sept. 1865; *Times*, 22 Sept. 1865; *Irishman*, 4 Apr. 1868; Michael H. Kane, 'American soldiers in Ireland, 1865–67', *The Irish Sword: The Journal of the Military History Society of Ireland*, vol. 23, no. 91, 125; *Irishman*, 7 Mar. 1868; *Express*, 23 Oct. 1865, Ms. 7,676; *Irish Times*, 20 Feb. 1866.

98. Col William Halpin to O'Mahony, 6 Oct. 1865, Fenian Brotherhood Collection, CUA.

99. *Irish Times*, 8 Feb. 1866; *Irishman*, 10 Feb. 1866; Habeas Corpus Suspension Act, 1866, (Transcript of abstracts), CSO/ICR/10, 464–5, 376, NAI.

100. Archibald, NY, to Lord Russell, 10 Oct. 1865, FO 5/1335, TNA.

101. Ibid., Consul Kortright to Russell, 30 Oct. 1865; Consul Edward Wilkins, St Louis, 7 Oct. 1865.

102. Ibid., Consul Kortright, Oct. 1865; *Irishman*, 2 June 1866. Figures for autumn 1865; Wilson, *Thomas D'Arcy McGee*, vol. ii, 249. By 1861 the Irish-born population of Britain amounted to 800,000.

103. *Irish People* (NY), 10 Mar. 1866; Consul Kortright, Oct. 1865, FO 5/1335, TNA.

104. Sir Frederick Bruce to Lord Russell, 31 Oct. 1865, FO 5/1335; Sim, *A Union Forever*, 88.

105. O'Mahony on Fenianism, *Irishman*, 7 Mar. 1868. The formation of a provisional government had been urged in 1865, *Proceedings of the Second National*, 14.

106. O'Mahony on Fenianism, *Irishman*, 7 Mar. 1868; Stephens had written to O'Mahony to engage Mitchel as their European agent, Stephens (alias J. Daly), 16 Sept. [1865], Fenian Brotherhood Collection, CUA; Sim, *A Union Forever*, 90.

107. Sim, *A Union Forever*, 88–9; O'Mahony on Fenianism', *Irishman*, 7 Mar. 1868.

108. O'Mahony on Fenianism, *Irishman*, 7 Mar. 1868; Morgan, *Through American*, 49.

109. Morgan, *Through American*, 108, 111–12; O'Mahony on Fenianism, *Irishman*, 28 Mar. 1868; O'Mahony's memoirs, *Irish People* (NY), 28 Mar. 1868.

110. Morgan, *Through American*, 112.

111. Col Halpin to O'Mahony, 6 Oct. 1865, Fenian Brotherhood Collection, CUA; O'Mahony on Fenianism, *Irishman*, 29 Feb. 1868; 30 Dec. 1865; O'Mahony on Fenianism, 21 Mar. 1868; 23 Feb. 1867.

112. Ibid., 21 Mar. 1868. O'Mahony's Requiem Mass was held nearby in 1877.

113. Ibid., O'Mahony on Fenianism, 14 Mar. 1868; 21 Mar. 1868.

114. Ibid., O'Mahony on Fenianism, 7 Mar. 1868; 28 Mar. 1868; Morgan, *Through American*, 112–13. See Appendix I.

115. O'Mahony on Fenianism, *Irishman*, 28 Mar. 1868; 4 Apr. 1868.

116. Ibid., 4 Apr. 1868; 28 Mar. 1868; T.W. Sweeny to O'Mahony, 12 Dec. 1865, Sweeny papers, NYPL; *New York Times*, 10 Dec. 1865.

117. *New York Times*, 10 Dec. 1865; O'Mahony on Fenianism, *Irishman*, 18 Apr., 4 Apr., 2 May & 9 May 1868.

118. F.F. Millen, 1831–89, *DIB*, vol. 6, 507; 'An account of Fenianism from April 1865 till April 1866', Larcom papers, Ms. 5,964, NLI.

119. *New York Times*, 10 Dec. 1865; 12 Dec. 1865; 13 Dec. 1865.

120. Ibid., 30 Dec. 1865.

121. Ibid., 15 Jan. 1866.

122. IRB letter of confidence, *Irishman*, 6 Jan. 1866.

123. *Irish Times*, 26 Jan. 1866; Mahony on Fenianism, *Irishman*, 9 May 1868.

124. Ibid., O'Mahony on Fenianism, 18 Apr. & 2 May 1868; 12 Aug. 1866, Larcom papers, Ms. 7,694; Rutherford, *The Secret History*, vol. ii, 64.

125. Ó Broin, *Fenian fever*, 12; Queen v. Charles McCarthy and others, CSORP 1866/23209, NAI.

126. Devoy, *Recollections*, 89–90; Maume, Maume & Casey, *The Galtee Boy*, 57, 60–3.

127. Hawkins, Powell, *The Journal of John Wodehouse*, 178; Devoy, *Recollections*, 87; Hanna R.M. to Sir Thomas Larcom, 4 Dec. 1865, Add. Ms. 42,821, BL; ibid., Thomas Talbot, 3 & 4 Dec. 1865. See Appendix I for Hetherington.

128. Ó Lúing, *Fremantle Mission*, 13–4; Devoy, *Recollections*, 90–2.

129. Devoy, *Recollections*, 91–3. The other members of the military council were Col Denis F. Burke, Col Thomas J. Kelly and Captain Doherty, while F.F. Millen had returned to New York. *Irish Times*, 9 Jan. 1866; 27 Feb. 1866; HCSA abstracts 1 (2), 464–5, NAI. See Appendix I.

130. Devoy, *Recollections*, 91, 105, 56, 363–4, 107; M. Moore, pike maker, *Irishman*, 7 Oct. 1865; 21 Oct 1865; Maume, Maume & Casey, *The Galtee Boy*, 18.

131. Mary C. Lynch & Seamus O'Donoghue, *O'Sullivan Burke Fenian* (Carrigadrohid 1999), 4; *Irishman*, 2 May 1868. Mulleda was amnestied in 1871, but committed suicide in Rossa's hotel in New York in 1876. Clan contacts ensured his Christian burial, attended by 3000 members. Ibid., 3 June 1876.

132. *Nation*, 2 May 1868; John Wyse Jackson and Peter Costello, *John Stanislaus Joyce* (London 1998), 26–7, 50. John Stanislaus Joyce, father of the more famous James, was related to the Daly family and knew the Casey brothers.

133. 26 Dec. 1865, Kimberley papers, Ms. Eng. c. 4,039, Bodleian.

134. Hawkins & Powell, *The Journal of John Wodehouse*, 181–2; *Irishman*, 6 Jan. 1866; 30 Dec. 1865; 10, 12, 16, 18 Dec. 1865, Strathnairn papers, BL Add. Mss. 42,824; ibid., 3 Jan. 1866. After Prime Minister Palmerston's death in October 1865, Lord John Russell succeeded him, while Chichester Fortescue replaced Sir Robert Peel as chief secretary.

135. *Irishman*, 18 July 1868.

5. FENIAN INFILTRATION OF THE ARMED FORCES, 1864–78

1. E.M. Spiers, 'Army organisation and society in the nineteenth century', Thomas Bartlett & Keith Jeffery (eds), *A Military History of Ireland* (Cambridge 1996), 337, 339; Kevin Kenny (ed.), *Ireland and the British Empire* (Oxford 2004), 106, suggests that up to 50 per cent of the army consisted of Irishmen in the early 1840s.

2. Map of military stations, 1 Dec. 1866, Ms. 43,887/1; Army returns, Larcom papers, Ms. 7,697, NLI; A.J. Semple, 'The Fenian Infiltration of the British Army', *Journal of the Society for Army Historical Research* (Autumn 1974), 149–50.

3. Elizabeth A. Muenger, *The British Military Dilemma in Ireland* (Kansas 1991), 3–4.

4. Sayers, 'The insurrection of 1848', *THJ* 2006, 111; Breen, *The Cappoquin Rebellion*, 41; Pigott, *Personal Recollections*, 146; Devoy, *Recollections*, 128, 140.

5. Devoy, *Recollections*, 140; Belchem, *Irish, Catholic and Scouse*, 170. See Arthur Anderson and Rody Kickham, Appendix I.

6. Devoy, *Recollections*, 140, 133–4; Quarterly returns, ending 31 June 1866, HO 8/168, TNA: No. 2665 John Murphy. See Appendix I.

7. Devoy, *Recollections*, 141. Not related to John O'Leary, he died in a US veterans' home in 1895.

8. Ibid., 141–2.

9. Semple, 'The Fenian Infiltration of the British Army', 136, 138; *FJ*, 8 Mar. 1865; quarterly returns ending June 1866, Woking Invalid Prison, Surrey, HO 8/168.

10. Devoy, *Recollections*, 142–4. William Walker, 1824–60, attempted to conquer various Latin-American regions and briefly became president of the Republic of Nicaragua before being executed by the Honduran government in 1860. Walker had hired European mercenaries to fight for him.

11. Devoy, *Recollections*, 63, 65–6.

12. Ibid., 130; Semple, 'The Fenian Infiltration of the British Army', 147, 155, 158; Larcom papers, Ms. 7,694, NLI; Pigott, *Personal recollections*, 144–5; Strathnairn to Duke of Cambridge, 20 Sept. 1865, BL Add. Ms. 42,821.

13. Devoy, *Recollections*, 152–3; No. 294 Corporal Thomas Chambers, joiner, enlisted on 8 Oct.1857, 61st foot 1865–6, WO 12/7146, TNA; *Times*, 22 June 1866.

14. Devoy, *Recollections*, 143, 65, 62; *Times*, 25 July 1866; *Nation*, 23 June 1866. See Appendix I.

15. *Irishman*, 23 Dec. 1865; Semple, 'The Fenian Infiltration of the British Army', 150–51.

16. Pilsworth St Clair was the son of an Irish NCO, born in Birmingham, while Maughan, also Mohan or Morgan, 1840–1920, a native of Moate, Co. Westmeath, migrated to Liverpool, Scotland and London: both belonged to the London IRB. Devoy, *Recollections*, 147, 333; *Nation*, 16 May 1868; 4 May 1867; 21 July 1866; *Liverpool Mercury*, 30 Apr. 1867.

17. Devoy, *Recollections*, 130; William O'Brien, *Recollections* (London & New York 1905), 52. William O'Brien, 1852–1928. Semple, 'The Fenian Infiltration of the British Army', 155; Liam Bolger, 'The military in Kilkenny', PhD thesis, NUI Maynooth, 2005, 129; 'Militia of Ireland, 23 Apr. 1866, return', Mayo papers, Ms. 11,188/10.

18. *Irish People* (NY), 17 Mar. 1866; 14 Apr. 1866; 8 Feb. 1868; 28 Mar. 1868; Archibald to Lord Clarendon, 20 & 26 Feb. 1866, FO 5/1336; Korthright to FO, 30 Oct. 1865, FO 5/1335, TNA.

19. Devoy, *Recollections*, 148–9.

20. *Irish Times*, 3 July 1866; 20 July 1866; Strathnairn papers, BL Add. Ms. 42,821; Rose to Duke of Cambridge, 6 Mar. 1866, BL Add. Ms. 42,822; Devoy, *Recollections*, 62; *Irish People* (NY), 7 Apr. 1866. Sir George Brown, 1790-1865, Commander-in-Chief since 1860; Montague fled to America, where he became an organizer.

21. Strathnairn to Duke of Cambridge, 3 Jan. 1866, Add. Ms. 42,824.

22. Strathnairn to Duke of Cambridge, 30 & 18 Aug. 1865, Add. Ms. 42,821; Strathnairn to Wodehouse, 13 Feb. 1866, [Add Ms. 42,822].

23. Strathnairn to Duke of Cambridge, 15 Feb. 1866, Add. Ms. 42,822.

24. *Nation*, 1 Sept. 1866; Strathnairn to Gen. Napier, 24 Feb. 1866, Add. Ms. 42,822; CSORP 1866/22285; *Kilkenny Journal*, 20 June 1866; *Irish Times*, 9 Feb. 1866. Gen. Sir Percy Feilding, 1827–1904, had distinguished himself in the Crimean War. Maher is sometimes given as Meara.

25. Devoy, *Recollections*, 60.

26. Inquiry as to the alleged ill-treatment of the convict Charles McCarthy, BPP 1878 [c. 1978], 7; *Irish Times*, 14 June 1866; *Irishman*, 16 June 1866; 19 Jan. 1878; 9 Mar. 1878.

27. Strathnairn to Duke of Cambridge, 1 Feb. 1866, Add. Ms. 42,824; 25 Feb. 1866, Add. Ms. 42,822; *Irishman*, 26 Jan. 1878.

28. Seán Ó Lúing, *Fremantle Mission*, 26; *Nation*, 3 Mar. 1866; Devoy, *Recollections*, 153.

29. *Nation*, 3 Mar. 1866.

30. Ibid.; Strathnairn to Duke of Cambridge, 27 Mar. 1866, Add. Ms. 42,822.

31. *Irish Times*, 20 Feb. 1866; 27 Feb. 1866; 2 Mar. 1866; 5 Mar. 1866.

32. *Irish Times*, 29 May 1866; *Irishman*, 2 June 1866; Stan McCormack, *Kilbeggan past and present* (Kilbeggan, n. d.), 73, 75–6; Strathnairn to Duke of Cambridge, 3 Jan. 1866. Add. Ms. 42,824.

33. Talbot, 17 Feb. 1866, CSORP 1866/23209, NAI; *Irishman*, 9 June 1866; Roger McHugh, *Trial at Green Street Courthouse* (Dublin 1946), vi; *Irish Times*, 29 May 1866.

34. Statement of Talbot, 17 Feb. 1866, CSORP 1866/23209; *Irish Times*, 10 June 1866.

35. Statement of Talbot, 17 Feb. 1866, CSORP 1866/23209.

36. *Irish Times*, 31 May 1866.

37. Ibid.; 1 June 1866; 29 May 1866.
38. Ibid., 4 June 1866; Statement of Talbot, 17 Feb. 1866, CSORP 1866/23209; *Irishman*, 9 June 1866.
39. Devoy, *Recollections*, 89–90, 113–4; Wodehouse to Sir George Grey, 14 Feb. 1866, Ms. Eng. c. 4,042, Kimberley papers, Bodleian. Appendix I.
40. Devoy, *Recollections*, 90.
41. Ibid., 90–3.
42. Ibid., 143. Appendix I.
43. Strathnairn to Duke of Cambridge, 3 & 26 Jan. 1866, Add. Ms. 42,824; Pigott, *Personal Recollections*, 368–9; McHugh, *Trial*, vi.
44. *Nation*, 23 June 1866.
45. Devoy, *Recollections*, 101.
46. Strathnairn to Wodehouse, 18 Feb. 1866, Add. Ms. 42,822.
47. Devoy, *Recollections*, 102–6.
48. Ibid., 101, 105–7, 109–11.
49. Strathnairn to Wodehouse, 17 Feb. 1866, Add. Ms. 42,822, BL.
50. Ibid., 18 Feb. 1866; Strathnairn to Cambridge, 23 Feb. 1866; Sir George Grey to Wodehouse, 16 Feb. 1866, Ms. Eng. c. 4,042, Kimberley papers, Bodleian; Devoy, *Recollections*, 184; 'Nation, 24 Feb. 1866.
51. *Times*, 24 Feb. 1866.
52. Strathnairn to Duke of Cambridge, 25 Feb. 1866, Add. Ms. 42,822. For Fennessy, 'centre' of the Buffs, see Appendix I.
53. Devoy, *Recollections*, 131, 156–7; Philip Fennell & Marie King (eds), *John Devoy's Catalpa Expedition* (New York & London 2006), 82–3.
54. Strathnairn to Gen. Cunynghame, 17 Feb. 1866; Strathnairn to Duke of Cambridge, 15, 18 & 25 Feb. 1866; Strathnairn to Gen. Napier, 16, 22 & 24 Feb. 1866, Add. Ms. 42,822; Strathnairn's confidential report, Mayo papers, Ms. 11,188/14, 13, NLI.
55. Strathnairn to Duke of Cambridge, 27 Mar. 1866, Add. Ms. 42,822.
56. Ibid., Strathnairn to Gen. Forster, 6 Apr. & 4 May 1866; Paul Walsh, *A History of Templemore and its environs* (Roscrea 1991), 58–60; *Nenagh Guardian*, 6 Jan. 1866; 27 Jan. 1866.
57. Strathnairn to Gen. Forster, 6 Apr. 1866, Add. Ms. 42,822; *Nation*, 17 Mar. 1866.
58. Strathnairn to Duke of Cambridge, 6 Mar, 25 Feb. & 31 Mar. 1866, Add. Ms. 42,822 ; *Times*, 5 June 1866.Thomas Emerson Headlam, 1813–75.
59. *Irish Times*, 29 Feb. 1866.
60. Ibid., 20 Feb. 1866; 26 Feb. 1866; 24 Feb. 1866; 5 Mar. 1866.
61. Ibid., 5 Mar. 1866; 27 Feb. 1866; *Irish Times*, 26 Feb. 1866. Geary became a prominent supporter of Roberts, *FJ*, 29 Dec. 1865.
62. Strathnairn to Duke of Cambridge, 6 & 31 Mar. 1866, Add. Ms. 42,822.
63. *Times*, 5 June 1866.
64. Strathnairn to Duke of Cambridge, 25 Feb. 1866, Add. Ms. 42,822; Jenkins, *The Fenian problem*, 59; *Irish Times*, 31 May 1866; 14 June 1866; See Appendix I.
65. Strathnairn to Duke of Cambridge, 4 Apr. 1866, Add. Ms. 42,822.
66. Ibid., 21 July 1866.
67. Ibid., Strathnairn to Gen. Cunynghame, 9 July 1866; Jenkins, *The Fenian problem*, 59–60.

68. *Irish Times*, 21 Aug 1866; *New York Herald*, 4 Nov. 1876; 5th Dragoons, 1866–7, quarter ending 31 Dec. 1866, WO 12/336, TNA: Foley, a labourer and native of Waterford, re-enlisted on 26 Nov. 1859. Devoy, *Recollections*, 157; Obituary, *New York Herald*, 4 Nov. 1876. See Appendix I.

69. *Irishman*, 6 Jan. 1866.

70. *Nation*, 10 Feb. 1866; *Irish Times*, 2 Apr. 1866; Strathnairn to Duke of Cambridge, 1 Feb. 1866, Add. Ms. 42,824; 23 Feb. 1866, Add. Ms. 42,822; 22 July 1867, Add. Ms. 42826.

71. Strathnairn to Wodehouse, 16 May 1866, Add. Ms. 42,822; J. Anthony Gaughan, *Austin Stack: Portrait of a Separatist* (Mount Merrion 1977), 11–13; *Irishman*, 15 Dec. 1866; William Moore Stack CSORP 1867/15695, NAI; *Liverpool Mercury*, 30 Jan. 1868; *Irish People* (NY), 28 Mar. 1868; ibid., 29 Feb. 1868; 17 Oct. 1868, which detailed arms thefts from the London Irish volunteers. See Appendix I for Dr Power.

72. Devoy, *Recollections*, 151–2; Register of suspects, vol. 2, CO 904/18/817, TNA; *Nation*, 12 Jan. 1867.

73. *Irishman*, 16 Mar. 1867; Devoy, *Recollections*, 63.

74. Devoy, *Recollections*, 77–8, 131–2, 93–4, 365; quoted in McCracken, *Inspector Mallon*, 147. A third brother was Niall Breslin, a 'centre', while John, chief marshal of the McManus funeral, was Michael O'Clohessy's brother.

75. Strathnairn to Wodehouse, 16 May 1866, Add. Ms. 42,822, BL.

76. Jerome Devitt, 'Bluster on One Side... Sound Preparation on the Other', http://www.britishnavalhistory.com/tag/2014-avml/; 'The "Navalization" of Ireland: The Royal Navy and Irish Insurrection in the 1840s', *The Mariner's Mirror, Journal of The Society for Nautical Research*, 101:4, 388–409; CSORP 1867/4237, NAI.

77. F 2228, Fenian Files, NAI.

78. Assorted reports and memoranda on Fenianism from resident magistrates, Mayo papers Ms. 43,887/8, NLI; *Irish Times*, 9 Feb. 1866. This is not the John Flood who was involved in Stephens's escape.

79. Patrick McCarthy, 'Conflicting loyalties – two Waterford Soldier-Fenians', *Decies* no. 53, 8; Devoy, *Recollections*, 182.

80. Strathnairn to Duke of Cambridge, 27 Jan.1866, Add. Ms. 42,824.

81. *FJ*, 28 Jan. 1878..

82. Pigott, *Personal Recollections*, 145.

83. Strathnairn to Duke of Cambridge, 27 Jan. 1866, Add. Ms. 42,824.

84. Devoy, *Recollections*, 149; *Irish Times*, 21 Mar. 1866; 25 Apr. 1866; Strathnairn to Duke of Cambridge, 4 Apr. 1866, Add. Ms. 42,824.

85. James Jeffrey Roche, *Life of John Boyle O'Reilly* (London 1891), 329.

86. Ms. 11,188/14, 1–4.

87. Ibid., 11.

88. Inquiry as to the alleged ill-treatment of the convict Charles McCarthy, BPP 1878 [c. 1978], 17.

89. Roche, *Life of John Boyle O'Reilly*, 56.

90. Inquiry as to the alleged ill-treatment of the convict Charles McCarthy, 16.

91. Ibid., 13.

92. Ibid., 13–4, 18.

93. *DPB i*, 303.

94. Ms. 11,188/14, 10.

95. Devoy, *Recollections*, 157–8, 251–2; Thomas Keneally, *The Great Shame*, 443.

96. *Times*, 2 June 1866; Devoy, *Recollections*, 67.

97. *Nation*, 30 Dec. 1865. After independence, Clonmel barracks was renamed Kickham Barracks, while its main square honoured McCarthy.

98. Devoy, *Recollections*, 143, 68; Strathnairn to Cambridge, 25 Feb. 1866, Add. Ms. 42,822.

6. TWO ATTEMPTED INVASIONS AND A PRELUDE TO INSURRECTION, 1866

1. O'Mahony on Fenianism, *Irishman*, 9 May 1868; *New York Times*, 12 Jan. 1866.

2. Mitchel to O'Mahony, 27 Jan. 1866, Fenian Brotherhood Collection, CUA; Stephens to O'Mahony, 10 Feb. 1866, Denieffe, *A Personal Narrative*, 216.

3. *New York Times*, 24 Feb. 1866; Morgan, *Through American*, 114–16; Mitchel's letter, *Irishman*, 14 Mar. 1868.

4. Secret memo from constabulary office, Dublin Castle, 1 Jan. 1866, Mayo papers. Ms. 43,887/2, NLI; *Irish Times*, 2 Feb. 1866; 5 Feb. 1867. Here I am indebted to Jerome Devitt.

5. Wodehouse to Strathnairn, 1 Feb. 1866, Kimberley papers, Ms. Eng. c. 4,041, Bodleian.

6. Ibid., Henry Arthur Herbert to Wodehouse, 11 Feb. 1866.

7. Ibid.

8. Ibid., Wodehouse to Lord Donegall, 2 Feb. 1866; Lord Bessborough to Wodehouse, 3 Feb. 1866; Lord Lurgan to Wodehouse, 7 Feb. 1866; Lord Sligo to Wodehouse, 9 Feb. 1866; Lord Courtown to Wodehouse, 10 Feb. 1866; Lord Dunraven to Wodehouse, 15 Feb. 1866, Ms. Eng. c. 4,042, Bodleian.

9. Lord Powerscourt to Wodehouse, 8 Feb. 1866, Ms. Eng. c. 4041; Hawkins & Powell, *The Journal of John Wodehouse*, 183.

10. Wodehouse to Gladstone, 12 Feb. 1866, Kimberley papers, Ms. Eng. c. 4,041.

11. Ibid.

12. Ibid., Gladstone to Wodehouse, 13 Feb. 1866.

13. Ibid., Strathnairn to Wodehouse, 13 Feb. 1866.

14. Ibid.

15. Ibid., Wodehouse to Sir George Grey, 14 Feb. 1866, Eng. c. 4,042.

16. Ibid.; ibid., Sir George Grey to Wodehouse, 16 Feb. 1866; Hawkins & Powell, *The Journal of John Wodehouse*, 183.

17. *Irish Times*, 29 Feb. 1866; *Times*, 21 Feb. 1866; HCSA abstracts vol. i (1), 119, NAI.

18. Ó Lúing, 'Aspects of the Fenian Rising in Kerry, 1867, I', 141; Seán Ó Suilleabháin, 'The Iveragh Fenians in oral tradition', Maurice Harmon (ed.), *Fenians and Fenianism* (Dublin 1968), 25.

19. Seoighe, *The Story of Kilmallock*, 206–8; *Irish Times*, 5 Apr. 1866; 1 Mar. 1866; 10 Mar. 1866; Sir George Grey to Wodehouse, 16 Feb. 1866, Ms. Eng. c. 4042. Appendix I.

20. Devoy, *Recollections*, 101, 105, 107, 111, 275; Denieffe, *A Personal Narrative*, 208–11; Hawkins & Powell, *The Journal of John Wodehouse*, 184; *Irish People* (NY), 17 Mar. 1866

21. Hawkins & Powell, *The Journal of John Wodehouse*, 185.

22. Ibid.; Devoy, *Recollections*, 87; Jenkins, *The Fenian problem*, 49, Letter from Col Kelly, *Irish People* (NY), 14 Apr. 1866.

23. Mitchel to O'Mahony, 10 Mar. 1866, Fenian Brotherhood Collection, CUA.

24. JM [John Mitchel] to ?, no date, Fenian Brotherhood Collection, CUA.

25. Mitchel to O'Mahony, 10 Mar. 1866, Fenian Brotherhood Collection, CUA.

26. CSO/ICR/10, 218, NAI.

27. *Irishman*, 24 Mar. 1866; 31 Mar. 1866.

28. Ó Broin, *Fenian Fever*, 29; Maume (ed.), *The Last Conquest*, 202.

29. *Irishman*, 2 June 1866; List of warrants issued, CSO/ICR/11 HCSA 1866, 52.

30. HCSA abstracts 1 (3), 533, NAI.

31. Ibid.; O'Donovan Rossa, *Recollections*, 65–6.

32. Edward Coyne, F 1182 NAI.

33. William Hort, 24 July 1866; petition of James Cody sen., 28 Apr. 1866, Fenian files, F 1224, NAI.

34. Ibid., 5 May 1866.

35. Edward Coyne, F 1182, NAI.

36. Ibid.; 31 July 1866, F 1224. See Appendix I.

37. CSO/ICR/10, 407, NAI.

38. Ibid. For other detained members of the Fogarty family, see John Fogarty, brother, ibid., 404; Johnny Fogarty of the Moat, Kilfeacle, cousin, 402; William Fogarty, cousin, 409. See Appendix I. *Gaelic American*, 17 Nov. 1923.

39. Jenkins, *Fenians and Anglo-American relations*, 35, 40–3; Sim, *A Union Forever*, 85–6. Henry Temple, Viscount Palmerston, 1784–1865.

40. Sir Frederick Bruce, 1814–67, youngest son of the Earl of Elgin.

41. Bruce to Clarendon, 4 Dec. 1865, quoted in James J. Barnes, *Private and Confidential: Letters from British Ministers in Washington to the Foreign Secretaries in London, 1844–67* (Selinsgrove 1993), 368.

42. Bruce to Lord Clarendon, 26 Mar. 1866, Canada, Fenian Affairs 1866–1869 Correspondence CO 537/466; Archibald to Lord Clarendon, 30 Jan. 1866, 20 & 26 Feb. 1866, FO 5/1336; Lord Monck to Carnarvon, 25 Jan. 1867, FO 5/1341, TNA.

43. Jenkins, *Fenians and Anglo-American relations*, 57–9, 63.

44. Adams to Seward, 22 Sept. 1865 in Whelan, *American Government in Ireland*, 158–9.

45. William Henry Seward, 1801–72; Bruce to Lord Clarendon, 16 Mar. 1866, quoted in Barnes, *Private and Confidential*, 374, 376; Sim, *A Union Forever*, 2.

46. Sim, *A Union Forever*, 98–102; *New York Times*, 5 Mar. 1866.

47. Whelan, *American Government in Ireland*, 170 -6, 189; *Cork Examiner*, 9 May 1866.

48. HCSA abstracts 1 (2), 465, NAI; Whelan, *American Government in Ireland*, 171–6, 187, 189; 18 July 1866, Larcom papers, Ms. 7,694, NLI.

49. Whelan, *American Government in Ireland*, 180, 182, 187–90; Wodehouse to Clarendon, 29 June 1866 & Clarendon to Wodehouse, 8 July 1866, Kimberley papers, Ms. Eng. c. 4,049, Bodleian; D'Arcy, *The Fenian Movement*, 368.

50. *Irishman*, 4 Apr. 1868.

51. Archibald to Lord Clarendon, 30 Jan. 1866, FO 5/1336. Circulation in 1869 was 9200, in comparison to the *Irish-American* with 35,000 and the *Boston Pilot* with 45,000, David Fitzpatrick, *Irish Times*, 11 July 2015.
52. Archibald to Lord Clarendon, 24 Jan. 1866, FO 5/1336.
53. Ibid., Bruce to Lord Clarendon, 8 Jan. 1866; *New York Times*, 19 Jan. 1866. Similar derision can be found in *New York Times*, 15 Jan. 1866; 1 Feb. 1866.
54. Archibald to Lord Clarendon, 13 Jan. 1866 & 6 Feb. 1866, FO 5/1336.
55. Ibid., 24 Jan. 1866; Archibald to Lord Clarendon, 6, 13, 20 Feb. 1866; 3 Mar. 1866.
56. Archibald to Lord Clarendon, 18 Apr. 1866, FO 5/1337, TNA; *Nation*, 26 May 1866; D'Arcy, *The Fenian Movement*, 135; Wilson, *Thomas D'Arcy McGee*, vol. ii, 224; McNamee to Mr Christian, 24 & 26 Mar. 1866, Sweeny papers, Ms. ZL–472, NYPL.
57. Bruce to Lord Clarendon, 26 Mar. 1866, Canada, Fenian Affairs 1866–69 Correspondence, CO 537/466; Murray to Bruce, 23 Mar. 1866; 20 Mar. 1866; 19 Mar. 1866.
58. *Nation*, 26 May 1866; *Irishman*, 2 Mar. 1867; Report from Clark to Murray & Bruce, 22 May 1866, CO 537/466; Archibald to Lord Clarendon, 18 Apr. 1866, FO 5/1337. The *E.H. Pray* is often misnamed the *Ocean Spray*.
59. Murray to Bruce, 17 May 1866, CO 537/466; Clark to Murray, 22 May 1866; Lieut-Gov. Arthur Gordon to Edward Cardwell, 20 Apr. 1866, FO 5/1337.
60. Gordon to Colonial Office, 18 Apr. 1866, FO 5/1337; Murray to Bruce, 17 May 1866, CO 537/466; Ker to Murray, 10 May 1866; Murray to Bruce, 4 May 1866; Clark to Murray & Bruce, 22 May 1866; Bruce to Lord Clarendon, 17 Apr. 1866, FO 5/1337.
61. Clark to Murray, 22 May 1866, CO 537/466; US Attorney Dart to Consul Hemans, 4 May 1866, Correspondence July to September 1866, FO 5/1339; Archibald to Lord Clarendon, 18 Apr. 1866, FO 5/1337.
62. *New York Times*, 6 May 1866.
63. Ibid.
64. O'Mahony to Francis Mandeville, 4 Dec. 1866, Maher, *Chief of the Comeraghs*, 98.
65. Denieffe, *A Personal Narrative*, 229–32.
66. Ibid., Stephens to O'Mahony, 12 Apr. 1866, 229; *New York Times*, 11 May 1866; *Nation*, 2 June 1866; Archibald to Lord Clarendon, 18 Apr. 1866, FO 5/1337; Stephens to 'my dear friend', 26 Apr. 1866, Fenian Brotherhood Collection, CUA.
67. *New York Times*, 12 May 1866.
68. A 145, 11 May 1866, Fenian files, NAI; *DPB i*, 9; *New York Times*, 18 May 1865; 29 May 1866; 'Edward Duffy', *Irishman*, 14 Mar. 1868.
69. Patrick Steward and Bryan McGovern, *The Fenians: Irish Rebellion in the North Atlantic World, 1858–1876* (Knoxville 2013), 117; Morgan, *Through American*, 122–3; Official report of Gen. John O'Neill (New York 1870).
70. Steward and McGovern, *The Fenians*, 118.
71. *New York Times*, 29 May 1866.
72. Official report of Gen. John O'Neill; Steward and McGovern, *The Fenians*, 122–3.
73. Official report of Gen. John O'Neill; John O'Keefe, ex-student St Patrick's College, Carlow, participant at Ridgeway, http://collections.mohistory.org/resource/174938.html; Steward and McGovern, *The Fenians*, 124–5.

74. Spear to Col John Mechan, 8 June 1866, Denieffe, *A Personal Narrative*, 252–3; Morgan, *Through American*, 134–6.

75. *New York Times*, 7 June 1866; Bruce to Lord Clarendon, 7 June 1866, FO 5/1338, TNA; Bruce to Lord Clarendon, 10 June 1866, quoted Barnes, *Private and Confidential*, 382.

76. D'Arcy McGee to Wodehouse, 11 June 1866, Kimberley papers, Ms. Eng. c. 4,049, Bodleian.

77. Bruce to Lord Clarendon, 7 June 1866, FO 5/1338; *New York Times*, 9 June 1866; Official report of General T.W. Sweeny, Sept. 1866, Denieffe, *A Personal Narrative*, 261.

78. Bruce to Stanley, 26 July 1866, Barnes, *Private and Confidential:*, 387.

79. D'Arcy McGee to Wodehouse, 11 June 1866, Kimberley papers, Ms. Eng. c. 4,049, Bodleian.

80. *To the Fenian Brotherhood of America. Official report of the investigating committee* (New York 1866).

81. *New York Times*, 29 Aug. 1866. Doran Killian was working as a lawyer by 1871, *Irish People* (NY), 8 July 1871.

82. *Memorandum by Thurlow, 16 Apr. 1866, FO 5/1337.*

83. Ibid.

84. *To the Fenian Brotherhood of America. Official report of the investigating committee.*

85. Ibid.

86. O'Mahony on Fenianism, *Irishman*, 14 Mar. 1868; Bruce to Clarendon, 21 May 1866, FO 5/1337; Bruce to Lord Stanley, 24 Sept. 1866, FO 5/1339; *Gaelic American*, 29 Nov. 1924.

87. O'Gorman to Smith O'Brien, 1 Jan. 1859, Ms. 446 in NLI, quoted Kerby A. Miller, *Ireland and Irish America*, 291–2.

88. O'Mahony to Francis Mandeville, 4 Dec. 1866; Maher, *Chief of the Comeraghs*, 97.

89. The unexpurgated original is in the possession of the Hanrahan family of Ballycurkeen House.

90. Ibid.

91. Ibid.

92. Jenkins, *Fenians and Anglo-American Relations*, 158–9, 178, 188, 200; Archibald to Lord Stanley, 8 Sept. 1866, FO 5/1339, TNA; Bruce to Stanley, 27 Aug. 1866; Sim, *A union forever*, 92.

93. Jenkins, *Fenians and Anglo-American Relations*, 168, 173; Bruce to Stanley, 5 Nov. & 17 Dec. 1866, Barnes, *Private and Confidential*, 390, 393.

94. 12 Aug. 1866, Larcom papers, Ms. 7,694, NLI.

95. Interview of Stephens by Eugene Davis, no date, Fenian Brotherhood Collection, CUA., Eugene Davis, 1857–97, journalist.

96. Jenkins, *Gladstone*, 262–3; Clarendon to Wodehouse, 8 July 1866, Kimberley papers, Ms. Eng. c. 4,049, Bodleian.

97. *Irish Times*, 19 Feb. 1868.

98. Habeas Corpus Suspension (Ireland) Act Continuance Bill, Hansard, House of Commons sitting, 31 July 1866; 19 Sept. & 15 Dec. 1866, Larcom papers, Ms. 7,694, NLI; *Irish Times*, 23 Feb. 1867; Fenian information from Corydon, Mayo papers, Ms. 11,188/10, NLI; Whelan, *American Government in Ireland*, 193.

99. *Irish Times*, 23 Feb. 1867; Anderson information, 26 Mar. 1867, Larcom papers, Ms. 7,594; Ó Broin, *Fenian Fever*, 101–3; Strathnairn to Lord Wodehouse, 24 Feb. 1866, Strathnairn papers BL Add. Ms. 42,822.

100. Strathnairn to Duke of Cambridge, 3 & 6 Dec. 1866, BL Add. Ms. 42,824. It was made from one gallon of refined coal oil, 2 oz. phosphate of carbon, 22 Jan. 1867, FO 5/1341, TNA.

101. *New York Times*, 28 Nov. 1866; 29 Oct. 1866; Ó Broin, *Fenian Fever*, 97–8; Strathnairn to Lord Abercorn, 1 Dec. 1866, BL Add. Ms. 42,822.

102. Archibald to Lord Stanley, 7 Dec. 1866, CO 537/466; *New York Times*, 7 Dec. 1866; 23 Dec. 1866.

103. *New York Times*, 28 Nov. 1866; 23 Dec. 1866; Bruce to Lord Stanley, 17 Dec. 1866, quoted Barnes, *Private and Confidential*, 393; Bruce to Lord Stanley, 8 Jan. 1867, CO 537/466, TNA; Official report of General Sweeny, Denieffe, *A Personal Narrative*, 262; Bruce, 8 Jan. 1867, Mayo papers, Ms. 43,888/5, NLI.

104. John Newsinger, 'Old Chartists, Fenians and New Socialists', *Eire-Ireland* xvii, 2 (Summer 1982), 31.

105. Confession of Fariola, Robert Anderson Papers, HO 144/1537/2, TNA; Stephens generally claimed to have 200,000 followers: *Irishman*, 2 June 1866.

106. HO 144/1537/2.

107. Ibid.; *Times*, 1 May 1868.

108. HO 144/1537/2. Appendix I.

109. HO 45/7799 part II, Case of Col Kelly, TNA. This was a son of Michael Doheny. See Appendix I.

110. Patrick Condon/Godfrey Massey, *DIB*, vol. 6, 415; Letter to Stephens, 20 Oct. 1866, Fenian Brotherhood Collection, CUA. Not to be confused with Capt. Patrick Joseph Condon, see Appendix I.

111. *Times*, 29 Apr. 1867; 'General Cluseret on Fenians', *Nation*, 5 July 1872.

112. Rutherford, *The Secret History*, vol. ii 266–7; Fenian headquarters, 7 Dec. 1866, CO 537/466; Edwards to Lord Stanley, 8 Jan. 1867, CO 537/466; *FJ*, 4 July 1872; James Stephens To "Brother & Friends"(?), January, Fenian Brotherhood Collection, CUA.

113. Edwards to Lord Stanley, 29 Jan. 1867, FO 5/1341; HO 144/1537/2; *Times*, 29 Apr. 1867. Stephens protested that he had not relinquished control over civilian Fenianism before retiring to Paris.

114. An analysis of 1086 HCSA files by Robert Anderson found that 47.8 per cent of Fenians were skilled workers, 6.4 per cent urban labourers, 9.1 per cent clerks and teachers, 3.6 per cent shop assistants and shopkeepers' sons, 8.2 shopkeepers and publicans, 5.3 per cent agricultural labourers, 6.9 per cent veterans of various armies and the police, but only 5.5 per cent farmers and their sons. Comerford, 'Patriotism as pastime', *Irish Historical Studies*, xxii, no. 87, 241.

7. THE RISING – 'A COUNSEL OF DESPAIR', 1867–8

1. Stopford A. Brooke & T.W. Rolleston, *A Treasury of Irish Poetry* (Norwood, Mass. 1915), 212–3.

2. Memorandum to Strathnairn, 6 Dec. 1866, Mayo papers, Ms 11,188 /17, NLI.

3. Government memo, June 1867, Larcom papers, Ms. 7,697, NLI.

4. Fariola, 'Amongst the Fenians', *Irishman*, 12 Sept. 1868; HO 144/1537/2, TNA; Keith Amos, *The Fenians in Australia 1865–1880* (Sydney 1988), 83; 'Col O'Connor on the Fenian Risings', *Irish People* (NY), 6 Feb. 1869. Flood, the son of a Dublin ship owner, had abandoned legal training under Isaac Butt. He accompanied Stephens on his escape from Dublin.

5. Precis of important police reports, 1867, HO 144/1537/1, TNA; Shin-Ichi Tagakami, 'The Fenian Rising in Dublin', *Irish Historical Studies*, vol. 29, no. 115, 341. O'Rourke was born in 1841. Nolan was probably a Manchester 'centre'. Nothing is known about Evans. Liddy/Leddy was arrested before the Rising.

6. Letter from O'Neill Fogarty, *Irish People* (NY), 18 Apr. 1868; 25 Apr. 1868; *Irishman*, 12 Sept. 1868.

7. Fariola, *Irishman*, 12 Sept. 1868; Ó Broin, *Charles Gavan Duffy*, 56.

8. *Irish Times*, 3 May 1867.

9. Fariola, *Irishman*, 12 Sept. 1868; HO 144/1537/2; McHale to Col Wood, 10 Feb. 1867, Mayo papers. 43,887/2, NLI; 'General Cluseret on Fenians', *Nation*, 5 July 1872.

10. 'Edward Duffy', *Irishman*, 14 Mar. 1868; 'Edward Duffy', *Irish People* (NY), 8 Feb. 1868; Letter from O'Neill Fogarty, 18 Apr. 1868. O'Neill Fogarty is not always mentioned, having fallen out with Col Kelly.

11. Fariola, *Irishman*, 12 Sept. 1868; *Times*, 29 Apr. 1867; Confession of Fariola, HO 144/1537/2; *Irish People* (NY), 25 Apr. 1868. See Appendix I.

12. Chief Constable, Liverpool, *Times*, 15 July 1872; *Liverpool Mercury*, 30 Apr. 1867; Devoy, *Recollections*, 187–9; John Denvir, *The Life Story of an Old Rebel* (Shannon 1972), 83.

13. *Irish Times*, 13 Feb. 1867; 6 Mar. 1867; Mayo papers, Ms. 43,888 /5, NLI.

14. Devoy, *Recollections*, 190; *Nation*, 23 Feb. 1867; Ó Lúing, 'Aspects of the Fenian Rising in Kerry, 1867', I, 142, 131–2; 'Aspects of the Fenian Rising in Kerry, 1867, II: Aftermath', *JKAHS* no. 4 (1971), 150–1. See Appendix I.

15. Devoy, *Recollections*, 190; Certificate, 20 July 1867, Mayo papers, Ms. 11,189/10; Ó Lúing, 'Aspects of the Fenian Rising in Kerry, 1867, I', 132–3, 146–7; 'Aspects of the Fenian Rising in Kerry, 1867, II', 140, 144; Letter from Col O'Connor, *Irish People* (NY), 18 Jan. 1868. The policeman survived. See Joseph Noonan, Appendix I.

16. *Nation*, 23 Feb. 1867; *Times*, 20 Feb. 1867.

17. *Irish Times*, 19 Feb. 1867; Ó Lúing, 'Aspects of the Fenian Rising in Kerry, 1867, II', 145.

18. Kieran O'Shea, 'David Moriarty (1814–77) I', *JKAHS* no. 3 (1970), 85–6, 98. Oliver Moriarty, born Lixnaw in 1821. For his reports see CSORP 1867/3675, NAI. Lord Castlerosse was the Earl of Kenmare's heir.

19. *Irish Times*, 19 Feb. 1867.

20. Ibid.

21. Ibid.

22. Ó Lúing, 'Aspects of the Fenian Rising in Kerry, 1867, II', 152–3; O'Shea, 'David Moriarty (1814–77) III Politics', 96; D'Arcy, *The Fenian Movement*, 235; 'Pastoral

of Cardinal Cullen', *FJ*, 4 Mar. 1867; Oliver P. Rafferty, 'The Catholic church and Fenianism', *History Ireland*, Nov./Dec. 2008, issue 6, vol. 16; Potter, *William Monsell*, 129–30. Monsell became Baron Emly of Tervoe, 1812–94.

23. *Irish Times*, 23 Feb. 1867. Dr Moriarty's relationship with the IRB was stormy. In 1862, when criticizing the 'Phoenix boys', he was told 'to shut up' during a public meeting.

24. *Irishman*, 23 Feb. 1867; Ó Lúing, 'Aspects of the Fenian Rising in Kerry, 1867, II', 149–50, 156; Mayo to Strathnairn, 4 Mar. 1867, Larcom papers, Ms. 7,594; *FJ*, 4 Mar. 1867.

25. John Newsinger, *Fenianism in Mid-Victorian Britain* (London & Boulder, Colorado 1994), 47–8; HO 144/1537/2. Edmond Beales, 1803–81, campaigning for working-class representation and president of the Reform League.

26. 'General Cluseret on Fenians', *Nation*, 5 July 1872; *FJ*, 4 July 1872; Newsinger, 'Old Chartists, Fenians and New Socialists', 33; Leon Ó Broin, 'Revolutionary nationalism in Ireland: the IRB, 1858–1924', T.W. Moody (ed.), *Nationality and the Pursuit of National Independence* (Belfast 1978), 104.

27. HO 144/1537/2; Charles Bradlaugh, politician and freethinker, 1833–91, H.C.G. Matthew & Brian Harrison, *Oxford Dictionary of National Biography* (Oxford 2004), vol. 7, 197; *Times*, 17 Jan. 1867; Hypatia Bonner, *Charles Bradlaugh: a record of his life and work* (London 1894), vol. i, 253; John Bedford Leno, *The Aftermath* (London 1892), 71–2.

28. Bonner, *Charles Bradlaugh*, vol. i, 253.

29. *Times*, 8 Mar. 1867.

30. Rutherford, *The Secret History*, vol. ii, 276–7; Shin-Ichi Takagami, 'The Fenian Rising in Dublin, March 1867', *Irish Historical Studies*, vol. 29 no. 115, 342.

31. HO 144/1537/2; K [Col Kelly] to 'my dear general' [Gleeson], 19 Mar. 1867, Fenian Brotherhood Collection, CUA.

32. Ibid.; *Irish People* (NY), 4 Apr. 1868; *FJ*, 4 July 1872; *Nation*, 5 July 1872; Devoy, *Recollections*, 234.

33. *FJ*, 4 July 1872; HO 144/1537/2; 'Edward Duffy', *Irishman*, 14 Mar. 1868; 'Edward Duffy', Irish People (NY), 8 February 1868. Ellen and Mary O'Leary, as well as an unnamed sister of Edward Duffy were facilitating the Rising.

34. HO 144/1537/2.

35. Ibid.

36. *Irish Times*, 30 May 1867; 1 May 1867; Anonymous, *The Voice of Freedom: a selection from* Irish Freedom *1910–1913* (Dublin 1913), 44. See Appendix I.

37. Larcom to Col Curzon, 3 & 4 Mar. 1867, Larcom papers, Ms. 7,594, NLI.

38. Ibid., Thomas Talbot, 3 Mar. 1867; Wood to Larcom, 3 Mar. 1867.

39. 'Mr James Francis Xavier O'Brien', *Weekly Freeman*, 29 June 1895; Regan-Lefebvre, *Autobiography of J.F.X. O'Brien*, 97–8, 100; Walter McGrath, 'The Fenian Rising in Cork', *Irish Sword*, vol. viii no. 33 (Winter 1968), 246.

40. Regan-Lefebvre, *Autobiography of J.F.X. O'Brien*, 100–06; McGrath, 'The Fenian Rising in Cork', 246 –7. O'Brien was arrested near Kilmallock.

41. CSO/ICR/10, 181A, NAI; McGrath, 'The Fenian Rising in Cork', 249; Devoy, *Recollections*, 218, 213. O'Sullivan had buried an ingeniously constructed, wooden cannon at the distillery, *Irishman*, 11 Apr. 1868.

42. Falvey, *The Chronicles of Midleton*, 55; Tomás Ó Ríordáin, *P.N. Fitzgerald: Forgotten Cork Fenian*, 8–9, 11–12. See Appendix I for Daly.

43. Falvey, *The Chronicles of Midleton*, 55–6; *FJ*, 9 Mar. 1867.

44. *FJ*, 9 Apr. 1867; 3 Apr. 1867; Devoy, *Recollections*, 213–14. O'Neill Crowley was born in 1832. See Appendix I.

45. Nicholas Ó Duinnin, 'A boycotted family in lone Kilclooney Wood 1867', *The Avondhu*, 23 May 2002; *FJ*, 9 Apr. 1867; 3 Apr. 1867; CSORP 1867/9163, NAI.

46. *FJ*, 3 Apr. 1867. Redmond 'regrett[ed] that we could not account for some more of these ruffians' to Larcom, 3 Apr. 1867, Larcom papers, Ms. 7,594.

47. Michael O'Connell, W.S. 1428, Bureau of Military History. See Appendix I.

48. P. O'Neill, Kinsale, *Weekly Free Press*, 28 Mar. 1914, quoted in Grove White, http://www.corkpastandpresent.ie/places/northcork/grovewhitenotes/kanturk-towntoknocknanuss/gw3_260_264.pdf, 262.

49. CSORP 1867/9163, NAI; Strathnairn to Lord Abercorn, 1 Apr. 1867, Strathnairn papers, BL Add. Ms. 42,824; *FJ*, 9 Apr. 1867; 3 Apr. 1867.

50. *FJ*, 3 Apr. 1867.

51. Ibid., 9 Apr. 1867. Similarly, the burial of an Invincible, while his comrades were awaiting trial, was dominated by women, 'Funeral of H. Rowles', *Cork Examiner*, 22 Mar. 1883.

52. Canon Sheehan as quoted Maher, *Chief of the Comeraghs*, 38.

53. Canon P.A. Sheehan, *The Graves at Kilmorna* (New York 1915), 154.

54. *FJ*, 9 Apr. 1867; Killeagh-Inch Historical Group, *Killeagh Parish Through the Ages* (Killeagh 2011), 322; Seoighe, *The Story of Kilmallock*, 217–8.

55. *Irish Times*, 7 Mar. 1867; List of warrants issued, CSO/ICR/11 HCSA 1866, 424B; Seoighe, *The Story of Kilmallock*, 205, 208–9; *Times*, 11 Mar. 1867.

56. *Cork Examiner*, 27 May 1929; *Times*, 11 Mar. 1867; Imelda O'Riordan, *Kilmallock Fenians. Retrieving their Story* (Kilmallock 2011), 28; Seoighe, *The Story of Kilmallock*, 209–11; Devoy, *Recollections*, 225–7.

57. Seoighe, *The Story of Kilmallock*, 210–11.

58. Ibid., 211–2; Devoy, *Recollections*, 226. W.H. O'Sullivan erected a Celtic cross with verses by Michael Hogan: 'Here lies one who loved his country well,/ And in her sacred cause untimely fell;/ Let every heart who reads this scroll,/ Pray God save Ireland and his immortal soul.' The IRA took the Kilmallock barracks on 28 May 1920. Some participants were descendants of the 1867 team.

59. Seoighe, *The Story of Kilmallock*, 212. *Irishman*, 12 Oct. 1867; Brian Dillon's mother had her licence withdrawn, McGrath, *A Cork Felon*, 47–9; *Irish Times*, 8 Mar. 1867.

60. *Nation*, 16 Mar. 1867.

61. Ibid. Dr Thomas Downes, PP, confirmed this report.

62. Aideen Carroll, *Seán Moylan: Rebel Leader* (Cork 2010), 15–6.

63. Stephen de Vere to Lord Dunraven, 11 May 1867, quoted Porter, *William Monsell*, 129–30; *Irish Times*, 24 Nov. 1866; CSORP 1867/3476, NAI; 'John Daly's Recollections, part III', *Irish Freedom*, Apr. 1912.

64. *Parish of Emly Journal 1990*, 10–11, 13; 'John Daly's Recollections', *Irish Freedom*, Apr. 1912; 'A '67 Hero', cutting from *Nationalist*, 1908, courtesy of Liam Ó Duibhir. See Appendix I. James Hogan, a schoolmaster for twenty-eight years, was dismissed by the board of education.

65. Michael & Liam Dwyer, 'The Fenian Rising 1867', *The Parish of Emly* (Emly 1987), 69; *Times*, 15 May 1867; CSORP 1867/3588; CSORP 1867/4783 *Times*, 9 Sept. 1867; *Munster Express*, 16 Mar. 1867.
66. 'The '67 Rising – report from an American veteran', *Parish of Emly Journal 1990*, 11.
67. Mainchín Seoighe, *Limerick Leader*, 20 Mar. 1948; *Times*, 9 Mar. 1867; CSORP 1867/3780 & CSORP 1867/3791, NAI.
68. 'John Daly's Recollections', *Irish Freedom*, Apr. 1912.
69. *Times*, 9 Mar. 1867; 13 Mar. 1867; CSORP 1867/3791; CSORP 1867/3675, NAI.
70. 'John Daly's Recollections', *Irish Freedom*, Apr. & May 1912; CSORP 1867/3780. An informer told the constabulary, who broke into the chapel to seize the pikes. The villagers held an indignation meeting at this desecration, accusing the police of having planted them: *Irishman*, 14 Mar. 1868; 21 Mar. 1868; *Times*, 16 Mar. 1868.
71. Mayo papers, Ms. 11,188/10, NLI; Fintan Lane, 'Labour lives no. 3: William Upton', *Saothar*, vol. 26 (2001), 89–90. See Appendix I.
72. HO 144/1537/2; Devoy, *Recollections*, 234; *Times*, 1 May 1868; *Irish Times*, 2 May 1867.
73. Michael O'Donnell, 'Thomas Francis Bourke (1840–1889)', *THJ* 1990, 27–31, 33; CSORP 1867/3178; Maher, *Chief of the Comeraghs*, iii. This is as unreliable as the report that the notably sober John O'Mahony had a drink problem. The disease is not mentioned in Bourke's prison record.
74. CSORP 1867/3475, NAI; 2–4 Mar. 1867, Larcom papers, Ms. 7,594, NLI.
75. CSORP 1867/3475; *Times*, 13 Mar. 1867.
76. Clare C. Murphy, 'North Tipperary in the year of the Fenian Rising (part 1)', *THJ* 1995, 109.
77. CSORP 1867/4537, NAI; Pigott, *Personal Recollections*, 243; William Rutherford, ''67 Retrospection' (Tipperary 1903), 12; CSORP 1867/3588, NAI; 'Col Kelly', *Irish People* (NY), 25 Apr. 1868.
78. Maher, *Chief of the Comeraghs*, 292; 'Death of Myles', *Tipperary Star*, 25 Jan. 1913; 'Death of J.J. Finnan', *Irish Freedom*, Feb.1913. His pen name was Myles the Slasher, see Appendix I.
79. Maher, *Chief of the Comeraghs*, 292; CSORP 1867/4783, NAI; Mayo papers Ms. 11,188/10, NLI; *Times*, 9 Sept. 1867.
80. *Nation*, 4 May 1867; Pigott, *Personal Recollections*, 243; CSORP 1867/4537, NAI; *Irish Times*, 11 Mar. 1867; Rutherford, '67 Retrospection, 18–19. See Appendix I. (Additional research by Tony Hocking).
81. CSORP 1867/4537, NAI.
82. *Nenagh Guardian*, 9 Mar. 1867; Devoy, *Recollections*, 219.
83. Walsh, *A history of Templemore and its Environs*, 82–3; CSORP 1867/8957; Fenian files, F 3597, NAI; *Irishman*, 25 Jan. 1868. See Appendix I.
84. CSORP 1867/8957, NAI.
85. Devoy, *Recollections*, 219–20; *Irishman*, 3 Aug. 1867; *Times*, 13 Mar. 1867; Larcom papers, Ms. 7,694; *Nenagh Guardian*, 3 Aug. 1867. See Appendix I.
86. John Rutter 'Woodcock' Carden, 1811–66, brother of Capt. Andrew Carden, *DIB*, vol. 2, 325; *Nenagh Guardian*, 9 Mar. 1867.
87. 5 Mar. 1867, Report 31st Regt., Kilmainham Ms. 1059, quoted Charles Townshend, *Political Violence in Ireland. Government and Resistance since 1848* (Oxford

2001), 89; E.H. Sheehan, *Nenagh and its Neighbourhood* (Bray n.d.), 63 –4. Baker, 1827–87, later a commander of the Ottoman Empire.

88. *Devoy, Recollections*, 228–30; O Cathaoir & Mac Fheorais, 'The Irish Republican Brotherhood in Clare 1858–1871', 460–1.

89. Ibid., 461–2, quoting Fr Patrick White, *History of Clare* (Dublin 1893).

90. *FJ*, 26 Mar. 1867; O Cathaoir, 'The Irish Republican Brotherhood in Clare', 462.

91. Takagami, 'The Fenian Rising in Dublin, March 1867', 344–9; Ryan's report, 4 Mar. 1867, Mayo papers, Ms. 11,188/10.

92. Takagami, 'The Fenian Rising in Dublin, March 1867' 349, 356–9. For casualties, see Appendix II.

93. Eva O Cathaoir, 'Patrick Lennon (1841–1901): Dublin Fenian Leader', *Dublin Historical Record*, vol. 44, no. 2 (Autumn 1991), 39.

94. Takagami, 'The Fenian Rising in Dublin, March 1867', 347, 351–4; Devoy, *Recollections*, 203–4, 199–201. O Cathaoir, 'Patrick Lennon', 39–40.

95. *FJ*, 9 Mar. 1867; Devoy, *Recollections*, 232–3; *Times*, 18 July 1867. Hugh O'Neill surrendered in Mellifont in 1603, unaware that Elizabeth I had died. Luke Fullam and his brother Laurence were sentenced to five years and transported to Western Australia.

96. CSORP 1867/4179; CSORP 1867/3658, NAI.

97. CSORP 1867/3571.

98. *Irish Times*, 9 Mar. 1867; 11 Mar. 1867; *Irishman*, 16 Mar. 1867.

99. CSORP 1867/7568, NAI; *FJ*, 11 Mar. 1867; 27 Mar. 1867.

100. *Irish Times*, 9 Mar. 1867. Continuing bad weather in Wicklow, Ulster and Munster: 13 & 14 Mar. 1867.

101. *Times*, 15 Mar. 1867.

102. Ibid.; ibid., 13 Mar. 1867; *Nation*, 23 Feb. 1867; Jenkins, *The Fenian Problem*, 90.

103. *New York Times*, 13 Mar. 1867.

104. Col Kelly to Gen. Gleeson, 19 Mar. 1867, Fenian Brotherhood Collection, CUA; Consulate to HO, 29 Mar. 1867, Ms. 43,888/5, NLI; ibid., Edwards to Larcom, 18 Mar. 1867; *New York Times*, 17 Mar. 1867; Larcom to Hamilton, 24 Mar. 1867, Larcom papers, Ms. 7,594.

105. K [Col Kelly] to 'My dear general [Gleeson]', 15 Mar. 1867, Fenian Brotherhood Collection, CUA.

106. Ibid.

107. Ibid.

108. Ibid., Col Kelly to Gen. Gleeson, 19 Mar. 1867, Fenian Brotherhood Collection, CUA.

109. Fariola to chief executive, Irish Republic, 26 Mar. 1867, Fenian Brotherhood Collection, CUA; Fariola to Anthony Griffin, chief executive, Irish Republic, 29 Mar. 1867; HO 144/1537/2; *Nation*, 13 Apr. 1867.

110. Belchem, *Irish, Catholic and Scouse*, 172; Col Kelly to Gen. Gleeson, 19 Mar. 1867, Fenian Brotherhood Collection, CUA; *Irishman*, 23 Mar. 1867; *FJ*, 27 Mar. 1867; Patrick McCormack, Cushendun, Co. Antrim, W.S. 339, BMH; Jenkins, *The Fenian Problem*, 93. During the Civil War the Confederacy used detonating mines, described as torpedoes.

111. *Nation*, 20 Apr. 1867; 20 Mar. 1867, CSORP 6339, NAI. See Appendix I.

112. *Irish People* (NY), 18 July 1868; *Irishman*, 4 July 1868; *Nation*, 27 June 1868; *Irish Times*, 3 July 1868. Appendix I.

113. CSORP 1867/7568, NAI; Townshend, *Political Violence in Ireland*, 93–4.

114. Castlerosse to Larcom, 26 Mar. 1867, Larcom papers, Ms. 7,594; MacDonnell to Larcom, 4 Apr. 1867.

115. *Times*, 13 Mar. 1867.

116. F 3,597, Fenian Files, NAI.

117. 'Capt. William Sweetman', *Southern Star*, 21 Sept. 1901.

118. Letter from O'Neill Fogarty, *Irish People* (NY), 18 Apr. 1868; Letter from Michael O'Rourke, 25 Apr. 1868; 23 May 1868; *Irishman*, 29 Aug. 1868.

119. Dr P.J. Kain to O'Donovan Rossa, 20 Nov. 1909, Fenian Brotherhood Collection, CUA. See Appendix I.

120. Return of Fenian prisoners, captured in the neighbourhood of Dungarvan, Mayo papers, Ms. 11,189/17, NLI; Bernadette Whelan, *American Government in Ireland*, 196–7; Devoy, *Recollections*, 235–6; D'Arcy, *The Fenian Movement*, 247, 272–3, 281–2. This issue concluded with the Anglo-American naturalization treaty, the 'Warren and Costello Act' (1870).

121. Edwards to Lord Stanley, 13 June 1867, Confidential reports and memoranda, Mayo papers Ms. 11,188/10, NLI; Report of senate, Fenian Brotherhood, 19 Jan. 1867, FO 5/1341, TNA; Edwards to Lord Stanley, 16 May 1867; Consulate, NY, to Lord Stanley, 10 Apr. 1867.

122. Edwards to Lord Stanley, 16 May 1867, FO 5/1341.

123. *Southern Star*, 24 Jan. 1903; Edwards to Lord Stanley, 13 June 1867, Ms. 11,188/10.

124. *Irish Times*, 31 Dec. 1867.

125. Ó Broin, *Fenian Fever*, 174; *Irishman*, 3 Aug. 1867; Districts proclaimed, Mayo papers, Ms. 11,188/10, NLI.

126. *Irish People* (NY), 23 May 1868; *FJ*, 30 Nov. 1867; *Irish Times*, 31 Dec. 1867; Telegram to Larcom, 27 Dec. 1867, Strathnairn papers, BL Add. Ms. 42,824; 'The Cork Men and New York Men', *Nation*, 4 Jan. 1868; Confidential to inspector general, 27 Feb. 1868, Mayo papers, Ms. 43,887/2, NLI.

127. Franks to Larcom, 1 Jan. 1868, Larcom papers, Ms. 7,596, NLI; De Gernon to Mayo, 3 Jan. 1868; De Gernon to Larcom, 2 Jan. 1868. As late as 9 Dec. 1869, the *Times* reported a large crowd drilling near Kilteely.

128. Ibid., De Gernon to Mayo, 3 Jan. 1868.

129. Ibid., R.M. Franks to Larcom, 1 Jan. 1868; Lord Mayo to Larcom, 18 Jan. 1868; Two notes from Lord Mayo, n.d.; enclosing report, *FJ*, 14 Feb. & *Mail*, 15 Feb. 1868; R.M. Moriarty to Larcom, 20 Feb. 1868; *Nation*, 1 Feb. 1868; 4 Apr. 1868; 25 July 1868; *Kerry Evening Post*, 26 Feb. 1868.

130. *Irish Times*, 21 Feb. 1868; 25 Feb. 1868; Lord Mayo to Larcom, 8, 10, 14, 16 Feb. 1868, Ms. 7,596; Telegram, 12 Feb. 1868; R.M. Hamilton to Larcom, 10 Feb. 1868. The informers were Michael Hartnett and a Mr 'Hunnan', a gentleman.

131. *Irishman*, 28 Mar. 1868.

132. Ibid.; O'Brien, *Recollections*, 77–8; Gavan Duffy, *My Life in Two Hemispheres*, vol. ii, 306–7.

133. Gavan Duffy, *My Life in Two Hemispheres*, vol. ii, 307.

134. *Irishman*, 28 Mar. 1868; *Times*, 23 Mar. 1868; O'Brien, *Recollections*, 138.

8. INCARCERATION OF THE LEADERS, 1865–8

1. Oscar Wilde, *The Ballad of Reading Gaol* (London 1996), 26.
2. Philip Priestley, *Victorian Prison Lives* (London 1999), x, 3–4, 33–4; Albert Crew, *London Prisons of Today and Yesterday* (London 1933), 103; A.W. Palmer, *A Dictionary of Modern History, 1789–1945* (Harmondsworth 1967), 45. Jeremy Bentham, 1748–1832.
3. Crew, *London Prisons*, 81–2; Priestley, *Victorian Prison Lives*, 37.
4. Priestley, *Victorian Prison Lives*, 37.
5. Crew, *London Prisons*, 84, 86.
6. Tim Carey, *Mountjoy. The Story of a Prison* (Cork 2000,), 42, 50–1; Priestley, *Victorian Prison Lives*, 38.
7. Henry Mathew & John Binny, *The criminal prisons of London, scenes of prison life* (London 1862), 114–5; Crew, *London Prisons*, 81.
8. Regan-Lefebvre, *Autobiography of J.F.X. O'Brien*, 116.
9. Jeremiah O'Donovan Rossa, *Irish Rebels in English Prisons* (Dingle, 1991), 82. See Breandán Mac Suibhne and Amy Martin, 'Fenians in the Frame: Photographing Irish political prisoners, 1865–68', https://oconnellhouse.nd.edu/assets/39749/macsuibhnemartinfDrpdf. Patrick Bryan, a native of Ballingarry, Co. Tipperary, refused, CSO/ICR/FP 36, NAI.
10. HO 45/9329/19461 part I, TNA; Measor to editor, *Times*, 18 Mar. 1867.
11. Maume, Maume & Casey, *The Galtee Boy*, 11–12; Editorial, *Times*, 20 Mar. 1867.
12. HO 45/9329/19461 part I, TNA; Whitty to Wodehouse, 18 June 1866, Kimberley papers, Ms. Eng. c. 4,049, Bodleian.
13. HO 45/9329/19461 part I, 27 Aug. 1866.
14. Ibid., Capt. Whitty, 20 Dec. 1865.
15. Maume, Maume & Casey, *The Galtee Boy*, 150.
16. O'Donovan Rossa, *Irish Rebels*, 87. Flannel underclothes could only be granted by the medical officer.
17. Ibid, 89.
18. Priestley, *Victorian Prison Lives*, 45; O'Donovan Rossa, *Irish Rebels*, 89–90; Maher, *The Valley Near Slievenamon*, 25.
19. Neil McKenna, *The Secret Life of Oscar Wilde* (London 2004), 536–7.
20. Anonymous letter to Pentonville Prison, 28 Sept. 1866, HO 45/9329/19461 part I, TNA.
21. 'Treatment of the Irish political prisoners', *Irishman*, 27 Feb. 1869, republished as pamphlet 'Things not generally known concerning England's treatment of the political prisoners', 13.
22. Michael Davitt, *Leaves from a Prison Diary* (New York 1885), 136–7.
23. Robert Anderson, *Criminals and crime: some facts and suggestions* (London 1907), 133–5.
24. Maher, *Chief of the Comeraghs*, 250, 247.
25. Pentonville Prison, directors' order book, 1863–85, PCOM 2/92, TNA.
26. Ibid., 2 Jan. 1866; 29 Aug. 1867, Millbank, letter from directors – Wm Moore Stack, letter as to Fenianism – 77261, HO 14/31, TNA; 15 & 23 Sept. 1866, Millbank,

James Keilly [sic] statement of Fenian plans, 73567, HO 14/29, TNA; Amos, *The Fenians in Australia*, 230–1.

27. Maume, Maume & Casey, *The Galtee Boy*, 157; Priestley, *Victorian Prison Lives*, 194–5, 131–2.
28. Newspaper cutting, HO 45/9329/19461 part I, TNA.
29. Letter from Col Henderson, 18 Apr. 1866, HO 45/9329/19461 part I.
30. Denieffe, *A Personal Narrative*, 46–7; Maume, Maume & Casey, *The Galtee Boy*, 189–90.
31. O'Donovan Rossa, *Irish Rebels*, 116.
32. Pamphlet 'Things not generally known', HO 45/9329/19461 part I; Report of the commissioners on the treatment of the treason-felony convicts, BPP 1867 [3880] xxxv. 673, 9. The pope had consecrated *Agnus Dei* wax discs since the middle ages to protect the faithful from illness and sudden death.
33. Pamphlet 'Things not generally known', 10.
34. Ibid.; O'Donovan Rossa, *Irish Rebels*, 111–12.
35. 17 Feb. 1867, governor's journals, Portland, 23 Sept. 1864–31 Mar. 1867, PCOM 2/361, TNA.
36. Ibid., 7 Feb. 1867; 24 Feb 1867; 2–5, 7 Mar. 1867.
37. Maume, Maume & Casey, *The Galtee Boy*, 135.
38. Michael O'Donnell, 'Thomas Francis Bourke – 1840–1889', *THJ* 1991, 112; Ryan, *The Phoenix Flame*, 203.
39. Account of a Fenian prisoner in newspaper cutting, HO 45/9329/19461 part I; Oscar Wilde recorded a similar experience, McKenna, *The Secret Life of Oscar Wilde*, 537–8.
40. Maume, Maume & Casey, *The Galtee Boy*, 156.
41. BPP 1871 [c. 319] [c. 319-1], 532; O'Donovan Rossa, *Irish Rebels*, 94.
42. O'Donovan Rossa, *Irish Rebels*, 94.
43. Priestley, *Victorian Prison Lives*, 267, 271, 258, 261–3; for punishment of warders, 1 May 1866, 5 June 1866, 3 July 1866, Director's visiting book, 1863–85, Pentonville Prison, PCOM 2/ 92; 4 Feb. 1867, Governor's journals, 23 Sept. 1864–31 Mar. 1867, Portland Prison, PCOM 2/ 361, TNA.
44. *Times*, 19 Jan. 1861; 15 Feb. 1861; 26 Mar. 1861.
45. O'Donovan Rossa, *Irish Rebels*, 158; O'Leary, *Recollections*, vol. i, 9–10; Crew, *London Prisons*, 81.
46. O'Donovan Rossa, *Irish Rebels*, 122–3; Mary Jane O'Donovan Rossa, *Irish Lyrical Poems* (New York 1868), 42.
47. O'Leary presented the shamrock to J.W. O'Beirne, a Dublin IRB man and founder of the NGA, in whose care it remains; O'Donovan Rossa, *Irish Rebels*, 123.
48. George Sigerson, *Political Prisoners at Home and Abroad* (London 1890), 51.
49. Sloan, *William Smith O'Brien*, 297; Richard Davis (ed.), *'To solitude consigned': the Tasmanian Journal of William Smith O'Brien* (Sydney 1995), 12.
50. Mitchel, *Jail Journal*, 9–10, 12; Davis, *'To solitude consigned'*, 31–3, 12.
51. *Nation*, 23 Sept. 1865; Bourke, *John O'Leary*, 5; Comerford, *Charles J. Kickham*, 17.
52. *Irishman*, 23 Dec. 1865; Pentonville Prison register, PCOM 2/71, TNA; Regan-Lefebvre, *Autobiography of J.F.X. O'Brien*, 1–2.
53. Maume, Maume & Casey, *The Galtee Boy*, 157, 188; Priestley, *Victorian Prison Lives*, 204.

54. Bourke, *John O'Leary*, 118.
55. Ibid.
56. W.B. Yeats, *Autobiographies*, 211; Quarterly returns for Portland, June 1866, HO 8/168, TNA.
57. Devoy, *Recollections*, 296; O'Donovan Rossa, *Irish Rebels*, 118.
58. O'Donovan Rossa, *Irish Rebels*, 82.
59. Ibid., 222.
60. Regan-Lefebvre, *Autobiography of J.F.X. O'Brien*, 113, 117.
61. O'Donovan Rossa, *Irish Rebels*, 115; Diary entry in unidentified newspaper, HO 45/9329/19461 part I, TNA.
62. Woking quarterly returns, ending 30 Sept. 1868, HO 8/177, TNA.
63. C.W. Sullivan (ed.), *Fenian Diary* (Dublin 2001), 137.
64. A.G. Evans, *Fanatic Heart: a Life of John Boyle O'Reilly* (Boston 1997), 44; O'Donovan Rossa, *Irish Rebels*, 159–60, 91–2.
65. *Times*, 20 Jan. 1866.
66. Edmund du Cane, Aug. 1873, HO 45/9293/17577, TNA.
67. O'Donovan Rossa, *Irish Rebels*, 128–9, 136.
68. Ibid., 168.
69. Malcolm Chase, *Chartism; a new history* (Manchester 2007), 359; *Irish People*, 5 Nov. 1864; Ian Kenneally, *From the earth, a cry. The story of John Boyle O'Reilly* (Cork 2011), 180–81. By the early 1850s, female Chartists had fallen silent under the influence of Victorian 'respectability'.
70. O'Leary, *Recollections*, vol. ii, 145.
71. Ibid.; *Irishman*, 23 Dec. 1865; Letter from E.E.C., *Irish People*, 15 July 1865; Emer Delaney, 'Women in the Risorgimento and the Irish independence movement', Colin Barr, Michele Finelli & Anne O'Connor (eds), *Nation/Nazione*, 220–1; Quinn, *Young Ireland*, 95–6.
72. Clarke, *My Life and Memories*, 57–9.
73. *Cork Examiner*, 23 Mar. 1867; *Irish People* (NY), 17 Feb. 1866; Eoghan Ó Néill, *The Golden Vale of Ivowen* (Dublin 2001), 493; Terry Golway, *Irish Rebel. John Devoy and America's Fight for Ireland's Freedom* (Sallins 2016), 148.
74. *FJ*, 6 Mar. 1866; *New York Times*, 24 Aug. 1865; Lehne, 'Fenianism', 105; *Brooklyn Eagle*, 18 May 1866. Ellen was not related to John O'Mahony.
75. Bishop Timon to Bishop Lefevere, 20 Feb. 1866, University of Notre Dame, 1866 calendar at http: //archives.nd.edu/calendar/c186602.htm.
76. *Kerry Evening Post*, 27 Sept. 1865.
77. Ibid.
78. *Irishman*, 14 Oct. 1865; 9 Feb. 1867; *Nation*, 30 Dec. 1865.
79. *New York Times*, 17 Dec. 1865; *Irish Times*, 7 Nov. 1865.
80. *FJ*, 18 Jan. 1866.
81. *Baltimore Daily Commercial*, 3 Jan. 1866; *New York Times*, 9 Mar. 1866; *Irishman*, 23 Feb. 1867; *Brooklyn Eagle*, 25 Apr. 1866; *Southern Star*, 24 Jan. 1903.
82. *Irish Times*, 13 Dec. 1866.
83. Ibid; *Brooklyn Eagle*, 29 Dec. 1866.
84. *Irishman*, 9 Feb. 1867.
85. Ibid., 2 May 1868.

86. *Times*, 27. Jan. 1868; Denieffe, *A Personal Narrative*, 130, 152–3; HO 144/1537/2, TNA; 'Edward Duffy', *Irishman*, 14 Mar. 1868. Mary O'Leary, 1841–72.

87. Edmund O'Leary to O'Mahony, 16 Nov. 1865, Fenian Brotherhood Collection, CUA; O'Leary, *Lays of Country, Home and Friends*, 17–8; Mitchel to O'Mahony, 7 Apr. 1866, Fenian Brotherhood Collection, CUA; Mitchel to O'Mahony, 10 Apr. 1866, Denieffe, *A Personal Narrative*, 227.

88. Letter from Ellen O'Leary, *Irishman*, 5 May 1866.

89. Ibid., 7 July 1866.

90. Ibid. The Fenians in Pentonville were attended by Canon Frederick Oakeley of St John's, Islington, a Catholic convert and former member of the Oxford movement. He opposed Fenianism, but, like Dr Manning, conceded that it was rooted in British misrule.

91. Ibid.

92. *Irishman*, 11 Nov. 1865; Devoy, *Recollections*, 113.

93. *Irishman*, 16 Dec. 1865.

94. Ibid., 11 Nov. 1865; 13 Jan. 1866; 23 June 1866; 9 June 1866.

95. *Irish People* (NY), 28 Apr. 1866; *Irishman*, 16 June 1866; 9 June 1866; 28 July 1866; 13 Oct. 1866; 11 Nov. 1865.

96. *New York Times*, 27 Dec. 1866; Leon Ó Broin, *The Prime Informer* (London 1971), 58.

97. *Irishman*, 9 Feb. 1867; *Nation*, 21 July 1867.

98. *Irishman*, 4 & 11 Apr. 1868; 30 May 1868; 20 Mar. 1869; *Nation*, 17 Aug. 1867.

99. Appeals in the *Irishman* for Mackey Lomasney's wife, 28 Mar. 1868; 4 Apr. 1868; Joseph Theobald Casey, also Denis D. Mulcahy, 18 July 1868; 6 Mar. 1869.

100. *Times*, 1 Nov. 1865; 21 Feb. 1866; *Irish People* (NY), 3 Mar. 1866; Ó Broin, *Fenian Fever*, 51. The press records only two, brief arrests of working-class Fenian women.

101. Mary Jane O'Donovan Rossa to Anna McDonald, Fenian Sisterhood, *Irishman*, 26 Jan. 1867; Denieffe, *A Personal Narrative*, 154–5; *New York Times*, 27 Dec. 1866; Lehne, 'Fenianism', 110; Chase, *Chartism*, 359.

102. *Irishman*, 13 June 1868; 4 July 1868; Lehne, 'Fenianism', 34–5.

103. Devoy, *Recollections*, 112–3.

104. The *Pall Mall Gazette*, 3 Feb. 1866. John Pope-Hennessy, 1834–91, MP King's Co., 1859–65, was a college contemporary of John O'Leary in Cork. A political maverick, Hennessy became a Home Ruler and MP for Kilkenny, 1890–91. The *Times* censured him as a colonial administrator for ignoring the upper classes in Barbados, while paying attention to the black majority, see *Irishman*, 29 Apr. 1876. O'Leary, *Recollections*, vol. ii, 164.

105. William Randall Cremer, 1828–1908, was awarded the Nobel Prize in 1903 and subsequently knighted.

106. 24 Feb. 1866, HO 45/9329/19461 part I, TNA; International Working Men's Association 1866, the Irish state prisoners, http://www.marxists.org/archive/marx/iwma/documents/1866/irish-state-prisoners.htm.

107. Mary Burns, 1823–63, *DIB*, vol. 2, 86. A mill hand, she toured Ireland with Engels. Lizzie Burns, 1827–78. Eleanor was the youngest daughter of Karl Marx. Jenny Marx-Longuet, her sister, publicized the plight of the Fenian prisoners in the

radical French paper, *La Marseillaise*, in 1870.

108. Quinlivan and Rose, *The Fenians in England 1865–1872* (London & New York 1982), 11–12, 66–7.

109. 'Charles J. Kickham', *Irishman*, 25 Nov. 1865; 9, 16, 30 Dec. 1865; 25 Aug. 1866.

110. Ibid., 16 June 1866 or 'Twilight on Slievenamon' in James Maher (ed.), *Dawn on the Irish Coast* (Mullinahone 1952).

111. Catherine Arnold, *Necropolis London and its Dead* (London 2007), 182–5.

112. *Irishman*, 28 Mar. 1868. Victor Hugo said that this reburial 'teems with omen' for Italy. The parallel with the McManus obsequies is obvious.

113. Ibid., 31 Mar. 1866; 9 June 1866; Prison returns for quarter ending June 1866, HO 8/168, TNA.

114. *Irishman*, 13 Oct. 1866; 9 June 1866; McGrath, *A Cork Felon*, 25. The author discovered Lynch's prison record in TNA. His grave was located by Charles McLauchlan of Manchester and the NGA erected a plaque to him at the Catholic Chapel in Brookwood Cemetery in 2004.

115. George Sigerson, *Modern Ireland: its vital questions, secret societies and government* (London 1869), 365–6; List of warrants issued, CSO/ICR/11 HCSA 1866, 149; *Irishman*, 28 Nov. 1868; 14 Nov. 1868; *Irish People* (NY), 19 & 5 Sept. 1868.

116. Sigerson, *Modern Ireland*, 376, 414; *Times*, 8 Jan. 1867. In September 1866, there had been 226 suspects in Mountjoy. *Irishman*, 20 Apr. 1867.

117. *Irishman*, 16 Mar. 1867; Michael H. Kane, 'American soldiers in Ireland, 1865–67', *The Irish Sword: The Journal of the Military History Society of Ireland*, vol. 23, no. 91, 119.

118. CSORP 1867/3178; List of warrants issued, CSO/ICR/11 HCSA, 1866, 64B, NAI; *Irishman*, 16 Mar. 1867. His large headstone in Rathcoole Cemetery, seen by the author twenty years ago, reads: 'He was through life an honourable, generous and brave patriot and gentleman.'

9. 'SUFFERING IN A GREAT AND NOBLE CAUSE', 1867–75

1. McGrath, *A Cork Felon*, 21.

2. *Cork Examiner*, 23 Mar. 1868.

3. *Irishman*, 20 Apr. 1867.

4. Ibid.; *Nation*, 20 Feb. 1867; Sigerson, *Modern Ireland*, 372–3.

5. Sigerson, *Modern Ireland*, 373.

6. Quotation from his monument in Glasnevin Cemetery, which was 'erected by his friends and associates to perpetuate the memory of his love of country, and his death, caused by a penal imprisonment, which ... could not extinguish his ardent aspirations for Ireland's freedom', *Irishman*, 23 May 1868.

7. Knox and Pollock were authorized to conduct this inquiry on 8 May 1867. Report of the commissioners on the treatment of the treason-felony convicts in the English convict prisons, BPP 1867 [3880] xxxv, 673; *Irishman*, 27 Feb. 1869.

8. *Irishman*, 20 Mar. 1869; Brendan Hughes, a twentieth-century Republican prisoner, believed that the strip-searches were frightening and 'an attempt to degrade

and brutalise'; see Ed Moloney, *Voices From the Grave* (New York 2010), 224.

9. Maher, *The Valley Near Slievenamon*, 248; *Irishman*, 20 Mar. 1869.

10. *Irishman*, 6 July 1867.

11. Knox and Pollock: report of the commissioners, BPP, 1867 [3880] xxxv. 673, 20, 4; *Irishman*, 6 July 1867.

12. *Nation*, 9 June 1866; *Irishman*, 6 July 1867.

13. McConville, *Irish Political Prisoners*.

14. O'Donovan Rossa, *Irish rebels in English prisons* (New York 1899), 212.

15. O'Donovan Rossa, *Irish Rebels in English Prisons* (Dingle, 1991), 139, 143.

16. Report of the commissioners, BPP 1867 [3880], 23.

17. Ibid., 4.

18. Ibid., 16.

19. Ibid., 14.

20. Ibid., 23–4.

21. Ibid., 24; *Irishman*, 17 Oct. 1868. See Appendix I.

22. *Irishman*, 27 July 1867; Sigerson, *Political Prisoners*, 159.

23. CSO/ICR/10, 497, NAI; *FJ*, 12 Sept. 1867; *Irish Times*, 18 Sept. 1867.

24. Report of town inspector of constabulary, Belfast, on 16 Sept. 1867, Robert Anderson papers, HO 144/1537/1, TNA; *Irishman*, 12 Oct. 1867.

25. Maher, *Chief of the Comeraghs*, ix.

26. *Irishman*, 29 Aug. 1868; *Irish People* (NY), 15 Feb. 1868; 23 May 1868; *Nation*, 27 Apr. 1867; 'Fenianism. A narrative by one who knows', *Contemporary Review*, Feb. & Apr. 1872, 638–9; Anthony Griffin, Fenian Brotherhood circular, 19 Sept. 1867, Fenian Brotherhood Collection, CUA.

27. *Nation*, 27 July 1867.

28. Anthony Griffin, Fenian Brotherhood circular, 19 Sept. 1867, Fenian Brotherhood Collection, CUA; Devoy, *Recollections*, 237–9; *DPB* i, 9.

29. Griffin, Fenian Brotherhood circular; *Irishman*, 29 Aug. 1868.

30. *Nation*, 21 Sept. 1867; Anthony Glynn, *High Upon the Gallows Tree* (Tralee c. 1970), 30–4; Wilson, *Thomas D'Arcy McGee*, vol. ii, 328; William Hogan, Fenianism, index of names, 1861–5, CSO/ICR/14. Much about the rescue remains unclear, due to later disagreements between Devoy and O'Meagher Condon. The Bolger brothers from Kilkenny, Timothy Featherstone of Kildorrery, County Cork, William Melville, John Neary and Peter Rice were among the participants. Rice fled to New York, where he was known as the man who had fired the fatal shot, which the Home Office considered possible. See Appendix I.

31. Glynn, *High Upon the Gallows Tree*, 34–8, 55, 41–3, 46–7; Devoy, *Recollections*, 245. Devoy later claimed that O'Meagher Condon had failed to bring the necessary tools. Report from Sub-Inspector Hamilton, Cork, 21 Sept. 1867, Robert Anderson papers, HO 144/1537/1, TNA.

32. Glynn, *High Upon the Gallows Tree*, 57–61, 111–5, 101; Quinlivan and Rose, *The Fenians in England*, 69–70. See, 'Grand musical celebration under the auspices of Clan na Gael in honour of the martyrdom of Allen, Larkin and O'Brien', 23 Nov. 1891, Villanova University website.

33. Glynn, *High Upon the Gallows Tree*, 127.

34. 'Last letter of Captain Michael O'Brien', *Irishman*, 30 Nov. 1867. This is echoed

in *Ulysses*, where Joyce writes of the 'waters of sorrow', which have made Ireland poignantly beautiful.

35. Ballymacoda & Ladysbridge Community Council, *Historical remains of Bally-macoda and Ladysbridge* (Ballymacoda & Ladysbridge n. d.), 71. This was brought to my attention by Michael O'Brien's relatives.

36. *Nation*, 16 Nov. 1867.

37. Glynn, *High Upon the Gallows Tree*, 112, 104–5; D'Arcy, *The Fenian Movement*, 269–70; Bruce to Stanley, 20 May 1867, FO 5/1341, TNA.

38. By 1861, 805,000 persons of Irish birth had migrated to Britain in search of a better life, settling in Liverpool, London, Glasgow, Edinburgh, Dundee, the Midlands and northern industrial towns, see Roger Swift, 'The outcast Irish in the British Victorian City: problems and perspectives', *IHS*, vol. 25, no. 99 (1987), 264. In 1861, 3.5 per cent of the population of Britain was Irish-born. Glynn, *High Upon the Gallows Tree*, 109–12. Jenkins, *The Fenian Problem*, 94–5; *Irish Times*, 6 Oct. 1867; 4 Nov. 1867; Hawkins & Powell, *The Journal of John Wodehouse*, 212–3.

39. Hawkins & Powell, *The Journal of John Wodehouse*, 213.

40. 'The holocaust', *Irishman*, 23 Nov. 1867. Dr Sigerson was the anonymous author.

41. Set to the Civil War tune 'Tramp, tramp, tramp the boys are marching', it was eventually replaced by the 'Soldier's Song'. Devoy, *Recollections*, 245–6. The present writer remembers that during the campaign to free the Birmingham Six, the Manchester martyrs were being recalled. Execution (of criminals): Fenians executed: Allen, O'Brien and Barrett; application for bodies refused, HO 45/7799, TNA; 'The Holocaust', *Irishman*, 23 Nov. 1867; also in Ken McGilloway, *George Sigerson* (Belfast 2011), 148.

42. *New York Times*, 17 Dec. 1867.

43. Kelly's letter to *Universal News*, *Irish People* (NY), 19 Oct. 1867.

44. *Irish People* (NY), 5 May 1866; *Irish World*, 10 Oct. 1874.

45. *Nation*, 28 Sept. 1867; 30 Nov. 1867; ; 'Letter from Col Kelly', *FJ*, 30 Oct. 1867; *Irish People* (NY), 18 Jan. 1868; 11 Apr. 1868.

46. 'Letter from Col Kelly', *Irish People* (NY), 4 Jan. 1868.

47. Mervyn Busteed, *The Irish in Manchester c. 1750–1921. Resistance, Adaptation and Identity* (Manchester 2016), 224–5; Breandán Mac Giolla Choille, 'Mourning the martyrs', *North Munster Antiquarian Journal* (1967), vol. x, no. 2, 175.

48. *Irishman*, 7 Dec. 1867.

49. Glynn, *High upon the Gallows Tree*, 132; *FJ*, 24 Feb. 1868; R.M. Hort to Larcom, 12 Jan. 1868, Larcom papers, Ms. 7,596; ibid., Wodehouse to Larcom, 8 Jan. 1868; T.D., A.M. & D.B. Sullivan, 'Guilty or not guilty?' Speeches from the dock, or protests of Irish patriotism (Dublin 1868); *Report of the trials of Alexander M. Sullivan and Richard Pigott: for seditious libel on the government* (Dublin 1868), 265–9.

50. *Irishman*, 7 Dec 1867; 14 Dec 1867; *Times*, 11 Oct. 1869; Chase, *Chartism*, 41.

51. *Irishman*, 7 & 14 Dec. 1867; *Irish Times*, 10 Dec. 1867.

52. *Irish Times*, 10 Dec. 1867; *Irishman*, 7 Dec. 1867.

53. Breandàn MacGiolla Choille, 'Mourning the martyrs', *North Munster Antiquarian Journal* (1967), vol. x, no. 2, 176, 180–3. Some years after he intervened to give focus to the Manchester Martyrs' procession in Linerick, Fr Patrick Quaid became

a supporter of Butt's home rule movement. Ignatius Murphy, *The Diocese of Killaloe 1850–1904* (Blackrock 1995), 459.

54. O'Shea, 'David Moriarty (1814–77): III politics', 97; Seán Ó Lúing, 'Aspects of the Fenian Rising in Kerry, 1867, V', *JKAHS* 1974, no. 7 (1974) 116 -8.

55. O'Shea, 'David Moriarty (1814–77): III politics', 98; *Irishman*, 4 July 1868.

56. Peter Berresford Ellis, *A History of the Irish Working Class* (Littlehampton 1972), 140; *Nation*, 30 Nov. 1867; *Irish Times*, 13 Dec. 1867; Quinlivan and Rose, *The Fenians in England*, 77, 82–7, 90.

57. *Times*, 14 Dec. 1867.

58. *Irish Times*, 16 Dec. 1867.

59. Ibid.; 9 Jan. 1868; *Daily Telegraph*, 17 Dec. 1867; *Irish Times*, 2 Jan. 1868; 15 Feb. 1868; 18 Dec. 1867; *Irish People* (NY), 18 Jan. 1868; *FJ*, 6 Jan. 1868; 28 Nov. 1867; Memo, 22 Dec. 1867, Mayo papers, Ms. 43,888/6, NLI.

60. Ryan, *The Phoenix Flame*, 197.

61. Letter from Colonel T.J. Kelly, *Nation*, 21 Dec. 1867; *Daily Telegraph*, 28 Dec. 1867; *Irish People* (NY), 11 Jan. 1868.

62. *Irish People* (NY), 25 Jan. 1868; 7 Mar. 1868; 4 Jan. 1868.

63. *Irish People* (NY), 18 Jan. 1868.

64. Ibid., 4 Jan. 1868; *Nation*, 28 Dec. 1867.

65. *Irish People* (NY), 4 Jan. 1868.

66. Ibid., 'The Clerkenwell explosion', 18 Jan. 1868; *Nation*, 18 Jan. 1868.

67. *Irish People* (NY), 18 Jan. 1868; 'Letter from Colonel Kelly', 4 Jan. 1868; Thomas Allsop, 1858, MEPO 3/27, TNA; Chase, *Chartism*, 299; George Jacob Holyoake, *Sixty years of an agitator's life* (London 1906), vol. i, 91; vol. ii, 19–23, 26–7, 31–2.

68. *Irish People* (NY), 4 Jan. 1868; 25 Jan. 1868; 3 Apr. 1869.

69. *Irish Times*, 2 & 17 Jan. 1868; Chronicle, 20 Dec. 1867; Archbishop Manning, *A Letter to Earl Grey* (London 1868), 4–5, 41.

70. Confidential memorandum & commission for James Murphy, Mayo papers, Ms. 43,888/6, NLI; Jenkins, *The Fenian Problem*, 162–3; Wilson, *Thomas D'Arcy McGee*, vol. ii, 337 ff.

71. Padraic C. Kennedy, 'The Secret Service Department: A British Intelligence Bureau in Mid-Victorian London, September 1867 to April 1868,' *Intelligence and National Security* 18, no. 3 (2003), 111–3; HO 45/7799, TNA.

72. Kennedy, 'The Secret Service Department', 103–7; *Daily Telegraph*, 17 Dec. 1867; J.W. Bazalgette, 21 Dec. 1867, HO 45/7799, part ii, TNA, also 23 Dec. 1867; *FJ*, 7 Oct. 1867. *Reynolds's Newspaper*, 2 Feb. 1868: London was threatened by 'a few tailors on strike, needy artisans, and the like', who struggled to raise a few shillings for the conspiracy.

73. *Irish Times*, 28 Dec. 1867; De Gernon to Mayo, 3 Jan. 1868, Larcom papers, Ms. 7,596, NLI.

74. Kennedy, 'The Secret Service Department', 100–2, 119–20.

75. HO 12/179/81780, TNA; *Irishman*, 2 May 1868; Quinlivan and Rose, *The Fenians in England*, 88–9; Devoy, *Recollections*, 248–9.

76. *Irishman*, 2 May 1868; 6 June 1868; 4 July 1868; 18 Dec. 1875; *Nation*, 28 Nov. 1868. Barrett did not fire the barrel.

77. *Irishman*, 4 Nov. 1865; 28 Sept. 1867; Petition of Andrew Kennedy, HO 12/78700; Licences: Andrew Kennedy, HO 14/30, TNA.
78. *Nation*, 25 Jan. 1868.
79. *Irishman*, 25 Jan. 1868; for his career, see 14 Mar. 1868; O'Donovan Rossa, *Irish Rebels in English Prisons* (Dingle 2001), 188–9; John Boyle O'Reilly, *The Poetry and Song of Ireland* (Kansas City n.d.), 781–2, 778. Tate Britain occupies the site of Millbank Prison.
80. 'The Lines written in Milbank Prison', *Nation*, 1 Jan. 1870.
81. Ryan, *Fenian Memories*, 75–6.
82. *Irishman*, 21 Nov. 1868; O'Leary, *Lays of Country, Home and Friends*, 57, 76. There are parallels between Duffy and Joseph Plunkett: though ill with consumption, both persisted in their revolutionary commitment.
83. O'Leary, *Lays of Country, Home and Friends*, 76.
84. *Times*, 27 Jan. 1868; *Nation*, 25 Jan. 1868.
85. *Irishman*, 23 May 1868; 27 June 1868; *Nation*, 27 June 1868.
86. Walter McGrath, *Evening Echo* (Cork), 1 Jan. 1969; *Irishman*, 5 Dec. 1868. See Appendix I.
87. *Nation*, 30 Apr. 1870; 9 July 1870.
88. Gladstone entry, *A Dictionary of Political Quotations* compiled by Robert Stewart (London 1984).
89. 'The Irish conspiracy by an American Fenian', *Nation*, 29 Feb. 1868; Jenkins, *Gladstone*, 314, 284; Anderson, *Sidelights*, 79; *Irishman*, 18 Apr. 1868.
90. *Irish People* (NY), 11 Apr. 1868.
91. *Irishman*, 18 Apr. 1868; 'Mr Mitchel's letters', *Nation*, 9 May 1868.
92. *Irishman*, 25 Apr. 1868; 18 Apr. 1868.
93. *Irishman*, 25 Apr. 1868; 23 May 1868; 10 Oct. 1868; David Thornley, *Isaac Butt and Home Rule* (London 1964), 55–6, 53.
94. HO 45/9329/19461 part I, TNA.
95. *Irishman*, 28 Nov. 1868; 12 Dec. 1868.
96. *Irish Times*, 13 Nov. 1868; Davitt, *Fall*, 83.
97. *Irish Times*, 13 Nov. 1868. Nolan's dedication to the prisoners earned him his middle name.
98. Sigerson, *Political prisoners*, 76; *Irishman*, 20 Feb. 1869; *FJ*, 30 Sept. 1869.
99. Charles Dickens, *Great Expectations* (Oxford 2008), 210.
100. O'Donovan Rossa, *Irish Rebels in English Prisons* (Dingle 1991), 196–7.
101. Ibid., 197, 200–1. This was Rossa's version of events. *Nation*, 14 Aug. 1869.
102. O'Donovan Rossa, *Irish Rebels in English Prisons* (Dingle 1991), 197–8, 208.
103. Gladstone entry, Robert Stewart, *A Dictionary of Political Quotations*.
104. *Irishman*, 27 Feb. 1869.
105. *Irish Times*, 9 Mar. 1869; *Irishman*, 27 Mar. 1869; Comerford, *The Fenians in Context*, 170.
106. *Irishman*, 20 Mar. 1869; Denieffe, *A Personal narrative*, 9; Maher, *The Valley Near Slievenamon*, 69; *Chief of the Comeraghs*, 105.
107. Amos, *The Fenians in Australia*, 185. C.W. Sullivan (ed.), *Fenian Diary*, 27; Devoy, *Recollections*, 253. Thomas Keneally, the writer, is a cousin of John Kenealy.
108. Amos, *The Fenians in Australia*, 187, 279–80, 194, 277. See Appendix I.

109. *Irishman*, 27 Feb. 1869; *Irish Times*, 9 Mar. 1869.
110. *Irish Times*, 29 Apr. 1869. O'Farrell, a native of Dublin, had been executed. It is unlikely that he was a Fenian.
111. Comerford, *The Fenians in Context*, 170; Quinlivan and Rose, *The Fenians in England*, 68, 171; Deputation to J. Bright, 12 Mar. 1870, HO 45/9331/19461 D, TNA.
112. Letter from McCarthy Downing, *Nation*, 14 Aug. 1869.
113. Ibid.; 7 Aug. 1869.
114. Ibid., 12 June 1869; Devon Commission, BPP 1871 [c. 319] [c. 319–1], 14. Rossa's action has modern parallels: 'some of the more hard-core of the Iraqi prisoners of war had thrown their own faeces and urine' at warders entering their cells in Guantanamo Bay in 2002, Frank Gardner, *Blood and Sand* (London 2007), 300.
115. There must have been a circulation war between Pigott and A.M. Sullivan. The former took care to remind his readers of Sullivan's alleged felon-setting in 1858, while his victim stated: 'It would be a weary task to follow Mr Pigott through the whole of his operations as the literary body-snatcher,' *Nation*, 7 Aug. 1869; Letter from McCarthy Downing, 14 Aug. 1869.
116. *Irish Times*, 28 June 1869; Comerford, *The Fenians in Context*, 174.
117. Davitt, *Fall*, 86; 30 Sept. 1869, Fenian files, 4869 R, NAI; Michael and Liam O'Dwyer, *The Parish of Emly* (Emly 1987), 69. See Appendix I.
118. *Nation*, 13 Nov. 1869; *Irishman*, 16 May 1868; Colman O'Mahony, 'Dominick O'Mahony', address to the O'Mahony Society at unveiling of headstone, 21 June 1993, Cork Central Library. See Appendix I.
119. 4869 R, Fenian files, NAI.
120. Ibid. Cornelius had been detained in Cashel after the Rising.
121. Ibid.; Quinlivan and Rose, *The Fenians in England*, 144, 148.
122. *Nation*, 6 Nov. 1869; Maume, Maume & Casey, *The Galtee Boy*, 145–6.
123. *Nation*, 13 Nov. 1869; *FJ*, 24 Dec. 1869; McConville, *Irish Political Prisoners*, 220. Richard O'Brien, 1809–85.
124. Regan-Lefebvre, *Autobiography of J.F.X. O'Brien*, 130–31; *Nation*, 20 Nov. 1869.
125. *Nation*, 20 Nov. 1869; Regan-Lefebvre, *Autobiography of J.F.X. O'Brien*, 132.
126. Regan-Lefebvre, *Autobiography of J.F.X. O'Brien*, 132–3; *Irishman*, 23 Sept. 1865.
127. List of warrants issued, CSO/ICR/11 HCSA 1866, 133, NAI; Gerard Moran, 'The Fenians and Tipperary Politics, 1868–1880', *THJ* 1994, 74.
128. CO 904/17/110, TNA; Kendal O'Brien', *Times*, 29 Nov. 1909. Here I am indebted to Liam Ó Duibhir. See Appendix I. *Nation*, 27 Nov. 1869.
129. 5297 R, Fenian files, NAI; *Times*, 12 Nov. 1869.
130. Gerard Moran 'The Fenians and Tipperary Politics, 1868–1880', 76.
131. *Nation*, 27 Nov. 1869; 4 Dec. 1869.
132. Ibid., 4 Dec. 1869.
133. Ibid., 11 Dec. 1869; 4 Dec. 1869.
134. Rachel Holmes, *Eleanor Marx: a Life* (London 2014), 98.
135. O'Donovan Rossa, *Irish Rebels in English Prisons* (Dingle 1991), 216–8; *Nation*, 4 Dec. 1869.
136. Hawkins & Powell (eds), *The Journal of John Wodehouse*, 243, 28; John Wodehouse, Camden third series, vol. 90, Royal Historical Society 1963, 10.

137. Moran, 'The Fenians and Tipperary politics, 77–8. Denis G. Marnane, 'Tipperary town one hundred years ago: issues of identity', *THJ* 2002, 172.
138. Marnane, 'Tipperary town one hundred years ago', 171, 173. William Hurley, 1835–99, sheltered Jeremiah J. Finnan after the Rising.
139. Comerford, *Charles J. Kickham*, 114–15; Moran, 'The Fenians and Tipperary politics', 75. This was later revised to thirteen votes.
140. Samuel Lee Anderson to Larcom, 19 Dec. 1869, Larcom papers, Ms. 7,694, NLI.
141. Ibid.
142. Ireland (Fenians): Commission on treatment of treason felony convicts in English prisons, HO 45/9330/19461A, TNA. Lord Devon's benevolence is still remembered in Templeglantine, Co. Limerick, according to the owner of the Devon Arms Hotel.
143. Ibid., John 'Amnesty' Nolan to HO, 7 May 1870.
144. Ibid., Letter from Butt, 2 June 1870.
145. Ibid.; ibid., 27 June 1870.
146. *Times*, 18 July 1870.
147. O'Donovan Rossa, *Irish Rebels in English Prisons* (Dingle 1991), 257, 259–60; Ireland (Fenians): Commission HO 45/9330/19461 A, TNA.
148. Report of the commissioners appointed to inquire into the treatment of treason-felony convicts, BPP 1871 [c. 319] [c. 319-1], 17, 24. For O'Connell, see Appendix I.
149. Ibid., 24–5. The administration was economizing by using convicts to build Woking Female Prison.
150. Ibid., 30, 22, 25.
151. *DPB i*, 1–2; *New York Times*,19 Jan. 1871; Jenkins, *Gladstone*, 321; O'Donovan Rossa, *Irish Rebels in English Prisons*, 276.
152. *FJ*, 6 Oct. 1876; *Times*, 15 Aug. 1877; Thomas Chambers file, HO 45/9324/17871, TNA.
153. Entry for 1873, HO 45/9324/17871.
154. Ibid., entry for 1877.
155. *Irish Times*, 15 Mar. 1875; *Nation*, 20 Mar. 1875. *Nation*, 5 Aug. 1876, when O'Connor Power stated in Parliament that these convictions were obtained by jury-packing and entrapment; *Times*, 5 Mar. 1878; 28 Mar. 1878; 15 Apr. 1878.
156. *FJ*, 3 Sept. 1872. Davitt's sustained interest in penal reform is evident in his testimony before the Kimberley Commission in 1878, see Laurence Marley, *Michael Davitt* (Dublin 2007), 33; Stanford, *That Irishman*, 20; Gerard Mac Atasney, *Tom Clarke* (Sallins 2013), 2.
157. F.S.L. Lyons, *Charles Stewart Parnell* (Dublin 2005), 43.
158. Denvir, *Life Story*, 183–4; McGee, *The IRB*, 54–5; *Irishman*, 21 Nov. 1874; 11 Dec. 1875; 11 & 18 Mar. 1876. See Appendix I.
159. Richard Fawkes, *Dion Boucicault. A Biography* (London 1979), 196–7; poster 'in memory of the Irish Political Prisoners', MEPO 3/3070, TNA.
160. Devoy, *Recollections*, 251–3; *DPB i*, 81; *Irishman*, 3 June 1876. George, Duke of Cambridge, 1819–1904; Amos, *The Fenians in Australia*, 85, mentions seventeen in Australia, but Boyle O'Reilly later escaped.
161. William O'Brien & Desmond Ryan (eds), *Devoy's Post Bag ii* (Dublin 1953), 566.

10. RESURGENCE AND DECLINE, 1868–78

1. Letter to the editor, *Irishman*, 29 Aug. 1868; T.W. Moody & Leon Ó Broin, 'The IRB Supreme Council, 1868–78', *IHS* vol. 19, no. 75, Mar. 1975, 299–300.
2. Ibid., 287–8, 299; *Nation*, 4 July 1868; *Irishman*, 14 Mar. 1868.
3. *Irishman*, 18 Apr. 1868; *Nation*, 18 Apr. 1868; Mayo papers, Ms. 11,189/17, NLI. The *Irish People* (NY) reported the theft of eighteen guns from a Cork armourer on 15 Aug. 1868. *Cork Examiner*, 18 June 1869; 2 July 1869.
4. Moody & Ó Broin, 'The IRB Supreme Council, 1868–78', 302–3, 288.
5. Ibid., 289, 304; 533/S, CBS 1890, NAI.
6. Ibid., 305–6, 309.
7. Michael MacDonagh, *The Home Rule movement* (Dublin & London 1920), 115–16; Moody, *Davitt and Irish Revolution*, 49–50, 53, 138–9; Comerford, *The Fenians in Context*, 166. John O'Connor Power, 1846–1919. Eva O Cathaoir, 'Edmond O'Donovan, Fenian and war correspondent, and his Circle', *Decies, Journal of the Waterford Archaelogical & Historical Society* no. 64 (2008); *Irish Times*, 21 Feb. 1889.
8. MacDonagh, *The Home Rule movement*, 112; Thornley, *Isaac Butt and Home Rule*, 90–1, 55; *Irishman*, 23 Nov. 1867; *DPB i*, 284.
9. *Knocknagow* appeared in the New York *Emerald* in serial form from March 1870. Comerford, *Charles J. Kickham*, 121–2; CO 904/17/151–2, TNA; *Irish Times*, 21 Feb. 1889. The 1871 amnesty obliged O'Leary to remain abroad until 1885. See Appendix I.
10. O'Brien, *Recollections*, 115–6; William O'Brien, *Evening Memories* (Dublin & London 1920), 444, 447.
11. Regan-Lefebvre, *Autobiography of J.F.X. O'Brien*, 129, 138.
12. Moody & Ó Broin, 'The IRB Supreme Council, 1868–78', 306–7.
13. Ibid., 310.
14. CO /904/17/251, TNA.
15. 'Long' John O'Connor, 1850–1928, not to be confused with John O'Connor, a native of County Wicklow, later secretary of the Supreme Council. MacDonagh, *The Home Rule movement*, 207.
16. *Nation*, 25 Dec. 1869; *Irishman*, 1 Jan. 1870; Devoy, *Recollections*, 366–7; John Augustus O'Shea, *Leaves from the life of a special correspondent* (London 1885), vol. ii, 161.
17. Devoy, *Recollections*, 366–7; *Nation*, 8 Jan. 1870; Thornley, *Isaac Butt and Home Rule*, 68.
18. Donnchadh Ó Corráin and Tomás O'Riordan (eds), *Ireland 1815–1870. Emancipation, Famine and Religion* (Dublin 2011), 31; Thornley, *Isaac Butt and Home Rule*, 77–80, 82.
19. Samuel Clark, *Social Origins of the Irish Land War* (Princeton 1979), 214–7 ; *Nation*, 6 Nov. 1869.
20. Ciarán Ó Gríofa, 'John Daly, the Fenian mayor of Limerick', David Lee (ed.), *Remembering Limerick* (Limerick 1997), 199.
21. Thornley, *Isaac Butt and Home Rule*, 98–9, 101, 87–8.

22. Brendan Cahir, 'Isaac Butt and the Limerick by-election of 1871', *North Munster Antiquarian Journal*, vol. x, no. 1 (1966), 60–1.

23. *Times*, 29 Oct. 1865: 'People were shocked, and many were incredulous, when Mr Barry, on the part of the Crown, stated that the plans of the Fenians embraced a general massacre of the owners of property and the Roman Catholic clergy.'

24. Devoy, *Recollections*, 287; *Irishman*, 26 Sept. 1868; 3 Oct. 1868.

25. Cahir, 'Isaac Butt and the Limerick by-election', 59, 56.

26. 'The Kerry "Home Rule" by-election, 1872', *JKAHS* no. 3 (1970), 154–5; *Nation*, 13 Jan. 1872.

27. *Nation*, 10 Feb. 1872; O'Shea, 'David Moriarty (1814–77): III politics', 101.

28. George Rice, 'Kerry's most exciting election', *Kerry Magazine*, Kerry Archaeological and Historical Society, 19 (2009), 20; O'Shea, 'David Moriarty (1814–77): III politics', 102.

29. Lord Kenmare to Lord Hartington, 13 Feb. 1872, Devonshire Papers 340,494, quoted Alan O'Day (ed.), *Reactions to Irish Nationalism* (London 1987), 54.

30. Carla King, *Michael Davitt* (Dublin 2009), xii.

31. *DPB i*, 75–6.

32. Moody & Ó Broin, 'The IRB Supreme Council, 1868–78', 314.

33. This makes the Rising of 1916 illegal; Comerford, *Charles J. Kickham*, 124.

34. Stanford, *That Irishman*, 50–1, 13, 16, 20; William Henry O'Sullivan, *DIB*, vol. 7, 984–5; O'Sullivan was derided as 'Whiskey Sullivan' for his defence of this Irish industry.

35. *DPB i*, 76.

36. Quinn, *John Mitchel*, 84; Fennell & King, *John Devoy's Catalpa Expedition*, 48.

37. 9013R, 3 July 1874, Fenian Files, NAI; *Irish Times*, 18 Feb. 1875; Lyons, *Charles Stewart Parnell*, 36.

38. Quinn, *John Mitchel*, 85–6.

39. Ibid., 86.

40. Herbert L. Sussman, *Masculine Identities: the History and Meaning of Manliness* (Santa Barbara, 2012), 86–7.

41. Denvir, *Life Story*, 125–6; Fenian suspects CSO/ICR/FP; Irish Crime Records, Fenian files, 5225 R, 7216 R, 7229 R, 7691 R; Index of names, 1861–5, CSO/ICR/14, NAI; Moody, *Davitt and Irish Revolution*, 101–2; *Irish Times*, 19 July 1870. See Appendix I.

42. Tomás Ó Siothcháin, 'The IRB raid on Mallow barracks', *Mallow Field Club Journal* no. 20 (2002), 7, 9, 10, 12, 18; according to O'Brien, *Recollections*, 205, James died of tuberculosis, 'murmuring something about the Mallow Bridge and the rifles'; *Irish Times*, 2 Aug. 1871. David Sheehy, *DIB* vol. 8, 886. A similar attempt involving Bandon barracks ended in utter disaster, *Irish Examiner*, 26 June 1873.

43. Regan-Lefebvre, *Autobiography of J.F.X. O'Brien*, 142–3, 137; A 612, Fenian files, NAI; O'Brien, *Recollections*, 116–7. The *Dundalk Democrat*, 6 June 1896, for instance, reported the discovery of five rusty rifles, bayonets and percussion caps under floorboards in Dublin, deposited any time after 1878.

44. Regan-Lefebvre, *Autobiography of J.F.X. O'Brien*, 138–9, 143–4. In 1879 Devoy discovered a similar reluctance to pay subscriptions, A 612, Fenian files, NAI.

45. HO 45/9329/19461 part I, TNA; *FJ*, 29 Mar. 1875; O'Brien, *Recollections*, 118–20; T.H. Ronayne to Devoy, 24 Sept. 1881, *DPB ii*, 101–2.

46. Regan-Lefebvre, *Autobiography of J.F.X. O'Brien*, 140, 143; Charles G. Doran to Devoy, 30 June 1875, *DPB i*, 114.

47. Devoy, *Gaelic American*, 29 Nov. 1924.

48. D'Arcy, *The Fenian Movement*, 297. Roberts was elected to Congress in 1869, lost his fortune in 1873, became US minister to Chile and died in 1897.

49. Henri Le Caron, *Twenty-five Years in the Secret Service: the Recollections of a Spy* (London 1892), 29, 36–8, 58–9.

50. Ibid., 60, 70–1, 73–5; *Report of General John O'Neill, President of the Fenian Brotherhood, on the attempt to invade Canada* (New York 1870), 4–6.

51. Archibald to Larcom, 26 May 1868, Larcom papers, Ms. 7,694; ibid., Const. Murphy, 10 Oct. 1868; 'Fenianism. A narrative by one who knows', *Contemporary Review*, Feb. & Apr. 1872, 640; *Irishman*, 10 Oct. 1868.

52. Michael Ruddy, *America's Irish Nationalists* (forthcoming); *Gaelic American*, 6 Dec. 1924.

53. *Proceedings of the Ninth General Convention of the Fenian Brotherhood* (New York 1870), 6.

54. Sir John Young to Lord Granville, 14 & 28 Apr. 1870; Ottawa, 9 Apr. 1870; *New York Times*, 25 Apr. 1870, Fenian raid on Canada, CO 880/6, TNA.

55. D'Arcy, *The Fenian Movement*, 350–5, 357, 362–3; Le Caron, *Twenty-five Years in the Secret Service*, 31–3; 'Address of General O'Neill', Fenian Brotherhood Collection, CUA; *New York Times*, 25 Apr. 1870; Young to Lord Granville, 26 & 28 May 1870, CO 880/6.

56. 'Address of General O'Neill', who denounced Meehan of the *Irish-American* as 'the evil genius of Fenianism'.

57. *DPB i*, 26–7, 30–1, Boyle O'Reilly to Devoy, 13 Feb. 1871; *Times* (New York), 25 Mar. 1871.

58. *Gaelic American* 6 Dec. 1924.

59. *DPB* i, 32–3; *Irish People* (NY), 30 Sept. 1871. Fitzgerald and Nicholson see Appendix 1.

60. Tenth general convention of the Fenian Brotherhood (New York 1871), CUA.

61. *New York Times*, 13, 16 & 19 Oct. 1871; Le Caron, *Twenty-five Years in the Secret Service*, 98–9. Louis Riel, 1844–85.

62. D'Arcy, *The Fenian Movement*, 385.

63. Ibid., 385–6, 388; Regan-Lefebvre, *Autobiography of J.F.X. O'Brien*, 139–40.

64. *Gaelic American*, 29 Nov. 1924; 22 Dec. 1923; *DPB i*, 97–8. Fr Sheehy, 1841–1917, uncle of Hanna Sheehy-Skeffington and a strong supporter of the Land League, joined both the Clan and the IRB, according to Devoy.

65. Ibid., 114–5, Charles G. Doran to Devoy, 30 June 1875; 130; *Gaelic American*, 6 Dec. 1924.

66. *Irishman*, 11 Dec. 1875.

67. Dr Carroll to Devoy, 24 Jan. 1876, *DPB i*, 131; 8 Feb. 1876, 134.

68. Ibid., Dr Carroll to Devoy, 10 Apr. 1876, 153; *Irishman*, 11 Mar. 1876.

69. *Nation*, 18 Mar. 1876; *DPB i*, 138.

70. Ibid., 139, Dr Carroll to Devoy, 24 Feb. 1876; 144–5.

71. *Nation*, 18 Mar. 1876.
72. *Gaelic American*, 29 Nov. 1924; Comerford, *Charles J. Kickham*, 130–1.
73. *Irishman*, 10 & 24 June 1876; 29 Apr. 1876; *Nation*, 30 Sept. 1876.
74. *Irishman*, 20 May 1876; 24 June 1876.
75. *FJ*, 20 Oct. 1877.
76. *Nation*, 22 Apr. 1876.
77. Ibid.
78. MacDonagh, *The Home Rule movement*, 114. In 1882 McInerney emigrated to the US, where he qualified as a medical doctor. *Nation*, 22 Apr. 1876; *Irish Times*, 18 Apr. 1876.
79. Moody & Ó Broin, 'The IRB Supreme Council, 1868–78', 293–5; Comerford, *Charles J. Kickham*, 132. According to Pigott, Egan had joined the Supreme Council around 1871–2.
80. *FJ*, 20 Oct. 1877.
81. *Nation*, 16 Sept. 1876.
82. Ibid.
83. Ibid., 16 & 23 Sept. 1876; MacDonagh, *The Home Rule movement*, 118.
84. *FJ*, 21 Sept. 1877.
85. Ibid.; MacDonagh, *The Home Rule movement*, 123.
86. MacDonagh, *The Home Rule movement*, 124; *Nation*, 29 Sept. 1877; *FJ*, 21 Sept. 1877.
87. *Nation*, 6 & 13 Oct. 1877.
88. *FJ*, 16 Oct. 1877; 18 Oct. 1877, where P. O'C. MacLoughlin hinted that O'Connor Power was illegitimate (untrue) and a workhouse child, sponsored by charitable people, whose political convictions he betrayed.
89. *Nation*, 27 Oct. 1877.
90. Carla King (ed.), *Michael Davitt: Jottings in Solitary* (Dublin 2003), 156.
91. Lyons, *Charles Stewart Parnell*, 49–51; Davitt, *Fall*, 108–9.
92. *DPB ii*, 568. The men serving life are named below, excepting Delany. Ibid., James Wilson to Devoy, 15 June 1874, 566–7. See Appendix I.
93. Fennell & King, *John Devoy's Catalpa Expedition*, 43, 52, 15–20; 23. After Breslin had been instrumental in the escape of Stephens from Richmond prison in 1865, he was nicknamed 'the Liberator'. See Appendix I.
94. Amos, *The Fenians in Australia*, 203, 220, 228, 230–1; *DPB i*, 219–220.
95. CO 904/17/58, TNA; Amos, *The Fenians in Australia*, 222; *Irish Times*, 21 Feb. 1889; Letter from John Walsh, 21 Dec. 1876, *DPB i*, 221–2; Amos, *The Fenians in Australia*, 225.
96. Amos, *The Fenians in Australia*, 233–4; Fennell & King, *John Devoy's Catalpa Expedition*, 102–5.
97. They included Anthony John Mundella, 1825–97, prominent Liberal MP for Sheffield, who attained cabinet rank; Samuel Plimsoll, 1824–98, who campaigned to make British shipping safer; Henry Fawcett, 1833–84, blinded in an accident, Liberal MP for Brighton, radical supporter of John Stuart Mill, Gladstone's postmaster general and husband of Millicent Garrett Fawcett; John Bright, 1811–91, MP for Manchester and Birmingham, a Quaker champion of religious liberty, who served in Gladstone's governments. *DPB i*, 173.

98. *Irishman*, 17 June 1876; *DPB i*, 173–4.

99. *DPB i*, 168; Obituary, *New York Herald*, 4 & 6 Nov. 1876; Devoy, *Recollections*, 157.

100. *New York Herald*, 6 Nov. 1876; register of 1st Calvary Cemetery, Queens, New York, which records Devoy as owner of Foley's grave; there is no headstone.

101. Archibald to Lord Derby, 27 Feb. & 9 Mar. 1877, FO 5/1599, TNA.

102. *Brooklyn Eagle*, 7 Feb. 1877. I am grateful to Dr Sayers for sharing his research.

103. *Irish World*, 17 Feb. 1877.

104. *New York Times*, 25 Feb. 1877; Personal Recollections of O'Mahony, *Irishman*, 10 Mar. 1877.

105. *Irishman*, 3 Mar. 1877; Obituary, *Brooklyn Eagle*, 7 Feb. 1877.

106. Archibald to Lord Derby, 27 Feb. 1877, FO 5/1599, TNA; *Brooklyn Eagle*, 7 Feb. 1877; *Nation*, 18 Mar. 1876.

107. *New York Times*, 9 Mar. 1877.

108. Ibid., 25 Feb. 1877.

109. Ibid.

110. *New York Times*, 9 Mar. 1877; 25 Feb. 1877; Recollections of O'Mahony, *Irishman*, 10 Mar. 1877. Dr Mulcahy had not been O'Mahony's regular physician.

111. *DPB i*, 252, 237, Dr Carroll to Devoy, 27 Feb. 1877.

112. *Brooklyn Eagle*, 14 Feb. 1877; 13 Aug. 1883; *Irish-American*, 24 Feb. 1877; *New York Times*, 12 Feb. 1877.

113. *Nation*, 17 Feb. 1877; *Irish Times*, 21 Feb. 1889. Sexton became a Parnellite MP, while Leavy was convicted of embezzlement and turned informer.

114. *Nation*, 24 Feb. 1877.

115. *New York Times*, 25 Feb. 1877.

116. *Nation*, 17 Feb. 1877.

117. Ibid., 24 Feb. 1877; *New York Times*, 26 Feb. 1877.

118. *Nation*, 3 Mar. 1877; *New York Times*, 26 Feb. 1877.

119. *Nation*, 3 Mar. 1877.

120. Ibid.; 24 Feb. 1877; *FJ*, 30 Oct. 1877.

121. *Nation*, 10 Mar. 1877.

122. *DPB i*, 234.

123. *New York Times*, 19 Mar. 1877. In Republican tradition those who suffer for Ireland have no need of clergy.

124. *Irishman*, 10 Mar. 1877. From the eponymous oratorio by Handel (1738). See Appendix I & II.

125. Dr Carroll to Devoy, 24 Oct. 1877, *DPB i*, 274; *New York Times*, 6 Jan. 1884; *Nation*, 29 Mar. 1884.

126. *DPB i*, 251–2.

127. *Irishman*, 9 Mar. 1878.

128. *Nation*, 19 Jan. 1878.

129. *Irishman*, 9 Mar. 1878.

130. *Nation*, 19 Jan. 1878.

131. Fr F. McCormack 'Voices from the past' (pamphlet), St Teresa's Church, Clarendon St, Dublin. Davitt, who made the arrangements, was so impressed by the Carmelites' tact that he booked them for his own funeral.

132. *Irish Times*, 16 & 17 Jan. 1878.

133. Fr F. McCormack 'Voices from the past'.

134. Letter from Archbishop of Cashel, *Nation*, 26 Jan. 1878.

135. Quoted Mark Tierney, *Croke of Cashel* (Dublin 1976), 91.

136. Thomas Chambers to Boyle O'Reilly, 18 Feb. 1878, *DPB i*, 304; Inquiry as to the alleged ill-treatment of the convict Charles McCarthy, BPP 1878 [c. 1978], 12.

137. *Irishman*, 2 Feb. 1878; Register of suspects, vol. 2, CO 904/18/817, TNA; Moody, *Davitt and Irish Revolution*, 201, 206. See Appendix I.

138. *Nation*, 9 & 23 Feb. 1878; 14 Sept. 1878; *Times*, 5 & 28 Mar. 1878; 15 Apr. 1878. Whitehall gave the US minister in London a negative reply re Condon Meagher, 6 July 1877, FO 55/1599, TNA.

139. *Nation*, 21 Sept. 1878. Devoy, *Recollections*, 247, claimed that Melody, a bad character, was convicted after boasting of his involvement. This gave him a patriotic reputation, which he later used for questionable financial transactions. Newspaper reports suggest psychological problems. *Times*, 8 & 15 Nov. 1878. Ahearn's heath was so poor that he was allowed to return to Ireland. Appendix I.

140. *DPB i*, 303; Chambers to Devoy, 28 Dec. 1885, *DPB ii*, 269–70; Roche, *Life of John Boyle O'Reilly*, 56.

141. Roche, *Life of John Boyle O'Reilly*, 328.

11. DYNAMITERS, LAND LEAGUERS AND THE RISE OF PARNELL, 1878–84

1. Le Caron, *Twenty-five Years in the Secret Service*, 102–3; *DPB i*, 316–7; *Irish World*, 4 Mar. 1876.

2. *Irish World*, 19 Sept. 1874; 10 Oct. 1874; 4 Dec. 1875; Whelehan, *The Dynamiters*, 76.

3. Whelehan, *The Dynamiters*, 139, 141–3, 145–8; 300; Shane Kenna, *War in the Shadows: the Irish-American Fenians who Bombed Victorian Britain* (Dublin 2014), 10, 15–6; Jeremiah O'Donovan Rossa, *Irish Rebels in English Prisons* (New York 1882), v.

4. Rossa, *Irish Rebels in English Prisons*, iii. This supplementary chapter summarizes Rossa's columns in the *Irish World*.

5. Ibid., vi, iii; *Irish World*, 4 Mar. 1876; *FJ*, 6 Apr. 1883.

6. Editorial, *Irish World*, 4 Mar. 1876.

7. Ibid., 25 Mar. 1876; McCafferty to O'Donovan Rossa, 27 Mar. 1876, Fenian Brotherhood Collection, CUA. See Appendix I.

8. *DPB i*, 251–2; *Irishman*, 1 Apr. 1876; O'Leary to Devoy, 28 Apr. 1876, *DPB i*, 161; *FJ*, 6 Apr. 1883; *Cork Examiner*, 28 Jan. 1885.

9. Rossa to Thomas Francis Bourke, undated, *DPB i*, 323.

10. Ibid., Devoy to ?, 1 Mar. 1876, 143; ibid., Dr Carroll to Devoy, 29 Mar. 1876, 151.

11. Robert Anderson, Home Office, 30 Mar.1881, Reports, Feb. 1881–Feb. 1884, Sir Robert Anderson Papers, HO 144/1537/1, TNA; *Irish World*, 21 Apr. 1877.

12. Davitt, *Fall*, 429, 432–3; Rossa to 'Skirmishing Fund' trustees, July 1880, *DPB i*, 540; *Brooklyn Eagle*, 8 July 1880.

13. Lyons, *Charles Stewart Parnell*, 36, 38–9, 44–7; O'Kelly to Devoy, 5 Aug. 1877,

DBP i, 267. Devoy's childhood friend, also referred to as J.J. O'Kelly.

14. Ibid., 21 Aug. 1877, 270; Donal McCartney & Pauric Travers (eds), *Words of the Dead Chief: Charles Stewart Parnell compiled by Jennie Wyse Power* (Dublin 2009),15–6; R. Barry O'Brien, *The Life of Charles Stewart Parnell* (London 1910), 82–3.

15. Dr Carroll to Devoy, 24 July 1906, *DPB i*, 298; Davitt, *Fall*, 125.

16. *DPB i*, 370; Le Caron, *Twenty-five Years in the Secret Service*, 145.

17. *FJ*, 11 Oct. 1878; Legg, *Webb*, 44–6; Robert Ensor, *England 1870–1914* (London 1968), 55; Llewellyn Woodward, *The Oxford History of England. The Age of Reform 1815–1870* (London 1962), 621–2.

18. *DPB i*, 384; Devoy, *Recollections*, 314.

19. *DPB i*, 401; ibid., Dr Carroll to Devoy, 16 Nov. 1879, 281; Lyons, *Charles Stewart Parnell*, 77–8, 118–9.

20. Ó Broin, 'The IRB Supreme Council, 1868–78', *IHS* vol. 19, no. 75, Mar. 1975, 293& 323; Dr Carroll to Devoy, 19 Jan. 1878, *DPB i*, 296; 12 Feb. 1878, 300; 27 Apr. 1876, 157.

21. Ó Broin, 'The IRB Supreme Council, 1868–78', 323; CO 904/17/151–2, TNA; Denieffe, *A Personal Narrative*, 151–2.

22. *Gaelic American*, 6 Dec. 1924.

23. Dr Carroll to Devoy, 4 Nov. 1878, *DPB i*, 367–8; ibid., *ii*, McInerney to Devoy, 12 July 1886, 285.

24. Ibid., *i*, 296, 384; A 612, Fenian files, NAI.

25. A 612, Fenian files.

26. Ibid.; *Weekly Irish Times*, 9 Feb. 1889.

27. A 612, Fenian files; Andrew Cook, *M: MI5's First Spymaster* (Stroud 2006), 56, Millen resumed spying in 1885; *DPB i*, 426–7.

28. Dr Carroll to Devoy, 16 Nov. 1879, *DPB i*, 279–80; A 612, Fenian files.

29. Devoy to James Reynolds, 24 Feb. 1879, *DPB i*, 406; Devoy report, Ms. 18,039, NLI; A 612.

30. Davitt described Harris as 'a local leader of conspicuous ability', *Fall*, 158; Patrick Egan, 163–4; P.W. Nally and John O'Kane, 147; O'Connor Power, 146; P.J. Sheridan, see Moody, *Davitt and Irish Revolution*, 312; Robert Johnson, 278. Only Johnston did not join the Land League.

31. Devoy's claim in 1879, that professionals and business people had joined the IRB, was exaggerated somewhat. A 612, Fenian files.

32. Lyons, *Charles Stewart Parnell*, 74–5; *FJ*, 17 Oct. 1878; 3 Dec. 1878.

33. Davitt, *Fall*, 141–2; Warwick-Haller, *William O'Brien and the Irish Land War*, 29–32.

34. Warwick-Haller, *William O'Brien and the Irish Land War*, 32.

35. Ibid., 33.

36. Davitt, *Fall*, 171, 160, 168–71, 193.

37. CO 904/17/103, TNA.

38. Ibid. These Clunes were the traditional Ribbon leaders in the Tulla district. John died in New York in 1920. O Cathaoir, 'The Irish Republican Brotherhood in Clare 1858–1871', 452–3.

39. Davitt to Devoy, 16 Dec. 1880, *DPB ii*, 21–2: 'Fitz is still distinguishing himself by inciting opposition to the Rival House [Land League]', getting 'the boys' to collapse the platforms in Clonmel and Athlone. Doran, CO 904/17/151, TNA.

40. *FJ*, 9 &10 July 1889.
41. Bourke, *John O'Leary*, 162, 199; Comerford, *Charles J. Kickham*, 212.
42. C.H. Rolleston, *Portrait of an Irishman* (London 1939), viii.
43. Dr Carroll to Devoy, 26 May 1876, *DPB i*, 170: O'Leary 'thinks all at home are frauds and imbeciles while here there is but little honesty and no capacity. He sees no hope for the cause and favours leaving it to future generations.' Ibid., Boyle O'Reilly to Devoy, 2 Aug. 1880, 545.
44. Ibid., Dr Carroll to Devoy, 16 Nov. 1879, 280; Dr Carroll to Patrick Mahon, 30 Mar. 1878, 325; *Gaelic American*, 23 June 1923.
45. O'Kelly to Devoy, 11 Feb. 1880, *DPB i*, 488–9.
46. Devoy, *Recollections*, 344; Le Caron, *Twenty-five Years in the Secret Service*, 153; *DPB ii*, 83; Warwick-Haller, *William O'Brien and the Irish Land War*, 18, 63; T.H. Ronayne to Devoy, 24 Sept. 1881, *DPB ii*, 101–2.
47. Ó Broin, *Revolutionary Underground: the Story of the Irish Republican Brotherhood, 1858–1924* (Dublin 1976), 20–1; Austin Stack, *DIB*, vol. 8, 1103; J.S. Casey, *DIB*, vol. 2, 411; Michael Power, CSORP 1881/1221, NAI; CO 904/17/129, TNA; Comerford, *Charles J. Kickham*, 173. See Appendix I.
48. Lyons, *Charles Stewart Parnell*, 124–5, 133–5, 140–1.
49. Le Caron, *Twenty-five Years in the Secret Service*, 135; Kenna, *War in the Shadows*, 14–5.
50. Whelehan, *The Dynamiters*, 207; Robert Anderson to Sir W. Vernon Harcourt, 30 Mar. 1881, Robert Anderson Papers, HO 144/1537/1, TNA.
51. Le Caron, *Twenty-five Years in the Secret Service*, 198; Mackey Lomasney to Devoy, 16 Dec. 1880, *DPB ii*, 25; 24 Dec. 1880, 27; 4 Jan. 1881, 31–2.
52. Le Caron, *Twenty-five Years in the Secret Service*, 100–2; Mackey Lomasney to Devoy, 24 Nov. 1880, *DPB ii*, 16–7; Devoy, *Recollections*, 211–2; 'Report of trial committee', Devoy papers, Ms. 18,019; Whelehan, *The Dynamiters*, 61.
53. Letter from Webb, *FJ*, 21 Oct. 1878; O'Donovan Rossa, *Irish Rebels in English Prisons*, iii.
54. O'Donovan Rossa, *Irish Rebels in English Prisons*, iii.
55. South Africa, the Cape mounted yeomanry, HC Deb 27 June 1879 vol 247 cc837–8.
56. South Africa, the Zulu War, HC Deb 12 June 1879 vol. 246 cc1708–18; Supply – army [estimates] HC deb 16 June 1879 vol 246 cc1919-2027; Report on operations involving use of dynamite, 1879, WO 32/7788, TNA.
57. Quinn, *Young Ireland*, 125–6.
58. John Mitchel, introduction, *The History of Ireland from the treaty of Limerick to the present time* (Glasgow & London n.d.).
59. *Brooklyn Eagle*, 14 Apr. 1883.
60. K.R.M. Short, *The Dynamite War* (New Jersey 1979), 50, 55, 64–5, 68; Mackey Lomasney to Devoy, 23 Feb. 1881, *DPB ii*, 44.
61. Mackey Lomasney to Devoy, 23 Feb. 1881, *DPB ii*, 45; ibid., Mar. 1881, 51–2; Devoy's *Recollections*, 212.
62. *FJ*, 9 July 1881.
63. Robert Anderson to Sir W. Vernon Harcourt, 29 Mar. 1881, Robert Anderson Papers, HO 144/1537/1, TNA; Le Caron, *Twenty-five Years in the Secret Service*, 193.
64. Le Caron, *Twenty-five Years in the Secret Service*, 187, 198–9, 192, 188–9.

65. Ibid., 62–5. Alexander Sullivan, 1847–1913.

66. Gillian O'Brien, *Blood Runs Green: The Murder that Transfixed Gilded Age Chicago* (Chicago 2015), 15–6, 57, 121; Le Caron, *Twenty-five Years in the Secret Service*, 191.

67. *DPB i*, 470–1; Letter from general military board of the Clan to S.C., IRB, 23 Dec. 1877, 288–90; 'Patrick Ford', *Gaelic American*, 23 June 1923; *New York Times*, 29 & 30 July 1881.

68. Ian Kenneally, *Courage and Conflict* (Cork 2009), 172–4; *DPB i*, 470.

69. *DPB ii*, 9; CO 904/17/130, TNA; Le Caron, *Twenty-five Years in the Secret Service*, 139.

70. *Irish Times*, 19 June 1882; 8 July 1882.

71. Liam Ó Sé, 'Gun-running in 1882', *The Other Clare*, vol. 29 (June, 2005), 67–8; HO 144/84/A7323 B Ireland – Fenians: conviction of Thomas Walsh, TNA; *Irish Times*, 10 Aug. 1882.

72. Davitt, *Fall*, 321; Lyons, *Charles Stewart Parnell*, 165–6.

73. Lyons, *Charles Stewart Parnell*, 169–70; Davitt, *Fall*, 335–40, 348.

74. Davitt, *Fall*, 356, 359.

75. Ibid., 357–9, 371–2, 377; *DPB ii*, 178; Le Caron, *Twenty-five Years in the Secret Service*, 207–8; Moody, *Davitt and Irish Revolution*, 536–7; Carla King, *Michael Davitt After the Land League* (Dublin 2016), 26–7; *New York Times*, 9 May 1882.

76. Short, *The Dynamite War*, 81–3. Sir Henry Brackenbury, *Some Memories of my Spare Time* (Edinburgh & London 1904), 312; Christopher Brice, 'The military career of General Sir Henry Brackenbury: the thinking man's soldier 1856–1904', PhD thesis, De Montfort University 2009, 145–7.

77. Richard Hawkins, 'Government versus secret societies: the Parnell era', T. Desmond Williams (ed.), *Secret Societies in Ireland* (Dublin 1973), 105; Short, *The Dynamite War*, 86-8.

78. Comerford, *Charles J. Kickham*, 173–5; James J. O'Kelly to Devoy, 21 Sept. 1882, *DPB ii*, 142.

79. *DPB ii*, 141.

80. Ibid., 142.

81. *Reynolds's Newspaper*, 10 Feb. 1895; Lindsay Clutterbuck, 'The evolution of counter terrorism methodology in the Metropolitan Police from 1829 to 1901', PhD thesis (Portsmouth University 2001), 218–9, 199.

82. Bernard Porter, *Plots and Paranoia: a History of Political Espionage in Britain 1790–1988* (London 1992), 104; *Reynolds's Newspaper*, 10 Feb. 1895. The hard-working Adolphus Frederick ('Dolly') Williamson, 1830–89, a protégé of Jonathan Whicher, the leading detective of the 1850s, was 'a quiet, middle-aged man' who rejected new methods. Something of an innocent abroad, he failed to notice that several senior officers were in league with white-collar criminals in 1877, which culminated in the scandal of the 'trial of the detectives'.

83. *DPB i*, 316, 318; *New York Times*, 28 Aug. 1882; 4 Sept. 1882; 14 Aug. 1884; 9 Dec. 1881; 8 Apr. 1883; Memorandum on John Daly, 27 Jan. 1885, CAB 37/14 1885 No. 5, TNA.

84. Short, *The Dynamite War*, 134. Tom Clarke was the son of Mary Palmer, a Protestant of Clogheen, Co. Tipperary, while his father James Clarke had joined the British army in 1847. Tom emigrated to the US from Dungannon, Co. Tyrone,

where he was the IRB 'centre', after shooting at the constabulary, which had attacked a Catholic procession, killing an unarmed civilian. For Curtin Kent, see Appendix I.

85. Ibid., 130–2; John D. McCarthy to O'Donovan Rossa, 9 Sept. 1883, *DPB ii*, 205; 'Scotland Yard. Its mysteries and methods', *Reynolds's Newspaper*, 24 Feb. 1895; *New York Times*, 14 Sept. 1894; Arthur Dowling, 'The forgotten Fenian', *The Avondhu*, 21 Dec. 2000.
86. Short, *The Dynamite War*, 148–9; *Irish Times*, 7 May 1883; *Brooklyn Eagle*, 14 Apr. 1883, explained they were being taught by the ubiquitous Professor Mezzeroff and gave the recipe for nitroglycerine. Dynamite 'is put into a freezer just like ice cream ... as easily made as ice cream' – 'an invention of heaven ... to help the poor man the world over to gain his freedom'.
87. Anderson to Home Secretary, 20 June 1883, Robert Anderson Papers, HO 144/1537/1, TNA.
88. *Brooklyn Eagle*, 13 & 26 Aug. 1883; *New York Times*, 31 Aug. 1883; Davitt, *Fall*, 429.
89. Devoy, *Recollections*, 240; *Irish Times*, 31 Mar. 1883; *Brooklyn Eagle*, 13 Aug. 1883. I am indebted to Jan Furtado, Featherstone's kinswoman, for tracing his origins.
90. Davitt, *Fall*, 431; *Irish Times*, 31 Mar. 1883; 7 Apr. 1883; *Nenagh Guardian*, 29 Feb. 1868.
91. *Nation*, 13 July 1889; *Irish Times*, 10 July 1889; *Brooklyn Eagle*, 13 Aug. 1883.
92. Davitt, *Fall*, 430–1; *Brooklyn Eagle*, 13 & 26 Aug. 1883.
93. *Irish Times*, 7 Apr. 1883; Queen v. Denis Deasy and others,30 July 1883, Assi 52/5, TNA.
94. Assi 52/5; Short, *The Dynamite War*, 151–2; *Nation*, 24 May 1884; 29 Nov. 1884; *New York Times*, 9 Aug. 1883; *Brooklyn Eagle*, 26 Aug. 1883.
95. *New York Times*, 25 Sept. 1890; 'Scotland Yard. Its mysteries and methods', *Reynolds's Newspaper*, 10 Mar. 1895.
96. *Brooklyn Eagle*, 13 Aug., 1883; Home Gordon, *The reminiscences of an Irish land agent being those of S.M. Hussey compiled by Home Gordon* (London 1904), 225–6.
97. *Brooklyn Eagle*, 13 Aug., 1883; The growth and prevention of crime in the district of Castleisland, HO 144/72/A19, TNA.
98. HO 144/72/A19; Home Gordon, *The reminiscences of an Irish land agent*, 237–9; *Brooklyn Eagle*, 7 Dec. 1884.
99. Robert Anderson to Harcourt, 30 Oct. 1883, c) Reports to secretary of state, Feb. 1881 – Feb. 1884, HO 144/1537/1, TNA; ibid.; Letter (unsigned), 29 Oct. 1883; Mary Noon Kasulaitis, 'A Fenian in the desert: Captain John McCafferty and the 1870s Arivaca Mining Boom', *Journal of Arizona History*, vol. 47, no. 1 (Spring 2006), 48; McCafferty to Devoy, 2 Oct. 1883, *DPB ii*, 212–3. See Appendix I.
100. Davitt, *Fall*, 434–7; *New York Times*, 11 Mar. 1884. See Appendix I.
101. *Nation*, 5 July 1884; Ryan, *The Fenian Chief*, 341. Patrick Casey, *DIB*, vol. 2, 413.
102. James Joyce, *Ulysses* (New York 1961), 43–4; Colm O Lochlainn, *Irish Street Ballads* (London 1984), 145, 'The Boys of Kilkenny'.
103. 'Scotland Yard. Its mysteries and methods', *Reynolds' Newspaper*, 10 & 17 Mar.

1895; *Irish Times*, 1 Sept. 1883; Davitt, *Fall*, 432; *Weekly Irish Times*, 5 May 1883.
104. Le Caron, *Twenty-five Years in the Secret Service*, 217–8; John Daly to John J. Breslin, 14 Feb. 1884, CAB 37/14 1885 No. 5, TNA. James Egan, 1839–1909.
105. 26 Jan. 1885, CAB 37/14 – 1885 No. 4, TNA; *Pall Mall Gazette*, 10 Mar. 1884; *New York Times*, 22 Apr. 1884; Home Gordon, *The reminiscences of an Irish land agent*, 235.
106. *DPB ii*, 242–3. Tom McDermott, O'Neill's son-in-law, had been Breslin's courier to Daly and a close associate of William McGuinness of the Supreme Council. After Daly's conviction, McDermott, unable to overcome IRB suspicions, succumbed to alcoholism.
107. 27 Jan. 1885, CAB 37/14 1885 No. 5.
108. *Nation*, 29 Mar. 1884; 5 Apr. 1884.
109. Ibid., 8 Aug. 1885; Davitt, *Fall*, 471. Jenkinson had Nally's trial relocated to obtain a convicting jury. By January 1884, he had spent £2725 on Crown witnesses and £6500 on general information, see O. McGee, 'Dublin Castle and the first Home Rule Bill: the Jenkinson – Spencer correspondence', *History Ireland* 5, vol. 15 (Sept./Oct. 2007).
110. *Glasgow Herald*, 14 Apr. 1884; *Irish Times*, 15 Apr. 1884; *Weekly Irish Times*, 19 Apr. 1884.
111. *Irish Times*, 15 Apr. 1884; 8 Nov. 1884; Secret Memorandum, Sept. 1890, CO 904/16, TNA. Sweeney died in 1892.
112. *Irish Times*, 4 Nov. 1884 revealed that Sweeney also used the names 'Philip Swan' and 'James Swan'; 'The Tubbercurry conspiracy case', 6 Nov. 1884; *Times*, 14 Nov. 1884.
113. *Nation*, 19 Apr. 1884; *Irish Times*, 15 Apr. 1884; *Weekly Irish Times*, 19 Apr. 1884.
114. *Pall Mall Gazette*, 12 Apr. 1884; *Weekly Irish Times*, 19 Apr. 1884; McGee, 'Dublin Castle and the first Home Rule Bill: the Jenkinson – Spencer correspondence'; *Glasgow Herald*, 14 Apr. 1884.
115. *Irish Times*, 15 Apr. 1884; 10 Sept. 1884; *Nation*, 8 Nov. 1884; Case of Mrs P.N. Fitzgerald, 26 June 1884 vol. 289 c 1405, House of Commons debates; *New York Times*, 11 May 1884; 1 June 1884; *Irish Times*, 26 Apr. 1884.
116. *New York Times*, 1 June 1884; 11 May 1884; 4 Nov. 1884. Ó Ríordáin, *P.N. Fitzgerald*, 23; *Irish Times*, 4 Nov. 1884.
117. *Nation*, 31 May 1884; Ó Broin, *The Prime Informer*, 76–7. Delaney later testified for the *Times* Commission; *Weekly Irish Times*, 8 Nov. 1884; *Nation*, 8 Nov. 1884.
118. *Irish Times*, 8 Nov. 1884; *Weekly Irish Times*, 15 Nov. 1884. By 1887, Dublin Castle had spent at least £500 on the emigration of informer John Moran to British Columbia, HO 144/162/A41646, TNA.
119. *Times*, 14 Nov. 1884; *Nation*, 13 Dec. 1884; Ó Ríordáin, *P.N. Fitzgerald*, 28–30.
120. *Nation*, 29 Nov. 1884.
121. O'Brien, *Blood Runs Green*, 42; *DPB ii*, 8–9; *New York Times*, 26 Apr. 1886.
122. *Times*, 24 Apr. 1886; Ireland–Fenians: Dynamite outrage at London Bridge, 1884–1891, HO 144/145/A38008, TNA.
123. W.B. Yeats, *Autobiographies*, 210.

12. LIVES OF THE INFORMERS, 1859–1908

1. *Irishman*, 4 Nov. 1865 recorded that Andrew Kennedy shook with fright in this position and his heels audibly drummed on the table, similar to Peter Carey, 'brother of James the immaculate', *Flag of Ireland*, 21 Apr. 1885.

2. Padraic Kennedy, 'The indispensable informer: Daniel O'Sullivan Goula and the Phoenix Society, 1858–59', *Eire-Ireland* 45, no. 3/ 4 (Autumn/Winter 2010), 148–52; Thomas Bartlett, 'Informers, informants and information', *History Ireland*, issue 2 (Summer 1998), vol. 6.

3. Kennedy, 'The indispensable informer', 152–8.

4. Frederick Moir Bussy, *Irish Conspiracies: recollections of John Mallon, the great Irish detective, and other reminiscences* (London 1910), 32.

5. Ibid., 38; Robert Johnson, *Spying for the Empire: the Great Game in Central and South Asia, 1757–1947* (London 2006), 81.

6. Kennedy, 'The Secret Service Department', 3–4, 6.

7. Ibid., 111, 113–5, 118, 120; Le Caron, *Twenty-five Years in the Secret Service*, 36–7. Hozier was probably the father of Clementine Churchill.

8. Gavan Duffy, *My Life in Two Hemispheres*, vol. ii, 278.

9. His original name was Herrmann Schoenfeld. A 7, Fenian files; ibid., 6954 R, NAI.

10. Ibid.; *Irish Times*, 6 Dec. 1865; *Irishman*, 2 Dec. 1865.

11. *Irishman*, 6 Jan. 1866; 6954 R, Fenian files, NAI. For Power, see Appendix I.

12. 6954 R, Fenian files.

13. Ibid., 8 Nov. 1870.

14. Ó Lúing, 'Aspects of the Fenian Rising in Kerry, 1867, I', 151; 'Aspects of the Fenian Rising in Kerry, 1867, II', 157–8; Daniel Cronin Coltsman and Thomas Gallwey, Killarney, 20 July 1867, Mayo papers, Ms. 11,189/10, NLI.

15. Mayo papers, Ms. 11,189/10 & 17.

16. Jenkinson, Activities of informants, 1892–1910, HO 317/38, TNA.

17. *Irishman*, 7 Oct. 1865; 27 Jan. 1866; O'Mahony on Fenianism, 4 Apr. 1868; 9 Dec. 1865; 30 Sept. 1865; CSORP 1865/7556, NAI; Larcom papers, Ms, 7,517, NLI.

18. *Irishman*, 4 Apr. 1868; *Nation*, 23 Nov. 1867. Mulleda was tried with O'Sullivan Burke for gun-running. He was amnestied in 1871.

19. *Nation*, 30 May 1868; 23 Nov. 1867; *Times*, 1 June 1868; 19 Nov. 1867.

20. *Times*, 18 Nov. 1867.

21. Ibid., 19 Nov. 1867; Special accounts, CO 904/6, TNA; Anderson to attorney general, 22 Sept. 1867, Official correspondence, Larcom papers, Ms. 7,596, NLI.

22. *Irishman*, 13 June 1868; *Nation*, 9 Nov. 1867; 'John Joseph Corydon', *Irish Times*, 6 Nov. 1867. The informer used 'Corridon'. Corridons with red hair still live in Kerry, according to Tom Casey, Ballyheigue. 'Corydon' is a shepherd in classical poetry.

23. *Irishman*, 3 Aug. 1867; Denvir, *Life Story*, 86; FamilySearch online resources, NLI.

24. *Irish Times*, 12 Feb. 1868; 19 July 1870; Michael H. Kane, 'American soldiers in Ireland, 1865–67', *The Irish Sword*, vol. 23, no. 91, 118; O'Mahony on Fenianism, Irishman, 4 Apr. 1868.

25. *Times*, 18 July 1870; 7 Nov. 1867; Bussy, *Irish Conspiracies*, 36.

26. *Times*, 7 Nov. 1867; 29 Apr. 1867; 7 May 1868; 4 Mar. 1868; *FJ*, 6 Nov. 1867; Head Const. McHale, Liverpool, 10 & 11 Feb. 1867, Robert Anderson Papers, HO 144/1537/1, TNA.

27. Denvir, *Life Story*, 85; *Nation*, 4 May 1867.

28. *Irish Times*, 2 Sept. 1867; *Irishman*, 1 Aug. 1868.

29. Case of Col Kelly, HO 45/7799, part II, TNA; *Times*, 29 Apr. 1867; Patrick Condon to T.J. Kelly, 13 Aug. 1866, Fenian Brotherhood Collection, CUA. Patrick Condon/ Massey is not to be confused with Patrick Joseph Condon, an honourable Fenian.

30. A Southern Fenian informant to Stephens, 20 Oct. 1866, Fenian Brotherhood Collection, CUA.

31. Ibid., Patrick Condon to P.J. Downing, 6 Jan. 1866.

32. Case of Col Kelly, HO 45/7799, part II; *Times*, 29 Apr. 1867; *Irish Times*, 1 May 1867.

33. Robert Anderson, *The lighter side of my official life* (London 1910), 18; *Sidelights on the Home Rule movement* (London 1906), 71.

34. Samuel Lee Anderson to attorney general, 22 Sept. 1868, Larcom papers, Ms. 7,596. Sir Samuel Lee Anderson, 1837–86, was dead by the time Robert's reminiscences appeared. Sir Robert Anderson, 1841–1918.

35. Ibid.

36. CSORP 1867/10079; CSORP 1867/10256, NAI; *Nation*, 4 May 1867.

37. *Times*, 29 Apr. 1867.

38. *Nation*, 4 May 1867.

39. http://hansard.millbanksystems.com/commons/1910/apr/21/sir-robert-anderson-and-the-times-1. The *Nation* agreed, 4 May 1867.

40. Report of R.M. Goold, Waterford, 14 June 1867, Précis of police reports, 1867, Robert Anderson Papers, HO 144/1537/1, TNA; *Times*, 17 June 1867; *FJ*, 18 June 1867.

41. *Irish Times*, 12 June 1867.

42. Ó Broin, *Fenian Fever*, 16; *Irishman*, 25 Apr. 1868.

43. http://www.waterfordcountymuseum.org/exhibit/web/Display/article/135/5/.

44. 'Nation, 15 Feb. 1868; *Irish People* (NY), 6 Feb. 1869.

45. Melbourne *Advocate*, quoted Amos, *The Fenians in Australia*, 274.

46. Devoy, *Recollections*, 59, 74; *Irish Times*, 20 Sept. 1865; 12 Oct. 1865; Denieffe, *A Personal Narrative*, 44–5; O'Leary, *Recollections*, vol. i, 95.

47. Ó Broin, *Fenian Fever*, 222; *Weekly Irish Times*, 1 Mar. 1884.

48. *Irish Times*, 8 Jan. 1866; 22 May 1866; 15 June 1866.

49. CSORP 1866/17567, NAI.

50. Ibid.

51. Devoy, *Recollections*, 239–40; Barry Kennerk, *Shadow of the Brotherhood: the Temple Bar Shootings* (Cork 2010), 33, 186.

52. *Times*, 30 Sept. 1867; 8 Oct. 1867; *Pall Mall Gazette*, 3 Mar. 1884; 26 Nov. 1867, HO 12/176/79701, TNA.

53. John Walsh, 1842–82, a native of Co. Kildare, married to Mary Fraser, youngest sister of Letitia Luby, was acquitted of the attempted assassination of an informer in 1868 and emigrated to US in 1875, where he died.

54. Kennerk, *Shadow of the Brotherhood*, 136, 139–140, 296–7, 299–301; Ó Broin, *Fenian Fever*, 223. See Appendix I for E. O'Donovan's involvement.

55. CBS 3/715/1, NAI; *FJ*, 22 Mar. 1883.

56. *Nation*, 23 Nov. 1867.

57. *Irishman*, 20 June 1868.

58. Ó Duinnin, 'A boycotted family', *The Avondhu*, 23 May 2002. The name of the actual informer is known locally.

59. Anderson, *The lighter side*, p.162; Ó Broin, *Fenian Fever*, 201; 'Capt. William Sweetman', *Southern Star*, 21 Sept. 1901.

60. Pierce Nagle to Larcom, 24 July 1866, CSORP 1866/14212, NAI.

61. Ibid.; CSORP 1866/20355, NAI; CO 904/6 Special accounts, TNA. £250 in 1867 is the equivalent of 150,000 today, see measuringworth.com.

62. 'Pierce Nagle', *Irishman*, 12 July 1873; *FJ*, 30 June 1873; 1 July 1879; *Times*, 7 July 1873; Pigott, *Personal Recollections*, 375; Census 1871 (England): 'Thomas Percival Kennedy'; Special accounts, CO 904/6.

63. Irishman, 20 June 1868; he had stolen from a constable, but the government prevented Ward's prosecution; 'however, it oozed out'.

64. Moody & Ó Broin, 'The IRB Supreme Council, 1868–78', *IHS* vol. 19, no. 75, Mar. 1975, 304, 289.

65. Letter from 'Slievenamon', *Irishman*, 26 Jan. 1878; *Nation*, 25 Nov. 1871; P440 Head Const. Talbot, special accounts, CO 904/6, TNA.

66. McHugh, *Trial*, vi–viii; *FJ*, 9 Nov. 1871; *Nation*, 15 & 22 July 1871; Pigott, *Personal Recollections*, 369; *Irish Times*, 13 & 17 July 1871; Sir William Wilde was among the surgeons summoned.

67. McHugh, *Trial*, ix, 71; Terence de Vere White, *The Road of Excess* (Dublin 1946), 254–5; *Irishman*, 28 Nov. 1874; Fintan Cullen & R.F. Foster, *Conquering England. Ireland in Victorian London* (London 2005), 20.

68. Special accounts, CO 904/6; Dublin Castle to A. Liddell, 8 & 12 Dec. 1868, CO 906/33, TNA.

69. Quinlivan and Rose, *The Fenians in England*, 128; Miscellaneous correspondence, 1867–1886, MEPO 3/3070, TNA; CSORP 1875/8334, NAI. This John Devany is not to be confused with a namesake, who turned informer during the trial of P.N. Fitzgerald in 1884.

70. Larcom to Sir James Ferguson, 15 June 1868, CO 906/33 – 1868, TNA.

71. Captain John Warneford Armstrong, a notorious *agent provocateur*, who had betrayed the Sheares brothers, received £461 p.a., living near Ballycumber, Co. Offaly, until 1858, denounced as 'Sheares Armstrong'. Special accounts, CO 904/6, TNA; *FJ*, 8 Mar. 1853; W.J. Fitzpatrick, *The Sham Squire; and the informers of 1798* (Dublin 1872), 226.

72. Special accounts, CO 904/6.

73. Ibid.

74. Ibid.

75. *Times*, 12 & 14 Oct. 1869; T.H.R. Cashmore, *The Mystery of Thomas Haydon Green: the Whitton Murder and the Cato Street Conspiracy* (Twickenham 1972), 13. It has not been possible to establish which of these two informers he was.

76. Census 1871 (England) Henry Johnson, Kyezor Place, Whitton, Twickenham, Middlesex, born Scotland about 1841, married to Mary, a native of Ireland, born about 1847. I am indebted to James Marshall, Local Studies Collection, Hounslow

Library, Middlesex, and Carol Davies Foster, Local Studies, Richmond-upon-Thames, Surrey.

77. *Times*, 14 Oct. 1869; 12 Apr. 1875, CSORP 1875/8334, NAI.

78. 15 & 13 May 1875, CSORP 1875/8334.

79. Cashmore, 'The mystery of Thomas Haydon Green', 2; *Nation*, 27 Sept. 1879; Census 1881 (England), Henry Johnson, Englefield Green, Egham, Surrey, courtesy Local Studies, Richmond-upon-Thames, Surrey.

80. Lindsay Clutterbuck, 'The evolution of counterterrorism methodology in the Metropolitan Police from 1829 to 1901, with particular reference to the influence of extreme Irish nationalist activity', Phd thesis (Portsmouth University 2001), 209; Special accounts, CO 904/6.

81. Patrick Foley, CSORP 1866/22285, NAI.

82. CSORP 1866/22285; Devoy, *Recollections*, 157; Special accounts, CO 904/6.

83. Gertrude Massey to Robert Anderson, Special accounts, CO 904/6; *Pall Mall Gazette*, 3 Mar. 1884.

84. Tom Corfe, *The Phoenix Park Murders: Conflict, Compromise and Tragedy in Ireland, 1879–1882* (London 1968), 187–8, 137–8, 141; Mary Noon Kasulaitis, 'A Fenian in the desert: Captain John McCafferty ', 47–9; 'John Walsh is dead', *New York Times*, 7 Mar. 1891. Kickham considered the Invincibles 'Fenians seduced by the Land League'.

85. McCracken, *Inspector Mallon*, 66, 86–7, 82; J.L. McCracken, 'The fate of an infamous informer', *History Ireland*, vol. 9 no. 2 (Summer 2001), 26; Corfe, *The Phoenix Park* Murders, 138–9; *Irish Times*, 21 Feb. 1889; *Irishman*, 26 Jan. 1878.

86. McCracken, *Inspector Mallon*, 88, 92–5, 97, 102–3.

87. Ibid., 108–9, 110–2, 114.

88. J.L. McCracken, 'The fate of an infamous informer', 27–9; McCracken, *Inspector Mallon*, 112; *Weekly Freeman*, 5 May 1883.

89. McCracken, *Inspector Mallon*, 125; Death of informer J. O'Loughlin, 9144/S 1892; Corfe, *The Phoenix Park* Murders, 255; *Flag of Ireland*, 16 May 1885.

90. CBS 1890, 1416/S, NAI; McGee, *The IRB*, 192–3.

91. Gosselin to Balfour, 22 Nov. 1887, Correspondence from Nicholas Gosselin to A.J. Balfour, T. Browning and Sir Matthew White Ridley, Home Secretary, PRO 30/60/13/2, TNA; Register of suspects, vol. 1, CO 904/17/351; Owen McGee, 'Keeping the lid on an Irish revolution: the Gosselin – Balfour correspondence', no. 6 (Nov. – Dec. 2007), vol. 15, *History Ireland*; *Belfast News-Letter*, 11 July 1889; Southwestern division: histories of J. Slattery, P.N. Fitzgerald & P.J. Hoctor, CBS 1890, 1128/S.

92. McGee, 'Keeping the lid on an Irish revolution'.

93. *FJ*, 28 Sept. 1894; 13 Aug. 1865; 12 Sept. 1890.

94. 16 Jan. 1887, Personnel of the Supreme Council, 1887–90, CBS 1890 533/S, NAI; Histories of J.C. Forde, Cork, F.B. Dineen etc., CBS 1892, 5483/S; CO 904/17/259, TNA.

95. *FJ*, 9 Mar. 1897; 21 June 1897; *Times*, 15 Sept. 1910; *Irish Times*, 23 Oct. 1900; *Weekly Irish Times*, 27 Oct. 1900; . Several of his controversies featured in the press. Hoctor, his mother and the typist continued to live together in 1901.

96. Register of suspects, vol. 2, CO 904/18/609.

97. Gosselin to Sir Matthew White Ridley, 7 Oct. 1896, PRO 30/60/13/2.

13. TOWARDS AN ALTERNATIVE REALITY, 1884–1908

1. Quoted Peter Hart (ed.) *British Intelligence in Ireland, 1920–21, The Final Reports* (Cork 2002), 97.
2. O'Brien, *The Life of Charles Stewart Parnell*, 317–8; Eugene J. Doyle, *Justin McCarthy* (Dublin 2012), 23, 35–6; Jenkins, *Gladstone*, 509–13; Lyons, *Charles Stewart Parnell*, 285.
3. Jenkins, *Gladstone*, 534–7; Lyons, *Charles Stewart Parnell*, 288–9, 351–2; Jenkinson to Spencer, 24 Sept. 1884; Stephen Ball (ed.), *Dublin Castle and the First Home Rule Crisis: the Political Journal of Sir George Fottrell, 1884–1887* (London 2008), 13, 29–30, 212; Ó Corráin and O'Riordan (eds), *Ireland 1815–1870*, 31–2.
4. James McConnel, 'Fenians at Westminster: The Edwardian Irish Parliamentary Party and the Legacy of the New Departure', *IHS*, vol. xxxiv, no. 133 (May, 2004), 42; Regan-Lefebvre, *Autobiography of J.F.X. O'Brien*, 145–6. O'Brien died MP for South Mayo in 1905. Jeremiah Condon, c. 1825–1908, whose son, Thomas, 1850–1943, remained the representative for Tipperary East until 1918. Harold Begbie, *The Lady Next Door* (Dublin 2006), xxiii; O'Brien, *Recollections*, 123–4; Register of suspects, vol. 1, CO 904/17/110 -1, TNA.
5. Begbie, *The Lady Next Door*, xxiii; Rolleston, *Portrait of an Irishman*, 50–1; Porter, *William Monsell*, 53–4.
6. Frank Callanan, *The Parnell Split 1890–91* (Cork 1992), 249; *Irish Times*, 10 July 1889; *FJ*, 10 July 1889; Lyons, *Charles Stewart Parnell*, 255.
7. Register of suspects, vol. 1, CO 904/17/151, TNA; IRB demonstration in Cork, CBS June 1890, 631/S, NAI.
8. Report of trial committee, Ms. 18,019 Devoy papers, NLI. A leading example was Luke Dillon, Philadelphia, born of Irish parents in 1850, who caused an explosion in the Commons. In 1900 Dillon was convicted of bombing the Welland Canal in Canada to hamper the British war effort against the Boers. Jenkinson also knew much about Captain Mackey, another dynamiter: CAB 37/14 – 1885 no. 4; Le Caron, *Twenty-five Years in the Secret Service*, 231–2.
9. Le Caron, *Twenty-five Years in the Secret Service*, 219–20; Memorandum on the organisation of the United Brotherhood, CAB 37/14 – 1885 no. 4, TNA; William O'Mulcahy to Devoy, 28 Dec. 1884, *DPB ii*, 258.
10. CAB 37/14 – 1885 no. 4; Devoy, *Recollections*, 392.
11. Richard Bennett to O'Donovan Rossa, 16 Dec. 1885, Fenian Brotherhood collection, CUA; Le Caron, *Twenty-five Years in the Secret Service*, 254; William O'Mulcahy to Devoy, 3 Apr. 1885, *DPB ii*, 261; Report of trial committee, Devoy papers, Ms. 18,018, NLI; *Gaelic American*, 10 Nov. 1923.
12. 'Michael Hogan's tribute', *Gaelic American*, 26 Dec.1908. See Appendix I. *Irish Times*, 6 Jan. 1887.
13. Consul Hoare to Lord Salisbury, 20 May 1887, Fenian Brotherhood, vol. 47, 1887–8, FO 5/2044; Letter McInerney to Devoy, 21 June 1887, Ms. 18,007/32/9; Le Caron, *Twenty-five Years in the Secret Service*, 220, 232. Cronin was born in Buttevant in 1846.
14. *DPB ii*, 233.

15. Consul Hoare to Lord Salisbury, 20 May 1887, Fenian Brotherhood, vol. 47, 1887–8, FO 5/2044, TNA; ibid., vol. 48, FO 5/2359, 1889–97, TNA.

16. Attempted revivals, see IRB in Cork in 1890, CBS 631/S, NAI; John Barry of Inagh in west Clare in 1896, Register of suspects, vol. 1, CO 904/17/59, TNA; Jeremiah Dunne, Carrigdrohid, chairman of the Macroom poor law guardians, to re-establish the local 'circle' in 1905. P.N. Fitzgerald asked William Lee of Newport and Michael Maher of Ballykinalee to revive the IRB in Newport, Co. Tipperary, Crime Special Branch, RIC, Apr. & Aug. 1905, CO 904/117, TNA; Register of suspects, vol. 1, CO 904/17/251; FJ, 28 Sept. 1886.

17. Progamme of YIS, 1884, Henry Dixon papers, Ms. 35,262/26, NLI; Quinn, Young Ireland, 129; FJ, 10 Mar. 1882; 28 Mar. 1882; Register of suspects, vol. 1, CO 904/17/1, TNA.

18. 20 June 1884, Progamme of YIS, Henry Dixon papers, Ms. 35,262/27, NLI; Nation, 2 Sept. 1882; 29 Aug. 1884, Minute book of YIS, Dublin, 1881–4, Ms. 16,095, NLI.

19. Nenagh Guardian, 18 Dec. 1909; 3 Dec. 1910; 30 Sept. 1881, Minutes of YIS, 1881–4, Ms. 16,095, NLI; CO 904/16/302, TNA; See Appendix I.

20. O'Brien, The Life of Charles Stewart Parnell, 318–9; 22 Oct. 1885, Minute book of YIS, 1885–6, Ms. 19,158; Young Ireland Society, Branches in Ireland and Scotland 188?, William O'Brien papers, Ms. 15,690, NLI.

21. Nation, 19 Sept. 1885; 27 Sept. 1884.

22. Ibid., 21 Mar. 1868; 28 Nov. 1868; 21 Sept. 1883 meeting & 29 Feb. 1884, Minute book of YIS, Dublin, 1881–4, Ms. 16,095; Frederick J. Allan and W.P. Barden to Devoy, 8 Nov. 1883, DPB ii, 221.

23. Irish Times, 18 Dec. 1885; Tierney, Croke of Cashel, 200; Nation, 18 June 1887; 3 Nov. 1883; 17 Nov. 1888; 11 Aug. 1888.

24. Unveiling of Lavin Memorial, 8 Sept. 1901, CBS 25302/S, NAI.

25. Hogan, 1828–99, wrote: 'Here lies one who loved his country well / And in her sacred cause untimely fell,' Nation, 5 Nov. 1870. Catholic clergy also blocked such monuments.

26. Nation, 28 Nov. 1885; 7 Aug. 1869; 19 July 1884; Weekly Irish Times, 28 Nov. 1885. Inscription in St Patrick's Graveyard, Kilkenny.

27. Irish Times, 26 Nov. 1888; History of suspects W. G. Fisher, Waterford, and P.J. O'Keeffe, Kilkenny, CBS 5404/S, NAI.

28. Gavan Duffy, My life in two hemispheres, vol. ii, 353–4.

29. Weekly Irish Times, 24 Jan. 1885; Bourke, John O'Leary, 174.

30. Times, 25 Aug. 1885; Bourke, John O'Leary, 177-8.

31. Letter from Luby to O'Leary, autumn 1885, O'Leary papers, Ms. 5,926, NLI.

32. Devoy's Recollections, 299; John O'Leary, What Irishmen should know. A lecture delivered at Cork, February 1886; How Irishmen should feel. Lecture delivered at Newcastle-on-Tyne (Dublin 1886), 9–11.

33. Bourke, John O'Leary, 184–5; Rolleston, Portrait of an Irishman, 17, 22.

34. O'Leary, What Irishmen, 5–9; 'Young Ireland: the old and the new', inaugural address to the Young Ireland Society (Dublin 1885), 10, 12; Bourke, John O'Leary, 228.

35. O'Leary, What Irishmen, 3, 5–6.

36. Half-yearly general meeting, 31 July 1885; & meeting of 30 Oct. 1885, Minute book of the Young Ireland Society, York St, Dublin, 1885–6, Ms. 19,158. Oldham and Rolleston, graduates of TCD, were founders of the *Dublin University Review*. Taylor, a talented orator and barrister, is mentioned in *Ulysses*.

37. *Weekly Irish Times*, 24 Jan. 1885; *New York Times*, 2 Feb. 1885.

38. Katharine Tynan, *Twenty-five years: Reminiscences* (London 1913), 131. Allan Wade (ed.), *The Letters of W.B. Yeats* (London 1954), 872.

39. Bourke, *John O'Leary*, 182–3, 192–3; Gonne MacBride, *A Servant of the Queen*, 84–7; Ken McGilloway, *George Sigerson*, 61; Wade, *The Letters of W. B. Yeats*, 109–10, 127–8, 139; *Nation*, 23 Nov. 1889.

40. Princess Edward of Saxe Meiningen, wife of commander of British army in Ireland. *Irish Times*, 3 Nov. 1888; 10 Nov. 1888; Gonne MacBride, *A Servant of the Queen*, 84, 89, 90–1; Davitt, *Fall*, 438–9; James O'Connor, HC Deb 26 Mar. 1897 vol. 47 cc1486-504, http://hansard.millbanksystems.com.

41. Gonne MacBride, *A Servant of the Queen*, 85; Adrian Frazier, *The Adulterous Muse. Maud Gonne, Lucien Millevoye and W.B. Yeats* (Dublin 2016), 66–7; *Irish Times*, 17 Oct. 1900.

42. *Irish Independent*, 27 Feb. 1933; 8 July 1933; Letter to editor, *Irish Press*, 29 May 1933; Shane O'Shea, *Death and Design in Victorian Glasnevin* (Dublin 2000), 167–8.

43. O'Shea, *Death and Design*, 168.

44. J.W. O'Beirne, a co-founder of the National Graves Association (1926), was one of two surviving NMC members, *Irish Press*, 27 Nov. 1933.

45. Marcus Bourke, *The GAA: a History* (Dublin 2000), 8, 28; Patrick William Nally, 1855–91, *DIB*, vol. 6, 852; Séamus Ó Riain, *Maurice Davin (1842–1927)* (Dublin 1994), 34; W.F. Mandle, 'The IRB and the beginnings of the GAA', *IHS*, vol. 20, no. 80, Sept. 1977, 419.

46. Bourke, *The GAA*, 13–4; Marcus Bourke, 'J.K. Bracken centenary: a reflection', *THJ* 2004, 263; Marie O'Neill, *From Parnell to de Valera: a Biography of Jennie Wyse Power* (Dublin 1991), 29–31; Mandle, 'The IRB and the beginnings of the GAA', 420. J.K. Bracken, 1852–1904, was the father of Brendan Bracken, protégé of Winston Churchill.

47. Register of suspects, vol. 1, CO 904/17/35; Connection between the GAA and the IRB, 17 Nov. 1887, CBS 12 Apr. 1890, 126/S.

48. *Nation*, 28 Nov. 1885; *FJ*, 16 Apr. 1889; McGee, *The IRB*, 85; Bourke, *The GAA*, 24; Ó Ríordáin, *P.N. Fitzgerald*, 37–8.

49. Register of suspects, vol. 2, CO 904/18/707; ibid., CO 904/18/955; Austin Stack, 'centre' for Kerry since 1908, *DIB*, vol. 8, 1103; CO 904/18/746.

50. Register of suspects, vol. 1, CO 904/17/103; Myles Dungan, *The Captain and the King* (Dublin 2009), 237.

51. *FJ*, 28 Sept. 1886; *Irish Times*, 26 July 1887; Patrick Hoctor, *DIB*, vol. 4, 733.

52. *FJ*, 27 July 1887; Bourke, *The GAA*, 28–31; Register of suspects, vol. 1, CO 904/17/351; Connection between the GAA and the IRB, 17 Nov. 1887, CBS 1890, 126/S, NAI; *Weekly Irish Times*, 31 Dec. 1887.

53. CBS 12 Apr. 1890, 126/S; CO 904/16/279, TNA.

54. Mark Tierney in *Irish Times*, 1 Sept. 1984; 2 Apr. 1888.

55. Le Caron, *Twenty-five Years in the Secret Service*, 235–6; Lyons, *Charles Stewart Parnell*, 353–4; O Broin, 'Revolutionary nationalism in Ireland: the IRB, 1858–1924', T.W. Moody (ed.) *Nationality and the Pursuit*, 113.

56. F.S.L. Lyons, *Ireland Since the Famine* (London 1971), 178–9; *Charles Stewart Parnell*, 371–5, 456; Jenkins, *Gladstone*, 553–6.

57. *Gaelic American*, 17 Nov. 1923; Sergeant Robb, 16 Jan. 1887 & Major Gosselin to RIC, 28 Jan. 1887, CBS 1890, 533/S, NAI.

58. Report of trial committee, Devoy papers, Ms. 18,018, NLI; Le Caron, *Twenty-five Years in the Secret Service*, 258–61. Sullivan served as head of the Irish National League of America from Apr. 1883. Although no longer Clan president, his successor Michael Boland acted as his proxy.

59. Le Caron, *Twenty-five Years in the Secret Service*, 260–3, 294–5; O'Brien, *Blood Runs Green*, 66–7; 30 June & 4 July 1888, FO 5/2044/317, TNA. The leaders had promised Mackey 'that his family would never want'.

60. 7 Apr. 1910, PRO HO 144/926/A49962, TNA; Le Caron, *Twenty-five Years in the Secret Service*, 269; O'Brien, *Blood Runs Green*, 70–1; *New York Times*, 12 Mar. 1894. Le Caron remained under guard in London, where he died in 1894.

61. O'Brien, *Blood Runs Green*, 195; *DPB ii*, 310. Three insignificant Clan members, Daniel Coughlin, Martin Burke and Patrick O'Sullivan, were sentenced to life. Coughlin was acquitted after retrial; *New York Times*, 17 July 1894. Sullivan became US ambassador for Chile. British consul, Chicago, to Lord Salisbury, 4 Dec. 1890, FO 5/2359, TNA.

62. 7 Apr. 1910, PRO HO 144/926/A49962, TNA; Ó Broin, *The Prime Informer*, 64; *Nation*, 24 Mar. 1889; Thomas J. Clarke, *Glimpses of an Irish Felon's Prison Life* (Cork 1970), 24–5, 54.

63. Porter, *Plots and Paranoia*, 112–3. Clarke first met Daly as an organizer in Ulster in 1878. Lyons, *Charles Stewart Parnell*, 434–9.

64. Luby to O'Leary, 7 Jan. 1887, O'Leary papers, Ms. 5,926, NLI.

65. Ibid., Luby to O'Leary, 13 Oct. 1889.

66. Porter, *Plots and Paranoia*, 108, 104–5; *Times*, 24 Apr. 1886; *Reynolds's Newspaper*, 10 Mar. 1895; *Pall Mall Gazette*, 15 Mar. 1884; PRO 30/6/62, TNA.

67. *Pall Mall Gazette*, 25 Feb. 1886; 8 Jan. 1887; Nicholas Gosselin, 7 Oct. 1896, PRO 30/60/13/2, TNA.

68. Ireland – Fenians: conviction of Fenians, HO 144/136/A35496C, TNA; *Times*, 24 Sept. 1890; Memorandum, 22 June 1885, HO 144/721/110757.

69. *Times*, 24 Sept. 1890; *Reynolds's Newspaper*, 4 Aug. 1895; Gonne MacBride, *A Servant of the Queen*, 148–9; *Times*, 24 Apr. 1886.

70. The amnesty movement, CO 904/16/413.

71. Register of suspects, vol. 2, CO 904/18/610. Afterwards Jones was banned from visiting Daly, who believed himself poisoned on purpose. *Irish Times*, 17 Mar. 1890.

72. *Irish Times*, 17 Mar. 1890; Register of suspects, vol. 1, CO 904/17/151; The amnesty movement, CO 904/16/413, TNA; *FJ*, 30 June 1890; 1 Sept. 1890.

73. Gosselin, 11 Apr. 1890, PRO 30/60/13/2.

74. Ibid.; Report on the Clan na Gael, 16 Apr. 1890, CBS 249/S, NAI.

75. Secret Memorandum, CO 904/16; The organisation of the United Brotherhood, CAB 37/14/4, TNA.

76. Jordan, *Kitty O'Shea*, 171; Lyons, *Charles Stewart Parnell*, 504–6, 521, 552–3, 574; Callanan, *The Parnell Split*, 246–9; Bourke, *John O'Leary*, 204.

77. Callanan, *The Parnell Split*, 77; Kilkenny election, CBS 1890, 2267/S, NAI; Wyse Jackson & Costello, *John Stanislaus Joyce*, 153; *Irish Times*, 25 Apr. 1896; *Nation*, 15 Nov. 1890. See Appendix I.

78. A brother of James Boland, Dublin, and uncle of Harry.

79. Quoted Lyons, *Charles Stewart Parnell*, 566.

80. Callanan, *The Parnell Split*, 67; 16 Dec. 1890, CBS 2220/S; Kilkenny election, CBS 1890, 2267/S, NAI; Lyons, *Charles Stewart Parnell*, 568; King, *Michael Davitt*, 315; Barry O'Brien to John O'Leary, 15 Mar. 1891, O'Leary papers, Ms. 5,927, NLI. The Parnellite candidate lost by 1165 votes, followed by defeats in North Sligo and Carlow.

81. Nationalist Organisations, 1890–3, CO 904/16/303, TNA.

82. Bourke, *John O'Leary*, 205; Register of suspects, vol. 2, CO 904/18/746; Register of suspects, vol. 1, CO 904/17/103; Register of suspects, vol. 2, CO 904/18/746.

83. Callanan, *The Parnell Split*, 244–5; The amnesty movement, CO 904/16/413.

84. *Irish Times*, 6 Apr. 1891; Davitt, *Fall*, 471: Nally 'died in prison when nearing the end of his sentence' in 1891. Register of suspects, vol. 1, CO 904/17/351.

85. http://hansard.millbanksystems.com/commons/1891/jul/27/class-iii;*FJ*,1Oct.1891; McConville, *Irish Political Prisoners*, 380.

86. The amnesty movement, CO 904/16/413, TNA; 5786/S, CBS 1892, NAI; *Times*, 8 Nov. 1892, HO 144/194/A46664C, TNA.

87. Jenkins, *Gladstone*, 606, 616, 601; Robert Ensor, *England 1870–1914*. Oxford History of England (Oxford 1992), 220–1, 381.

88. Figures for 1893, CBS 7928/S, NAI.

89. 12 Dec. 1892, CBS 5996/S; 15 Nov. 1894, CBS 9246/S, NAI. Mallon's experience went back to the 1860s.

90. CBS 31 July 1894, 8806/S; CBS 1904, 29274/S. This split is confusing; IRB leaders who joined the INA fudged the issue in their memoirs.

91. *New York Times*, 28 Sept. 1894; 'Dr Clarke', CBS 1894, 9273/S, NAI.

92. *New York Times*, 27 Sept. 1895; 18 Nov. 1895, Correspondence and memoranda from Nicholas Gosselin to A.J. Balfour, T. Browning and Sir Matthew White Ridley, Home Secretary, PRO 30/60/13/2, TNA.

93. 18 Nov. 1895, Correspondence and memoranda from Nicholas Gosselin, PRO 30/60/13/2; ibid., Gosselin to Sir Matthew White Ridley, 7 Oct. 1896.

94. Ibid., 18 Nov. 1895.

95. Ibid.; CBS 10819/S, NAI.

96. Unity between IRB and INB, CBS 1895, 11067/S; 13 Nov. 1895, Amnesty split in Limerick between Fitz & Hoctor, CBS 1895, 10819/S, NAI.

97. Register of suspects, vol. 1, CO 904/17/64; Ó Broin, *Revolutionary Underground*, 74.

98. Register of suspects, vol. 1, CO 904/17/109; 5786/S, CBS 1892, NAI; *Nation*, 27 June 1896 & 25 July 1896.

99. *Reynolds's Newspaper*, 4 Aug. 1895; 3 Mar. 1895. This is confirmed by official documentation: Ireland – Fenians: Treason felony. Seven cases, 1883–1893, HO 144/116A26493, TNA; 'Scotland Yard', *Reynolds's Newspaper*, 10 Mar. 1895.

100. Thomas J. Clarke, *Glimpses*, 13.

101. Ibid., 14, 16. They had arrived in Birmingham in March 1883 with Tom Clarke among this team.

102. Ibid.,16–7; Summary of prisoners' health, HO 144/195/A46664D; http://hansard. millbanksystems.com/commons/1891/aug/03/second-reading; *Brooklyn Eagle*, 20 June 1895; 6 Apr. 1896; 18 May 1896; Letter from Foreign Office to Home Office, 28 Oct. 1892, HO 144/116 A26493.

103. *Brooklyn Eagle*, 7 Oct. 1895; HO 144/116 A26493; Summary of prisoners' health, HO 144/195/A46664D; ibid., 29 July 1896; *Brooklyn Eagle*, 6 Sept. 1896; *New York Times*, 5 Sept. 1896.

104. 2 Sept. 1896, case of A. Whitehead, medical reports, HO 144/195/A46664D; *Brooklyn Eagle*, 11 Sept. 1896; *New York Times*, 8 & 19 Sept. 1896. Dr Gallagher died in 1925.

105. Kathleen Clarke, *Revolutionary Woman* (Dublin 1991), 19–21.

106. *New York Times*, 12 Sept. 1896.

107. Ibid.; Precis of medical reports, HO 144/195/A46664D; Ó Broin, *Revolutionary Underground*, 87.

108. Clarke, *Revolutionary Woman*, 21; Karen Steele (ed.), *Maud Gonne's Irish Nationalist Writings, 1895–1946* (Dublin 2004), 10; *FJ*, 12 Jan. 1897; Ms. 33,576, NLI.

109. Clarke, *Revolutionary Woman*, 21–2; Devoy, *Gaelic American*, 8 Nov. 1924. Probably Treacy of Gibbinstown, Appendix I.

110. Ibid; Anna MacBride White and A. Norman Jeffares (eds), *Always your friend. The Gonne–Yeats letters 1893–1938* (London 1993), 79; *New York Times*, 25 Oct. 1897.

111. MacBride White and Jeffares, *The Gonne-Yeats letters*, 80; W.B. Yeats, *Autobiographies*, 353–4; Gosselin to HO, 20 Nov. 1900, Miss Maud Gonne CO 904/202/166 pt. A, TNA; Gonne MacBride, *A Servant of the Queen*, 180, 186–7.

112. McConville, *Irish Political Prisoners, 403–4*; Clarke, *Revolutionary Woman*, 24, 26–7; MacBride White and Jeffares, *The Gonne–Yeats letters*, 107; Mac Atasney, *Tom Clarke*, 51.

113. 'Maud Gonne', *Gaelic American*, 8 Nov. 1924; CBS 4 Aug. 1899 19717/S, NAI; Ó Broin, *Revolutionary Underground*, 95.

114. Confidential reports, Feb. – July 1898, CO 904/68, TNA.

115. *FJ*, 15 July 1897; Confidential reports, Feb. – July 1898, CO 904/68; Gonne MacBride, *A Servant of the Queen*, 270.

116. Gonne MacBride, *A Servant of the Queen*, 269; Feb. 1896, Register of suspects, vol. 2, CO 904/18/818; 18 Dec. 1900, 23634/S, NAI.

117. Ó Broin, *Revolutionary Underground*, 86; Marnane,'Tipperary town one hundred years ago: issues of identity', *THJ* 2002, 184; *Southern Star*, 23 Apr. 1898.

118. Confidential report, May 1898, CO 904/68, TNA.

119. *Southern Star*, 21 May 1898; Confidential report, May 1898, CO 904/68, TNA; Ó Ríordáin, *P.N. Fitzgerald*, 56. An eternal light burns in memory of Michael Lonergan, John Shinnick and John Casey 'shot to death in Mitchelstown on the 9th September 1887' to this day. See Appendix I, Felix O'Neill.

120. Confidential reports, Feb. to July 1898, CO 904/68; William O'Brien, *Who fears to speak of ninety-eight?* (Dublin 1898), 31–2.

121. *Southern Star*, 20 Aug. 1898; Ó Broin, *Revolutionary Underground*, 90; Owen McGee, 'Frederick James Allan (1861–1937), Fenian & civil servant', *History Ireland* (Spring 2002).

122. The foundation stone was removed during the 1930s. President de Valera unveiled a statue of Tone nearby in 1967, which was blown up by Loyalist paramilitaries in 1971, but later restored.

123. Orlaith Mannion, '"Silent but eloquent reminders": the nationalist monuments in Cork and Skibbereen', Laurence M. Geary (ed.), *Rebellion and Remembrance*, 185; Mathúin Mac Fheorais, 'J.K. Bracken – the Kilrush Connection', *Clare Association Yearbook 2011*.

124. Ó Broin, *Revolutionary Underground*, 92; Confidential report, May 1898, CO 904/68.

125. Bulmer Hobson, 1883–1969, *DIB*, vol. 4, 726; Dr Patrick McCartan, 1878–1963, 'Extracts from the papers of the late Dr Patrick McCartan', *Clogher Record* vol. 5 no. 1 (1963), 30; Seán Moylan, *Seán Moylan: In His Own Words: His Memoir of the Irish War of Independence* (Aubane 2009), 21; William Henry, *Supreme Sacrifice* (Cork 2005), 9–10.

126. Alice Milligan, 1866–1953. Henry Mangan (ed.), *Poems by Alice Milligan* (Dublin 1954), xviii.

127. Mangan (ed.) *Poems*, 103, 99–100.

128. Catherine Morris, 'Alice Milligan: Republican tableaux and the revival', *Field Day Review*, vol. 6, 2010, 145; William Rooney, *Poems and Ballads* (Dublin & Waterford 1902), xxiii–iv, 200. Rooney, 1873–1901.

129. Luby to O'Leary, 19 July 1890, O'Leary papers, Ms. 5,926; Dermot Meleady, *Redmond the Parnellite* (Cork 2008), 239, 376.

130. *FJ*, 28 May 1894.

131. *Times*, 21 Nov. 1904; Mannion, 'Silent but eloquent reminders', 188–90; *Times*, 7 Dec. 1904.

132. 'Myles [the slasher]' to editor, *Tipperary People*, 20 July 1906.

133. 6882 R & 7599 R, Fenian files; Transcripts of abstracts of cases, CSO/ICR/10, HCSA 1866, 408; Leaflet 'The veterans of the IRB', 30 May 1889, courtesy of Jeanne Ahearn Mogayzel, New York.

134. *Nation*, 8 Feb. 1873.

135. Ó Lúing, 'Aspects of the Fenian Rising in Kerry, 1867 II', 162–3; *Irish People* (New York), 10 Dec. 1870, 164. See Appendix I.

136. Denieffe, *A personal narrative*, 46; *New York Times*, 12 Sept. 1900; Dr Denis Dowling Mulcahy, sale catalogue of books and furniture, New York Public Library; *The Irish book lover*, vol. i, 169, July 1910. The dictionary was never completed.

137. See his law case against Rossa, Luby and Devoy in *Brooklyn Eagle*, 6 Jan. 1884, also *New York Times*, 29 Aug. 1888. One of Mulcahy's relatives had married into the Spanish aristocracy; her trustee attempted to pocket the inheritance: *New York Times*, 30 July 1887; 25 Oct. 1892; Mulcahy to O'Leary, 2 Sept. 1896, O'Leary papers, Ms. 5,926, NLI; *New York Tribune*, 12 Sept. 1900.

138. Mulcahy to O'Leary, 20 Feb. & 28 Nov. 1890, O'Leary papers, Ms. 5,926.

139. Ibid., Mulcahy to O'Leary, 8 Oct. 1896.

140. Ibid., letter from Luby household to O'Leary, 28 Oct. 1900. *New York Tribune*, 25 Feb. 1900; *New York Times*, 12 Sept. 1900.

141. *New York Tribune*, 2 Aug. 1897; Luby household to O'Leary, 28 Oct. 1900, O'Leary papers, Ms. 5,926.

142. *New York Tribune*, 16 Sept.1900; *New York Times*, 9 May 1901.

143. Dr Carroll to Devoy, 4 Nov. 1878, *DPB i*, 368; James O'Connor to Devoy, 26 Feb. 1909, *DPB ii*, 378; *Gaelic American*, 5 Dec. 1908.

144. George Lyons, W.S.104, BMH; Gonne MacBride, *A Servant of the Queen*, 280–1.

145. Gonne MacBride, *A Servant of the Queen*, 278; Catherine Morris, *Booklet for El Lissitzky: The Artist and the State Exhibition*, IMMA, 2015; Nell Regan, *Helena Molony: a Radical Life, 1883–1967* (Dublin 2017), 41.

146. Lyons, W.S.104, BMH.

147. Ibid.; CBS 29274/S & 26693/S, NAI.

148. *Times*, 30 Mar. 1901.

149. Ibid.; *Southern Star*, 6 Apr. 1901; Mallon's report, CBS 1901, 24423/S.

150. CBS 1901, 24423/S; *Southern Star*, 6 Apr. 1901; *Irish Times*, 6 Apr. 1901. Dineen's relations had attempted to shelter O'Neill Crowley in 1867.

151. *FJ*, 1 Apr. 1901; CBS 1901, 24423/S; Ryan, *Fenian Memories*, 70.

152. Balfour Papers PRO 30/60/28, TNA; Eunan O'Halpin, 'The Secret Service Vote and Ireland, 1868–1922', *IHS*, vol. 23, no. 92 (1983), 351.

153. Memorandum from inspector general, RIC, 6 Jan. 1900, PRO 30/60/28. Seamus MacManus, husband of Anna Johnston, agreed, W.S.283, BMH.

154. Memorandum, 6 & 8 Jan. 1900, PRO 30/60/28. Andrew Reed, 1837–1914.

155. O'Donoghue, *Tomás MacCurtain* (Tralee 1958), 12; Bulmer Hobson, *Ireland Yesterday and Tomorrow* (Tralee 1968), 2; Richard Kirkland, *Cathal O'Byrne and the Northern Revival in Ireland, 1890–1960* (Liverpool 2006), 132; Sean Cronin, *The McGarrity Papers* (Tralee 1972), 19; Mac Atasney, *Seán MacDiarmada*, 13–5.

156. Padraic Colum, *Arthur Griffith* (Dublin 1959), 57–8, 62; Bulmer Hobson, *Ireland Yesterday*, 2, 7–8; Arthur Griffith, *The Resurrection of Hungary: a parallel for Ireland* (Dublin 1904), 91–2; D.J. Hickey and J.E. Doherty, *A New Dictionary of Irish History from 1800* (Dublin 2005), 98.

157. P.S. O'Hegarty, *The IRB 1902–14*, W.S.026, BMH.

158. Ibid.

159. Diarmuid Lynch, *The IRB and the 1916 Insurrection* (ed. Florence O'Donoghue), (Cork 1957).

160. Précis of information 1908–1909, CO 904/118; P.S. O'Hegarty, W.S.026, BMH; O'Donoghue, *Tomás MacCurtain*, 9–10.

161. P.S. O'Hegarty, W.S.026, BMH.

162. Ibid.; Gonne MacBride, *A Servant of the Queen*, 278–9; Des Ryan, 'Opposition to the Boer War, Limerick, 1899–1902', *Old Limerick Journal* (Winter 2004).

163. May 1905, Précis of information received by CSB, RIC, Apr. 1905 – Sept. 1906; Oct. – Dec. 1907, CO 904/117; ibid., Nov. 1905; May 1908, Précis of information, RIC, 1908–1909, CO 904/118, TNA; ibid., Nov. 1908; 15 Dec. 1900, Miss Maud Gonne CO 904/202/ 166 pt. A, TNA. See also statements of Thomas Barry, Knockbrack, Cork, and Liam de Roiste, BMH.

164. W.E.H. Lecky, 'Ireland in the light of history', *Historical and Political Essays* (London 1910), 79–80; Rolleston, *Portrait of an Irishman*, 51.

165. Rolleston, *Portrait of an Irishman*, 118–21.

166. Ibid., 117.
167. Feb.–Mar. 1905, July 1906, Précis of information and reports, DMP district, Mar. 1905 – Dec. 1908, CO 904/11, TNA; CBS 1904, 29274/S, NAI; Gosselin Obituary, *Times*, 6 Feb. 1917.
168. W. Alison Phillips, *The Revolution in Ireland* (London 1923), 46; Begbie, *The Lady Next Door*, 72, 64–6. John Belchem recorded similar official misjudgments regarding the IRB in Liverpool.
169. 'Fenianism: the last Fenian', Kevin Barry (ed.), *James Joyce: Occasional, Critical, and Political Writings* (Oxford 2000), 138.
170. *Irish Independent*, 20 Mar. 1907.
171. Ibid., 7 Oct. 1907; Feb. 1905 & Nov. 1907, Information and reports, Mar. 1905 – Dec. 1908, CO 904/11; 14 Dec. 1903, 29186/S, NAI. Daly was the rising star after 1903 until caught for embezzling IRB funds in 1910.
172. P.S. O'Hegarty, W.S.026, BMH.
173. Griffith to John O'Leary in 1901, Padraig Colum, *Arthur Griffith*, 62.
174. Dec. 1907, Precis of information and reports relating to the DMP district, Mar. 1905 – Dec. 1908, CO 904/11; Clarke, *Revolutionary Woman*, 35–6; Clarke, *Glimpses*, 40–1; Cronin, *The McGarrity Papers*, 36.
175. Hobson, *Ireland Yesterday*, 35; for instance, witness statements of John Flanagan, commandant, 2nd Battalion, Mid-Clare Brigade, Tullycrine and Joseph Barrett, brigade operations officer, Mid-Clare Brigade, Thomas McInerney, Ardrahan and Martin Newell, Loughrea, Bureau of Military History.

APPENDIX I

1. Main sources are the Dublin Castle Fenian papers, Fenian records in the TNA, the writings of John Devoy, the Fenian Brotherhood Collection of the CUA, especially the roster of officers, various Irish, British and American newspapers, local history journals and Bureau of Military History statements. Age of suspects as recorded at first arrest. FP: Fenian photograph index, NAI.
2. CSO/ICR 14, NAI.
3. Roster of the military officers of the Fenian Brotherhood, NY, 1865, 33, Fenian Brotherhood records, CUA.
4. *Irish Times*, 9 & 10 Dec. 1887; *FJ*, 7 Dec. 1887.
5. CSO/ICR 14, NAI.
6. *Irishman*, 21 Mar. 1868.
7. Roster of the military officers of the Fenian Brotherhood, 114.
8. Ibid., 56.
9. Ibid., 172.
10. FP 140, NAI.
11. Roster of the military officers of the Fenian Brotherhood, 118.
12. Mary Noon Kasulaitis, 'Captain John McCafferty: mine promoter', *The Connection, Open Forum Monthly Journal*, vol. xx no. 4, May 2004.
13. CSO/ICR 14, NAI.
14. Roster of the military officers of the Fenian Brotherhood, 114.

15. CSO/ICR 11, NAI.
16. *Skibbereen Eagle*, 7 Nov. 1914.
17. *Nation*, 24 Feb. 1866.
18. *Southern Star*, 11 Mar. 1995.
19. CSO/ICR 10, 69, NAI.
20. Roster of the military officers of the Fenian Brotherhood, 53.
21. Seán Ó Súilleabháin, 'The Iveragh Fenians in Oral Tradition', *University Review*, vol. 4, no. 3, 1967, 217.
22. Ibid., 222.
23. 'Dunne, of Callan', 3 Feb. 1872, *Irish People* (NY).
24. CSO/ICR 10, 161A.
25. Kathleen Clarke, *Revolutionary Woman*, 18.
26. Richard Eaton R.M. to U.S., CSORP 1867/4314.
27. Abstracts of cases under Habeas Corpus Suspension Act, 1866, vol. 1, 300, NAI.
28. *Irishman*, 4 July 1868.
29. *Nation*, 4 Apr. 1873.
30. *Cork Examiner*, 16 Dec. 1929.
31. *Irish People* (NY), 11 Feb. 1871.
32. Seoighe, *The Story of Kilmallock*, 206–7.
33. CSORP 1867/3323, NAI.
34. CSO/ICR 10, 294, NAI.
35. F 3529 Attack on barracks at Emly, County Tipperary, Fenian files, NAI.
36. Précis of information and reports, Mar. 1905–Dec. 1908, CO 904/11; *Nenagh Guardian*, 1 Jan. 1910; 3 Dec. 1910; *Weekly Irish Times*, 26 June 1915.
37. CSO/ICR 11 HCSA 1866, 393, NAI.
38. 'A wreath of prison flowers', *Nation*, 17 July 1869; *Irish book lover*, vol. xiv, 109–10, July–Aug. 1924.
39. *Nation*, 18 Jan. 1868.
40. *Irishman*, 16 Mar. 1867.
41. List of warrants issued, CSO/ICR 11 HCSA 1866, 373, NAI.
42. Ibid., 540.
43. Ibid., 571.
44. 'Death of Edward Walsh, of Tipperary', cutting from *Sunday Citizen*, courtesy of Jeanne Ahearn Mogayzel, New York.
45. List of warrants issued, CSO/ICR 11 HCSA 1866, 648.

APPENDIX II

1. In Killeagh, Co. Cork, roads have been named after Laurence Kelly and Timothy Daly.

Index

Page numbers in *italics* refer to illustrations; page numbers in **bold** refer to entries in Appendix I and Appendix II.